Correctional Perspectives

Views From Academics, Practitioners, and Prisoners

Leanne Fiftal Ala
University of Missouri–Ka.

Paul F. Cromwell
Wichita State University

Roxbury Publishing Company
Los Angeles, California

Library of Congress Cataloging-in-Publication Data
Alarid, Leanne Fiftal, 1967–
Correctional perspectives: views from academics, practitioners, and prisoners /
Leanne Fiftal Alarid, Paul Cromwell
p. cm.
Includes bibliographical references.
ISBN 1-891487-74-4
1. Correctional institutions. 2. Criminals—Rehabilitation. I. Cromwell, Paul F.
II. Title

HV8665 .A463 2002
365—dc21   2001031871

Publisher: Claude Teweles
Managing Editor: Dawn VanDercreek
Production Editors: Monica Gomez, Carla Max-Ryan
Production Assistant: Josh Levine
Typography: Synergistic Data Systems
Cover Design: Marnie Kenney

Printed on acid-free paper in the United States of America. This book meets the standards for
recycling of the Environmental Protection Agency.

ISBN 1-891487-74-4

ROXBURY PUBLISHING COMPANY
P. O. Box 491044
Los Angeles, California 90049-9044
Voice: (310) 473-3312 • Fax: (310) 473-4490
E-mail: roxbury@roxbury.net
Website: www.roxbury.net

Contents

Part One: Effects of Sentencing Changes

Chapter I: Institutional Crowding

Academic Perspective

Gerald G. Gaes

Gaes suggests that prison crowding is rarely the sole cause of serious problems related to prisoner health, violence, recidivism, and prison riots.

Practitioner Perspective

Michael S. Vaughn

Vaughn identifies the factors that correctional administrators believe have contributed to prison crowding and suggests how institutional overpopulation can be reduced.

Prisoner Perspective

Dannie M. Martin and Peter Y. Sussman

Martin and Sussman link crowding with increased institutional stress, which encourages a climate of increased violence, secretiveness, clique mentality, violence, and deceit.

Chapter II: Growth in the Number of Women Prisoners

Academic Perspective

Meda Chesney-Lind

Chesney-Lind considers whether the cause for the large increase in female prisoners is a change in the nature of female offending or whether it arises from a shift in the criminal justice response to women offenders.

Practitioner Perspective

Elaine Lord

Lord provides details on issues that women face during incarceration and shows how the criminal justice system is responding differently to women offenders, often in misguided ways.

Ex-Prisoner Perspective

Susan Dearing

Dearing shares perspectives from women prisoners and former prisoners to explain how changes in laws and law enforcement have affected the growth of women in prison, and she details the incarceration experience, including the lack of services available in prison.

Part Two: Treatment of Offenders

Chapter III: Elements of Correctional Rehabilitation

Academic Perspective

Paul Gendreau

By analyzing commonalities of effective and ineffective intervention programs, Gendreau examines how far researchers have come since the Martinson study in determining what works in the treatment of prisoners.

Chapter IV: Medical Treatment: HIV/AIDS in Corrections

Part Three: Prison Security Issues

Chapter V: Prison Gangs

Academic Perspective

Geoffrey Hunt, Stephanie Riegel, Tomas Morales, and Dan Waldorf
Using in-depth interviews of ex-prisoners in California, this selection measures changes in prison life due to the infiltration of prison gangs.

Practitioner Perspective

Michael P. Phelan and Scott A. Hunt
Phelan and Hunt examine the meaning of tattoos belonging to *La Nuestra Familia,* a Latino prison gang with roots in California.

Prisoner Perspective

Victor Hassine
Hassine demonstrates how the existence of prison gangs and racial separatism can actually be beneficial to prison administrators.

Chapter VI: Prison Violence

Academic Perspective

Michael Welch
Welch introduces various causes and levels of prison violence throughout history.

Practitioner Perspective

JoAnne Page
On the basis of 25 years of experience working in prisons and jails, Page concludes that correctional institutions breed anger, violence, and destructiveness.

Chapter VII: Security Housing Units: Supermax Prisons

Chapter VIII: Women Guarding Men

Part Four: Special Issues Facing Corrections

Chapter IX: Correctional Privatization

Chapter X: Juveniles in Adult Corrections

Chapter XI: On Death Row

Part Five: Getting Out

Foreword

Thirty years ago I began a career linked to the prison system as it was called then, and rightfully should be called today. Soon after this system started to be called a "correctional system." After working for eight years in a maximum-security prison, and 23 years of studying and teaching about prisons, it is a pleasure to see that the idea of multiple perspectives is finally taking hold. The framework for the readings in this collection reflects something I realized shortly after I started my prison-related career. For those living and working in prisons, they are hyper-reality—a reality reflected in struggles to survive. However, *when trying to understand prisons there is no reality, there is only perspective*. A perspective is a way of looking at things, of deriving meaning and understanding from the events that surround you. Personal experiences and the experiences of one's peers shape perspective. Expectations shape perspective. An individual's role and place in the structure of organizations shapes his or her perspective as demands, rules, evaluations and organizational cultures limit the information and ways of living and working available for success. This is true whether a person is a politician making a career out of being "tough on crime," an academic attempting to get materials published through the peer review process, a correctional officer working to establish a reputation with prisoners and win the respect of his or her peers, a journalist seeking the "big story" and a move to a more prominent media venue, or a prisoner simply seeking to survive years of incarceration. Each perspective brings something of "reality," though each is very different.

Discussions about any specific perspective is a discourse—a conversation written by those who reflect a particular perspective. Academics have these conversations through articles in academic journals and books. Correctional practitioners hold these conversations at meetings of professional associations and conferences, and their professional journals. Prisoners, alas, rarely have these conversations in public and only get to make their feelings public when good fortune and astute publishers manage to come together to secure publication of their words.

These various discourses or conversations about prisons committed to writing have histories. As with any collection there are limitations of space and cost that force a limited time perspective. But every issue covered in this collection has a history of discourse. The history of these conversations and discussions is something which students are well advised to pursue. This history will add context to the conversations the prisoners, academics, and practitioners provide in this collection.

Though this collection of readings allows students to see what scholars, practitioners, and prisoners have to say about specific topics, it is clear that no one person speaks for all prisoners', practitioners', or academics' experiences. It is important that students as citizens and voters, and those involved in shaping the future of correctional policy, began to understand that there is no truth here, there is only perspective. That the answers are always works in progress, not hyperbolic statements-of-fact and assuredness that the "political" perspective of the politician involved in corrections often provides.

The chapter introductions and the discussions of assumptions and "realities" portrayed in the readings are especially useful in helping students integrate and synthesize what the prisoner, practitioner, and academic perspectives bring to a particular issue. Readers should use these to situate themselves in the middle of the "correctional world," using each perspective as a filter and counterpoint for the others. In this way, a more realistic and complex understanding of the human dilemmas that are at the base of correctional policy and practice can emerge. Justice and injustice, punishment and reform, doing good and doing harm, individual choice and environmental influences on behavior, social meaning and individual lives, all merge in the world of corrections. The choices we as a society and polity make, and perspectives we use to make these choices, will be better understood by paying attention to what everyone brings to the table of experience. We should not limit ourselves to narrow one-sided views. This is the challenge that this valuable collection brings to the reader.

—Lucien X. Lombardo, Professor
Department of Sociology
and Criminal Justice
Old Dominion University
June 3, 2001

Lucien X. Lombardo, Professor, Department of Sociology and Criminal Justice, Old Dominion University, Norfolk, VA. Dr. Lombardo has been working in, studying, teaching and writing about correctional issues since 1969. He is the author of two editions of *Guards Imprisoned: Correctional Officers at Work*, co-editor of *Prison Violence in America*, and author of numerous articles relating to prison life and collective violence.

Preface

Academic researchers and legal scholars have studied and recorded the bulk of what is known about corrections in America today. The scholarly view is important, in that researchers participate in knowledge acquisition through trained observation in prison, sampling, interviews, and survey methodology. Correctional research is thus presented in terms of issue significance, previous research findings over time, and new results. The scholarly view is considered to be more objective in the sense that the social scientist studies the entire criminal justice system from an outside perspective. The scholarly view, however, is limited to what participants allow the researcher to see.

On the other hand, "insider" correctional perspectives, such as those from practitioners and prisoners, offer unique insights that are sometimes missed by the outside researcher. Practitioners and prisoners are considered to hold more subjective views because they live and work daily inside prison. Insiders might not be familiar with the correctional literature, but they view the system with a more meticulous and critical lens. The insider perspective has been historically neglected in correctional research.

In putting this book together, we decided to present the outsider and insider roles within the same text to provide a comparison of these viewpoints. This text examines twelve critical issues currently facing prisons and jails all over America. Each of the twelve topics will be systematically examined from three different perspectives: academic, practitioner, and prisoner.

The Academic Perspective: The academic perspective consists of contemporary writings and/or research by outside correctional experts, agency researchers, and professors who have studied the issue. The academic selections were chosen to introduce and describe each issue.

The Practitioner Perspective: The practitioner perspective focuses on what it is like to work in the field or how one or more workers view a particular correctional issue based on firsthand experience. We selected practitioners as authors or academics who surveyed practitioners on their views.

The Prisoner Perspective: The prisoner perspective depicts how prisoners view each correctional issue. We selected works authored by prisoners, ex-prisoners, or academics who surveyed offenders on specific correctional topics.

Using each of the three perspectives, we have chosen to examine twelve contemporary correctional issues. The text is divided into five parts. Part One examines some effects of recent sentencing changes, such as institutional crowding and how sentencing has impacted the growth of women prisoners. Part Two describes the treatment of offenders through correctional counseling and rehabilitation as well as the medical treatment of HIV (human immunodeficiency virus) in prison. Part Three explores various intertwined prison security issues: prison gangs, prison violence, and security housing units/supermax. The question of women correctional officers working in all-male prisons is also considered. Part Four identifies special issues facing corrections today. These include privatization, juveniles in adult corrections, and living and working on death row. Finally, Part Five portrays the current state of parole and the perspectives of prison release.

Each correctional topic in the text was selected to encourage critical thinking and classroom discussion, particularly as it relates to how the three perspectives compare and contrast. The editors introduce each chapter by identifying a common assumption about the topic, explaining where the assumption originated, and presenting evidence to dispel any erroneous assumptions. The three perspectives are then presented as separate readings. Focus questions appear at the beginning of each reading so that the students have some idea of what they should be looking for as they read. We view this collection as a supplemental text to an introduction to corrections course or an institutional corrections course, and our aim is to present the viewpoints of those who study, work, and live in the corrections system. (The articles chosen for each perspective do not necessarily represent the viewpoints of all individuals within that perspective.)

***

We wish to thank the proposal reviewers who provided useful comments that greatly improved the text. These reviewers include: Martha Elin Blomquist, Florida State University; Susan F. Brinkley, University of Tampa; Chuck Fields, Eastern Kentucky University; Jessie L. Krienert, Illinois State University; Harvey W. Kushner, Long Island State University; Faith E. Lutze, Washington State University; Mary Parker, University of Arkansas-Little Rock; Joycelyn Pollock, Southwest Texas State University; Philip L. Reichel, University of Northern Colorado; and Larry Travis, University of Cincinnati.

We extend a special debt of gratitude to Dee Pritchett at Wichita State University and to Claude Teweles at Roxbury Publishing Company.

About the Editors

Leanne Fiftal Alarid graduated with a Ph.D. in criminal justice from Sam Houston State University in 1996. She is currently assistant professor and program coordinator of criminal justice/criminology in the Department of Sociology/Criminal Justice and Criminology at the University of Missouri–Kansas City. Her areas of expertise are in institutional and community corrections, women and crime, and criminal justice policy. Dr. Alarid has authored fifteen journal articles and recently completed the fifth edition of *Community-Based Corrections* with Paul Cromwell and Rolando del Carmen. She is currently co-editing (with Scott Decker and Charles Katz) another Roxbury Publishing book on controversial issues in criminal justice. She has also worked for a juvenile group home and an adult halfway house for almost three years.

Paul Cromwell received a Ph.D. in 1986 from Florida State University. As a scholar and former practitioner in the corrections and criminal justice field, he has authored four books, twenty-six journal articles, and fourteen book chapters. He has also edited eleven books. Dr. Cromwell has over twenty years of combined work experience in the criminal justice field as Director of Drug and Alcohol Programs, Director of Juvenile Services/Chief Juvenile Probation Officer, Parole Board Member, Federal Probation Officer, and Juvenile Probation Officer. He continues to teach corrections and criminal justice courses at Wichita State University, where he is Professor of Criminal Justice and Director of the School of Community Affairs.

About the Contributors

Ronald Burns is assistant professor at Texas Christian University.

Meda Chesney-Lind is professor and director of women's studies at the University of Hawaii at Manoa. The author of over fifty monographs and papers on women and crime, she has written *Girls, Delinquency, and Juvenile Justice* with Randall G. Shelden. In 1992, she was awarded the American Society of Criminology's Michael J. Hindelang Award for outstanding contribution to criminology.

Susan Dearing earned a B.A. in sociology from Central Methodist College in Fayette, Missouri, and is currently the director/program coordinator of a group home for mentally retarded/developmentally disabled adults. She is completing her M.A. in sociology from the University of Arkansas–Fayetteville.

Anne S. De Groot is an assistant professor of medicine and community health at Brown University and is on the HIV/AIDS program staff at the Lemuel Shattuck Hospital in Jamaica Plain, Massachusetts.

Gerald G. Gaes is director of the Office of Research and Evaluation within the Federal Bureau of Prisons.

Paul Gendreau is professor of psychology and director of the graduate program in the Department of Psychology at the University of New Brunswick in Canada. He received his Ph.D. in psychology from Queen's University, Kingston, Ontario. He has worked in criminal justice and correctional settings since 1961 and developed (with Don Andrews) the widely used Correctional Program Assessment Inventory.

Antonio A. Gilbreath is serving time at the Eastham Unit; a state prison in Texas.

Craig Haney is a professor of psychology and director of the Program in Legal Studies at the University of California, Santa Cruz. He received a Ph.D. in social psychology and a J.D. degree from Stanford University. He has studied and written extensively on the psychological effects of working and living in maximum security prisons.

Victor Hassine has a J.D. from New York Law School. He is currently serving time for murder in a state prison in Pennsylvania. In 1990, he received Pennsylvania Prison Society's Inmate of the Year Award.

Martha L. Henderson is an assistant professor at Southern Illinois University. She teaches and conducts research in the areas of corrections and community corrections. Her research interests also include an examination of the impact of race and class on criminal justice processing.

Rodney J. Henningsen is professor in the College of Criminal Justice at Sam Houston State University. His current research focuses on community corrections management.

Norman Holt is employed by the California Department of Corrections.

Geoffrey Hunt is a Senior Research Associate at the Institute for Scientific Analysis in San Francisco, California. He is a social anthropologist by training.

Scott A. Hunt is associate professor of sociology and director of graduate studies at the University of Kentucky. He received his Ph.D. in 1991 from the University of Nebraska.

Denise L. Jenne teaches at Montclair State University.

Robert Johnson teaches in the Department of Justice, Law, and Society at the American University. He is the author of numerous journal articles and books in the area of corrections.

W. Wesley Johnson is associate professor and the associate dean of faculty at Sam Houston State University. His current research focuses on imprisonment and community corrections. His recent publications have appeared in *Crime and Delinquency, Justice Quarterly,* and *Corrections Management Quarterly.*

Robert C. Kersting teaches at Westfield State College.

Patrick Kinkade is director of criminal justice and associate professor at Texas Christian University.

Richard Lawrence teaches in the Department of Criminal Justice at St. Cloud State University.

Matthew C. Leone is associate professor at the University of Nevada–Reno.

Douglas S. Lipton is senior research fellow at National Development and Research Institutes in New York City, where he previously served as director of research. He has authored more than 200 publications including six books, one of which is *The Effectiveness of Correctional Treatment* (1975), coauthored with the late Robert Martinson and Judith Wilks.

Elaine Lord is superintendent of Bedford Hills Correctional Facility, a position she has held since 1984.

Calbraith MacLeod has spent time in five state correctional facilities and four federal institutions. During his incarceration, he participated in numerous rehabilitation programs and accumulated college course credits. He is the author of *Practical Reformation* and is currently serving a 40-year Vermont state prison term.

Sue Mahan is associate professor at the University of Central Florida. She conducts research in the area of women and crime.

Dannie M. Martin is an ex-convict who did federal time for bank robbery and was paroled in 1991. While incarcerated, he wrote articles that appeared in the "Sunday Punch" section of the *San Francisco Chronicle*.

Kevin I. Minor is professor and chair of the Department of Correctional and Juvenile Justice Studies at Eastern Kentucky University. Dr. Minor has co-authored two books and over 30 articles and book chapters. His areas of interest include institutional and community corrections, juvenile delinquency and justice, and evaluation research.

Alan C. Mobley is a Ph.D. candidate in the Department of Criminology, Law, and Society at the University of California, Irvine.

Tomas Morales is employed by the Institute for Scientific Analysis in San Francisco, California.

John H. Morris III has served time as a prisoner in Pelican Bay State Prison, a supermax prison in Northern California.

Daniel S. Murphy is currently a doctoral candidate in the Department of Sociology at Iowa State University. In 1992, he went to federal prison for five years for cultivating marijuana and went on to earn his M.A. in sociology from the University of Wisconsin–Milwaukee in 1999.

Patricia O'Brien is assistant professor at the University of Illinois at Chicago in the Jane Addams College of Social Work.

JoAnne Page is the executive director of The Fortune Society, a position she has held since 1989. She graduated from Yale Law School with a J.D. degree in 1980. Between 1972 and 1986, she taught in New York state prisons, worked as a criminal defense attorney with the Legal Aid Society, and developed programs that provided alternatives to incarceration for felony defendants through the Court Employment Project.

Michael P. Phelan is employed in the Department of Sociology at the University of Kentucky in Lexington. He worked as a correctional officer for the California state prison system from 1984 to 1990.

Scott Phillips is a doctoral student at Louisiana State University.

Frances P. Reddington is associate professor in the Department of Criminal Justice at Central Missouri State University. She publishes in the juvenile justice area.

Stephen C. Richards is an associate professor of sociology and criminology at Northern Kentucky University. He served five years in federal prison for conspiracy to distribute marijuana. Following his release, he completed an M.A. in sociology from the University of Wisconsin–Milwaukee in 1989 and a Ph.D. in sociology from Iowa State University in 1992.

Stephanie Riegel is employed by the Institute for Scientific Analysis in San Francisco, California.

Joshua D. M. Rogers IV is serving time in the Texas Department of Criminal Justice–Institutional Division.

Mike Rolland is the author of *Descent Into Madness* and served time as a prisoner during the Santa Fe, New Mexico state prison riot.

Anthony Ross is currently on death row in San Quentin State Prison in California. He is an avid reader and writer and is attempting to publish an anthology of his own fiction and death row writings.

Allen D. Sapp is a professor in the Department of Criminal Justice at Central Missouri State University.

Vincent Schiraldi is director of the Justice Policy Institute.

David Shichor is professor emeritus in the Department of Criminal Justice at California State University–Fullerton.

Steven F. Singer is founder and former director of the nationally recognized program called Doin' Time Gettin' Straight, a prison-based therapeutic community operative at Marion Correctional Institution in Lowell, Florida.

Emmitt L. Sparkman is warden of the Marshall County Correctional Facility, a 1,000-bed medium security prison for men operated by Wackenhut Corrections Corporation for the Mississippi Department of Corrections. Mr. Sparkman holds an M.S. degree from Eastern Kentucky University and has over 25 years of experience in juvenile and adult corrections in treatment, security, and administrative positions.

Peter Y. Sussman is a journalist and editor for the "Sunday Punch" section of the *San Francisco Chronicle*. He is co-author with Dannie Martin of the book titled *Committing Journalism: The Prison Writings of Red Hog*.

Charles M. Terry is assistant professor of criminal justice at the University of Michigan–Flint. He spent over twelve years in correctional custody for crimes including burglary, shoplifting, and the possession and sale of heroin. Following his release from

prison in 1990, he completed a B.A. in sociology from the University of California–Santa Barbara, and a Ph.D. from the University of California, Irvine.

Morris L. Thigpen is former commissioner of the Alabama Department of Corrections.

Michael S. Vaughn is associate professor of criminal justice at Georgia State University. He has published numerous scholarly articles and is the current editor of *Criminal Justice Review*.

Dan Waldorf is employed by the Institute for Scientific Analysis in San Francisco, California.

Michael Welch is associate professor in administration of justice at Rutgers University, New Brunswick, New Jersey. He is the author of four books and dozens of book chapters and scholarly articles.

James B. Wells is professor of Correctional and Juvenile Justice Studies and director of the Center for Criminal Justice Education and Research at Eastern Kentucky University. He received his Ph.D. in Research, Measurement, and Statistics from Georgia State University. His main areas of research include criminal and juvenile justice, evaluation research, and the improvement of criminal justice training and university-level teaching through multimedia instruction.

Terry L. Wells is assistant professor of criminal justice in the Department of Government and Sociology at Georgia College and State University. His current research focuses on community corrections, juvenile justice, and probation officer stress. He has recently published in *Corrections Management Quarterly, Journal of Contemporary Criminal Justice,* and *Federal Probation*.

Jason Ziedenberg is a researcher with the Justice Policy Institute.

Part One
Effects of
Sentencing Changes

Chapter I
Introduction

Institutional Crowding

Common Assumptions	Reality
• Prison crowding causes riots, substandard medical care, and other unsafe prison conditions. • An overcrowded correctional institution automatically violates the Constitution.	• There is no clear-cut evidence that crowding causes riots, violence, and other unsafe prison hazards (Gaes 1994; Klofas and Stojkovic 1996). • Institutional crowding, by itself, can no longer be used as a constitutional violation in inmate lawsuits. The courts are now focused on alleviating the problems that cause cruel and unusual punishment. Such changes include improving medical care and increasing staff ratios, before focusing on reducing the number of offenders (Call 1995).

Over the last decade, American jails and prisons have experienced unprecedented growth in the numbers of convicted offenders who are incarcerated. This growth resulted in part from perceptual changes in how the criminal justice system processed and punished juveniles, women, violent offenders, and drug offenders. Prison expansion intensified with "get tough" legislation that decreased judicial and parole authority using sentencing guidelines, mandatory minimums, and three strikes laws. As a result of the "war on drugs" and new sentencing policies, the United States currently has 6.3 million persons, or nearly 3 percent of the total adult population, under the supervision of the criminal justice system. More than 2 million offenders are incarcerated in local, state, and federal prison and jail institutions (Beck 2000).

Increased funding for prison construction has been mandated to support sentencing changes that are resulting in longer sentences and decreased opportunities for early release. Meanwhile, correctional crowding is the result when the system fails to keep pace with changes in arrest and sentencing policies.

Initial inquiry into the effects of institutional crowding occurred many years ago, shortly after administrators began "double-bunking" (prisoners were required to share their cells). Correctional reformers were concerned that double-bunking and allowing prisoners to sleep on mattresses in the gymnasium disintegrated the safety and control of the prison environment. Correctional officers were believed to have less control over inmates. Crowded prison conditions were believed to cause higher illness rates, stress, violence, and prison uprisings. However, research on the causes of prison riots has shown that prison mismanagement and perceived unfair treatment were primary causes (Useem and Kimball 1989). Furthermore, early crowding research has been criticized for not taking other intervening variables (e.g., custody level, housing assignment, proliferation of gangs, and racial tension), individual factors (e.g., age, prior criminal history, and propensity toward violence) into account (Klofas and Stojkovic 1996). Institutional crowding can be a *contributing* factor to increased stress, noise, and lack of privacy, but recent evidence indicates that crowding is rarely a direct cause.

In interpreting the Eighth Amendment of the Constitution, the courts have also distinguished between crowding as a cause and as a contributing factor. The Eighth Amendment guarantees that prisoners will not be exposed to cruel and unusual punishment. A crowded institution, by itself, is not a constitutional violation. Cruel and unusual punishment arises when crowded conditions cause "unnecessary or wanton pain" or if the conditions are "grossly disproportionate to the crime for which the offender is incarcerated" (*Rhodes v. Chapman* 1981).

In *Wilson v. Seiter* (1991), the Supreme Court found that for crowding to be a violation of the eighth amendment, the grievance must demonstrate "deliberate indifference" to basic offender needs by prison staff and/or administrators. In other words, a prison can operate above its "rated capacity" (i.e., the number of beds per institution), but prison staff cannot intentionally ignore the offender's basic needs of food, warmth, safety, medical needs, and exercise. The court does not believe that by simply reducing the number of offenders, the services provided will improve. Jack Call (1995) predicted that recent court rulings will likely make it more difficult for a case to be substantiated against the prison. He also stated, however,

that lower courts were still willing to rule in favor of prisoners who could show "that they were subjected to severely overcrowded conditions with harmful effects under circumstances where prison officials knew or must have known about the conditions and their likely effects" (p. 403).

It is unclear whether offenders confined in jails may be more adversely affected by institutional crowding than those in prisons. Michael Welch (1994) points out that jails were designed to detain suspects and convicted misdemeanants for a year or less (although some jails held individuals for up to two years because of prison crowding). Because of this, jails provide less opportunity for offenders to occupy their time through participation in treatment programs and other services. A recent government report stated that jails remain crowded even with an additional 26,000 beds in the last year and 250,000 since 1990 (Bureau of Justice Assistance 2000).

Jails continue to be holding facilities for offenders who have been arrested by police under mandatory arrest policies for domestic violence or for driving under the influence of drugs or alcohol. Jail populations have increased substantially, particularly in states that enforce mandatory minimums, truth-in-sentencing laws, and habitual offender laws. Pretrial detainees who face long sentences or life without parole under three strikes are more likely to request a trial and to be detained in jail waiting for their trial date (Bureau of Justice Assistance 2000). On the other hand, offenders in prison are incarcerated for longer periods of time than individuals in jail. Given the unsubstantiated relationship between unconstitutional prison conditions and institutional crowding, future research should focus on other potential causes that lead to hazardous prison settings.

Recommended Readings

Beck, Allen J. 2000. *Prisoners in 1999*. Washington, DC: U.S. Department of Justice.

Bureau of Justice Assistance. (2000). *A Second Look at Alleviating Jail Crowding: A Systems*

Perspective. Washington, DC: U.S. Department of Justice.

Call, Jack E. (1995). "Prison Overcrowding Cases in the Aftermath of *Wilson v. Seiter*." *The Prison Journal* 75 (3): 390–405.

Gaes, Gerald G. (1994). "Prison Crowding Research Reexamined." *The Prison Journal* 74: 329–363.

Klofas, John M., and Stan Stojkovic. (1996). "Correctional Crowding: The Half-Life of an Idea in the Social Sciences." *Social Pathology* 2 (1): 23–31.

Paulus, Paul B. (1988). *Prison Crowding: A Psychological Perspective*. New York: Springer-Verlag.

Ruback, R. Barry, and Christopher A. Innes. (1988). "The Relevance and Irrelevance of Psychological Research: The Example of Prison Crowding." *American Psychologist* 43 (9): 683–693.

Useem, Burt, and Peter Kimball. (1989). *States of Siege: U.S. Prison Riots, 1971–1986*. New York: Oxford University Press.

Welch, Michael. (1994). "Jail Overcrowding: Social Sanitation and the Warehousing of the Urban Underclass." In *Critical Issues in Crime and Justice* (Albert Roberts, editor). Thousand Oaks, CA: Sage.

Wooldredge, John. (1996). "Research Note: A State-level Analysis of Sentencing Policies and Inmate Crowding in State Prisons." *Crime and Delinquency* 42 (3): 456–466.

Court Cases

Rhodes v. Chapman, 452 U.S. 337, 101 S.Ct. 2392, 69 L.Ed.2d 59 (1981).

Wilson v. Seiter, 501 U.S. 294, 111 S. Ct. 2321, 115 L.Ed.2d 1 (1991).

Internet Websites

A quarter-million mentally ill Americans behind bars, study finds. (1999, 11 July). Available: *http://www.cnn.com/US/9907/11/inmate.mental.health.ap/index.html*

Krane, J. (1999a, 12 April). Demographic revolution rocks U.S. prisons. Available: *http://www.apbnews.com/cjsystem/behind_bars/oldprisoners/mainpris0412.html*

Krane, J. (1999b, 20 August). Crowded prisons, plummeting crime rates. Available: *http://www.apbnews.com/cjsystem/behind_bars/1999/08/20/prison0820_01.html*

The Prison Population Bomb. Shows the extent to which prison populations have increased nationwide. Available: *http://www.demographics.com/publications/AD/96_AD/AD880.htm*

Schlosser, Eric. (1998). "The Prison Industrial Complex." *Atlantic Monthly* (December). Available: *http://www.theatlantic.com/issues/98dec/prisons.htm*

1
Challenging Beliefs About Prison Crowding

Gerald G. Gaes

Focus Questions

1. What is Gaes' position on the relationship between prison crowding and prisoner health, violence, and recidivism?

2. Does Gaes believe that prison crowding contributes to prison riots?

3. According to Gaes, which has a more significant effect on violence—individual or institutional factors?

4. What allegations are made about the problems of academic research that focus on correctional crowding?

Many people suppose that crowding is the primary cause of most problems in prisons, a belief that is echoed in media accounts of prison disturbances. When a sensational prison incident occurs, media coverage usually suggests that crowding was one of the root causes. However, it is not just the media that seem to have adopted this premise as conventional wisdom. As Jeff Bleich (1989) has pointed out in his recent article, "The Politics of Prison Crowding," almost every participant in the crowding debate has a vested interest in promoting the idea that overcrowding will inevitably result in serious inmate management problems or a degeneration in inmate quality of life. This be-

lief serves the interests of all parties—prison administrators, correctional officers and their unions, prisoners' rights advocates. prison reformers, and the inmates themselves.

Bleich cites three reasons why prison administrators might promote the crowding-leads-to-pathology doctrine:

- They can request more resources.

- They can exercise more control over the prison environment.

- They can explain incidents that occur within the prison.

Thus, an administrator can buffer criticism by warning of impending problems that might be caused by crowding or may even avert criticism of a crisis by basing an explanation on crowding.

I propose an alternative viewpoint to bring some balance back into the debate over the relative contribution of crowding compared to *other* causes of prison problems. I am not ruling out the possibility that prison crowding can lead to fewer services available to inmates, a deterioration in inmates' quality of life, and poorer working conditions for staff. However, I would like to bring into perspective the many other conditions that can lead to prison problems.

Is Crowding the Major Source of Prison Problems?

Let me start with a proposition that many correctional administrators and criminologists would consider misguided, if not patently false: *prison crowding is rarely the sole cause of serious inmate problems.* I will consider three main objections to this proposition, then conclude with suggestions for future research on crowding and other institutional factors.

The Argument Based on Conventional Wisdom

Sceptics might reply that it is intuitively obvious that my assertion is wrong. The conventional wisdom among administrators, jurists, prisoners' rights advocates, and others is that crowding must eventually result in some kind of problem. They point to the numerous successful suits against crowded state prisons and to prison riots, some of which have occurred in crowded state prisons and local jails.

In December 1988, the American Civil Liberties Union (ACLU) reported that 10 entire prison systems and 30 other jurisdictions with a major prison were under a court order or consent decree in which crowding was cited as a primary issue. To give some perspective to crowding litigation, we must rely on data collected by the Bureau of Justice Statistics (BJS). In the most recent BJS census of state prisons, administered in 1984, 123 out of 694 prisons were under court order or consent decree for crowding. No federal prisons were involved in such litigation. If we add federal prisons to the 1984 total, 123 out of 739 prisons, or 16.6 percent, were under court order or consent decree.

There are several reasons why the extent of litigation should not be taken as evidence that crowding is the primary cause of a decline in prison conditions. In prison crowding suits, the aim of the litigation is to demonstrate that prison conditions have deteriorated to the point that they should be considered cruel and unusual. Thus, what is often demonstrated is not the causal relationship between crowding and poor conditions, but the fact that prison conditions have become unconstitutional.

In fact, relief of these conditions usually goes beyond setting population caps or reducing the population. In the extensive Texas crowding suit, relief involved specific remedies concerning medical care, grievance procedures, and other inmate issues. Because it is necessary to bring relief to these types of prison systems, I do not question these court interventions; rather, the issue here is determining cause and effect. Many prisons have been well managed with equally high or even higher populations than those under court order or consent decree. If prisons are poorly managed, or if administrators and staff are deliberately indifferent to inmate needs, egregious conditions can exist in the absence of crowding. Thus, the fact that judicial intervention has been at least in part based on crowding is not proof that crowding has been the basis of the prison problems. Judicial intervention, even if based on false assumptions and naive theories of crowding, can still improve inmate conditions.

The second intuitive assumption is that prison disturbances are primarily the result of crowding, a notion that has been popularized in media accounts. Bert Useem and Peter Kimball (1989) have studied some of the major prison riots in the last two decades, including Attica, Santa Fe, and Joliet. They contend that many of the tensions and deprivations that existed in these prisons prior to the riot, including the level of crowding, were also present in many other prisons throughout the country. Useem and Kimball (1989) argue that the major causes of such riots were breakdowns in the administrative control and operation of the prison, the conviction among the rioting inmates that their demands were legitimate, and the perception that state authorities were likely to capitulate to at least some inmate demands.

A Prison Can House Only So Many Inmates!

A second objection is the argument that there must certainly be some level of crowding at which an institution can no longer deliver services, and staff can no longer ensure inmate safety, or even their own safety. Those on both sides of the debate about the extent to which prison should be used as punishment often agree with this presumption. Proponents argue for increased prison construction. Opponents argue for increases in alternative sanctions.

When the argument is stated this way, and it often is, it is a proposition no one can disagree with—it is in fact tautological. It assumes that some level of crowding, by definition, will result in poorer prison conditions, and it circumvents the more difficult practical problem of determining the level of crowding that inevitably leads to inhumane conditions. Social scientists have tried to study this more difficult problem by analyzing the relationship between levels of crowding and variables that measure the decline in quality of life, such as assault rates or health deterioration.

The real issue can be posed in the language of economists. What is the *marginal effect* of increased density on prison problems? Or, for each additional unit of inmate density, what is the unit decrease in inmate quality of life? There are two theoretical approaches to this problem. Some advocate the "critical mass" theory, which says that each additional inmate degrades the system only slightly, until there is a level of population density—the critical mass that results in a precipitous decline in quality of life. It may be that the population density has to remain high for a long time before problems ensue. Others argue that each additional inmate degrades the system. Perhaps the decline in services becomes more severe as higher levels of density occur, but there is no specific level of crowding at which the system precipitously disintegrates.

Although reasonable people will agree that there is some level of crowding that will bring any correctional system to its knees, it is difficult to establish the precise level at which a decline begins. There is no evidence showing a consistent relationship between institutional levels of crowding and measures of inmate quality of life. My sense is that in most prison systems, as crowding increases, management responds with additional resources or different program approaches. There are instances in which prison populations have doubled or even tripled with no appreciable changes in the quality of inmate care or safety.

However, responses to population increases may be limited by a variety of factors. With regard to infrastructure, some prisons may be designed with very little flexibility for expanding operations such as sanitation, dining, and medical care. Further-

more, some prisons operate under tight budget constraints that restrict their flexibility. Finally, the higher the custody level of the inmate population, the more difficult it is to counter population increases. These factors will determine the relative responsiveness of different prison systems to population increases, which, in turn, affects the population level at which additional inmates might cause a problem. The search for this magical level is further complicated by staff attitudes and the administrative will to cope with increased density.

Because all of these factors confound our analysis of the relationship between density and inmate conditions, it is extremely difficult to demonstrate a relationship between the two and even more difficult to set some standard of "maximum population capacity" appropriate for every institution. If prison density, regardless of these other factors, was the most important determinant of inmate safety and care, it is likely that research would have demonstrated the impact of crowding in spite of the variations in the other factors I've discussed. Thus, to return to the argument that some level of crowding *must* cause problems, the counter-argument says that the maximum population capacity of an institution is variable and depends on factors other than the particular rated or design capacity of its housing space. The implication of this argument for prison conditions suits is that future litigation must continue to emphasize all aspects of prison life. Furthermore, the population cap imposed by the court should be based on the specific institution's capability to ensure inmate safety and to provide all other important services.

Crowding Effects are Real, but Difficult to Uncover

A third objection to my proposition is that crowding does cause many problems; however, the reason that it is difficult to find a relationship between density and a decline in quality of life is that crowding is difficult to define and is not measured consistently, either across different institutions or over time. I have some sympathy for this argument. There is indeed great variability in the definitions of rated or design capacity and there is probably some error in their measurement. Crowding has also been defined as the difference between inmates housed in single-bunked cells versus double-bunked cells or dormitories. There are many other definitions and measurement issues as well.

I have recently completed a review of all prison crowding studies (Gaes 1990). I concluded that even when some attempt at precision in measurement is made, there is no very convincing evidence that crowding is related to serious degradation in the quality of inmate life. Thus, the failure to date to find convincing research evidence for the effects of crowding is not just a problem of definition and measurement. To emphasize this point, there are studies that minimize the definition and measurement errors associated with comparing different institutions using different crowding criteria by examining the quality of life in a specific institution that has undergone a large population increase. Even in such institutions, there is no consistent research evidence indicating serious effects of crowding.

Crowding Research and Its Implication for Managing Prisons

While social scientists who study prisons and the administrators who manage them have a common interest in the topic, they rarely share perspectives. Prison managers approach the administration of a prison as a series of strategies that allow them to maintain order, fulfill program goals, and provide basic services. Social scientists are interested in causal relationships that may or may not meet the information demands of managers.

I will briefly summarize crowding research issues from the perspective of both administrators and social scientists. Research on crowding has thus far focused on three main themes: inmate health, inmate violence, and recidivism. There have been many secondary themes, such as the perception of crowding and other quality-of-life issues; however, these have usually been studied either to explain the primary themes or to bolster researchers' confidence in the results concerning health, violence, and recidivism.

By far the most studied parameter of inmate health has been the rate at which inmates use the prison clinic or report for sick call. Some studies have looked at blood pressure and other biological indicators of health; however, in my opinion, results from these studies are not convincing due to poor methodology or reliance on small inmate samples.

In my research review of the crowding literature, I concluded that there is no consistent evidence that crowding affects any of the three major variables: health, violence, and recidivism. Other researchers would disagree. However, regardless of which side's arguments you find compelling, on this issue, social scientists rarely address matters that most concern prison administrators: the strategies and procedures that are useful in managing institutions having more inmates than their rated capacity.

As institutions become more crowded, the primary response of managers is to extend services—food, medical, training, and case management—to the larger populations. This must be done in coordination with the concern for both inmate safety and continued public safety. Social scientists seem uninterested in the strategies administrators adopt and focus instead on the problems, as if the managers were sitting still while their institutions were deluged by additional inmates. A survey and site visits conducted by George and Camille Camp attempted to examine the strategies used by administrators to manage crowded prisons. These authors found that institutions were adopting procedures that allowed them to continue providing standard services to inmates despite the increase in population. Prison administrators accommodated increases in population through different strategies; for example, some suggested tighter internal security, such as a pass system, while others suggested improvements in grievance procedures. However, despite the Camp study's documentation of these issues, none is currently being studied by social scientists involved in crowding research.

What Do We Know About the Determinants of Prison Violence and Inmate Health?

As a practical matter, crowding research has contributed very little to our understanding of the relationship between population density and quality of life. It has not, however, been a fruitless exercise. Psychological research on prison clinic utilization and crowding has taught us that inmates who first arrive at an institution and inmates who change housing units within an institution are more likely to seek health care in a prison clinic. This fact alone can be used to anticipate clinic demand and is leading to a better understanding of why inmates use the clinic for reasons independent of or only marginally related to their health.

As regards violence, one of the lessons learned from crowding research is that individual factors seem to have a much more potent effect on inmate violence than do institutional factors. This needs further exploration. Many environmental factors other than crowding—age, size, direct versus indirect supervision, type of institution control, type of internal inmate classification system, staffing ratios, inmate turnover, program participation, and even management style—should be studied in relation to inmate characteristics and their combined effect on violence. This distinction between the effect of crowding and other institutional and inmate characteristics on the quality of inmate life is not an academic exercise. A focus on specific crowding levels, if it diverts attention from crucial management variables, may interfere not only with our *understanding* of the quality of inmate life, but with the *actual* quality of inmate life.

Bridging research and practice

By challenging some of our commonly held assumptions about the nature of prison crowding, I hope to broaden our understanding of the issues. The debate and research on prison crowding will, no doubt, continue. Both perspectives, the political and the analytical, are necessary. The political perspective, as represented by Bleich's paper, brings to bear different views on the purposes of incarceration and forces us to reevaluate correctional objectives. Crowding research may eventually lead to a more definitive answer on the nature and effects of crowding.

It is also important to realize that many other environmental or management influences may have a more dramatic influence on the quality of inmate life. These should not be excluded from either the political debate or the research efforts. Researchers need to take advantage of this opportunity to provide practitioners with the type of information they want and need to do their jobs effectively. Such studies will not only help forge a stronger bridge between research and practice, but may also provide important and unexpected answers concerning the effects of crowding.

References

Bleich, Jeff. 1989. "The politics of prison crowding." *California Law Review*, 77(5), October.

Gaes, Gerald G. 1990. "Prison crowding re-examined." Washington, DC: Office of Research, Federal Bureau of Prisons.

Useem, Bert and Kimball, Peter. 1989. *States of Siege: U.S. Prison Riots, 1971–1986*. New York: Oxford University Press.

Reprinted from: Gerald G. Gaes, Director of Research, Federal Bureau of Prisons, "Challenging Beliefs About Prison Crowding." In *Federal Prisons Journal*, 2(3): 19–23. Copyright © 1991 Department of Justice, Federal Bureau of Prisons. Reprinted by permission of the author.

2

A National Study of Correctional Administrators' Views on Prison Crowding

Michael S. Vaughn

Focus Questions

1. What factors do correctional administrators believe have contributed to crowding?

2. How can crowding be reduced?

3. How have administrators responded to prison crowding?

4. According to corrections officials, what alternatives to prison would work but are not currently being implemented?

5. What do correctional administrators think the public wants?

... One of the primary problems with contemporary correctional policy is that it is usually created by politicians who talk tough, judges and legislators who have never set foot inside a prison, and governors who are driven by the desire to cut budgets. Correctional administrators have been neglected by the bureaucratic apparatus that makes policy, inasmuch as legislators, governors, and the courts rarely tap their practical

experience when policy is formulated. Policies are intended to respond to public fears about crime, but problems arise when too little focus is given to the long-term implications of such policies. Correctional administrators' views should be instructive, albeit not imperative, in the formulation of public policy because they are the professionals who ultimately translate policy into action. It is with these matters that the research reported in this paper was concerned.

By examining the level of acceptance and the implementation of these philosophies, this paper will explore how each philosophy has contributed to prison overcrowding. Survey data will be presented from the 50 state correctional directors, who were asked about the extent of overcrowding in their systems and their policies directed at alleviating overpopulation. This paper will also explore the use of alternatives to incarceration, the issue of which offenders are perceived to be eligible for incarceration options, and the question of whether the use of alternatives has reduced prison overcrowding. In conclusion, the paper argues that correctional administrators should play a more active role in the formulation of public policy than they have in the last 20 years.

Methodology

This paper deals with the findings of a larger research project that examined administrative responses to overcrowding in adult institutional facilities. It expands on previous efforts by Holbert and Call (1989) and Sapp (1983a, 1983b, 1984). The purpose of this study was to identify the factors that correctional administrators believe have contributed to overcrowding in institutions and the administrative responses that they have adopted to alleviate overpopulation. Additional information was obtained about the directors' actions that had alleviated

11

prison overcrowding and the tactics that were not currently in use but that the administrators believed could reduce overpopulation. Punishment philosophies of the correctional directors were also sought for the purpose of gauging (a) each director's perception of the views of the citizens in his or her state, (b) each director's understanding of his or her state's current official philosophy, and (c) each director's views on the philosophy that his or her state should adopt in order to reduce overpopulation most effectively. The study also sought to determine the administrators' perceptions of the factors that they believed were causing overpopulation and the solutions that could help resolve the problem. Correctional directors were selected as subjects of study because they manage the social organizations that represent the fastest-growing item in many state budgets. It is appropriate to solicit the opinions and views of correctional managers on public policy formulation because they are ultimately charged with policy implementation.

During the summer of 1990, questionnaires were mailed to the commissioners of corrections in all 50 states as part of a study on administrative responses to overcrowding in adult institutional facilities. Follow-up questionnaires were mailed to those administrators who did not return the initial survey. Usable questionnaires were returned from all 50 states.

Although each survey was addressed to the prison system's director, the persons who returned the questionnaires held a variety of posts, including deputy director, administrative assistant, research adviser, and planning official. If the commissioner did not fill out the survey, the respondent to whom this task was delegated was encouraged to convey the philosophy of the top executive. In each instance in which an individual other than the correctional administrator completed the survey, the respondent held a high-level management position within the agency. This maximized the likelihood that respondents held opinions and positions that were similar to those of the directors on the questions solicited. Moreover, most prison directors, following policy, personally reviewed the completed survey.

The respondents in this study were asked about the extent of overcrowding in their institutions and, in addition, about the operational capacities of all adult institutions. Each administrator was also asked to estimate the rankings that would be assigned to four philosophies of punishment (deterrence, incapacitation, rehabilitation, and retribution) by citizens and by state officials and to indicate his or her own opinions or judgments as to the punishment philosophy that ought to be adopted by his or her state.

Findings

The Prevalence of Overcrowding

Officials in 48 states (96 percent) believed that their institutions suffered from overcrowding. There were two north central states (4 percent) that were said by their administrators not to be plagued by overpopulated institutions. There were 23 states (46 percent) that were under some type of court order to reduce prison overcrowding. Of the 27 states (54 percent) that were not under such a court order, three were under a court-imposed population cap, and six additional states had emergency release laws; both of these mechanisms limit intake of new inmates. Administrators in four states (8 percent) responded that they had previously been under court order to reduce overpopulation in correctional institutions.

Factors Contributing to Overcrowded Institutions

Overall, an average of 8.76 factors were said to contribute to overcrowding. Three-quarters (74 percent) of these factors linked crowding to increased sentence length, the drug problem, and public pressure to get tough on crime. Approximately 34 percent were related to changes in sentencing laws, 28 percent were a result of legislative discretion in altering applicable statutes, 22 percent were a result of court actions, and 16 percent were a result of correctional administrative decisions.

Of the 50 respondents, 46 (92 percent) reported that longer sentences were the primary factor contributing to the overpopulation of adult correctional facilities. Nearly as many, 45 (90 percent), believed that public demand for increased sentences contributed to overpopulation, and 44 (88 percent) cited the incarceration of drug offenders. There were also 44 respondents (88 percent) who believed that legislative responses to public demand contributed to overcrowding, and 37 (74 percent) said that both mandatory sentences and increases in minimum sentence length were contributing to the problem. In addition, 35 respondents (70 percent) reported that more effective law enforcement practices and techniques were responsible for overpopulated prisons, and 26 (52 percent) reported that stringent parole requirements were restricting early release of inmates. There were 23 respondents (46 percent) who maintained that determinate sentencing was a contributing factor. A shift in public policy from rehabilitation to incapacitation and an increase in the incidence of criminal activities were each cited by 21 respondents (42 percent). Although 13 respondents (26 percent) cited the abolition of good time and the same number held paroling authorities liable for previously released inmates, only 10 (20 percent) cited the abolition of parole as contributing to the problem. Both demographic factors and presumptive sentencing were reported by nine respondents (18 percent). Only six respondents (12 percent) reported that the abolition of gain time led to prison overcrowding.

Administrative Responses to Overpopulated Prisons

Each state had adopted, on average, approximately eight responses in an attempt to alleviate overcrowding. Of all the administrative responses, 38 percent were related in some way to increasing the operational capacity of adult institutions. Of the 50 states, 47 (94 percent) were embarking on construction programs to build new prisons or to increase the number of cell blocks. There were 42 states (84 percent) that were double- or triple-bunking, 29 (58 percent) were converting nonprison properties such as motels, office buildings, mental hospitals, and juvenile facilities to correctional use, and 27 states (54 percent) were converting existing

prison facilities (such as gyms, chapels, auditoriums, and warehouses) to create additional bed space.

Although the primary administrative response to overpopulated adult institutions involved increasing the existing design capacity, keeping inmates or releasing inmates back into the community was another popular alternative, representing 33 percent of all administrative responses. There were 41 states (82 percent), for example, that were using community service programs (such as furlough, educational and work release, and halfway houses). This tactic appeared to be a safety valve by which directors shifted inmates to other locations when operational capacities reached court or statutory limits. In addition, intensive probation supervision and house arrest or electronic monitoring were used in, respectively, 36 states (72 percent) and 35 states (70 percent) as methods of reducing crowding.

Whereas 20 states (40 percent) were increasing their use of traditional probation, respondents in 19 states (38 percent) reported the use of graduated release programs involving an increase in good time, growth in gain time, additional prison labor credits, and accelerated early release by paroling officials. Prison officials in 18 states (36 percent) were using both shock probation and boot camp retreats to reduce crowding. There were 14 states (28 percent) that reported implementation of emergency release laws, and 12 (24 percent) had adopted either direct imposition of a mixed sentence or incarceration as a condition of probation. Respondents in only eight states (16 percent) reported the use of intermittent incarceration, and six states (12 percent) cited reductions in intake. Court-mandated early release and drug testing in lieu of incarceration were used in, respectively, four states (8 percent) and three states (6 percent).

Additional Administrative Responses

Each respondent was asked whether there were administrative responses or alternatives to incarceration that were not currently in use in his or her state but that could reduce overpopulation. . . . Thirty respondents believed that supplemental administrative responses could be adopted. Respondents in 16 states (32 percent) wished that lawmakers would conduct sentencing impact studies before enacting stiffer criminal penalties. Prison directors in 14 states (28 percent) advocated increased use of diversion programs, and the same number advocated expansion of intensive probation supervision. Administrators in 13 states (26 percent) believed that a greater reliance on community resources and services should be attempted, and respondents in five states (10 percent) wanted to increase the applications of electronic monitoring and house arrest. Reinstitution of parole, enlargement of operational capacity, implementation of more boot camp retreats, and reliance on shock incarceration were supported by administrators in four states (8 percent).

Administrative Responses That Have Reduced Crowding

Respondents were also asked which administrative responses, if any, had actually alleviated prison crowding. . . . In brief, the findings show that, on the basis of the implementation of administrative responses, no apparent differences exist between states that reported reductions in crowding and those that did not. This finding is predictable because states have differing correctional policies and disparate levels of intake. . . .

Types of Offenders Eligible for Alternatives to Incarceration

The questionnaire asked which inmates should be eligible for alternatives to incarceration. Respondents in 45 states (90 percent) answered that property offenders should be eligible for such alternatives; only two (4 percent) would offer alternatives to violent offenders. In a similar vein, no respondent suggested that repeat or habitual felony offenders should be eligible for alternatives to incarceration, and only 14 (28 percent) believed that repeat misdemeanor offenders should qualify. There were 47 respondents (94 percent) who said that first-time misdemeanor offenders should be placed in alternatives, but only 38 (76 percent) expressed a desire to offer alternatives to first-time fel-

ony offenders. Finally, according to 22 respondents (44 percent), those offenders who traditionally receive no sanction should be eligible for alternatives. This last finding suggests that, as more inmates become involved in diversion programs, the influence of the criminal justice system increases over offenders who previously would have received no sanction.

Philosophy of Punishment

. . . Respondents stated that, if prisons are to become less crowded, incapacitation should not be a primary concern. For a system ideally tailored to reduce crowding, directors cited deterrence as the preferred philosophy, implying that society ought first to attempt to prevent crimes from occurring; in the event that crimes continue to be committed, rehabilitation should become the secondary goal. In case crimes cannot be prevented and criminals cannot be rehabilitated, incapacitation should be the tertiary goal. Although prison officials said that the citizens of their states favored retribution, they themselves ranked retribution as least important. Overall, responses reflected a desire to reduce incapacitation as the primary philosophy of punishment.

Discussion

Administrative Strategies and Punishment Philosophies

Although Skovron, Scott, and Cullen (1988) showed that states used front-door strategies, back-door strategies, and expansion of capacity to reduce overcrowding (Austin, 1986), the respondents in this study reported that states relied most frequently on increasing operational capacity and reducing the number of inmates to be incarcerated. . . .

Which Punishment Philosophy Controls Decisions?

For both the current state punishment philosophy and the ideal punishment philosophy to reduce overcrowding, the respondents ranked incapacitation as the highest priority and retribution as the lowest priority. If incapacitation were truly a state's primary philosophy, violent offenders should be more eligible for incarceration alternatives than property offenders, because violent offenders are less likely to recidivate (Graber, 1980). Yet, in response to the question about which inmates should be eligible for alternatives to incarceration, prison administrators replied that property offenders should receive alternatives more often than violent offenders. Assuming inmates who are potentially eligible for alternatives are perceived as less threatening, prison directors apparently believe that violent offenders are more of a threat to society than property offenders. However, this hypothesis is not supported by recent research (Roberts & Gebotys, 1989), which shows that offenders who are convicted of very serious violent crimes, if they are not habitual or repeat offenders, are less likely to recidivate than those who are convicted of property crimes.

Even though prison directors cited retribution as high among their perception of citizens' preferences, they also stated that retribution was the least important objective for their states' current philosophies and for their ideal philosophy to reduce crowding. However, the respondents' answers to the question about incarceration alternatives support the view that prison administrators, concurring with their perceptions of society at large, support retributive purposes of punishment. If this supposition is accurate, retribution and punishment may be the real goals of policymakers and correctional officials, whereas other punishment philosophies such as incapacitation, deterrence, and rehabilitation are the stated goals.

Not all research, however, supports the hypothesis that the public harbors negative attitudes toward rehabilitation. Gottfredson, Warner, and Taylor (1988) found that correctional administrators overestimated the public's punitive views. Their investigation suggested that the public favored deterrence and rehabilitation as the primary objectives of punishment and cited nonutilitarian objectives less frequently: Retribution was ranked lowest, and incapacitation was ranked only third. Similar findings have been reported by other researchers, who

found public support for community corrections and rehabilitative programs (Cullen, Clark, & Wozniak, 1985; Riley & McNickle-Rose, 1980).

Although this paper was not designed to determine whether prison administrators were conversant with citizens' views of punishment, it supports earlier research showing that corrections officials perceived a punitive public. If earlier research reporting public support for utilitarian goals of punishment is correct, it would appear that prison administrators have misperceived public opinion. Indeed, there is mounting evidence suggesting that policymakers overestimate the public's punitiveness and misunderstand the community's needs (Murphy & Pilotta, 1987). This disturbing finding highlights the complex nature of correctional policy formulation and points to the need for additional research in this developing area.

Conclusion

"Most experts argue that a prison is crowded when more than 85 percent of its cells are occupied" (Toch, 1985, p. 64). In stark contrast, this study found that the 50 state prison systems were operating, on average, at 122 percent of their current capacity: 613,046 inmates were being housed in facilities designed to accommodate 501,070. Although a plethora of research on prison crowding has been conducted, Gaes (1991) has pointed out that criminologists show little interest in studying administrative strategies and procedures; most of the research on prison crowding has focused on the institutional conditions, the pains of imprisonment, and the problems associated with the crowded conditions (Ruback & Innes, 1988). This paper, however, has addressed an issue that is of top concern to prison administrators—the strategies and procedures used to manage facilities that possess more inmates than they are designed to hold.

This paper has indicated that states currently rely on incapacitation as the primary justification for punishment, but it must be noted that it is difficult to separate incapacitation from retribution. Political support for retribution and incapacitation is demonstrated by America's incarceration of vast numbers of individuals (Gibbons, 1988; Travis, 1989). The implementation of these punishment philosophies requires a major infusion of financial resources, and maximum security construction estimates range from $70,000 (Reed, 1984) to $155,000 (Zawitz, 1988) per cell. In addition, this paper has revealed that, although incapacitation is the dominant philosophy, correctional officials believe that deterrence and rehabilitation should receive more support.

Competent professionals and staff are not consistently providing input into correctional policy, even though they are capable of contributing valuable information to the debate. Public policy is frequently shaped by politicians who pay little attention to correctional experts. With the shift in policy over the last 20 years, politicians and policymakers have become polarized into "an endless cycle of recriminations" against the correctional system (Murphy & Dison, 1990, p. 163). Many seem to be unwilling to face the political pressures of special interest groups and depart from conventional techniques to sketch a fresh route for correctional reform. This paper has argued that correctional administrators should influence the formulation of public policy by playing an active role in the correctional policy debate. If correctional administrators do not enter the public policy debate, correctional policy will continue to be manipulated by political demagogues.

Although this paper has argued that correctional administrators must be given larger roles in the formulation of public policy, this does not mean that administrators should create public policy simply because they have practical experience. Rather, administrators should be permitted to provide rational input into public policy. This can be effected by giving correctional administrators the opportunity to participate along with politicians, judges, journalists, researchers, and special interest groups in the debate on prison crowding.

References

Austin, J. (1986). Using early release to relieve prison crowding: A dilemma in public policy. *Crime and Delinquency, 32,* 404–502.

Cullen, F. T., Clark, G. A., & Wozniak, J. F. (1985). Explaining the get tough movement: Can the public be blamed? *Federal Probation, 49*(2), 16–24.

Gaes, G. G. (1991). Challenging beliefs about prison crowding. *Federal Prisons Journal, 2*(3), 19–23.

Gibbons, D. C. (1988). *The limits of punishment as social policy.* San Francisco, CA: National Council on Crime and Delinquency.

Gottfredson, S. D., Warner, B. D., & Taylor, R. B. (1988). Conflict and consensus about criminal justice in Maryland. In N. Walker & M. Hough (Eds.), *Public attitudes to sentencing: Surveys from five countries* (pp. 16–55). Aldershot, England: Gower Publishing.

Graber, D. A. (1980). *Crime, news, and the public.* New York, NY: Praeger.

Holbert, F., & Call, J. E. (1989). The perspective of state correctional officials on prison overcrowding: Causes, court orders, and solutions. *Federal Probation, 53*(1), 25–32.

Langan, P. A. (1991). America's soaring prison population. *Science, 251,* 1568–1573.

Murphy, J. W., & Dison, J. E. (1990). Conclusion. In J. W. Murphy & J. E. Dison (Eds.), *Are prisons any better? Twenty years of correctional reform* (pp. 163–172). Newbury Park, CA: Sage.

Murphy, J. W., & Pilotta, J. J. (1987). Research note: Identifying at risk persons in community based research. *Sociology of Health and Illness, 9,* 62–75.

Reed, R. J. (1984). Prison overcrowding: The Connecticut response. *Western New England Law Review, 7,* 389–396.

Riley, P. J., & McNickle-Rose, V. (1980). Public vs. elite opinion on correctional reform: Implications for social policy. *Journal of Criminal Justice, 8,* 345–356.

Roberts, J. V., & Gebotys, R. J. (1989). The purposes of sentencing: Public support for competing aims. *Behavioral Sciences and the Law, 7,* 387–402.

Ruback, R. B., & Innes, C. A. (1988). The relevance and irrelevance of psychological research: The example of prison crowding. *American Psychologist, 43,* 683–693.

Sapp, A. D. (1983a). *Administration responses to prison overcrowding: A survey of prison administrators.* Unpublished manuscript, Central Missouri State University, Center for Criminal Justice Research, Warrensburg.

——. (1983b). *Correctional administrators' perceptions of contributory factors and effects of prison overpopulation.* Unpublished manuscript, Central Missouri State University, Center for Criminal Justice Research, Warrensburg.

——. (1984). Prison overcrowding: A survey. In D. N. Travisono (Ed.), *Vital statistics in corrections* (pp. 54–55). College Park, MD: American Correctional Association.

Skovron, S. E., Scott, J. E., & Cullen, F. T. (1988). Prison crowding: Public attitudes toward strategies of population control. *Journal of Research in Crime and Delinquency, 25,* 150–169.

Toch, H. (1985). Warehouses for people? *The Annals of the American Academy of Political and Social Science, 478,* 58–72.

Travis, L. F. (1989). Crowding in American prisons and jails: Causes, effects, and possible solutions. *The Justice Professional, 4,* 257–278.

Zawitz, M. W. (Ed.). (1988). *Report to the nation on crime and justice* (2nd ed.). Washington, DC: U.S. Department of Justice, Bureau of Justice Statistics.

3
Report From an Overcrowded Maze

Dannie M. Martin
Peter Y. Sussman

Focus Questions

1. What is the purpose of developing a caged mentality?

2. What are the effects of crowding inside the prison, in Martin and Sussman's view?

3. How might prison crowding affect a prisoner's reintegration to society upon release from prison?

4. How do the revised federal sentencing laws contribute to crowding?

Phoenix, Ariz. (Sept. 3, 1989)—A man was stabbed in the chest in a noisy mess hall as we ate lunch one day in Lompoc penitentiary in California. He ran by the table where I was eating with three other men. Dark arterial blood was pumping out of his chest and splashing onto the floor within three feet of our table.

We watched him leave the dining room and then finished our lunch. After the meal, I remarked to one of the cons I'd been eating with that it seemed to me we should at least have lost our appetite.

"I don't see why we should've," he replied. "It was his problem, not ours."

I had been in prison for seven years at that time, and I began to realize that something drastic had happened to me. I had divorced my feelings from the things I could see about me, and my senses had withdrawn to a world that had nothing much to do with my environment.

As I pass the nine-year mark this month, I wonder how wide the chasm between my vision and my senses will be in two more years, when I am due to be paroled.

It isn't a reassuring line of thought. But I also understand that while living in a crowded cage awash in a sea of noise, I must acquire a caged mentality or I won't survive.

The two most devastating aspects of modern prisons are noise and overcrowding. Prisons are noisy places anyway, but when they become overcrowded, as most are now, the noise becomes unbearable, and there's no escape from it.

The din of an overcrowded prison puts a heavy burden of stress on us all. We become, among other things, tense, irritable, introverted, bitter, paranoid, and violent.

A study of overcrowding done on a colony of laboratory mice back in the '50s uncovered many types of abnormal behavior. Cannibalism, self-mutilation, aggressive behavior (to the point of attacking any moving object), sexual ambiguity, and introversion. Those characteristics were brought about by overcrowding, not by deprivation of food or other necessities.

Looking about me, I can see stark examples of those mouse aberrations manifesting themselves in closely confined men. Much of that overcrowding results from legislative changes, and the effects on individuals can be painful to behold.

A twenty-year-old man came here recently from the East Coast. He was sentenced to fifteen years with no possibility of parole under the new federal sentencing code. He was convicted of bank robbery, and it's his first trip to prison. The new sentencing code allows very little credit for good time, and he will have to serve about thirteen years before his release.

Not long after he arrived here, he was placed in Isolation by mistake when the authorities confused his name with that of a notorious stool pigeon. Soon after that incident, he was assigned a cell with a weight lifter twice his size who tried to force him into a homosexual act, then beat him within an inch of his life when he refused.

He approached a guard with one eye swollen shut, and through mangled, swollen lips, he mumbled that he'd like a cell change.

"There's no room," the guard replied. "You'll have to stay where you were assigned."

The young man then violated another rule so that he could be put back in Isolation in order to get a cell change and a new cell partner.

"I never thought prison was this bad," he told me in the yard when he was released from Isolation.

I assured him that this prison is not as bad as maximum-security prisons like Leavenworth and Lompoc. He didn't seem to take much consolation from that fact.

Stories like that young man's will become more common as bewildered newcomers and cage-wise cons are pressed ever tighter because of tough new sentencing laws.

The small cellblock I live in was designed for 60 men in single cells. There are more than 120 of us in here now, with all the cells doubled up. We don't choose our cell partners. When a bunk becomes vacant, another convict is moved in.

When you live in a small cell with another convict, his presence is always there, whether you're using the toilet, writing a letter, or reading a book. It's a much closer relationship than a marriage. But it's between two people who usually don't want to live with each other.

Outside the cell, the lines and lists go on forever. We stand in a long line three times a day in order to eat. At the prison store, we wait in a raucous crowd until our name is called. We stand in line to be strip-searched before visits with people on the outside, then stand in line to be strip-searched after the visit. We line up at the laundry and line up to sign up for a phone call.

Anyone who wants to work in hobbycraft finds there's a three- or four-month waiting list for a hobby card. When the prison is overcrowded, all the lines and lists are longer.

I've seen convicts go crazy while standing in a line; they begin hitting and kicking everyone they can reach. For someone with an aversion to lines, this aspect of prison is hell on Earth.

Many prisoners in this pressure-cooker environment develop antisocial coping mechanisms.

When people tour a prison, they see convicts nonchalantly making their way to jobs or standing patiently in chow lines waiting to eat. In the cellblocks, they see us playing pinochle or lying in a cell reading a book. They go away thinking that we live a calm existence.

But the real world of convicts lies hidden from the view of a tourist. These crowds of seemingly uniform prisoners are banded together in groups that work against the laws of the prison system itself.

Some convicts like to drink, and four or five of them will get together and make wine regularly. Others gamble and run betting pools. Stolen food and government merchandise are bought and sold. Drug users band together in schemes to obtain their drug of choice.

The guards don't see much more of our real world than the tourists, unless they happen to stumble upon someone using drugs or gambling.

We've developed codes and signals to protect our world. I can look at a convict across the building from me and put my right index finger under my eye, and he will nod his head and remain standing where he is while I go back into my cell.

I've just told him to watch for the guard, and he will stand there and watch until I come out and signal him that I'm finished with whatever I'm doing. A convict will do that for someone he doesn't even know, and we all know the signal. It's only one of many we use to communicate in our own world.

By nurturing our hidden life and being loyal to it, we find some relief from the crowds and the noise. Even if it's only a drunk, a high, or an exciting wager, it helps. The best of it all is that it's hidden from view and belongs to us alone.

Naturally, some of this goes on all the time in all prisons, but overcrowding encourages the climate of lawlessness; it spurs us to develop our subterranean activities.

When a 60-man cellblock is made into a 120-man cellblock, there is still only one guard. His job becomes twice as hard, even as the extra convicts help to develop more schemes.

The overcrowding pushes us further toward introversion, secretiveness, clique mentality, violence, and deceit. Those aren't the traits society wants to foster in a man headed back to the "free world" someday.

The new federal sentencing law, approved by the Supreme Court early this year, is adding another dimension of madness in already overcrowded prisons. Because of the "get-tough" legislation, judges will no longer have much of a say in sentencing. Whatever the circumstances of the crime, the sentence is definite and final. Parole is abolished. The basic unfairness of those harsh new sentences is hard to believe.

Every week, people are coming in here with twenty-five and thirty-year sentences with no chance of parole. Many of them are as young as nineteen and twenty. They are more abusive toward guards and violent toward fellow convicts. They don't have anything to lose. The courts have tattooed the term "criminal" on the foreheads of young men who might still have had a chance to take other routes.

Recently, at a 4:00 P.M. standing count here, a guard walked by a convict's cell and told him to stand up.

"Fuck you!" was the reply.

The guard asked him again to stand up.

"I said fuck you!" the man replied and remained sitting down.

After the count, some guards came and led him off to Isolation. A few days later, when he was released from the hole, I asked him why he had done that.

"I have a ten-year sentence with no parole," he told me. "I only get one year good time, so I have to do nine years if I'm a good boy. Well, I'd rather lose that year of good time right now and do ten years my way than nine their way. I'll stand up when I feel like it, and I meant exactly what I said: Fuck him!"

Older convicts are in a state of shock right now because of the heavy impact on them of the new sentencing law. A forty-five-year-old man whom I've known for years just received a thirty-year sentence for possession of a gun. His prior crimes were two second degree burglaries and an assault that didn't involve a weapon. He will have to serve twenty-five years in prison before he's eligible to be released.

"I can't believe this," he says. "People don't do this much time for murder. If I do survive this sentence, I will be seventy years old when I get out."

"What if you do live through it?" I asked him. "What will you do at that age when you are released?"

"Man, if I have to do all that time and finally get back out, the only thing I'll want to know is if that judge and that prosecutor are still alive," he replied.

A man here from Seattle pleaded guilty to a conspiracy to sell cocaine. It was a plea bargain, and he received twenty years, of which he will have to serve eighteen years in prison. He is forty-seven years old.

I told him I couldn't understand how someone could plead guilty in exchange for eighteen years in prison. I would take my chances in court.

"They held back another charge," he said. "If I refused the plea bargain, they were going to add that charge as well and give me thirty years."

Members of gangs from the inner cities are already arriving here in large numbers. Most of them were sentenced to long, non-paroleable terms under the new sentencing guidelines. These are kids who grew up in ghettos bumming quarters to play Pac Man machines.

They've heard the slogans "War on Drugs" and "War on Crime" used so often that now they believe it. When people go down on their turf, they are war casualties to them, not victims.

They wear their gang colors in prison yards now, and their young eyes burn with an old, hard look of having nothing much more to lose. It's as if they are saying: "Well, you got tough on us. Now what?"

Not long ago at Phoenix, the isolation building became so full that convicts had to be put on a waiting list to go to the hole. Often, when a man finishes his isolation time, he has to languish in there another two weeks until a mainline cell comes open.

I sometimes wonder what happened to those deranged mice when the overcrowding study was completed. I doubt they were turned loose to roam in an innocent colony of field mice.

But most of these convicts with unnaturally long sentences will survive and eventually be released. After fifteen or twenty years in a noisy, violent, overcrowded prison, some of them are going to make Freddy Kreuger look like an Eagle Scout.

Chapter I
Discussion

Institutional Crowding

Gerald Gaes questions the validity of previous prison crowding research and attempts to dispel the myth that crowding is a root cause of most prison problems. He provides evidence that crowding may be linked to but does not directly cause unconstitutional prison conditions. He mentions that crowding has been used over the last two decades as an excuse for courts to intervene in prison management. Further, crowding has been used by correctional administrators as a reason to increase funding and to mask poor prison management. Gaes underscores the need to examine factors other than crowding that contribute to problems in prison.

In contrast to Gaes, the selection by Martin and Sussman establishes a clear connection between crowded conditions and undesirable character traits, such as "introversion, secretiveness, clique mentality, violence, and deceit." These traits are what some prison observers refer to as the "prisoner's code of conduct," which rewards individuals for violence as the primary form of communication. One conclusion that could be drawn from the Martin and Sussman article is individuals who become "prisonized" feel more comfortable living within the prison world and are less capable of handling the stressors of daily life outside the prison walls. The "caged mentality" the authors describe develops as a coping mechanism to deal with the noise and lack of privacy. An argument might be made that the caged mentality exists to a higher degree in supermax prisons where everyone has his or her own cell. This is because prisoners in the most secure prison units remain locked in their cell 23 hours per day. Overcrowding is thus not an issue, but the unbearable noise remains.

Vaughn's study of correctional officials showed that administrators recognize the importance of crime prevention and rehabilitation, but they believe that prisons function to incarcerate people who have not been deterred from crime. Prison administrators felt that correctional crowding resulted primarily from a change in sentencing laws, longer sentences, and a reliance on incapacitation as a response to drug use and other types of criminal behavior. Although most states were increasing the capacities of prison institutions or converting existing buildings into prisons, many administrators favored utilizing more community corrections programs as alternatives to incarceration, especially for property offenders.

Chapter II
Introduction

Growth in the Number of Women Prisoners

Common Assumptions	Reality
• Women prisoners encompass a small and inconsequential segment of the entire prisoner population.	• Even though women prisoners comprise only 6.6 percent of all prisoners, the increase in women prisoners is proportionally greater than that of men prisoners (Beck and Harrison 2001).
• Women are committing more violent crimes and are increasingly becoming a threat to public safety.	• Most women are incarcerated for drug-related and nonviolent crimes that are related to being economically and socially disadvantaged. The vast majority of women criminals are not a threat to public safety and may not require incarceration as punishment (Stanko 2001).

In 2001, over 91,600 women, representing 6.6 percent of the total prisoner population, were housed in adult correctional institutions (Beck and Harrison 2001). This represents twice the number of incarcerated women held in jails and prisons one decade ago. Likewise, arrest and conviction trends show that the criminal justice system is less lenient toward women than it did in the past.

As an example, the war on drugs has changed the way that drug offenders are processed and punished. That is, mandatory sentencing laws and sentencing guidelines have reduced the amount of judicial discretion. For instance, Pollock (1999, 96) notes that federal sentencing guidelines do not allow for caretaker status to be used as a mitigating circumstance during sentencing. Because many women are primary caretakers

(and often sole caretakers) of dependent children, a larger number of children grow up in homes of extended family members. Although recent laws have increased sentence lengths for male and female drug users and lower-level drug dealers alike, women have been affected in greater proportions by the societal trend to get tough on crime.

Statistical data show that women and men have different criminal behavior patterns (Pollock 1999). This evidence is supported by qualitative interviews that depict many women as followers in a criminal event. Women were influenced by men to commit crimes, but women more often played secondary roles in group criminal behavior (Alarid et al. 1996). Female criminality was intertwined with poverty, drug use, and lack of skills and education (Sanchez

2001). Furthermore, many women prisoners were victimized physically, sexually, and emotionally prior to their incarceration (Stanko 2001).

Jails and prisons were built initially to incarcerate people who threatened public safety and who required rehabilitation to reform their behavior. Many treatment opportunities today exist within the community, and a community corrections sentence allows women to maintain close ties with their dependent children. The majority of women prisoners do not exhibit predatory behavior requiring imprisonment and are able to complete a sentence in the community.

Recommended Readings

Alarid, Leanne F., James W. Marquart, Velmer S. Burton, Francis T. Cullen, and Steven J. Cuvelier. (1996). "Women's Roles in Serious Offenses: A Study of Adult Felons." *Justice Quarterly* 13 (3): 431–454.

Beck, Allen J., and Paige M. Harrison. (2001). *Prisoners in 2000.* Washington, DC: U.S. Department of Justice, Bureau of Justice Statistics.

Maher, Lisa, and Kathleen Daly. (1996). "Women in the Street Level Drug Economy: Continuity or Change?" *Criminology* 34 (4): 465–498.

Miller, Eleanor. (1985). *Street Woman.* Philadelphia, PA: Temple University Press.

Pollock, Joycelyn M. (1999). *Criminal Women.* Cincinnati, OH: Anderson.

Pollock-Byrne, Joycelyn M. (1990). *Women, Prison, and Crime.* Pacific Grove, CA: Brooks/Cole.

Sanchez, Lisa. (2001). "Gender Troubles: The Entanglement of Agency, Violence, and Law in the Lives of Women in Prostitution.. In C. M. Renzetti and L. Goodstein (eds.), *Women, Crime, and Criminal Justice* (pp. 60–76). Los Angeles: Roxbury Publishing.

Simpson, Sally, and L. Elis. (1995). "Doing Gender: Sorting out the Caste and Crime Conundrum." *Criminology* 33 (1): 47–81.

Stanko, Elizabeth A. (2001). "Women, Danger, and Criminology," Pp. 13–26 in In C. M. Renzetti and L. Goodstein (eds.), *Women, Crime, and Criminal Justice* (pp. 13–26). Los Angeles: Roxbury Publishing.

Steffensmeier, Darryl, J. Kramer, and Cathy Streifel. (1993). "Gender and Imprisonment Decisions." *Criminology* 31 (3): 411–446.

Internet Websites

Amnesty International. The Impact of the War on Drugs on Women. Available: *http://www.amnesty-usa.org/rightsforall/women/factsheets/drugs.html*

Amnesty International. Mothers behind bars. Available: *http://www.amnesty-usa.org/rightsforall/women/report/women-101.html*

The February 2001 issue of *Corrections Today* is devoted to correctional issues of female offenders. Available: *http://www.corrections.com/aca/cortoday/index.html*

Kalfrin, V. (1999, 21 September). Girls chase boys in lives of crime. *APB News* [Online]. Available: *http://www.apbnews.com/newscenter/breakingnews/1999/09/21/juveniles0921_01.html*

Kurshan, N. (n.d.). Women and imprisonment in the U.S. Available: *http://www.prisonactivist.org/women-and-imprisonment.html*

Women's Federal Prison Camp, Pekin, Illinois. Available: *http://www.drcnet.org/pubs/guide/10-95/visit.html*

4
Examining Trends in Female Incarceration

Meda Chesney-Lind

Focus Questions

1. According to Chesney-Lind, what factors contribute to the tremendous growth in the number of women prisoners in the last two decades?

2. What evidence does the author provide for her assertions?

3. What background characteristics do many women in prison have, according to the American Correctional Association national survey?

4. What solutions are proposed to decrease the growth of the number of women in prison?

Since 1980, the number of women imprisoned in the United States has tripled. Now, on any given day, over 80,000 women are locked up in American jails and prisons. Increases in the rates of women incarcerated surpassed male rate increases every year in the last decade, and an unprecedented number of expensive prison cells are being built for women (Bureau of Justice Statistics, 1991a:2; Bureau of Justice Statistics, 1991b:4).

It is now clear that while the notion that the women's movement produced a flood of female crime, which received extensive publicity in the 1970s, has been largely discredited (see Chesney-Lind, 1986, for a review of this debate), another trend—that of skyrocketing increases in the numbers of women in prison—is an incontrovertible fact, and yet this situation has met with far less media attention.

This chapter will attempt to make sense of this dramatic shift in the pattern of women's imprisonment. In particular, this is an effort to determine whether the increase in women's imprisonment is a product of a change in women's crime or a shift in the criminal justice system's response to women offenders.

Discussing the situation of women offenders, including women in prison, has historically attracted far less interest in both mainstream and feminist criminology than considerations of women as victims. As a consequence, there has been little effort made by feminist as well as traditional scholars to interpret this unprecedented interest in the imprisoning of women. Such has not been true of the correctional establishment, whose primary response to overcrowding in women's prisons has been a rush to build more prison space, often at an enormous cost. Such a willingness to spend millions of dollars—per state—incarcerating women stands, of course, in stark contrast to the paucity of resources made available to other women's programs.

Given these patterns, this chapter contends that the feminist movement and feminist scholars must make the decarceration of women a part of their political agendas. Since, as this chapter attempts to show, there are clear indications that the extraordinary increases in women's imprisonment have been a product of criminal justice policy shifts rather than significant changes in women's criminal behavior, equally dramatic reductions in women's prison populations ought to be within reach. Indeed, this paper contends that the decarceration of women is a viable political strategy and might well be a model for reducing our reliance on imprisoning men as well.

Imprisoning Women

Stark increases in the number of women held in state and federal prisons marked each year of the last decade. In 1980, there were 12,331 women in our nation's prisons. By 1990, that number had grown to 43,845, an increase of 256 percent. In 1980, there were 303,643 males in prison. This number grew to 727,398 in 1990, an increase of 139.6 percent (Bureau of Justice Statistics, 1991b:1). Clearly, while the numbers of incarcerated men far exceed the numbers of incarcerated women (women are 5.5 percent of the state prison population, 7.5 percent of the federal prison population, and 9.5 percent of the jail population) (Bureau of Justice Statistics, 1991a:2; Bureau of Justice Statistics, 1991b:4), the increase in the number of incarcerated women is alarming and deserves our a attention. In fact, the United States now imprisons more people than at any other time in its history. According to a recent study by the Sentencing Project (LaFranier, 1991:A-3), the United States has the highest rate of incarceration in the world.

These trends have triggered two types of responses. First, among those in the correctional bureaucracies across the United States there has been a "boom" in the creation of new women's institutions. Second, among many in the media, and some in academia, there has again been speculation that these numbers signal the emergence of a new, tougher female criminal whose appearance has necessitated increased reliance on imprisonment. . . . Are the women currently doing time in U.S. prisons there because their offenses were so serious that no choice but imprisonment was possible?

New, Tougher Women Criminals?

Increases in women's imprisonment surpassed increases experienced by men every year between 1981 and 1989—a pattern that was finally broken in 1990 when the male rate of increase edged slightly ahead of the women's rate (8.3 percent compared with 7.9 percent). This pattern was not found in the commitments to federal prisons, however; here women's incarceration jumped 36.8 percent between 1989 and 1990, compared with only 13 percent for men. It must be recalled, however, that the male rate of incarceration is still substantially higher than that of women. In 1990, for example, the male incarceration rate was 566 per 100,000, compared with 31 per 100,000 for women (Bureau of Justice Statistics, 1991b:4).

Some may suggest that the dramatic percentage increases in women's incarceration are simply an artifact of the smaller base numbers involved in women's imprisonment. For this reason, the increases in the jailing of women should be placed in historical context. Women made up 4 percent of the nation's imprisoned population shortly after the turn of the century. By 1970, the figure had dropped to 3 percent. By 1990, however, more than 5.7 percent of those incarcerated were women. In addition, the rate of women's imprisonment grew from 6 per 100,000 in 1925 to 31 per 100,000 in 1990 (Cahalan, 1986; Bureau of Justice Statistics, 1991b). Finally, the base numbers involved in women's imprisonment are no longer small, and large increases continue. In 1990, for example, the relatively "small" increase in the number of women incarcerated in federal and state prisons meant that the number of women behind bars climbed from 40,566 to 43,855.

By contrast, total arrests of women (which might be seen as a measure of women's criminal activity) increased by 60 percent between 1981 and 1990. The FBI reports that Part 1 arrests (including arrests for murder, rape, aggravated assault, robbery, burglary, larceny-theft, motor vehicle theft, and arson) of women increased by about 46 percent during the same time period, while Part 1 arrests of men increased by about 26 percent (Federal Bureau of Investigation, 1991:178). While these trends in women's crime may appear to be serious, it should be noted that most of the increase in women's arrests is accounted for by more arrests of women for nonviolent property offenses, such as shoplifting, check forgery, and welfare fraud, as well as for substance abuse offenses such as driving under the influence of alcohol and drug offenses.

... In one five-year period (1986–1990) arrests of women increased by about 29.3 percent, while arrests of men increased by 19.5 percent. Arrests of women for Part 1, or crime index, offenses showed a slightly smaller increase (21.2 percent), while male arrests for these offenses increased by 17.4 percent (Federal Bureau of Investigation, 1991:181). Jail populations for both men and women grew significantly during the same time–the women's jail population increased by 73 percent, while the men's grew by 45.6 percent (Bureau of Justice Statistics, 1991a: 2). The prison population grew by 76.9 percent for women and a lesser 46.2 percent for men (Bureau of Justice Statistics, 1991b:4). These figures suggest that increases in women's imprisonment cannot be explained by increases in women's crime, at least as measured by the number of arrests; the figures also show that the increases in women's imprisonment far outstrip those seen in the imprisonment of males.

Profiles of Women in Prison

A look at national data on the characteristics of women in state prisons confirms that women are not being imprisoned because of a jump in the seriousness of their offenses. In fact, the proportion of women imprisoned for violent offenses actually dropped during the 1980s; in 1979, nearly half (48.9 percent) of the women in prison were incarcerated for a violent offense, but by 1986, this figure had fallen to 40.7 percent. By contrast, the number of women incarcerated for property offenses increased from 36.8 percent of women's commitments in 1979 to 41.2 percent in 1986, with most of the increase accounted for by a jump in the number of women committed for larceny-theft. Increases were also noted in the percentage of women imprisoned for public order offenses (e.g., gambling, carrying weapons, and pros-

titution). Women were also slightly more likely to be incarcerated for drug offenses, but the Bureau of Justice Statistics reports that the increase was explained by a jump in the number of women incarcerated for possession of drugs rather than drug trafficking. Finally, while these same statistics also show that the majority of women in prison for drug offenses are sentenced for "trafficking" (7.3 percent compared with 4.0 percent in 1986) (Bureau of Justice Statistics, 1988), other research notes that women tend to cluster near the bottom of the drug distribution network, since, in the words of one researcher, "the serious business of trafficking, i.e. smuggling and bulk sales, is controlled and conducted by men" (Simpson, 1992; see also Steffensmeier, 1983).

Perhaps the clearest evidence that the United States is not seeing a shift in the character of women's crime comes from a recent national study on the backgrounds of women under lock and key. This research both challenges the image of a new, "tougher" inmate and begins to hint at the real causes of women's crime.

The American Correctional Association (ACA) recently conducted a national survey of imprisoned women in the United States and found that overwhelmingly they were young, economically marginalized women of color (57 percent) and mothers of children (75 percent), although only a third were married at the time of the survey (American Correctional Association, 1990). This portrait is remarkably similar to the profile found by Glick and Neto (1977) in their national study of women inmates nearly a decade and a half earlier. They found that the typical woman inmate was young, poor, nonwhite, and unmarried and was also a high school dropout and a mother.

The backgrounds of the women in the ACA study, as well as their current status, clearly show the price they have paid for being poor. About half of them ran away from home as youths, about a quarter of them had attempted suicide, and a sizable number had serious drug problems. One-half of the women used cocaine; about a quarter of them used it daily. One-fifth said they used heroin daily. Indeed, about a quarter of the adult female offenders said they committed the crime for which they were incarcerated to pay for drugs.

The ACA survey found that over half of the women surveyed were victims of physical abuse, and 36 percent had been sexually abused. Another study of women in prison in Massachusetts suggests that if anything, these figures are conservative. Mary Gilfus (1988) found that when childhood physical abuse, childhood sexual abuse, and adult rape and battering were combined, fully 88 percent of her sample had experienced at least one major form of violent victimization. About one-third of the women in the ACA study never completed high school; of those, 34 percent failed to graduate because they were pregnant.

Twenty-two percent had been unemployed in the three years before they went to prison. Just 29 percent had only one employer in that period. Generally, they had worked in traditional women's service, clerical, and sales jobs. Two-thirds had never earned more than $6.50 an hour for their labor.

Most of these women were first imprisoned for larceny-theft or drug offenses. At the time of the survey, they were serving time for drug offenses, murder, larceny-theft, and robbery. While these latter offenses sound serious, like all other crimes they are heavily gendered. Research indicates, for example, that of women convicted of murder or manslaughter, many had killed husbands or boyfriends who repeatedly and violently abused them (Browne, 1987; Ewing, 1987). One early national investigation into homicide in the United States, for example, concluded that homicides committed by women were seven times as likely as male homicides to be in self-defense ("Causes of Violence," 1969, cited in Browne, 1987). Other studies confirm the importance of this. A 1977 study (Lindsey, 1978) of women in prison in Chicago found that 40 percent of those serving time for murder or manslaughter had killed lovers or husbands who had repeatedly attacked them. In New York, of the women committed to the state's prisons for homicide in 1986, 49 percent had been the victims of abuse at some point in their lives, and 59

percent of the women who killed someone close to them were being abused at the time of the offense. For half of the women committed for homicide, it was their first and only offense (Huling, 1991). Earlier studies of women charged with robbery often show that they were less active participants and noninitiators of these crimes (Fenster, 1977; Ward et al., 1968). One recent study takes some issue with this image of women's passivity and instead stresses the role that drug addiction and prior history of prostitution play in women's robberies (Sommers and Baskin, 1991).

Other recent figures from several states suggest more strongly that the "war on drugs" has translated into a war on women. A study done by the Rhode Island Justice Alliance noted that in their state (which has seen the number of women imprisoned there jump from 25 to 250 in the last five years), 33 percent of the women imprisoned were incarcerated for a drug crime (Rhode Island Justice Alliance, 1990). Finally, nearly half (47 percent) of women held as state-sentenced offenders in Massachusetts prisons are there for drug offenses (LeClair, 1990).

Huling reports that in New York's prisons, only 23.3 percent of women inmates were incarcerated for drug offenses between 1980 and 1986. By February 1991, that proportion had risen to 62 percent (Huling, 1991). In Hawaii, 24 percent of the sentenced felons in 1987 and 1988 were doing time for a drug related offense, according to the official records; interviews with women in prison in Hawaii, however, put the figure far higher (Nowak, 1990). Finally, a study comparing Connecticut women awaiting trial or sentenced in 1983 with those in 1986 (Daly, 1987:3) found that, in three years, the proportion of women incarcerated for drug sale or possession had increased from 13 percent to 22 percent.

Another criminal offense, that of driving under the influence (DUI), has recently been the subject of much debate, and the penalties have escalated. Coles reviewed arrest trends in California, a state that now has the largest incarcerated female population in the world. She notes that California has seen a shift in women's arrests for DUI. Previously, women were rarely arrested for this offense unless the DUI involved a traffic accident or they physically or verbally abused an officer. But that pattern appears to be eroding. Coles found that while female misdemeanor DUI arrests have decreased, the felony arrest rate for this offense has increased; she also notes that women's share of these arrests appears to be increasing, at least in California (Coles, 1991). Coles's findings suggest that women's traditional insulation from certain forms of arrest has been eroded in the wave of get-tough legislation in the last 10 years. . . .

The war on drugs, coupled with the development of new technologies for determining drug use (e.g., urinalysis), plays another, less obvious role in increasing women's imprisonment. In Hawaii, a recent study of women felons revealed that fully half were in prison because they had been returned there for violating the conditions of their parole by failing to pass random drug tests (Kassebaum and Chandler, 1992). In California, 40,460 parole violators were returned to prison in 1991. This figure clearly helped that state earn the dubious distinction of having over 100,000 people in prison, or the highest incarceration rate in the world (Garnett and Schiraldi, 1991:2). Many of these returns, especially those of women inmates, were the result of failed urinalysis (Garnett, 1991).

The profiles of women under lock and key suggest that crime among women has not gotten more serious. Rather, it appears—especially in small states—that what has happened is that incarceration is being used where other forms of nonincarcerative responses previously were utilized.

Getting Tough on Women's Crime

Data on the characteristics of women in prison suggest that factors other than a shift in the nature of women's crime are involved in the dramatic increases in women's imprisonment. Simply put, it appears that the criminal justice system now seems more willing to incarcerate women. Other evidence on the sentences women receive also supports this interpretation. A recent California study found that the proportion of females who received prison sentences for the commission of felonies increased from 54 percent to 79 percent between 1978 and 1987 (California Department of Justice, 1988).

What exactly has happened in the last decade? While explanations are necessarily speculative, some reasonable suggestions can be advanced. First, it appears that mandatory sentencing for particular offenses at both the state and federal levels has affected women's incarceration, particularly in the area of drug offenses. Sentencing "reform," especially the development of sentencing guidelines, also has been a problem for women. As noted earlier, in California this has resulted in increasing the number of prison sentences for women (Blumstein et al., 1983). Sentencing reform has created problems in part because the reforms address issues that have developed in the handling of male offenders and are now being applied to women offenders.

Daly's (1991) review of this problem notes, for example, that federal sentencing guidelines ordinarily do not permit a defendant's employment or family ties/familial responsibilities to be used as a factor in sentencing. She notes that these guidelines probably were intended to reduce class and race disparities in sentencing, but their impact on women's sentencing was not considered.

Finally, the criminal justice system has simply become tougher at every level of decision making. Langan notes that the chances of a prison sentence following arrest have risen for all types of offenses (not simply those typically targeted by mandatory sentencing programs) (Langan, 1991:1569). Such a pattern is specifically relevant to women, since mandatory sentencing laws (with the exception of those regarding prostitution and drug offenses) typically have targeted predominantly male offenses such as sexual assault, murder, and weapons offenses. In essence, Langan's research confirms that the whole system is now "tougher" on all offenses, including those that women traditionally have committed.

A careful review of the evidence on the current surge in women's incarceration suggests that this explosion may have little to do with a major change in women's behavior.

This stands in stark contrast to the earlier growth in women's imprisonment, particularly to the other great growth of women's incarceration at the turn of the twentieth century.

Perhaps the best way to place the current wave of women's imprisonment in perspective is to recall earlier approaches to women's incarceration. Historically, women prisoners were few in number and were, it seemed, an afterthought in a system devoted to the imprisonment of men. In fact, early women's facilities were often an outgrowth of men's prisons. In those early days, women inmates were seen as "more depraved" than their male counterparts because they were acting in contradiction to their whole "moral organization" (Rafter, 1990:13).

The first large-scale and organized imprisonment of women occurred in the United States between 1870 and 1900, when many women's reformatories were established. Women's imprisonment then was justified not because the women posed a public safety risk but rather because women were seen to be in need of moral revision and protection. It is important to note, however, that the reformatory movement that resulted in the incarceration of large numbers of white working-class girls and women for largely noncriminal or deportment offenses did not extend to women of color. Instead, as Rafter has carefully documented, African-American women, particularly in the southern states, continued to be incarcerated in prisons, where they were treated much like the male inmates. They not infrequently ended up on chain gangs and were not shielded from beatings if they did not keep up with the work (Rafter, 1990:150-151). This racist legacy, the exclusion of black women from the "chivalry" accorded white women, should be kept in mind when the current explosion of women's prison populations is considered.

Indeed, the current trend in adult women's imprisonment seems to signal a return to the older approaches to women offenders: women are once again an afterthought in a correctional process that is punitive rather than corrective. Women also are no longer being accorded the benefits, however dubious, of the chivalry that characterized earlier periods. Rather, they are increasingly likely to be incarcerated not because the society has decided to crack down on women's crime specifically but because women are being swept up in a societal move to "get tough on crime" that is driven by images of violent criminals (almost always male) "getting away with murder."

This public mood, coupled with a legal system that now espouses "equality" for women with a vengeance when it comes to the punishment of crime and rationality in sentencing, has resulted in a much greater use of imprisonment in response to women's crime. There also seems to be a return to the imagery of depraved women from earlier periods—women whose crimes put them outside of the ranks of "true womanhood." As evidence of this, consider the new hostility signaled by the bringing of child-abuse charges against women who use drugs, even before the birth of their children (Noble, 1988; Chavkin, 1990:483–487). The fact that many of the women currently doing time in U.S. prisons are women of color further distances them from images of womanhood in which women are seen as requiring protection from prison life. All of this noted, it still seems that the escalation in women's imprisonment is largely the indirect and unanticipated consequence of the mood of a society bent on punishment.

Discussion and Conclusion

We must begin to take seriously a moratorium on construction of women's prisons and consider the need to decarcerate women, while we provide more and better options for women. The standard correctional response to an influx of new female inmates has been to crowd women into existing facilities and then to propose building out of the trouble caused by overcrowding. Ironically, the construction response often follows being sued or threatened with litigation (by prisoners and feminists) regarding the inadequacy of existing facilities. For this reason, those concerned about the situation of women inmates must be somewhat cautious about litigation as a sole response to the problem of conditions in women's prisons, since their work can ultimately fuel the development of new, larger women's prisons (see Chesney-Lind, 1991).

Unfortunately, legislators propose spending enormous sums of money to build prison beds for women (e.g., $200,000/bed for 96 beds in my own state of Hawaii) at the same time that they cut hundreds of thousands of dollars out of services to women—especially funds for shelters and domestic violence programs. This trade-off has surfaced in many states. In California, prison construction, funded by $6.2 billion in bond issues passed during the 1980s, has continued despite drastic budget cuts in other departments. The University of California and California State University systems face, for example, possible campus closures and budget cuts of $255 million, and welfare aid to families with dependent children in the same state was cut by $225 million in fiscal year 1991. New York State has just spent $180,000 per bed to add 1,394 new prison spaces for women. Yet 12,433 women and children were denied needed shelter in 1990, and nearly three-quarters of these denials were because of lack of space (Huling, 1991:6).

Such skewed priorities are particularly tragic, since the availability of welfare assistance and shelters is clearly related to women's crime. For example, an analysis of partner homicide from 1976 to 1984 in the United States revealed a "sharp decline" of 25 percent in the numbers of women killing male partners during that period—a decline linked by researchers to the passage of domestic violence legislation and the growth of legal resources for abused women (Browne, 1990). Every dollar that is spent locking women up could be spent far better on services which would prevent women from becoming so desperate that they resort to some form of criminal activity, sometimes to outright violence.

Besides examining priorities that appear to be misplaced, we must also question who benefits from the incarceration of women. This requires a shift in focus from simply studying the offender to studying the system that locks up women. What role, for example, do political contributions play in the enthusiasm with which lawmakers embrace the building of prisons? In Hawaii, many of the companies and individuals who build prisons are also heavy contributors to political campaigns (Lind, 1991). Every year, the engineering firms and the architectural firms (who may get these "jobs" without even bidding) give the governor and others in the state thousands of dollars. As the prison construction industry becomes a major component of many local economies, we must document its structure and politics. We must also challenge the politics of prison location, where legislators see the establishment of a prison in their jurisdiction, particularly if it has been hard-hit economically, as pork barrel politics for their constituents (e.g., Immarigeon, 1992).

This willingness to spend millions of dollars—per state—incarcerating women stands, of course, in stark contrast to the paucity of resources made available to other needed community-based programs to assist women in their everyday lives. Given these patterns, it seems essential that the feminist movement and feminist scholars make the decarceration of women a part of their political agendas. Since the extraordinary increases in women's imprisonment have been a product of criminal justice policy shifts rather than significant changes in women's criminal behavior, equally dramatic reductions in women's prison populations ought to be within reach. Indeed, the decarceration of women, and the investment of the dollars saved in opportunities and services for people on the economic margins of our society, might well serve as a model for challenging America's "ideology of incarceration" (Immarigeon, 1991).

References

American Correctional Association. 1990. *The Female Offender: What Does the Future Hold?* Washington, D.C.: St. Mary's Press.

Austin, Jim, and Aaron McVey. 1989. "The NCCD Prison Population Forecast: The Impact of the War on Drugs." *NCCD Focus*. San Francisco: National Council on Crime and Delinquency.

Blumstein, Alfred, Jacqueline Cohen, Susan E. Martin, and Michael H. Tonry (eds.). 1983. *Research on Sentencing: The Search for Reform*. Vols. 1 and 2. Washington, D.C.: National Academy Press.

Browne, Angela. 1987. *When Battered Women Kill*. New York: The Free Press.

———. 1990. "Assaults Between Intimate Partners in the United States." (December 11, 1990.) Washington, D.C.: Testimony before the United States Senate, Committee on the Judiciary.

Bureau of Justice Statistics. 1988. *Profile of State Prison Inmates, 1986*. Washington, D.C.: U.S. Department of Justice.

———. 1991a. *Jail Inmates 1990*. Washington, D.C.: U.S. Department of Justice.

———. 1991b. *Prisoners in 1990*. Washington, D.C.: U.S. Department of Justice.

Cahalan, M. W. 1986: *Historical Corrections Statistics in the United States 1950–1984*. Washington, D.C.: U.S. Department of Justice.

California Department of Justice. 1988. "Women in Crime: The Sentencing of Female Defendants." Sacramento: Bureau of Criminal Statistics.

"Causes of Violence." 1969. A staff report to the National Commission on the Causes and Prevention of Violence. Washington, D.C.: U.S. Government Printing Office.

Chavkin, Wendy. 1990. "Drug Addiction and Pregnancy: Policy Crossroads." *American Journal of Public Health*. 80:4 (April): 483–487.

Chesney-Lind, Meda. 1986. "Women and Crime: The Female Offender." *Signs* 12 (Autumn): 78–96.

———. 1991. "Patriarchy, Prisons, and Jails: A Critical Look at Trends in Women's Incarceration." *The Prison Journal LXXI* (Spring–Summer): 51–67.

Coles, Frances S. 1991. "Women, Alcohol and Automobiles: A Deadly Cocktail." Paper presented at the Western Society of Criminology Meetings, Berkeley, Calif., February.

Crites, Laura (ed.). 1975. *The Female Offender*. Lexington, Mass.: Lexington Books.

Daly, Kathleen. 1987. "Survey Results of the Niantic Interviews, December 1983 and May 1986." Mimeographed, January.

———. 1991. "Gender and Race in the Penal Process: Statistical Research, Interpretive Gaps, and the Multiple Meanings of Justice." Mimeographed, April.

Ewing, C. 1987. *Battered Women Who Kill*. Lexington, Mass.: Lexington Books.

Federal Bureau of Investigation. 1991. *Uniform Crime Reports 1990*. Washington, D.C.: U.S. Department of Justice.

Fenster, C. 1977. "Differential Dispositions: A Preliminary Study of Male-Female Partners in Crime." Unpublished paper presented to the annual meeting of the American Society of Criminology.

Garnett, Rick. 1991. Personal communication with the author.

Garnett, Rick and Vincent Schiraldi. 1991. "Concrete and Crowds: 100,000 Prisoners of the State." San Francisco: The Center on Juvenile and Criminal Justice.

Gilfus, Mary. 1988. "Seasoned by Violence/Tempered by Law: A Qualitative Study of Women and Crime." A dissertation presented to the faculty of the Florence Heller School for Advanced Studies in Social Welfare at Brandeis University, Waltham, Mass.

Glick, Ruth, and Virginia Neto. 1977. *National Study of Women's Correctional Programs*. Washington, D.C.: U.S. Department of Justice.

Huling, Tracy. 1991. "Breaking the Silence." Correctional Association of New York. Mimeographed, March 4.

Immarigeon, Russ. 1991. "Instead of Prisons: Observations from Elsewhere." Paper presented at the annual meeting of the Movement for Alternatives to Prison, Auckland, New Zealand.

———. 1992. Personal communication with the author.

Kassebaum, Gene, and Susan Chandler. 1992. "Polydrug Use and Self-Control Among Men and Women in Prison." Paper presented at the Hawaii Sociological Association Meetings, Honolulu.

LaFranier, Susan. 1991. "U.S. Has Most Prisoners Per Capita in the World." *Washington Post* (Jan. 5): A-3.

Langan, Patrick A. 1991. "America's Soaring Prison Population." *Science*. Vol. 251 (Mar. 29):1569.

LeClair, Daniel. 1990. "The Incarcerated Female Offender: Victim or Villain?" Research Division, Massachusetts Department of Correction, October.

Lind, Ian. 1991. "Campaign Finance Practices Create Industry Outlaws." *Building Industry Magazine* (December). Honolulu: Honolulu Trade Publishing Co.

Lindsey, Karen. 1978. "When Battered Women Strike Back: Murder or Self Defense?" *Viva* (September): 5859, 66, 74.

Mauer, M. 1992. *Americans Behind Bars: One Year Later*. Washington, D.C.: The Sentencing Project.

Noble, Amanda. 1988. "Criminalize or Medicalize: Social and Political Definitions of the Problem of Substance Use During Pregnancy." Report prepared for the Maternal and Child Health Branch of the Department of Health Services, University of California, Davis.

Nowak, Carol. 1990. "A Psychological Investigation of Women's Decisions to Participate in Criminal Activities." Dissertation submitted to Saybrook Institute, San Francisco.

Rafter, Nicole Hahn. 1990. *Partial Justice: Women, Prisons and Social Control*. New Brunswick, NJ.: Transaction Books.

Rhode Island Justice Alliance. 1990. "Female Offender Survey, Rhode Island Adult Correctional Institution, Women's Division." Mimeographed.

Simpson, Sally S. 1992. "Distinguishing Drug Involvement by Gender." Paper presented at the annual meeting of the American Society of Criminology, San Francisco, November.

Sommers, I., and D. R. Baskin. 1991. "The Situational Context of Violent Female Offending." Paper presented at the American Society of Criminology Meetings, San Francisco.

Steffensmeier, Darrell. 1983. "Organizational Properties and Sex-Segregation in the Underworld." *Social Forces*, 61:1010–1032.

Ward, David, et al. 1968. "Crimes of Violence by Women," in Donald J. Mulvihil et al. (eds.). *Crimes of Violence*. Vol. 13. Staff report to the National Commission on the Causes and Prevention of Violence. Washington, D.C.: U.S. Government Printing Office.

5

A Prison Superintendent's Perspective on Women in Prison

Elaine Lord

Focus Questions

1. What impact does incarceration have on women and their dependent children?

2. What is the author's view on prison programs for mothers with children?

3. What is the nature of the relationship among family violence, drug abuse, and crime?

4. In what ways are men prisoners different from women prisoners in how they "do time"?

5. What is Lord's view of women being seen as "special needs offenders"?

Bedford Hills Correctional Facility is New York State's maximum-security prison for women. Many of the women housed within its electronically secure fences are long termers, having six or more years to serve on their minimum sentences before they can even appear before the parole board for release consideration. Bedford Hills is also the state's reception and classification center for women, accepting into the state prison sys-

tem more than 3,000 women a year, sorting and distributing these new women between various prison facilities across the state. As the superintendent (or warden) of Bedford Hills, I have overall responsibility for the security, administration, and programs provided at this facility and have acted in this capacity since 1984. During the early 1980s, the reception center for women received closer to 250 new women a year, and the Bedford facility's capacity was about 400—a phenomenal rate of growth that has been felt throughout the prisons and jails in this country. In March 1995, 720 women were confined at Bedford Hills. . . .

Impact of Incarceration on Women and Children

The ACA's [American Correctional Association] Task Force on the Female Offender (1990) found that the average woman offender is responsible for young children and is usually a single parent/primary caretaker of the children. The average woman offender comes from a single-parent home and often has other incarcerated family members. The most difficult consequence of imprisonment for women is to endure the pain of separation from their children. Many women feel tremendous guilt over this separation, and children, in their way, wonder what they have done to create a situation where their mothers are taken or sent away. It is clear that both mothers and children grapple with how to maintain their bonds while separated. They discuss sending kisses through the mail or watching the same moon at night, and some run away to talk to their mothers. Children just do not give up on their mothers because they are in prison.

It is important to support parenting by listening to mothers, by getting mothers talking about their experiences, by providing educational experiences about parenting issues, and by providing opportunities for mothers to talk to teachers and school counselors. In the visiting room, it is important to provide child care givers so that a woman can have some time outside of a child's hearing to discuss problems/issues with other adults or perhaps to have some individual time with one of her children. The play area, which takes up one third of the visiting room, provides a more normal setting for a mother and child. And because a mother's absence has so deep an impact on a child, mothers now tape-record stories to send to their children so that they can be played whenever the children are lonely or just to help them sleep.

Sister Elaine Roulet, the director of our extensive parenting and children focused programming, has developed a vast network of support for the women and their children. There is a nursery program for women and their babies at Bedford Hills with a prenatal education component. There is a program in which children are transported unescorted to visit their mothers. In the host family program, children spend a week during the summer and weekends during the rest of the year with their mothers. And there are numbers of parenting courses available for the mothers, including a course to assist women in assessing their own needs in parenting themselves. There are many supports for enhancing and strengthening the bonds between women and their children.

However, if we are ever going to effectively intervene in the intergenerational connections of crime, abuse, drugs, and incarceration, we must recognize that these are families at risk. To effect change and enhance the healthy nurturing potential of these mother/child relationships, we must face that this can occur only in the context of consistent relationships and cannot occur in isolation. These relationships cannot thrive on two hours a week or a month, and they cannot thrive on one week a year—they cannot thrive in prison. Everything that we are doing in prison to address family issues we can do better in free society and at considerably less cost. And maybe even more basic, why is it necessary to separate these women from their children? A free society should

strive to use the least restrictive response to transgression. For most women and children, this is certainly not prison. It is important to remember that parenting is a learned skill. Birthing is biological, mothering is not. And, all too frequently, these mothers come from families that were themselves in crises or that are still in crises—that were mired in poverty, drugs, violence, and homelessness. We need to divert funds from prisons that are exorbitantly expensive and move those funds to assist families with young children at risk before they are caught up in the criminal justice system.

Of course, it would be naive not to understand that these are families in great stress and in need of support. For some women, getting off the street is critical to getting away from drugs. However, there are alternatives to prison that already exist and that would not have so horrendous an impact on the family unit. Imprisonment should be the absolute last resort for use when all else has failed and when there is concern for the safety of others. This is not the case for the majority of women who are sent to prison. They would be expected to do well in settings where they could be with their children and where the majority of the budget is not spent on staff or sophisticated security paraphernalia—where direct and necessary services are provided.

Please do not get me wrong; I believe strongly that programs for mothers and children are critical when the mothers are in prison. I think that parenting programs are an important aspect of programs for women offenders. Of course, I also believe that they should be a standard and required component of every school curriculum from elementary school through high school. Parenting is a skill, a critical one that addresses our futures in a most literal sense. But, and it is a big but, parenting is not a panacea. It does not address the issues that bring women to prison in the first place, and it may increase the burden they feel on returning to society instead of lessening it. In fact, child-related issues are a significant source of the guilt for women in prison. We need to be very cognizant that we do not build into these concerns for parenting a return to old ways of dealing with women by limiting their roles to those of mother.

We need to assist women in understanding the dynamics of their own families in relation to their drug abuse, violence, or other criminal behaviors. We need to find ways to build supports for dealing with sometimes dysfunctional family relations that can help to insulate the women, even on their release, and help them to accept the limitations of the families they have. There is a wonderful staff person at Bedford Hills that puts it the following way.

> Remember the old story of Mother Hubbard and her cupboard. Well, there may have been times in your life that your mother turned around to get something from the cupboard for you, but the cupboard was bare. But she always gave you everything she had. And when you turn to your child, sometimes your cupboard may be bare, too. What is important is that we give what we have and that she gave you everything that she could.

Women's Experiences of Family Violence and Drug Abuse

Two-thirds of incarcerated women ran away from home at some time as children, and about one-fourth attempted suicide previously. About 65 percent of incarcerated women were victims of severe and prolonged physical and sexual abuse primarily as children, but for many continuing into adulthood. For most of these women, the abuse occurred before the age of 14 and was perpetrated by a male member of the family. Three-quarters had histories of alcohol abuse, and one-half had histories of drug abuse. Many had previously participated in drug and alcohol treatment programs (ACA Task Force on the Female Offender, 1990, pp. 17–19).

Cain (1990) writes that we need to move beyond the traditional approaches of feminist criminology, namely unequal treatment, the nature of female criminality and women as victims that measures women in terms of men. She suggests that we must begin from women's experiences and help women to for-

mulate their own experiences in a way that makes sense to them. . . . In sum, our questions need to be about women, not about crime or prisons, and about who the women are and how they become who they are.

Work with women involves "bearing witness" so that they can examine their life histories in a safe setting in which they can sort out the pathways that took them to prison, come to be aware of themselves in terms of those life histories, and finally accept and examine their own responsibility for their own actions. According to Judith Herman (1992),

> The core experiences of psychological trauma are disempowerment and disconnection from others. Recovery, therefore, is based upon the empowerment of the survivor and the creation of new connections. Recovery can take place only within the context of relationships; it cannot occur in isolation. (p. 133)

There is a need, therefore, to reconnect to other people and discover once again capacities for trust, autonomy, initiative, competence, identity, and intimacy. These would seem to be basic essentials to guard against returning to prison. They do not grow out of traditional therapy visits but rather grow out of real-life situations and real interactions. Prisons are not fertile ground for such work. The rigidity and authoritarianism of prisons by their very nature can be yet another experience of power and control as belonging to others, not the women. Prison does not allow women to experiment with their own decision making but rather reduces them to an immature state in which most decisions of consequence are made for them.

When the experience of family is one of "pervasive terror, in which ordinary caretaking relationships have been profoundly disrupted," what we see described is "a characteristic pattern of totalitarian control, enforced by means of violence and death threats, capricious enforcement of petty rules, intermittent rewards, and destruction of all competing relationships through isolation, secrecy, and betrayal" (Herman, 1992, p. 98). (Some scholars would argue that this description fits our fortress prisons as well as dysfunctional families.) And, certainly, some of the clear long-term effects when children develop in a climate of domination are "pathological attachments to those who abuse and neglect them, attachments that they will strive to maintain even at the sacrifice of their own welfare, their own reality, or their lives" (p. 99).

As a result of their experiences, some women may replicate the violence they have experienced, whereas others may numb themselves or seek a false aura of power with drugs. Drug use, then, is a manifestation and, again, we must look beyond the substance abuse itself to the real story. Drug use becomes a way to numb pain, to take oneself out of a painful and hopeless world. The drug use, in and of itself, is not the problem that needs to be addressed but is only a symptom—of feelings that must be kept in check to ensure survival. In fact, research has shown a link between violent victimization experiences and alcohol and drug use among women (Miller, Downs, & Joyce, 1993, p. 1). This is currently a population that is in large measure finding its way to prison. Yet, residential drug treatment costs between $17,000 and $20,000 per year, and outpatient treatment costs $2,700 per year. All of these figures are well below costs of imprisonment for these same women, coupled with foster care costs for their children. Prison costs between $20,000 and $30,000 per year, whereas foster care adds another $4,000 to $14,000 per year, excluding administrative costs. Miller and her coauthors suggest that "women who use drugs should be placed in treatment programs specifically designed for dealing with the woman and her children. This can be accomplished at a fraction of the cost of incarceration" (p. 7). Certainly, treatment programs are designed as such—for substance abuse treatment. Prisons, on the other hand, are designed to keep inmates out of the community at large. Prisons may have substance abuse programs, but they are not the main business of the prison. Security takes precedence over all other functions and absorbs the majority of the funding. Thus, a drug program in prison functions in and around the daily regime of security. In prison, it will always remain a secondary function to security. That is simple reality.

We need to be more honest with ourselves that the vast majority of women receiving prison sentences are not the business operatives of the drug networks. We need to stop deluding ourselves that we are putting pushers in prison. The glass ceiling appears to operate for women whether we are talking about legitimate or illegitimate business. Women sell drugs in small quantities to maintain their own habits or, sometimes, they move large amounts of drugs as "mules" for males who control sophisticated drug businesses. They are very small cogs in a very large system, not the organizers or the backers of illegal drug empires. This, coupled with a growing mood among the American public reportedly concerned about early intervention with troubled kids and more drug treatment in preference to more prisons, should give us the opening needed to look at better and more cost-effective ways of dealing with women offenders. . . .

Long Termers

Bedford Hills Correctional Facility is both a maximum-security female facility and the reception center for the state. It is a community of about 700 women, of which approximately 600 are considered general population. The majority of women are in their late 20s to early 30s, primarily women of color, and from New York City. About 49 percent of the women at Bedford Hills are imprisoned for what are categorized as violent felonies (34 percent with murder, manslaughter, or attempted murder convictions). The average minimum sentence being served by women in general population is eight and one-third years, but even more startling is the reality that close to 200 women are serving sentences in excess of 10-year minimums and that close to 100 women will be imprisoned for at least 10 years of their lives (New York State DOCS, 1992).

I feel compelled to share that the picture is not much different in many jurisdictions across this country. We are facing a time, not far into the future, when the greatest problem facing our prisons may be the need for geriatric care. The United States sentences people to prison for far longer terms than are rendered in many other countries of the world. We seem to have a need to destroy hope right now, whereas other countries see hope as critical to prisoners and prison systems. We need to begin to look at how punitive we really are and come to some decisions as a society in terms of what we want. The cost of our current actions is extremely high and will weigh down not only this generation but many generations to come.

Difference

There are differences between men and women, in physical ways and in psychosocial ways. Men and women see the world through different eyes and different cultural experiences, and they react differently to it. Researchers have found that women attribute their success to luck, whereas men attribute their success to skill (Deaux, White, & Farris, 1975), that women smile more than do men (Mehrabian, 1971), and that men interrupt women more frequently than women interrupt men (Frieze & Ramsey, 1976).

In the same way, women "do time" differently from how men do time. Men concentrate on "doing their own time," relying on their feelings of inner strength and their ability to withstand outside pressures to get themselves through their time in prison. Women, on the other hand, remain interwoven into the lives of their significant others, primarily their children and their own mothers, who usually take over the care of the children. Yet, the inmate generally continues in a significant caretaking role even while incarcerated. All anyone has to do to see a major difference is to observe prison visiting rooms to see the difference. A woman's most frequent visitors are grandma with the kids, whereas a man's are his wife and the kids. In American society, we trap ourselves when making "special" arrangements—in essence, we try to make everything identical for different groups and then decide what is special that needs to be addressed about one group. Generally, this gets us into trouble.

I cringe when I hear about the "special" needs of women—and, in my case, of incarcerated women. In America, we have gotten caught up in arguments of equality but seldom can define equality or even identify *equal* to what. In the case of prisoners, equal generally means equal to men prisoners. Maybe what we should be addressing is the inequality of women. Why? Why don't we make it a policy to do programs for mothers and then add programs for fathers. I see no reason that they should not be included. Elizabeth Cady Stanton believed that instead of any recognition of their value as mothers, women generally were excluded from many sectors of life because they were mothers (Einsenstein, 1987, p. 92). She saw the ability to mother as an essential difference between men and women and believed that "there would be more sense in insisting on man's limitations because he can not be a mother than on woman's because she can be" (p. 92).

The problem with understanding equality in terms of identicalness is simply that the sexes are not identical. Men and women are different, even in terms of the crimes they commit, their roles, their risks of being violent, their victims, their risks of recidivism. Yet, to make women "equal," many jurisdictions have gone on building programs to make women's prisons like or equal to men's prisons. Prison security classification systems are designed for male prisoners who present substantially different risks to society and to the prison managers. It is almost unknown to create classification systems for women that would factor in their own particular realities and characteristics. Rather, to be "equal," we simply use instruments designed to assess the dangerousness of men and overbuild or oversecure for women at significant cost but little real gain in increased safety. . . .

Fear of Crime

It is important that we separate the difference between our fears of crime and a real understanding of what prisons can do and who prisoners are. Prisons keep people off the streets and out of our communities and, overall, they do that job quite well. But the financial cost is enormous. To build a traditional maximum-security prison costs about $100,000 per cell. Instead of high brick or stone walls, prisons now depend more on sophisticated electronic equipment that is still costly and always in need of maintenance.

Dealing with crime is truly everyone's business. It demands a clear law enforcement response from government *combined* with significant efforts to address the root causes of crime, particularly poverty, racism, and overwhelmed families. To do this effectively, we cannot spend the bulk of our resources on incarceration, which is the most expensive response.

Conclusion

Working with and supporting families is probably the most effective thing that we can do in addressing crime. We cannot be afraid to work at instilling in children basic ethics of respect, pride, honesty, and especially responsibility for one's own actions. We need to learn to celebrate and understand differences while creating community around larger issues such as safety and hope for the future of all children. But building community requires that we include people, not exclude them. Otherwise, the cycle will continue to spiral, as youngsters have little or no stake in our communities. We have to come to understand the costs of our present course of actions, not only in dollars and cents but also in the lives and futures of our children. As a society, we need to accept that alternatives to imprisonment do not diminish individual responsibility for one's actions. We do not need to put people in prison to make them feel the weight of wrongful actions. Indeed, we have become willing to incarcerate ever larger numbers of our population with little result and a heavy cost burden. As a result, the United States has the highest rate of incarceration in the world. That means that we are willing to put more people in prison in proportion to our population than is any other country. I, for one, do not like that image of America.

Crime is an act, not a way of being; it is not a steady state. We need to take firm action against crime and criminals, but the action we need to take has to be thoughtful and meaningful, has to be tailored to the harm, and has to be geared to prevent further injury. It is during such periods of stress that we can sometimes be most creative. There are no "good" prisons; some are simply more humane than others. Small changes can make large differences. It is in our hands to stop the cycle.

References

American Correctional Association Task Force on the Female Offender. (1990). *The female offender. What does the future hold?* Washington, DC: St. Mary.

Cain, M. (1990). Towards transgression: New directions in feminist criminology. *International Journal of the Sociology of Law 18*, 1–18.

Deaux, K., White, L., & Farris, E. (1975). "Skill versus luck: Field and laboratory studies of male and female preferences." *Journal of Personality and Social Psychology, 32*, 629–36.

Einsenstein, Z. (1987). Elizabeth Cady Stanton: Racial-feminist analysis and liberal-feminist strategy. In A. Phillips (Ed.), *Feminism and equality* (pp. 77–102). New York: New York University Press.

Frieze, L, & Ramsey, S. J. (1976). Nonverbal maintenance of traditional sex roles. *Journal of Social Issues, 3*(2), 133–141.

Herman, J. (1992). *Trauma and recovery.* New York: Basic Books.

Mehrabian, A. (1971). "Verbal and nonverbal interaction of strangers in a waiting situation." *Journal of Experimental Research in Personality, 5*, 127–38.

Miller, B. A., Downs, W. R., & Joyce, K. (1993, March). Victimization of drug women. Paper presented at the Fourth International Conference on the Reduction of Drug Related Harm, Rotterdam.

New York State Department of Correctional Services. (1992). *Statistical summary of females under custody as of December 12, 1992.* Albany, NY: Author.

Excerpts from: Elaine Lord, "A Prison Superintendent's Perspective on Women in Prison." In *The Prison Journal,* 75(2): 257–269. Copyright © 1995 by Sage Publications, Inc. Reprinted by permission.

6

The War on Drugs and Women Prisoners

Susan Dearing

Focus Questions

1. What has been the effect of the war on drugs on the growth of the number of women in prison?

2. What pre-prison experiences do most women prisoners share?

3. How do media and politicians portray the image of the criminal or the felon?

4. According to Dearing, why do many women return to self-destructive relationships and abusive men?

5. What were some of the things that Dearing witnessed and experienced in prison?

6. What does Dearing mean when she says that parolees are set up to fail?

Although we live in an historical era in which all aspects of everyday life are mediated by the logic of commodities, everyday life is the source of social change and transformation. Everyday life is, indeed, of consequence. The lived experience—shared with others—is our social reality. And it is the only reality we can know.

—Richard Quinney 1998

I am a former prisoner of the Department of Corrections of the State of Missouri. I am not a woman who was living an ordinary life and suddenly found herself incarcerated because of a mistake. My life before prison was replete with a consistent pattern of self-destructive choices, and I asserted, like most other inmates, that I always seemed to be in trouble and did not understand why. I was arrested for the first time when I was sixteen or seventeen and continued to be arrested off and on until I went to prison at age thirty-six. Because of my history and lifestyle, I was a typical inmate.

In this work, I will share perspectives from inmates and former inmates, including my own. I will attempt to explain how changes in laws and law enforcement have affected the population growth of women in prison. I will describe the initial experience of incarceration, the lack of services available in prison, and how incarcerated women's self-perceptions and their future options change after release.

I have changed the names of the women who graciously allowed me to tape a few of our conversations. A brief biography of each woman appears at the end of this work. We visited and shared our experiences, thoughts, and feelings. We talked to each other from the depths of ourselves without fear of judgment or condemnation. We did not have a need to prove ourselves to each other by peppering our conversations with innuendoes implying "progress."

During our discussions, no one masqueraded as a "victim," which does not mean that we had not been victimized. Victimization is an experience, not an identity, just as conviction and incarceration were experiences, not identities. Those of us who have willingly accepted (and embellished upon) the identities and labels meted out by "experts" and professionals did so because of the seduction of approval. Peer pressure and the seduction of approval are not synonymous, and we (former inmates) considered anyone other than (which meant "better than") ourselves to be an "expert." The following is common ground to us, as well as to most of the women with whom we spent time in prison.

Perspectives Through Time

When I was incarcerated in January of 1991, the "war on crime" and "war on drugs" had been declared several years prior, and everyone with whom I was associated was aware of it. We did not consider ourselves to be criminals; we imagined we had immunity to the new laws and tried not to participate. That means we tried to keep from getting arrested. The "get tough on crime" strategy of incarceration and long sentences was not a deterrent to anyone living a chaotic, rebellious life. As a matter of fact, the overcrowding created by new definitions of crime and sentencing policies often meant (in the beginning) that an officer had to think twice about making an arrest.

Women believed they would not be arrested because, prior to the "war," officers had been reluctant to arrest them. The belief in that advantage (by both men and women), whether real or imagined, was based on a variety of factors. Was there a place to lodge women in the jail? Did the officer believe that women were powerless waifs, incapable of performing criminal acts, especially those of violence? Because of our backgrounds and lifestyles of poverty, violence, and addiction, female defendants in the criminal justice system knew the answers to those questions long before their first personal encounter with legal authorities. We had learned local and regional mores from the experience of bailing associates (usually men) out of jail.

Gina's point of view is expressed by most people in her generational cohort:

> You know, I didn't feel like I had low self-esteem when I was sellin' drugs. I didn't feel, you know I didn't! I felt like Miss Queen Bee, and I was well-kept. The way I was raised, though, you know it was a way of life. In the seventies, everybody was gettin' high. I mean, you know, that

was cool. That was the only thing to do. So then, the eighties, when Reagan came into office, that was all changed up.

As politicians and "victims' rights" groups espoused messages of hatred and retribution through the media, the public's definition of crime and those who commit crime became distorted. Today, the word *felon* evokes images of serial murderers, sexual predators, and dangerous animals. Overcrowding in jails and prisons ceased to be addressed as a human rights issue in the United States, and inhumane treatment of prisoners was (and continues to be) rationalized as "just deserts." The criminal justice system shifted its focus from rehabilitation to revenge, and the resultant overcrowding changed the focus of prison administrators from monitoring the progress of individuals to emergency management of a contained and theoretically dangerous crowd.

Some people are most assuredly dangerous, out of control, or both; they have been emotionally damaged to such an extent that they would pose a menace to others under any circumstance. Very few inmates would go along with the idea of releasing all prisoners from jails and prisons. Most female prisoners are serving sentences not for violent crimes, but for drug-related and property offenses.

Today, women know they are going to be arrested, charged, and incarcerated for activities that at one time merited probation or assistance with their problematic lives. Women complain bitterly of "profiling," harassment, and discrimination in low-income housing areas—not racial discrimination, but discrimination on the basis of economic class.

The increased prevalence of violence is an inevitable result of the "war," and women are more likely to express themselves in violent terms as they personally experience the elimination or downsizing of rehabilitation, treatment, and education programs that once offered them and their children hope for a better life. They believe their children have become the latest targets of a vengeful system out of control, and they are distressed that their adolescent offspring may use the "war" and entry into it as a rite of passage into adulthood. Because of the images evoked by the term "war," and because of harsher sentences imposed, the stakes have become much higher to those violating the law.

Prisoners and those living in poverty have not been the only people victimized by the "tough on crime" politically (in)correct agenda. Police officers have been influenced to react in violent and inhumane ways toward fellow human beings, and some are not afraid to assert their disdain for new laws while booking "offenders." Judges have expressed outrage over mandatory sentencing. Politicians have been intimidated by their colleagues and constituencies for questioning policies or daring to sign pardons or commute sentences. Children are left vulnerable, helpless, and ostracized by their peers while their only caregivers serve time. All are victims of a war they did not start and do not understand.

Our Common Ground

Social Standards and Values

I did not see any criminals while I was in prison. I saw women just like me. The majority of inmates had been molested or raped and were addicted to drugs. I couldn't judge them because we had so much in common. Most women in prison were not bad people. Paula candidly expressed what most female inmates already know:

> I guess I used to judge people that were in prison as different. I used to think I was superior, till I went down. An' I thought, "You know? We're not any different than other people out there." An' the guards would tell me, "Paula, the only difference between me an' you is that you got caught and I didn't." An' it was like, yeah that's true, an' they would tell me, "Hell, we smoke pot. We do this, we do that." Except they get stopped by the cops for speeding, and the guards still wouldn't get a ticket. An' they'd tell me about it, an' brag about it, like the title really gave 'em something. I don't know what it is. Protection, that's what it is [laughter]. Protection from the state.

Although it is currently popular to research and write about the intersections of sex, race, and class effects on life chances, these factors by themselves have nothing whatsoever to do with life chances. Rather, *attitudes* people have about sex, race, and class have everything to do with life chances. Many female prisoners have been beaten, raped, tortured, locked in closets, bought, sold, demeaned, and used in ways the larger (polite) society cannot imagine. Some of us suffered those atrocities before we were adolescents, and thus we were convinced that we deserved them. Donna's childhood experience is typical:

> I was molested. My older brother molested (raped) me when I was twelve.

How old was he?

> Sixteen. My mom said that I deserved it. My dad said it was "in the family. Don't worry about it." My aunt and uncle grounded me for a month. They said it was my fault.

The experience of childhood assault, sexual or otherwise, when blamed on the child, creates a shame-based individual. People do not like to talk about experiences they have been made to feel ashamed of. Many of us do not divulge those experiences to even the most sympathetic of social workers, researchers, or best friends. We think it is not worth the degradation and humiliation. Our common thought is, "What can a person do that is so terrible as to deserve that kind of treatment from anyone?" We are terrified someone will give us an answer that will increase the self-hatred we already feel. When we are honest about our experiences and are asked why we have lived under such grim circumstances, we usually regurgitate answers suggested to us in sessions with psychologists. The truth is often much simpler than that. We do not know how to live any other way, and no amount of time with a counselor changes the environment we face when we leave prison.

Lying on my cell bunk in the Chillicothe, Missouri, women's prison, listening to conversations in the hall, I mused about the "reality" of what women were saying and was

The War on Drugs and Women Prisoners

horrified by the way women, including me, viewed themselves. For example, Mandy bragged, "My man (pimp) said I *[sic]* the best woman he ever have. I can stand on the street corner, eat lunch, and make money all at the same time."

For the first time in my life, I saw the truth about most of us. We would do anything for approval and attention, no matter how self-destructive and/or demeaning our actions. Tragically, the objects of our self-imposed servitude, sacrifice, and self-debasement were almost always abusive men, so-called friends, whose loyalties and affections changed from moment to moment, depending on what they thought they could get from various women. Honest, open, decent human beings frightened us. We used and abandoned people who were devoted to us and pursued love, approval, and loyalty from people incapable of giving it. We had no idea how to interact outside of the chaotic environments we came from. No matter how much we suffered, we returned again and again to the familiar.

Almost everyone who has been victimized or has experienced tragedy at some time in his or her life gains attention by playing the role of the long-suffering, self-righteous, indignant "victim." Prisoners are no different. In a group of incarcerated women or men, inmates cannot resist the urge to outdo each other in telling their personal tragic circumstances or how they have been personally wronged. After a few days in jail or prison, one becomes keenly aware of the resistance to shift the conversation away from the "sad tale." On the one hand, we seem to have a need to convince ourselves and others that we are innocent victims of situations beyond our control. On the other, we often change roles from innocent victim to *best* booster, robber, dealer, whore, fighter, or whatever charge led to our convictions. The change of perspective often takes place in the same conversation, which is confusing to a listener who happens to be an outsider. We insist to outsiders that we have "changed," even though we have not been asked that question. We make that assertion because one thing has *not* changed: the seduction of and intense need for approval.

Political Impressions

Almost all of us who have served time believe that the "otherness" and alienation created by socially constructed definitions of crime and criminals, as well as sexism and racism, are ideologies used by the powerful (wealthy) to continue to divide, control, and exclude the economically disadvantaged. Some of us are more conscious than others of that unspoken and sometimes unconscious intent, but all of us have a definite sense that something is not quite right. Although most inmates are disadvantaged economically, socially, and educationally, they are bright enough to notice a practice Jeffrey Reiman (1996, 99) refers to as "weeding out of the wealthy" during arrest, charging, and sentencing. Why are jails and prisons full of economically disadvantaged people, while economically advantaged criminals get probation? Many inmates in jails and prison have not been consistently exposed to social mores and alternative paths that meet normative standards of "socially acceptable behavior." This is why prisoners and former prisoners feel like victims even though many take responsibility for their actions.

New definitions of crime give inmates a clearer picture of class stratification techniques than the view available to the rest of society. According to political and media rhetoric, a felon is a felon is a felon. For instance, I was convicted of technical possession of more than 35 grams of marijuana, a Class C felony, first offense. My "significant other" grew five plants for his yearly "stash." I did not smoke pot, but I lived in the house where one plant was found after it was harvested and stripped, thus I was guilty of possession and was sentenced to three years in prison. My first cellmate was serving a life sentence for a brutal murder with no link to domestic violence (which would have been a mitigating factor). Failure to classify and separate prisoners according to the seriousness of their crimes leaves inmates with a lasting impression of jails and prisons as warehouses for the poor, a garbage heap of humanity.

The Experience of Incarceration

In 1991, females remanded to the Department of Corrections in Missouri were initially sent to Renz Correctional Center. The "Renz Farm" was a men's prison, located near the Missouri River and had at one time been self-supported by inmate labor with vegetable gardens and livestock. When the Renz facility was condemned (leaking roof, dank odors, and stark deprivation), male prisoners were transferred to newer facilites, while the department of corrections continued to use Renz as a diagnostic and classification facility for women. The damage caused by the flood of 1993 forced the permanent closure of the Renz prison, and a new prison was built in Vandalia. Renz still stands and looks just as it did the day I entered it—formidable, cold, and depressing.

After women were classified, a process that usually took two weeks, they served their sentence at Renz or were transferred to the prison in Chillicothe. The sudden increase in the female prison population slowed the diagnostic and classification process considerably. As a result, women were staying longer in lock-down or crowded into dorms with the general population for a month or more. The lock-down was half underground like a split-level basement. We were locked in cells, two women per cell, 23 hours a day. The lock-down was overcrowded, with cots placed along the walls outside the cells to accommodate the overflow. As more women entered, those in the cells the longest were moved to cots. When the room would hold no more, women were moved to a dormitory on top bunks in cubicles with the general population.

I lay on my upper bunk in lock-down the first three weeks, trying to deal with the closed-in feeling. Next to me, protruding from the wall, was a bare light bulb. Directly beneath it was an old iron toilet. I mused that if I unscrewed the bulb, stood in the water in the toilet, and stuck my finger in the socket, I could electrocute myself. Or, I could unscrew the bulb, break it, and cut my throat with it. Or, I could climb the bars, hook my knees in them, hang upside down, then suddenly straighten my legs and fall to the con-crete floor on my head. Those thoughts were a way of convincing myself that I could leave any time I decided to leave, and I would be all right as long as I thought so. It was a strategy of emotional survival, not suicide.

The morning we were transported to the diagnostic center in Fulton for evaluation, I stood outside in the dark, cold, and sleet, waiting to board the van. I was dressed in an orange jumpsuit five sizes too large, a tattered state-issued coat, handcuffs attached to waist chains, and shackles. I thought, "This is not what I envisioned for my life. I am ashamed that anyone has ever known me."

Meals were served in another building, and we walked outside, crossed an asphalt area, and ascended ten open narrow concrete steps to enter the room. There was no rail to hold on to. One of the inmates had a seizure halfway down those steps one day after lunch. The inmates in front of and behind her held her arms and legs to keep her from falling to the asphalt, while guards looked on in boredom. Life and death of inmates mean nothing to most guards.

Programs and Services

Medical care. Medical care in most prisons can only be described as egregious. Until the fall of 1998, the majority of doctors hired (by a private "for profit" company) to work in the Department of Corrections in Missouri could not practice medicine in the public sector because their licenses had been revoked or they had been sanctioned by the American Medical Association (Allen and Bell 1998). Deaths from neglect or error are commonly described as deaths from "natural causes"—if they are acknowledged at all.

After the first mandatory physical examination in the Department of Corrections, inmates pray that they do not become ill and die in prison. Paula spent her entire sentence in a medical dorm because she was pregnant. Experiences with medical staff and the health crises of fellow inmates still haunt her:

> There was that ol' lady that was goin' to Chillicothe. I can't say how old she was. She used to [vomit] everything she ate. She used to shit everything she ate. [An-

other] inmate helped this lady clean up her bowel movement, her [vomit]. She helped out as much as she could. An' Emma kept goin' back to the doctors. They kept sending her back to the dorm. They said there was nothing wrong with her. They transferred her out. The lady had no family members, so there was nobody they could contact, so they were transferring the lady to Chillicothe an' the lady died going to Chillicothe.

Other shared experiences among us are more graphic than I care to include. Inmates are forbidden to take food from the dining room. Pregnant women often risk "hole time" for sneaking fresh fruit.

Vocational training and education. It astounds me to hear that women have "special needs," but even though almost total responsibility for child rearing is forced on women, a way to make a decent living isn't listed as one of those "special needs." Quite the opposite is true, and women are given educational/vocational options that force them to be economically dependent on men and/or the state. For example, in the Missouri Department of Corrections women's prison in Chillicothe, "job training" consists of certified nurse's aid training, secretarial skills, and cosmetology. Most "women's jobs" do not pay a living wage, and women are compelled either to seek a man to help support them, even at great physical peril to themselves and their children, or to obtain money in illegal ways.

Many state departments of corrections maintain that women's prisons are smaller than men's and that budgets do not accommodate the cost of establishing a full range of training programs. This argument is flimsy and illogical. If money is a problem, then why aren't men's vocational programs adjusted to the less expensive programs, such as certified nurse's assistants, secretaries, and cosmetologists? The taxpayers would be spared millions. When viewed in that light, sexist stereotyping and oppression become obvious. Women do not have "special needs." Men and women have the same needs: to support themselves and their children in a safe, meaningful, and dignified way.

Vandalia women's prison (1,460 beds) opened in 1998 to replace the Renz unit. Although the facility in Chillicothe offers the same programs it did a decade ago, Vandalia is attempting to offer nontraditional job training, such as skills in clothing manufacture, textiles, and upholstery, or in industrial technology. Instructors are difficult to recruit because of the wage offered, but the supervisors are committed to crafting and staffing programs designed to teach women skills that can be used to earn a living wage.

Educational programs consist of Adult Basic Education (ABE), Special Education, and General Equivalency Diploma (GED). Inmates without high school diplomas or GEDs are mandated to work toward obtaining a GED. Progress must be evident to qualify for parole. Prisoners must pay to enroll in college classes. In Vandalia, the inmate must be 25 years or age of younger and incarcerated for a short term to attend college classes. No reason was given for that policy.

I tutored for the ABE and Special Education programs while serving time. Rosie said she did not like to read. I found a book by Maya Angelou in the library and asked her to read the first few pages. The next morning, Rosie grabbed me and asked, "Is there any more of these books in there!?" She had read the entire book the night before. Her language test scores soared, and her eyes sparkled with anticipation for more. It is during those times that inmates envision their futures in the outside world as ones of thrilling promise. They are certain their lives will be different and wonderful because the learning process causes them to *feel* different and wonderful about the world.

Conclusion

Most people do not realize what our lives were like before the prison experience. No matter what we have suffered in or out of prison, most of us are filled with anticipation of a "fresh start" when we think about returning to the outside world. I make that statement tongue in cheek because some of us think about new strategies to avoid getting caught at what we were doing. But most of us think about living in ways we have never known—as responsible, law-abiding contributors in a community.

When I was released on parole, I discovered that no matter my outlook or my efforts, the world seemed to be closed. I was denied jobs and housing because of my convicted felon status, and I felt like damaged goods. I walked to the river, sat on the bank, and watched the ferry go back and forth. I thought about the excited look on Rosie's face while she read Maya Angelou in the prison school, unaware of what she would face "out here." And I cried because I couldn't do anything about any of it, no matter how hard I tried. I could not change public opinion. The experience of living in a society closed off to me changed my opinion. I realized that all the honest endeavors in the world would not help me gain entry, and I thought I no longer had a place "out here." I wanted to get on a bus, go back to the prison, bang on the gates, and yell, "Let me in!!"

We can research and write about how women get to prison and what goes on there. It is fascinating and helps us develop strategies toward prevention. We can do many things to help inmates prepare for a different and better life on the outside. But if we do not acknowledge and address the "set up to fail" situation that parolees currently face, we are tilting at windmills.

References

Allen, William, and Kim Bell. (1998, Septmeber 17)."Death, Neglect, and the Bottom Line," in the *St. Louis Post-Dispatch*, p. G1.

Reiman, Jeffrey. 1996. *. . . And the Poor Get Prison: Economic Bias in American Criminal Justice*. Boston: Allyn and Bacon.

Quinney, Richard. 1998. *For the Time Being: Ethnography of Everyday Life*. Albany: State University of New York Press.

Appendix

The problems I have encountered in this writing are twofold. First, my life since incarceration has not been static. I have been student, worker, manager, director, colleague, instructor, board member, neighbor.

I perform a variety of roles in the community. Pronouns in this writing have created much confusion. Who are "us, them, we, they?" Second, what is meant by the terms "criminal" and "crime"? The definitions change with the coming and going of popular legislators and the ideologies they espouse. It is my intent to avoid participating in the "blame game" so prevalent in literature. No one ever did anything to me. Many people (including me) did things for themselves out of self-interest, and others were harmed as a result. When I recognized that simple fact, I ceased to live under the delusion that I was anyone's intended victim.

Who We Are

Paula is Hispanic, in her late twenties, and has four children ranging in age from two to eleven. She was incarcerated while she was pregnant with her fourth child. I met her six months prior to her sentencing and have maintained contact. Her story is particularly poignant because she exposes the travesty of health care in the prison system. Her situation today also reveals the United States' unconscionable indifference to children. Paula was deported to Mexico as a result of the 1996 bill mandating deportation of anyone convicted of a felony who is not a U.S. citizen. Mexico is a country with which she is unfamiliar. She had lived in the United States since the age of three and was a legal permanent resident. Her children are currently motherless and located in two different places in the United States, separated by almost two thousand miles. Paula was not permitted to hug them goodbye, was put on a plane, and literally dumped on the other side of the Mexican border.

Gina is Caucasian, forty years old, has a one-year-old daughter, and is looking for work. I met her while we were both incarcerated. We became friends in prison, shared the same work detail for a time in the dining room, and lived across the hall from each other. I did not see her for nine years and met her again recently while I was processing applications for energy, housing, and cooling assistance. She lives in a trailer park where most of the residents are either on parole, "on the run," or waiting for a significant other to get out of prison. Gina's perspective is important because her experiences in and out of prison are common to the majority of female offenders, regardless of ethnicity.

Mary is black, in her mid-twenties, has three children, and is pregnant. She is on parole and homeless. Convicted felons are denied housing assistance in most areas of the country. Homeless children do not influence the decisions of the Housing Authority or Section 8 representatives. Felons often have restricted employment choices. Mary obtained her Nurse's Aid certification while serving time, but because her felony was manslaughter, she cannot work in the health care field. Like Gina, Mary's situation is common to women who have served time.

Sharon is in her mid-forties, has no children, and often finds herself on the edge of poverty, although after her release she obtained a B.A. in addition to certifications for CPR, first aid, nonviolent crisis intervention,

and Medication Technician Level I. Education, experience, references, and social skills have not offset the felony question on job applications.

Melanie is Caucasian, in her late thirties, has three children, and works in a convenience store. Melanie and I met in a city jail while waiting for trial dates, unable to post bond. We served time in the same prisons. When she was granted parole in Missouri, she was extradited to Illinois to serve another year and a half for a drug charge. Melanie survived the Department of Corrections but was nearly beaten to death by a man she became involved with after she was released. I had not seen her for eight years and met her again in a seminar she presented as a professional in a drug treatment center.

Chapter II
Discussion

Growth in the Number of Women Prisoners

The three perspectives in this section are strikingly consistent in the reasons they give for the growth of the number of women in prison. First, Chesney-Lind explains that one of the primary factors contributing to the increase of women prisoners is a change in the criminal justice system's response to women offenders. The author provides statistical data showing that women have not become more violent and are not committing crimes at a greater rate. Chesney-Lind proposes to discontinue prison construction and argues that most women offenders should be provided with more treatment options in the community.

Both Lord and Dearing mention the similar background characteristics of women prisoners as marginalized offenders and victims. The commonalties of female preprison experiences include poverty, drug abuse, physical and sexual abuse, exposure to violence, dysfunctional relationships, and lack of skills. Lord's experience as a warden since 1984 has provided her the opportunity to discuss policy alternatives that help women offenders deal with the links between crime and preprison variables. Lord discusses the impact of incarceration on women and their dependent children. Lord would agree with Chesney-Lind that family issues could be addressed more effectively in the community.

Dearing shares personal perspectives about her experiences with the criminal justice system and focuses on various factors that have played a part in the creation of a more conservative attitude toward crime. These factors include changes in sentencing laws, strong advocates of victims rights groups, the use of crime policy as a political issue, and increased media coverage of crime. These media images carry over into crime policy through legislation designed to further alienate and marginalize offenders. Dearing concludes by asking an important question: Why does society further stigmatize ex-prisoners after they have completed their sentence? Dearing challenges researchers to further examine the link between stigmatization, lack of opportunity, and return to criminal behavior as a factor in the continued growth in the number of women prisoners.

Part Two
Treatment of Offenders

Chapter III
Introduction

Elements of Correctional Rehabilitation

Common Assumptions	Reality
• Offender treatment programs do not work.	• Some treatment programs and skills classes, targeted for the appropriate offenders, are effective in assisting offenders to avoid future criminal activity altogether or at least reduce the frequency and severity of criminal behavior. Some successful counseling programs focus on behavior modification and operant conditioning of unacceptable behaviors that are related to an individual's involvement with the criminal justice system, such as uncontrollable anger, drug and alcohol addiction, or sexual deviance. Other programs focus on rehabilitating offenders through such activities as a formal education, learning a new trade or skill, or parenting classes (Kratcoski 1994).
• The public supports getting tough on criminals.	• Public opinion surveys have consistently shown that the public supports correctional rehabilitation and early intervention efforts along with punishment in either community-based or institutional settings (Applegate, Cullen, and Fisher 1997; Cullen et al. 1998). Apparently, the public is not as punitive as the media and politicians make it seem.

If the public has continuously supported the use of correctional treatment, and if some programs have demonstrated effectiveness in rehabilitating prisoners, why is the usefulness of rehabilitative methods in question? To answer this we must look briefly at the origins of the assumption that correctional treatment does not work. Early efforts at correctional rehabilitation did not become fully realized until the 1950s, when rehabilitation dominated community and institutional corrections until the early 1970s. In many state prisons, offenders could seek out the programs inside the walls that they felt would benefit them most. Release from prison on parole depended, in part, on what programs offenders participated in while incarcerated.

The rehabilitation era was short-lived as a result of three main factors. First, the crime rate continued to rise in the 1960s and 1970s. This led to an increase in fear of crime and concern about community safety. Second, correctional practitioners were ill-equipped to "diagnose and cure" criminality. At that time, there was very little knowledge and available information about causes of criminal behavior or how prisoners should be classified. Although the knowledge base was expanding, there were few contemporary evaluations to gauge program effectiveness (Irwin 1980). Finally, a study conducted by Martinson and his colleagues captured widespread attention and permanently changed the course of correctional rehabilitation programs. Martinson's team reviewed over 200 evaluations of correctional rehabilitative programs between 1945 and 1967 and reported positive outcomes in 48 percent of all programs evaluated. (Lipton, Martinson, and Wilks 1975). However, one year before that study was published, Martinson (1974, 25) published a condensed version, in which he concluded: "With few and isolated exceptions, the rehabilitative efforts that have been reported so far had no appreciable effect on rehabilitation." Although Martinson (1979) later revised his conclusions from the 1974 study, the damage had already been done. The Martinson study was interpreted as "nothing works" and was used as ammunition to decrease funding for prison rehabilitation programs. Although rehabilitation never completely disappeared from prison, program budgets were cut and prisoners were left with few treatment options. The "nothing works" slogan seems to have a continued effect on current media depictions of crime and crime policy.

Today, correctional treatment programs are different in five important ways. First, offenders are expected to take more responsibility for their actions. Although the purpose of correctional treatment is to deal with individuals' conditions and actions that may have contributed to their involvement in crime, offenders must also learn that they are accountable for their own future behavior. Second, many treatments and programs are involuntary, in the sense that treatment

is a stipulation of sentence completion. Third, many more treatment programs are administered in the community for offenders sentenced to probation or some other form of community corrections program. Although some prisoners have access to treatment while incarcerated, some critics have questioned whether prison is the appropriate environment for such programs (Mathiesen 1990; Wright 1997). Fourth, the concept of "rehabilitation" has been replaced by "habilitation." Dora Schriro, former director of the Missouri Department of Corrections, differentiates these two concepts:

> I do not want to rehabilitate inmates, which means return them to what they were. I want to *habilitate* them. My focus is on mandatory education that results in high school equivalency, and mandatory industry work to have a vocation. I want them to have the basic tools for citizenship—literacy, employability, sobriety. (Gavzer 1995, 5)

Finally, contemporary correctional counseling pays close attention to assessment, classification, and referral of offenders to programs that best meet their needs (Kratcoski 1994, 2). Because there are many factors contributing to why people commit crimes and become involved with the criminal justice system—and only a limited number of resources—each individual's treatment plan focuses on the key problems.

Recommended Readings

Applegate, Brandon K., Francis T. Cullen, and Bonnie Fisher. (1997). "Public Support for Correctional Treatment: The Continuing Appeal of the Rehabilitative Ideal." *The Prison Journal* 77: 237–258.

Cullen, Francis T., and Karen Gilbert. (1982). *Reaffirming Rehabilitation*. Cincinnati, OH: Anderson.

Cullen, Francis T., John P. Wright, Shayna Brown, Melissa Moon, Michael B. Blankenship, and Brandon K. Applegate. (1998). "Public Support for Early Intervention Programs: Implications for a Progressive Policy Agenda." *Crime and Delinquency* 44: 187–204.

Currie, Elliott. (1985). *Confronting Crime: An American Challenge.* New York: Pantheon.

Gavzer, B. (1995, August 13). "Life Behind Bars." *Chicago Tribune,* Parade, 4–7.

Irwin, John. (1980). *Prisons in Turmoil.* Boston: Little, Brown.

Kratcoski, Peter C. (1994). *Correctional Counseling and Treatment,* 3rd edition. Prospect Heights, IL: Waveland.

Lipton, Doug, Robert M. Martinson, and J. Wilks. (1975). *The Effectiveness of Correctional Treatment.* New York: Praeger.

Martinson, Robert M. (1974). "What Works: Questions and Answers About Prison Reform." *Public Interest* 35: 22–54.

——. (1979). "New Findings, New Views: A Note of Caution Regarding Sentencing and Reform." *Hofstra Law Review* 7: 243–258.

Mathiesen, Thomas. (1990). *Prison on Trial.* Newbury Park, CA: Sage.

Wright, Richard A. (1997). "The Evidence in Favor of Prisons." Pp. 95–108 in M. D. Schwartz and L. F. Travis (eds.), *Corrections: An Issues Approach.* Cincinnati, OH: Anderson.

Internet Websites

Adult and Correctional Education site. Provides information on correctional education and substance abuse treatment. Available: *http://www.io.com/~ellie/*

Centre Inc. Example of a substance abuse and mental health facility for the Federal Bureau of Prisons. Available: *http://rrnet.com/~centre/*

A Convict's View—Confessions of a Jailhouse Drug Addict. Available: *http://www.prisonzone.com/writers/ghost.html*

Field, G. (1998, February). Continuity of offender treatment: Institution to the community. Available: *http://www.whitehousedrugpolicy. gov/treat/consensus/field.pdf*

Shapiro, C. (1998, February). Family-focused drug treatment: A natural resource for the criminal justice system. Available: *http://www.whitehousedrugpolicy.gov/treat/consensus/shapiro.pdf*

Other websites that examine inmate treatment in prisons and jails: *http://www.ibr.tcu.edu/projects/crimjust/pta.html* and *http://members.aol.com/MacFlap/Geesetheatre.html*

7

The Principles of Effective Intervention With Offenders

Paul Gendreau

Focus Questions

1. What information sources does Gendreau use as a basis for his conclusions?

2. What are the eight principles of effective treatment interventions for offenders?

3. What strategies are considered ineffective?

4. Why are intensive supervision programs (ISPs) considered ineffective?

Criminal justice practitioners and policymakers have been repeatedly informed that offender rehabilitation has been a failure; in the words of Martinson (1974), "Nothing works." Even though Martinson (1979) eventually recanted his views, the anti-rehabilitation rhetoric took firm hold, particularly in the United States, for a variety of sociopolitical reasons (Cullen & Gendreau, 1989). Many state jurisdictions subsequently embraced the new epoch of deterrence (Martinson, 1976), which was presumed to have considerable promise in reducing offender recidivism.

But the data have continued to accumulate testifying to the potency of offender rehabilitation programs. This evidence is readily accessible in a variety of published offender treatment outcome literature reviews since the nothing works credo became fashionable in the later 1970s. . . . What are the broad results emanating from this literature? If one surveys all studies that include control group comparisons, as Lipsey (1992) did in his impressive overview of 443 programs, 64 percent of the studies reported reductions in favor of the treatment group. The average reduction in recidivism was 10 percent. When the results were categorized by the general type of the program, for example, employment, reductions in recidivism were as high as 18 percent.

The thrust of my work and that of my colleagues, such as Don Andrews and Jim Bonta, has been to look into the "black box" of treatment programs. Unlike Martinson and his followers, we believe it is not sufficient just to sum across studies or file them into general categories. The salient question is what are the principles that distinguish between effective and ineffective programs? What does it means that an employment program was offered?—what exactly was accomplished under the name of "employment"? As a result of endorsing the perspective of opening the black box, we have been able to generate a number of principles of effective and ineffective intervention. Our analyses in this regard have revealed that programs that adhered to many of the characteristics described in the next section reduced recidivism in the range of 25 percent to 80 percent with an average of about 50 percent (Andrews, Zinger, et al., 1990).

Information Sources

The principles are based on three types of information: (a) narrative reviews of the offender treatment literature, (b) meta-analytic reviews of this literature, and (c) individual studies and insights garnered from my clinical experience in the field, and that of colleagues, who have designed and run successful programs.

Exemplary Programs

Space does not permit a detailed review of all the individual programs that, in my view, are particularly meritorious. For those readers who wish to go beyond the principles discussed here to inspect at firsthand some of the primary source material, several of the best programs can be located in Ross and Gendreau (1980), an edited volume with commentary on the studies by the editors and updates of some of the original studies by the program designers themselves. More recently, Andrews, Zinger, et al. (1990, Table 1, pp. 403–404) have supplied the references to 35 program evaluations designated "appropriate correctional service." All but 2 of the 35 studies found reduced recidivism; 20 of these programs lowered offender recidivism rates by at least 25 percent compared to their control groups (some studies involved more than one treatment-control comparison).

There are at least a dozen programs that I believe satisfy most of the effective principles described later and that can be recommended as good models for future program development. Family therapy programs for juveniles of either the family systems or multisystemic type have been noteworthy for their therapeutic integrity.... Some innovative probation-based adult programs that featured cognitive behavioral strategies and matching of client, treatment service, and treatment provider characteristics were those of Andrews and Kiessling (1980) and Ross, Fabiano, and Ewles (1988). There are, unfortunately, few good examples forthcoming from adult institution samples; two exceptions were Jesness (1975) and Wexler, Falkin, and Lipton (1990).

I now turn to the principles of effective and ineffective programs. They are set forth as succinctly as possible; in a few instances,

however, clarification is required. It should be noted that meta-analysis is the principal source of information for "effective" Principles 1(b), 2, 3 and "ineffective" Principles 1 through 6. The rest are based on a combination of narrative reviews, selected experimental studies, and clinical knowledge.

Principles of Effective Intervention

1. Services

Services should be intensive and behavioral in nature.

   a. Intensive services occupy 40 percent to 70 percent of the offenders' time while in a program and are of 3 to 9 months' duration.

   b. Behavioral strategies are essential to effective service delivery.

Interested readers might wish to consult two highly recommended texts on the theories underlying behavioral programs (Liebert & Spiegler, 1990) and the what and how of various behavioral interventions (Spiegler & Guevremont, 1993). Because I often find confusion among practitioners as to what is meant by the term *behavioral*, here follows a thumbnail sketch of behavioral program principles.

Virtually all offender behavioral programs are based on the principles of operant conditioning. At the core of operant conditioning is the concept of *reinforcement*, which refers to the strengthening or increasing of a behavior so that it will continue to be performed in the future. The most efficient and ethically defensible way to achieve this goal is to use positive reinforcers (something prosocial the offender considers pleasant or desirable) and to ensure that reinforcers are contingent (contingency management) on the behavior being enacted. In contrast, punishment, which is used much less frequently by behavioral therapists, attempts to weaken or suppress behavior by providing unpleasant or harmful consequences.

Three types of positive reinforcers are used to strengthen behavior. They may be tangible (money, material goods) or activities (shopping, sports, music, television, socializing) or social (attention, praise, approval). Behavior modifiers usually employ the last two types of reinforcers because they are natural consequences of a person's life. Positive reinforcers fit nicely into a powerful concept called the Premack principle, which simply states that making a high-probability behavior contingent on a lower-probability behavior will increase the frequency of the latter. Social reinforcers are much to be preferred because they are cost-effective and require little effort to satisfy contingency management practices. Most programs include a general menu of reinforcers, with efforts made to individualize them where possible.

There are many types of behavioral programs. The three described next are prevalent in the offender behavioral treatment literature. A well-designed program will employ at least two of the following, as each overlaps to some degree with the others.

    a. *Token economies*—A reinforcement system for motivating offenders to perform prosocial behaviors. Tokens can be tangible or symbolic, that is, points. They are most often used with groups.

    b. *Modeling*—The offender observes another person demonstrating a behavior that he or she can benefit from imitating. Andrews and Bonta (1994, pp. 202–203) include an excellent summary of how modeling should be carried out with offenders.

    c. *Cognitive behavioral*—There are several schools of cognitive behavioral therapy (see Spiegler & Guevremont, 1993). Fundamentally, they are intended to change the offender's cognitions, attitudes, values, and expectations that maintain antisocial behavior. Problem solving, reasoning, self-control, and self-instructional training are frequently used techniques. Cognitive therapists stress that a good therapeutic relationship, involving empathy, openness, and warmth, is necessary for effective cognitive therapy.

2. Behavioral Programs

Behavioral programs should target the criminogenic needs of high-risk offenders. Treatment is more effective when it is matched with the offender's risk level. Higher-risk offenders are much more likely to benefit from treatment than low-risk offenders.

There are two types of risk factors—static and dynamic. A static risk factor is any aspect of an offender's past criminal history that is fixed in time (e.g., number of previous convictions). Dynamic risk factors are those aspects of the offender's everyday functioning that are amenable to change. Gendreau, Little, and Goggin (1995) have listed those dynamic risk factors that are the best predictors of recidivism and therefore the most promising targets for intervention—Andrews and Bonta (1994) refer to them as criminogenic needs. If these factors undergo positive changes, the offender's criminal behavior will be reduced. Some of these criminogenic needs involve antisocial attitudes, styles of thinking and behavior, peer associations, chemical dependencies, and self-control issues. There are also dynamic factors (or noncriminogenic needs) that if targeted for treatment will not lead to reductions in antisocial behavior (e.g., lack of self-esteem and feelings of personal inadequacy, such as anxiety and depression; Andrews, Bonta, & Hoge, 1990).

It is critical that behavioral programs employ risk assessment measures that measure a wide range of criminogenic need factors. Of the measures in widespread use that have been identified as comprehensive, reliable, and valid (Gendreau et al., 1995), the measure with the best predicted validities is the Level of Supervision Inventory (Andrews & Bonta, 1994).

3. Characteristics of Offenders, Therapists, and Programs

Characteristics of offenders, therapists, and programs should be matched. The responsivity principle is rooted in the notion that there can be potent interactions between the characteristics of individuals and their settings or situations (Gendreau, 1981;

Gendreau & Ross, 1979). These authors have decried the simple-minded rationale of the time that programs should be limited to one treatment modality, for example, using only a token economy and ignoring all other behavioral strategies, and treating all offenders as if they all had identical personality traits, attitudes, and beliefs. We are indebted to Andrews, Bonta, and Hoge (1990) for developing and refining the concept of responsivity to guide treatment interventions. Their review provides summaries of intervention studies demonstrating that substantial variations in recidivism result from paying attention to responsivity factors. Andrews has also generated some impressive data of his own in this regard (see Andrews & Kiessling, 1980; Andrews, Kiessling, Robinson, & Mickus, 1986).

The principle of responsivity simply states that treatment programs should be delivered in a manner that facilitates the learning of new prosocial skills by the offender. Failure to do so means that programs can easily fail, as Arbuthnot and Gordon (1986) demonstrated when they found some of their clients did not succeed because they did not have the cognitive skills to understand the program material. Essentially, the responsivity principle is one of matching treatment x offender type x therapist's style. The three components of responsivity are the following:

a. Matching the treatment approach with the learning style and personality of the offender. As a case in point, offenders who prefer high degrees of structure or who are impulsive are likely to function better in programs such as graduated token economics, which initially provide considerable external control with concrete rules for appropriate behavior. Psychiatrically troubled offenders, on the other hand, will often perform more adequately in low-pressure, sheltered-living environments.

b. Matching the characteristics of the offender with those of the therapist. For example, offenders who are more "anxious" respond best to therapists exhibiting higher levels of interpersonal sensitivity.

c. Matching the skills of the therapist with the type of program. Therapists who have a concrete conceptual-level problem-solving style function best in a program that is highly structured.

4. Program Contingencies and Behavioral Strategies

Program contingencies and behavioral strategies should be enforced in a firm but fair manner.

a. Reinforcement contingencies must be under the control of the therapists.

b. Staff, with meaningful input from offenders, design, maintain, and enforce contingencies.

c. Positive reinforcers exceed punishers by at least 4:1.

d. Internal controls, for example, drug testing for substance abuse, are judiciously used to detect possible antisocial activities of clients.

5. Relating to Offenders

Therapists should relate to offenders in interpersonally sensitive and constructive ways and should be trained and supervised appropriately. Interpersonal skills have all but been ignored in the nothing works debate. This principle was initially formulated in 1979 (Gendreau & Ross, 1979) in the following words:

To what extent do treatment personnel actually adhere to the principles and employ the techniques of therapy they purport to provide? To what extent are the treatment staff competent? How hard do they work? How much is treatment diluted in the correctional environment so that it becomes treatment in name only?

It is an essential component of what is called therapeutic integrity (Gendreau & Ross, 1983–1984). Most of the exemplary studies noted previously make mention of some of the four criteria described next; few of the studies that report no reductions in recidivism comment in this regard.

   a. Therapists are selected on the basis of interpersonal skills associated with effective counseling. Some of these factors are clarity in communication, warmth, humor, openness, and the ability to relate affect to behavior and set appropriate limits. With these sorts of skills, therapists can be effective sources of reinforcement and can competently model prosocial skills.

   b. Therapists have at least an undergraduate degree or equivalent with training in theories of criminal behavior and the prediction and treatment of criminal behavior.

   c. Therapists receive 3 to 6 months' formal and on-the-job or internship training in the application of behavioral interventions both in general and specific to the program.

   d. Therapists are assessed periodically on the quality of their service delivery.

   e. Therapists monitor offender change on intermediate targets of treatment.

6. Designing Program Structure and Activities

Program structure and activities should be designed to disrupt the delinquency network by placing offenders in situations (people and places) where prosocial activities predominate.

7. Providing Relapse Prevention Strategies

Relapse prevention strategies should be provided in the community to the extent possible. Relapse prevention is a strategy that originated in the alcoholism field and has begun to be adapted to offender populations such as sex offenders (Maletzsky, 1991). It is essentially an outpatient model of service delivery applied after the offender has completed the formal phase of a treatment program in prison or a community residential center. Elements of the strategy include the following:

   a. Plan and rehearse alternative prosocial responses.

   b. Monitor and anticipate problem situations.

   c. Practice new prosocial behaviors in increasingly difficult situations and reward improved competencies.

   d. Train significant others, such as family and friends, to provide reinforcement for prosocial behavior.

   e. Provide booster sessions to offenders after they have completed the formal phase of treatment.

8. Advocacy and Brokerage

A high level of advocacy and brokerage should be attempted as long as community agencies offer appropriate services. Where possible, it is desirable to refer offenders to community-based services that provide quality services applicable to offenders and their problems. Therefore, it is vital that community services be assessed in this light in as objective a manner as possible (see, e.g., Correctional Program Assessment Inventory [CPAI]; Gendreau & Andrews, 1994). The reality, regrettably, is that many programs are lacking in most of the effective components noted earlier. As a case in point, a recent survey of 112 offender substance abuse programs using the CPAI reported that only 10 percent of the programs had programmatic elements that would indicate an effective service was being provided (Gendreau, Goggin, & Annis, 1990). A similar result, again using the CPAI, was found for a similar number of juvenile offender programs (Hoge, Leschied, & Andrews, 1993).

Principles of Ineffective Intervention

The first three principles of ineffective intervention are grounded in therapeutic approaches that have little in common with or are antagonistic to behavioral methods.

1. Traditional "Freudian" Psychodynamic and "Rogerian" Nondirective or Client-Centered Therapies

Offender treatment programs that have been based on these two approaches have emphasized the following processes:

a. "Talking" cures

b. Good relationship with client as a primary goal

c. Unraveling the unconscious and gaining insight

d. Fostering positive self-regard

e. Self-actualization through self-discovery

f. Externalizing blame to parents, society

g. Ventilating anger

2. "Medical Model" Approaches

a. Change in diet

b. Plastic surgery

c. Pharmacological, for example, testosterone suppressants

3. Subcultural and Labeling Approaches

. . . Subcultural theory emphasizes respecting the offender's culture and "doing good for the disadvantaged" by providing access to legitimate opportunities. Labeling theory operates on the principle that the criminal justice system stigmatizes youth and therefore offenders should be diverted from the system.

Neither approach favors behavioral-style interventions for offenders. If a program must be offered, nondirective therapies are preferred, and in the case of labeling theory, sanctions such as restitution are considered to be worthwhile alternatives.

4. Programs, Including Behavioral, That Target Low-Risk Offenders

5. Programs, Including Behavioral, That Target Offender Need Factors That Are Weak Predictors of Criminal Behavior (e.g., anxiety and depression)

6. "Punishing Smarter" Strategies

The so-called punishing smarter strategies became popular in community corrections in the mid-1980s. In the classic paper of the time, it was stated, "we are in the business of increasing the heat on probationers . . . satisfying the public's demand for just punishment . . . criminals must be punished for their misdeeds" (Erwin, 1986, p. 17). The programs that resulted are commonly known as intensive supervision programs (ISPs). ISPs usually include some or all of the following components:

a. Greatly increasing contact between supervisors and offenders

b. Home confinement

c. Frequent drug testing

d. Restitution

e. Electronic monitoring

f. Shock incarceration

g. Boot camps

Because punishing smarter strategies have become so popular in the United States—that they are not in other comparable Western societies is an interesting question in itself—the following data will be of interest. Gendreau and Little (1993) completed a preliminary meta-analysis of the punishing smarter literature. The analysis consisted of 174 comparisons between a punishment group and a control group. The authors found that these programs produced, on average, a slight increase of recidivism of 2 percent. . . .

Indeed, of the entire punishing smarter literature, only two studies have been found that reported reductions in recidivism of more than 20 percent (Gendreau, Paparozzi, Little, & Goddard, 1993; Pearson, 1987). Both were programs in New Jersey; one was evaluated by Frank Pearson and the other was Mario Paparozzi's Bureau of Parole program. Their distinguishing feature is that each attempted to provide as much treatment services as possible. The Bureau of Parole evaluation is of particular interest, because it used a carefully chosen matched control group. In addition, this program deliberately targeted high-risk offenders, provided significantly more treatment services to the ISP than the regular probation control group, and examined the quality of implementation of the program and probation officer supervision style. Unfortunately, the quality of services provided in either New Jersey program could not be determined.

With colleagues, I have addressed the matter in detail elsewhere of why punishment and punishing smarter programs have been failures (Gendreau & Goddard, 1995; Gendreau & Ross, 1981). . . . Briefly, the conclusions are as follows:

1. There is no experimental evidence that most of the sanctions currently in use are effective punishers that reliably suppress behavior. The exception to the list is fines, which are rarely used in ISPs. As well, ISPs almost invariably target behaviors that are not predictors of criminal behavior, such as fitness or obeisance. Only five reliable and potent punishing stimuli have been experimentally identified: electric shock, some forms of drug-induced aversion, overcorrection, time-out, and fines.

2. For any of the effective punishing stimuli to work, the following rules must apply without exception:

   a. Escape from the punishing stimuli is impossible.

   b. The punishing stimulus is applied immediately and at maximum intensity. Also, it is applied at the earliest point in the deviant response chain and after every occurrence of the deviant behavior.

   c. The punishers should not be spread out and should be varied.

Obviously, it is virtually impossible to meet these criteria in the real world in which offenders live, unless some sort of unbelievably efficient Orwellian environment is envisioned by adherents of punishing smarter programs.

3. Punishment only trains a person what not to do.

4. When punishment is inappropriately applied, several negative consequences can occur, such as producing unwanted emotional reactions, aggression, or withdrawal—or an increase in the frequency of the behavior that is punished!

5. People who appear to be resistant to punishment are psychopathic risk takers, not neurotic or under the influence of a substance, or have a previous history of being frequently punished. All of these characteristics are to be found, in varying degrees, among offenders more than other clinical groups.

6. The social psychology of attitudes and attitude change nicely documents how many people inoculate themselves from threats and coercion by the way they choose to interpret "evidence," employing self-relevant reasons that disregard negative consequences, and have affective schema, that is, free-will arguments or ego defenses, that are resistant to attitude change. The social-psychological literature on influence has established that the principles of reciprocity, liking, authority, and commitment, among others, are necessary to change behavior (see Cialdini, 1993). The means by which these principles operate make it a rather doubtful proposition that they could be employed effectively, given the way sanctions programs are structured (Gendreau & Goddard, 1995). The reader is also reminded that behavioral programs require therapists to establish an open, trusting, and empathic relationship.

When proponents of sanctions try to justify the use of sanctions as umbrellas under which effective treatment programs might reside, they minimize the fact that a surround of sanctions can create a miasma in which it is difficult to establish supportive relationships or sustain the predominant use of positive reinforcers vis-à-vis punishers. The offender behavior modification literature is replete with examples of the disastrous consequences that befall programs in which punishment and control are emphasized over all else (Ross & McKay, 1978).

Conclusion

In conclusion, the evidence is persuasive that specific styles of service delivery can reduce offenders' criminal behavior to a degree that has profound policy implications. We also have a clear idea as to what doesn't work. In fact, some of the programs that do not work, such as ISPs, have also been shown to be very costly and contribute to prison overcrowding (Gendreau et al., 1993). The next goal of the rehabilitative agenda, besides adding to the principles as more data accrue, is to address how we can overcome the sociopolitical and professional barriers to the implementation of high-quality offender services that have been found to be effective in reducing offenders' criminal behavior (Gendreau, 1996; Gendreau & Ross, 1987).

References

Andrews, D. & Bonta, J. (1994). *The psychology of criminal conduct.* Cincinnati, OH: Anderson.

Andrews, D., Bonta, J., & Hoge, R. (1990). Classification for effective rehabilitation: Rediscovering psychology. *Criminal Justice and Behavior, 17,* 19–52.

Andrews, D. & Kiessling, J. (1980). Program structure and effective correctional practices: A summary of the CaVIC research. In R. Ross & P. Gendreau (Eds.), *Effective correctional treatment* (pp. 441–463). Toronto: Butterworths.

Andrews, D., Kiessling, J., Robinson, D., & Mickus, S. (1986). The risk principle of case classification: An outcome evaluation with young adult probationers. *Canadian Journal of Criminology, 28,* 377–384.

Andrews, D., Zinger, I., Hoge, R., Bonta, J., Gendreau, P., & Cullen, F. (1990). Does correctional treatment work? A clinically-relevant and psychologically-informed meta-analysis. *Criminology, 28,* 369–404.

Arbuthnot, J. & Gordon, D. (1986). Behavioral and cognitive effects of a moral reasoning development intervention of high-risk behavior disordered adolescents. *Journal of Consulting and Clinical Psychology, 54,* 208–216.

Cialdini, R. (1993). *Influence: Science and practice.* New York: Harper Collins.

Cullen, F. & Gendreau, P. (1989) "The effectiveness of correctional rehabiliatation: Reconsidering the 'Nothing Works' doctrine." In L.

Goodstein & D. L. MacKenzie (Eds.), *The American Prison: Issues in Research Policy* (pp. 23–44). New York: Plenum.

Cullen, F. & Gilbert, K. (1982). *Reaffirming rehabilitation.* Cincinnati, OH: Anderson.

Erwin, B. (1986). Turning up the heat on probationers in Georgia. *Federal Probation, 50*(2), 17–24.

Gendreau, P. (1981). Treatment in corrections: Martinson was wrong. *Canadian Psychology, 22,* 332–338.

——. (1996). Offender rehabilitation: What we know and what needs to be done. *Criminal Justice and Behavior, 23*(1), 144–61.

Gendreau, P. and Andrews, D. (1994). *The Correctional Program Assessment Inventory* (4th ed.) Saint John, Canada: University of New Brunswick Press.

Gendreau, P., & Goddard, M. (1995). *Community corrections in the U.S.: A decade of punishing stupidly.* Manuscript submitted for publication.

Gendreau, P., Goggin, C., & Annis, H. (1990). Survey of existing substance abuse programs. *Forum on Corrections Research, 2,* 608.

Gendreau, P., & Little, T. (1993). *A meta-analysis of the effectiveness of sanctions on offender recidivism.* Unpublished manuscript.

Gendreau, P., Little, T. & Goggin, C. (1995). A meta-analysis of the predictors of adult offender recidivism: Assessment guidelines for classification and treatment. Ottawa: Ministry Secretariat, Solicitor General of Canada.

Gendreau, P., Paparozzi, M., Little, T., & Goddard, M. (1993). Does "punishing smarter" work? An assessment of the new generation of alternative sanctions in probation. *Forum on Corrections Research, 5,* 31–34.

Gendreau, P. & Ross, R. (1979). Effective correctional treatment: Bibliotherapy for cynics. *Journal of Research in Crime and Delinquency, 25,* 463–489.

——. (1981). Correctional potency: Treatment and deterrence on trial. In R. Roesch & R. Corrado (Eds.), *Evaluation and criminal justice policy* (pp. 29–57). Beverly Hills, CA: Sage.

——. (1983–1984). Correctional treatment: Some recommendations for successful intervention. *Juvenile and Family Court Journal, 34,* 31–40.

——. (1987). Revivification of rehabilitation: Evidence from the 1980s. *Justice Quarterly, 4,* 349–407.

Hoge, R., Leschied, A., & Andrews, D. (1993). *An investigation of young offender services in the* province of Ontario: A report of the repeat offender project. Toronto: Ontario Ministry of Community and Social Services.

Jesness, C. (1975). Comparative effectiveness of behavior modification and transactional analysis programs for delinquents. *Journal of Consulting and Clinical Psychology, 43,* 758–779.

Liebert, R., & Spiegler, M. (1990). *Personality: Strategies and issues* (6th ed.). Pacific Grove, CA: Brooks/Cole.

Lipsey, M. (1992). Juvenile delinquency treatment: A meta-analytic inquiry into the variability of effects. In T. Cook, H. Cooper, D. Cordray, H. Harmann, L. Hedges, R. Light, T. Louis, & F. Mosteller (Eds.), *Meta-analysis for explanation* (pp. 83–127). New York: Russell Sage.

Maletzky, B. (1991). *Treating the sexual offender.* Newbury Park, CA: Sage.

Martinson, R. (1974). What works? Questions and answers about prison reform. *Public Interest, 35,* 22–54.

——. (1976). California research at the crossroads. *Crime and Delinquency, 22,* 178–191.

——. (1979). New findings, new views: A note of caution regarding sentencing reform. *Hofstra Law Review, 7,* 243–258.

Pearson, F. (1987). Evaluation of New Jersey's intensive supervision program. *Crime & Delinquency, 34*(4), 437–448.

Ross, R. Fabiano, E., & Ewles, C. (1988). Reasoning and rehabilitation. *International Journal Offender Therapy and Comparative Criminology, 20,* 165–173.

Ross, R., & Gendreau, P. (Eds.) (1980). *Effective correctional treatment.* Toronto: Butterworths.

Ross, R., & McKay, H.B. (1978). Behavioral approaches to treatment in corrections: Requiem for a panacea. *Canadian Journal of Criminology, 20,* 279–295.

Spiegler, M. & Guevremont, D. (1993). *Contemporary behavior therapy* (2nd ed.). Pacific Grove, CA: Brooks/Cole.

Wexler, H., Falkin, G., & Lipton, D. (1990). Outcome evaluation of a prison therapeutic community for substance abuse treatment. *Criminal Justice and Behavior, 17,* 71–92.

8
Essential Elements of the Effective Therapeutic Community in the Correctional Institution: A Director's Perspective

Steven F. Singer

Focus Questions

1. What is a therapeutic community (TC)?

2. How is a TC different from a regular prison setting?

3. What elements of the TC are essential to successful treatment intervention?

4. Which elements to successful intervention were mentioned in this reading by Singer and in the previous reading by Gendreau?

Today is Wednesday, a fairly typical Wednesday. This is orientation day at Marion Correctional Institution, a major correctional institution in north central Florida. On this day newly arriving inmates will be familiarized with institutional procedure and introduced to available program services. It is 2:15 P.M.; the substance abuse treatment program will now address the group that typically includes 15 to 20 inmates displaying a variety of affects. There is definitely a sense of uneasiness as the director of the substance abuse treatment program and a group of program graduates take the podium. "Good afternoon, welcome to Marion Correctional Institution," the program director begins. "For the next 30 minutes we will be speaking about Doin' Time Gettin' Straight, a program that could very well save your life."

Oh yes, it is clear from their faces. No sooner had the "blue bird" (the Department of Corrections inmate transport bus) arrived and had the newcomers' feet hit the pavement were they besieged by awful rumors of what takes place in the drug program. "Don't sign up," admonish the voices of those angry offenders summarily discharged from treatment for a myriad of reasons, "they're nothin' but a bunch of snitches and faggots."

Following brief introductory remarks, the group is quickly polled to determine the number of first offenders present as compared with those whose incarceration represents a recommitment. Invariably, the majority includes second- or third-time repeaters. The group is again polled as to the number of offenders present who are in prison as a result of choice. Virtual silence fills the room. Not one hand is raised. The speaker is immediately viewed as suspect. Hearing such a nonsensical question from the program director, they immediately begin to reflect on the rumors. "Yes, perhaps there is something wrong with the director; they're right, I should not sign up. Don't have to worry about that one." The director then explains that if indeed they are in prison and not by choice, many for the second or third time, perhaps that which is in need of scrutiny is not the director or the drug program but their own mental stability. It is asserted that their incarceration is more than likely premised on the presence of serious emotional disturbance which has resulted in completely unacceptable behavior. Left unaddressed, such impairment usually escalates resulting in further imprisonment, be it under lock and key or otherwise.

In a forceful manner the director makes it abundantly clear that treatment is of necessity to intervene in their cycle of destruction, that hope exists, and that they need not see themselves as worthless entities. Such notions have no doubt been previously suggested to them. They are told that the ingredient essential to the pursuit of hope is courage.

Following testimonials from model program inmates, the director relates that over the course of his 17 years in corrections, he has never met one inmate who was convinced that he was returning to prison. Yet, shortly subsequent to release, they find themselves huddled elbow to elbow at the iron gates of the county jail awaiting a return to prison, self-styled habits that will control them for years to come.

This chapter is an account of what has "worked" at Doin' Time Gettin' Straight, a 9-to-12-month prison-based therapeutic community (TC) at Marion Correctional Institution. . . .

The Treatment Setting

Basic to the effective delivery of treatment services is the availability of a reasonable treatment setting. The ideal situation includes the presence of a self-sustaining environment that is totally isolated from inmates uninvolved with the program. If this is not possible, at minimum, those in treatment must have separate living quarters. It should be asserted that although it is undesirable and certainly a challenge, it is entirely possible to operate effectively if the treatment facility is not separate from the general population. However, because of the average offender's resistance to committing himself to intrusive treatment involvement, the absence of separation mandates accessibility

of program inmates to all of the amenities and services available to nonprogram inmates.

The treatment environment should ensure the privacy of program participants as well as provide ample space to accommodate individual therapy and groups of all sizes. The setting should be clean, motivational, and abound with data slogans and other materials that in a reinforcing fashion exhort one toward recovery. Counselors should have their own private space, supplies, and an abundance of resource materials available to allow for the dynamic delivery of treatment services. Ongoing staff exposure to quality correctional training experiences is a must. Staff members new to corrections must be properly oriented. They should be observed for indication of inadvertent breaches of security. They should be encouraged and made welcome to ask questions and otherwise make use of the experience of their colleagues. Whatever is necessary to minimize a staff member's vulnerability to the cunning manipulations of the inmate is worthy of pursuit.

A Healthy Partnership

Following appropriate treatment staff selection, which is discussed later, another priority is creating a sound foundation for a workable relationship with custodial staff. Within correctional institutions, programs are often poorly developed due to institutional resistance and shifting institutional priorities. A supportive relationship with administrative and custodial staff is essential for successful program operation.

It must be understood that change is and of itself uncomfortable and that treatment is foreign to correctional personnel, particularly those who have worked within the closed correctional system for years. The concept of treatment in prison is relatively new. It tends to be highly scrutinized initially and resisted, if not totally rejected. There are those in corrections with careers spanning 20 or more years whose ideas of "what works" simply do not include the viability of treatment. To embrace a new philosophy entails a perception of having been "wrong" for the better part of a career.

Equally problematic is the fact that, historically, in the prison setting, treatment staff have not enjoyed the best of reputations. They have been referred to as "liberal, bleeding hearts" and "easy marks." In the early 1970s the services of many treatment professionals were imposed on the correctional system in line with legal mandates. They were therefore viewed with resentment, and tolerated at best. Resentment stemmed from the idea of inmates being provided with expensive social services that were cost prohibitive to the law-abiding citizen.

Regardless of the rationale behind the foregoing perceptions, treatment personnel must be sensitive to custodial concerns, be able to convey that those offenders in treatment are not considered "special" or "privileged," and understand that the development of rapport takes time and patience. Establishing reasonable interdepartmental rapport is facilitated by an existing working relationship with the program director. The program director must demand a spirit of cooperation from her staff and custodial personnel. "Turf wars" should not be tolerated if the staff is to function as a unified team with different but complementary functions.

Treatment staff must understand that because the program is operative within prison walls, custody and security are the top priorities. Custodial personnel need to view the program not as a threat but rather as another facet of inmate management. Both custodial and program personnel should agree that the long-term benefits of treatment, specifically a reduction in societal victimization, is a common goal worth striving toward. Each department must be sensitive to the other's needs. Relationships between department members should be cordial and professional with open lines of communication.

Custodial personnel need not understand the intricacies of treatment principles in order to work in concert with the program. However, it is recommended that the program's philosophy be shared in general terms, preferably available in written form. Custodial personnel should occasionally be invited into the treatment arena during those times when violation of confidentiality

guidelines is not at issue. Custodial staff should also be observed in the execution of their duties.

Although preferable for purposes of continuity and training, it is not absolutely necessary that the treatment program be routinely staffed by the same correctional officers. While shift rotations resulting in the placement of a variety of officers in the program may create extra effort, it has proven to be an excellent public relations tool. If the treatment program is operating appropriately, there will be consistency in decision making, accountability, discipline, and scheduling. At minimum, even in a fledgling program, such regimentation should manifest itself in an attitude of respectfulness among participants and notable cleanliness in the dormitories and program quarters. Should treatment personnel not interfere with vital custodial functions, and in the absence of any significant patterns of program errors, a comfortable and trusting working relationship between custodial and treatment staff should begin to emerge.

A Solid Referral Base

The success of any program is dependent on the ability to identify appropriate program participants for referral to treatment. Candidates should be transferred to proper treatment settings on a priority basis. Candidates should include those with a history of drug abuse or addiction. Although a serious concern, in the TC we need not get into the business of attempting to treat the "pusher" if the offender was not seriously using. However, our experience has been that most offenders involved in the business of selling were also using.

At the referring facility the written (hopefully factual) history of each inmate received should be closely scrutinized for indication of treatment need. Each inmate entering the system should also be interviewed with [the] same [information] being compared to their histories. The potential candidate should also be subjected to reliable assessment instruments indicating not only need but also readiness and willingness to engage in the treatment process. Only the most motivated should be referred initially, and, even then, their motivation should be reevaluated close to their expected date of transfer.

Upon arrival at the treating facility, as a matter of routine all referrals should again be evaluated as to their treatment suitability. All routine arrivals should likewise be screened for possible inclusion in treatment should their sentence structure allow. An appropriate referral includes not only a significant history of abuse but also the sentence length. Although treatment at the beginning of an inmate's lengthy prison term is by no means harmful and certainly can have educative value, maximum therapeutic gains are accrued via treatment toward the end of an inmate's prison term. This is because much of what is learned in treatment is incompatible with life in the hostile, predatory post-treatment prison setting.

Although the ideal treatment candidate is one who is motivated, it is possible to effectively treat those who have volunteered solely to gain access to the such fringe benefits as community work release. Intervention by other TC members may help the unmotivated offender embrace recovery and realize that treatment is critical to his future survival. In my experience, most inmates simply have no interest in treatment. Therefore, the more substantial the inducements available to those in treatment the better. Consistently denying these "carrots" to those who refuse to engage in the treatment process is critical. In Florida the privilege of access to community work release can be withheld. I advocate imposing more substantial consequences, such as denying parole. The withholding of privileges, and their reinstatement, can be used as leverage to persuade even the most resistant inmates to give treatment options serious consideration.

The prospect of treatment in the TC, typically foreign to the offender, can be intimidating, and the unfounded rumors circulating from the general prison population further serves to complicate matters. Such negativity seems to be fairly common, as was demonstrated in this chapter's initial discussion of the program Doin' Time Gettin' Straight. To combat these negative percep-

tions, those awaiting screening for potential enrollment should be exposed to a solid introductory program that includes tours and opportunities for casual conversation with program participants. Program candidates should be allowed to ask questions and voice concerns in order to allay their anxieties.

An intensive treatment program must be sold hard, particularly during its first 30 days when the dropout rate seems to be the highest. Such attrition can be especially problematic for a program that is under the vigilant eye of the legislature or other monitoring agencies. Program operation should not be tempered by an inordinate number of empty beds, and a treatment waiting list is essential. The program must operate from a position of strength, power, and control if it is to be respected by the inmates.

An excellent source of recruitment on a local level is the actual program participant. As a matter of social interest and as part of the recovery process, those in treatment should always be encouraged to refer a friend in need. Inmates exert terrific influence over one another. Another source of program recognition and strength is the area of competitive sports. Athletic achievement is typically held in high esteem by inmates, and this forum allows for the display of one's individual talent as well as team solidarity and friendship. Many rumors have been dispelled on the "rec yard" and many lasting treatment alliances have been formed.

The Program Director

Fundamental to the sound health of the TC is the performance of the program director. Not only should this individual have a firm understanding of the correctional environment, she should have a good working knowledge of treatment and the dynamics of the TC. The director must be patient and understand that the effective delivery of treatment services may on occasion be compromised because of the security needs of the institution. Finally, the director should be aptly prepared for the inherent stresses of the job.

The program director should be a model of recovery, with high standards of performance. She should be approachable, flexible, and willing to try innovative ideas. The lead person should be sensitive to feedback from line staff and the administration, have a healthy capacity to withstand frustration, and, last but not least, have a good sense of humor.

The director must be attentive to counselor performance. She must be sensitive to indication of burnout and do all that is necessary to minimize its destructive effects. On a regular basis the director should provide opportunities for staff to attend professional meetings and receive training as well as allow staff to vent frustration and offer ideas for program enhancement. The message should be clear that the future success of the program is theirs to mold and to own. The director should be sensitive to staff conflict, isolation, or counselors functioning at odds with the program's interest or philosophy. Attention should likewise be paid to the possibility of staff over involvement or identification with an inmate that typically stems from unresolved issues in the practitioner.

The Substance Abuse Counselor

Serious attention and time must be devoted to appropriate counselor selection. Applicants should not only have the requisite counseling skills but also be comfortable operating within a locked prison setting with inmates who can be unpleasant and dangerous. Counselors must be prepared to aggressively engage the offender in treatment and be mindful that a history of abuse will sometimes surface during the participant's struggle toward recovery.

Counselors must have a strong belief in the viability of treatment in the correctional setting. They must be committed, consistent, and conservative in decision making. Counselor selection should be guided by the facilitative effects of having several recovering addicts on board who have been stable themselves for a period of three or more years. The presence of some ex-offenders who have demonstrated stability for a shorter period of time is also desirable.

Treatment staff should be composed of a racial and cultural mix representative of those in the treatment population. Despite the gender of program participants, staff should be both male and female.

Because treatment needs vary, contrasting therapeutic styles can be of value. They should, of course, be complementary and certainly not at odds with the program's theoretical orientation or philosophy. Generally, regardless of the therapist's approach, progress can be made if the offender views the therapist as genuine, consistent in application of principles, competent, and caring. Finally, in an effort to broaden the treatment experience for the offender, and possibly to offset the effects of counselor burnout, each program participant should be assigned a different counselor at the close of a period not exceeding six months.

If the foregoing recommendations are followed, the staff should provide sufficient depth and expertise to address the needs of subjects with a myriad of complex treatment issues. Staff resources will be maximized if close attention is paid to suitably matching the counselor with the participant. Prudence should be exercised when assigning offenders with special pathological conditions, for example, sexual addicts. Although many substance abuse programs contain sexual addicts, who are often treated by both male and female counselors, the offender need not be assigned to female counselors if the offender's preference is adult female victims.

The Program Participant

Appropriate selection of program participants is vital to a successful program. An acceptable screening process will, at minimum, ensure that the participants have a history of substance abuse, are treatment motivated, and have sufficient time available to complete the program. Applicants should be intelligent enough to understand the principles presented. They should be free of physical or mental disorders and be able to withstand the effects of intrusive treatment techniques without suffering damage or losing emotional control. Applicants must not have a recent history of behavior incidents suggestive of gross immaturity or behavioral instability.

Those engaged in the process of inmate screening and selection will have the arduous, redundant, time-consuming task of reviewing factual written documentation available on the offender, counteracting denial, and otherwise selling the program. This work is critical to reaching the resistant interviewee. Because change on any level is typically unsettling to the offender, newly arriving inmates should be quickly screened so as to prevent them from becoming too comfortable with their setting and routine. They should not be allowed sufficient time to fortify the defense mechanisms that serve to refute their need for treatment.

One obstacle to a program's ability to bring inmates into treatment is a general prison population whose disinterest and distrust can be fueled by the anger generated from program participants who have been terminated for one reason or another. Inmates are typically more prone to listen to, take guidance from, and trust other inmates than staff. If program participants interface with the general population, it is highly recommended that terminated inmates be transferred quickly so as to minimize disruption and not dissuade the possible ambitions of others who may have expressed an initial interest in treatment.

A large part of the negativity found in the general population is related to the intrusive nature of the program. Those who have been discharged as non-amenable for treatment seem to have a sense that what was provided them was indeed what they needed, but that the program was too intimidating or demanding of their time and effort. Instead of openly admitting to this, however, they tend to condemn the program. Because they are now considered treatment failures by the institution, they typically have a limited chance of securing a community work release placement. These inmates often engage in a campaign to discredit the program, hoping to find a renewed access to work release.

Other elements responsible for inmates resisting entry into treatment or for spreading harmful rumors about the program relate to their false sense of pride, profound anxiety regarding the treatment experience,

feelings of shame, and their misperceptions that they have already accomplished without treatment that which is necessary to avoid a recommitment. Many inmates display a newly found religiosity. Also operative is a preference to pursue immediate comforts, a fundamental lack of discipline, inertia, the feeling that exposing oneself to additional rules is further imprisoning, and that "going to the state" for anything is acquiescence. Finally, it is inconceivable for average offenders to consider having to break the convict code, particularly when the state may be making money on them in exchange for their being exposed to the "horrors" of treatment.

Offenders who do well in treatment parallel those who are willing to surrender and are otherwise "sick and tired of being sick and tired." They firmly realize that their lives were out of control "on the streets" and that they are in need of professional intervention to break their cycle of recidivism. They feel privileged to be a part of a recovery program, a position that the program should promote. Successful participants are patient and understand that treatment is painful, intense work. They understand that the more of themselves they invest and the more risks they take, the faster their recovery. Finally, successful participants have respect for the integrity of the program and their fellow participants. They do not lose sight of the fact that although they live in a TC, they also live within a prison, the security of which is a top priority.

The Treatment Experience

Involvement in the TC must be voluntary. This does not mean that incentives for treatment should not be offered. However, it is clear that treatment will not be effective for offenders placed in a program against their will, regardless of provision of incentives. The treatment experience should be minimally of 9-to-12-months duration on a full-time basis. Participants should be exposed to the program's entire treatment curriculum. Because offenders have different levels of motivation, maturity, intellect, and degrees of pathology, actual treatment length should be open-ended.

The program should have a clearly defined mission, philosophy, and theoretical orientation that is monitored for consistency in practice. A handbook should be available to participants that includes program expectations, rules, and the standard state and federal consent forms necessary for residential treatment programs operating in the correctional setting. To ensure that these materials are properly understood, an orientation program and a mentoring system should be employed.

Discipline should be enforced. Program rules should be of limited number and easily understood. They should contain cardinal rules, which, if violated, result in immediate expulsion. The rules should make it clear that the program is a no-nonsense arena of recovery. From the first day, violations must be dealt with strictly, consistently, and expediently.

Program participants must understand that there is "no free lunch." Status in the community is earned. Hope is for sale, but it can only be purchased with serious and committed involvement. Participants should feel uncomfortable in the treatment environment, and staff should be suspicious of happy, relaxed participants. While balance, peace, and recovery can only result from hard work, a successful program will promote a sense of family and belonging. Tremendous feelings of security are generated by being a part of something bigger than oneself. For many, the TC is providing the very first experience of family. "Family members" are required to be empathic and otherwise available to each other.

A sense of spirituality is critical to the recovery process. However, it is important to ensure that spirituality does not involve a particular set of religious beliefs. The program should in no uncertain terms advocate or condone the imposition of a staff member's religious beliefs on participants.

The cleanliness of dormitories and program space should be an essential component of the treatment process. The program should, without question, be a showplace. All bunks should be impeccably maintained. Program participants should likewise be fastidious in hygiene and grooming, which will facilitate the development of self-esteem, pride, dignity, and respect. Standards designed to measure cleanliness should be established as the maintenance of personal living space tends to be an important indicator of attitude.

The rationale behind a clean environment and strict regimentation is to provide a setting of heightened awareness to teach offenders to routinely monitor and order their world.

Fundamental to a healthy TC is a climate where participants can take risks and freely confront themselves and others without fear. In the treatment setting, to confront is to care.

The treatment environment is not a forum to focus on racial issues, religion, and so on. Participants in the TC who are genuinely uninterested in treatment tend to bring up such issues in an effort to entertain themselves, disrupt the program, or shift focus away from themselves. The program should be absolutely intolerant of such activity. The only color in the Doin' Time Gettin' Straight program is orange, the color of the participants' name tags.

Treatment staff should be sensitive to the nature of the offenders' convictions and not require them to publicly divulge this information unless they choose to do so. Revelations of such sensitive information could prove problematic if leaked to those outside of the TC. Accordingly, the program should avoid specialty group treatment for same-crime offenders. An effective treatment program not only tightly manages offenders' time, it also deters substance abuse by screening urine on a random but consistent basis. I believe that twice-a-month screenings are sufficient. Urinalysis can yield both positive indication of use and also give a reasonably accurate indication of suspected use. Those with positive indication of use should be met with harsh consequences if not immediate discharge, and the prison's disciplinary process might be used to augment program sanctions.

It is important to note that the TC has a life of its own. Its health and momentum are integrally tied to the committed efforts of staff as well as the consistency and expediency with which problems are handled. The program's health should be constantly monitored, perhaps by the program's internal structure, a group of participants or graduates with earned positions of leadership. These individuals should be a highly motivated group who facilitate and otherwise oversee the program's operation. It should be stressed that they have absolutely no authority over the other participants. By program design these individuals are held in high esteem and are otherwise seen as worthy of respect. Those in the most senior positions in the structure need not remain there for periods of more than a year. Such term limits, as well as other checks and balances, can help to prevent abuse and corruption among inmate leaders.

In a sizable program, the internal program structure can be quite large and complex. The demands of this job and the accompanying emotional strain are great. Daily effort must be exerted in examining program trends, monitoring for procedural compliance (a never-ending process), and otherwise interfacing with the director and counselors. The rigors of this full-time position dictate an annual rotation of this duty, provided the program has enough qualified staff to do so.

Treatment is conducted both individually and in group by professional counselors. Caseloads should ideally not exceed a ratio of 15:1. Effective delivery of treatment services can only be accomplished subsequent to a review of all available records and the development of comprehensive psychosocial histories and individualized written treatment plans. Because of the manipulative skills of some program participants, it cannot be stressed enough that review of all available factual historical data is essential prior to engaging in the treatment process. Failure to do so can easily result in a therapist being happily manipulated into feeling that he is making significant gains with a client when the reality is that it is the therapist who is being "treated."

I have found that the most effective treatment approach with the convicted male addict in the TC is one that is uniformly hardnosed, intrusive, and emotionally evocative. In high-impact group treatment experiences, keeping the offender off balance emotionally is particularly fruitful. The overall treatment approach should be responsibility based. It should principally focus on that disordered thinking responsible for the offender's behavior that has resulted in his incarceration. Such issues usually include limited self-esteem; excessive anger and resentment; depression; shame; disturbance in interpersonal relationships; and an inability to achieve a state of calm, particularly in critical situations.

It is revealing how much stress offenders are willing to endure if they are satisfied with their treatment gains and are confident in their therapist. Existing rapport can be enhanced by involving significant members of the participant's family in the treatment experience, as this reinforces commitment, establishes a channel of communication, and typically results in access to information otherwise unavailable to the therapist.

An effective treatment program should offer a variety of treatment experiences, most of which will be of the group variety. The standard fare includes the encounter group, which is designed to orient, affirm, emote, and, ultimately, shatter denial. The support and fellowship offered by such groups as Alcoholics Anonymous and Narcotics Anonymous is indispensable. Participants who routinely attend these meetings often incorporate these support systems into their postrelease lives outside prison walls.

In the correctional setting, groups of all sizes and intensity can be monitored by staff. It is also critical that sufficient time and resources be given to those participants in emotional turmoil related to an intense treatment experience. The assignment of "pit crews" (a team of at least five group participants used to assist individuals to focus on the healing process) and "shadows" (individuals with whom trust and confidence has been established) for follow-up work is particularly effective.

A program of merit boasts a solid academic curriculum that focuses on a myriad of core issues related to the offender's substance abuse and criminality. Because previous exposure to basic substance abuse educational material is not uncommon to offenders in Florida, such programming is kept to a minimum. It is necessary that staff ensure that participants understand the material that has been presented. Should participants experience difficulty with the material, every effort should be made to provide them access to in-program tutorial opportunities.

All program participants should be routinely provided feedback on progress made in treatment. This feedback should be incorporated into the treatment file along with weekly case notes. Treatment progress should be measurable. A fixed set of criteria, all of which are performance based, should exist for program advancement. Because a host of offenders experience difficulty in delaying gratification and tend to have a low tolerance for frustration, all achievements, no matter how small, should be celebrated. These may very well be the first achievements of consequence in an offender's life.

The inmate that is not achieving, is borderline in performance, or outright obstreperous, poses a unique challenge for staff. Every effort should be made to gain rapport with and effectively treat the difficult participant. A variety of creative techniques, including transactional analysis, psychodrama, and branch groups, is employed to do so. Those who are problematic or unwilling or unable to perform can always be put on notice. Barring extraordinary circumstances, dismissal from the program should never come as a surprise. In the absence of unusual circumstances, the participant should be afforded an opportunity to return to treatment subsequent to the lapse of a prescribed period.

Vital to sound treatment programming is the appropriate clinical staffing of all important decisions made by the practitioner. There exists tremendous strength and comfort in the availability of such a forum. Such a process is of value when program decisions are tested either locally or in a court of law.

A major component of a dynamic treatment program includes motivational elements. For example, on a daily basis all program participants should begin their treatment day with a short meeting designed to do nothing more than inspire and elevate moods. This is especially important as the struggle toward recovery is a strenuous one. Such meetings typically include the partici-

pants' singing, dancing, reciting of inspirational messages, and so forth. These meetings effectively serve to offset depressive feelings related to incarceration and the negativity projected by those inmates who are not in the program, and they provide an ideal way to build camaraderie and program solidarity. The program should also provide a daily meeting that takes place toward the close of the work day during which announcements are made and behavioral problems are attended to. This meeting also provides participants an opportunity to reflect on and share their day's achievements.

Vital to an offender's success as a program graduate is the smooth transition to additional treatment services that are compatible with those of the program from which he has graduated. Discharge plans, which should have been under consideration early in the offender's treatment, should be solidified well before program completion. Following execution of appropriate releases prior to graduation, upon program completion the treatment file should be transferred to the receiving facility with treatment areas in need of further attention being clearly delineated. As mentioned earlier, offenders should be treated toward the end of their term in order to prevent a return to a hostile setting. Likewise, end-of-sentence treatment can prevent return to the often dysfunctional support systems from which they came.

Doin' Time Gettin' Straight's treatment process does not claim to cure but rather to educate. The value of such education has repeatedly been demonstrated in populations who have experienced similar treatment. Monies previously available to build bigger and more secure prisons are a thing of the past. Treatment works! Let's get busy.

Excerpts from: Steven F. Singer, "Essential Elements of the Effective Therapeutic Community in the Correctional Institution: A Director's Perspective." In *Drug Treatment Behind Bars: Prison-Based Strategies for Change*, Kevin E. Early, (ed.), pp. 75–88. Copyright © 1996 Kevin E. Early. Reprinted by permission of Praeger Publishers, an imprint of Greenwood Publishing Group, Inc.

9

Through the Narrow Gate

Calbraith MacLeod

Focus Questions

1. What childhood experiences influenced MacLeod's behaviors as an adult?

2. What did MacLeod do to be sentenced to prison the first time? Why did he return?

3. Why are some correctional treatment programs ineffective, according to the author?

4. What steps did MacLeod take to change his own attitudes and behavior?

5. Do you think MacLeod is rehabilitated?

I'm a machinist by trade. I live in one of a range of prison cells housing the former owner of an industrial supply business, a truck driver, an apartment manager, a baker, a building contractor, a coordinator of a day center for the developmentally disabled, a scientist who's worked for NASA, a window glazer, an auto-body technician, a radio disc jockey, a professional piano tuner, a house painter and a cabinet builder. Four of my neighbors have general education diplomas, five graduated [from] high school and four hold college degrees. Seven of my neighbors are veterans. We've all been married. We all have children who love and miss us, and all but two of us owned homes. All of us owned cars when we were free—cars that were reg-

istered, inspected and insured. We didn't steal them. . . .

As convicted people, it is important we remember we came from a social world so we have some chance of returning to live in it, relate to it and leave it with the dignity of human-beings. No matter what the media, our captors or their agents refer to us as, it is important that we do not think of ourselves as scum, predators and animals. It is important we do not adopt the idea—they treat me like an animal so I will act like one. For the moment we give in to either of these temptations, we dramatically reduce the chance we will be able to get back on track toward the wholesome visions we all once harbored about how our lives as human beings are supposed to unfold.

None of us wanted to be criminals. We did not sit in our fifth grade social studies classes and dream of spending our lives in conflict with the law. We dreamed of having homes and jobs and grown-up toys. We dreamed of leading serene, sane, nondestructive lives. Although many people, both in and out of prison, do not want convicts to be at peace in prison, it is our early dreams of serenity we as prisoners need to rediscover if we are to transform our lives into demonstrations worthy of self-respect. Further, it is only in developing a feeling of inner peace that we who will be released from prison can hope to live in society for long as nondestructive citizens. In fact, regardless of our optimistic fantasies of being able to control ourselves "this time" when we get out, if we do not develop a sense of serenity in prison, there exists small chance our behavior as free people will be any different than before we were imprisoned. The inability to create a feeling of serenity while living with society is what initially sparked many a convicted person's criminal exploits.

Fortunately, even when we've fallen far from the mark and face the hatred of a billion people, as long as we remember we're humans, we maintain the capacity for self-respect. I believe the fact that we each own the ability to lead ourselves to a place of serenity while under any adversity is the most awesome power we as humans possess. I hope, by the end of this chapter, you will understand how that can occur.

I am the third child of six born to married parents. My childhood occurred during the late 50s and throughout the 60s. My family owned a home and a little land, but not much else. My father was a WWII veteran, as patriotic as a man can be. But I don't think the war did him any favors. I've seen him leap, startled as a rabbit, at the sound of fireworks on the 4th of July. I've also seen him stand by with punctured lungs after an auto accident and refuse medical treatment until the doctor had examined his son's injuries. I've also watched him rape my mother. He ordered me to watch. It was a game: he'd rape her, he said, because she beat me. I'd watch as the humiliation part of her punishment, then she'd beat me when my father was at work.

I don't think my mother was ever able to love children. She held me in a loving manner twice in my life. Maybe she just didn't know how to be loving. Her own mother died when she was young, so maybe that had something to do with it. I know she hated me. I can't really blame her given the recurring circumstances. Still, I hated her for not showing me the affection I deserved and I hated her for beating me. She once threw me with such fury, my head struck a bureau hard enough to knock me unconscious. I can imagine my father lifting my limp body from the floor, screaming at my mother for having killed me. But of course I didn't die.

My father died of tuberculosis when I was twelve. For the next two years, my mother beat me every night upon her return from her second-shift job, except one night when my sister hid my father's leather belt, my mom's weapon of choice. After a year or so, I got so used to "the belt," it just didn't hurt anymore; I couldn't even cry. It was as though my tears were all used up. The only problem was that when I didn't cry, my mother became so furious and out of breath from swinging the belt, I was afraid she would give herself a heart attack. So I started to fake crying. After I turned 14, my mother

struck me with the buckle end of the belt one night. She'd never done that before; there had always been an unspoken rule against it. That night I took the belt away from her and told her it was over, she would hit me no more. She went to her room and cried for a couple of hours and never raised a hand to me again.

I entered adulthood with no self-respect, no concrete values and enough hatred to have fueled a world war. I felt like an intruder in a world belonging to other people. I believed something was wrong with me. Other people always seemed happy; they appeared to easily understand how to act, what to do and when to do it. I, however, felt a need to plan how to act from moment to moment. Life presented a continuous struggle to be what I thought others wanted me to be. I felt relaxed only when drunk, high or with people I'd already learned how to please. The people I spent time with were not my friends. I looked a part of the group, but secretly I felt alone. I thought other people controlled my life and hated them for controlling me and myself for not stopping them. My inability to control my life filled me with rage. . . .

I married a beautiful woman. I bought a wonderful country home. I fathered lovely children. I built the quickest car in my town. I acquired credit galore and money to waste, and I consumed more alcohol than ever before. I smoked marijuana, took speed, snorted cocaine and ate acid. I lied without guilt or reason, stole anything I could and took pride in my thievery. Fear of one thing or another became my constant companion. My prospects of solving any problem grew remote. I lost any clear identity, ideals or self-respect. My conduct wavered from aggressive to assaultive as I worked to frighten, humiliate and control the world around me. I immersed myself in orgies of sex and drugs and perversity. My beautiful wife became an object of utility to me. I neglected my lovely children. I abused my creditors and I damaged my wonderful home. . . .

I reasoned that working the night shift would create more time to spend with my family; however, when I worked at night, I slept all day. I thought if I invited other people to live at my home, I'd stop abusing my wife, but I continued to psychologically abuse her. I imagined if I stockpiled fruit juice I'd drink that instead of beer, but I continued to get drunk. I supposed staying away from people who stole would help me quit stealing, but my thievery continued. I believed if I gave my wife the money for creditors, she'd keep it safe, but after a few drinks I'd frighten her enough to return the money to me.

I understood I was destroying my relationships, property, reputation, health and finances. In spite of it all, I continued in my destructive ways.

Finally, my cruel behavior towards my wife erupted into hurtful violence, and I was charged with aggravated assault and sentenced to five years in prison. In prison, I was asked to participate in a newly developed program for sex offenders. I wasn't required to do the program, because I wasn't convicted of a sex crime. Nevertheless, I agreed to do what the program coordinator instructed. I would have done whatever necessary to shorten my time in prison.

The program I attended consisted of three meetings each week—a unit meeting where inmates voiced their gripes about prison conditions and restrictions; a group meeting where several of us would discuss various aspects of our crimes; and a one-on-one meeting with a student of psychology. After six months of going to these meetings, I was released from prison and placed on parole. I didn't feel any different than when I'd gone into the program, but I told myself—they are professionals, perhaps they know something I don't. Perhaps, I thought, all will now be well and I can get on with a good life.

The conditions of my release included continuing to see a therapist once every two weeks, to attend one group meeting each week and to meet my parole officer once a month. My sessions with my therapist consisted of discussions of the weather. The therapist really didn't seem to care what we talked about. My group meetings were discussions of how things were going for everyone and, according to the participants, everything was always going well. No one was about to expose any problems for fear of their parole being violated. My meetings

with my parole officer occurred as scheduled for the first few months, then three months at a time would pass and I would need to call her to find out if she was interested in seeing me.

My parole officer told me she would not violate my parole for drinking or for losing my job, but she would violate my parole if both these things occurred. Since I had been released in a strange town and since, according to her assessment, I was "not an alcoholic," my parole officer agreed with me that bars were a good place for me to meet people. So I went to a different bar every night. I must have wanted to meet a lot of people!

The sad part is that even if my parole officer had not allowed me to drink, I would have. Even if my parole officer had been attentive, I would have abused my wife. Even if the group meeting had been a place I could have told the truth, and even if my therapist had been caring, I would have still participated in destructive conduct. The prison program I had attended was not designed to heal my broken persona. It had done nothing to reduce my fears, self-pity, selfishness or hatred towards myself, others and the world.

I met my second wife in a bar. We got an apartment within a few months. I wanted to love her and provide a decent life for us both, but mixed in with my wish to be a good husband to her were reoccurring desires to dominate and humiliate her. She was strong willed, and I seriously injured her twice during my attempts to force her to do my bidding.

My wife had stayed with me because I had manipulated her into being so dependent upon me she had nowhere to turn. Fortunately, I was placed in prison for leaving the scene of an accident. My incarceration granted her the freedom to become somewhat independent and, courageously, to tell the police of my mistreatment of her. I was sentenced to serve 20 to 40 years in prison for abusing her and causing her injury.

I returned to prison consumed by more hatred than ever towards myself and towards the entire world. I'd felt like I could have blown the entire planet out of space if I'd had the ability. I hated myself, I hated others, I hated animals, I hated flowers or anything of beauty. The Vermont State prison administration was so frightened by me, they contracted a place for me in a federal penitentiary. . . .

Unfortunately, I found the federal and the Vermont prison systems offered only partial answers. The federal prison offered an alcohol/drug abuse program, but it was strictly a program of information, a critical ingredient in a successful alcohol/drug program, but only one ingredient of many necessary and absent. Vermont corrections offered violent offender and sex offender programs which basically operated in the same ways. One is asked to write "thinking reports" when he encounters situations that did or could lead him to victimize someone. The report consists of describing the situation and listing the thoughts, feelings and behavior patterns one experienced. The object of the exercise is to recognize and change distorted thinking patterns and to become able to identify in advance when one is heading toward victimizing behavior so he can intervene in the process. It is thought that the earlier one can recognize he is heading for trouble, the easier it will be for him to intervene.

While the self-awareness this exercise delivers can be useful as a small part of a rehabilitation whole, it is not a whole unto itself. The problem I experienced with the intervention method of rehabilitation is it did nothing to address the underlying desires and hostilities I was experiencing. Though I was able to keep myself from being violent for a short time, I remained as burdened by a lack of self-respect, by hatred and by compulsions to commit crime as I had ever been. I am one of many who confirm it will not be long before a person full of hostility and burdened by compulsions to commit crimes says to heck with this intervention exercise. It just isn't practical, for one so burdened, to live his life in this way. The intervention approach is like telling an alcoholic who is repeatedly arrested for driving drunk that all he needs to do is recognize when he is drunk and get someone to drive him home. This does nothing to address his underlying problems; how long will it be before he can't find someone to drive him home or just doesn't feel like bothering with the exercise?

With the exception of the Chapman University program I attended at the Lompoc Penitentiary, the correctional programs I have been involved with in federal prison and in the Vermont state prison system have been, as least for me, incomplete programs without a realistic agenda.

1. The programs utilize embarrassment on a group scale, group viewing or listening to personal thinking reports and tape recordings of fantasies as a tool of therapy.

Problem: Most convicted people are convicts partly because they were humiliated as children. But we are not children anymore; we can now choose, and few of us are willing to subject ourselves to what we once suffered when we had no choice in the matter. Most of us made a silent pact years ago that no one would ever humiliate us again.

2. The programs incorporate strategies aimed at getting the convicted person to know how his victim felt.

Problem: We know how our victims felt. We wanted them to feel that way. We were trying to have them feel like we'd felt all our lives. By telling a convicted person that his victim felt frightened, humiliated, hurt and powerless, the program directors are telling him crime holds great power and that his criminal efforts were a success.

3. The correctional programs I've attended have been billed as something one should do because his or her previous behavior was bad for other people and for society.

Problem: While still ensnared in a destructive lifestyle, a convict's first concern is not other people and society. We care about ourselves. We are for the most part egocentric people and need programs designed to utilize that egocentricity. We need programs billed as good for us.

4. The intervention approach includes the expectation that a convicted person will use the methods because of the threat of a return to prison.

Problem: The threat of prison never stopped us from committing crimes before, and now we are familiar, therefore less frightened, of the concept.

5. As a part of one's intervention in destructive behaviors, one is expected to disclose any risky thoughts, behaviors or feelings to a program counselor on the street.

Problem: We do need someone to disclose such things to on the street if we hope to maintain a crime free life. However, we need someone we can trust not to "flip out" or get frightened by what we tell them, else we will never be able to be honest, and such a counselor will be of no use whatsoever. Every convict knows if he told the state counselors the true thoughts or desires he encounters while living on house arrest, probation or parole, the counselor would quickly have him back inside prison. We need someone outside we can tell anything to and get constructive feedback.

The therapeutic strategies I have experienced in corrections contain the view that the only important thing is to stop the convicted person from committing more crime, no matter how the convict feels, no matter how he must suffer through life, no matter what kind of destructive medication, continuous supervision or continuous fear it takes to ensure nondestructive behaviors. But this approach only encourages convicts, especially younger ones, to develop unrealistic expectations regarding how they, after treatment, are going to be able to lead normal lives. The discouragement that follows will have them saying, "What's the use?" Implying that fear and supervision will keep one on the right track, irrespective of his personal happiness, is a position that causes heartache, frustration and pain, because it promises something it can't deliver—long-term non-destructive conduct. It leads the falsely guided to a gradual build-up of anger and resentment, setting themselves and others they care greatly about up for eventual harm. Then, when the harm does come, when the convict re-offends, the program directors declare, "See what happens when you don't follow our recommendations!" To imply that all program participants who re-offend didn't develop the ability to stop committing crimes merely because they hadn't tried hard enough and long enough and because they didn't have a sufficiently positive attitude is a gross insult. I'm but one of the countless number of typical convicts who have applied themselves to numerous correctional programs with dedication and diligence enough to match any recipient of a doctorate degree. Don't tell us that we didn't try hard enough!

What is particularly infuriating is when a program facilitator moans about how hard he found it to fight a particular character flaw. He neglects to say that the character defect was never really an integral part of his make-up. The person who initially developed into a nondestructive lifestyle simply can't understand the criminal lifestyle. If I had a magic wand, I would put some program directors in the shoes of a typical criminal weighted down with compulsions, unstable emotions and no self-respect. After he's struggled to become able to just stop hating himself for a few minutes each day after years of determined effort and many setbacks, then he might begin to understand what I mean. If I could then wish him into the shoes of the person with an obsession for sex, drugs, money or power so strong that he repeatedly hurts those he most cares for, he would, when feeling suicidal, finally get the full message that how we feel on the inside matters a heck of a lot.

All of us can transform ourselves and develop serenity and self-command enough to lead us to living a nondestructive lifestyle. However, we can never, ever gain control over our lives or truly enter into lasting non-destructive lifestyles solely through the methods of supervision, fear and staged intervention.

It is true that to enter a nondestructive lifestyle, we convicted people need a combination of various helps. Some need job skills, some need to learn how to read and write, some need to end their substance abuse, some need medicinal aid to overcome depression. However, we all need the ability to love and respect ourselves, and to do this we need to acquire command of our own lives. Believe me, there is not one person who is repeatedly acting the part of a criminal who has command of his or her own life, and there is no criminal who has not gained a considerable degree of control of his or her own life who will ever be anywhere except on the verge of committing another crime. This is not an effort to be discouraging, just factual.

When I entered prison, I already possessed an education, job skills, mental health (as in brain chemistry) and physical health. However, I could not respect or love or even like myself, and I did not possess any self-command. All my plans lay subject to the arbitrary rule of my emotions, to the likes and dislikes of other people, and to the various compulsions that appeared at unexpected moments and ordered me away from meaningful activities to seek out power and sex, and money and notoriety. What I needed from a rehabilitation program was the means to gain control of my own life. What I was offered by Vermont corrections was a way to intervene in the things which were still controlling my life. I was offered a box of Band-Aids for a reoccurring wound, not a way to stop being wounded.

My placement in the federal penitentiary at Lompoc, California, was one of the best things that had ever happened to me. I was exposed to relatively normal people there. The drug dealers in federal prison had not suffered the emotional damage many men in the state prison had. They were angry at the judicial system, but not at other people or the world in general. Most importantly, I became exposed to the Chapman University program at Lompoc. The education teachers in the Vermont prison system, well meaning as they were, had continually commented on how brilliant I was. However, when I began taking college courses, I found the Chapman University professors were not easily impressed.

The professors who came to the prison treated me like a person. It amazed me— they weren't a bit afraid of me. I admired their courage and nonjudgmental attitude. Theirs was not the challenging false courage I was used to encountering. The professors

took the stance of "We know there's something of value inside of you and if you don't destroy us in the process, we're going to help you retrieve it." They weren't frightened of being harmed; they were not offended by insults. I had never seen such self-command. For some reason, I knew it was the type of courage and self-command I had been searching for [for] a very long time.

One night I read a small book containing the description of a person whom I could only think detestable. In the morning, I awoke to the sight of the book laying on my nightstand, and I suddenly realized I was no different from the person described in the book. I gained a very clear view of my true self and I didn't like what I saw.

I met three other inmates who were also searching for a viable way to change their lives. I realized there were people more intelligent than myself in the world and that I may not be able to figure out how to straighten out my own life and become like the professors by my own methods. With these insights, I joined the three inmates I'd met in searching for methods that would have some real rehabilitative impact upon us. We were not searching for ways to look good, we were searching for ways to extinguish our hatred of ourselves and others and to become truly self-commanding, courageous, self-respecting individuals.

After a few years in federal prison in California, I was returned to state prison. When I was returned to Vermont, I was allowed to enter the Violent Offender program, a program designed to help people intervene in their violent behaviors. Unfortunately, prison policy soon changed and it was determined one could only enter a program while within two years of his minimum release date. Thus, I was stopped from completing that program.

Left to my own devices, I looked in other places to find ideas about how I could really change my life. I went to church, but the people there didn't have time to change their lives; they were too busy discussing what was wrong with other religions to study what was right about theirs. I started going to Alcoholics Anonymous meetings; right away I found that many of the volunteers had all the attributes I'd previously observed only in the university professors. Over time, I listened to many people who once had many of my own characteristics explain to me how they had changed their lives. Finally, I understood I needed to do many of the things they had done to see if they would work as well on myself.

What follows are, in a condensed version, the viewpoints I adopted, the actions I took and the results I obtained. I did not invent, develop or otherwise think of any of these viewpoints or methods; I just utilized them because of the liberty and serenity other people told me they'd derived from them.

1. I ended my drug and alcohol use. I did this by seeking those who had ended their own use of these substances and by doing what they told me they had done.

2. Instead of judging behavior, thought or speech as good or bad in a moral sense, I began to view and judge all personal conduct from the singular standpoint of whether it empowered me, debilitated me or concerned me at all. I am of the mind that conduct empowers me when it allows me to remain in reality and when it diminishes feelings of hostility and shame.

3. I came to understand that my ability to respect myself and therefore my ability to love myself rested not on an accumulation of wealth and skills and knowledge, but on the bedrock of appropriate conduct. How I choose to act determines whether or not I can respect and love myself. This was a radical idea! In one moment it changed my traditional thinking of 40 years from "what will or do they think of me" to "what do or will I think of myself?"

4. I differentiated hostility from anger. By hostility, I'm stating I intend to wage war and punish offending parties until they surrender or until I'm satisfied they've suffered at least as much as I have. Through the lens of hostility, I view people as enemies and disguise my cruelty as righteous. By anger, I am saying I disapprove of a particular behavior or event, and I intend to defend my goods, services, resources, serenity and security from theft, but I don't desire to punish the offending party. Through the lens of anger, I see victimizers as errant siblings in need of practicable methods to liberate themselves from the influence of a destructive lifestyle.

I looked back over all the years of my life and listed all the hostilities I still harbored towards various people, groups and institutions. I looked at what part I had played in the situations. I realized I have never gotten away with any mean or dishonest action without the consequence of increased hostility and of further reducing my control over myself, and that people who act with a hurtful motive suffer similar punishment. Lastly, I offered up all of my old hostilities to this system and got out of the punishment business.

5. I listed all the hostilities I harbored towards natural events and realized it was laughable for me to assume I was important enough for the natural world to single me out for special treatment. It was I who had been adopting goals and expectations in opposition to natural events.

6. I listed all the hostilities I harbored towards myself. I tried to think of everything I'd ever done or not done that would allow me to dislike myself, and I assembled a list of the negative character traits I'd exhibited, i.e. dishonesty, selfishness, etc. I came to understand that my destructive behaviors posed no lasting quality and were not as powerful as I'd liked to imagine, and I stopped equating criminal conduct with power.

7. I found someone with a closed mouth and a nonjudgmental nature and disclosed all the hostilities I'd listed against myself. As a result, recollections of the humiliating thoughts and behaviors lost their ability to emotionally disturb me to any great degree. That in itself was quite liberating.

8. I wrote down all the things I feared and collected them into categories. I found the vast majority of my fears pertained to my image, to the ways I'd wanted other people to view me. Others pertained to my hesitation to accept responsibility for my own choices, my dislike of unpredictable events and my view of success as unobtainable.

   I combated my fears of other's thoughts about me by realizing people had better things to do than think about me. Further, I redoubled my efforts to stop using the opinions of other people as a source of self-respect. I moved instead towards the possession of personal character traits I, myself, could respect myself for. My quest for empowerment required me to find the courage to move onward to a lifestyle of reality, readily accepting blame for my own actions. I strove to recognize when I was blaming my own behavior on an outside source and to redirect my viewpoint. I discovered that my visions of success always contained the element of serenity. Unfortunately, I had been searching for serenity by collecting wealth, things, power over people and events, and by impressing others with my skills and intelligence. Working to acquire self-respect and reduce fear and hostility was instead the route to lead me to serenity. I combated my fears of unpredictable events by restraining myself from trying to control events I have no real control over and abandoning my efforts to predict the future to any great extent. I do plan for the future, but I concentrate on what I can do today to create the tomorrow I want. I have found that as long as I work to separate myself from the tools and deceptions of my old lifestyle, what the future delivers will always be better than what I'd had before.

9. I came to understand one cannot fully respect himself simply by acting in appropriate ways; one must also make reparation for past harmful conduct. Towards this end, I listed all the people, (including business owners and others effected by my behaviors), I had harmed in any way over my entire life. I reviewed each situation and estimated and noted the dollar figure of the monetary losses I'd caused others to suffer. Having completed my list, I wrote letters to every person and group I'd identified as having harmed. I apologized for my trespasses and accepted responsibility for my debts. Some of the smaller debts I paid right away, some will need to wait, some can be repaid in other ways. For example, I owe the taxpayers a large sum of money, but if I inspire one person to turn away from a life of crime, I will have repaid even this huge obligation.

10. I revisited the list of shame-producing character traits I'd assembled while exploring my hostility towards myself, and I assembled a list of character traits opposite to those I'd identified. I studied each character trait and made an effort to clarify what each meant to me. I was assembling a personal, moral base from which to direct my thoughts and actions.

11. I began a campaign to be helpful to others. This errand is as helpful to me as to others, because it lends my life a perceptible purpose and keeps my conduct appropriate; I would not be helpful if I demonstrated and modeled hurtful conduct.

12 I recognized that the cognitive and intervention strategies currently employed by Vermont corrections constitute wonderfully useful methods to maintain one's new lifestyle, after it is effected, and availed myself of the appropriate programs.

As a result of these actions I followed, my sessions of punitive self-hatred regarding my past actions have all but ended. My self-respect is no longer contingent upon what people think about me. I enjoy freedom from the futile labor of trying to persuade the world to conform to my will, and I seldom experience the necessity to try to convince anyone of anything or to change them. I possess no need to frighten people or to present myself as dangerous, crazy, hot tempered or intimidating. I've acquired the ability to form honest relationships with all types of people, and I welcome friendly relations, but it's no longer imperative I secure the friendship of any specific person. I seldom feel lonely and I no longer entertain thoughts of suicide. My life is as though I've stopped racing around a track and entered the calm of the infield. I can see people still struggling to outperform me and one another, but I no longer feel any need to be in the race. Life for me has stopped being a competition. I have come to understand there is nothing of value I can steal from people and no grand prize for being "the best." I enjoy a new ability to maintain my composure even while faced with difficult situations and confronted by the most obnoxious of people, no longer afraid that my emotions will force me to act destructively. I enjoy the liberty to use the wisdom and knowledge of yesterday's and today's people; this no longer threatens my independence and is a gift of incredible value to me.

Most important to me, by taking the actions I've described, my compulsions to commit crime have miraculously diminished to a point where a little willingness on my part easily keeps them at bay.

The thoughts pulling many convicted people toward destructive conduct are akin to the way excuses to smoke enter the mind of one who is trying to quit, or in line with the thoughts of a depressed individual who entertains the notion, "I should just kill myself," until he finally does try. These yearnings seem to emerge out of nowhere and become feared and ever-lurking opponents. Even knowing the almost certain consequences that follow destructive conduct are not enough to push the thoughts of it out of our minds. We are like the person who repeatedly tries to solve his problems by getting drunk, and discovering they are worse when he sobers, begins yet another drunken spree. Why does the alcoholic or cigarette smoker not just quit? Why does the overweight person simply stop eating so much food?

Those who say, "He could stop committing crimes if he really wanted to," are mis-

taken. Wanting to stop is not enough. Many people want to live normal, nondestructive lives, just as many people want to lose weight, stop smoking cigarettes and stop contemplating suicide. The program of Alcoholics Anonymous exists because people who wanted to stop drinking found they could not do so. Is anyone ready to tell the over two million people in that organization that they hadn't really wanted to stop?

It is here I have good news for those who suffer as I did from recurring destructive thoughts. After taking the decisive actions I've described above, the thought of participating in destructive conduct has not overridden the command of my thoughts in three years. Before that time, I cannot remember three months passing in which destructive desires did not seize command of my thoughts. This new self-command is not unlike that enjoyed by the smoker who, years after quitting, may encounter the desire to smoke, but can now easily brush the thought aside. There are thousands of recovered alcoholics who had previously suffered from mental obsessions to drink. After doing their Twelve Steps, the obsession to drink was lifted.

I don't know why the methods I followed liberated me from the mental messages to be destructive. I didn't ask a "higher power" to do it. I just took the actions I've described and the destructive mental messages became infrequent and lost power over my self-direction. This strategy represents the missing link between corrections' current cognitive and intervention strategies and long-term nondestructive conduct By turning criminal compulsions into the less intense form of a habit, the intervention and cognitive restructuring approaches then become viable rehabilitation strategies.

I could not have stayed out of prison before I took the actions I did. My emotions had been extremely unstable and I'd been consumed by hatred towards myself and others. I'd been addicted to alcohol and drugs and plagued by compulsions. I am none of these things now. Still, the lifestyle I lived for so long lurks, waiting for me to become so comfortable in my new lifestyle that I backslide. Even though I have built for myself a new style of living, I will need several things to stay out of prison when released. I will need to remain active in Alcoholics Anonymous to keep from returning to the use of alcohol, drugs and fantasy. I will need a support system in place, consisting of people I can be honest with without fear of them over-reacting. I will need to be sure I do not get involved in any codependent relationships—to do this, I may need to forgo intimate relationships altogether. I will need to rebuild financial stability without getting caught up in the need to buy things, and I will need to remain active in doing voluntary service work to help others. Of course, I will need a job and an apartment, but I have never experienced difficulty with being employed or finding a place to live. I will need to maintain my new lifestyle by developing intervention techniques, and this is where it would be helpful to be involved in a group situation such as the programs many prisons utilize today, where other members of the group point out places one's thinking may yet be distorted and where intervention techniques are developed.

I have come a long way along a difficult route. It is as though I began what was supposed to be a constructive journey through life by first losing the equipment I needed to see me through. Then I found need to turn around, retrace the trail, pick up the gear and brush it off. Some of the equipment is bent and dented and can be patched up and used with care; some of the gear is damaged beyond repair. Nevertheless, I am now capable of moving forward. Today my life is filled with purpose and meaning and direction and power. I have been shown how to be of real help to people like myself. My life has become greatly simplified, and I have no desire to flee from reality or to act out the part of a criminal. Today, without resignation, apathy or undue effort, I've finally stopped hurting others and myself.

Reprinted from: Calbraith MacLeod, "Through the Narrow Gate." In *Frontiers of Justice, Volume 3: The Crime Zone*, Claudia Whitman and Julie Zimmerman (eds.), pp. 24–38. Copyright © 2000 by Biddle Publishing Company. Reprinted by permission.

Chapter III
Discussion

Elements of Correctional Rehabilitation

The three readings in this section provide concrete examples of what can work in correctional rehabilitation and treatment. For example, the therapeutic community model at Marion emphasizes individual responsibility for future behavior. Many of Gendreau's and Singer's principles of effective intervention are comprehensive, in part because they were written to help service providers and counselors. While inside prison, MacLeod developed his list of what he needed to do to heal and change his life. He gained knowledge of how to do this from the wisdom of various people. MacLeod's list is much more simplistic than Gendreau's and Singer's and focuses on using a cognitive-behavioral model to find inner peace and forgiveness. MacLeod is also in the process of repaying victims and serving as a mentor to other offenders to prevent them from recidivism. MacLeod's experience is a reminder of how much others may be mistaken in assuming what offenders know about how to treat other people. It remains to be seen how involvement or lack of involvement in prison rehabilitation programs may affect recidivism.

Most prisoners are not as fortunate (in terms of participation in treatment and gaining insight from treatment) as MacLeod, for a number of reasons. First, most prison rehabilitation programs have entry waiting lists. Many prisoners are not able to take advantage of treatment for the full duration of their sentence. Second, most long-term offenders are not eligible for many programs, because participation is restricted to those who are within two years (typically) of release. Third, security concerns prevail over treatment needs. Treatment may be disrupted as a result of cell moves or sudden transfers to another prison. Transfers are conducted in the interest of risk level and institutional security. Fourth, as Gendreau mentioned, high-risk prisoners are the best candidates for treatment. With the exception of programs like Marion, however, the bulk of programs are offered in minimum- and medium-level security units. Finally, through emotional exertion and independent self-exploration, offenders must be genuinely willing to open themselves to the idea of change and must follow through to establish healthy attitudes and behaviors. This is difficult and terrifying for some convicts to do in a sober state of mind, but a few manage to succeed.

Chapter IV
Introduction

Medical Treatment: HIV/AIDS in Corrections

Common Assumptions	Reality
• Infectious diseases in jail and prison do not concern the general public.	• Correctional facilities receive and release large numbers of individuals who have engaged in behaviors that place them at risk for carrying and spreading hepatitis, tuberculosis (TB), human immunodeficiency virus (HIV), and a number of other communicable diseases. Most prisoners will eventually be released to the families and the communities from which they came. Failure to treat and educate prisoners about their medical problems will only contribute to further spread of certain diseases to people outside of prison (Flanigan, Rich, and Spaulding 1999)
• Taxpayers should not be paying for prisoners to receive comprehensive medical treatment while incarcerated.	• Correctional institutions are bound by legal precedent to provide prisoners with adequate medical care for all their medical needs (*Estelle v. Gamble* 1976). At the same time, not responding to prisoner medical needs in the management and treatment of infectious diseases such as HIV/AIDS may constitute "deliberate indifference"—a violation of the Eighth Amendment.

Prisoner health care is perhaps one of the most pressing problems facing corrections today. Rising health care costs, the expansion in the prisoner population, elderly prisoners, and longer mandatory sentences all contribute to a higher per prisoner cost to ensure that prisoners, as they age, receive adequate medical care throughout their sentence.

Many prisoners enter prison in poor health for a number of reasons:

- No health insurance
- Years of cigarette smoking and drug and alcohol abuse

- Poor nutritional habits
- No exercise regimen

A disproportionate number of prisoners have high blood pressure, kidney failure, cirrhosis, diabetes, and hepatitis. Health care issues vary from surgical procedures, pregnancy, and dialysis to treatment for mental illness, contagious diseases, and impairments that affect vision, hearing, speech, learning, and physical movement (for a discussion on general health issues for prisoners, see Maruschak and Beck 2001; Ross and Lawrence 1998).

This chapter discusses correctional medical issues related to the prevention and treatment of HIV/AIDS. The prevalence of HIV infection is disproportionately higher among incarcerated persons compared with the rate in the general population. In 1996, new AIDS cases among incarcerated persons were over six times the national rate, and women prisoners' cases were 23 times over the national rate (Flanigan, Rich, and Spalding 1999).

This high rate of HIV and AIDS is because incarcerated persons have engaged disproportionately in behaviors that place them at risk of contracting HIV. These behaviors include needle sharing during intravenous drug use, unprotected sex, multiple partners, and other situations involving exchange of bodily fluids (Alarid and Marquart 1999). At the same time, incarceration is an optimal environment in which to undertake new and existing intervention strategies (see Hogben and St. Lawrence 2000 for detailed discussion on HIV risk reduction approaches in prison).

Some of the concerns about the prevention and treatment of HIV and AIDS are discussed in the three readings that follow. These issues include mandatory HIV testing of all prisoners, condom distribution upon request, and housing for seropositive (HIV-positive) prisoners separate from the general prisoner population. Although HIV-positive prisoners' immune systems have maintained an adequate level of T-cells, separate housing is recommended to protect prisoners with full-blown AIDS (prisoners whose T-cells level have dropped so low that the prisoner is confined to a bed) from contracting other diseases and illnesses.

People who are HIV-positive are also more likely to become infected with airborne diseases such as pneumonia and tuberculosis (TB). TB is spread when an infected person coughs, sneezes, or talks, and air-borne particles are breathed in by another person. Most TB strains are treatable with antibiotics taken for up to one year, but there are newer drug-resistant strains of TB that have recently been discovered in prisons. The drug-resistant TB may be fatal (Faiver 1998, 5).

It is important both to initiate medical care when an individual is incarcerated and to continue community aftercare (medical treatment and drug treatment) when HIV-infected prisoners are released from prison (Flanigan et al. 1999). Medical costs and treatment needs of prisoners will certainly be important issues facing corrections administrators in the next decade.

Recommended Readings

Alarid, Leanne F., and James W. Marquart. (1999). "HIV/AIDS Knowledge and Risk Perception of Adult Women in an Urban Area Jail." *Journal of Correctional Health Care* 6(1):97–127.

DeLeon, George. (1996). "Therapeutic Communities: AIDS/HIV Risk and Harm Reduction." *Journal of Substance Abuse Treatment* 13 (5): 411–420.

Faiver, Kenneth L. (1998). *Health Care Management Issues in Corrections*. Lanham, MD: American Correctional Association.

Flanigan, Timothy P., Josiah D. Rich, and Anne Spaulding. (1999). "HIV Care Among Incarcerated Persons: A Missed Opportunity." *AIDS* 13: 2475–2476.

Hogben, Matthew, and Janet S. St. Lawrence. (2000). "HIV/STD Risk Reduction Interventions in Prison Settings," *Journal of Women's Health and Gender-Based Medicine* 9(6): 587–592.

Maruschak, Laura M., and Allen J. Beck. (2001). "Medical Problems of Inmates, 1997." Washington, DC: U.S. Department of Justice, Bureau of Justice Statistics.

Ross, Phyllis Harrison, and James E. Lawrence. (1998). "Health Care for Women Offenders," *Corrections Today* (December): 122–129.

Court Cases

Estelle v. Gamble, 429 U.S. 97, 97 S. Ct. 285, 50 L.Ed.2d 251 (1976).

Internet Websites

The AIDS Knowledge Base: Issues on HIV in Prisons. Available: *http://hivinsite.ucsf.edu/akb/current/01pris/*

Canadian AIDS Legal Network. Available: *http://www.aidslaw.ca/durban2000/e-durban-crimlaw.htm*

Correctional HIV Consortium. A national, non-profit organization providing information and services regarding HIV/AIDS and TB in corrections. Available: *http://www.silcom.com/~chc/*

A Convict's View of Healthcare Behind Bars—The Story of Jimmy Goodner's Fight with Cancer. Available: *http://www.prisonzone.com/writers/goodner.html*

The Journal of Prisoners on Prisons. A journal written by prison inmates on perspectives on prison. Available: *http://www.synapse.net/~arrakis/jpp/jpp.html*

10
HIV/AIDS and the Correctional System

Douglas S. Lipton

Focus Questions

1. What evidence exists suggesting that HIV/AIDS is a primary medical concern in corrections institutions?

2. What controversial practices and policies affect the rate of HIV transmission inside prison?

3. What are the advantages and disadvantages to mandatory HIV testing?

4. What are the arguments for and against segregating the HIV-positive prisoner?

5. What factors contribute to the increase in tuberculosis inside correctional facilities?

6. What policy recommendations are made?

This paper deals with the prevalence and transmission of HIV within correctional settings, and the serious concern that this growing phenomenon generates. This concern about HIV/AIDS flows from several considerations.

- Prisons in the U.S. have higher concentrations of injection drug users (IDUs) than any other kinds of institutions;

- Rates of HIV are high among new entrants to prison;

- IDUs are the second largest group at risk for HIV infection in the U.S.

- High-risk methods of transmission (such as anal sex and needle sharing) occur with some frequency within prisons;

- Prisons and jails are hives of potential infection; [and]

- The potential cost for HIV/AIDS medical services in this population is likely to exceed the fiscal resources for the system itself.

This paper will also note the opportunity that incarceration affords to deliver HIV prevention/education, to test different models for such prevention/education, and, as vaccines become available, to test them with seropositive and high-risk persons in a relatively controlled environment. The paper also points out the parallel increases in tuberculosis and related perils for the correctional setting. This is in hope of not only reducing seroincidence and seroprevalence of HIV within this population, as well as the transmission of TB, especially of the multiresistant variety, but also to reduce the likelihood of the transmission of these two plagues to others as parolees return to their communities.

Before presenting the epidemiology and consequences of human immunodeficiency virus (HIV) within the correctional setting, and their relevance for drug abuse treatment within correctional settings, some general statistics regarding the injecting drug user (IDU) and HIV disease can set a context.

IDUs account for approximately 30 percent of Acquired Immune Deficiency Syndrome (AIDS) cases among adults in the U.S. (CDC 1992). In New York City, IDUs comprise 41 percent of the adult cases, and among cases of AIDS in men, the incidence of cases with the risk factor of drug injection exceeds new cases with the risk factor of men who have sex with men (NYC Department of Health 1992). The seroprevalence of HIV infection among IDUs entering drug abuse treatment in Manhattan, New York City has been stabilized at approximately 50 percent (Des Jarlais et al. 1989; iterated in 1995). Current studies of out-of-treatment IDU populations in Manhattan indicate similar rates, e.g., a study in Bushwick, Brooklyn has found a rate of 43 percent (Friedman 1992) and based on a study in East Harlem (Deren in press), the seroprevalence rate for IDUs not in treatment is 47 percent.

Epidemiology in Prison Settings

Among prison inmates, a 1992/93 survey by NIJ (Hammett et al. 1994) reflected an AIDS incidence rate among prisoners that was 20 times higher than the 1992 U.S. general population. HIV infection rates in prisons exceeded the general population by about 6 to 1 based on sero-epidemiological surveys reported by Lurigio (1991). According to the Bureau of Justice Statistics (1994), 52.4 percent of drug offenders in state prisons in 1991 (78, 729) were tested for the HIV virus; 3.2 percent of that amount were positive for the HIV virus (HIV positive). (Of all offenders, about 2.2 percent or 17,479 were HIV positive.) Drug-using offenders have a higher risk for HIV infection—4.9 percent of IDUs tested positive, and 7.1 percent who shared needles tested HIV positive. Of the total prison inmates, 2.2 percent were infected with AIDS virus in 1991. Almost 10 percent of these persons had progressed to full-blown AIDS (Harrow 1993). Geographically, the northeastern region of the United States had most of the HIV positive inmates. Data from the recent Survey of State Prison Inmates shows that 2.2 percent of inmates who reported the results of the test for the virus that causes AIDS said they were HIV positive (BJS 1993b). Among all inmates, 51 percent reported HIV test results, 32 percent had never been tested, 9 percent did not know if they had been tested, 7.5 percent said they had been tested but never found out the results, and only .1 per-

cent refused to report test results. Of those who were tested for the presence of HIV, and who reported the results: females (3.3 percent) were more likely than males (2.1 percent) to test HIV positive. The predominant (by more than three to one) method of transmission for these inmates was injection drug use. The probability of becoming HIV positive is directly related to the frequency of needle sharing and using needles to inject drugs.

In the national Survey of State Prison Inmates, 25 percent admitted injecting drugs for nonmedical purposes, and 12 percent admitted sharing a needle. Fully 40 percent of inmates who used drugs in the month before the offense had in the past used a needle to inject drugs, half of these self-reported sharing needles. Thus, there is a large portion of inmates at risk of developing HIV. In the years since HIV has been identified, in New York State's correctional facilities alone, 1,488 inmates have died of AIDS-related causes (through July 31, 1993, per NYS Department of Health 1993), and currently 17.8 percent of the state's 67,000 inmates are HIV positive—this is generally considered a conservative estimate (Mahon and Machon 1993).

Although national data on this point have not been fully assembled, a distinct trend is clear: about 450 cases of AIDS had been reported among prison inmates in the U.S. at the end of 1985; by the following October the number of cases had increased to 1232. In 1985, 51 percent of the state and federal systems in the U.S. reported no cases; in 1989, only 10 percent reported no cases; now, six years later, none do. A recent review article indicates that inmate populations, with their high proportion of IDUs, are at considerable risk for developing (and subsequently spreading) HIV (Brewer and Derrickson 1992) especially in areas where high seropositivity rates, high STD rates, and substantial populations of IDUs already exist, such as in the New York metropolitan area. It should be noted that it is not only the concentration of IDUs among prisoners that increases the likelihood of HIV infection, but it is also the high proportion of crack users who are of considerable risk for HIV infection since this form of drug abuse has been linked with high-risk sexual behaviors (Inciardi 1989). The primary risk factor for transmission of AIDS among prisoners, however, has always been injection drug use (Brewer and Derrickson 1992). Homosexual contact alone accounts for very few cases of AIDS among inmates—2.2 percent (NYS Dept. of Health 1987).

In contrast to New York's statistics, in the states of Wisconsin and Oregon, for example, where such research has been conducted; the rates of HIV infection are low (0.56 percent in Wisconsin in 1988 and 1.2 percent in Oregon in 1987). In Vlahov et al.'s (1991) study of ten states' correctional systems, 10,944 inmates were assessed and seroprevalence rates ranged from 2.1 percent to 7.6 percent for males—in states with moderate to high seroprevalence rates.

McCullough et al. (1993) examined the correlates of seropositivity and reports that of NYS male inmates who were IV drug users, who had shared needles, injected at a shooting gallery, were homosexual/bisexual, had a sexually transmitted disease, and who were sex partners of an IV drug user or an HIV positive person, about fifty-two percent were seropositive.

Ethnicity and Gender

Data from the recent *Survey of State Prison Inmates* reveals that about 3.7 percent of Hispanic inmates were HIV positive as compared to 2.6 percent of African-American inmates and 1.1 percent of white inmates. Hispanic women (6.8 percent) had higher HIV-positive rates than white women (1.9 percent) and African-American women (3.5 percent) (BJS 1993b).

Interestingly, among incarcerated populations, in contrast to populations outside of prisons, women have shown higher seroprevalence rates, and this is exemplified in the ethnicity section above. In his 1989 update for U.S. correctional systems, Hammett (1989) reported that, of the seven correctional systems reporting seropositivity rates of more than one percent, all but one reported higher seroprevalence for women. In

1991, Vlahov et al. reported that the 10 high prevalence correctional systems (unidentified) showed the same gender-specific trend, and 9 of 10 reported higher rates for women. While the actual causes are unknown, the high rates of prostitution, needle sharing, and unprotected sex appear to be likely causes (Vlahov and Polk 1991). HIV infection among women entering NYS prisons was first measured in the fall of 1988. This study yielded a rate of 18 percent (N = 480). In the fall of 1992, the seropositivity rate had risen among NYS women offenders to 20 percent even though there were 10 percent fewer drug injectors. The latter cohort had higher proportions of women who practiced risky sex, exchanged sex for drugs or money, and who had a positive syphilis serology. Overall, however, the HIV-positivity rate for entering women appears now to be stable at about 20 percent (Mikl, Smith, & Greifinger 1993).

Women in correctional facilities, a population that has tripled nationwide in the last decade, certainly are at high risk for becoming infected with HIV. HIV seroprevalence rates vary widely, from 3.2 percent to 35 percent, concordant with HIV rates associated with drug use and heterosexual transmission (Schilling et al. 1994). In Massachusetts, for example, in 1988–1989, women inmates tested positive at three times the rate of men (Waring & Smith 1991). At Rikers Island in NYC, the corresponding HIV seroprevalence rates were 25.8 percent for women versus 16.1 percent for men (Florio et al. 1992). Moreover, 15 to 25 percent of new admissions test positive for TB. Among incarcerated women in Quebec province (N = 394), 6.9 percent were found positive (13 percent among those with histories of injection drug use). Predictors were history of injection drug use, sexual or needle contact with seropositive person, self-reported genital herpes, and having had a regular sexual partner who injected drugs, but not related to prostitution (Hankins et al. 1994).

The question of how frequently HIV is transmitted among inmates has been examined in several studies. The most comprehensive study to date found that only 0.3 percent of a sample of Illinois inmates who had been seronegative subsequently tested positive after one year in prison (Hammett et al. 1994: 28). In Maryland, similar results were reported (0.4 percent per year—Brewer, Vlahov et al. 1988) and in Nevada (0.2 percent per year—Horsburgh, Jarvis et al. 1990). There are likely to be considerable differences in rates of in-prison HIV infection based on four main factors: the seropositivity rate of the inmate population; the seropositivity rate of the catchment area from which they mainly come; the rate at which high risk activities occur among the inmates, i.e., high risk sex and needle sharing; and the policies and practices of the institutional administration and staff regarding these risky activities.

Three of the related, but controversial, policies and practices of the institutional administration and staff regarding these risky activities are described below: Mandatory screening or testing incoming inmates for HIV; segregating HIV-infected inmates; and in consideration of illicit, but existing male-on-male sexual activity, making condoms available.

Screening for HIV

There is also considerable variance in the degree to which states and local jurisdictions require HIV screening of inmates. In the U.S., public health officials have attempted to control the spread of HIV through education, voluntary testing and counseling of persons who may be at high risk of HIV. Most testing is voluntary with the exception of immigrants, Job Corps applicants and military personnel. The public has largely supported mandatory testing of prisoners (Bayer 1989, 166) and the issue still is being strongly debated (Blumberg 1994). Nevertheless, the majority of the states (80 percent) and the federal government also still test for HIV only on a voluntary informed consent basis (as do most countries, Australia excepted). In the U.S., only sixteen states require arriving inmates to be tested for seropositivity. Other methods employed include: targeting risk groups, routine testing unless inmate declines, testing upon suspicion of symptoms, and "incident testing"—testing when inmates or staff are exposed to body fluids. The judiciary itself sometimes requires HIV testing as it has in Arizona, California, Kansas and Washington (Lillis 1993).

The purported advantages to mandatory HIV testing include: (1) efficient targeting of prevention and education; (2) placing HIV-positive inmates under special supervision, reducing potential transmission risks; (3) projecting future AIDS cases more accurately, producing better fiscal and staffing projections; (4) insuring appropriate medical treatment/prophylaxis. The opponents to mandatory testing argue: (1) education and prevention should be for all inmates; (2) segregating infected individuals is unwarranted as well as discriminatory, creating pariahs subject to harassment, violence and post-release discrimination; (3) current medical technologies cannot identify all infectious individuals, and cannot treat them effectively; (4) an isolation policy risks inadvertently encouraging risky behavior by creating the false perception that the remaining inmates are uninfected; (5) anonymous testing can satisfactorily achieve epidemiological projections; (6) inmates with a history of high risk behaviors have a medical incentive to come forward to receive treatment (e.g., AZT); (7) expenses connected with mandatory testing are better directed toward education and medical care.

Segregating the HIV-positive Inmate

What about segregation? Proponents argue segregation is necessary to prevent in-prison transmission of HIV since (1) homosexual activity occurs in every prison; (2) STDs are transmitted; (3) tattooing is common; (4) illicit drug use among IDUs occurs; (5) anal rape occurs. Opponents say: (1) HIV is not spread through casual contact; (2) segregation undermines the public health message that HIV is not transmitted except through certain "high risk" behaviors; (3) infected inmates are placed in substandard living quarters, denied participation in work assignments, work release, rehab groups, and recreation programs. They also may miss out on opportunities to earn "good time" by not participating in such programming; (4) in prison communities with many HIV positive inmates, it may be necessary to develop duplicate services, straining correctional budgets; (5) lowered likelihood of voluntarily seeking HIV testing knowing it will result in segregated housing. Most prisons in U.S. mainstream inmates who are HIV positive. In 1992, only eight percent of the state (and federal) prisons (Alabama and Mississippi) and no jails segregated inmates. This shift towards allowing HIV infected inmates into the general population was not due to increased compassion or policies of nondiscrimination. Rather, the shift stemmed from overcrowding concerns and law suits by HIV-positive inmates challenging the actions of correctional administrators to segregate them. (See, e.g., *Cordero v. Coughlin, Dunn v. White, Harris v. Thigpen, Judd v. Packard, Powell v. Dept of Corrections*).

Special housing needs for these inmates primarily occur now only when full-blown AIDS is evident, and this typically takes the form of a special AIDS ward in the infirmary or in a long-term care facility. Early release policies have also emerged wherein afflicted inmates who are deemed terminally ill are released to be at home in the last weeks before death. In instances, however, where inmates do not have a home, they cannot be released to a hospice because of the expense, so they usually stay in the prison infirmary until death (Tesoriero & LaChance-McCullough 1995).

Condom Distribution

Condoms have been distributed in high risk communities for almost ten years. Some public health offcials have suggested that correctional administrators should make condoms available in order to protect inmates from infection because of the level of sexual activity in prison (Blumberg 1994). No epidemiologic data exist in the literature, however, regarding the extent of male-to-male sex in prison. Nonetheless, anecdotal and prison autobiographical literature consistently proclaim both facultative homosex-

ual contact as well as anal rape. Despite the general awareness of this risky behavior, very few jurisdictions have elected to distribute condoms, mainly on the basis that such distribution implies tacit approval of an illicit sexual activity. Other objections are based on the notions that condoms would facilitate smuggling of contraband; they could be used in the manufacture of weapons, and the doubt that they offer significant protection against infection during anal intercourse.

Six jurisdictions currently offer condoms to inmates—New York City, Philadelphia, San Francisco, Washington, DC, and the states of Mississippi and Vermont, and few problems have been reported. The fears underlying the objections noted above have not been justified by experience. (It should be noted that the method of condom distribution varies across these jurisdictions: Philadelphia provides condoms in connection with HIV counseling sessions following HIV testing; similarly, in San Francisco an inmate may obtain condoms as part of their AIDS educational program, as does Washington, DC which also allows an inmate to get them [condoms] from the infirmary; New York City and Vermont distribute only one condom to a requesting inmate upon a visit to the medical unit; and, in contrast, in Mississippi, inmates may purchase an unlimited quantity at the canteen.) Although many jurisdictions have considered making condoms available to inmates, most have no plans to do so currently. Incidentally, no system provides bleach for needle cleaning (Hammett et al. 1994).

Medical Treatment for HIV-positive Inmates

Once identified, HIV positive inmates are entitled to adequate medical care and treatment. (See *Estelle v. Gamble* 1976.) "Adequacy" here means that it must meet community standards, not necessarily the latest technology, and be provided in a less restrictive environment bearing in mind security needs. Medical care for HIV positive inmates and AIDS patients varies considerably across the country's prisons. Access to experimental drugs has been extremely limited. This is mainly because of Federal restrictions on using prisoners in clinical trials, which in turn is based on a protecting inmates from exploitation. Less than 20 percent of state correctional systems offer experimental HIV therapies (Hammett et al. 1994). Although drug related treatment is very expensive, and inmates are not offered AZT, for example, until their CD4 cell count is below 500 per the FDA criteria, fully 98 percent of the correctional systems make AZT available (Hammett et al. 1994). In Hammett's (1994) survey he also found that about 80 percent offer ddI and Bactrim/Septra or aerosolized pentamidine to treat PCP or pneumocystis carinii pneumonia, AIDS' most common opportunistic infectious manifestation.

All these pharmaceutical agents and the HIV/AIDS-related medical services, as well as the extensive prevention efforts are expensive. Although there has been some fiscal respite from the CDC's partial funding of these efforts, costs continue to rise. In mid-1993 a report was issued showing that 76 percent of the state correctional systems reported substantial increases in health care costs, and that more than 10 percent of the total correctional budgets were now allocated to health care (Lillis 1993). These direct health care cost increases omit the psychological care and social service costs associated with HIV positivity and AIDS, as well as the costs associated with HIV education and prevention.

HIV Education and Prevention

Hammett's (1994) survey of the nation's correctional systems reveals that 48 states have some form of HIV/AIDS education for inmates, with 94 percent having it on intake, and 50 percent also having it at discharge. Most often, such programming is delivered by institutional health staff or by outside contractors "live" in group sessions, in addition to taped sessions.

Content typically includes modes of transmission, signs of infection, markers of disease progression, HIV testing and its impli-

cations, infection control procedures, confidentiality requirements, resources for assistance for incarcerated HIV positive inmates as well as when they get out. Safe sex information is provided in most (96 percent) institutions, and prevention through cleaning paraphernalia in 71 percent of them. Peer education programs are now available in one-third of the states (Hammett et al. 1994).

All states offer HIV/AIDS education to correctional staff. Content-wise it is the same as the inmates' program except it adds training in security and care of HIV positive inmates. Despite early fear of danger to officers, no reported inmate-to-officer transmission has yet occurred (Hammett et al. 1994). The rank order of reasons for implementing prevention programming are as follows: (1) institutional safety for inmates and staff; (2) public health reasons; (3) prison environment, and (4) forestalling inmate litigation (Martin, Zimmerman, and Long 1993).

Tuberculosis

The increase in HIV has been paralleled with an increase in tuberculosis (TB), STDs, and other HIV-related conditions. Since 1980, the rate of TB in N.Y.C. has increased from 19.9 per 100,000 to 49.8 per 100,000 in 1990, more than five times the national case rate. The highest case rates were found for African Americans and Hispanics, with a case rate of 129.0 per 100,000 among African-Americans (Bureau of Tuberculosis Control, n.d.). This increase in TB is directly related to the HIV epidemic, and it is estimated that 40 to 60 percent of IDUs with HIV also have TB (United Hospital Fund of New York 1992).

The problem of tuberculosis in correctional facilities is not a new one. From 1944–1948, for example, the prevalence of TB in New York State institutions was 1.2 percent for men and 0.7 percent for women—a significantly higher rate than in the general population of 0.3 percent (Katz and Plunkett 1950). Twenty years later Hans Abeles, then head of health services for the New York City Department of Corrections, reported active tuberculosis among newly admitted inmates to Rikers Island to be 0.2 percent (Abeles et al. 1970). Braun (1989) reports that the incidence of TB increased from 15.4 per 100,000 in 1976–1978 to 105.5 per 100,000 in 1986. Outside of New York, correctional facilities surveyed in 1984–1985 revealed that of 15,379 TB cases in 29 states, 1.2 percent were reported as living in prison or jail at the time of diagnosis. Inmate TB incidence was 30.94 per 100,000 and the relative risk of TB among inmates compared with the rate in the general population was 3.9 (Centers for Disease Control, unpublished data, 1988)—in other words the risk of having/contracting TB for inmates was almost four times greater than for ordinary citizens.

There are three factors responsible at the current time for the increase in TB seen in inmate populations: (1) in prisons and jails there is an overrepresentation of population groups (minority groups and lower socioeconomic groups) at high risk for TB (Snider and Hutton 1989); (2) the close living conditions with a 'critical mass' of persons promote the transmission of TB infection—about 40 percent of cases convert while in their facilities (Stead 1978); (3) the high rate of HIV infection among prisoners (MMWR 1987)—Pitchenik et al. (1987) found the seroprevalence of HIV antibodies in 71 consecutive TB patients to be 31 percent. Because the prevalence of HIV infection is so high in correctional facilities (because of the concentration of IDUs), there is little question that the TB problem will be increasing. Braun (1989) found in NYS that 56 percent of the TB cases in the prison system reported in 1985–1986 had AIDS or HIV infection. In just one year recently, Hammett (1988) reported the increase of AIDS cases to be 59 percent among correctional inmates in the U.S. The prevalence of HIV infection in prisons is unknown but would be expected to be 50 to 100 times higher (Snider and Hutton 1989). Not only is the prevalence likely to be higher but the progression of the TB outbreak is likely to be accelerated by the presence of HIV in the population. According to Zoloth et al. (1993), the problem is made more complicated first by the fact that much of the current TB problem in the state prisons is due to a multidrug-resistant variety of TB—recently eight deaths due to this form of TB were reported in NYS prisons. Second, anergy may occur in groups at high risk for tuberculosis compromising the identification of TB by the standard Mantoux (tuberculin) skin testing.

Conclusions

In brief, there are five main points in this paper. The rate of HIV infection has been steadily climbing in U.S. institutions, and although the rate of increase has slowed, it is still likely to climb more before leveling. Similarly, TB rates, and most importantly, rates of multi-drug resistant TB, are rising as well in prison populations. Both these phenomena present risk for infectious spread among the inmate population, and to the communities to which released inmates return, and in which the correction officers reside. In addition, HIV disease or AIDS and treatment of active TB involve very high medical costs—costs which correctional or health department budgets will soon be unlikely to meet.

These costs are necessarily increased by the costs of social services, psychological care, and prevention programming. Such programming in jails and prisons needs to develop content congruent with the sensitivities and issues of people of color, women and IDUs who are at particularly high risk to develop HIV. Making drug abuse treatment generally available to all inmates and combining it with HIV-prevention appears to be a significant opportunity to deal with two important problems efficiently. Moreover, the correctional setting is in many ways an ideal environment within which to test various HIV prevention strategies using methodologically sound evaluation designs, and to try new vaccines because it has "high" retention, it is relatively controlled, and there are sufficient numbers to obtain stable results.

Recommendations

- HIV testing available on request for all inmates.

- Pretest counseling focusing on the meaning and significance of possible outcomes.
- Condom distribution upon request for HIV positive inmates.
- Risky behavior/risk reduction education for all.
- Ready access for medical/prevention services for HIV positive inmates.
- Confidentiality assurance for all.
- Medical, mental and social service access for HIV-positive inmates.
- Post-test counseling and support services for all.
- Pre-release counseling for HIV/AIDS services in community.
- Counseling/services for family of HIV positive inmates available on request.
- Methodologically sound evaluation research into efficacy of prison-based HIV education at stimulating risk reduction.

References

Abeles, H., Feibes, H., Mandel, E. et al. (1970). The Large City Prison: A Reservoir of Tuberculosis. *American Review of Respiratory Disease*, 101, 706–709.

Bayer, R. (1989). *Private Acts, Social Consequences: AIDS and the Politics of Public Health*. New York: The Free Press.

Blumberg, M., & Langston, D. (1995). The Impact of HIV/AIDS and Tuberculosis on Corrections. In K. C. Haas & G. P. Alpert (Eds.) *The Dilemmas of Corrections: Contemporary Readings* (3rd Ed.) Waveland Press (forthcoming).

Braun, M. M., Truman, B. I., Maguire, B., DiFernando, G. T., Wormser, G., Broaddus, R., Morse, D. (1989). Increasing Incidence of Tuberculosis in a Prison Population: Association with HIV Infection. *J.A.M.A.* 261, 393–397.

Brewer, T. F. and Derrickson, J. (1992). AIDS in Prison: A Review of Epidemiology and Preventive Policy. *AIDS*, 6(7), 623–628.

Brewer, T. F., Vlahov, D., Taylor, E., Hall, D., Munoz, A., & Polk, B. F. (1988). Transmission of HIV Within a Statewide Prison System. *AIDS*, 2(8), 363–366.

Bureau of Justice Statistics. (1993a). *Drugs and Crime Facts, 1992*. Washington, DC: US Department of Justice.

———. Bureau of Justice Statistics. (1993b). *Survey of Inmates in State Prison, 1991*. Washington, DC: US Department of Justice.

———. (1994). *Drugs and Crime Facts, 1991*. Washington, DC: US Department of Justice.

Bureau of Tuberculosis Control, n.d. *Tuberculosis in New York City: 1990*. N.Y.C. Department of Health.

Centers for Disease Control, unpublished data, 1988 cited in Snider and Hutton, *J.A.M.A.*, 1989.

Centers for Disease Control, 1992. Unpublished data.

Deren, S., Friedman, S., Tross, S., Des Jarlais, D. C., Sufian, M., Davis, W. R., Abdul-Quader, A., Sotheran, J. Neaigus, A. 1989. Hispanics in NYC: AIDS Risk Behaviors Among Intravenous Drug Users and Sex Partners. Presented at the NIMH-NIDA Technical Review on Facilitating HIV Related Behavior Change Among Latinos and Native Americans, Albuquerque, NM, Nov. 1989.

Deren, S., Tortu, S., Davis, W. R. (1997, forthcoming). An AIDS Risk Reduction Project with Inner City Women. In Squire, T. (ed.) *Women, Psychology and AIDS*. Sage Publications (in press).

Des Jarlais, D. C., Friedman, S. R., Novick, D. M. Sotheran, J. L. Thomas, P., Yancovitz, S. R., Mildvan, D., Weber, J., Kreek, M. J., Maslansky, R., Bartelme, S., Spira, T., Mannor, M. (1989). HIV-1 Infection Among Intravenous Drug Users in Manhattan, New York City 1977–1987. *J.A.M.A.* 261, 1008–1012.

Des Jarlais, D. C. (1995). Personal communication with the author.

Florio, S. et al. (1992). HIV infection in the New York City jails: a voluntary program. Presented at the VIII International Conference on AIDS, Amsterdam, July 1992.

Friedman, S. R., Sotheran, J., Abdul-Quader, A., Primm, B., Des Jarlais, D. C. et al. (1987). The AIDS Epidemic among Blacks and Hispanics. *The Milbank Quarterly* 65 (Supp.). 2, 455–499.

Friedman, S. R., Des Jarlais, D. C., Neaigus, A., Jose, B., Suftan, M., et al. (1992). Organizing Drug Injectors Against AIDS: Preliminary Data on Behavioral Outcomes. *Psychology of Addictive Behaviors*, 6(2), 100–106.

Hammett, T. M. (1988). *AIDS in Correctional Facilities: Issues and options*. 3rd Edition. Washington, DC: National Institute of Justice (NIJ).

———. (1989). *1988 Update: AIDS in Correctional Facilities*, Washington, DC: NIJ.

——. (1990). *1989 Update: AIDS in Correctional Facilities.* Washington, DC: NIJ.

Hammett, T. M., Harrold, L., Gross, M., & Epstein, J. (1994). *1992 Update: HIV/AIDS in Correctional Facilities, Issues and Options.* Washington, DC: NIJ.

Hankins, C. A., Gendron, S., Handley, M., Richard, C., LaiTung, M. T., & O'Shaughnessy, M. (1994). HIV Infection among women in prison: An assessment of risk factors using a nonnominal methodology. *American J. Public Health* 84(10), 1637–1640.

Harwood, A. (1981). *Ethnicity and Medical Care.* Cambridge, MA: Harvard Univ. Press.

Heckler, M. M. (1985). *Report of the Secretary, Task Force on Black and Minority Health.* Washington, DC: U.S. Department of Health and Human Services.

Horsburgh, C. R., Jarvis, J. Q., McArther, T., Ignacio, T., & Stock, P. (1990). Seroconversion to Human Immunodeficiency Virus in Prison Inmates. *American J. Public Health*, 80(2), 209–210.

Inciardi, J. (1989). Trading Sex for Crack Among Juvenile Drug Users: A Research Note. *Contemporary Drug Problems*, 16, 167–178.

Katz, J., & Plunkett, R. E. (1950). Prevalence of Clinically Significant Pulmonary Tuberculosis Among Inmates of New York State Penal Institutions. *American Review of Tuberculosis*, 61, 51–56.

Lillis, J. (1993). Dealing with HIV/AIDS-Positive Inmates. *Corrections Compendium*, 18(6), 1–3.

Lurigio, A. J., Petraitis, J., & Johnson, B. (1991). HIV Education for Probation for Probation Officers: An Implementation and Evaluative Program. *Crime and Delinquency*, 37(1), 125–134.

Mahon, N., & Machon, S. (1993). When HIV Is Not The Issue: Assessment of the HIV and Non HIV Related Needs of Prisoners and Former Prisoners. Presented at the IX International Conference on AIDS, Berlin, Germany.

Martin, R., Zimmerman, S., & Long, B. (1993). AIDS Education in U. S. Prisons: A Survey of Inmate Programs. *The Prison Journal*, 73(1), 103–129.

McCullough, M. L., Tesoriero, J. M., Sorin, M. D., & Lee, C. (1993). Correlates of HIV Seroprevalence Among Male New York State Prison Inmates: Results from the New York State AIDS Institute Criminal Justice Initiative. *J. Prison & Jail Health*, 12(2), 103–134.

Mikl, J., Smith, P. F., & Greifinger, R. B. (1993). *HIV Seroprevalence Among New York State Prison Entrants.* Poster presentation at IX International Conference on AIDS, Berlin, Germany.

MMWR (1987). Tuberculosis and Acquired Immunodeficiency Syndrome–New York City. *Mortality and Morbidity Weekly Report* (MMWR), 36, 785–795.

N.Y.C. Department of Health. (1992). *AIDS Surveillance Annual Update, 1991.* NYC: Bureau of Communicable Disease Control.

N.Y.S. Department of Health. (1987). *AIDS Surveillance Monthly Update*, NYC: Bureau of Communicable Disease Control.

——. Department of Health. (1993). Personal communication from Karen Kelly, D. o. H. AIDS Surveillance Unit, August 31, 1993.

Pitchenik, A. E., Burr, J., & Suarez, M. et al. (1987). Human T-Cell Lymphotropic Virus-III Seropositivity and Related Disease Among 71 Consecutive Patients in Whom Tuberculosis Was Diagnosed: A Prospective Study. *American Review of Respiratory Disease*, 135, 875–879.

Pounds, M. B., & Delaney, P. (1992). Barriers To Care: Redefining Access for Ryan White CARE ACT Special Populations. Presented at 120th Annual Meeting, American Public Health Association.

Schilling, R., El-Bassel, N., Ivanoff, A., & Gilbert, L. et al. (1994). Sexual risk behavior of incarcerated drug-using women, 1992. *Public Health Reports*, 109(4), 539–547.

Selik, R. M., Castro, K. G., & Pappioanou, M. (1988). Racial/Ethnic Differences in the Risks of AIDS in the United States. *American J. Public Health*, 78(12), 1539–1545.

Snider, D. E. Jr. and Hutton, M. D. (1989). Tuberculosis in Correctional Institutions. *J.A.M.A.*, 261 (3), 436–437.

Stead, W. W. (1978). Undetected Tuberculosis in Prison (Source of Infection for Community at Large). *J.A.M.A.*, 240, 2544–2547.

Sufian, M., Friedman, S. R., Neaigus, A., Stepherson, B., & Rivera-Beckmann, J. (1990). Impact of AIDS on Puerto Rican Drug Users. *Hispanic J. Behavioral Sciences*, 12(2), 122–134.

Tesoriero, J. M., & LaChance-McCullough, M. L. (1995). *Substance Abuse, HIV/AIDS, Tuberculosis in American Prisons: Key Factors in Today's Health Care Crisis.* Unpublished Report, New York State Department of Health, Albany, NY.

United Hospital Fund of New York. (1992). *The Tuberculosis Revival: Individual Rights and Societal Obligations in a Time of AIDS.* New York City.

Vlahov, D., Brewer, F., & Castro, K. et al. (1991). Prevalence of Antibody to HIV Among Entrants to U.S. Correctional Facilities. *J.A.M.A.*, 265, 1129–1132.

Vlahov, D., & Polk, F. (1988). Intravenous Drug Use and HIV Infection in Prison, *AIDS Public Policy J.*, 3, 42–46.

Waring, N., & Smith, B. (1991). The AIDS epidemic: Impact on women prisoners in Massachusetts—an assessment with recommendations. *Women Criminal Justice*, 2, 117–143.

Zoloth, S. R., Safyer, S., Rosen, J., Michaels, D., Alcabes, P, Bellin, E., & Braslow, C. (1993). Anergy Compromises Screening for Tuberculosis in High-Risk Populations. *American J. Public Health*, 83(5), 749–751.

11

Women Prisoners with HIV: A Letter From a Prison Doctor

Anne S. De Groot

Focus Questions

1. Why is it important for De Groot to understand her female HIV patients?

2. What has the author learned about the link between childhood incest, drug use, and HIV?

3. Why do women prisoners who are HIV positive return to the same abusive household upon release from prison?

4. How can incest and sexual abuse be prevented from occurring?

I *have been providing medical care to HIV infected women who are incarcerated at a prison in Massachusetts since May 1, 1992. Working with the HIV-infected women at that clinic opened my eyes to their struggles. I am amazed that they have been able to survive such difficult lives, and I have been deeply affected by their strength, their joys and their sorrows. I wrote this short piece on Friday night, July 28, 1995, after attending HIV clinic at the prison. Some of the details of this story have been changed, to protect my patients.*

It is Friday night after HIV clinic. I am lying in bed holding my daughter in my arms. Her face is moonshaped and turned up to the light coming through the windows. She is beautiful, she is two, she is a small but precious vessel of joy. During the daytime her joy spills over and over as she laughs and plays.

I cannot sleep. It is not because the heat is oppressive, it is not because the sprinklers outside are turning incessantly, it is not because the trees make scary shadows on the wall. I cannot sleep because I cannot forget what X told me about her father today.

"When I went home at Thanksgiving, he grabbed my breasts and my ass" and "it happened again at Easter." She told me it started when she was three "but it was only oral sex," and it continued until she was 13. She said "he never penetrated me" . . . except one time, he almost did, in the toolshed, and she doesn't remember exactly what happened, but it stopped after that.

There was a divorce and a custody battle and she ran away to Florida to live a different kind of life when she was in her early teens. She returned to her father's house when she was seventeen, and one day, when her stepmother and stepsister had left the house, he tried to get her to do it again. He walked into the kitchen "you know like that" (making a gesture to show a man who had nothing on below his waist). She said that she laughed nervously and said, "No, Dad, I really don't want to do that now" (I wish I could make you hear the voice that she used to say this last sentence because it sounded so childlike and pleading and I felt that I was standing in the kitchen watching this happen) and he said, "Why not? You would do it if I paid you."

In my clinic today, she said "When I found out I had HIV I was happy, because I thought he would never touch me again." She said, "I thought if I got fat and really ugly, nobody would want to touch me." She told her father that she had HIV—she even said she had AIDS, but it didn't make a difference at Thanksgiving.

I can't get this out of my head tonight. X had just finished a post-incarceration drug abuse recovery program and had returned home for Thanksgiving, when her father touched her again. She had just finished the program, she felt safer and stronger, she thought she was protected by her HIV, and he invaded her space anyway. After Thanksgiving she started eating to keep from using drugs again, and purging to get clean, and eating and purging. She didn't pick up drugging again, even though her self-esteem had hit rock bottom. Her father tried to touch her again at the next family reunion.

Just a few weeks later she went along with some friends who had decided to start using drugs again, and she ended up back in prison, where I saw her looking huge and not at all HIV positive but bruised and ashamed to be back inside. She couldn't say, at that time, why she came back (now she says that she was still "too much inside of it"), even though I tried very hard to learn from her where the weakness lay, in someone I knew to be resolved to recover and dedicated to avoiding reincarceration. Today, after she finally told me about her reasons for returning, she said that she felt a huge weight leave her. I asked her if I could write it all down, especially this part that just happened, so that we could use her story as a tool to change this terrible world.

How do I keep X safe from her father? How do I repair the damages that have been done to the women that share their stories with me? Questions fill my head. How do I keep my children safe from this? How can I keep it from happening to the child next door, to the child across the street, to the children in my city? I lie awake listening for cries and tears around me, feeling powerless to keep this harm from happening. Tonight, in the heat and in the dark, the danger to women and children overwhelms me. I sit down at my computer to write it out, to bring it into the light, to purge it from me. I don't know where this writing will go. This is X's story, and my own. If we bring our fears and our wounds out into the light, will writing these stories make a difference in women's lives?

And how this conversation with X came about today? Some people think I go dredging for these stories. In this case, I had asked her to see the dietitian to talk about her eating disorder. I sent her to the dietitian for two reasons—to find some way to draw attention to her bulimia and to get some assistance with it, and also to illustrate to the prison dietitian the complexity of the dietary issues involved in caring for HIV-seropositive women. Many, too many, of the women I see in my clinic have eating disorders: How am I to be sure that they get their HIV medicine if it is purged with their food? My experience at work confirms what is known about eating disorders: bulimia has been linked to childhood sexual abuse.

Today X told me that the session with the dietitian was helpful, because she actually confessed that her bulimia was worse during the past winter, and because she finally realized the connection between her father's actions and her reincarceration. To tell me this, she had to tell me that her father had abused her again, and that is how the whole story came out. We talked at length, and she smiled through her tears as she left my clinic. Her terrible sadness, fear, and anger remained with me.

So what does all of this have to do with running an HIV clinic for women? Nothing at all, if you ask prison officials and prison health care corporations. Nothing at all, if you ask my medical colleagues who wonder why I don't do "my work" and stop seeking answers to my questions. But I can't separate listening to these stories and seeking to understand my patients from my work. If my work is to "take care" of HIV-infected women, then understanding why these women use drugs, do sex work, don't go to their HIV clinic appointments that I set up for them on the outside, and end up coming back to see me in the HIV clinic at the prison is part of the work that I have to do. Understanding why my patients have eating disorders will enable me to intervene effectively, so that the medications they are taking for their HIV disease are absorbed. Learning more about my patients helps me set priorities: Is it more important to find safe housing, away from an abusive spouse, or start a new anti-viral drug? Is it more important to reunite them with their families than to urge them to move to a city where they might have access to HIV care? Which intervention will save the life of my patient?

A case in point: Y returned to prison at the same time as X. Y was also a recent graduate of the postincarceration drug recovery program. The story that she lives with, the story that was untold until she came to my clinic the first time, is this one: her son is also her brother. Her relationship to her son/brother has never been discussed within her family. Is it a surprise that she left home at an early age and spent many years on the street drinking, drugging, and doing sex work to support her habit? Why did she tell me and no one else her story? Because I asked her why (not how or when) she started using drugs. I have learned from my experience at the prison that many of my patients left home as teenagers because of childhood sexual abuse, turning to drugs for comfort and sex work to support their drug habits. Unless the cycle of abuse is broken, these women will never be free to choose a healthier lifestyle—whether they are already living with HIV, or at risk of becoming infected.

Y spent many hours talking about her son/brother with me at the clinic and in sessions with counselors in the drug recovery program. As part of her drug treatment program after she was released from prison, she wrote down all of the things her father did to her. She says now, after returning to prison for using drugs again, that telling her story at the drug treatment program made her feel strong enough to go home to see her son, at last. She thought she might tell him that she was HIV positive, but wasn't sure that she could tell him the truth about their kinship. He still thought she was his sister, and she didn't think that he was ready to learn the truth she had been living with every day, all 17 years of his life.

When she returned home, she found that her son had a newborn son, and that she was now a grandmother, and an aunt, all at once. Her son had named this new child after his father, her abuser. She spent many hours

that weekend holding the baby. Then she went off to find her friends, so that she could get high and forget about the whole thing.

Another case in point: Z is 25. Last year, Z moved back to her mother's house after her husband died of AIDS, and her mother moved her stepfather back into her room with her. That was the way they lived when she left home at 16. She says that she protested, that she ran out into the yard crying about incest, but they sat her down at the kitchen table and told her that it couldn't be incest because he was not her real father. I try to imagine this scene in my head—I see the kitchen table, the stepfather, the mother. How can this be? I ask her why her mother does this to her. She says her stepfather doesn't care that she is HIV positive, he doesn't wear a condom when he sleeps with her, and she thinks that her mother is "getting him back" this way. She wears her hair long, in two big pony tails set high on her head like a little girl. She talks in a little-girl voice and won't look me in the eye when she tells me that she has to go home when she gets out, to her mother and stepfather, because she has no other place to go.

For so many of the women I take care of, there is no safe place to go. X tells me about "running away" from her father, running from room to room, and running away from home. Running from the hero of her life. The stories the women tell are all different but all the same: The abuser is always the person they love the most. Recovery involves calling the abuse by its name and losing that love. For some, this loss is the largest one, bigger even than the initial loss of trust. And for women who are HIV seropositive, the urge to return home to find comfort can be heartbreaking. There is no other place to go, no safe place to find love.

I am told that incest has been a part of human behavior for a long, long time. Through my work at the prison, I am learning the terrible consequences of incest. Women who have been forced to have sex as children, who have never been able to speak about their experiences, bear the scars forever. For women who have no access to professional counseling and psychotherapy, drugs and alcohol numb the pain and diminish the terror of sexual intimacy. Blame is internalized, and self-esteem is destroyed. The links to drug use and sex work are clear, and now HIV has entered the equation. These links, between childhood losses, failure of support systems, lack of access to means of recovery from abuse, drug use, sex work, and HIV infection are illustrated over and over again by the women who come sit with me in my HIV clinic at the prison and speak to me about their lives. Because I ask them about their lives and because I choose to spend the time listening, I have learned that every other woman who comes through my doors at that prison clinic is a survivor of childhood sexual abuse.

I ask: What comes before? How does it start? What unhinges that taboo, allows men to begin to damage their daughters, their granddaughters, their nieces, and their sisters? I don't know the answer. What can we change about our society to prevent this from happening to women? A student of mine wrote me the one answer that I think is valid: We must not tolerate sexual abuse of children. There must be no acceptance, no excuse, for valuing the lives of women and children less than sexual pleasure. I have come to know the newest consequence of childhood sexual abuse: To damaged self-esteem and troubled hearts is now added the burden of HIV. For my child, I don't know which way the danger lies, and that is why I sit here writing, wondering if I will be heard, wondering how I can protect my moonlit daughter, wondering how I can change women's lives.

Author's Note

The stories of patients X, Y, Z have been changed to protect their identities. Any resemblance to any one individual's life story is coincidental. This work would not be possible without the support and encouragement of S. Zierler , C. C. J. Carpenter, K. H. Mayer, and APT; and my Directors Joe Cohen and Rochelle Scheib at the Lemuel Shattuck Hospital, Jamaica Plain, MA.

References

Anne S. De Groot and Debi Cuccinelli. (1996). "Put her in a cage: Childhood sexual abuse, incarceration, and HIV infection," in J. Manlowe and N. Goldstein, eds., *The Gender Politics of HIV in Women: Perspectives on the Pandemic in the United States.* New York University Press.

Jessica Stevens, Sally Zierler, Virginia Cram, Diane Dean, Ken H. Mayer, and Anne S. De Groot. (1995). "Risks for HIV Infection in incarcerated women." *Journal of Women's Health* Volume 5(4): 1–7.

Reprinted from: Anne S. De Groot, "Women Prisoners with HIV: An Open Letter From a Prison Doctor." (Written February 2, 1996). Available: *http://www.wco.com/~aerick/hiv.htm*. Reprinted by permission of the author.

12
'Til Death Do Us Part: The Deadly Game of AIDS in Prison

Antonio A. Gilbreath
Joshua D. M. Rogers IV

Focus Questions

1. What does it mean to be a participant in "The Game"?

2. What are the different reasons that prisoners join the game?

3. How do prisoners feel about contracting AIDS from same-sex relations?

4. What do prisoners do to protect themselves from contracting HIV in prison?

5. Can you name policies that prison administrators could impose that would decrease the rate at which prisoners contract HIV?

Since the beginning of the AIDS epidemic, the number of reported HIV and AIDS cases has risen dramatically, while the number of Americans dying from HIV disease has slowly but steadily begun to decline, largely as a result of powerful new AIDS medications. In our nation's prisons and jails, however, where the highest concentration of people living with AIDS exists, the AIDS mortality rate continues to soar. In the Texas Department of Criminal Justice, which has more prison beds than any other prison system in the free world, the epidemic is so severe that AIDS-related illnesses are the leading cause of death among prisoners.

Texas prisoners no longer appear to be afraid of being infected with HIV, the virus that causes AIDS. Contrarily, there is a disturbing growth in the number of prisoners who knowingly infect willing partners and, more alarmingly, prisoners who actually want to become infected with the virus. Motivated by a preternatural thirst for love and affection in an impersonal and violent world, prisoners may underestimate the certainty with which this silent assassin kills. They play a deadly game of chance in a game in which they will often become the losers.

When asked to think of America's prisoners, most people may think of our nation's refuse locked away in small dank cells designed to protect our citizens and communities from society's reprobates. These men and women, castaways from a world where human needs can easily be satisfied, are left to survive in ways that many would consider abhorrent.

Prisoners have the same needs and desires as men and women who are free to go home nightly to their husbands, wives, or sweethearts. In prison, however, the comfort of a lover's touch is one of the many privileges denied to those whose sexual needs and yearnings for compassion and companionship remain unfulfilled.

Same-sex behavior, homosexuality to most, was shown to exist even in the early annals of prisons. Being in "The Game" is a phrase used by Texas prisoners to describe the ritual of sexual conquest. In prison, "The Game" is a way of life and, for far too many, it is a precursor to death.

The Game is a way of reaching out to satisfy unmet needs for love, companionship, and, unfortunately for some, domination. The victor's spoils come tainted with a deadly prize. For whoever plays the game, for whatever it is that they seek, the unwanted prize is often HIV. This indiscriminate killer has already claimed thousands of lives and, if left unchecked, it will continue to consume untold numbers.

There are many reasons to explain or justify why both adult and juvenile prisoners join the game. The justification for the risks they take varies from person to person. Some of the most common reasons are shared in the following personal stories. Chief among the reasons are survival sex, sexual servitude, recreational sex or, for most, the need for a companion's love and affection.

Regardless of the reasons that lead them to the game's arena, men quickly learn that "The Game" is not a game of amusement. The fun is short-lived; the consequences can be potentially deadly.

The following are two personal accounts from prisoners who are incarcerated in the Texas Department of Criminal Justice.

Sergio's Story

Ten years ago, when I was a young and dumb 19-year-old kid, I had never dreamed of ending up in prison, let alone falling in love with another man. Okay, sure, I'd messed around with a few friends when I was younger. That was just curious hormones wanting to take the equipment for a test drive. I had always considered myself "100 percent man." I have two kids to prove it! From what I now know of myself, you could describe me as bisexual.

As I got into my twenties, for some reason I couldn't get my life together. Well, I guess I do know why. I was a drug addict. I still am. What got me sent to prison was breaking into houses to pay for the methamphetamine or marijuana high that I love so much. Man, I shot so much meth that a couple of my veins had collapsed.

All of that led me here to the Texas prison system. This is my fourth time down. I've been here seven years on a 25-year sentence. My first three times I didn't stay long enough to explore the seedy side of prison life. But this time, I knew I was going to be here for a

while. I made up my mind that I should get comfortable. I'd be all right so long as I had my sex, drugs, and rock n' roll. I really enjoy sex, and my hand can't replace that feeling of something warm between my legs.

You would never have guessed that I was shy and quiet when I first came down. I usually stayed in my cell, which could get pretty lonely. I had decided to do my time on a protection wing, where I had heard that sex is easier to get. I had heard right. There were plenty of offers not just for me to "do" them, but some also wanted to "do" me. I wasn't interested in being "done." I tried it as a kid and it hurt too much.

I did have a few casual encounters. Nothing serious at first; just some hand and blow jobs every once in a while. Then I met Carl. Man, he was special. We stayed together for four and a half years. That was my first real relationship, and it lasted longer than any that I had had in the world.

I never gave AIDS a whole lot of thought then. I wasn't worried about it. I thought that I couldn't get it because I wasn't gay. The only thing I was worried about was giving Carl, my "wife," herpes. As it turned out, we both had genital herpes but we were too afraid to be honest with each other. I think neither of us wanted honesty to keep us from having what we both wanted—sex.

After four and a half unforgettable years, Carl finally went home, leaving me feeling all alone. At first, I had been using Carl for the sex, food, and favors. Isn't that what "The Game" is all about? Everybody is just using everybody else to get what they want. Except I fell in love with Carl and I got myself hurt when he left. I told myself that I wasn't going to put my heart or feelings into a relationship anymore, if I ever had another one. It's just a game. We're supposed to have fun, right? Wrong! That was the way I felt before I met Victor.

I thought that I knew what love was. I thought Carl and I loved each other because something kept us together for all those years. Then, wham! Victor turned my world upside down. He wasn't like any punk I'd ever met. He was like a real woman! You could tell by his voice, skin, actions, and the way that he dressed. This Mexican was very much a woman to me. Victor had everything that I could possibly want; except he also had AIDS.

As much as I wanted to, Victor and I never got "married" or officially became a couple. He was already "married" to Bobby. That didn't stop us, though, from becoming best friends. Even as friends, Victor was a sex freak. He wanted to sample every young, good-looking white guy that came onto our wing. Occasionally, there would be three-somes or foursomes going on in his cell. If I wasn't a part of it, it would drive me insanely jealous. I wanted to be the only one who had sex with him. Victor had this weird hypnotic effect on guys. He could literally drive you crazy. One guy tried to cut his own throat over him. Others fought or tried to cross each other out. But nothing bothered Victor. He would just keep on humping away like that pink battery bunny. He didn't seem to care that he had AIDS. He just liked turning guys out.

I lived for the moment when it was my turn to have sex with him. I stayed aroused all day. I wanted him bad and I didn't care what it took. I'd be lying if I said I wasn't worried about getting AIDS. I know that who-ever was catching (receiving) had a better chance of getting it than the pitcher, right? At least, that's what I've been told.

My unforgettable first time didn't last long enough. After it was over, once back in my cell, the high of the orgasm was replaced by a sudden wave of panic. What if everything that I'd heard about AIDS was wrong? I started feeling my neck and under my arm-pits, expecting my glands to have become swollen in less than an hour. What did I know? I just knew that I wasn't supposed to be able to get this stuff.

After a frantic self-examination that re-vealed nothing wrong, I gave myself a clean bill of health and probably a false sense of immunity against HIV. Feeling relieved that I had escaped from that close call, I switched back to wondering when I could have him again. He was so good that I couldn't leave him alone.

Apparently, Victor liked having sex with me. After Bobby was transferred to an AIDS care unit, we had sex every day, sometimes a couple of times a day. I'd fallen in love again, this time with Victor, and I knew that I would be willing to die for him.

I could never get Victor to be with just me. He wanted everyone, and it drove me blind with rage if someone else was in his cell. I didn't want to share him with anyone.

I tried every trick I knew to get moved in with Victor. Since the Texas Department of Corrections only allows HIV-positive people to live together, it wasn't going to happen. Vernon, Victor's old boyfriend before Bobby, moved in instead. I was pissed!! He thought that he was so in love with Victor that he had taken a diabetics syringe and had injected himself with Victor's blood so that he could become HIV positive. It worked.

Despite that, I still had sex with Victor. So did a lot of other guys who got snagged in this "Black Widow's" web. I can't count how many guys he might have given HIV to. He didn't hide the fact that if we were dumb enough to mess with him, then we deserved what we got.

We began to argue all the time over other guys. But our biggest disagreement was that he wouldn't "marry" me and make Vernon move out. Victor began treating me like dirt most of the time. He would deny me sex until I was a "good boy." It worked. I would be good so that I could get back into the saddle. Someone finally pulled me aside and helped me to see the misery that I was bringing on myself. I came to realize that drugs weren't my only addiction: sex and Victor were too.

I tried to find the willpower to leave him alone, especially as my fears about getting HIV increased. It seems like everyone was getting it now. But his hold on me was too strong, or else I was too weak. My life was getting way out of control again. I was ob-sessed! What little judgment I had left kept leading to Victor's drawers. I felt like I'd sold my soul to the devil for sex, and when he asked me to dance, I was powerless to say no.

Hoping to rejoin Bobby, Victor applied for a trade school so he could get transferred. Actually, I was glad that he was leaving. With him on his way elsewhere, I could start fight-ing the devil's hold. But before he left, my hormones would demand satisfaction, and win. I knew it wasn't going to be easy leaving him alone. Hell, I loved him!! I guess I really was willing to die for him.

I have finally regained enough of my senses to find the courage to confront the question that was burning fiercely in my mind. I've never taken an HIV test. Something told me that it's time to know the truth. I'm worried as hell. Actually, I'm scared shitless! Too many people have HIV or AIDS now. Others have it but are too scared to find out. I've got to know.

I've said a few times that I'd be willing to die for Victor. I have this sick feeling that soon the devil might get paid.

Barry's Story

I'm an inmate at the Texas Department of Criminal Justice. I'm probably going to die here. No, I'm not on Texas' infamous death row. No judge or jury has condemned me to death. No prison gang has put out a contract on my life. My death sentence was self-imposed. You see, I deliberately allowed myself to be infected with the virus that causes AIDS. I have HIV.

I guess that sounds pretty crazy, but I'm not crazy. I did it because I was in love. I loved this dude so much that I let him kill me.

I'm not much different than the thousands of guys who come here carrying a lot of time with them. I was 18 years old when I was given two stacked life sentences. I supposed that it was better to forget about the outside world and any chance for a normal life. That also meant that I had to give up women.

Now I'm 32 years old and it's been 15 years since I've felt the warmth of a woman's touch, unless you count being searched by women guards. As you might have guessed, all my sexual pleasure has been with other men. I've lost count of how many men I've had sex with while here in prison. I like sex. It's as simple as that. Although I wasn't gay when I got here, it's no big deal that I am now. I'm still a man.

Back in the early days of "The Game," nobody gave a damn about AIDS. Hell, we weren't exactly sure what it was. We knew from reading the newspapers or watching television that a whole lot of people were afraid of whatever it was. We might have been, too, if we thought that it had something to do with us. Back then, only gays got AIDS. I never considered myself gay until some years later.

Anyone who's been to prison knows that it can get pretty lonely. My cousin was on the same wing with me, but because we didn't always get along, I wished for someone closer. I would jump in and out of relationships looking for love in all the wrong places, never finding that special someone. I wanted someone who would be more than just a bed warmer on those cold Texas nights. Just like I can't tell you how many men I've been with, neither can I tell you how many times I thought that I was in love.

Mitchell was an awesome lover. He had a great sense of humor and he knew how to make me feel special and needed. I loved taking care of him. Man, we had so many good times together, even though I knew he had AIDS. I suppose you can say that I had waited all of my life for someone like him to come along. You couldn't see his illness. Since I'd been with lots of people that I knew had HIV, being with Mitchell was no big deal.

The more time I spent with Mitchell, the more I wanted to be cellmates with him. The only way that they were going to let us live together, though, was if both of us had HIV. I still hadn't gotten it yet, but I had a plan.

By the time I had a good idea of what HIV or AIDS was, a lot of people in prison had it. There was something strange, though, about all those people who supposedly had AIDS. I've never actually seen someone who was really sick or dying from AIDS. I mean, yeah, I know it can kill you, but what I'm saying is that I personally hadn't seen anybody like that. So just maybe this thing wasn't as bad as everyone said. So I got this idea that if I were to get it, as long as I keep working out and taking those new AIDS drugs, I'd probably be all right.

Mitchell and I talked about how to do this for several weeks. Surprisingly, he didn't really mind going along with what I had proposed. We both wanted to be cellies and we knew that this was probably the only way. Mitchell got a tattoo of my name on his neck right after we got married. Although that was a symbolic expression of our love, we both felt that by going through with this plan, we would be bound together for all eternity.

Believe it or not, we weren't the first to do something this desperate. I personally know three other guys who did the same thing. They all now have HIV. One guy shot up with a needle full of his lover's blood. Another did it by rubbing bleeding cuts together. The other guy did it the way that I did—screwed himself to death. I did Mitchell every way that you could imagine. It took three or four months for it to work, but it did. What helped, I think, was that Mitchell bled heavily from his rectum during sex. So don't think just because you're pitching, you can't get it—you can.

I've seen lots of guys dragging their asses back to the cellblock, all long in the face because they had just found out that they had that "shit." Man, I was happy when that nurse told me that I had it! It must have tripped her out. I couldn't get to Classification fast enough so we could get moved. To our great disappointment, they weren't buying it at first. It took a little grease, but we eventually got it done.

We hadn't been shacked up three weeks before Mitchell and I began fighting. We argued over little stuff at first. You know how it is when you spend all of your time under somebody. Not only did we live together, but we worked at the same place, too. The only time I got to myself was when I was in the craft shop.

The main reason that things started falling apart was that I was jealous. I would find out that he was accepting stuff from someone or maybe he was being a little too friendly in the dayroom. When I heard stuff like that, it always made me mad. I've always had a bad temper; that's what got me in prison in the first place. But I really hate people who mess around with what's mine. Even though Mitchell was taller and outweighed me, I wasn't afraid of any man, punk or otherwise.

Our arguing started getting physical. We'd fight in the dayroom. We'd fight in our cell. We'd fight in the chow hall. It didn't matter where; we'd just fight. But we always made up by having sex. That was the only good thing about our fights.

After several months, I began to realize that maybe this relationship wasn't going to last forever. We'd be doing good to make it into next week. The sex was all right. Sex is sex. I just didn't feel the same inside anymore. I knew we were drifting apart. Sex wasn't even about pleasing him anymore. I just wanted to get off.

We had one final argument that pushed me over the edge. The details really aren't important. I just wanted to beat the pressure, to make this whole thing go away. The rest of the cell block was getting sick of our yelling or of being dragged into our battles. I was tired of fighting. I had sores inside and out. Love isn't suppose to hurt this way, is it? I had a feeling that Mitchell wanted to hang on. He would get all sexy and affectionate, hoping that I would change my mind. It almost worked. Almost.

Eventually, Mitchell had had enough too. He decided that he wanted to move out. I sort of expected it, but it still hurt to lose him. And I had to face reality—it was over. There was nothing left to hold us together, except the virus that we shared.

The event that signaled the end for us was the final argument that led to a bloodbath in the dayroom. Mitchell started talking shit about stuff that was history. He was trying to push me into fighting so we would go to jail. He was making me mad, but I didn't want to fight him. That was, until he tried to slap me. No man, I don't care who he is, is going to slap me like some whore. When I snapped, so did my cousin; we both started punching and kicking Mitchell all over the dayroom, though he got in a few pretty good licks himself. That was our bloodiest fight ever. Blood, our infected blood, was splattering everywhere. We fought for what must have been ten minutes before the guards took us to lock-up in handcuffs.

As I sat in solitary, waiting for my wounds to heal and my fate to be decided, I thought about how at one time this person meant so much to me that it was worth taking the risk of HIV. 'Til death do us part. I thought that I would love him forever. I knew that I was taking a big risk and I'd give anything if I could give back this disease.

I'm sure that they're going to see to it that we stay separated from now on. One of us may even get shipped to another unit. No matter where I end up, I'll always have a memento of our fatal attraction—I'll always have HIV. . . .

During the writing of this essay, some changes occurred in the lives of the people who shared their experiences with us. After eleven agonizing days awaiting his test results, Sergio learned that he had been infected with HIV. Despite his emotional but short-lived exit from "The Game," his thirst for sex and his longing for companionship foreordained his return. Wanting desperately not to expose anyone else to this disease, he hoped to find an HIV-positive partner. He found instead a partner who is uninfected, and with whom he struggles daily to withstand his almost insurmountable urges to have sex.

After serving time in solitary to atone for their fight, Barry and Mitchell remained on the same unit and, surprisingly, even returned to living in the same cell. To some extent, they have reconciled their relationship, despite occasional skirmishes. In truth, Barry would like to move out and end the relationship, but neither party relishes seeing the other with someone else. Declaring a stalemate, Barry has acquiesced to this fatal attraction and has opted to bide his time until Mitchell is paroled in the not-too-distant future.

Chapter IV
Medical Treatment: HIV/AIDS in Corrections

Discussion

The first reading by Lipton relates to in-prison prevalence and transmission of HIV. Lipton discusses the fact that prisons have a disproportionate number of people who have engaged in behaviors on the street that place them at high risk for HIV. These behaviors include intravenous drug use, needle sharing, unprotected sex, multiple partners, and anal sex. The reading by prisoners Gilbreath and Rogers indicates that many sexual at-risk behaviors continue inside prison. Lipton would likely agree with Gilbreath and Rogers that prisons should distribute condoms to prisoners on request.

There are two troubling aspects discussed in these readings. First, researchers are aware of the close connection between HIV (and other diseases), drug use, and unprotected sex. Yet, as the readings show, many prison systems could be doing more to prevent the spread of disease. Some prisoners will contract HIV inside prison and may spread the disease to their spouses or partners after their release in the community. Another example that De Groot points out is that most prison medical staff are not encouraged to better understand how to prevent HIV among women prisoners.

A second disturbing issue is that some prisoners have naïve and carefree attitudes regarding HIV. Although some prisoners will literally die to have sex, most prisoners are extremely concerned with remaining HIV-negative. Some prisoners remain celibate and uninvolved in "The Game" for fear of contracting hepatitis, HIV, and other sexually transmitted diseases. Some uninfected prisoners have filed lawsuits against the prison because these prisoners do not feel adequately protected against assaults from prisoners who *are* infected with HIV. Prisoners also seem divided on the issue of mandatory HIV testing, so the issue is much more complex and has yet to be decided by the courts.

Lipton cautions that potential costs to correctional systems for HIV and AIDS medical services will soon exceed system resources. However, incarceration affords opportunities for some prisoners to remain clean and sober, so they can receive information on HIV prevention. Prisons can also function to test different models for HIV prevention in a relatively controlled environment, and to test vaccines voluntarily.

Part Three
Prison Security Issues

Chapter V
Introduction

Prison Gangs

Common Assumptions	Reality
• Prison gangs are unorganized groups of prisoners who just like to hang out together.	• Prison gangs are, by definition, a type of organized "security threat group"; most gangs have a formalized constitution of rules and regulations, a paramilitary hierarchy of authority, requirements for recruitment and membership, and no affiliation with other legitimate prison organizations.
• Prison gangs exist only in prison, while street gangs exist outside of prison.	• Prison gangs originated inside prison for the purpose of self-protection and control of drug trafficking and other illegal goods and services. Prison gang membership has expanded to other state and federal prison systems as well as outside of prison. Although street gangs originated on the street, many members get sentenced to prison. While incarcerated, street gang members fully retain their membership and associate with others in their gang, or an "alliance" group, also known as a "set."
• Prison gangs can be eradicated by dividing them—transferring members to different prisons.	• Prison gangs can never be completely eliminated because of their significance for members. For example, most gangs have a strict "blood in/blood out" obligation. This means that once prospects meet the initial requirements of membership (blood in), they are in the group for life. The gang member either dies defending the gang or is killed if others discover that he or she is trying to get out of the gang (blood out). Transferring known gang members to other prisons contributes to the further spread of gangs throughout the United States. Active prison members will simply begin recruiting prospects to continue their illegitimate profiteering. Thus, prisons that had no notable gang problem before will likely experience gang activity if gang members are spread around.

Prison gang formation has had a snowball effect since groups originated in the 1950s in Washington State penitentiary and became more organized throughout the 1960s in California and Illinois state prisons. For example, an early prison gang, the *Mexikanemi* (Mexican Mafia), was first discovered by California prison officials in 1957. Urban Hispanic inmates from east Los Angeles formed the gang to control drugs and other contraband that entered the facility. With the formation of the Mexican Mafia, other convicts in the prison needed to protect themselves from victimization, and they formed their own groups in response. One such prison gang was *La Nuestra Familia*, a group of rural Hispanic convicts.

A noticeable characteristic about most prison gangs is that they are racially segregated and from a particular neighborhood or city. As more prison gangs formed, recruitment became more active so that prison gangs could sustain their numbers. Alliances were created as smaller gangs combined to increase their strength against larger enemy groups.

Currently, prison gangs are classified as a type of security threat group (STG). Other categories of STGs include white supremacy groups, street gangs, cults, and outlaw motorcycle gangs. A security threat group by definition jeopardizes the safety and security of the prison institution. This is because STGs typically have a profit orientation and an ideology built around racial hatred and self-protection. Most STGs desire to earn a profit through intimidation, violence, and illegitimate activities while incarcerated. These activities are designed to give the group money, power, position, and a more comfortable prison existence. These behaviors include drug trafficking, prostitution, gambling, extortion, and theft. Groups who compete for this profit are at war with each other inside the prison, and they are closely connected with people who reside outside the walls.

Despite their existence for over forty years, little is known about prison gangs for a number of reasons. First, members are secretive about their membership and activities related to the gang. This secrecy has been a key to sustaining their existence. Second, the gang checks out its members carefully to ensure loyalty. The "blood in/blood out" expectation makes it difficult for outsiders to infiltrate the gang. Third, prison gangs go to great lengths to avoid detection. STGs constantly change their codes, signs, and methods of operation. Finally, the small amount of information gained about STGs is typically collected by a few gang intelligence officers inside the prison. With the exception of a few journal articles in the early 1990s, prison gang information has not been often publicized.

Recommended Readings

American Correctional Association. (1994). *Gangs in Correctional Facilities: A National Assessment*. Washington, DC: National Institute of Justice.

Camp, George M., and Camille Graham Camp. (1988). *Management Strategies for Combating Prison Gang Violence*. South Salem, NY: Criminal Justice Institute.

Carroll, Leo. (1974). *Hacks, Blacks, and Cons: Race Relations in a Maximum Security Prison*. Lexington, MA: Lexington Books.

Pelz, Mary E. (1996). "Gangs" Pp. 213–218 in *Encyclopedia of American Prisons*, edited by Marilyn McShane and Frank P. Williams. New York: Garland.

Pelz, Mary E., James W. Marquart, and C. T. Pelz. (1991). "Right-Wing Extremism in the Texas Prisons: The Rise and Fall of the Aryan Brotherhood of Texas." *Prison Journal* 71 (2):23–37.

Internet Websites

California Gang Investigator Association. Available: *http://www.cgiaonline.org/*

Florida Department of Corrections Security Threat Group Intelligence Unit. Available: *http://www.dc.state.fl.us/pub/gangs/prison.html*

Gangs OR Us, a service dedicated to gang education and criminal justice training. Available: *http://www.gangsorus.com/*

Information about some of the prison gangs in California prisons. Available: *http://members.tripod.com/malo_pvn/id18.htm*

Texas Gang Investigator Association. Available: *http://www.tgia.net*

13
Changes in Prison Culture: Prison Gangs and the Case of the 'Pepsi Generation'

Geoffrey Hunt
Stephanie Riegel
Tomas Morales
Dan Waldorf

Focus Questions

1. Which established prison gangs existed at the time of this study?
2. How were confidential informants used?
3. How has the prison environment changed over time?
4. What newer prison gangs have emerged?
5. How have prison authorities attempted to control prison gang behavior?

Since Clemmer (1958) published *The Prison Community* in 1940, sociologists and criminologists have sought to explain the culture of prisons. A key debate in this literature centers on the extent to which inmate culture is either a product of the prison environment or an extension of external subcultures. Those in the former camp, such as Sykes and Messinger (1977), Cloward

(1977), and Goffman (1961), have argued that the inmate social system is formed "as a reaction to various 'pains of imprisonment' and deprivation inmates suffer in captivity" (Leger and Stratton 1977:93). These writers saw the prison as a total institution in which the individual, through a series of "status degradation ceremonies," gradually became socialized into prison life. Analysts such as Irwin and Cressey (1977) challenged this view of prison life, arguing that it tended to underestimate the importance of the culture that convicts brought with them from the outside. They identified two dominant subcultures within the prison—that of the thief and the convict—both of which had their origins in the outside world.

Our interview material did not clearly support one or the other of these opposing views and instead suggested that other dynamics of prison life were key to understanding inmates' experiences. Salient in inmate interviews was a greater degree of turmoil than was common to prison life in the past. The reasons for this turmoil were complex and included newly formed gangs, changes in prison population demographics, and new developments in prison policy, especially in relation to gangs. All these elements coalesced to create an increasingly unpredictable world in which prior loyalties, allegiances, and friendships were disrupted. Even some of the experienced prisoners from the "old school" were at a loss as to how to negotiate this new situation. Existing theories were not helpful in explaining our findings, for the current dynamics could not be attributed solely to forces emanating from inside the prison or outside it. . . .

The Established California Prison Gangs

According to various accounts (Camp and Camp 1985; Davidson 1974; Irwin 1980;

Moore 1978; Porter 1982), the first California prison gang was the Mexican Mafia—a Chicano gang, believed to have originated in 1957 in the Dueul Vocational Institution prison. This Chicano group began to intimidate other Chicanos from the northern part of the state. The non-aligned, predominantly rural Chicanos organized themselves together for protection. They initially called themselves "Blooming Flower," but soon changed their name to *La Nuestra Familia*. Like the Mexican Mafia, *La Nuestra Familia* adopted a military style structure, with a general, captains, lieutenants, and soldiers. However, unlike the Mexican Mafia, *La Nuestra Familia* had a written constitution consisting of rules of discipline and conduct.

The Texas Syndicate, a third Chicano gang, followed the model of the Mexican Mafia and *La Nuestra Familia* and utilized a paramilitary system with a president at its head. Its members are mainly Mexican-American inmates, originally from Texas, who see themselves in opposition to the other Chicano groups, especially those from Los Angeles, who they perceive as being soft and too "Americanized."

Both black and white prisoners are also organized. The general view on the origins of the Black Guerilla Family (B.G.F.)—the leading black gang—is that it developed as a splinter group of the Black Family, an organization reportedly created by George Jackson. The authorities were particularly wary of this group, both because of its revolutionary language and reports that its members, unlike those of other gangs, regularly assaulted prison guards.

The Aryan Brotherhood—the only white gang identified in California prisons—originated in the late 1960s. It is said to be governed by a three-man commission and a nine-man council who recruit from white supremacist and outlawed motorcycle groups. According to prison authorities, it is a "Nazi-oriented gang, anti-black, [which] adheres to violence to gain prestige and compliance to their creed" (Camp and Camp 1985:105).

The available sociological literature on older prison gangs is divided on the issue of their relationship to street gangs. On the one hand, Moore, in discussing Chicano gangs, argues that they were started by "state-raised youths and 'psychos'" (1978:114) inside the prisons, while Jacobson sees them as an extension of street gangs. Although Moore sees the gangs as initially prison inspired, she describes a strong symbiotic relationship between the street and the prison. In fact, she notes that once the gangs were established inside the prisons, they attempted to influence the street scene. "The Mafia attempted to use its prison-based organization to move into the narcotics market in East Los Angeles, and also, reputedly, into some legitimate pinto-serving community agencies" (1978:115).

Institutional Attempts to Control the Gangs

Prison authorities see gangs as highly undesirable and have argued that an increase in extortion, intimidation, violence, and drug trafficking can be directly attributed to their rise. In responding to prison gangs, the California Department of Corrections (CDC) introduced a number of strategies and policies, for example, using "confidential informants," segregating gang members in different buildings and prisons, intercepting gang communications, setting up task forces to monitor and track gang members, locking up gang leaders in high security prisons, and "locking down" entire institutions. These changes were perceived by our respondents who saw the CDC as increasingly tightening its control over the prison system and the gangs.

Prison Guards

In spite of the "official" view that gangs should be eradicated, many prison authorities hold a more pragmatic view and feel that the gangs have "had little negative impact on the regular running of prison operations" (Camp and Camp 1985:xii). Moreover, as Cummins (1991) has noted, there is often a considerable discrepancy between the official stance and what takes place within particular prisons. This point was emphasized by our respondents who portrayed guards' attitudes toward the gangs as complex and devious and saw the guards as often accepting prison gangs and in some cases even encouraging them. In supporting this view, they gave three reasons why guards would allow gangs to develop or continue.

First, some noted guards' financial incentive to encourage gang behavior. They suggested that guards are keen to create "threats to security" which necessitate increased surveillance and, consequently, lead to overtime work.

> They have a financial interest in getting overtime. . . . Anything that was "security" meant that there were no restrictions in the budget. So if there are gangs, and there are associations, if there is some threat in that focus of security, they make more money. (Case 17)

Others went even further and told us that some guards benefitted from gangs' illegal activities.

> Well, you know the guards, aren't . . . you'd be surprised who the guards affiliated with. Guards have friends that's in there. They have their friends outside, you know. Guards'll bring drugs in. Sell 'em. Guards will bring knives in, weapons, food. The guards play a major role. (Case 7)

Not only were guards involved in illegal activities, but the practice was often overlooked by other guards. For example, as one respondent philosophically replied in answer to our question: "Were individual guards involved in illegal gang activities?"

> Well, I think you have guards that are human beings that . . . don't really want to do more than they have to. So if they see a guard doing something a little shady, it's easy to turn a blind eye because of the hassle it would take to pursue it. (Case 16)

Finally, in addition to these financial incentives, some believed that guards encouraged gang activities and conflict in order to control the prison inmates more effectively and "keep the peace out of prisons" (Case 32).

> They perpetuated the friction because, for instance, what they would do is . . . give false information to different

groups. . . . Something to put the fear so that then the Latino would prepare himself for a conflict. . . . And so everybody's on point and the next thing you know a fight would break out and the shit would come down. So it was to their interest to perpetuate division amongst the inmates so that they would be able to better control the institution. Because, if you are spending your time fighting each other, you have no time . . . to fight the establishment. (Case 34)

This divide-and-rule policy was emphasized by many of our respondents and was seen as a major contributory factor in prisoner conflicts.

Jacketing and the Use of Confidential Informants

According to our respondents, another prison administration tactic was "jacketing"—officially noting in a prisoner's file that he was a suspected gang member. Once identified as a gang member, a prisoner could be transferred to a high security prison or placed in a special housing unit. "Jacketing," which is similar to the "dirty jacket" procedure outlined by Davidson (1974), was seen by our respondents as a particularly arbitrary process and one in which the prisoner had little or no recourse.

> Like I said, if you're a sympathizer, you could be easily jacketed as a gang member. You hang around with 'em. You might not do nothing. But hang out with 'em. Drive iron with 'em. Go to lunch with 'em. (Case 1)

Many respondents felt the process was particularly unfair because it meant that a prisoner could be identified as gang member and "jacketed" purely on the basis of information from a confidential informant. Confidential informants or "snitches" supplied intelligence information to prison authorities about inmate activities, especially gang-related activities.

> Now let's say you and I are both inmates at San Quentin. And your cellie gets in a fight and gets stabbed. So all of a sudden, the Chicano who is a friend of your cellie says that he'll get the boys and deal with this. They talk about it but nothing hap-

pens. All of a sudden one of the snitches, or rats, says I think something is cooking, and people are going to make a move to the administration. What will happen is that they [the administration] will gaffel up you and me and whoever else you associate with and put us all on a bus straight to Pelican Bay. They will say we have confidential reliable information that you guys are planning an assault on Billy Bob or his gang. . . . And you're wondering, you've never received a disciplinary infraction. But by God now, information is in your central file that you are gang affiliated, that you're involved in gang violence. (Case 16)

Our respondents distinguished between two types of snitching: dry and hard.

Dry snitching is a guy who will have a conversation with a guard and the guard is just smart enough. He'll say you talk to Joe, don't ya? You say, oh, yeah, Joe's a pretty good ol' boy, I heard he's doing drugs but don't believe it. He might smoke a few joints on the yard, but nothing hard. He just dry snitched. He indirectly dropped a lug on Joe. And then you got the guy who gets himself in a jam and goes out and points out other inmates. (Case 16)

Dry snitching could also refer to a prisoner supplying general information to guards without implicating anyone by name. This allowed the prisoner to develop a "juice card" or a form of credit with the guard.

A "juice card" is that you have juice [credit] with a particular guard, a lieutenant, a sergeant or somebody that is part of staff. . . . Let's say that somebody is dry snitching. By dry snitching I mean that they might come up to their juice man that has a "juice card," let's say it is a sergeant of the yard, and they might go up there and say, "Hey, I hear that there is a rumble coming down. I can't tell you more than that but some shit is going to come down tonight." So they alert the sergeant, right. The sergeant tells him, "I owe you one." Now the guy might come up to the sergeant and say, "Hey remember you owe me one, hey, I got this 115 [infraction] squash it." "Okay, I will squash it." That is the "juice card." (Case 34)

Many of our respondents felt there was a growing number of snitches (also see Stojkovic 1986). A key factor promoting this growth was the pressure exerted by the guards—a point denied by the prison authorities in Stojkovic's research.

Pressure could be applied in a number of ways. First, if for example a prisoner was in a high security unit, he often found himself unable to get out unless he "debriefed"; i.e., provided information on other gang members. Many respondents felt that this was an impossible situation because if they didn't snitch, their chances of getting out were minimal. As one respondent remarked:

They [the guards] wanted some information on other people. . . . So I was put between a rock and a hard place. So I decided I would rather do extra time than ending up saying something I would later regret. (Case 10)

Second, if the guards knew that a prisoner was an ex-gang member, they might threaten to send him to a particular prison, where he would be attacked by his own ex-gang.

See, there is a lot of guys in there that are dropouts from whatever gang they were in, and they are afraid to be sent to a joint where some other tip might be. They even get threatened by staff that if they don't cooperate with them, they will be sent to either Tracy or Soledad and they are liable to get hit by their own ex-gang, so they cooperate. (Case 40)

However, it would be inaccurate to suggest respondents accused only the prison authorities, since many also pointed out other developments within the prison system, and especially within the prison population, to explain what they described as a deteriorating situation.

Prison Crowding, the New Gangs, and the 'Pepsi Generation'

Since 1980, the California prison population has increased dramatically from 24,569 to 97,309 (California Department of Corrections 1991). The net effect of this expansion has been severe overcrowding in the prisons. In 1970, prison institutions and camps were slightly underutilized and the occupancy rate stood at 98 percent. By 1980, they were full, and in 1990, the rate had risen dramatically to 180 percent of capacity. Currently, the inmate population stands at 91,892, while bed capacity is only 51,013. In order to cope with this overcrowding, institutions have been obliged to use all available space, including gymnasiums and dayrooms.

Many respondents graphically described the problems created by this situation and complained about the deterioration in prison services. However, in talking about prison overcrowding they tended to concentrate more on the changes in the characteristics of the inmates currently arriving. Specifically, they focused on the growth of new gangs, the immaturity of new inmates, and the problems they caused within the prison. Respondents felt this change in prison population characteristics had a major effect on day-to-day activities and contributed to the fragmentary nature of prison life.

The New Gangs

According to our respondents, although all five of the older gangs still exist, their importance has diminished. The reasons for this appear to be twofold. First, many of the older gang members have either dropped out, gone undercover, or have been segregated from the rest of the prison population. Second, a new crop of gangs has taken center stage. In other words, prison authorities' efforts to contain the spread of gangs led, unintentionally, to a vacuum within the prison population within which new prison groupings developed.

Information on these new gangs is relatively limited in comparison with information on the older gangs. Thus it is difficult to be precise about their structure and composition. Moreover, a further complication is whether or not these groups fit current definitions of what constitutes a gang. For instance, if we adapt Klein and Maxson's (1989) definition of a street gang—community recognition as a group or collectivity, recognition by the group itself as a distinct group, and activities which consistently result in negative responses from law enforcement—then these new groupings constitute gangs if the prison is considered the community. However, if we compare them with the Mexican Mafia, *La Nuestra Familia*, or the Black Guerilla Family, which have developed hierarchies or clearly articulated constitutions, they constitute instead territorial alliances which demand loyalties and provide security and protection. Regardless of whether these groups fit traditional definitions, respondents made it clear they had a significant impact on the traditional prison loyalties and allegiances and contributed to conflicts amongst the prisoners.

Chicano and Latino gangs. Among Chicanos, the Nortenos and the Surenos are the most important groupings or gangs. These two groups are divided regionally between the North and South of California, with Fresno as the dividing line. Although regional loyalties were also important for the Mexican Mafia and *La Nuestra Familia*, the regional separation between North and South was not as rigid as it is today for Surenos and Nortenos.

In addition to the Nortenos and the Surenos, two other groups were mentioned—the New Structure and the Border Brothers. Our respondents provided differing interpretations of the New Structure. For instance, some noted it was a new Chicano group made up of Nortenos which started in San Francisco, while others implied it was an offshoot of *La Nuestra Familia*. Opinions differed as to its precise relationship to *La Nuestra Familia*.

The Border Brothers are surrounded by less controversy. Their members are from Mexico, they speak only Spanish and, consequently, keep to themselves. Most of our respondents agreed this was a large group constantly increasing in size, and that most members had been arrested for trafficking heroin or cocaine.

Although, there was little disagreement as to the Border Brothers' increasing importance, which was partly attributed to their not "claiming territory," there was, nevertheless, some dispute as to their impact on the North/South issue. Some respondents saw the Border Brothers as keeping strictly to themselves.

> The Border Brothers don't want to have anything to do with the Surenos-Nortenos—they keep out of that 'cause it's not our fighting and all of that is stupid.... Either you are a Chicano or you're not. There is no sense of being separated. (Case 3)

Others predicted that in the future, the Border Brothers will become involved in the conflict and will align themselves with the Surenos against the Nortenos.

> It used to be Border Brothers over there and Sureno and Norteno, stay apart from each other. . . . But now what I see that's coming out is that the Border Brothers are starting to claim Trece now. What I think is going to happen, to the best of my knowledge, is that the Surenos instead of them knockin' ass with the Nortenos, they're going to have the Border Brothers lock ass with the Nortenos due to the fact that they're South and all that. Maybe in a few years we will see if my prediction is true or not. (Case 36)

Black gangs. The Crips, originally a street gang from South Central Los Angeles, are the largest of the new black gangs. It is basically a neighborhood group.

> Interviewer: So the Crips is more a neighborhood thing than a racial thing?

> Respondent: Oh yeah! That's what it stems from. It stems from a neighborhood thing. There's one thing about the Crips collectively, their neighborhoods are important factors in their gang structures. (Case 5)

The Bloods are the traditional rivals of the Crips. Although, like the Crips, they are a neighborhood group, they do not attribute the same importance to the neighborhood.

> They're structured geographically in the neighborhood, but it's not as important as it is for the Crips. Only in LA is it that important. Bloods from LA, it's important for them but they don't have as many neighborhoods as the Crips. But anywhere else in Southern California the neighborhoods are not that important. Only in LA. (Case 5)

The 415s are a third black prison gang emerging recently. The group is made up of individuals living within the 415 San Francisco Bay area telephone code. Although the group's visibility is high, especially in the Bay area, the organization appears to be loosely structured, so much so that one of our respondents suggested that the 415s were more an affiliation rather than a gang.

All of these gangs are said to be producing a significant impact on prison life. Whereas previously, there were four or five major gangs, today there are nine or ten new groupings, each with its own network of alliances and loyalties. These crosscutting and often conflicting allegiances have a significant impact on prison life. They produce a confusing, disruptive situation for many prisoners and can even produce problems for existing friendships. As one Puerto Rican respondent noted, "When I first started going to the joints . . . it wasn't as bad to associate with a guy from the North and the South. It wasn't that big of a deal" (Case 39). But as the fragmentation increased and dividing lines became more rigid, this type of friendship was much less acceptable. According to many of our respondents, another consequence of fragmentation was an increase in intraethnic conflict, especially amongst the black population.

> Back then there was no Crips, there was no Bloods, or 415s. It is a lot different now. The blacks hit the blacks. When the blacks at one time were like the B.G.F., where the blacks would stick together, now they are hitting each other, from the Crips, to the Bloods, to the 415, are pretty much all enemies. (Case 39)

The picture provided by our respondents is one of an increasing splintering of prison groupings. Allegiances to particular groups, which had previously seemed relatively entrenched, are now questioned. Friendships developed over long prison terms are now disrupted, and where previously prisoners made choices about joining a gang, membership has now become more automatic, especially for Chicanos. Today, what counts is the region of the state where the prisoner comes from; if he comes from south of Fresno, he is automatically a Sureno, if he is from north of Fresno, he becomes a Norteno.

'Pepsi Generation'

Respondents not only described the conflict arising from the new divisions within the prison population, but also attributed this conflict to new prison inmates. They emphasized that the new generation of prisoners differed from their generation—in their dress, attitudes, and behavior toward other prisoners and the prison authorities. Respondents described themselves as convicts who represented the "old school."

> In my point of view there is what is called the old school. . . . And the old school goes back to where there is traditions and customs, there is this whole thing of holding your mud, and there is something you don't violate. For instance, you don't snitch, you are a convict in the sense that you go in and you know that you are there to do time. And there is two sides. There is the Department of Corrections and there is you as the convict. (Case 34)

A convict, in this sense, was very different from the present day "inmate" who they described as not having

> a juvenile record or anything like that, and so that when they come in, they have no sense of what it is to do time. . . . The inmate goes in there and he goes in not realizing that, so that they are doing everybody else's number or expect somebody else to do their number. Which means, for instance, that if they can get out of something they will go ahead and give somebody up or they will go against the code. Say for instance, the food is real bad and the convict would say, look, we have to do something about this so let's make up a protest about the food and present it to the warden. And the convict will go along with it because it is for the betterment of the convicts. The inmate will go and go against it because he wants to be a good inmate and, therefore, he is thinking about himself and not the whole population. (Case 32)

The prisons were full of younger prisoners who were described disparagingly by our respondents as "boys trying to become men," and the "Pepsi Generation," defined as

the young shuck and jive energized generation. The CYA [California Youth Authority] mentality guys in a man's body and muscles can really go out and bang if they want. They are the youngsters that want to prove something—how tough and macho and strong they are. This is their whole attitude. Very extreme power trip and machismo. The youngsters want to prove something. How tough they are. And there is really very little remorse. (Case 16)

According to our respondents, the "Pepsi Generation" went around wearing "their pants down below their ass" (Case 40) and showing little or no respect for the older inmates, many of whom had long histories of prison life which normally would have provided them with a high degree of status. Disrespect was exhibited even in such seemingly small things as the way that the younger prisoners approached the older inmates.

> They'll come up and ask you where you are from. I had problems with that. They come with total disrespect. It seems like they send the smallest, youngest punk around and he comes and tries to jam you. You know, you've been around for a long time, you know, you've got your respect already established and you have no business with this bullshit. . . . And here you have some youngster coming in your face, talking about "Hey man, where you from?" (Case 2)

This view was graphically corroborated by a 38-year-old *Familia* member who described the young inmates in the following way:

> They're actors. Put it this way, they're gangsters until their fuckin' wheels fall off. . . . I'm a gangster too. But there is a limitation to everything. See, I can be a gangster with class and style and finesse and respect. Get respect and get it back. That's my motto, my principle in life. Do unto another as you would like to have done to you. These kids don't have respect for the old timers. They disrespect the old men now. (Case 36)

The "younger generation" was not only criticized for its disrespect, but for its general behavior as well. They were seen as needlessly violent and erratic and not "TBYAS"—thinking before you act and speak.

> I think they're more violent. They are more spontaneous. I think they are very spontaneous. They certainly don't use TBYAS. I think their motivation is shallower than it was years ago. (Case 16)

Their behavior had the effect of making prison life, in general, more unpredictable, a feature many of our respondents disliked.

> They have nothing but younger guys in prison now. And, ah, it has just changed. I don't even consider it prison now anymore. I think it is just a punishment. It is just a place to go to do time. Which now, since there are so many children and kids in prison, it is hard to do time now. It is not like it used to be where you can wake up one morning and know what to expect. But now you wake up and you don't know what to expect; anything might happen. (Case 12)

Inmate Culture Reassessed

Inmates' picture of prison life is of increasing uncertainty and unpredictability; more traditional groupings and loyalties are called into question as new groups come to the fore. Whereas previously, prisoners believed a clear dividing line existed between convicts and authorities, today they see this simple division disintegrating. This occurs because, in their attempt to control the spread of prison gangs, authorities introduced a series of measures which contained the gangs, but also unexpectedly created a vacuum within the organizational structure of the prison populations—a vacuum soon filled by new groups. Group membership was taken from newer inmates, who, according to our respondents, had not been socialized into the convict culture. The dominance of these groups soon led to an environment where the rules and codes of behavior were no longer adhered to and even the more experienced prisoners felt like newcomers. Moreover, the ability of prisoners to remain nonaligned was hampered both by develop-

ments amongst the prisoners and by the actions of the authorities. For example, a Norteno arrested in the South and sentenced to a southern prison would find himself in a very difficult and potentially dangerous situation.

> You'll see some poor northern dude land in a southern pen, they ride on [harass] him. Five, six, seven, ten deep. You know, vice versa—some poor southern kid comes to a northern spot and these northern kids will do the same thing. They ride deep on them. (Case 2)

Study respondents portrayed prison culture as changing, but the change elements they identified were both inside and outside the institution. The available theoretical approaches, which have tended to dichotomize the source of change, fail to capture the complexity and the interconnectedness of the current situation. Furthermore, the information we received produced no conclusive evidence to prove whether or not the street scene determined the structure of gangs inside the prison or vice versa. For example, in the case of the Crips and the Bloods, at first glance we have a development which supports the approaches of Jacobs (1974) and Irwin and Cressey (1977). The Crips and the Bloods originated in the neighborhoods of Los Angeles and transferred their conflicts into the prison environment. In fact, according to one respondent, once in prison, they bury their intragang conflicts in order to strengthen their identities as Crips and Bloods.

> Even when they are "out there" they may fight amongst themselves, just over their territory. . . . But when they get to prison they are wise enough to know, we gotta join collectively to fend off everyone else. (Case 5)

However, although the Crips and Bloods fit neatly into Jacobs' perspective, when we consider the case of the 415s and the Nortenos and the Surenos, we find their origins fit more easily into Cloward's (1977) alternative perspective. According to two accounts, the 415s began in prison as a defense group against the threatening behavior of the Bloods and the Crips.

It [the 415s] got started back in prison. In prison there is a lot of prison gangs . . . and they were put together a lot. They got LA gangs like the Bloods and the Crips, and they are putting a lot of pressure on the people from the Bay area. And we all got together, we got together and organized our own group. (Case G189)

Originally, the Nortenos and Surenos existed neither on the streets nor in the adult prisons but within the California Youth Authority institutions. Gradually this division spread to the adult prisons and soon became powerful enough to disrupt the traditional loyalties of more established gangs. Furthermore, in-prison conflicts soon spread to the outside and, according to information from our San Francisco study, Norteno/Sureno conflicts are beginning to have a significant impact on the streets.

Conclusion

As Irwin (1980) noted over ten years ago, prisons today are in a turmoil. From both the Department of Corrections' perspective and the interview material, it is clear that the prison system is under immense pressures. As the prison population expands and the Department of Corrections attempts to find more bed space, the problems within the prisons multiply. The impact of this situation on the inmates is clear from the interviews—they complain about the increased fragmentation and disorganization that they now experience. Life in prison is no longer organized but instead is viewed as both capricious and dangerous.

For many, returning to prison after spending time outside means being confronted by a world which they do not understand even though they have been in prison many times before. Where once they experienced an orderly culture, today they find a world which operates around arbitrary and ad hoc events, and decisions seem to arise not merely from the behavior of their fellow prisoners but also from prison authorities' official and unofficial decisions. Where before they understood the dominant prison divisions—prisoners versus guards and black versus white

inmates—today they find new clefts and competing allegiances. The Chicanos are split not only between the Mexican Mafia and *La Nuestra Familia* but also North versus South. A relatively unified black population is divided into different warring camps of Crips, Bloods, and 415s.

The world portrayed by our respondents is an important corrective both to the criminal justice literature, which portrays prison life in very simplistic terms, and to those theoretical approaches which attempt to explain prison culture solely in terms of internal or external influences. Our interviews have shown that the linkages between street activities and prison activities are complex and are the result of developments in both arenas. Therefore, instead of attributing primacy to one set of factors as opposed to the other, it may be more useful and more accurate to see the culture and organization of prison and street life as inextricably intertwined, with lines of influence flowing in both directions.

References

California Department of Corrections (1991) *Historical Trends: Institution and Parole Population, 1970-1990.* Offender Information Services Branch. Data Analysis Unit. Sacramento.

Camp, George, M., and Camille, G. Camp (1985) *Prison Gangs: Their Extent, Nature and Impact on Prisons.* U.S. Department of Justice, Office of Legal Policy, Federal Justice Research Program. Washington, D.C.

Clemmer, Donald (1958) *The Prison Community.* New York: Rinehart and Co.

Cloward, Richard (1977) "Social control in the prison." In *The Sociology of Corrections*, Robert G. Leger and John R. Stratton (eds.), 110–132. New York: John Wiley and Sons.

Cummins, Eric (1991) "History of gang development in California prisons." Unpublished paper.

Davidson, R. Theodore (1974) *Chicano Prisoners: The Key to San Quentin.* Prospect Heights, IL.: Waveland Press, Inc.

Goffman, Erving (1961) *Asylums.* Garden City, N.J.: Anchor.

Irwin, John (1980) *Prisons in Turmoil.* Boston: Little, Brown and Company.

Irwin, John, and Donald Cressey (1977) "Thieves, convicts, and the inmate culture. In *The Sociology of Corrections*, Robert G. Leger and John R. Stratton (eds.), 133–147. New York: John Wiley and Sons.

Jacobs, James (1974) "Street gangs behind bars." *Social Problems* 21:395–409.

Klein, Malcolm W., and Cheryl L. Maxson (1989) "Street gang violence." In *Violent Crime, Violent Criminals,* Neil Allen Weiner and Marvin E. Wolfgang (eds.). Newbury Park, Calif.: Sage.

Leger, Robert G., and John R. Stratton (1977) *The Sociology of Corrections: A Book of Readings.* New York: John Wiley and Sons.

Moore, Joan W. (1978) *Homeboys: Gangs Drugs, and Prison in the Barrios of Los Angeles.* Philadelphia: Temple University Press.

Porter, Bruce (1982) "California prison gangs: The price of control." *Corrections Magazine* 8: 6–19.

Stojkovic, Stan (1986) "Social bases of power and control mechanisms among correctional administrators in a prison organization." *Journal of Criminal Justice* 14:157–166.

Sykes, Gresham M., and Sheldon L Messinger (1977) "The inmate social system." In *The Sociology of Corrections,* Robert G. Leger and John R. Stratton (eds.), 97–109. New York: John Wiley and Sons.

14
The Meaning of Prison Gang Tattoos

Michael P. Phelan
Scott A. Hunt

Focus Questions

1. How do prison gang tattoos define an individual's past and future?

2. What phases exist in prison gang membership?

3. How did Phelan collect data about prison gang tattoos?

4. How are prison gang tattoos different from tattoos worn by the general public?

. . . Bodily markings, such as tattoos, can communicate one or more of the following: (1) personal identity, (2) cultural values and practices, and (3) membership in subgroups within societies that are rebellious, peripheral, marginalized, or otherwise set apart from the "mainstream" (Grumet 1983; Hambly 1925; Mead 1928; Sanders 1988). Concerning inmate populations, Bronnikov (1993, p. 53) points out that tattoos are a "kind of secret language, understandable only to the initiate," and used, in part, to situate identities. . . .

Gang members use tattoos to communicate their membership, rank, specializations, and personal accomplishments, which typically revolve around murder, drug trafficking, and other crimes. With tattoos, gang members ally themselves with their "nefarious business" in a way that cannot be mistaken (Hambly 1925). As pictorial life-histories, expressions of cultural values and practices, and announcements of group solidarity, tattoos can be conceptualized as a form of identity work. Moreover, gang tattoos, inasmuch as they portray group initiations, memberships, and notable personal feats accomplished in the service of their gangs, represent efforts at symbolic self-completion that communicate moral careers.

Data and Research Setting

This study of prison gang tattoos is the result of opportunistic research (Adler and Adler 1987). Phelan collected data while acting as a full participant in the California State prison system from 1984 to 1990. Over those six years, as a standard occupational practice, Phelan collected hundreds of official and unofficial documents, including training manuals and texts, records of disciplinary actions, bed assignments, his and other officers' notes pertaining to actual or potential problematic situations, and, most central for this study, sketches of inmates' tattoos. Here, we elaborate upon our data sources to suggest the cultural context in which the identified tattoos were worn and interpreted.

As part of the hiring process, Phelan underwent a mandatory six-week training course for newly hired correctional officers. The course provided academic instruction, physical conditioning, weapons qualifications, and training in observational skills. During this instruction, novice correctional officers were educated on matters of prison environment (e.g. prison gangs), search and seizure practices, discretionary decision making, criminal law, and inmate/staff relationships. The basic training course was followed by continuous in-service training and workshops that were intended to provide information about issues of immediate concern (e.g., increased gang violence), develop proficiency in various job tasks, disseminate and update informational materials (e.g., descriptions of toxic and explosive agents), and improve officers' communication and morale. For the officers and their administrators, this training was important in that it provided current information concerning institutional procedures, gang identification, and other details from intelligence sources. From a sociological standpoint, the basic and subsequent on-site training constructed a cultural knowledge base that allowed correctional officers to function as such. More specific to our present concern, the frequent classes, presentations, and in-service training sessions provided some of the data on gangs and tattoos used in this article.

While formal training provided data on prison gangs and tattoos, the bulk of the data came from Phelan's daily interactions with hundreds of male inmates and other prison personnel. The observations of the prison environment were experienced, at the time, as a correctional officer, not a sociologist. Nonetheless, over the six years of correctional work, Phelan meticulously generated numerous files pertaining to a wide range of topics, such as signed disciplinary actions, post orders (i.e., detailed job descriptions), and sketches of actual tattoos worn by various gang members. Phelan was able to make sense of the highly symbolic meanings of gang tattoos (not to mention myriad other aspects of prison life) due to the socialization efforts of "elders" (both officers and inmates) who made him prison "wise" (Goffman 1963). The importance of becoming prison wise is emphasized by Webb and Morris (1985, pp. 205–206): "Merely being hired does not make one a guard in the truest sense of the word. The new guard must first become 'con-wise.' That is, he must come to have an understanding of the inmate culture, certain expectations of inmates, and a method of interacting with them that is common to guards."

The tattoo sketches and Phelan's personal files, along with classroom notes, training handouts, handbooks, and other official and unofficial documents function as empirical materials for this article. The interpretations of prison gang tattoos in this article are based on a negotiated understanding of the tattoos that emerged from observations, written documents, as well as interactions with inmates and other prison personnel. To a certain degree, recollection of these experiences and observations, now a decade old, are necessarily relied upon for our analysis. Naturally, this introduces the possibility of biased or otherwise distorted data being produced by faulty or selective recollection. However, this potential shortcoming of opportunistic research is minimized by relying most heavily on original written documents and sketches.

Our data and interpretations were influenced by the context of prison culture, including the activities and organization of gangs within the correctional facility. In prison and out, gang members use symbols and signs to communicate group affiliation, such as distinctive colors, hats, hand signals, and tattoos. Among prison gang members and those who are "wise," there is agreement as to what the various symbols represent. Interactionally competent correctional officers could recognize the gang with which a person was affiliated, the part of the state from which the inmate hailed, and even what street he had lived on and defended (Demello 1993, p. 11). From tattoos and other non-verbal symbols, Phelan learned inmates' religious beliefs, ethnic culture, girlfriends' names, number of kills, and criminal specialization. Knowing this information made it easier for correctional officers to house inmates (i.e., this knowledge helped correctional officers to avoid housing members of hostile gangs together).[1] This information was gathered despite a basic tenet in the prison code that prevented correctional officers from fraternizing with inmates. Similarly, inmate elites insisted that prisoners were not allowed to fraternize with the guards. In these ways, both prison officials and inmate elites attempted to control the channels of communication, an important source of power in the prison system. To a certain degree, these nonfraternization rules were successful. Ironically, though, both correctional officers and prisoners attempted to learn each other's ways so as to carry out their tasks more efficiently and with reduced risks.

Sketches of the tattoos collected by Phelan were associated with four major prison gangs: the Mexican Mafia, *Nuestra Familia*, Aryan Brotherhood, and Black Guerrilla Family. These four California prison gangs are felt to be of major importance because of their power within prison and on the streets (Carter, Glaser, and Wilkins 1985; California 1984; Clark 1992; Goodgame 1985; Lane 1989; Ralph 1997; Sandza and Shannon 1982) For the purposes of our analysis, we concentrate on *Nuestra Familia* tattoos. To better understand the symbols and tattoos of this gang, a general overview of its history and organizational structure, as they were commonly understood by prison personnel and inmates, is in order.

The *Nuestra Familia* was believed to have been formed at San Quentin in 1968 by the ten most wanted inmates on the Mexican Mafia hit list for self-protection (California 1984; Sandza and Shannon 1982). Today, membership is drawn heavily from northern Californian Mexican Americans, particularly from San Jose, Santa Clara, Gilroy, Salinas, Santa Barbara, Oxnard, Stockton, and Fresno (Carter et al. 1985). The northern regional identification of the *Nuestra Familia* and the southern identification of the Mexican Mafia is a powerful symbolic source of their violent conflict.

Since the early conflict with the Mexican Mafia, the *Nuestra Familia* has developed into a highly structured, military-like organization (Carter et al.1985). The *Nuestra Familia* has a constitution patterned after the Sicilian Mafia Constitution of 1912 (California 1984) and is ruled by a General whose power is unlimited and absolute (Carter et al. 1985). There are ten Captains, ranked from one to ten in descending order. The first Captain is the successor to the General. Underneath the Captains are Lieutenants and soldiers. A soldier must have three "kills"

(i.e., must have murdered three people) to be eligible for promotion to Lieutenant and five kills to be put up for Captain (Carter et al. 1985). In terms of recruitment, an individual who is interested in joining must have a current member act as a sponsor. Requests for membership can be made by any member directly to a Captain. The member who acts as sponsor is held accountable for the recruit. The final membership decision is not given for 30 days, and it must be approved by the governing body. Membership in the *Nuestra Familia* demands a high degree of loyalty, and it is assumed to be a lifelong commitment (Carter et al. 1985). These sentiments are suggested in the *Nuestra Familia* oath: "If I go forward, follow me; if I hesitate, push me; if they kill me, avenge me; if I am a traitor, kill me" (California 1984; Sandza and Shannon 1982).

Prison Gang Tattoos as Symbolic Self-Completion

Tattoos generally, and those worn by *Nuestra Familia* members in particular, are symbols that represent commitment to self-defining goals and lines of action (see Sanders 1988). Because tattoos are relatively permanent modifications to the body, their presence is an expression of a deeply felt and enduring identity. They can be used to symbolically complete an identity by closing off or resolving identity ambivalence (cf. Davis 1992; Kaiser et al.1991). They are marks for life. Based on her study of tattoos worn by inmates at Folsom Prison, Demello (1993, p.12) discusses inmates' perceptions of the seriousness of tattoos that convey commitment to convict status and enlarge the scope of individuals who would potentially recognize the completeness of this self-definition:

> Older convicts feel that younger prisoners should not get tattooed if they don't already have any tattoos, and many tattooists in prison will simply refuse to be the first to tattoo a new prisoner. . . . An "honorable" prison tattooist doesn't want to be responsible for helping to ruin a young prisoner's life, particularly if that individual is going to be getting out of

prison any time soon. By acquiring tattoos during his incarceration, he would be making concrete his identity as a convict, and may regret his decision to become tattooed.

Given that many gangs, including the *Nuestra Familia*, expect life-long association from their members, tattoos announcing gang affiliation symbolically demonstrate the wearer's commitment to these terms of membership. The type of tattoo and its location also convey different levels of commitment (Sanders 1988). Large and ornate tattoos are intended to attract more attention and announce the features to which the wearer is most committed. For instance, tattoos worn on the face and neck are the most visible, and thus suggest a higher level of commitment than tattoos on other less visible parts of the body.

In this article, we use *Nuestra Familia* tattoos to illustrate the identity work of symbolic self-completion, particularly the visual communication of moral careers. We organize our presentation around five career stages that we refer to as pre-initiate, initiate, member, veteran, and superior. These stages reflect an etic analysis of prison gang tattoos in that we attempt to formulate a conceptual framework that would be useful for understanding symbolic self-completion and the visual communication of moral careers across social, cultural, and temporal contexts (see Ulin 1984). Given the military language used by the *Nuestra Familia*, a strictly emic framework would limit generalizability and the possibility of comparative analysis. Our etic analytical categories were grounded in and inductively derived from the values and meanings given to tattoos by prison gang and correctional staff members (see Glaser and Strauss 1967).

Pre-initiate

The pre-initiate phase refers to that period *before* an individual is allowed to claim rudimentary group affiliation. During this stage, an individual may experience a sense of identity incompleteness or ambivalence, in that he has an affinity toward gang membership, but has not yet been identified by a *Nuestra Familia* member as a person available for recruitment. Simple tattoos can symbolically complete the wearer's identity as someone interested in gang membership, thereby resolving the problem of ambivalent allegiance. As Lane (1989, p. 126) puts it, "the process of gang identification begins long before the inmate arrives at the doors of the prison." Announcing an affinity toward gang membership can be accomplished by such mimetic behavior as wearing "appropriate" gang colors or clothing. Rudimentary pre-initiate tattoos communicate basic in-group/out-group distinctions, often based on ethnic differences and geographic locations.

In terms of gang tattoos, those desiring to be aligned with the *Nuestra Familia* may engrave some symbol that announces a "northern" identity (e.g., "Norte," Spanish for North), which is the traditional territory of the *Nuestra Familia*. The important point here is that these tattoos do not convey actual recruitment or group membership, but rather only signify a sense of possible compatibility and interest. . . .

[A] pre-initiate status is communicated by an elaborate tattoo worn by some Mexican juveniles who espouse a Northern identity. The tattoo depicts a young, Latina revolutionary, clad in a sombrero and bandolier, and armed with a rifle and flag. In the bottom left corner and in the bottom right corner are the letters "CYA." These letters stand for the California Youth Authority, a system of correctional facilities for juveniles. Just as academic vitae announce the prestige of institutional affiliation, prison gang tattoos often include symbols of the facilities where inmates have done their time. . . .

According to Demello (1993, p 10; see also Govenar 1988), "tattoos can range from technologically primitive to relatively advanced":

> The most primitive method of tattooing is hand plucking or hand picking. Here, the individual typically takes a sewing needle, wraps it in string, and dips it into ink. The needle is then stuck into the skin over and over until a line is achieved, and then the design is shaded in (the string acts as a reservoir for the ink). These tattoos usually look more primitive than tat-

toos created with a machine, because a continuous line is difficult to achieve with a hand picked tattoo. . . . These tattoos are clearly homemade, are usually self-inflicted, and are thus usually on a hand or lower arm. Thus not only does the method of execution signify that the wearer is of a low socio-economic status in that he cannot afford, or has no access to, professional tattoos, but the tattoos themselves are usually on extremely public areas of the body where they can be easily read by others. . . .

Initiate

In contrast to pre-initiate status, the initiate stage suggests greater commitment to gang activities. Because tattoos depicting pre-initiate status merely suggest an affinity or interest in gang membership, they create an identity ambivalence in terms of commitment. Tattoos indicating an initiate position move the wearer toward symbolic completion of a gang identity by suggesting the beginning of a gang career that involves recruitment, sponsorship, and a period of apprenticeship. In a *Newsweek* article, Art Serrato, a former *Nuestra Familia* member, describes the initiate phase as involving a mastering of rules and the gang's constitution: "They drilled us eight hours a day. . . . It was brainwashing" (Press, Sandza, and Shannon 1983). The initiate phase resolves identity ambivalence by requiring a public pledge of commitment to group membership and a readiness to enact certain classes of behavior. However, another form of identity ambivalence emerges in that commitment has been professed but not demonstrated. Since the initiate has yet to prove himself, he is not entitled to all of the benefits of group membership; the construction and affirmation of his gang identity is relatively incomplete.

The *Nuestra Familia* provides an example of a specific tattoo associated with the initiate phase of one's moral career. *Nuestra Familia* initiates typically wear a delicately engraved rose. . . . The wearing of this rose symbolizes potent moral commitments that pre-initiate announcements do not carry. Wearing the rose suggests that the individual has agreed to all of the moral obligations that *Nuestra Familia* membership entails. Further, in terms of impressions "given off" (Goffman 1959), the rose, without more advanced *Nuestra Familia* markings, suggests to correctional officers that the individual wearing such a tattoo might be actively seeking to prove himself. This leads "wise" correctional officers to approach such an inmate with increased caution, thereby attempting to limit the opportunities an inmate might have to demonstrate his worthiness for full gang membership. . . . As Demello (1993, p. 10) points out, this can mark career passage from juvenile correctional facilities to adult prisons: "In the [California] Youth Authority system, by far the most common method of applying tattoos is by hand, and by the time an individual graduates from the juvenile justice system into adult prison, he usually graduates to machine-made tattoos as well, and often begins to cover up his old hand plucked tattoos with better quality, machine tattoos."

Member

The initiation phase ends when an individual's membership in the *Nuestra Familia* has been approved by the governing body. We refer to this as the member phase. A degree of identity ambivalence emerges at this point which leads to symbolic self-completion efforts. Specifically, identity ambivalence exists because the member has successfully demonstrated his ability to fulfill the requisite moral obligations, but has not necessarily accomplished any remarkable deeds on behalf of the gang that warrant advanced status. . . .

Veteran

Unlike pre-initiate, initiate, and member tattoos, veteran tattoos provide more detailed information about a wearer's personal accomplishments, thus removing some of the ambivalence associated with earlier stages in his moral career. Veteran tattoos indicate some of an individual's most significant achievements while in the service of his gang. In this way, they are similar to military medals, providing decorations as rewards to "deserving" individuals and lifting up role models for the rest of the group.

The *Nuestra Familia* had veteran tattoos that communicated personal honors. For instance, . . . teardrops which are always worn under the left eye. Each teardrop represents an occasion when the wearer "has been down" (i.e., served a prison sentence) or has killed a person (Demello 1993). Compare this to . . . the cross under the left eye. While the cross under the left eye merely conveys membership status, the tears . . . announce the veteran status of the wearer in that he has either "been down" twice or killed two people. Another tattoo used by the *Nuestra Familia* to communicate veteran status is a simple star. . . . When this star is worn on the arm or body, it means that the wearer has one "hit" to his credit. If this same symbol is worn on the face, it implies that the wearer has two hits to his credit. In terms of impressions "given off," a "wise," correctional officer who sees an individual with a star tattooed on his face knows that inmate needs only one kill to become a *Nuestra Familia* officer. A "wise" correctional officer in that situation might take precautions to avoid giving such an inmate a chance to move up in rank.

Superior

While veteran tattoos distinguish between members and those who have accomplished remarkable deeds in the service of their gangs, they do not announce the rank of elite gang members. This identity ambivalence is symbolically addressed by the use of tattoos reserved for high ranking officers in the gang. Because there are only a few elite officers in the *Neustra Familia*, recorded tattoos of superior rank are rare. However, we have evidence of such tattoos from the *Nuestra Familia*. The tattoo . . . is worn only by Lieutenants, Captains, and the General. It is a tattoo of a Mexican male with a large moustache, rifle, bandolier, and a sombrero that covers his face and hides his identity. The number of bullets tattooed on the bandolier represent how many kills the person has to his credit. The individual who wore the tattoo . . . had three kills. In this case, someone "wise" to prison life would recognize the wearer of this tattoo as a *Nuestra Familia* Lieutenant. Furthermore, the "wise" would

know that the wearer of this tattoo needed two more kills to be eligible for possible promotion to Captain. In other words, this tattoo communicates information about the wearer's past career as well as his possible future career trajectory.

Discussion

We have tried to demonstrate that tattoos are a form of identity work that involves symbolic self-completion and conveys a sense of a wearer's moral career. Our data on prison gang tattoos suggests that tattoos visually communicate an individual's past accomplishments, present status, and possible future behavior. Focusing on the symbols of the *Nuestra Familia* has enabled us to show that tattoos are more than reflections of fad, fashion, and playful deviance. They are significant symbols that allow others to place or situate the tattooed person in appropriate social locations (see Stone 1962). In prison, information concerning identity can literally be a matter of life or death.

In addition to augmenting an identity work perspective, our analysis has implications for a sociological understanding of tattoos. Some similarities exist between tattoos found among inmates and those worn by the general public. For example, aesthetic, political, gendered, religious, and in-group/outgroup boundary dimensions are found in the tattoos worn by both prison and non-prison populations (cf. Demello 1993; Sanders 1988). However, our study suggests that some tattoos have additional meanings and functions for prisoners and ex-prisoners.

One of the biggest differences is that inmates have extremely limited material resources with which to communicate their identities. For the most part, clothes, hairstyles, jewelry, eye wear, and other adornments are more available to those on the outside than they are to inmates. As a result, the body is the primary material used to convey self-definitions to others (Bronnikov 1993; Demello 1993; Seaton 1987). Tattoos function as one kind of secret language for the initiated in prison (Bronnikov 1993). Also, due to a lack of material resources (e.g., tattoo inks and professional tattooing machines), prison tattoos tend to be monochromatic (i.e., black only), whereas professional tattooists on the outside have access to a range of colors and precision tools from supply houses (Demello 1993). Monochromatic tattoos etched by homemade tattoo guns are distinctive and communicate inmate or (when seen on the streets) ex-convict status.

Another difference is that tattoos are more frequently found on the neck and facial areas among inmates (cf. Demello 1993; Sanders 1988). Tattoos on these areas "make the body especially obvious, and more importantly, express, to the convict, other prisoners, and the outside world, the social position which that body occupies" (Demello 1993, p.10). In contrast, on the outside, tattoos are often etched in less conspicuous places and even in relatively private areas to be shared only with intimates (Sanders 1988). This suggests that tattoos play a more prominent public role in the symbolic self-completion of prisoners' identities.

A third difference centers on the issue of social order in prisons. Inmates as well as correctional staff take active roles in establishing, negotiating, and maintaining norms and social order (Ralph 1997). Uniforms, which have symbols designating specific roles and ranks, communicate correctional officers' experience, status, and their nominal obligations for maintaining an orderly existence (see Stone 1962). Certain tattoos are the functional equivalent of uniforms for inmates, especially those reserved for prison gang elites. Because bodies and the tattoos they wear are valued material resources among prisoners, inmates have developed sanctions for the improper display of certain symbols. Our analysis suggests that some tattoos reflect an individual's accomplishments, and they must be earned. Discussing tattoos found in Russian prisons, Bronnikov (1993, p. 54) makes the same point: "The pictures and symbols are supposed to correspond with the criminal's deeds. Punishment for a person wearing incorrect symbols is extremely severe, sometimes even death" In addition to other forms of communication, tattoos help to announce to inmates and correctional staff which prisoners are in positions of power and authority.

Note

1. Another important piece of information is an inmate's alias or street name. These names are considered highly secret, and, as such, they are difficult to discover. One time, Phelan's Lieutenant called, wanting a Crip from his building who was a suspect in an assault that occurred earlier that day in the yard. All the information the Lieutenant had was the alias, E-Rock. Phelan told one of "his" Crips (i.e., a Crip with whom he had established rapport) that he had a message for E-Rock. Phelan asked, "Have you seen him?" The friendly Crip replied, "He's standing right over there, Phelan, are you blind?" After joking about his failing eyesight in his old age, Phelan thanked "his" Crip and maneuvered E-Rock around the corner to escort him unnoticed to the Lieutenant's office. Phelan was careful not to 'front off' the Crip who had unknowingly given E-Rock up (i.e., Phelan ensured that he did not embarrass "his" Crip publically by apprehending E-Rock and thus exposing the correctional officer's con). Care was taken in this matter so as not to damage the rapport that had been established.

References

Adler, Peter and Patricia Adler. 1987. *Membership Roles in Field Research*. Newbury Park, CA: Sage.

Bronnikov, Arkady G. 1993. "Telltale Tattoos in Russian Prisons," *Natural History* 102: 50–59.

California. 1984. Texts and Handouts from Richard A. McGee Correctional Training Center.

Carter, Robert M., Daniel Glaser, and Leslie T. Wilkins. 1985. *Correctional Institutions*. New York: Harper and Row.

Clark, Harold. 1992. "From the Streets to Our Prisons." *Corrections Today* 54:8.

Davis, Fred. 1992. *Fashion, Culture, and Identity*. Chicago: University of Chicago Press.

Demello, Margo. 1993. "The Convict Body: Tattooing Among Male American Prisoners." *Anthropology Today* 9:10–13.

Glaser, Barney G. and Anselm Strauss. 1967. *The Discovery of Grounded Theory*. Chicago: Aldine.

Goffman, Erving. 1959. *The Presentation of Self in Everyday Life*. Garden City, NY: Doubleday.

——. 1963. *Stigma: Notes on the Management of Spoiled Identities*. New York: Free Press.

Goodgame, Gerald W. 1985. "Mayhem in the Cellblocks: Gangs Terrorize Folsom and Other Overcrowded Prisons." *Time*, August 12:20.

Govenar, A. 1988. "The Variable Context of Chicano Tattooing." Pp. 209–218 in *Marks of Civilization*, edited by Arnold Rubin. Los Angeles: UCLA Museum of Cultural History.

Grumet, Gerald W. 1983. "Psychodynamic Implications of Tattoos." *American Journal of Orthopsychiatry* 53:482–492.

Hambly. 1925. *History of Tattooing and Its Significance*. London: F. H. & G. Witherby.

Kaiser, Susan B., Richard H. Nagasawa, and Sandra S. Hutton. 1991. "Fashion, Postmodernity, and Personal Appearance: A Symbolic Interactionist Formulation." *Symbolic Interaction* 14:165–185.

Lane, Michael P. 1989. "Inmate Gangs." *Corrections Today* 51:98.

Mead, Margaret. 1928. *An Inquiry Into the Question of Cultural Stability in Polynesia*. New York: AMS Press.

Press, Aric, Richard Sandza, and Elaine Shannon. 1983. "California's Prison Gang." *Newsweek*, February 1:74–75.

Ralph, Paige H. 1997. "From Self-Preservation to Organized Crime: The Evolution of Inmate Gangs." Pp. 182–186 in *Correctional Contexts: Contemporary and Classical Readings*, edited by James W. Marquart and Jonathan R. Sorensen. Los Angeles: Roxbury.

Sanders, Clinton R. 1988. "Marks of Mischief: Becoming and Being Tattooed." *Journal Of Contemporary Ethnography* 16:395–432.

Sandza, Richard and Elaine Shannon. 1982. "California's Prison Gang." *Newsweek* February 1:74.

Seaton, Elizabeth. 1987. "Profaned Bodies and Purloined Looks: The Prisoner's Tattoo and the Researcher Gaze." *Journal of Communication Inquiry* 11:17–25.

Stone, Gregory P. 1962. "Appearance and the Self." Pp. 86–118 in *Human Behavior and Social Processes*, edited by Arnold M. Rose. Boston: Houghton Mifflin.

Ulin, Robert C. 1984. *Understanding Cultures: Perspectives in Anthropology and Social Theory*. Austin, TX: University of Texas Press.

Webb, O. L. and David G. Morris. 1985, "Prison Guards." Pp. 204–214 in *Correctional Institutions*, edited by Robert M. Carter, Daniel Glaser, and Leslie T. Wilkins. New York: Harper and Row.

Excerpts from: Michael P. Phelan and Scott A. Hunt, "Prison Gang Members' Tattoos as Identity Work: The Visual Communication of Moral Careers." In *Symbolic Interaction*, 21(3): 277–298. Copyright © 1998 by JAI Press, Inc. Reprinted by permission of University of California Press.

15
Prison Gangs: Racial Separatism as a Form of Social Control

Victor Hassine

Focus Questions

1. How did the ratio between white officers and black inmates affect prison race relations?

2. Why were the various prison gangs at Graterford prison established?

3. What were the differences between black and white prison gangs at Graterford?

4. What was Omar's view about the game of race relations in prison?

Every Pennsylvania prison that I have been to, regardless of the ratio between black and white inmates, was operated by an almost entirely white staff. In Graterford between 1981 and 1982, over 80 percent of the staff were white, while over 80 percent of the inmates were black. By July 1987, according to two Pennsylvania Department of Corrections surveys on a racial breakdown of inmates and a corrections-workforce comparison, the disparity remained relatively the same with 76 percent white staff and 76 percent black inmates. To its credit, however, Graterford employed the highest percentage of minority employees out of all Pennsylvania's state prisons.

Though the prison had been desegregated since the late 1960s, the inmates of Graterford continued to impose their own form of segregation. For example, it was an unspoken rule that the dining hall be divided into a black section and a white section. The administration did its part as well, for example, by refusing to double-cell white inmates with black inmates. De facto segregation was very much alive in those days, as it is today.

At Graterford I observed that many of the new white guards had little experience interacting with people of different races. Presumably due to feelings of intimidation or discomfort with inmates of other races, they tended to be much stricter with those of their own race.

During my initial classification period at Graterford, I was required to identify myself as either white or black. There were no other options. Hispanics and Native Americans were classified as white or black at their own choosing. It wasn't until the mid-1980s that the racial classification process at Graterford allowed inmates to designate themselves as anything other than black or white.

Among the African-American population at Graterford was a large and well-established Black Muslim community, the vast majority of which came from Philadelphia. On the other hand, most of the white prison staff were Christians, many of whom were raised in the rural communities around the prison. This extreme imbalance between the racial, regional, and religious composition of staff and inmates vividly reflected the general dysfunction of the prison that prevailed throughout my years there.

Though non-white inmates were usually embraced by the prison population, they were often considered suspect by the white staff who seemed to reserve the benefit of the rehabilitative doubt only for white inmates. This racial bias at Graterford did not result in favoritism by staff but rather provoked a divisive and relentless competition between the inmates themselves for the staff's favor. Everyone in the prison system was forced to play the bias game, because the only group identity available to inmates was based on skin color.

As a rule, a prison administration is reluctant to promote any group activity or identity that might evolve into a clique of gangs. Graterford was solely in the business of confinement, so its entire security force was geared toward discouraging and punishing any group affiliations. All inmates were issued identical uniforms, and there were strictly enforced rules against any congregation of more than five inmates. While some social and religious organizations were permitted to operate, the administration made the rules of participation so cumbersome that these groups constituted an organization in name only. Though the prison could not punish an inmate for belonging to a legitimate group, it could try to weaken his desire to belong. One of the ways in which this was accomplished was to influence every inmate, including myself, in the direction of racial polarization.

Black and White Prison Gangs

Generally, black gangs in Graterford were extensions of Philadelphia's neighborhood street gangs. They bore names based on their urban location; for example, the 21st and Norris Gang, the 60th and Market Gang, the 10th Street Gang, etc. Many of their members had belonged to the original street gang before they were incarcerated. Once sent to Graterford, they joined their prison counterpart to carry on the gang's traditions. As more and more street-gang members arrived, their growing strength in numbers enabled them to conduct a wider array of prison-gang activities.

The moment any African-American Philadelphian entered the prison, scouts immediately approached him to determine which part of the city he came from and whether he had been a member of a street gang. This sorting of incoming blacks based on geography dictated the character of black prison gangs, giving rise to the often-used term "homey" for those who hailed from the same neighborhood or hometown. Homeys were the most common recruits for black gang membership.

Black gangs competed vigorously with each other for turf and the control of contraband sales. While this competition often resulted in violent battles, gangs on many occasions merged their enterprises and worked together. For example, rival gangs had been known to fight each other over the business of selling drugs, yet they frequently cooperated in bringing the drugs into the prison.

Those black gangs formed by inmates from areas other than Philadelphia differed considerably from the black Philly gangs in that, for the most part, they had no counterparts on the streets. Such non-Philly gangs usually originated in the prison and their members were often strangers who happened to be from the same county or city. The competition between regional gangs and Philly gangs tended to be very hostile and violent. There was seldom any trust or cooperation between them. Numerically, Philly gangs greatly outnumbered other gangs, which allowed them to dominate the population and completely exclude outsiders from joint ventures.

Regardless of their numerical superiority, it is highly probable that Philly gangs still would have had more control, because their carry-over from street gangs gave them the distinct advantage of functioning under well-established rules, organizational structures, leadership systems, and ideologies. In contrast, regional or prison-based gangs tended to be weakened internally by frequent power struggles, uncertain leadership, and untested organizational processes.

Because Graterford's black gangs were determined almost exclusively by geography, gang membership was widely diverse. In any one gang you could expect to find drug addicts, thieves, murderers, and hustlers of every ethnic influence, including Muslims, Christians, and atheists. This amalgam of homeys provided black gang members with a sense of commonality so dynamic that the administration was very hard pressed to break them apart.

Black gangs at Graterford primarily operated as money-making enterprises. While geography helped to bring prison gang members together, it was money and drugs that kept them together. The goal of every gang was to earn money, which meant selling anything that anyone was willing to buy. As in a corporation, gang profits were then reinvested to buy more contraband for further distribution. Gang members gauged their individual value by the amount of money they were able to make. What they did with their earnings was of no consequence, since the hustle itself seemed to be all that mattered. Money earned was merely an indicator of how good a hustler an inmate could be.

White gangs at Graterford were a completely different story. These gangs almost always originated in prison and, like the non-Philly gangs, were not as well structured or established. They, too, were comprised of members who were often strangers to each other, most of them brought together by the simple chance of their skin color.

Statistically, white gangs in Graterford were strictly a minority, usually formed for their own protection from other gangs. While they might be involved in some hustling, they were limited by their inability to protect their turf or business interests against the larger black gangs. They were more likely to be the buyers of drugs and contraband than the sellers.

Furthermore, most white gang members were not brought together by geography but rather out of a need to protect their mutual interests. White drug addicts tended to join together in order to pool their funds to buy drugs at a volume discount. Some white gangs were formed because of ethnic bonds, such as Catholics, Italians, and Protestants, or because of special interests, such as gamblers and bodybuilders.

White gangs at Graterford were more likely to be small, improvised groups rather than organized teams with specific agendas and were generally much less diverse than their black counterparts. Whereas black gangs required large memberships to generate income and protect their turf, white

gangs preferred to have as few members as possible in an effort to stretch their resources. Any white gang that grew too large would promptly be challenged by the dominant black gangs.

The exceptions in Graterford were the outlaw motorcycle gangs that successfully managed to entrench themselves within the prison system. Like the Hell's Angels who had already established themselves on the street, they were far more business-oriented and could compete directly with black gangs in the sale of contraband, drugs in particular. Despite their relatively small numbers in the prison, their connections to the much larger street gangs made them resourceful money-makers and a power to be reckoned with.

The Muslim and the Jew

Not long after my first Lifers meeting, Omar became my closest friend and my window into the workings of prison life. He knew many of the inmates at Graterford and understood better than I the language, games, players, and dangers of the prison system. Most importantly, he was willing to share his wisdom with me. His profound insight into the system helped me to grope my way through a foreign country of which I had had no inkling before I arrived at Graterford. Thus, Omar became my Old Head and I became his eager disciple.

A few months after I had lost my job in the Major's office, Omar was hired to take my place. Since he now lived on the same block as I did, I often visited him in his cell. We ate meals together, walked the yard together, and exchanged a lot of jailhouse philosophy to kill time. We became inseparable and were one of the more unusual sights in Graterford: the veteran black Muslim from Philadelphia and the young Jewish rookie from New Jersey. We were constantly arguing about one issue or another.

I would often find my Old Head sitting on the cold, hard concrete floor of his cell, deeply absorbed in writing a letter to his family but never turning his back to the doorway, always keeping one cautious eye on the inmate traffic a few feet away. His cell was drab and spartan, containing little more than state-issued clothing, bedding, and some old newspapers. I once asked Omar why he chose to have so few possessions.

"I don't like people taking things away from me," he replied. "If I don't have anything in here that's mine, then the authorities can't take away any more than they already have. Besides, I don't think it's healthy for a man to get too comfortable in the slammer."

On one occasion I had just returned from a prison basketball game that had ended in a vicious melee between a black and a white gang. Often one prison gang would field a team to play against a team backed by another gang, and the rivalry on the court usually led to violence. Watching who won the game was only half as exciting as watching who won the fight *after* the game.

But today I was particularly disturbed by the rampant hatred and racism between black and white inmates, so I posed a naive question to Omar: "Why do they hate and hurt each other so much? Why don't they just get together and channel their hatred toward the guards?"

Omar's ubiquitous grin vanished. After a long stare that was pregnant with pause, he finally said: "It's all a game."

"What, that's it?" I protested. "All the beatings, stabbings, and killings are just a game? It's no game. Men dying is no game."

Omar regarded me with some amazement. I must have been a bit more excited than I had intended. With a gentle but serious tone he cautioned, "Are you going to argue with me or are you going to listen?"

I sat quietly, waiting for him to share his view of the restless shadow we lived in. Just outside his cell, silent, unfriendly faces glided past, glancing inside, never smiling. It was this kind of backdrop that kept a man alert in his cell at all times. Occasionally a prison guard would look in on us and then move on. Though I was not allowed to enter another man's cell, the rule was never enforced.

"Most of the hate and anger in here is all a game," Omar emphasized again. "It's a hustle, just another way for people to make money. Anger and hatred are a prison's cash crop."

"When whites hate blacks, they're stealing the sympathy and favor of a mostly white Christian administration. When blacks hate whites, they're strong-arming appeasements and concessions. The administration, they get the most out of it all. Violence and hatred in prison means more money, more guards, more overtime, and more prisons. What incentive is there to keep prisons safe and humane? All staff has to do is sit back and let the men here tear each other apart. Then they can cry to the legislatures and tell them how much more money they need to control their prison. Just like with the prison swag men, dope boys, and laundry men, there's something being sold and money being made. Only it's a lot more money than most of the guys in here can ever imagine. It's a lot easier for everyone to profit from hatred than it is to help the poor and ignorant do something positive with their lives."

I couldn't believe what I was hearing. "Come on, Omar, you can't believe that stuff. You're sounding real paranoid, like there's a conspiracy everywhere." His views were similar to those of Double D, who believed the administration was actually encouraging gang activity. But I wasn't ready to believe either one of them. The prison system was too chaotic to be that deliberate.

Omar replied, "Well, then you tell me why, with all the guards, guns, locks, gates, walls, and money, they still can't stop what's going on in here?"

I had no answer to that. "Okay, if this is all a game and everybody knows it, then why do the men in here play it? Why do they play when it can get them hurt and even killed?"

Omar smiled assuredly. "It's like a Dodge City crap game in here, Victor. Everyone who plays it knows it's crooked, but they play it anyway—because it's the only game in town."

Reprinted from: Victor Hassine, "Race Relations in Prison." In *Life Without Parole: Living in Prison Today*, 2nd Edition, Thomas J. Bernard, Richard McCleary, and Richard A. Wright (eds.), pp. 71–78. Copyright © 1999 by Roxbury Publishing Company. All rights reserved.

Chapter V
Discussion

Prison Gangs

Hunt and colleagues interviewed convicts to determine how prison gangs and elements of the prisoner subculture have changed over the years. One of the more notable facets was how the entire prisoner subculture has become more dangerous, uncertain, and disorganized as a whole. Yet, prison gangs are arguably more organized today than in the past. Gang life is further intertwined between prison and the street, and it is interesting how some of the smaller street gangs suspend their rivalries in prison and join together to avoid victimization from larger and more influential groups. The paradox is that these smaller gangs join together not because they want to, but because they have to for self-protection.

As Phelan and Hunt indicate, tattoos remain a symbolic and lasting part of identity and past accomplishments for gang members. Some STGs intentionally apply tattoos in obvious areas of the body, such as the face and neck. These tattoos can be more readily seen by other inmates. Other gang members have tattoos with meanings that must be interpreted by gang intelligence officers. Some tattoos reveal the rank and position in the gang. Despite the alliances or sets formed while in prison, increased fragmentation and violence would seem to be a natural by-product of protecting profits.

Hassine focuses on race relations between correctional officers and prisoners. He states that the race/ethnic breakdown of staff in most prison systems around the country does not represent the race/ethnicity of the prisoners. This situation has improved in some areas of the country. The race relations between officers and prisoners currently seem overshadowed by the racial hatred and violence among prison gangs. Most violent incidents in prison are gang-related, and they are more often between two or more inmates than between an officer and a prisoner. It is evident that Hassine is most likely not a gang member and has learned what he knows about gang conflicts through other prisoners, such as Omar. One interesting observation made in this reading is that prison gang behavior may serve a purpose. We may wish to question whether the violence from prison gang behavior has replaced prison riots as both a form of change and as a form of social control. In other words, have prison gangs at war (to enhance their group status) drawn away the focus from prisoners as a whole trying to better their conditions?

Chapter VI
Introduction

Prison Violence

Common Assumptions	Reality
Individual-Level Violence	
• Violent incidents between two prisoners tend to be interracial (between two different races).	• Although inmate violence can be interracial, violent incidents between two prisoners are more often intraracial (among the same race). Causes of individual-level violence include disputes over drugs, failure to pay gambling debts, a discovery of theft, spreading false rumors, or lovers' quarrels.
Collective Violence	
• Prison riots tend to be large-scale takeovers by prisoners who seize hostages. Prison riots are caused by prisoner confrontation with staff.	• According to Montgomery and Crews (1998), over 70 percent of prison riots involve between 15 and 200 prisoners in a small, contained area of the prison. Most riots do not involve any hostages and dissipate within 9 hours. These contained riots do not result in large-scale takeovers by prisoners. The vast majority of riots are caused by confrontations between prisoners (racial tension, gang-related, and rules violations), while only a small number are related to staff confrontation (4 percent) or occur as a result of correctional officers' carelessness (3 percent).

Violence exists as a fundamental part of the daily prison environment. Silberman (1995) discusses how prisons are magnified versions of the violence that exists in some inner-city neighborhoods. The reasons for prison violence are similar to those for inner-city violence: racial inequality, scarce resources, and economic instability. Compared to the outside world, of course, prison society contains a significantly higher proportion of people who exhibit predatory behavior. Many individuals with violent tendencies have been socialized within a culture of violence and have experienced violence from both sides—as victims and as offenders.

Furthermore, life in prison for all offenders is more stressful than life in the outside world, because daily existence in prison is more regulated, noisier, and less private.

Prisoners live in a world where their behaviors are constantly being watched by someone else—either other prisoners or correctional officers. Thus, every prisoner must maintain a public reputation to avoid being targeted by others exhibiting predatory behavior (Lombardo 1994). Individual-level violence in prison is committed by people who seek to solve personal conflicts (no matter how seemingly small or petty) through violent means or who attempt to establish a reputation by intentionally victimizing another prisoner (as in the case of sexual assault). Prisoners who are repeatedly victimized while incarcerated tend to have few associates, are more likely to exhibit timid behavior, do not respond with violence when victimized, and tend to be addicted to gambling, sex, illegal drugs, or a combination of these.

While individual-level violence is a conflict between two prisoners or between a prisoner and a correctional officer, collective violence involves two or more groups in conflict. The groups in conflict typically vary by race or ethnicity (for example, black prisoners and white prisoners having racial conflict), gang membership (for example, Mexican Mafia and *La Nuestra Familia* fighting about drugs or territorial issues), or by prisoners protesting against prison administrators. Collective violence occurs primarily because of interpersonal conflict among "connected" inmates. Connected prisoners have many close friends or associates who are present to provide back-up support during the conflict. A prison gang "hit" (when one or more gang members repeatedly stabs or attempts to kill a member of a rival gang) is an example of this type of collective violence.

Riots are yet another type of collective violence. A riot has been characterized by researchers as involving "the seizure of control over part or all of the prison through violence or force, the destruction of property, and the presentation of demands by a group of inmates" (Martin and Zimmerman 1990, 712). In most prison riots, prisoners take over a small area of the prison, which prison staff contain to prevent the riot from spreading; prison staff remain in control of the rest of the prison. In only a few riots (e.g., Attica, New York and Santa Fe, New Mexico) have prison staff lost control of the entire prison. Riots have multiple causes; the most common is confrontation between prisoners. The number of riots has increased since the 1960s, but this increase may reflect the expansion of correctional institutions nationally (Montgomery and Crews 1998).

Recommended Readings

Alarid, Leanne Fiftal. (2000). "Sexual Assault and Coercion Among Incarcerated Women Prisoners: Excerpts From Prison Letters." *The Prison Journal* 80(4).

Fleisher, Mark S. (1989). *Warehousing Violence.* Newbury Park, CA: Sage.

Larsen, N. (1988). "The Utility of Prison Violence: An A-Causal Approach to Prison Riots." *Criminal Justice Review* 13(1):29–38.

Lombardo, Lucien X. (1994). "Stress, Change, and Collective Violence in Prison." Pp. 291–305 in *Prison Violence in America,* 2nd ed., edited by Michael C. Braswell, Reid H. Montgomery, and Lucien X. Lombardo. Cincinnati, OH: Anderson.

Martin, Randy, and Sherwood Zimmerman. (1990). "A Typology of the Causes of Prison Riots and an Analytical Extension to the 1986 West Virginia Riot." *Justice Quarterly* 7(4): 711–737.

May, John P., (ed.) (2000). *Building Violence: How America's Rush to Incarcerate Creates More Violence.* Thousand Oaks, CA: Sage.

Montgomery, Reid H., and Gordon A. Crews. (1998). *A History of Correctional Violence: An Examination of Reported Causes of Riots and Disturbances.* Lanham, MD: American Correctional Association.

Silberman, Matthew. (1995). *A World of Violence: Corrections in America.* Belmont, CA: Wadsworth.

Internet Websites

Attica: The Prison Revolt of 1971. Available: *http://home.earthlink.net/~dwgsht/attica2.html*

Chen, H. H. (1999, 11 January). The 'big house' of the future. Available: *http://www.*

apbonline.com/safestreets/1999/01/11/ fence0111_01.html

California prison at the center of violent accusations. Available: *http://www.cnn.com/US/ 9611/22/prison.shooting/*

Donohue, Brian (January 23, 2000), "Harsh Unit Is Prison's Answer to Violence." Available: *The Star Ledger http://www.nj.com/jersey/ledger/ e4992f.html*

Prison Activist Resource Center, a non-profit group dedicated to changing prison conditions. Available: *http://www.prisonactivists. org/*

Prison Rape. Available: *http://www.fsu.edu/ ~crimdo/losch.html*

Prison Violence links. Available: *http:// www.io.com/~ellie/violence.html*

Useem, Burt, Camille Graham Camp, George M. Camp, and Renie Dugan (1995) "The Revolution of Prison Riots." Available: *http:// www.ncjrs.org/txtfiles/prisriot.txt*

16
The Reproduction of Violence in U.S. Prisons

Michael Welch

Focus Questions

1. What are the differences between collective and individual levels of prison violence?

2. What are the sources of prison violence?

3. What characteristics did the Attica and New Mexico prison riots have in common? How were these riots different?

4. How prevalent is sexual assault in prison?

5. What strategies does Welch propose to reduce violence in prison?

Introduction

The first major prison riot recorded in American history was in 1774 at the Simsbury prison, a primitive institution that was constructed over an abandoned copper mine in Connecticut (Dillingham and Montgomery, 1985). Hence, the history of prison violence is as old as the nation itself. Between 1900 and 1985, more than 300 riots were documented in U.S. corrections (Dillingham and Montgomery, 1985). Although not all of these disturbances resulted in deaths and major destruction, some riots are remembered as devastating events: in particular, the uprisings at Attica prison in New York and at the penitentiary at New Mexico.

Since incarceration involves the practice of warehousing criminals (many of whom are violent) in overcrowded and understaffed institutions, it stands to reason that prisons continue to be among the most dangerous places in society. Indeed, danger is intimately associated with life in prison, where both inmates and staff struggle to avert victimization.

In this chapter, various levels (collective versus individual) and forms (inmates versus inmates, inmates versus staff, staff versus inmates) of institutional violence are discussed. In addition to describing theories of violence, the riots at Attica and the penitentiary at New Mexico are presented. In doing so, we explore institutional violence in the past and present, especially as they relate to future trends.

Motives and Goals of Prison Violence

Recognizing and identifying the types of prison violence are crucial to our understanding of why and how violence emerges. Just as there are different levels and forms of violence, there also exist various motives or goals. At the most fundamental level of analysis, the motives and goals of prison violence are characterized as either *instrumental* or *expressive* (Bowker, 1985).

Instrumental Violence

Instrumental violence is rational or calculative because it sets out to achieve a particular goal. This is especially true of inmate-inmate violence, in which an inmate assaults a fellow prisoner physically or sexually for the purpose of garnering power and status within the prison society. In pursuit of dominance, an inmate may employ violence (or the threat of violence) to get what he wants: a more desirable living situation, sexual satisfaction, commodities (sneakers, junk food), contraband (drugs, weapons), and various services (laundry tasks, paperwork for legal matters). By way of instrumental violence, the aggressor may enhance his self-image (Bowker, 1985). Instrumental violence is not restricted to individual violence; it also emerges within collective disturbances, especially when goals, usually in the form of demands, are pronounced (Welch, 1995, 1996).

Expressive Violence

Expressive violence is not rational, insofar as goals are not consciously pursued. Rather, such violence is expressive in the emotional sense, such as a spontaneous release of tension. Expressive violence is apparent in individual outbursts of violence as well as in collective disturbances, as depicted by a "mob mentality." In either case, expressive violence requires a psychological state of readiness coupled with a conducive situation, or precipitating event.

It needs to be emphasized that instrumental and expressive violence are not mutually exclusive; many violent incidents involve a combination of the two. For instance, in the hostile world of prison, inmates have consciously engaged in assaults so that others would perceive them as being savagely violent. Such displays of expressive violence are instrumental because [violence] bolsters the inmates' reputation, thereby enhancing their power and status. For example, in the years leading up to the riot at the penitentiary at New Mexico, inmates felt vulnerable to snitches and other violent cliques of prisoners. Consequently, some inmates reinforced their own "macho" reputations by unleashing emotional outbursts of violence. Bolstering a violent reputation among one's peers serves as a form of self-protection (Colvin, 1982; Welch, 1995, 1996; see also Abbott, 1981).

Sources of Prison Violence

Although there are literally dozens of factors attributed to prison violence, we are served best by concentrating on three of the most instrumental sources of institutional disturbances: the violent inmate, the social climate of violence, and overcrowding. We should stress that these factors are regarded as *sources* and not *causes*, since they are not solely responsible for violence.

The Violent Inmate

It stands to reason that prisons are violent places because they house violent offenders. Indeed, that is one of the purposes of prisons in society—to protect nonviolent citizens from those who are violent. This line of reasoning is especially true of maximum-security penitentiaries, which hold the most violent criminals. Therefore, violence in prisons is, in part, explained by the fact that inmates attempt to settle their disputes in a manner which they are accustomed to—through violence.

However, prison violence is not the domain of maximum-security penitentiaries housing violent offenders. Prison violence also takes place in medium- and some minimum-security facilities. Moreover, violence also arises among prisoners who do not have violent histories. Considering this, we must look to other sources of violence, such as the social climate of violence and overcrowding.

The Social Climate of Violence

A major axiom in sociology is that some actions are *motivated*, whereas others are *situated*. Applying this notion to prisons, it is proposed that inmates (even those who are generally nonviolent) may resort to violence because of the contextual features of their environment. Toch (1985) examined the social climate of violence in prisons and concluded that the situational context is not the sole producer of violence but may enhance or reduce the likelihood of occurrence. Toch identifies a number of contextual features that contribute to prison violence:

- *By providing payoffs.* Acting violently in prison has rewards, such as peer admiration or the creation of fear (which

The Reproduction of Violence in U.S. Prisons **139**

may be instrumental by serving as a form of protection).

- *By providing immunity or protection.* Violence in prison is perpetuated because victims generally adhere to a code of silence by not "ratting" on the aggressor(s).
- *By providing opportunities.* Due to the institutional routine and internal architecture, there are numerous opportunities for assaults. Violence often takes place when the risk of being seen by staff is minimal and in places that conceal the attack.
- *By providing temptations, challenges, and provocations.* The climate of violence is replete with temptations, challenges, and provocations to engage in violence against inmates who are regarded as deserving an assault.
- *By providing justificatory premise.* Since prisons are viewed as violent places, especially by inmates themselves, violence is justified because the norms permit it.

As we shall see in the section on intervention, the prevalence of violence can be reduced by attending to each of these contextual features of the prison climate.

Does Overcrowding Contribute to Violence?

At a glance, it makes sense that overcrowding contributes to prison violence. However, we must remain mindful that almost all correctional facilities are overcrowded, and violence varies from institution to institution. Therefore, it is important to determine more precisely what effect overcrowding (in addition to other factors) has on institutional violence. A report by the Bureau of Justice Statistics (1989) finds little evidence that prison population density is *directly* associated with inmate-inmate assaults and other disturbances. Nevertheless, most forms of aggression are *indirectly* fueled and exacerbated by overcrowding. The Bureau of Justice Statistics emphasizes that violence occurs more frequently in maximum-security facilities, irrespective of their population densities. However, other studies have found that overcrowding is an important factor affecting institutional violence (Farrington and Nutall, 1985; Gaes and McGuire, 1985). Clearly, additional research is needed to assess more precisely the impact that overcrowding has on prison violence; moreover, this knowledge should be taken into account to formulate preventive measures.

The Riot at Attica

Perhaps no other prison riot has received as much notoriety as the uprising at Attica (New York). From the onset, Attica became a metaphor for numerous social problems, including racism, oppression, and injustice. Yet metaphors aside, in-depth investigations of Attica have concluded that racism, oppression, and injustice were salient features before, during, and after the riot (*Attica: The Official Report*, 1972; Wicker, 1975; Mahan, 1985; Useem, 1985; Useem and Kimball, 1987, 1989; see also Oswald, 1972, and the 1991 Commemorative Issue of *Social Justice*, devoted to Attica).

Between September 9 and 13, 1971, 43 persons died at the upstate New York maximum-security prison. Most alarmingly, 39 were killed and more than 80 others were wounded by gunfire during the 15 minutes it took the state police to retake the institution. "With the exception of Indian massacres in the late 19th century, the State Police assault which ended the four-day prison uprising was the bloodiest one-day encounter between Americans since the Civil War" (*Attica: The Official Report*, 1972:130).

The storming of the prison did not end the violence; for many inmates, it was the beginning. Hundreds of inmates were subsequently stripped naked and beaten by correction officers, troopers, and sheriffs' deputies. The agony was prolonged because prison officials withheld immediate medical care for those suffering from gunshot wounds and injuries stemming from the widespread reprisals. In fact, when the shooting stopped, there were only 10 medical personnel available to treat more than 120 seriously wounded inmates and hostages, and only two of them were physicians. Doctors at local hospitals who could have assisted the wounded were not dispatched by prison officials until four hours later.

Reprisals by officers against inmates were characterized as brutal displays of humiliation (from *Inmates of Attica v. Rockefeller*, 1971, quoted in Deutsch et al., 1991:22):

> Injured prisoners, some on stretchers, were struck, prodded or beaten with sticks, belts, bats, or other weapons. Others were forced to strip and run naked through gauntlets of guards armed with clubs which they used to strike inmates as they passed. Some were dragged on the ground, some marked with an "X" on their backs, some spat upon or burned with matches, others poked in the genitals or arms with sticks.

The Prisoners' Class Action Suit

On February 27, 1991, the U.S. Court of Appeals for the Second Circuit removed the final obstacle, which permitted a class action civil rights suit to proceed. The suit (*Al-Jundi v. Mancusi*, 1991) was filed on behalf of the 1,200 prisoners who were killed, wounded, denied medical care (following the storming of the prison), and beaten by officers. Following years of legal resistance, the case went to trial on September 30, 1991, in Buffalo, New York. The suit sought to hold liable four top supervisory officials: Russell Oswald (Commissioner of Corrections), Major John Monahan (commander of the assault force), Vincent Mancusi (Attica's prison warden), and Karl Pfeil (deputy warden).

The jury found Deputy Warden Pfeil liable for violent reprisals following the riot for permitting police and guards to beat and torture inmates. The jury deadlocked on the liability of the three other state officials (Oswald and Monahan are deceased). Additional litigation has also stemmed in the aftermath of the uprising. For example, in 1989, seven former Attica inmates and their families were awarded nearly $1.3 million for injuries suffered during the storming of the prison. Such legal action demonstrates that state prison officials are not above the law, even during such horrific situations as large-scale riots.

It should be noted that due to litigation and the prisoners' rights movement, a new breed of prison administrators have emerged. Both today and while looking toward the twenty-first century, an increasingly larger number of corrections commissioners, directors, superintendents, and wardens are now expected to be proficient in law. In fact, many newly recruited administrators are themselves attorneys. It is understood that a good administrator can spot legally problematic issues quickly and resolve them before they surface as law suits (Welch, 1996).

The New Mexico State Prison Riot

Whereas Attica symbolizes the political struggles that often occur between inmates and staff (and administration), the uprising at the New Mexico State Prison (February 2, 1980) stands as an example of sheer brutality among inmates. In a most accurate characterization, Mahan (1994) refers to the New Mexico riot as a "killing ground."

Similar to the riot at Attica, the officials at New Mexico were not prepared to deal with a large-scale riot. In fact, the institution was inexcusably understaffed: At the time of the riot there were only 22 guards supervising 1157 inmates in a prison built to hold 800. Moreover, the riot might have been prevented from spreading, but other officers were unable to produce a complete set of prison keys. Perhaps the worst institutional flaw of all, though, was the failure of "shatterproof" glass installed at the control center, the prison's lifeline. When the inmates broke the protective glass and seized the control center, they had full access to the facility. Here they pushed buttons that opened all interior gates. The violence quickly spread, but the degree of brutality that awaited other inmates was simply horrible (Saenz, 1986).

Small cliques of inmates sought revenge against snitches and other prison outcasts, including convicted child molesters, known as "diddlers" or "short-eyes." The string of violent encounters that erupted were preceded by several preparatory events. First, prisoners stormed the institution's pharmacy, where they consumed massive doses of drugs such as amphetamines, or "speed." Such a "high" generated 36 hours of frantic and savage destruction. Others preferred alternative sources of mood alteration; for example, some inmates broke into the shoe shop, where they sniffed the intoxicating fumes of glue (Anon., 1980).

To further prepare themselves for the impending acts of revenge, inmates confiscated prison records identifying informers and those convicted of sex offenses, the two most despised criminal types in the prison society. Finally, inmates added to their arsenal of shanks by equipping themselves with tools and blowtorches stolen from the prison maintenance supply room. Now they were ready to create a nightmare that would shock even the most jaded prison expert. The impending rampage would exceed the typical forms of beatings characteristic of prisons. For the next several hours, inmates unleashed their rage by raping, burning, decapitating, castrating, and eviscerating fellow prisoners (Stone, 1982).

Unlike Attica, the riot had no identified course of action; it simply constituted a series of independent acts of revenge. There was no carnival atmosphere, no leadership, no lists of grievances, no organization, nothing. Only unspeakable brutality (Mahan, 1994). In large part, the violence was the direct work of small cliques of prisoners, mostly Chicano (58 percent of the inmate population), who took full advantage of the uprising to settle their differences with rival Chicano inmates (Colvin, 1982, 1992). Additional acts of brutality consisted of the following: A snitch had a steel rod driven through one ear and out the other; another was stomped to death and a perpetrator carved "rat" into his abdomen; seven inmates were found slashed to death in their cells; a rope was tied to the neck of an inmate who was nearly decapitated when his body was thrown off the tier; and a prisoner whose eyes were nearly gouged out was beheaded with a shovel (Anon., 1980). In 36 hours, $36 million of damage was incurred; all the more tragic though, 33 inmates were killed at the hands of other prisoners (Office of the Attorney General of the State of New Mexico, 1980).

By examining the Attica and New Mexico riots, numerous lessons present themselves; for example, the relationship that exists within institutional conditions, inmate-staff/administration relations, and violence. Although uprisings are relatively rare events, conditions that contribute to riots are often ignored in most prisons. Other large-scale riots have since erupted in prisons and jails across the nation over the past 25 years. For example, when George Jackson was shot in San Quentin in 1971, three inmates and three guards were killed during a riot. In 1978, three officers were murdered during an uprising in Pontiac Correctional Center (Illinois) and two prisoners and a guard were killed at Georgia State Prison (Reidsville). Other violent disruptions have occurred in the State Prison at Southern Michigan, Joliet Correctional Center (Illinois), Marion Federal Penitentiary (Illinois), Rikers Island (New York), Atlanta Federal Penitentiary, and Oakdale Detention Center, just to name a few. In each of the institutions, the conditions for a riot had existed for a considerable length of time, but few meaningful attempts had been made to alter them.

Inmate-Inmate Violence

A careful examination of riots helps us understand collective violence, whether that aggression transpires among inmates or staff. Whereas riots are relatively uncommon events, physical assaults between inmates constitute a daily problem in most prisons and jails. Several institutional features contribute to such violence. First and foremost, violence is attributed to lack of adequate supervision by officers. That is, as overcrowding outpaces the hiring of guards, violence becomes increasingly imminent. For example, leaders of the corrections officers' union at Rikers Island (New York) report that more than 3000 assaults on inmates and staff occur each year (Welch, 1991 a). Assaults are more likely to take place in facilities that do not have adequate supervision, especially if the interior architecture limits supervision. The proliferation of weapons in an institution is also the result of security lapses, and when officers feel that they do not have the ability to control inmates, they often permit prisoners to protect themselves by any means necessary (Colvin, 1982; Welch, 1995, 1996).

Sexual Assault in Prison

A particularly alarming form of violence among inmates is sexual assault. However, the issue of sexual assault in prison is complicated because while brutal attacks do take place, we must not be led to believe that rape in correctional institutions is a common occurrence. In fact, research demonstrates that the frequency of sexual assault in prisons (and jails) is exaggerated (Lockwood, 1980, 1982, 1985; Nacci, 1982; Nacci and Kane, 1984).

Lockwood (1980, 1982) systematically examined sexual assault in correctional institutions and found that sexual violence falls into two groups. In the first category, sexual violence is a form of domination that is used to coerce one's victim. "The primary causes of violence are sub-cultural values upholding men's rights to use force to gain sexual access" (Lockwood, 1982:257). The other category includes cases in which the target reacts violently to propositions perceived as threatening; therefore, sexual assault emerges as a form of self-protection.

What is far more common than homosexual rape in correctional institutions is *sexual harassment,* in which the *threat* of sexual assault by one inmate over another is used as a form of dominance. Moreover, it is the frequency of sexual harassment (insults and offensive propositions) that may lead some observers to believe that rape is rampant in prisons, largely attributable to the level of fear generated. Accordingly, Nacci's (1982) study of sexual assault in the federal prison system found that only 2 out of 330 inmates surveyed had been compelled to perform undesired sex acts, but 29 percent had been propositioned by other inmates. Similarly, Lockwood's (1980) examination of sexual assault in the New York State prison system

found 28 percent of the inmates surveyed had been aggressively approached by inmates seeking sexual favors. Lockwood (1985:90) concludes: "The problems caused by sexual propositions in prison affect far more men than those suffering the devastating consequences of sexual assault." Problems stemming from sexual assault include fights, social isolation, racism, fear, and crisis (also see Lockwood, 1991).

Although some research endeavors to explore sexual assault in prisons (Chonco, 1989; Jones and Schmid, 1989; Tewksbury, 1989), future studies are necessary to further establish the prevalence and dynamics of sexual victimization, especially in light of the emergence of AIDS/HIV.

Inmate-Staff Violence

Because work as a correctional officer is characterized as hazardous duty, most officers are reminded routinely of the dangers of working in a tense atmosphere. Officers must supervise inmates who have the potential to direct and vent their anger at the staff. For safety purposes, most guards prefer to work alongside a fellow officer. Due to overcrowding and budgetary constraints, however, such arrangements are difficult to maintain. Today, officers are guarding increasingly more inmates; the potential for violence has increased proportionately as well.

Whereas systematic examinations of prison riots are plentiful, few researchers have explored patterns of individual assaults on correctional officers by inmates. Bowker (1980) offered two categories that help us to distinguish between fundamentally different types of assaults on officers. First, assaults are sometimes *patterned spontaneous attacks* which occur during volatile situations: for example, an officer being assaulted when intervening between fighting inmates. Second, some assaults may be categorized as *spontaneous attacks*. Unlike the former, these assaults do not take place "in the heat of the moment"; they are premeditated. Consequently, officers have difficulty anticipating such violence.

Light (1990a, b, 1991) investigated patterns of assaults on officers and found numerous interactional themes which help explain the motives of violence. One interactional theme encompasses assaults ensuing from an officer's command that the inmate objects to. The following case illustrates this type of assault (Light, 1991:251): "Inmate was standing on stairs leading to the gym and correctional officer told him to move. Inmate refused and correctional officer repeated his order. Inmate punched correctional officer on side of face."

Inmates may also lash out against staff to express their protest of being unjustly treated. Similarly, prisoners may react violently to an officer's attempt to search an inmate's person, cell, or property. Light (1991: 253) recorded the following incident from staff records: "CO was pursuing inmate who had fled from [the] area to avoid being frisked before entering the mess hall, when inmate turned around and punched CO in the mouth." Officers also run the risk of assault when approaching emotionally unstable inmates. For example: "As inmate was entering mess hall, he broke from line and struck correction officer with his fists. As he was being subdued by CO, inmate slashed him with a razor blade on left arm and side of face (report cites 'apparent psychotic episode' as cause, and refers to inmate's 'catatonic state')" (Light, 1991: 256–257). Other assaults are categorized according to the following interactional themes: inmates fighting, movement, restraint, contraband, sexual and remaining categories. Light's study found that most assaults on officers are reported as having unexplained motives, or taking place for no apparent reason. For instance: "While checking that inmate's cell door was locked on rounds, correctional officer received urine thrown in his face by inmate. Inmate then attempted to hit CO with broom and glass jar" (Light, 1990b:249).

While officers cannot expect to work in prisons that are completely free of violence, they can exercise caution in dealing with inmates. Training helps officers deal effectively with violent inmates and to identify volatile situations (or "hot spots"), thereby reducing the risk of assault. Just as important, present and future prison administrations have the responsibility to improve those institutional conditions that engender violence (see Fleisher, 1989).

Future Strategies to Reduce Violence

It is unreasonable to presume that all incidents of prison and jail violence can be prevented. However, policymakers and administrators can employ measures to make correctional institutions safer places for officers to work and for inmates to live. We must acknowledge that all levels and forms of prison and jail violence are associated with institutional conditions. While overcrowding has been cited as one factor, there are multiple sources of stress and frustration (poor food services, inadequate health care, lack of meaningful programs, etc.) that, left unchecked, may lead to violence (Welch, 1995, 1996).

Administrators need to focus on staff training that addresses both levels of violence. At the individual level, officers must learn skills (i.e., conflict resolution) that permit them to deal effectively with frustrated and angry inmates. At the collective level, officers must be prepared to prevent and control large-scale disturbances. Explicit policies and procedures ranging from strategies for containing the disturbance to the appropriate use of force are necessary components of institutional control (American Correctional Association, 1991).

Other preventive measures focus on the following: better screening of inmates to determine who is more likely to resort to aggression; the introduction of ombudsmen, formal procedures of filing grievances, and dispute resolutions that are taken seriously by inmates, staff, and administration; and neutralizing the impact of gangs by denying them the recognition they need to generate power.

Architecture and the New Generation Philosophy

Since the future of corrections entails the construction of additional institutions, it is imperative that more attention be given to architectural designs. Zupan (1991) emphasizes the importance of architecture in corrections by pointing out that better-designed correctional facilities can lead to safer and more humane environments. The traditional architecture of correctional institutions feature the linear/intermittent surveillance design, which has serious limitations. For example, the linear/intermittent design limits supervision, thereby contributing to violence and misconduct because it provides more opportunities for these acts with less fear of detection (Welch, 1991b). Zupan proposes greater use of New Generation jails to reduce violence. "Underlying the New Generation philosophy is the assumption that inmates engage in violent and destructive behavior in order to control and manipulate a physical environment and organizational operations which fail to provide for their critical human needs" (Zupan, 1991:5).

The New Generation philosophy is driven by widely accepted assertions regarding human (not necessarily criminal) behavior. Individuals tend to engage in violence and misconduct when their critical needs (such as safety, privacy, personal space, activity, familial contact, social relations, and dignity) are not met. In attempting to meet these critical needs in the New Generation jail, inmates are divided into manageable groups (between 16 and 46) and housed in modules in which the correctional staff has maximum observation, supervision, and interaction with inmates (Welch, 1991b; Zupan 1991).

Critics, however, argue that New Generation jails are limited because they can only control "softer prisons," not hard-core violent offenders. Yet the New Generation approach has never been tested systematically with a high-security inmate population. Instead, current and future trends suggest that more attention is being given to technological advances to improve supervision (e.g., monitors, videotaping, etc.) as well as traditional "nuts and bolts" and "bricks and mortar."

Conclusions

Institutional violence has remained a problem throughout the history of U.S. cor-

rections and is likely to remain a critical issue in the near and distant future. Yet even though prison officials are aware that the necessary conditions for riots exist within their institutional walls, they continue to play the game of chance. More often than not, they win, because large-scale riots and major disturbances are relatively rare events (refer to Martin and Zimmerman, 1990). However, in terms of other forms of violence, it is expected that assaults among inmates (and between inmates and staff) will continue to proliferate throughout the next decade. As prison and jail populations continue to grow, institutional programs, services, and security will fail to keep pace with demand, thereby ensuring that institutions will remain dangerous for inmates and staff alike.

Reiman (1990) raises several key questions about the role of corrections in society, and in the context of prison violence, he helps us identify and confront the institutional conditions and effects of incarceration. Reiman proposes that prisons should be both civilized and civilizing. One can hardly conclude that violent prisons are civilized, a point that should concern us because most inmates eventually return to society. If prisoners do not become more civilized during their incarceration, how can citizens feel safe when inmates are released?

Insofar as single incidents of victimization rarely transform a nonviolent person into a dangerous marauder, we should be concerned about the impact that persistent assaults have on individuals. Even for those who have not been assaulted in prison, the experience of incarceration is profound. Yet for those who have endured violence, the effects of prison are all the more dramatic. It is no exaggeration to say that these inmates suffer a level of punishment exceeding the sentence imposed by the courts (Welch, 1995, 1996). And the future will see little change.

References

Abbott, J. H. (1981). *In the Belly of the Beast: Letters from Prison.* New York: Vintage Books.

American Correctional Association (1991). *Riots and Disturbances in Correctional Institutions.*

College Park, MD: American Correctional Association.

Anon. (1980). The killing ground. *Newsweek*, February 18, pp. 66–76.

Attica: The Official Report of the New York State Commission (1972). New York: Bantam Books.

Bowker, L. (1980). *Prison Victimization*. New York: Elsevier.

——. (1985). An essay on prison violence. In M. Braswell, S. Dillingham, and R. Montgomery (eds.), *Prison Violence in America*. Cincinnati, OH: Anderson Publishing.

Bureau of Justice Statistics (1989). *Prison Rule Violators*. Washington, DC: U.S. Department of Justice.

Chonco, N. (1989). Sexual assaults among male inmates: A descriptive study. *Prison Journal* 69(1):72–82.

Colvin, M. (1982). The New Mexico prison riot. *Social Problems* 29(5):449–463.

——. (1992). *The Penitentiary in Crisis: From Accommodation to Riot in New Mexico*. Albany, NY: State University of New York Press.

Deutsch, M., D. Cunningham, and E. Fink (1991). Twenty years later: Attica civil rights case finally. *Social Justice* 18(3):13–25.

Dillingham, S., and R. Montgomery (1985). Prison riots: A corrections nightmare since 1774. In M. Braswell, S. Dillingham, and R. Montgomery (eds.), *Prison Violence in America*. Cincinnati, OH: Anderson Publishing.

Farrington, D., and C. Nutall (1985). Prison size, overcrowding, prison violence, and recidivism. In M. Braswell, S. Dillingham, and R. Montgomery (eds.), *Prison Violence in America*. Cincinnati, OH: Anderson Publishing.

Fleisher, M. (1989). *Warehousing Violence*. Thousand Oaks, CA: Sage Publications.

Gaes, G., and W. McGuire (1985). Prison violence: The contribution of crowding and other determinants of prison assault rates. *Journal of Research in Crime and Delinquency* 22(1):41–65.

Jones, R., and T. Schmid (1989). Inmates' conceptions of prison sexual assault. *Prison Journal* 69(1):53–61.

Light, K. C. (1990a). Measurement error in official statistics: Prison infraction data. *Federal Probation* 52:63–68.

——. (1990b). The severity of assaults on prison officers: A contextual study. *Social Science Quarterly* 71:267–284.

——. (1991). Assaults on prison officers: Interactional themes. *Justice Quarterly* 8(2): 243–262.

Lockwood, D. (1980). *Prison Sexual Violence*. New York: Elsevier Books.

——. (1982). Contribution of sexual harassment to stress and coping in confinement. In N. Parisi (ed.), *Coping With Imprisonment*. Thousand Oaks, CA: Sage Publications.

——. (1985). Issues in prison sexual violence. In M. Braswell, S. Dillingham, and R. Montgomery (eds.), *Prison Violence in America*. Cincinnati, OH: Anderson Publishing.

——. (1991). Target violence. In K. C. Haas and G. P Alpert (eds.), *The Dilemmas of Corrections*. Prospect Heights, IL: Waveland Press.

Mahan, S. (1994). "An orgy of brutality" at Attica and the "killing ground" at Santa Fe. In M. Braswell, S. Dillingham, and R. Montgomery (eds.), *Prison Violence in America*, 2d ed. Cincinnati, OH: Anderson Publishing.

Martin, R., and S. Zimmerman (1990). A typology of the causes of prison riots and an analytical extension to the 1986 West Virginia riot. *Justice Quarterly* 7(4):711–737.

Nacci, P. L. (1982). Sex and sexual aggression in federal prisons. Unpublished manuscript, U.S. Federal Prison System, Office of Research, Washington, DC.

Nacci, P. L., and T. R. Kane (1982). *Sexual Aggression in Federal Prisons*. Washington, DC: U.S. Department of Justice, Federal Prison System.

——. (1984). Sex and sexual aggression in federal prisons: Inmate involvement and employee impact. *Federal Probation*, 8, March, 46–53.

Office of the Attorney General of the State of New Mexico (1980). *Report of the Attorney General on the February 2 and 3, 1980 Riot at the Penitentiary of New Mexico*. Santa Fe, NM: Office of the Attorney General of the State of New Mexico.

Oswald, R. B. (1972). *Attica: My Story*. New York: Doubleday.

Reiman, J. (1990) *The Rich Get Richer and the Poor Get Prison*, 3rd ed. New York: Macmillan.

Saenz A. (1986). *Politics of a Riot*. Washington, DC: American Correctional Association.

Social Justice (1991). Attica: 1971–1991, A Commemorative Issue, 18:3.

Stone, W. G. (1982). *The Hate Factory: The Story of the New Mexico Penitentiary Riot*. New York: Dell Books.

Tewksbury, R. (1989). The fear of sexual assault in prison inmates. *Prison Journal* 69(1):62–71.

Toch, H. (1985). Social climate and prison violence. In M. Braswell, S. Dillingham, and R.

Montgomery (eds.), *Prison Violence in America*. Cincinnati, OH: Anderson Publishing.

Useem, B. (1985). Disorganization and the New Mexico prison riot. *American Sociological Review* 50(5):677–688.

Useem, B., and P. A. Kimball (1987). A theory of prison riots. *Theory and Society* 16, pp. 87–122.

——. (1989). *States of Siege: U.S. Prison Riots, 1971–1986*. New York: Oxford University Press.

Welch, M. (1991a). Institutional conflict in jail: The crisis at Rikers Island during the summer of 1990. Presented at the Annual Meeting of the Academy of Criminal Justice Sciences, Nashville, TN.

——. (1991b). A review of jails: Reform and the new generation philosophy. *American Jails* March–April, 132–135.

——. (1995) A sociopolitical approach to the reproduction of violence in Canadian prisons. In J. I. Ross (ed.), *Violence in Canada: Sociopolitical Perspectives*. Toronto: Oxford University Press.

——. (1996). *Corrections: A Critical Approach.* New York: McGraw-Hill.

Wicker, T. (1975). *A Time to Die.* New York: Quandrangle.

Zupan, L. L. (1991). *Jails: Reform and the New Generation Philosophy*. Cincinnati, OH: Anderson Publishing.

Cases

Al-Jundi v. Mancusi, 90 F.2d (1991)

Inmates of Attica v. Rockefeller, 453 F.2d. (1971)

17

Violence and Incarceration: A Personal Observation

JoAnne Page

Focus Questions

1. What precipitating factors influence prison violence?

2. How is weakness viewed in prison?

3. Why is violence seen as a normal part of prison life?

4. Why is the cycle of violence difficult to break once a prisoner is released?

Violence is a dominant and defining thread running through the fabric of jail and prison life. It shapes the culture of the institution and the fears, behaviors, and values of the prisoners within the walls. The violence of the jail and prison world is often a reinforcement of violence in the lives of prisoners who were abused as children and grew up on streets where their lives were not safe or valued by the larger society. The culture of violence, whether it is reinforced or learned for the first time in jail and prison, leaves the institution walls in the souls and the internal scar tissue of prisoners upon their release, and is brought home with them to their families and communities.

Norwegian criminologist Nils Christie has described prisons as factories of pain; just as societies are careful about how much money they put into circulation, they should be equally careful about how much pain they choose to circulate. Jails and prisons are also factories and catalysts of violence. The United States is decades into an experiment of escalating incarceration, striking in the extent of its reach into the fabric of the lives of its citizens and its communities. Its profound consequences in terms of individual and community impact upon generations, civil liberties, and use of resources are simply not discussed enough as incarceration continues to grow. The time for such a discussion is now.

For 25 years, I have had experience in jails and prisons and with released prisoners. I have many stories from inside and outside correctional walls, many of which reflect the insidious damage of prison culture. One of my first experiences occurred at the Green Haven Correctional Facility in New York. I learned that one of the quiet, male offenders in my group had been the victim of a prison gang rape. I was stunned by the information, but even more by the casual way in which it was conveyed and the way he was treated by other members of the group. He was disrespected, shunned, and harassed. The other prisoners viewed the rape as his fault because he was unable to effectively defend himself. The blame that he received hit me harder than the fact of the rape itself.

I went home that night and asked my father, a concentration camp survivor, for an explanation, having previously used his experience as a way of understanding the culture of confinement. He told me that, in the concentration camp, the weak were feared and seen as a danger to the survival of others. Having grown up in a culture that protected weakness, I had stepped into a culture in which weakness was a crime punishable by violence up to and including death. I never forgot that first harsh awakening into the reality of the world I was visiting.

Other stories are worth sharing. I remember sitting in the back of a car driven by several ex-offenders and hearing them talk about their friend who had just been released. He was locked up again on a homicide charge, "gotten for a body" they related matter-of-factly. While I was teaching one of my prison classes, an extremely polite student came in late. He apologized profusely for his lateness, explaining that someone had been stabbed on his prison tier and it had taken a while to mop up the mess. It was clear from his explanation that the stabbing was troubling and worthy of note only because it had made him late.

I remember teaching another class deep within Sing Sing prison and discovering that most of my students were carrying knives because stabbings regularly occurred in the corridor through which they had to pass on the way to class. I walked into Green Haven one day and heard allegations that an inmate patient had been beaten to death by correction officers. I tried to conduct business as usual while the ex-offenders with me collected personal statements from prisoners who were jeopardizing their own safety by coming forward about the details. I remember their rage and sense of helplessness at the end of the day but, even more, I remember their shock that I still had the capacity to be surprised at such a killing.

Prison stories blend with stories I have heard from ex-offenders after their release. One man who had served almost 20 years described what it was like for him to step into a subway and be shoved by another rider. He began swinging to attack in an automatic move that he learned behind bars, only to stop short upon seeing that the person who had shoved him was a little old lady with shopping bags. Had the person been male and anywhere near his age, violence would have resulted, and he would have viewed his actions as self-defensive, based on the conduct code he had learned behind bars. Another man, also released after many years, described to me how he was walking down the street and heard running footsteps behind him. Swinging around to attack or defend, he saw a jogger coming at him and put his fists down in embarrassment.

It is natural, upon release, to bring the culture of prison to the street. It is easy, translating through a prison context, to see behavior that is innocent within the larger society as requiring self-defense through attack.

I have spent many years working with people behind bars. I have seen the profound lessons that incarceration teaches and reinforces. The lessons include an ability to shut off emotion, the definition of weakness as a justification for violence and exploitation, the casualness with which violence is regarded as a daily part of living, and a culture in which preemptive full-force attack is a necessary means of self-defense when hostility is anticipated. Triggers for such anticipation can include the pushing, staring, and rude comments that are part of the pattern of daily urban life. Incarceration also breeds and fosters "global rage," an impulsive and explosive anger so great that a minor incident can trigger an uncontrolled response.

I have seen the struggle of those who have been socialized to prison life as they attempt the difficult transition from a world of criminals, violence, and incarceration to a world of wage earners, caring families, and a free society. I have seen how the values and life skills learned while incarcerated, and the accumulated pain and rage, jeopardize such a transition. They are further handicapped if the communities to which they return are saturated with violence, drugs, and poverty. Often the slide back into the destructive and violent street world, and eventual reincarceration or death, is the path of least resistance. The way out of the cycle of crime and incarceration is uphill, and all too many cannot break out of the pattern that they have learned so well.

After 25 years of working in jails and prisons, and with ex-offenders who have survived them, there are some things I know. I know that people have a powerful will toward health and hope, and I have seen that will used to transform lives that looked damaged and destructive beyond salvaging. I have had the extraordinary privilege of being able to witness and support such transformation. I have heard my prisoner students say that, in growing up, they saw their future options as dying or being locked up. I know that it is a terrible crime at an unacceptable cost to allow so many young people to grow up with such a bleak sense of the future.

There are things that I do not know, and they scare me. I do not know what the United States will become as it continues locking up more and more of its young people. Certainly not the "land of the free." I do not know what happens to the soul and the future of communities most hard-hit by incarceration, communities that see their young people achieve their formative acculturation in handcuffs and behind bars. Or what happens when states spend more money on incarceration than on education. Or what the children of the women being incarcerated in record numbers will look like in 10 years. Or

whether the casualty rate among young black men will keep escalating.

For 25 years I have worked with people doing time in prisons and jails. I have seen the anger and destructiveness that these institutions breed and foster. We live in a very small world; our lives are connected by a fragile and intimate weave. We are increasingly choosing to build factories of rage and pain and violence. We are choosing to destroy lives and communities, to plant dragon seeds. And if there is any lesson that we know, it is that we reap what we sow.

18
Realities of Fear

Mike Rolland

Focus Questions

1. What dilemmas do the prisoners face during the riot?

2. Why don't the prisoners run or turn themselves over to authorities?

3. How does Rolland's view of the New Mexico riot differ from Welch's view?

4. What were the precursors or causes of the riot?

Editor's note: *The following reading is an account of specific events that occurred during the New Mexico State prison riot. The author is one of the prisoners who was present along with seven other prisoners. The riot lasted a total of 36 hours. At the time of this account, the prisoners had had control of the prison for over 24 hours, and some small groups of prisoners (like Rolland's) had been assigned to stay in one area of the prison and keep one guard hostage (Diego).*

February 3, 1980—9:50 A.M.

The shouting and screaming from outside subsided a little. A few distant voices could still be heard. Someone out there demanded the State Police-National Guard take action. "Do something," the voice bellowed. "What are you afraid of . . . why don't you storm the prison . . . shoot 'em all . . . kill 'em . . . kill 'em!" The words heard in the lobby were

chilling. Everyone inside listened in rapt attention. A new wave of fear passed through me. I imagined the forces outside gearing up at that moment to rush in to save the rest of the guards. They now had their justification and I could feel what was imminent.

Then someone in front of me laughed and shouted, "Let's set one on fire. Let him run to the gate and see what they say about that." Others around the lobby started laughing at the idea, but I knew some of these guys were serious about it. All that was needed now was someone to co-sign the idea and it would happen. Most of the convicts in this room had nothing to lose, or felt they had nothing. Being confined outcasts of society gave everyone in the room at that moment a tangible goal and power. For some, it was a determination to force our keepers to deal with us honestly. For others, it was just entertainment and opportunity to inflict agony and terror for the moment and to hell with the consequences. More and more I could feel the second group was just a hair's breath from getting us all killed. Other ideas were shouted out with a building exuberance around the crowded lobby and Felix, Lucky, Bear, and others in that crew stepped into the center of the floor.

Felix told everyone, "Shut the fuck up!!" and he pointed to individuals around the room telling them the same thing. The room got suddenly quiet again. He glared around the room at the head runners and said, "No one does anything to the hostages unless I say so." Everyone stayed silent and he continued, "We're gonna see what they do out front about the negotiations. Anyone that has hostages, go to 'em. Stay with 'em and don't hurt 'em." Very menacingly he growled, "And if any of you motor mouths don't like it, I'm right here," and he slapped his hand against his chest. Still, no one said anything and no one moved. Then he and his whole crew stalked out in the direction of the prison center.

I let out the breath I was unconsciously holding, when Frank said, "I'll catch up with you guys later;" and as Felix passed us, he fell in step beside him. I glanced around the room and saw Stanley with Boots by the overturned pop machine. Strolling over to them I said, "Let's get out of here." Others were leaving the lobby in groups of three and four. We moved through the visiting room and toward the control center. I could hear voices of others in front and behind heading in the same direction.

As we passed through the control gates and started down the long hallway, Frank materialized out of the swirling smoke saying, "I knew it was you guys 'cuz I heard your shoe flapping." He chuckled and waded in behind Stanley and me heading for guard's mess hall. The kitchen and two chow halls were now the regular routes around the gym fire. In the main dining room Stanley took the lead and we filed in line behind him. Half listening to Frank behind me, I concentrated on navigating through thick, smothering smoke and Stanley's back. Frank said something about Felix finding out who was making those threats on the radio. Strangely I could hear him and not the roar of the gym fire. Since the roof had fallen in on the gym floor, the fire didn't sound as intense but this smoke was even worse. Stanley guided us around the tables and obstacles laying in the swamp and we made it to the corridor again.

Wading toward the cellblock, the smoke thinned quite a bit. It blew over our heads going in the opposite direction. There must be a draft pulling air and smoke to the gym fire. Amazingly, when we reached Cellhouse 1, it was clear of smoke and I pulled my gas mask off. I didn't know how long this would last, but it was a bit of relief, for a change.

As soon as we reached the cell, Weasel was anxious for answers to his many questions. Frank went into his doctor mode and started checking the crusty burns on the guard and questioning him about how he felt. Weasel kept asking what was going on out front. I didn't want to talk in front of the hostage, so after I used the tape again to repair my shoe, I waved everyone out on the tier. We left Frank smearing salve on the guard's burns and the rest of us went to the TV room.

Once there I explained to Weasel that the officials had lied about the exchange of hostages for the television interview. I told him about the last guard sent out with the stick and the special message he took to the gate.

We sat on the bench watching the TV. The commentator mentioned the recent hostage released. The scene on the TV screen was of the front gate and the forces gathering around the little building outside the gate. We discussed the possibilities of what the officials would do next. Weasel asked about the threats he'd heard over the radio and Boots said he'd heard Felix say that he'd deal with it. I asked Weasel how the guard was and Weasel just shrugged his shoulders and said, "He doesn't believe he'll be released." I nodded my head, not saying anything.

Stanley got our attention by angrily saying, "What the fuck are we supposed to do now?" He stood up by the windows watching the gym fire next door. When I said, "All we can do now is wait," he blew off a disdainful, "Phew!" and turned back to watching out in the cellblock. "The damn smoke is coming back in again," he said and looked at me as if this is all my fault. I knew what was on his mind, or I thought I did. None of us really knows what's coming next. With that last hostage sent out impaled and Felix off searching for the idiots making those threats, it all felt like something was about to happen that we couldn't control. Everything seemed to be heading for a climax of doom. I felt it but I didn't want to say anything about it and tried to keep the conversation on the facts with a positive outcome. It seemed to me that if we talked about the worst happening, that would just give the worst credibility to becoming real. While Boots and Weasel watched the TV screen, I stood up and moved over to Stanley by the window.

When I stood up, I could see the smoke pouring into the cellblock from the hallway. It wouldn't be long until it filled the block again. At the window I saw black smoke and sparks rolling skyward as parts of the remaining gym roof continued to collapse in on the floor. All the glass in the huge gym windows was gone on this side of the gym wall. From where we stood we could see down through the bars to the gym floor. The fire looked like it had a life of its own and it looked like it was regenerating itself.

I glanced at Stanley beside me and said, "What's the deal, brother? You know as well . . ." He wouldn't look at me and stalked away to the table and sat down between Boots and Weasel on the bench. I turned and looked at him startled and angry. "What the fuck is your problem?" I mumbled.

As he sat down he said, "We've got to leave that fuckin' hostage on his own. We can't stay with him anymore." He pounded his fist on the bench with every word. "We gotta find another place to hide until all this bullshit is over." Weasel and Boots had turned sideways in their seats watching him. I stood by the window looking at him with astonishment, listening to his breathless rush of words, waiting for him to finish. He kept on, "None of this hostage watching has been my idea. I didn't like it from the beginning and I don't like it now. We can't help him, we can't, we can't . . ." He suddenly stopped talking and looked at each of us for a response. Weasel and Boots didn't say anything. They just glanced away, dumbfounded at the outburst. I couldn't let it hang and had to say something. "Man, you know we can't leave the hostage on his own, not now. We've committed ourselves to this side and if we try to run out, we'll be treated just like those we hauled to the gym." I waved my arm at the fire behind me and we glared at each other across the space between us. Surely he knew what he was suggesting. If we were to attempt to bail out now we'd just get ourselves killed. In prison a person can't get away with committing to one side, be involved in what we had already seen and done, and then try to run out. He scowled at me as if I should co-sign his ludicrous rambling—as if I'm being unloyal to our friendship by my not agreeing with him. I can't scoff his words, no matter how ridiculous they sound. I tried to mellow the glower on my face and said, "Brother, I don't like this shit any more than you do . . . none of us do." I pointed at Boots and Stanley, "But man, we're committed to see this through. Let me get Frank and let's see what he says." I held my hands up. "Just stay right there. I'll go get Frank," and I moved toward the door.

As I walked out of the room, I couldn't help but notice the clouds of smoke rolling in the block. It had already filled the front half of the cellblock and moved toward the TV room.

I ambled down the tier with thoughts flashing on Stanley. I'd known him since I stepped off the bus three years ago, when I'd arrived here. He worked in the reception building for new prisoners that came in the joint. From day one we'd become friends and partners. I thought I knew him pretty well. I'd never seen him run from trouble or ever thought he would. It's way out of character for him to suggest it. No-no, not now. And even though I'm not sure we're gonna come out on top with the road I've committed us to, we can't run now. I couldn't bring myself to agree with him on running. At the same time, he's my partner and I gotta give him all the room that I can—but still, I don't want to see him end up like John.

When I reached the cell door I walked right in, hesitated for a moment and then asked, "Anything on the radio?" Frank looked up from the bed beside the guard, wrapping his arms, and just shook his head no. I moved to the desk, adjusted the volume and squelch knobs on the radio that sat in the battery charger. It worked all right and I slowly sauntered back to the door. I hadn't thought out what I'd say to Frank and I didn't want to talk in front of Diego. He was paranoid already and I didn't want to frighten him any more than he already was. I said to the guard, "We're gonna have to leave you for a minute." Then I said to Frank, "Come out here and see this man. You gotta check this out." I pushed on the door and went out on the tier to wait against the railing.

Smoke had already filled the block past the cell door and I stood outside waiting and watching it sock us in again. Frank walked out behind me and he said, "Did you know he was in the Tet offensive (in South Vietnam) in '68?" He pointed over his shoulder at the cell with the guard, Diego, still inside. "Yeah, I know," I said. "He was in 'Nam in '68 and '69." Frank leaned on the railing beside me and said, "What's the deal? What did you want to show me? Man, this smoke is bad." He coughed, and pulled his towel over his nose and mouth. "Come on, we gotta talk in the TV room," I said and headed down the tier. He followed and we walked out of the wall of moving smoke that had filled two-thirds of the cellblock. I hadn't bothered to pull my gas mask on yet and we walked into the TV room together. I went to the television and turned the volume down. Frank plopped down on the bench beside Boots.

I stood beside the television, glanced at Stanley, Weasel, and Boots. Then I spoke to Frank. "Some of us think that things have gotten way out of control." I looked at Frank for some kind of reaction—but he just stared at me over his towel wrap and I continued. "We all know what Felix and his crew are trying to get done, but what if it doesn't work? What next? I'm not ready to sacrifice myself for this fuckin' joint." Frank gave no indication that my words made the slightest impression on him. Stanley started to say something and I looked over at him, but Frank interrupted by saying, "It's not gonna come to that. Those suit-wearing officials aren't gonna let the negotiations fail, not on their part. They won't let things get any more out of control than they already are." He pointed to the television screen and went on. "There's too much media coverage out there. Oh, if we were behind a wall where they could be hidden from view we'd be in big trouble. But with those fences out there, they can't be sure that they aren't being seen by those television cameras." He pulled his towel off and kept talking without missing a beat. "So far no hostages have been killed, so the Governor can't risk his political career on sending in troops and getting a lot more people killed. So far, all the killings have been done by us. Yeah, and they probably know about the bodies in the gym. But they don't care about us. And they actually don't care what happens to these guards 'cuz the guards are just cannon fodder for the state. But you can bet the Governor is keeping track of what goes on here and his concern isn't this fuckin' place. His concern is his political future. You'll see. Those officials at the gate will agree to anything Felix says now. They'll probably let him talk live on the TV. They'll stand out there at the gate and look reasonable and accommodating for the media. But in the end, they'll lie and smile and just cover their asses." His last words trailed off and left images in my mind of peaceful settlement and agreements to change and everything will be fine and we'll all be alive tomorrow.

Then Stanley said, "I still think we should hide until the National Guard comes in." He sat on the bench looking as if we should agree with him. The expression on his face said he'd already made up his mind about all this. I looked at him and at Weasel next to him. Then Frank asked matter-of-factly, "Where can you hide? Tell me and I'll go with you. Where can we hide in here?" He leaned forward and looked at Stanley. "Come on, man. Get real . . . you know we couldn't get away with running out now. If anyone runs out now they'll be considered a rat and end up with the rest of the rats." No one said anything for a long few seconds. I glanced at Stanley, then at Frank, waiting for one or the other to say something to relieve the tension. Stanley sat there fumbling with his gas mask, looking at the floor. Finally I said, "What you said about the media makes sense and there's no place anyone can hide in here." Frank nodded his head and I glanced over at Stanley and he slowly raised up looking at me. He didn't say anything but I could see the haunted eyes that said he was unconvinced about anything Frank said. And now I'd have to worry about him slipping off somewhere and trying to hide and probably getting himself killed in the process.

Frank pointed at the television and said, "Turn it up. Let's hear what they're doing." I reached for the volume control and stepped over to sit next to Stanley on the bench. The smoke had drifted in the room but it was insignificant to what showed on the TV screen. Everyone sat glued to the unfolding drama. The scene was of the front of the joint, the sidewalk and doors of the lobby entrance, the fancy lettering above the entrance naming the asylum, and movement inside, but it was too dark to make anyone out distinctly. Then Felix and Lucky appeared at the doors. They shuffled down the two steps, hesitated, and strided down the sidewalk toward the camera. It refocused and the commentator's voice said, "We'll switch live to the negotiations at the front of the prison now." This is what we should have seen an hour ago. This scene on TV probably would have saved that last guard from being impaled.

I was riveted to the TV screen, but it kept blurring and my ears popped as if I was on an airplane. The figures on the screen were talking, but I couldn't hear what they were saying. I turned my head, looking around the TV room, and everything looked surreal. The television, the walls, the table kept blurring and refocusing and blurring again. I shook my head hard trying to clear it, but that didn't help. Suddenly I thought about the smoke. There's something in the smoke, something I'm breathing. I groped for the gas mask on top of my head, pulled it down over my face and blew out to clear it. Then I took a couple of slow deep breaths but that didn't help either. Everything around the edge of my vision fogged over and I croaked, "Ahhh fuck . . ." and leaped to my feet. I glanced around and everything still looked unfocused and blurred. I glanced down at Stanley and he was watching me with a puzzled expression. I lightly pushed off away from the table and stumbled backwards into the wall. My head spun and I bent over groaning and my stomach flipped. I saw sparks burst white and tasted something foul that filled my mouth and just got my mask off in time to spew a yellowish brown liquid that splashed on the floor at my feet. I groaned again and, amazingly, my head cleared and I felt better. Actually I felt clammy. Hot, but better. I raised up slowly, wiping my mouth on my left sleeve and Stanley and Frank were in front of me. They were both looking at me as if I was a patient. Stanley spoke first. "Are you all right, man?" I looked at him and attempted a smile and said, "I don't, shit, I don't know," and turned my head to spit more of the nasty taste from my mouth. Then before I could move, Stanley had my left arm and Frank grabbed my right and they pulled and directed me to the bench. I told them that I was okay, and I actually did feel all right. My vision had cleared and my stomach quieted. My legs felt a little shaky and I could still taste whatever I spit on the floor but no matter, Frank had me as his patient now. He said down beside me and

took my left arm, pressing his fingers into my wrist. I glanced up to see Stanley and Weasel looking at me as if I was dying or something.

I told Frank again, "I'm all right . . ." and tried to pull my arm away from him. He just held it tighter saying, "Wait a minute." So I sat back down and let him get a full measure of my pulse. Finally he released my arm and announced my heartbeat normal. I started to stand and said, "I need some water," but before I could raise off the bench, Frank pulled me back down. Weasel looked on and said, "I'll get some water," and he took off at a trot out of the TV room. I had a sudden flash of anger because it was irritating to be treated like an invalid. But then I just smiled at my friends around me and sat back. Frank asked in his gravel voice, "When's the last time you ate something?" I opened my mouth to say, but I really couldn't remember when I had eaten last. Stanley piped in with, "We ate some Fritos two days ago." I looked up at him and nodded my head, remembering that we had eaten some of those chips from that pile of stolen items. Then Weasel was back and handed me a tumbler of water that I immediately drafted down. Frank and Stanley continued their discussion of my strange behavior as if I wasn't there. I smiled at Weasel, and Frank turned and pointed a serious finger at my chest. With all the authority of his medical opinion, he announced that I'd had an anxiety attack. He said, "With all this madness going on, and in combination with not eating anything for so long, you had an attack of nerves." And he was serious. I took a dubious sip from the cup of water and said, "Come on, man . . . the next thing you'll be telling me is I'm pregnant and this was just morning sickness." I glanced over at Stanley, wanting him to confirm my assessment of Frank's quackery. He and Weasel were talking in low tones, looking at me suspiciously. I heard Stanley say, "Don't let him out of your sight." He was telling Weasel to watch me and I had to grin at them. They were actually concerned. I could see it in their faces but that wasn't necessary. I said to Weasel, "Yeah, you better keep a close eye on me," and I lunged to the left and passed Frank and bounded to the TV room door before they could react. As I walked out I heard Frank say, "This is serious shit, Banker (Rolland's nickname in prison)—you shouldn't . . ." and I was around the end of the tier before I looked back and saw Weasel walking out the door after me.

I continued down the tier to the cell. At the door I stopped and turned on him, "Man, you ain't gotta watch me or follow me. I'm all right!" He just walked up to me, not saying anything. The smug expression on his face told me that he was given a mission by Stanley and nothing I said made a bit of difference.

When I pulled on the door to go inside, I saw the guard spin around from watching something out the back cell window. I moved on in the cell and said to him, "What's out there man?" He pointed out the window saying, "There's another fire next door." I stepped past him to the desk and saw fires in the Dorm A-2 next door. It looked like it had just been started 'cuz there wasn't any smoke coming out the windows yet. Then as I watched, another fire flared up and I could see some guys scurry away from it. "Hey, check it out," I said. "The crazy bastards are starting more fires." Behind me Weasel peered out over my shoulder. "Do you think they'll set everything on fire?" he asked with concern. I nodded my head and said, "Yeah, they'll probably try . . . but we don't have to worry 'cuz there's nothing that'll burn in the cellblocks." I kept watching the guys next door move through the dorm with their bottles of dry-cleaning fluid. I hoped they couldn't set the cellblocks on fire, but with that fluid . . . anything was possible. And with enough determination, this whole joint could be burned to a blackened husk.

Author's Note

The incidents described in this book and those 36 hours in 1980 have haunted this writer to the point that something had to be said about it. For the obvious reasons, all names of the living had to be changed, but I'm sure for those who were there and survived the riot, they know and remember these individuals.

Through a tragedy of errors, the officials at the prison ignored the rumors of an impending takeover and riot. Those same officials believed they had effectively intimidated and demoralized the prisoners to the point that none would have the courage to rebel. And even though the rumors had been circulating through the prisons for months before February 2, 1980, the rumors were laughed off and it was business as usual. But, it should be noted, there was nothing the officials could have done to prevent this takeover. The stage had been set long before the rumors began. Prisons are full of routine and mundane regularity where prisoners can wait for the perfect moment that a guard is lax in judgment or not paying attention.

The group of guards and officials who perfected and perpetuated the ongoing fear and hatred before the riot were eventually identified. The months of investigation after the riot by the Attorney General concluded with removing the deputy warden, head of security, and other middle-management prison officials. The Attorney General's report placed the primary blame for the riot on mismanagement of the prison and years of corruption.

Felix, Lucky, Bear, Frank, and many others were charged in the investigation for leadership in the riot. They were all shipped to federal prison facilities. I don't know what became of these individuals. Stanley, Weasel, and Boots were eventually paroled or released. I was able to maintain contact with Stanley for a short while, but as with most prison friendships, we lost contact with and track of each other. Attempts were made to contact Captain Francisco Vasquez, but at the time he was confined to a hospital bed and unable to remember anything of the riot. Donald V. Diego, the burned guard, recovered from his injuries. Since the riot, I have been in contact with Diego. He is doing well and running his own construction business.

Of the numerous dead—independent investigators confirmed that 33 prisoners perished in the riot. An additional prisoner died several months later of his wounds. A team of forensic experts found only three bodies in the burned-out gym, so investigators dispute that bodies were taken to the gym and burned. I do not know how many prisoners were murdered or how many died from overdosing on drugs. But it should be made clear as to why so many were killed. Most of those murdered were thought to be or in fact were informers. In prison, an informer or rat is the most loathed and hated by prisoners. The police use informers to set up and catch criminals. The courts use informers to prosecute their criminal cases, and guards and prison officials use informers to snitch on other prisoners. It shouldn't be surprising that these individuals were the center of attention and retribution once the prison was wide open and without restraint. What was unique in this case is the "snitch game" the officials used to control prisoners.

The hate that permeated this prison was not unique. In most prisons across this country, inmates exceed the capacity by two to three times that for which they were designed. In most American prisons, there are guards and officials who believe that it's part of their job to make those confined as miserable as possible. These guards and officials routinely place the lives of those confined and those who work in these facilities in danger. The spark to light the madness is ahead for all these prisons. The only thing that has changed is the prisoners' attitudes. The prison takeovers and riots of the future won't be to negotiate change or to improve the conditions of those confined. The prisoners of today know this is an exercise in futility. The riots and takeovers of the future will be for one purpose only—REVENGE.

In understanding the events of this story, read it not with the intentions to ask why these horrendous events could have happened in the past. But understand it is still happening and will continue until society realizes that the whole idea of locking a person in a box to repent is a dismal failure. The entire concept of sentencing a person to reform/rehabilitate has not worked and will not work with the present antiquated justice system on which our society relies. When warehousing and abusing a person passes the point that it insults the good senses of what is just and moral, then when that individual is released into society again, he has only learned a deeper hatred and disrespect for society and the laws that have abused him.

Chapter VI
Discussion

Prison Violence

Her experiences working in prison allow Page to observe how violence is considered to be a normal part of prison life and how victims are blamed for not being able to defend themselves. Page argues that prisons are places that give rise to pain, anger, and violence. She reminds us that it is difficult for prisoners to let go of the survival mechanisms inherent in the convict subculture after their release to the outside world.

Welch discusses the various levels and types of prison violence, as well as what might be done to reduce violent incidents. He predicts that prison violence will continue to escalate as long as the offender population grows faster than the proportion of institutional staff and spaces for services and treatment. Both Page and Welch question the civility of the prison environment and how the incarceration experience may have a negative effect on prisoner reintegration. Prison violence may not only slow the progression of rehabilitation, but it may also contribute to recidivism and citizens' fear of prisoner reintegration.

In his summary discussion of the New Mexico state prison riot, Welch sets up the scene for a firsthand account of the riot, which was witnessed by Mike Rolland. This riot is considered the most destructive and bloodiest riot in U.S. prison history. The New Mexico riot was an extreme example of an "expressive" prison riot, in which various gangs and factions struggled for power. The riot in New Mexico was much different than the more controlled and politicized riot at Attica, which had convict leaders who tried to negotiate for the best interests of all inmates. The Attica riot, though not as destructive, was officially handled by the state in a poor manner. 39 people, including 10 hostages, died at Attica—all by gunshot wounds fired by state officials. Rolland's experience in Santa Fe exemplifies the unchecked anger, gang divisions, and violent capabilities that exist (but are usually controlled) in most prison environments.

Chapter VII
Introduction

Security Housing Units: Supermax Prisons

Common Assumptions	Reality
• Prisoners are sent to supermax units because of the severity of the crime they committed on the streets or because they have been sentenced to life without parole.	• Prisoners are sent to supermax units because they have committed violent acts *while incarcerated;* they pose a danger to the safety of the institution or to others within the institution; they have escaped or attempted an escape; and/or they are identified gang members.
• Supermax prisoners have the same privileges and freedoms as other prisoners.	• Because of the security threats they pose, prisoners in supermax facilities have *fewer* privileges and freedoms than any other prisoners. Supermax prisoners are kept locked down in a single cell for 23 hours per day, whereas prisoners in maximum security prisons are locked down for only 8 to 12 hours.

Alcatraz Federal Penitentiary, the forerunner of today's supermax prisons, housed the most dangerous and disruptive federal prisoners from 1932 to 1963. Prisoners on "The Rock" (Alcatraz's nickname) were able to eat, work, and enjoy recreation outside of their cells. After Alcatraz closed its doors, these prisoners were dispersed throughout the federal system in hopes that they would be able to live among the general prison population (Hershberger 1998). Many of these prisoners were placed in the United States Penitentiary (USP) in Marion, Illinois (when it opened in 1972), where they continued to have some freedom of movement outside their cells. Marion was considered to be a "control unit," the name used by the federal system in 1972 to refer to a part of the prison, or an entire prison, that functioned as the most secure facility in the system (Dowker and Good 1993). However, it wasn't until 1983, when two correctional officers and one prisoner at Marion USP were murdered within one week, that prison officials instituted a permanent lockdown at Marion USP, which continues to this day. The most violent and disruptive inmates were once again consolidated into one unit and given the highest security measures and staff specially trained to handle violent incidents (Hershberger 1998). These prisoners were not allowed out of their cells, except for one hour each day to shower and exercise. This new way of managing the most violent and disruptive prisoners, isolating them for 23 hours in their own cells, became known as "super-maximium" custody prisons, or "supermax."

Supermax prisons are also known by the following terms: administrative segregation, administrative maximum security (ADX), closed maximum security unit (CMAX), control unit, high security, restrictive housing, secure housing unit (SHU), special management, and "maxi-maxi." Between 57 and 108 facilities house approximately 1.8 percent of the total felony offender population (over 20,000 offenders) in cells designed for supermax custody level prisoners (King 1999). The number of supermax facilities is increasing, but the current number varies because many older maximum security facilities also house prisoners in administrative segregation (e.g., 10–15 percent of their entire population) in one area or wing within the prison. On the other hand, some technologically advanced prisons have been built in the last decade to house only prisoners of supermax status (for example, Florence ADX).

Supermax prison is not officially considered to be a punishment, but a correctional tool to safely manage the most violent and disruptive prisoners who have demonstrated that they cannot live among the general prisoner population. The hope is that violence can ultimately be reduced. Violence reduction has so far not fully materialized. From 1991 to 1995, the number of prisoner assaults on staff has reportedly increased (Henningsen, Johnson, and Wells 1999). Despite these setbacks, some prison administrators argue the importance of keeping supermax prisoners isolated because they endanger the safety of prison staff and prisoners, and they jeopardize institutional security. As previously discussed, supermax prisoners have worked their way to the highest custody level because, while behind bars, they caused serious injury or death to another prisoner or correctional officer; they escaped or attempted a serious escape; or they are high-ranking members of a prison gang. Supermax prisoners may not have committed a violent crime on the streets, but because of their violent behavior inside prison, they are isolated from other prisoners and have limited staff interaction. We wish to emphasize that many prisoners who have done time in a supermax facility will return to less secure prisons and will one day be released into the community. As you read about the conditions inside a supermax prison in the following readings, pay attention to the controversies that surround the use of prolonged isolation. Ask yourself the following question: What would a prisoner be like upon release to the community after spending his or her entire sentence in a supermax facility?

Recommended Readings

Dowker, Fay, and Glenn Good. (1993). "The Proliferation of Control Unit Prisons in the United States." *Journal of Prisoners on Prisons* 4 (2):1–16.

Fellner, J., and J. Mariner. (1997). *Cold Storage: Super-Maximum Security Confinement in Indiana.* New York: Human Rights Watch.

Haney, Craig, and Mona Lynch. (1997). "Regulating Prisons of the Future: A Psychological Analysis of Supermax and Solitary Confinement." *Review of Law and Social Change* 23: 477–570.

Harrington, Spencer P. M. (1997). "Caging the Crazy: Supermax Confinement Under Attack." *The Humanist* 57 (1):14–20.

Henningsen, Rodney J., W. Wesley Johnson, and Terry Wells. (1999). "Supermax Prisons: Panacea or Desperation?" *Corrections Management Quarterly* 3(2):53–59.

Hershberger, Gregory L. (1998). "To the Max." *Corrections Today* 60 (1):54–57.

King, Roy D.. (1999). "The Rise and Rise of Supermax." *Punishment and Society* 1(2): 163–186.

Reid, Larry, Pam Ploughe, Rick Wright, and Wes Lehman. (2000). "The Colorado State Penitentiary Progressive Reintegration Opportunity Unit." *Corrections Today* (June).

Riveland, Chase. (1999). *Supermax Prisons: Overview and General Considerations.* Washington, D.C.: National Institute of Corrections, U.S. Department of Justice.

Internet Websites

American Civil Liberties Union. (1997, 8 August). 'Super-max' prisons minimize humanity. Available: *http://www.aclu.org/news/ w080897a.html*

The June 2000 issue of *Corrections Today* has an article about a supermax facility in Colorado. Available: *http://www.corrections.com/aca/ cortoday/june00/colorado.html*

Gazis-Sax, J. (1997). American Siberia: The purpose of Alcatraz. Available: *http://www. alsirat.com/alcatraz/purpose.html*

For another look at the history of Alcatraz Penitentiary. Available: *http://www.nps.gov/ alcatraz/*

Links to more Federal and State prison agencies. Available: *http://www.statecorrections.com/ links/*

Prison Activist Resource Center—a group devoted to improving prison conditions. Available: *http://www.prisonactivist.org/control- unit/*

San Francisco Chronicle article in 1998 on Colorado's ADX federal supermaximum prison in Florence, Colorado. Available: *http:// www.mapinc.org/drugnews/v98.n1200. a06.html*

19

Infamous Punishment: The Psychological Consequences of Isolation

Craig Haney

Focus Questions

1. What types of privileges and services are provided to prisoners at Pelican Bay?

2. What are the psychological consequences of isolation?

3. What happens when prisoners with pre-existing psychiatric disorders enter supermax facilities?

4. What is Haney's general view of secure housing institutions like Pelican Bay state prison?

Since the discovery of the asylum, prisons have been used to isolate inmates from the outside world, and often from each other. As most students of the American penitentiary know, the first real prisons in the United States were characterized by the regimen of extreme isolation that they imposed upon their prisoners. Although both the Auburn and Pennsylvania models (which varied only in the degree of isolation they imposed)

eventually were abandoned, in part because of their harmful effects upon prisoners,[1] most prison systems have retained and employed—however sparingly—some form of punitive solitary confinement. Yet, because of the technological spin that they put on institutional design and procedure, the new super-maximum security prisons are unique in the modern history of American corrections. These prisons represent the application of sophisticated, modern technology dedicated entirely to the task of social control, and they isolate, regulate, and surveil more effectively than anything that has preceded them.

The Pelican Bay SHU

The Security Housing Unit at California's Pelican Bay State Prison is the prototype for this marriage of technology and total control.[2] The design of the Security Housing Unit—where well over a thousand prisoners are confined for periods of six months to several years—is starkly austere. Indeed Pelican Bay's low, windowless, slate-gray exterior gives no hint to outsiders that this is a place where human beings live. But the barrenness of the prison's interior is what is most startling. On each visit to this prison I have been struck by the harsh, visual sameness and monotony of the physical design and the layout of these units. Architects and corrections officials have created living environments that are devoid of social stimulation. The atmosphere is antiseptic and sterile; you search in vain for humanizing touches or physical traces that human activity takes place here. The "pods" where prisoners live are virtually identical; there is little inside to mark location or give prisoners a sense of place. Prisoners who are housed inside these units are completely isolated from the natural environment and from most of the natural rhythms of life. SHU prisoners, whose housing units have no windows, get only a glimpse of natural light. One prisoner captured the feeling created here when he told me, "When I first got here I felt like I was underground." Prisoners at Pelican Bay are not even permitted to see grass, trees, or shrubbery. Indeed, little or none exists within the perimeters of the prison grounds, which are covered instead by gray gravel stones. This is no small accomplishment since the prison sits adjacent to the Redwood National Forest and the surrounding landscape is lush enough to support some of the oldest living things on earth. Yet here is where the California Department of Corrections has chosen to create the most lifeless environment in its—or any—correctional system.

When prisoners do get out of their cells for "yard," they are released into a barren concrete encasement that contains no exercise equipment, not even a ball. They cannot see any of the surrounding landscape because of the solid concrete walls that extend up some 20 feet around them.

Overhead, an opaque roof covers half the yard; the other half, although covered with a wire screen, provides prisoners with their only view of the open sky. When outside conditions are not intolerably inclement (the weather at Pelican Bay often brings harsh cold and driving rain), prisoners may exercise in this concrete cage for approximately an hour-and-a-half a day. Their movements are monitored by video camera, watched by control officers on overhead television screens. In the control booth, the televised images of several inmates, each in separate exercise cages, show them walking around and around the perimeter of their concrete yards, like laboratory animals engaged in mindless and repetitive activity. Prisoners in these units endure an unprecedented degree of involuntary, enforced idleness. Put simply: Prisoners here have virtually nothing to *do*. Although prisoners who can afford them are permitted to have radios and small, regulation-size televisions in their cells, there is no *activity* in which they may engage. Except for the limited exercise I have described and showers (three times a week), there are no prison routines that regularly take them out of their cells. All prisoners are "cell fed"—

twice a day meals are placed on tray slots in the cell doors to be eaten by the prisoners inside. (Indeed, on my first tour of the institution one guard told me that this was the only flaw in the design of the prison—that they had not figured out a way to feed the prisoners "automatically," thus eliminating the need for any contact with them.) Prisoners are not permitted to do work of any kind, and they have no opportunities for educational or vocational training. They are never permitted out on their tiers unless they are moving to and from showers or yard or being escorted—in chains and accompanied by two baton-wielding correctional officers per inmate—to the law library or infirmary outside the unit. Thus, with minor and insignificant exceptions, a prisoner's entire life is lived within the parameters of his 80 square-foot cell, a space that is typically shared with another prisoner whose life is similarly circumscribed.

All movement within these units is tightly regulated and controlled and takes place under constant surveillance. Prisoners are permitted to initiate little or no meaningful behavior of their own. When they go to shower or "yard," they do so at prescribed times and in a prescribed manner and the procedure is elaborate. Guards must first unlock the padlocks on the steel doors to their cells. Once the guards have left the tier (they are never permitted on the tier when an unchained prisoner is out of his cell), the control officer opens the cell door by remote control. The prisoner must appear naked at the front of the control booth and submit to a routinized visual strip search before going to yard and, afterwards, before returning to his cell. Some prisoners are embarrassed by this public display of nudity (which takes place not only in front of control officers and other prisoners, but whomever else happens to be in the open area around the outside of the control booth.) As might be expected, many inmates forego the privilege of taking "bard" because of the humiliating procedures to which they must submit and the draconian conditions under which they are required to exercise. Whenever prisoners are in the presence of another human being (except for those who have cellmates), they are placed in chains, at both their waist and ankles. Indeed, they are chained even *before* they are permitted to exit their cells. There are also special holding cages in which prisoners are often left when they are being moved from one place to another. Prisoners are kept chained even during their classification hearings. I witnessed one prisoner, who was apparently new to the process, stumble as he attempted to sit down at the start of his hearing. Because he was chained with his hands behind his back, the correctional counselor had to instruct him to "sit on the chair like it was a horse"—unstable, with the back of the chair flush against his chest.

The cells themselves are designed so that a perforated metal screen, instead of a door, covers the entrance to the cells. This permits open, around-the-dock surveillance whenever guards enter the tiers. In addition, television cameras have been placed at strategic locations inside the cellblocks and elsewhere within the prison.

Because the individual "pods" are small (four cells on each of two floors), both visual and auditory surveillance are facilitated. Speakers and microphones have been placed in each cell to permit contact with control booth officers. Many prisoners believe that the microphones are used to monitor their conversations. There is little or no personal privacy that prisoners may maintain in these units.

Psychological Consequences

The overall level of long-term social deprivation within these units is nearly total and, in many ways, represents the destructive essence of this kind of confinement. Men in these units are deprived of human contact, touch, and affection for years on end. They are denied the opportunity for contact visits of any kind; even attorneys and experts must interview them in visiting cells that prohibit contact. They cannot embrace or shake hands, even with visitors who have traveled long distances to see them. Many of these prisoners have not had visits from the outside world in years. They are not permitted to make phone calls except for emergencies

or other extraordinary circumstances. As one prisoner told me: "Family and friends, after the years, they just start dropping off. Plus, the mail here is real irregular. We can't even take pictures of ourselves" to send to loved ones.[3] Their isolation from the social world, a world to which most of them will return, could hardly be more complete.

The operational procedures employed within the units themselves insure that even interactions with correctional staff occur infrequently and on highly distorted, unnatural terms. The institutional routines are structured so that prisoners are within close proximity of staff only when they are being fed, visually searched through the window of the control booth before going to "yard," being placed in chains and escorted elsewhere within the institution. There is always a physical barrier or mechanical restraint between them and other human beings.

The only exceptions occur for prisoners who are double-celled. Yet double-celling under these conditions hardly constitutes normal social contact. In fact, it is difficult to conceptualize a more strained and perverse form of intense and intrusive social interaction. For many prisoners, this kind of forced, invasive contact becomes a source of conflict and pain. They are thrust into intimate, constant co-living with another person—typically a total stranger—whose entire existence is similarly and unavoidably co-mingled with their own. Such pressurized contact can become the occasion for explosive violence. It also fails to provide any semblance of social "reality testing" that is intrinsic to human social existence.[4]

The psychological significance of this level of long-term social deprivation cannot be overstated. The destructive consequences can only be understood in terms of the profound importance of social contact and social context in providing an interpretive framework for all human experience, no matter how personal and seemingly private. Human identity formation occurs by virtue of social contact with others. As one SHU prisoner explained: "I liked to be around people. I'm happy and I enjoy people. They take that away from you [here]. It's like we're dead. As the Catholics say, in purgatory.

They've taken away everything that might give a little purpose to your life." Moreover, when our reality is not grounded in social context, the internal stimuli and beliefs that we generate are impossible to test against the reactions of others. For this reason, the first step in any program of extreme social influence—ranging from police interrogation to indoctrination and "brainwashing"—is to isolate the intended targets from others and to create a context in which social reality testing is controlled by those who would shape their thoughts, beliefs, emotions, and behavior. Most people are so disoriented by the loss of social context that they become highly malleable, unnaturally sensitive, and vulnerable to the influence of those who control the environment around them. Indeed, this may be its very purpose. As one SHU prisoner told me: "You're going to be what the place wants you to be or you're going to be nothing."

Long-term confinement under these conditions has several predictable psychological consequences. Although not everyone will manifest negative psychological effects to the same degree, and it is difficult to specify the point in time at which the destructive consequences will manifest themselves, few escape unscathed. The norms of prison life require prisoners to struggle to conceal weakness, to minimize admissions of psychic damage or pain. It is part of a prisoner ethic in which preserving dignity and autonomy, and minimizing vulnerability, is highly valued. Thus, the early stages of these destructive processes are often effectively concealed. They will not be apparent to untrained or casual observers, nor will they be revealed to persons whom the prisoners do not trust. But over time, the more damaging parts of adaptation to this kind of environment begin to emerge and become more obvious.[5]

The first adaptation derives from the totality of control that is created inside a place like Pelican Bay. Incarceration itself makes prisoners dependent to some degree upon institutional routines to guide and organize their behavior. However, the totality of control imposed in a place like Pelican Bay is extreme enough to produce a qualitatively different adaptation. Eventually, many prisoners become entirely dependent upon the structure and routines of the institution for the control of their behavior. There are two related components to this adaptation. Some prisoners become dependent upon the institution to *limit* their behavior. That is, because their behavior is so carefully and completely circumscribed during their confinement in lockup, they begin to lose the ability to set limits for themselves. Some report becoming uncomfortable with even small amounts of freedom because they have lost the sense of how to behave without the constantly enforced restrictions, tight external structure, and totality of behavioral restraints.

Other prisoners suffer an opposite but related reaction caused by the same set of circumstances. These prisoners lose the ability to *initiate* behavior of any kind—to organize their own lives around activity and purpose—because they have been stripped of any opportunity to do so for such prolonged periods of time. Apathy and lethargy set in. They report being tired all the time, despite the fact that they have been allowed to do nothing. They find it difficult to focus their attention, their minds wander, they cannot concentrate or organize thoughts or actions in a coherent way. In extreme cases, a sense of profound despair and hopelessness is created.

The experience of total social isolation can lead, paradoxically, to social withdrawal. That is, some prisoners in isolation draw further into themselves as a way of adjusting to the deprivation of meaningful social contact imposed upon them. They become uncomfortable in the course of the little social contact they are permitted. They take steps to avoid even that—by refusing to go to "yard," refraining from conversation with staff, discouraging any visits from family members or friends, and ceasing correspondence with the outside world. They move from being starved for social contact to being frightened by it. Of course, as they become increasingly unfamiliar and uncomfortable with social interaction, they are further alienated from others and disoriented in their presence.

The absence of social contact and social context creates an air of unreality to one's existence in these units. Some prisoners act out as a way of getting a reaction from their environment, proving to themselves that they still exist, that they are still alive and capable of eliciting a human response—however hostile—from other human beings. This is the context in which seemingly irrational refusals of prisoners to "cuff up" take place—which occur in the Pelican Bay SHU with some regularity, in spite of the knowledge that such refusals invariably result in brutal "cell extractions" in which they are physically subdued, struck with a large shield and special cell extraction baton, and likely to be shot with a taser gun or wooden or rubber bullets before being placed in leg irons and handcuffs.[6] In some cases, another pattern emerges. The line between their own thought processes and the bizarre reality around them becomes increasingly tenuous. Social contact grounds and anchors us; when it is gone, there is nothing to take its place. Moreover, for some, the environment around them is so painful and so painfully impossible to make sense of, that they create their own reality, one seemingly "crazy" but easier for them to tolerate and make sense of. Thus, they live in world of fantasy instead of the world of control, surveillance, and inhumanity that has been imposed upon them by the explicit and conscious policies of the correctional authorities.

For others, the deprivations, the restrictions, and the totality of control fills them with intolerable levels of frustration. Combined with the complete absence of activity or meaningful outlets through which they can vent this frustration, it can lead to outright anger and then to rage. This rage is a reaction against, not a justification for, their oppressive confinement. Such anger cannot be abated by intensifying the very deprivations that have produced it. They will fight against the system that they perceive only as having surrounded and oppressed them. Some will lash out violently against the people whom they hold responsible for the frustration and deprivation that fills their lives. Ultimately, the outward expression of this violent frustration is marked by its irrational-

ity, primarily because of the way in which it leads prisoners into courses of action that further insure their continued mistreatment. But the levels of deprivation are so profound, and the resulting frustration so immediate and overwhelming, that for some this lesson is unlikely ever to be learned. The pattern can only be broken through drastic changes in the nature of the environment, changes that produce more habitable and less painful conditions of confinement. The magnitude and extremity of oppressive control that exists in these units helps to explain another feature of confinement in the Pelican Bay SHU that, in my experience, is unique in modern American corrections. Prisoners there have repeatedly voiced fears of physical mistreatment and brutality on a widespread and frequent basis. They speak of physical intimidation and the fear of violence at the hands of correctional officers. These concerns extend beyond the physical intimidation that is structured into the design of the units themselves—the totality of restraint, the presence of guards who are all clad in heavy flak jackets inside the units, the use of chains to move prisoners out of their cells, and the constant presence of control officers armed with assault rifles slung across their chests as they monitor prisoners within their housing units. Beyond this, prisoners speak of the frequency of "cell extractions" which they describe in frightening terms. Most have witnessed extractions in which groups of correctional officers (the previously described "cell extraction team") have entered prisoners' cells, fired wooden or rubber bullets and electrical tasers at prisoners, forcibly chained and removed them from their cells, sometimes for the slightest provocation (such as the failure to return food trays on command). And many note that this mistreatment may be precipitated by prisoners whose obvious psychiatric problems preclude them from conforming to SHU rules or responding to commands issued by correctional officers.[7] One prisoner reported being constantly frightened that guards were going to hurt him. The day I interviewed him, he told me that he had been sure the correctional staff was "going to come get him." He stuck his toothbrush in the door of his cell so they couldn't come inside. He vowed "to hang myself or stop eating [and) starve to death" in order to get out of the SHU.

I believe that the existence of such brutality can be attributed in part to the psychology of oppression that has been created in and around this prison. Correctional staff, themselves isolated from more diverse and conflicting points of view that they might encounter in more urban or cosmopolitan environments, have been encouraged to create their own unique worldview at Pelican Bay. Nothing counters the prefabricated ideology into which they step at Pelican Bay, a prison that was designated as a place for the "worst of the worst," even before the first prisoners ever arrived. They work daily in an environment whose very structure powerfully conveys the message that these prisoners are not human beings. There is no reciprocity to their perverse and limited interactions with prisoners—who are always in cages or chains, seen through screens or windows or television cameras or protective helmets—and who are given no opportunities to act like human beings. Pelican Bay has become a massive self-fulfilling prophecy. Violence is one mechanism with which to accommodate to the fear inevitably generated on both sides of the bars.

Psychiatric Disorders

The psychological consequences of living in these units for long periods of time are predictably destructive, and the potential for these psychic stressors to precipitate various forms of psychopathology is clear-cut. When prisoners who are deprived of meaningful social contact begin to shun all forms of interaction, withdraw more deeply into themselves, and cease initiating social interaction, they are in pain and require psychiatric attention. They get little or none.[8] Prisoners who have become uncomfortable in the presence of others will be unable to adjust to housing in a mainline prison population, not to mention free society. They are also at risk of developing disabling, clinical psychiatric symptoms. Thus, numerous studies have un-

derscored the role of social isolation as a correlate of mental illness. Similarly, when prisoners become profoundly lethargic in the face of their monotonous, empty existence, the potential exists for this lethargy to shade into despondency and, finally, to clinical depression. For others who feel the frustration of the totality of control more acutely, their frustration may become increasingly difficult to control and manage. Long-term problems of impulse control may develop that are psychiatric in nature.

This kind of environment is capable of creating clinical syndromes in even healthy personalities and can be psychologically destructive for anyone who enters and endures it for significant periods of time. However, prisoners who enter these places with *pre-existing* psychiatric disorders suffer more acutely. The psychic pain and vulnerability that they bring into the lockup unit may grow and fester if unattended to. In the absence of psychiatric help, there is nothing to keep many of these prisoners from entering the abyss of psychosis.

Indeed, in the course of my interviews at Pelican Bay, numerous prisoners spoke to me about their inability to handle the stress of SHU confinement. Some who entered the unit with pre-existing problems could perceive that they had gotten worse. Others had decompensated so badly that they had no memory of ever having functioned well, or had little awareness that their present level of functioning was tenuous, fragile, and psychotic. More than a few expressed concerns about what they would do when released— either from the SHU into mainline housing or directly into free society (as a number are). One prisoner who was housed in the unit that is reserved for those who are maintained on psychotropic medication told me that he was sure that the guards in this unit were putting poison in his food. He was concerned because when released (this year), he told me "I know I won't be able to work or be normal."

Many SHU prisoners also reported being suicidal or self-mutilating. A number of them showed me scars on their arms and necks where they had attempted to cut themselves. One prisoner told me matter-of-factly,

"I've been slicing on my arms for years, sometimes four times a day, just to see the blood flow." One suicidal prisoner who is also deaf reported being cell extracted because he was unable to hear the correctional officers call count (or "show skin"—a procedure used so that staff knows a prisoner is in his cell). He now sleeps on the floor of his cell "so that the officers can see my skin." Another prisoner, who has reported hearing voices in the past and seeing "little furry things," has slashed his wrists on more than one occasion. Instead of being transferred to a facility where he could receive mental health treatment—since obviously none is available at Pelican Bay—he has been moved back and forth between the VCU and SHU units. While in the VCU, he saw a demon who knew his name and frequently spoke to him. As I interviewed him, he told me that the voices were cursing at him for talking to me. In the course of our discussion, he was clearly distracted by these voices and, periodically, he laughed inappropriately. One psychotic SHU prisoner announced to me at the start of our interview that he was a "super-power man" who could not only fly, but see through steel and hear things that were being said about him from great distances. He had lived in a board-and-care home and been maintained on Thorazine before his incarceration. Although he had attempted suicide three times while at Pelican Bay, he was confident that when he was placed back in the mainline he would not have to attempt to kill himself again—because he thought he could convince his cellmate to do it for him. Another flagrantly psychotic SHU prisoner talked about a miniature implant that the Department of Corrections had placed inside his head, connected to their "main computer," which they were using to control him electronically, by programming him to say and do things that would continually get him into trouble. When I asked him whether or not he had seen any of the mental health staff, he became agitated and earnestly explained to me that his problem was medical—the computer implant inserted into his brain—not psychiatric. He offered to show me the paperwork from a lawsuit he had filed protesting this unauthorized medical procedure.

When prison systems become seriously overcrowded—as California's is (operating now at more than 180 percent of capacity)—psychiatric resources become increasingly scarce and disturbed prisoners are handled poorly, if at all. Often, behavior that is caused primarily by psychiatric dysfunction results in placement in punitive solitary confinement, where little or no psychiatric precautions are taken to protect or treat them. They are transferred from one such punitive isolation unit to another, in what has been derisively labeled "bus therapy."[9] In fact, I have come to the conclusion that the Pelican Bay SHU has become a kind of "dumping ground" of last resort for many psychiatrically disturbed prisoners who were inappropriately housed and poorly treated—because of their psychiatric disorders—in other SHU units. Because such prisoners were unable to manage their disorders in these other units—in the face of psychologically destructive conditions of confinement and in the absence of appropriate treatment—their continued rules violations, which in many cases were the direct product of their psychiatric disorders, have resulted in their transfer to Pelican Bay. Thus, their placement in the Pelican Bay SHU is all the more inappropriate because of the process by which they got there. Their inability to adjust to the harsh conditions that prevailed at these other units should disqualify them for placement in this most harsh and destructive environment, yet, the opposite appears to be the case.

Conclusions

Although I have seen conditions elsewhere that approximate those at the Pelican Bay SHU, and have testified about their harmful psychological effects, I have never seen long-term social deprivation so totally and completely enforced. Neither have I seen prisoner movements so completely regimented and controlled. Never have I seen the technology of social control used to this degree to deprive captive human beings of the opportunity to initiate meaningful activity, nor have I seen such an array of deliberate practices designed for the sole purpose of preventing prisoners from engaging in any semblance of normal social intercourse. The technological structure of this environment adds to its impersonality and anonymity. Prisoners interact with their captors over microphones, in chains, or through thick windows, peering into the shields that hide the faces of cell extraction teams as they move in coordinated violence. It is axiomatic among those who study human behavior that social connectedness and social support are the prerequisites to long-term social adjustment. Yet, persons who have been wrenched from a human community of any kind risk profound and chronic alienation and asociality. A century and a half ago, social commentators like Dickens and de Tocqueville marveled at the willingness of American society to incarcerate its least favored citizens in "despotic" places of solitary confinement.[10] De Tocqueville understood that complete isolation from others "produces a deeper effect on the soul of the convict," an effect that he worried might prove disabling when the convict was released into free society. Although he admired the power that American penitentiaries wielded over prisoners, he did not have the tools to measure their long-term effects nor the benefit of more than a hundred years of experience and humane intelligence that has led us away from these destructive interventions. Ignoring all of this, places like Pelican Bay appear to have brought us full circle. And then some.

Notes

1. In words it appears to have long since forgotten, the United States Supreme Court, more than a century ago, characterized solitary confinement as an 'infamous punishment' and provided this explanation for its abandonment: '[E]xperience demonstrated that there were serious objections to it. A considerable number of the prisoners fell, after even a short confinement, into a semi-fatuous condition, from which it was next to impossible to arouse them, and others became violently insane; others still, committed suicide; while those who stood the ordeal better were not generally reformed, and in most cases did not recover sufficient mental activity to be of any subsequent service.' . . . [I]t is within the memory of many persons interested in prison discipline that some 30 or 40 years ago the whole subject attracted the general public attention, and its main feature of solitary confinement was found to be too severe.' *In re Medley*, 134 U.S. 160, 168 (1890).

2. Its predecessor, the federal prison at Marion, Illinois, is now more than 25 years old and a technological generation behind Pelican Bay. Although many of the same oppressive conditions and restrictive procedures are approximated at Marion, these comments are focused on Pelican Bay, where my observations and interviews are more recent and where conditions are more severe and extreme. In addition to some of the descriptive comments that follow, conditions at the Pelican Bay SHU have been described in Elvin, J. "Isolation, Excessive Force Under Attack at California's Supermax," *NPP Journal*, Vol. 7, No. 4, (1992), and White, L. "Inside the Alcatraz of the '90s," *California Lawyer* 42–48 (1992). The unique nature of this environment has also generated some media attention. E.g., Hentoff, N., "Buried Alive in American Prisons," *The Washington Post*, January 9, 1993; Mintz, H., "Is Pelican Bay Too Tough?" 182 *The Recorder*, p. 1, September 19,1991; Roemer, J. "High-Tech Deprivation," *San Jose Mercury News*, June 7, 1992; Ross, J. "High-tech dungeon," *The Bay Guardian* 15–17, 1992. The creation of such a unit in California is particularly unfortunate in light of fully 20 years of federal litigation over conditions of confinement in the "lockup" units in four of the state's maximum security prisons (Deuel Vocational Institution, Folsom, San Quentin, and Soledad). E.g., *Bright v. Enomoto*, 462 F. Supp. 397 (N.D. Cal. 1976). In a lengthy evidentiary hearing conducted before Judge Stanley Weigel, the state's attorneys and corrections officials were present during expert testimony from numerous witnesses concerning the harmful dens of the punitive solitary confinement they were imposing upon prisoners in these units. Except for some disagreement offered up by Department of Corrections employees, this testimony went unanswered and unrebutted. *Toussaint v. Rusben*, 553 F. Supp. 1365 (N.D. Cal. 1983), aff'd in part *Toussaint v. Yockey*, 722 F.2d 1490 (9th Cir.1984). Only a few years after this hearing, and while a federal monitor was still in place to oversee the conditions in these

other units, the Department of Corrections began construction of Pelican Bay in apparent deliberate indifference to this extensive record and seemingly without seeking any outside opinions on the psychological consequences of housing prisoners. In a unit like the one they intended to create or engaging in public debate over the wisdom of such a project, they proceeded to commit over $200 million in state funds to construct a prison whose conditions were in many ways worse than those at the other prisons, whose harmful effect had been litigated over the preceding decade.

3. Most corrections experts understand the significance of maintaining social connectedness and social ties for long-term adjustment, in and out of prison. See, e.g., Schafer, N. "Prison Visiting: Is It Time to Review the Rules?" *Federal Probation* 25–30 (1989). This simple lesson has been completely ignored at Pelican Bay.

4. Indeed, in my opinion, double-celling in Security Housing Units like those at Pelican Bay constitutes a clear form of overcrowding. As such, it can be expected to produce its own, independently harmful effects, as the literature on the negative consequences of overcrowding attests.

5. Although not extensive, the literature on the negative psychological effects of solitary confinement and related situations is useful in interpreting contemporary observations and interview data from prisoners placed in punitive isolation like Pelican Bay. See, e.g., Heron, W. "The Pathology of Boredom," *Scientific American*, 196 (1957); Burney, C. "Solitary Confinement," London: Macmillan (1961); Cormier, B., & Williams, P. "Excessive Deprivation of Liberty," 11 *Canadian Psychiatric Association Journal* 470–484 (1966); Scott, G., & Gendreau. P. "Psychiatric Implications of Sensory Deprivation In a Maximum Security Prison," 12 *Canadian Pyschiatric Association Journal* 337–341 (1969); Cohen. S., & Taylor, L. *Psychological Survival* Harmondsworth: Penguin (1972); Grassian, S. "Psychopathological Effects of Solitary Confinement," 140 *American Journal of Psychiatry* 1450—1454 (1983); Jackson. M. *Prisoners of Isolation: Solitary Confinement in Canada.* Toronto: University of Toronto Press (1983); Grassian, S. & Friedman, N. "Effects of Sensory Deprivation in Psychiatric Seclusion and Solitary Confinement" 8 *International Journal of Law and Psychiatry* 49–65 (1986); Slater, R. "Psychiatric Intervention in

an Atmosphere of Terror," 7 *American Journal of Forensic Psychiatry* 6–12 (1986); Brodsky, S., & Scogin, F. "Inmates In Protective Custody—First Data on Emotional Effects," 1 *Forensic Reports* 267–280 (1988); and Cooke, D. "Containing Violent Prisoners: An Analysis of the Barlinnie Special Unit" 29 *British Journal of Criminology,* 129–143 (1989).

6. This description of cell extraction practices is corroborated not only by numerous prisoner accounts of the process but also by explicit Department of Corrections procedures. Once a decision has been made to "extract" a prisoner from his cell, this is how the five-man cell extraction team proceeds: the first member of the team is to enter the cell carrying a large shield, which is used to push the prisoner back into a corner of the cell; the second member follows closely, wielding a special cell extraction baton, which is used to strike the inmate on the upper part of his body so that he will raise his arms in self-protection; thus unsteadied, the inmate is pulled off balance by another member of the team whose job is to place leg irons around his ankles; once downed, a fourth member of the team places him in handcuffs; the fifth member stands ready to fire a taser gun or rifle that shoots wooden or rubber bullets at the resistant inmate.

7. One of the basic principles of any unit premised on domination and punitive control—as the Pelican Bay Security Housing Unit is—is that a worse, more punitive and degrading place always must be created in order to punish those prisoners who still commit rule infractions. At Pelican Bay, that place is termed the "Violence Control Unit" (which the prisoners refer to as "Bedrock"). From my observations and interviews, some of the most psychiatrically disturbed prisoners are kept in the VCU. Prisoners in this unit are not permitted televisions or radios, and they are the only ones chained and escorted to the door of the outside exercise cage (despite the fact that no prisoner is more than four cells away from this door). In addition, there are Plexiglas coverings on the entire outside facing of the VCU cells, which results in a significant distortion of vision into and out of the cell itself. Indeed, because of the bright light reflected off this Plexiglas covering, I found it difficult to see clearly into any of the upper-level VCU cells I observed, or even to look clearly into the faces of prisoners who were standing right in front of me on the other side of this Plexiglas shield. Inside, the perception of

confinement is intensified because of this added barrier placed on the front of each cell.

8. In the first several years of its operation, Pelican Bay State Prison had one full-time mental health staff member, and not a single PhD psychologist or psychiatrist, to administer to the needs of the entire prison population, which included over 1,000 SHU prisoners, as well as over 2,000 prisoners in the general population of the prison. Although the size of the mental health staff has been increased somewhat in recent years, it is still the case that no advance screening is done by mental health staff on prisoners admitted to the SHUs to determine pre-existing psychiatric disorders or suicide risk, and no regular monitoring is performed by mental health staff to assess the negative psychological conse-

quences of exposure to this toxic environment.

9. Cf. Toch, H., "The Disturbed Disruptive Inmate: Where Does the Bus Stop?" 10 *Journal of Psychiatry and Law* 327–350, (1982).

10. Dickens, C., *American Notes for General Circulation.* London: Chapman and Hall (1842); Beaumont, G., & de Tocqueville, A. *On the Penitentiary System in the United States and Its Application In France.* Montclair, NJ: (1833; 1976).

20

Attitudes of Prison Wardens Toward Administrative Segregation and Supermax Prisons

Terry L. Wells
W. Wesley Johnson
Rodney J. Henningsen

Focus Questions

1. What labels are synonymous in naming supermax facilities?

2. What opinions do wardens have about the utility of supermax prisons?

3. What do wardens think about increasing the numbers of supermax facilities?

4. What privileges and services are provided to prisoners in administrative segregation and supermax facilities?

In efforts to deal with an increasingly volatile inmate population, many jurisdictions have turned to high-security units, widely know as supermax prisons. The National Institute of Corrections (NIC 1999) cites these units as being "political symbols of how 'tough' a jurisdiction has become"; supermax prisons reflect a distinctly new inmate management policy, which Feely and

Simon (1992) have termed the "new penology." As is often the case in correctional practices, knowledge concerning the necessity, utility, and method of operation has not kept pace with the increased growth of facilities. The growing number of inmates confined in these high-security environments argues for an increase in research to examine their operation and effects.

This article examines the development of supermaximum incarceration and its link to past penal policies. Results from a national survey of state prison wardens regarding conditions in supermax facilities in their own institutions are presented and discussed in relation to the development of correctional practice in the United States. Wardens' opinions of supermax are summarized and discussed in light of emerging correctional practices.

Historical Development and Issues Associated With the Use of Supermax

Although not everyone agrees about the origins of supermax (King 1999; Ward 1995; Ward and Carlson 1995; National Institute of Corrections, 1999), Ward and Carlson (1995) assert that the consolidation of offenders in the federal system at Alcatraz Island in San Francisco signaled the beginning of efforts by correctional systems to deal with the worst offenders. Following the close of Alcatraz and major inmate disturbances at federal prisons in the 1970s, federal prison administrators moved the most recalcitrant inmates to the federal penitentiary in Marion, Illinois, and placed them under permanent "lockdown." In this "new" high-security environment, inmates had limited access to amenities and privileges and little direct contact with visitors or staff. This attempt to respond to the most difficult inmates received national and international attention and was soon implemented at other federal and state correctional institutions.

Facilities have been specifically constructed for the purpose of holding disruptive or violent offenders. The Administrative Maximum Security (ADX) facility in Florence, Colorado, is now the primary institution that houses federal inmates considered dangerous and aggressive (NIC 1997). At the state level, Pelican Bay (California) and the Estelle High Security Unit (Texas) are examples of state supermax facilities that have recently been examined (Henningsen, Johnson, and Wells 1999). At both the federal and state level there is an emphasis on security and isolation through the use of state-of-the-art technology and institutional design to provide "extended control" of inmates who are considered too disruptive for the general prison population (NIC 1999).

Defining a Supermax

Currently, there are no strict guidelines for determining whether a facility or unit qualifies as supermax. Various names have been assigned to facilities that operate under similar conditions and hold similar offender types. Administrative Maximum Security (ADX) is the term for federal facilities such as in Florence, Colorado. Across the United States, names such as Protective Custody, Special Management, High Security, Administrative Segregation (ad-seg), or Administrative Separation are used. Defining what is representative of this particular type of confinement has been problematic, and only recently have there been attempts to identify the characteristics that qualify a form of incarceration as supermax. In a national survey conducted by the National Institute of Corrections (1997) one definition of supermax housing is the following:

A free-standing facility or a distinct unit within a facility that provides for the management and secure control of inmates who have been officially designated as exhibiting violent or serious and disruptive behavior while incarcerated.

Such inmates have been determined to be a threat to safety and security in traditional high-security facilities, and only separation, restricted movement, and limited direct access to staff and other inmates can control their behavior. (p. 1)

King (1999) summarized the definition offered by the National Institute of Corrections (NIC) as containing three elements that characterize a supermax facility or unit: (1) inmates are physically separated from other units or facilities; (2) inmates' movements are restricted, and they are separated from staff and other inmates for safety and security; and (3) prisoners to be thus confined are selected by an administrative, rather than a disciplinary process and have been identified as needing control because of their violent and disruptive behavior in prison.

A later report by the NIC (1999) describes supermax as a

Highly restrictive, high-custody housing unit within a secure facility, or an entire secure facility, that isolates inmates from the general prison population and from each other due to grievous crimes, repetitive assaultive behavior, the threat of escape or actual escape from high-custody facility(s), or inciting or threatening to incite disturbances in a correctional institution. (p. 6)

The lack of a clear definition earlier raised several questions and concerns for research into supermax prisons. Is it the behavior of the inmate, the institutional design, or the conditions of confinement that should determine if a unit or facility should be labeled a supermax? Because of the differing definitions, the NIC (1997) report questioned whether the term "supermax" should describe the correctional architecture, the institution's security designation, or whether it should be based on the custody or confinement status of the inmate.

Research on Supermax

Research on the growth and effects of conditions related to supermax is sparse but generally involves two areas. One recent area of research has focused on the number of facilities, the number of offenders, and the characteristics of operation and conditions of incarceration. A second area has looked into the potential damage to an offender's mental health or psychological well-being in supermax confinement. The second area of research, briefly discussed here, is beyond the scope of the current study, although there is a growing body of research into the impact of isolation on inmates, as more correctional systems institute conditions similar to those at supermax prisons (Haney 1993; Fellner and Mariner 1997).

Characteristics of Supermax Facilities

Most of the available information about conditions of confinement in supermax facilities comes from government reports and from a national survey conducted by the National Institute of Corrections in 1996. The survey results contained information from the Federal Bureau of Prisons and state departments of corrections in all 50 states and the District of Columbia. In addition, the NIC survey included one facility in New York City, New York, one county facility in Cook County, Illinois, and the Correctional Services in Canada (NIC 1997). Much of the information that follows comes from the NIC report.

Findings from the NIC national survey indicate that there are 34 states operating approximately 57 supermax facilities or units nationwide. Many states reported the need for additional institutions in the near future. Thirty-six of the reporting departments of corrections cited the need to better manage violent and seriously disruptive inmates as the reason for new construction of supermax facilities. In addition, another 17 departments listed the need for managing gang activities as a major factor (NIC 1997). Although the exact number of inmates currently confined in supermax facilities is not known, King (1999) suggests that in 1998 more than 20,000 offenders were held under supermax conditions. This represented 1.8 percent of offenders serving more than one year.

The NIC survey also sought information about the criteria correctional systems use to place offenders in supermax, the method of release, and the level at which these decisions are made. According to the report, more than 20 departments of corrections (DOCs) use an objective classification system and a predetermined method for earning transfer out of supermax. The authority for decisions involving placement or removal rests at the institutional level in approximately half of the departments that maintain supermax facilities. In the remaining DOCs reporting, such decisions are made by the central office, by the director, or by an immediate subordinate. Over 20 of the departments reported that inmates can complete their sentences while in supermax. Concerning other conditions of confinement, 16 supermax facilities allow for physical contact with staff, usually during recreation, while 13 did not allow contact. In all facilities, inmates spend most of their time in-cell. Twenty DOCs indicated that inmates spend approximately 23 hours per day in their cells.

The NIC survey found that correctional departments with programs for inmates use a variety of methods to deliver services such as mental health care, access to law library materials, and religion. Fifteen departments reported that no programs are provided to inmates outside of their cells. Few of the DOCs reported a dedicated staff for mental health needs. Likewise, law materials are generally delivered to the cell upon request or are contained within a satellite or mini-library on the unit. The NIC reported that religious observance and materials are available, with 17 DOCs offering in-cell chaplain visitation.

Effects of Confinement on Inmates

In an overview of issues and considerations involving supermax prison, a recent report suggests several areas of concern for correctional systems (NIC 1999). Legal issues associated with long-term isolation, lack of standards for admission or release, and inadequate delivery of services were cited as potential problems. An additional and perhaps more important issue focused on the confinement of offenders, who may suffer from mental illness and the potential effects of isolation upon current and future mental health.

Various groups concerned with humane treatment of prisoners have harshly criticized supermax facilities for the potential ill effects of such confinement. These opponents suggest that supermax facilities house many inmates with psychological problems who may receive inadequate care and that the conditions of confinement create problems for otherwise mentally healthy individuals. Psychological side-effects of total isolation range from total dependency, pervasive hostility, spontaneous fits of rage, and unbearable levels of frustration to delusions, schizophrenia, and paranoia (Haney 1993; Grassian 1983; Fellner and Mariner 1997). Other critics question the causal order of the relationship between isolation and sanity—does control create psychological dysfunction or does the dysfunction cause the control?

Many of the arguments against the increased use of supermax prisons question both the possible effects of long-term confinement with limited human contact and the constitutionality of an environment associated with facilities of this type. According to a former warden of the ADX in Florence, the challenge of "operating a supermax facility is to properly balance staff and inmate safety needs against important constitutional and correctional management principles that govern prison life" (Hershberger 1998). The United States Federal Court in the 1995 case of *Madrid v. Gomez*, while noting the conditions in California's Pelican Bay as potentially damaging psychologically, failed to rule that such confinement had reached the level of cruel and unusual punishment.

The National Corrections Executive Survey 1998

The NIC's national survey (1997) initially provided most of what is currently known about the administration and conditions existing in supermax facilities. The data collected by the authors in the National Corrections Executive Survey (NCES) in 1998 provide a more current assessment of conditions within supermax facilities. The survey, while similar to that conducted by NIC, differs in two distinct ways. First, the NCES targets wardens and administrators of prisons. Second, the survey solicited opinions from respondents concerning issues such as the costs and benefits of confining offenders under conditions similar to supermax. By questioning individuals who are involved in the day-to-day operation of facilities characteristic of supermax institutions, a more complete summary of "extended control" correctional practices is provided. The methods in the collection of this data, methodological problems associated with conducting research in this area, and a general overview of the findings from the survey are presented here.

Terms such as supermax, admax, high security, special housing, and other such descriptives have emerged as "call names" to identify a new breed of correctional institution in the United States. They reflect the development of more restrictive types of custody facilities, designed to hold numbers of criminal offenders. Questions concerning the nature and number of institutions and the variety of conditions under which inmates are confined has made it difficult to evaluate what these institutions are doing and how well they are meeting their goals. Increasing the knowledge in the area of supermax facilities is important for at least three reasons.

First, more information about facilities that go by these various names will allow for an improved definition; currently, units that are often dissimilar in many aspects of operation share the same name. By collecting data that assist in describing common characteristics of and distinct differences between correctional systems and individual units, both practitioners and scholars can discuss issues consistent with their particular institution.

The second reason for increasing our knowledge arises from the growth in the overall national correctional system. As the number of offenders contained within supermax facilities increases, it is important to explore both the organizational outcomes and the effects of the nature of confinement on offenders' future behavior and mental health. Research in this direction is currently sparse and often involves controversial findings. More data and research information are needed to provide a better understanding of the association between characteristics of confinement and various outcomes.

A third reason for the need to collect data on facilities of this type concerns legal issues and incarceration. Confinement under the unique conditions related to supermax units triggers a concern for humane treatment of offenders. Questions surrounding the Eighth Amendment's prohibition against cruel and unusual punishment and other constitutional issues require that research projects collect and share information on the characteristics and operation of supermax prisons, perhaps for the preparation of guidelines for commitment to a supermax facility or unit and for the types of medical services and amenities to be provided to inmates.

Methodology

The data in this analysis are part of an ongoing project conducted by Sam Houston State University designed to address issues of confinement and the conditions under which inmates serve their sentences. The initial NCES was administered in 1995 (see Johnson, Bennett, and Flanagan 1996) and attempted, in a national survey, to assess the opinions of wardens on the impact and importance of programs and services provided to offenders during incarceration. As a follow-up to the 1995 study, the 1998 NCES was designed to target facilities that were said to confine inmates under conditions similar to those in supermax institutions.

The targeted sample was derived from a listing of all maximum-security facilities within the United States. The surveys were administered by mail, followed by an additional inquiry and second survey several weeks later. Each warden of a state institution was asked if his or her facility contained a specialized administrative segregation supervision area within the prison unit. Only wardens who responded positively to this question are included in this analysis. From the initial sample of 275 institutions, 140 surveys were returned, a response rate of approximately 51 percent. Of these 140 surveys, 108 reported that they confined inmates under conditions similar to those suggested by the literature to fit the definition of supermax prisons (King 1999). The analysis here contains the responses from wardens at the 108 state prison facilities; however, because of confusion over what exactly constitutes a supermax facility or unit, the authors suggest caution in data interpretation. One example of this need for caution is a report in the literature that no more than 60 facilities can be designated as supermax. This discrepancy suggests that the survey data may include responses from institutions that are not truly characteristic of these facilities. The NIC (1997) survey noted that definitional problems such as this had the effect of keeping some of the correctional departments from responding to its survey and resulted in information being presented on facilities or units not having comparable custody levels or types of housing.

Questionnaire and Sample Characteristics

The survey sought the opinions of wardens about the amount of privileges and rights that inmates are afforded and the characteristics of confinement in the administrative segregation units. The majority of wardens are white (77 percent) males (89 percent) who possess an average of 22 years of correction experience, seven years of which has been in their present position. A majority of Wardens (73.8 percent) reported education at the baccalaureate college level or beyond. Political party affiliation was fairly evenly divided, with slightly more (33 percent) belonging to the Republican party than the Democratic (26.2 percent) or Inde-

Table 20.1
Characteristics of Administrative Segregation Institutions
(Percentages in parentheses)

Variable	n (%)	Mean	Total N
Inmate Population (Institution)		1459	105
Inmate Gender (Institution)			
Male	91 (87.5)		
Female	0 (0.0)		104
Both male and female	13 (12.5)		
Percent population confined in ad-seg		(12.0)	97
Average age of inmate in ad-seg		28	97
Daily ad-seg count		133	102
Percent by race in ad-seg			
Anglo		(39.0)	93
African-American		(46.0)	91
Hispanic		(19.0)	66
Other		(8.0)	31
Percent identified as gang member in ad-seg		(23.4)	93
Length of stay in ad-seg (months)		9.5	95
Hours lockdown per day		22.7	104
Most common offense for offenders in ad-seg			
Rule violation	38 (40.4)		
Assault on inmate	23 (24.5)		
Assault on staff	16 (17.0)		94
Protection	10 (10.6)		
Gang membership	2 (2.1)		
Other	5 (5.3)		
Function of Administrative Segregation			
Institutional safety	66 (64.1)		
Separation	22 (21.4)		103
Incapacitation	6 (5.8)		
Discipline	5 (4.9)		
Isolation	2 (1.9)		
Allow two or more in single cell in ad-seg			
Yes	36 (34.0)		
No	70 (66.0)		106
Require periods of silence in ad-seg			
Yes	24 (22.9)		105
No	81 (77.1)		
Common area in ad-seg unit			
Yes	39 (36.8)		106
No	67 (63.2)		

pendent (31 percent) party. More than a third of the wardens reported prior military service, with 50 percent in the Army.

Findings

Characteristics of the reporting institutions are presented in Table 20.1. The name given to the specialized unit varies among the respondents. Only 5 wardens gave "supermax" as the name of the institution; "administrative segregation" is the label used in over 50 percent of the institutions reporting. Wardens listed "special management" as the term used in 12 institutions. Asked to select the most important function of administrative segregation, two-thirds reported that institutional safety is the primary concern. Discipline and isolation are the main functions in only seven institutions responding to the question.

Institutions in the sample maintained an average prison population of nearly 1,500 offenders—mostly male. Twelve percent of the inmate population, averaging 28 years of age, are confined in administrative segregation. Twenty-eight wardens reported that over 10 percent of their population were in administrative segregation, and 14 respondents reported over 30 percent of the popula-

Table 20.2
Warden Opinion of Administrative Segregation and Supermax Prisons
(Percentages in parentheses)

Variable	Strongly Disagree	Disagree	Agree	Strongly Agree	Total N
Ad-seg/supermax inmates have too many privileges/rights	3 (2.9)	54 (51.9)	41 (39.4)	6 (5.8)	104
Our state needs more ad-seg units/space	17 (16.2)	49 (46.7)	39 (37.1)	_____	105
I believe we need more supermax high-technology prison units	1 (1.0)	21 (20.2)	57 (54.8)	25 (24.0)	104
I do not believe that supermax high-technology prison units are worth the extra taxpayer dollars it takes to build such units	36 (35.0)	55 (53.4)	10 (9.7)	2 (1.9)	103

Table 20.3
Current Privileges in Administrative Segregation Units
(Percentages in parentheses)

Variable	YES n (%)	NO n (%)	Total N
In-Cell Privileges			
Commode	106 (100.0)	_____	106
Intercom	28 (27.7)	73 (72.3)	101
Shower	11 (11.0)	89 (89.0)	100
Inmate Control in Cell			
Commode	100 (95.2)	5 (04.8)	105
Water	89 (84.8)	16(15.2)	105
Lights	54 (54.0)	46 (46.0)	100
Intercom	22 (23.2)	73 (76.8)	95
Shower	18 (18.0)	82 (82.0)	100
Subject to Restriction/Reduction			
Recreation Time	97 (91.5)	8 (7.5)	106
Telephone	97 (91.5)	9 (8.5)	106
Visitations	94 (88.7)	12 (11.3)	106
Television time	76 (76.0)	24 (24.0)	100
Mail	23 (23.3)	79 (76.7)	103
Allowed to Keep in Cell			
Reading Material	105 (99.1)	1 (.09)	106
Sexually oriented reading material	66 (62.9)	39 (37.1)	105
Radios	65 (62.5)	39 (37.5)	104
CD or tape players	26 (24.5)	80 (75.5)	106
Non-uniform clothing	21 (20.0)	84 (80.0)	105

tion confined in administrative segregation. The approximate cell size is about 71 square feet and ranged from 32 to 158 square feet. Of inmates confined in administrative segregation, 46 percent are identified as African American. Although nearly a fourth of the offenders are identified as gang members, only two wardens reported that gang membership itself is sufficient for commitment to administrative segregation.

The survey contained four questions directed at the opinion of wardens in areas of privileges afforded inmates and the need for bed space or new facilities. Table 20.2 reports the opinions of the wardens in these areas.

The wardens' responses are mixed concerning the privileges and rights afforded to inmates. While a slight majority do not believe that offenders have too many liberties (54.8 percent), over 45 percent suggest that inmates have enjoyed more privileges than required. When considering the need for more bed space and construction, wardens overwhelmingly support building more supermax prisons (78.8 percent) but suggest that their individual states do not require additional administrative segregation facilities or units. Over 88 percent of the wardens agreed that the new high-tech prisons, characteristic of supermax, are worth spending taxpayer dollars.

Table 20.3 presents the results from questions concerning the privileges provided to inmates confined in administrative segregation units. In the area of basic needs, only commodes are provided in the inmate's cell in all institutions. Inmates have the ability to control water in most of the facilities, but only a slight majority of wardens reported that offenders have control of lights in the cell. Services such as visitation, television viewing, and recreation are all subject to restrictions in most facilities. In addition, the majority of wardens reported that inmates are not allowed to keep items such as non-uniform clothing and CD or tape players. Most facilities allow radios and, with the exception of one facility, all provide reading material.

Table 20.4 reports on the provision of services such as education, legal assistance, physical and mental health care, recreation, and availability of religious observances.

With the exception of library services (which most provide), vocational training (which only one provides), and college education (which 13 percent provide), respondents are split over offering educational services. Slightly more than half reported that their facility provides high school education and basic literacy education. Concerning the offering of legal services, most wardens reported that offenders have access to law materials and legal assistance. Only visits to the library are prohibited in the majority of facilities.

The majority of wardens also reported that their facilities provide health-care screening, AIDS treatment, dental care, and individualized medical care. Over 61 percent of the wardens reported that their facility provides a dedicated health-care staff. In the area of mental health care, a large percentage provide a dedicated psychiatric staff and routine screening, but less than a third have a psychiatric clinic on the unit.

Recreational opportunities are limited in the facilities reporting. Although most provide an exercise yard and 40 percent allow basketball, all other activities are extremely limited. With limited time out of their cells, prisoners have few options for recreation. Religious observances, such as chaplain cell visits and the providing of religious material, are available in over 90 percent of the facilities, and cell-front services are conducted in nearly half the units.

Summary and Conclusions

The present study has attempted to contribute to a description of services provided inside supermax facilites. While many of the findings in this study are supportive of those presented by the National Institute of Corrections (1997), this study has attempted to expand the amount of knowledge on supermax prisons by exploring the opinions of wardens and current conditions at an institutional level. The majority of wardens responding to the survey supported the construction of new supermax prisons but are divided over whether inmates receive too many privileges and rights. Using taxpayer money for building supermax facilities was

Table 20.4
Current Amenities and Activities in Administrative Segregation Units
(Percentages in parentheses)

Variable	YES n (%)	Total N	Variable	YES n (%)	Total N
Educational Services			**Other Amenities**		
Vocational training	1 (01.0)	100	Special diet (religion/health related)	101 (97.1)	104
High school education	47 (45.6)	103	Air conditioning	39 (37.5)	104
College education	13 (12.9)	101	Telephone calls (emergency basis)	78 (74.3)	105
Basic literacy education	45 (45.0)	100	Mail privileges	105 (99.1)	106
Library services	93 (90.3)	103			
Legal Services			**Recreation Programs/Equipment**		
Access to law library material	90 (87.4)	103	Weightlifting	8 (07.7)	104
Copy legal materials	85 (85.0)	100	Exercise yard	101 (95.3)	106
Legal aid visits available	60 (58.3)	103	Basketball	43 (40.6)	106
State-funded legal services	65 (64.4)	101	Access to jogging track	6 (05.8)	104
Materials delivered to cell	91 (88.3)	103			
Satellite/mini-library on unit	40 (38.8)	103	**Religious Observances**		
Inmates escorted to library	23 (22.5)	102	Chaplain cell visits	98 (93.3)	105
Access to legal help	85 (84.2)	101	Closed-circuit TV/recorded	22 (21.2)	104
			Religious material available	105 (99.1)	105
Physical Health Care			Cell-front services	50 (48.1)	104
Routine screening (on unit)	93 (88.6)	105	Services at a counselor cubicle	18 (17.5)	103
Clinic in ad-seg unit	44 (42.3)	104			
Healthcare staff (dedicated)	63 (61.2)	103	**Other Programs**		
AIDS Treatment/AZT	84 (83.2)	101	Anger management	43 (41.0)	105
Condom distribution	4 (03.9)	103	Substance abuse	39 (37.5)	104
Surgery (nondental)	62 (61.4)	101	Recreation (except physical)	23 (22.1)	104
Dental care	87 (83.7)	104			
One-on-one medical care	101 (96.2)	105			
Mental Health Care			**Television Privileges**		
Psychiatric staff (dedicated)	62 (60.2)	103	TV viewing	50 (49.0)	102
Routine screening (on unit)	88 (84.6)	104	TV in individual cells	38 (36.5)	104
Psychiatric clinic (on unit)	33 (31.7)	104	TV viewing restricted by content	19 (18.8)	101
Closed circuit monitoring	26 (25.2)	103	TV viewing restricted by day/time	20 (20.0)	100
Crisis intervention available	20 (20.8)	96			

also deemed appropriate by more than 80 percent of the respondents. Concern for safety was the number one reason cited by the wardens for isolating offenders.

Current conditions of confinement were also examined. The wardens reported that, on average, 12 percent of their institution population is confined in isolation. Educational and vocational opportunities are limited, and offenders spend a large majority of time in their cells. Recreation is limited and inmates are often restricted in materials they are allowed to possess. Cell-front religious observance is available in approximately half the institutions, and many provide a dedicated staff for physical and mental health.

Little is currently known about the characteristics, operation, and effects of supermax prisons. Difficulties with conducting research and specific areas of concern about their use are well documented (Ward 1995). A clear definition of such facilities has not been fully developed, and requirements for commitment or release vary across correctional systems. As individual systems move toward the increased use of supermax facilities, more in-depth investigation is warranted.

References

Feely, M. M., and J. Simon. (1992). "The New Penology: Notes on the Emerging Strategy of Corrections and its Implications." *Criminology* 30(4):449–473.

Fellner, J., and J. Mariner. (1997). *Cold Storage: Super-Maximum Security Confinement in Indiana.* New York: Human Rights Watch.

Flanagan, T. J., W. W. Johnson, and K. Bennett. (1996). "Job Satisfaction Among Correctional Executives: A Contemporary Portrait of Wardens of State Prisons for Adults." *The Prison Journal* 76(4):385–397.

Grassian, S. (1983). "Psychopathological Effects of Solitary Confinement." *American Journal of Psychiatry* 140(11):1450–1454.

Haney, C. (1993). "Infamous Punishment: The Psychological Consequences of Isolation." *The National Prison Project Journal*, Spring, 3–21.

Henningsen, R. J., W. W. Johnson, and T. Wells. (1999). "Supermax Prisons: Panacea or Desperation?" *Corrections Management Quarterly* 3(2):53–59.

Hershberger, G. (1998). "To the Max." *Corrections Today* 60(1):54–57.

Johnson, W. W., K. Bennett, and T. J. Flanagan. (1997). "Getting Tough on Prisoners: A National Survey of Prison Administrators." *Crime and Delinquency* 43(1):24–41.

King, R. (1999). "The Rise and Rise of Supermax." *Punishment & Society* 1(2):163–186.

Madrid v. Gomez, 889 F. Supp. 1146 N.D. Calif. (1995).

National Institute of Corrections. (1997). *Supermax Housing: A Survey of Current Practice.* Washington, DC: U.S. Department of Justice.

——. (1999). *Supermax Prisons: Overview and General Considerations.* Washington, DC: U.S. Department of Justice.

Ward, D. A. (1995). "A Corrections Dilemma: How to Evaluate Super-Max Regimes." *Corrections Today* 57(4):104—108.

Ward, D. A., and N. A. Carlson. (1995). "Super-Maximum Custody Prisons in the United States." *Prison Service Journal* 97:27–34.

21
It's a Form of Warfare: A Description of Pelican Bay State Prison

John H. Morris III

Focus Questions

1. What are the conditions in Pelican Bay State Prison according to Morris's experience?

2. Why do prisoners come to Pelican Bay State Prison?

3. How does Morris's view of Pelican differ from Haney's view? How are Haney's and Morris's views similar?

The bus ride from Folsom State Prison to Pelican Bay State Prison is breathtakingly beautiful. You pass through Clear Lake with its raised boathouses, wander up Highway 101 through towering redwoods and alongside the Eel River until you reach Eureka and the Pacific Ocean. You stare, mesmerized, at crashing waves on glorious California beaches and at pretty women in shorts and miniskirts enjoying this warm May day. You cannot get enough of the sights, sounds, and smells; then you reach Smith River and the prison.

At first glance, there is nothing remarkable. It is just like all the other new California prisons (Ione, Corcoran, Tehachapi, etc.) built in the mid 1980s. That perception changes as you are escorted off your bus by two baton-wielding correctional officers, down a long, enclosed hallway to your new home.

California's newest prison, Pelican Bay, is also touted as its most secure and innovative, technologically speaking. It is home to the supposedly strongest 'hole' in the United States. The Security Housing Unit (or S.H.U.) is literally and figuratively a world unto itself.

There are two facilities, called C and O. Each facility is divided into ten units. The units are subdivided into six pods. These pods contain eight two-man cells. Not all the pods are double-celled, although they will be shortly as the S.H.U. fills. Each pod has a 'yard' with approximately 200 square feet of space, with twenty-foot walls. There is no exercise equipment. Nothing but you and a camera mounted behind thick steel mesh that covers the 'open sky' portion of the yard. Each prisoner is allowed an hour and a half of yard each day. There is one shower per tier. You are given ten minutes to shower and shave (without a mirror) and return to your cell.

The doors, run pneumatically, are opened and closed by a guard in a centrally located booth in each unit. Since the guard controls the doors and all traffic s/he is called 'control.' This guard has a rifle, usually a 9mm semi-automatic assault type. All prisoners are strip searched and handcuffed before a door is opened to allow you to go to or from the yard, the law library, the doctor or dentist, and elsewhere. Each prisoner is escorted by two guards carrying their nightclubs at all times.

Visiting is via phone and behind a thick Plexiglass partition only. There are no contact visits or conjugal visits ('family visits') for S.H.U. prisoners, as the rest of the state's prisoners enjoy. Even the law library is caged. Working behind glass are the free-person-law-librarian and his/her guard. You knock on the window and your order is filled. Books cannot be checked out. The library, which is only a law library, is understaffed and the collection is not up to even the simplified standards for a S.H.U.

Personal clothing that belongs to the prisoner is limited to the basics: running shoes, T-shirts, socks, shorts, and thermal underwear (all white). All other clothing is 'state issue' and consists of a mustard yellow jumpsuit which ties instead of zips or snaps (for metal control), white socks, T-shirts, shorts and so forth. Items such as deodorant, shampoo, and soap are either what you brought from your sending institution or what you purchased here at the canteen. The toiletries are placed in bags or paper containers after being removed from their original wrappings. Deodorant is taken out of its plastic housing. Things evaporate or dry up quickly or go stale in the case of cookies or chips. Coffee, tea, and Koolaid are sold, but no tobacco items. There is no smoking in S.H.U., no 'dip' or 'chew' either, no matches. Staff routinely smokes or 'dips' in front of you, but I haven't been able to smoke since I arrived, nor will I.

You are forced to send any other personal property home. If you are unlucky enough to be alone, you can either donate your property or destroy it. You cannot have your property set aside for you when (hopefully) you reach a 'mainline' prison after your S.H.U. stay is up. There are no rules which allow this practice and it only applies to S.H.U. prisoners. So you send all your personal belongings home; stuff it has taken you years to accumulate: your photos (you can only keep fifteen), books, tapes, headphones, levis, sweatshirts, pants, all the stuff which over the last ten years has made doing twenty-one-to-life bearable.

Mail comes every day except Sunday. It often takes nine days or more to reach you even from close by. It is either the Post Office's routing or the delay is here; you cannot find out which.

The former Governor of California, George Deukmejian, and the Director of the California Department of Corrections, James Rowland, both claimed that this new S.H.U. is only for California's worst prisoners, but you know that this is patently untrue. It is home to whomever a warden or program administrator wishes to send here. Although the majority of prisoners are here for either violent acts inside prison or for gang membership, gang association, or both, there are many prisoners who are not here for these reasons. Some are drug users/dealers inside the prison, and some are merely the unfortunate ones who have run afoul of some officer or staff member and were shipped up here.

The criteria for being housed here are specific, but not always followed. Like all prisons, there are prisoners who simply 'fall through the cracks' in the rules, and there are ones who get shipped 'just because.' Either way, the prisoners here are placed in S.H.U. for either a set term (e.g. fifteen months) or 'indeterminate.' Indeterminate is supposedly designed to control the gangs, gang associates, and anyone the Department of Corrections deems dangerous. It is to keep anyone named 'indeterminate' from ever going to a mainline prison until he breaks and 'debriefs.' Debriefing is a euphemism for 'snitching.' Until the prisoner debriefs and tells on himself and his comrades, he is here for 'life' or until he is deemed 'okay' by a judgment which is entirely arbitrary.

The whole setup is designed to cause mental, physical, and emotional stress. First off, the prison is located in a remote corner of the state near the Oregon border. Most of the prisoners are from the southern section of California, like Los Angeles and San Diego. This means that visitors must travel more than a thousand miles to get to the prison. Most prisoners and their families are poor. Travel costs present a hardship for these families. That is why visitors are rare.

The isolation goes on even inside the prison. Contact with staff is kept to a minimum and what occurs is formal. You cannot see out from your cell as in other prisons. The 'sky' in the yard is your one source of 'outside.' Even your senses are kept dulled.

Colors, when used, are muted, mostly just white, off-white, and grey. Although the food is outstanding in taste and warmth, the menu is unaltered and soon becomes predictable. These things taken separately mean little or nothing, but when placed together they take on an altogether sinister form.

Television is an example. To those few who are lucky enough to own a personal television, the situation is bizarre. The speaker wires are cut to facilitate the use of earphones because headphones are prohibited. Even though the region surrounding the prison uses local cable television or satellite broadcast, this prison points its dish at (of all places) Denver, Colorado. Satellite dishes are not taxed according to where they are pointed; therefore, there is no fiscal advantage to the prison for tuning—in Denver. Denver is at least 1500 miles and a couple of time zones away. Even the guards cannot explain it. I suggest that the reason is to isolate us from local events. Again, by itself this is nothing, but along with the grey walls, the limited personal property, and similar restrictions (e.g. you are given one book a week to read) the intent seems quite clear. Most people simply 'zone out' on Denver television or become exercise freaks, or both.

Even the cells are eerie. There are no mirrors. The only time you can see yourself is on the little knob in the shower. You shave on your knees looking at the one-inch reflection. There is very little for you to control in your cell. The light switch is a silver bump and no one seems to knows how it works. You have, of course, the usual sink/toilet combination to play in. Since showers are every other day, 'bird baths' are the order of the day. There is a weird, overly cemented table/desk/seat arrangement, which is uncomfortable at best, and a couple of cement bunks. The lower bunk has a couple of 'lockers' or shelves which are very poorly designed. They are so deep that anything pushed back is almost beyond salvage and requires a pole or whatever to drag, push, or pull it out. Though the cells are more than 80 square feet, with or without a 'cellie' (cell mate), they quickly shrink when you are inside them for 22 hours a day.

It is a physical and psychological form of warfare being carried out against you. No one could honestly say it is by accident that all these things 'just happened' at once. This is done to break you, to punish you, to ruin you. After spending years in here, what comes out will not be quite 'right.' But, of course, the California Department of Corrections has that solved. When or if you are released from S.H.U., you are sent to Pelican Bay's mainline. They have a semi-lockdown type of 'step' program there. If you screw up (an entirely arbitrary decision by some staff member who may have taken a disliking to you), you return to S.H.U.; if not, you are sent to another equally strict prison.

I lay there in my bunk thinking. Fairly soon, with all of California's prison building, this state will surpass all of the country's prison systems for sheer volume and will pass Russia's also. This is the thought that passes through your head as you lie thinking in your Pelican Bay Security Housing Unit bunk; this and a few stray ones of beautiful redwoods, pretty women in shorts and miniskirts, and northern California beaches with big Pacific waves rolling in.

References

Elvin, J. (Winter 1991). "U.S. Now Leads World in Rate of Incarceration." *The National Prison Project Journal* 6 (1):1–2.

McConnell, J. V. (April 1970). "Criminals Can Be Brainwashed—Now." *Psychology Today*.

Chapter VII
Discussion

Supermax Prisons

It is clear from the readings that there are concerns about the psychological consequences and the legality of conditions of some supermax prisons. Haney describes the conditions he observed and recorded while interviewing inmates housed at Pelican Bay State Prison. Haney describes the sensory deprivation and stress that exacerbates mental illness and the lack of emotional control that likely caused or contributed to why prisoners were transferred to supermax in the first place. What is most interesting is that for many prisoners, the problems they have with lack of self-control, violent tendencies, and so forth, are intensified in supermax rather than helped through treatment.

It is important to note that not all supermax prisons are the same. Although some supermax prisons have minimal treatment programs (e.g., Texas), others have experimented with rehabilitation and with ways of providing inmates a chance to work their way out of supermax. For example, the Colorado State Penitentiary, Colorado's supermax prison—which opened in 1993 and houses over 500 inmates—has two programs. First, the "quality of life behavioral modification program" aids convicts in holding themselves accountable for irresponsible behavior and learning how to act responsibly and appropriately. In addition, Colorado has a five-level transitional unit to aid supermax prisoners in eventual transfer to a less secure prison. As of March 2000, 226 prisoners had been accepted into the program. Of this number, 188 (83 percent) completed all five levels of the program, and only seven people have returned to the supermax

facility—a recidivism rate of 3.7 percent (Reid et al. 2000).

Even within the supermax prison, there are different levels of freedoms and privileges. Wells, Johnson, and Henningsen found in their national survey of wardens that a wide array of programs and services was offered to prisoners in supermax units. It appeared that the majority of inmates had access to legal services, library services, medical care, routine health screening, AIDS treatment, religious materials, a chaplain, and an outdoor exercise yard. All inmates were fed inside their cells and had mail privileges. It was somewhat disconcerting that only 60 percent of all supermax prisons had psychiatric staff dedicated to the unit, and just over 40 percent provided anger management classes.

Morris describes many of the same conditions that Haney observed at Pelican Bay. A few years following the publication of Haney's and Morris' articles, one case (*Madrid v. Gomez* 1995) was decided by the Federal District court that forced Pelican Bay State Prison to improve the medical care afforded to prisoners in supermax, but it had little effect on facility operations as a whole. Supermax facilities remain characterized by video surveillance, sensory deprivation, and minimal contact between correctional officers and prisoners.

The problem with most research on supermax facilities is that it has narrowly focused on the conditions of confinement. Criticisms of supermax prisons would be better substantiated if studies were conducted to compare long-term psychological consequences upon release and recidivism rates of supermax prisoners with those of prisoners having similar characteristics who were confined in maximum security prisons. Future research should also investigate whether violent incidents are reduced because of supermax facilities and whether supermax deters other prisoners (who are not in supermax) from committing violent acts.

Reference

Reid, Larry, Pam Ploughe, Rick Wright, and Wes Lehman. (2000, June). "The Colorado State Penitentiary Progressive Reintegration Opportunity Unit." *Corrections Today.*

Chapter VIII
Introduction

Women Guarding Men

Common Assumptions	Reality
• Because they are (usually) smaller in physical size than male prisoners, women correctional officers are ineffective.	• Correctional officers rely primarily on their communication skills rather than on physical force in their encounters with prisoners. When physical force is necessary, men and women correctional officers support each other as a team. With proper restraint and take-down training, physical size becomes irrelevant.
• Friendships or romantic relationships between women correctional officers and male prisoners are tolerated.	• Correctional officers are trained that all relationships with prisoners must remain professional. Any attempt by male or female officers to extend or redefine this relationship threatens the security of the institution, and the officer may lose his/her job. In some states, a sexual relationship can result in a criminal charge.

Prior to the 1970s, women worked only in clerical positions in male prisons. Women began working as correctional officers in male prisons as a direct result of Title VII, a 1972 amendment to the Civil Rights Act that prohibited sex discrimination by state and local governments. Many states initially limited female officers to working in noncontact positions, or in minimum and medium security institutions. Legislation forced the government to allow women to work in prisons of all custody levels. For example, 1991 was the first year that women were allowed to work as correctional officers in United States Penitentiaries (USPs), the highest security prisons in the federal system at that time. As of 1999, nearly 22 percent of all uniformed correctional officers nationwide were women, ranging from a low of 7 percent in Maine to a high of 50 percent in Mississippi (Camp and Camp 1999, 134).

During the 1980s and 1990s, a sizable body of research assessed the attitudes and perceptions of cross-gender supervision. These studies reveal that male coworkers generally oppose the presence of female officers in male prisons (see Zupan 1992); women were seen by their coworkers as less assertive and too personal (Farkas 1999), and female officers report being sexually harassed by their coworkers (Pogrebin and Poole, 1997). The addition of women correctional officers has made no measurable difference in the amount of prison violence, nor has the presence of women increased assaults on male staff (Shawver and Dickover 1986). Other research found no gender differences in officer attitudes toward prisoners; in other words, women officers were no more sensitive to prisoner needs than male officers (Zupan 1986).

Despite these results, in a male prison, like in all other traditional male occupations, women are still defined first by their sex role and second by their capabilities (Pogrebin and Poole 1997). Future studies should focus more on integrating perceptions with work behaviors of female and male officers that include and exclude them in the guard subculture. For example, are women excluded from working in certain positions in the prison, or do women exclude themselves from working in these positions? Are women excluded from participation in breaking up an inmate fight, or do women refuse to be involved in physical confrontations? Measurable variables include number of incidents involving use of force, officer turnover rates, assault rates, and promotional patterns.

In sum, the weight of the evidence on women working in men's prisons shows that women have yet to be fully accepted and integrated into the prison environment.

Recommended Readings

Camp, Camille Graham, and George M. Camp. (1999). *The Corrections Yearbook 1999.* Middletown, CT: Criminal Justice Institute.

Farkas, Mary Ann. (1999). "Inmate Supervisory Style: Does Gender Make a Difference?" *Women and Criminal Justice* 10(4):25–45.

Pogrebin, Mark R., and Eric D. Poole. (1997). "The Sexualized Work Environment: A Look at Women Jail Officers." *The Prison Journal* 77 (1):41–57.

Shawver, Lois, and Robert Dickover. (1986). "Research Perspectives: Exploding a Myth." *Corrections Today* (August):30–34.

Zimmer, Lynn E. (1986). *Women Guarding Men.* Chicago: University of Chicago Press.

Zupan, Linda L. (1986). "Gender-Related Differences in Correctional Officers' Perceptions and Attitudes." *Journal of Criminal Justice* 14: 349–361.

———. (1992). "The Progress of Women Correctional Officers in All-Male Prisons." Pp. 323–343 in *The Changing Roles of Women in the Criminal Justice System*, 2nd edition, Imogene L. Moyer (ed.), Prospect Heights, IL: Waveland.

Internet Websites

Johnson v. Phelan (1995) decision: "Should women correctional officers be barred from certain areas of men's prisons?" Available: *http://www.kentlaw.edu/7circuit/1995/93-3753.html*

Jurado, Rebecca "The Essence of Her Womanhood: Defining the Privacy Rights of Women Prisoners and the Employment of Women Guards." *Journal of Gender, Social Policy, and the Law.* Available: *http://www.wcl.american.edu/pub/journals/genderlaw/archives/v.7/v.7.1/jurado.pdf*

Miniclier, Kit. Women Wardens Unlock New Perspectives, *The Denver Post*, December 4, 2000. Available: *http://www.denverpost.com/news/news1204i.htm*

Pollard, Jacinta, and Laura Sorbello. "Whore to Madonna and Back: The Challenge of being a Female Therapist in a Male Prison." A paper presented at the Women in Corrections Conference, Adelaide, Australia; November 2000. Available: *http://www.caraniche.com.au/wtm.htm*

22
Women Corrections Officers in Men's Prisons: Acceptance and Perceived Job Performance

Richard Lawrence
Sue Mahan

Focus questions

1. What assumptions have been made in the past about women correctional officers working in men's prisons?

2. Which group was most resistant to women working in men's prisons?

3. What perceptions did male correctional officers hold in this study about prison as a dangerous place for women?

4. Was a gender difference present in perceived job performance?

... Research studies have been conducted on the role of women officers in prisons, but the studies were either focused on women's prisons or included only a small number of women officers working in men's prisons. Other studies were based on interviews or observations of women officers, but the exact measures or bases for comparing women and men officers were not clear. There was a need for more research on women officers (see Philliber, 1987) that examined their acceptance and perceived job performance. That was the purpose of this study. It includes a review of previous research on women officers and findings of survey data from a sample of men and women officers working in men's prisons.

Research on Women in Corrections

Morris and Hawkins (1970) were among the first to recommend hiring women as officers in men's prisons. They argued that women would "bring a softening influence to the prison society" (1970, p. 133). Petersen (1982) suggested that the presence of women might have a "normalizing" effect on men's prisons, encouraging inmates to re-examine their overall view of women and increasing the likelihood of favorable adjustment upon release. Others have observed that women COs appear better able to diffuse potentially violent situations through non-violent interventions (Kissel and Katsamples, 1980; Zimmer, 1986), eliminating the aggressive confrontational tendency noted by researchers in the traditional male corrections officer. Inmate status from "taking out" an officer was no longer gained in the presence of women officers. Some have suggested that women COs were able to perform the job while being less intimidating, less competitive, and less physical than most men officers (Zimmer, 1987), and they could redefine officer-inmate relations, thus reducing tensions and improving the prison environment (Crouch, 1985).

Differences between men and women COs in styles of supervising inmates have been reported in a number of studies. Graham (1981) reported that women officers have a calming effect on male prisoners. Peterson (1982) found that a majority of a sample of male inmates felt that the presence of women officers improved the atmosphere of the institution, and nearly half of them believed that the presence of women COs tended to reduce tension and hostility within the institution. Crouch and Alpert (1982) found that women officers in women's prisons hold less "tough-minded" views than men COs working in men's prisons. Zimmer (1987) suggested that women bring their own unique style to the corrections officer role, gaining voluntary compliance from inmates not through threats or physical force but through mutual accommodations and friendly relationships with inmates. Pollock (1986) claimed that women often interact with male inmates as they would other men: friendly, understanding, and supportive.

A common expectation was that women officers would have more positive attitudes toward inmates' needs, or greater tolerance and understanding of inmate problems. However, Jurik (1985b) found no differences in men and women officers' attitudes toward inmates. In a study of 31 county jails in the state of Washington, Zupan (1986) found no differences between men and women officers' perceptions of inmate needs. Officers with more experience had less support for rehabilitation, but neither gender nor education was significantly related to officers' rehabilitative orientation (Cullen et al., 1989, p. 39; Van Voorhis et al., 1991, p. 493). Walters (1992) reported that women COs had significantly lower scores on a custody orientation scale than men COs (indicating less support for the traditional custodial role), but most of the women COs in the sample were employed at a minimum security institution.

Acceptance of Women as Corrections Officers

Corrections departments in virtually all states faced some resistance from men officers and supervisors when they began to hire women to work in men's prisons. The resistance ranged from subtle to overt. The single

greatest obstacle reported by most women officers was being accepted by men officers and being allowed to perform comparable job responsibilities (Szockyj, 1989; Jurik, 1985a). Women officers faced more resistance from men officers than from male inmates (Holland, Levi, Beckett and Holt, 1979; Petersen, 1982; Holeman and Krepps-Hess, 1983). Petersen (1982) studied women corrections officers in Wisconsin and found that men officers were more hostile to women officers and caused more problems for them than did male inmates. Women were more likely than men COs to accept other women as corrections officers (Simpson and White, 1985), and women COs reported better work relationships with other officers (both men and other women) than men did (Walters, 1992, p. 186).

Some of the earlier studies on women COs suggested that resistance to women officers derived from men's perception that women were inappropriate for the traditional all-male prison role. Some researchers suggested that the presence of women officers in men's prisons might have threatened the "macho" image and norms of behavior which often characterized the prison officer subculture (Crouch, 1985; Horne, 1985; Owen, 1985). Physical strength, along with threat or use of physical force to gain control and punish unruly or disrespectful inmates, had been an accepted role of the traditional corrections officer (Crouch, 1980; Marquart, 1986). However, there was evidence that the role orientation of corrections officers was more diverse and multidimensional in the late 1980s, with many officers supportive of rehabilitation and of adopting a human service approach (see Toch and Klofas, 1982; Cullen et al., 1989; Van Voorhis et al., 1991). Corrections officers who were new to the field held more positive attitudes toward rehabilitation of inmates (Cullen et al., 1989; Van Voorhis, 1991). The more favorable attitudes of newer officers may reflect the corrections system's recruitment strategies that were attracting officers who reacted more favorably to inmates. Positive attitudes toward rehabilitation may also result from new training programs for corrections officers (Jurik, 1985b, p. 537; Clear and Cole,

1994, p. 336). Changes in recruitment, training, and officer orientations may have led to a reduction in the resistance to women officers in men's prisons. Horne (1985) found that some of the initial strong hostility of men toward women officers decreased after women had been employed for a period of time. There was evidence that as women demonstrated their abilities in men's prisons, men officers became more accepting of them (Crouch, 1985; Walters, 1990).

There was also evidence that the roles and responsibilities to which women were assigned were not comparable to men officers. Researchers reported that women officers in California prisons were less likely than men officers to be assigned to the full range of officer responsibilities (Holeman and Krepps-Hess, 1983). Chapman et al. (1983) noted that most prison administrators had not developed legitimate roles for women comparable to those for men.

The introduction of women as officers in men's prisons met with resistance from many male employees (Peterson, 1982; Holeman and Krepps-Hess, 1983; Horne, 1985; Jurik, 1985a; Owen, 1985; Zimmer, 1986). As a consequence of their smaller numbers in men's prisons, women officers were minorities or "tokens" within the prisons and as such were closely observed but not completely accepted or assimilated into the prison organizations (Zupan, 1992, p. 330).

Additional burdens faced by women COs included problems of overgeneralization. All women officers tended to be judged by the actions and job performance of a few. Supervisors tended to limit women's job assignments within prisons. There was also evidence of discrimination by men supervisors in their formal evaluations of women officers' job performance (see Zupan, 1992, pp. 331–332).

Issues of Danger and Personal Safety

The need to maintain a controlled, safe environment was an issue for many who questioned women's role as officers. Many male prison employees believed that women COs presented a greater risk of being assaulted in a men's prison, and they doubted whether women had the physical and mental toughness deemed necessary for dealing with the dangerous prison environment (Jurik, 1985a; Parisi, 1984). Some men officers believed that women were more susceptible to victimization by inmates or were unable to back up the men officers in a potentially violent situation (Holeman and Krepps-Hess, 1983; Jurik, 1985a; Parisi, 1984; Simpson and White, 1985). Szockyj (1989) found that less than a third of men officers were comfortable with female backup during a violent confrontation (1989, p. 223). This perception led some men to believe that they must be over-protective of women officers (Bowersox, 1981; Zimmer, 1986). The available research evidence, however, indicated that women were not assaulted more frequently nor seriously than men officers. Holeman and Krepps-Hess (1983) found no differences in inmate-officer assaults between men and women COs in California prisons. Shawver and Dickover examined data from California prisons and found that women officers were assaulted significantly less frequently than men officers and they found no evidence that men officers were assaulted more frequently when there were more women working in the prisons (1986, p. 32).

Some resistance to women working in men's prisons revolved around issues of sexual vulnerability. Some men feared that women COs were vulnerable to sexual assaults by inmates. Findings that women officers were no more susceptible to assault than men officers should have dispelled this fear (Jacobs, 1981; Parisi, 1984; Crouch, 1985). Related concerns were that voluntary sexual activity with inmates or men officers would jeopardize the security and safety of the institution (Peterson, 1982; Jurik, 1985a; Zimmer, 1986), or that women officers might use sexual relationships with supervisors or administrators to gain professional advancements (Jurik, 1985a). A review of the available research literature indicates no evidence to support concerns about women officers' greater risk of sexual exploitation.

Perception of Job Performance

Many women officers believed they must work extra hard to overcome men officers' beliefs that women cannot perform adequately in a men's prison (Nicolai, 1981). Women officers were often given low-risk assignments away from cell-blocks in areas such as control rooms, visitation, and clerical areas where they had little inmate contact (see Jurik 1985a, pp. 384–385; and Zimmer, 1986, pp. 86–88). Few studies had been conducted in which researchers compared the job performance of men and women COs, but available research indicated that gender was not a significant factor in adjustment, attitudes, or performance of corrections officers (see Zupan, 1992, pp. 334–338).

Most women COs were confident of their ability to work in men's prisons. Kissel and Katsamples (1980) reported that women officers in their sample were "completely" (8 percent) or "for the most part" (92 percent) satisfied with their job performance, and all believed their job performance was equal to that of the men officers (1980, p. 226). In their study of corrections officers in California, Holeman and Krepps-Hess (1983) found no differences between men and women on job performance measures. Fry and Glaser (1987) found no significant differences between men and women officers in their adjustment to prison work or in their ability to perform job responsibilities in men's prisons. Results showing comparable job performance of women COs were noteworthy considering that women were more often tested by inmates and scrutinized more critically by men officers. It was common for inmates and veteran staff to test new employees, and Horne (1985) found that new women officers in men's prisons believed they were being tested more intensely than new men officers. Zimmer suggested that because women were more recently hired to work in men's prisons, they were scrutinized more carefully and more was expected of them than of men officers (1986, p. 105).

Individual and Organizational Factors

Corrections officers' age and years of experience and the security level of the prison in which they worked were identified as significant individual and organizational factors related to attitudes toward inmates and

professional orientations. Jurik (1985b) found age to be correlated with officers' attitudes toward inmates, but in the opposite direction from that expected. Older COs held more optimistic attitudes toward inmates (1985b, p. 535). Cullen et al. (1989) found correctional experience to be negatively related to a rehabilitative orientation. Tenure on the job tended to diminish belief in rehabilitation and perhaps heighten a custodial response to inmates. In contrast, Van Voorhis et al. (1991) found that older officers were significantly more likely to have a rehabilitative focus.

In a study of corrections officers working in newer minimum and medium-security facilities in the western United States, Jurik (1985b) found that assignment to a minimum security prison was associated with more positive attitudes toward inmates (p. 526). She suggested that the relationship between attitudes and security level could also result from a selection bias in the recruitment of more positively-oriented officers to work in minimum-security units. Cullen et al. (1989) found that working in a maximum-security prison was not significant in explaining rehabilitation or custody orientations of officers, but Van Voorhis et al. (1991) found that maximum-security officers reported significantly greater levels of work stress and perceptions of dangerousness. The research focus in these studies was on the determinants of corrections officer attitudes toward inmates and officers' professional orientations, but the findings suggested that age, years of experience, and security level may also have influenced officers' resistance to women working in men's prisons and officers' perception of safety and dangerousness in the prison environment.

Purpose of the Study

The results of previous research studies revealed differences between men and women officers in their acceptance of women as COs in men's prisons, in perceived danger and safety risks posed by women COs, and in perceived job performance. Some researchers claimed that women employ different supervision styles in adapting to mens' prisons; others found no differences in attitudes or correctional orientations between men and women COs. Researchers noted some changes in the traditional corrections officer subculture and differences in younger and older officers' attitudes and correctional orientation. Age, years of experience, and prison security level were among the individual and organizational factors that were found to affect officers' attitudes and work orientations, but the findings were not clear and consistent. The inconsistencies in the methods and findings of previous studies indicated that there was a need for further research on women in corrections. Some studies included only small samples of women officers; others were conducted only in women's prisons, and some researchers did not clearly specify the sample sizes or the methods on which their conclusions were based.

The present study represented an effort to extend the three areas of research on women corrections officers. First, the present analysis examined whether there were significant gender differences in the acceptance of women officers in men's prisons. Previous findings led to expectations of gender differences in acceptance of women COs and that newer, less experienced men officers might be more accepting of women. The second objective was to examine gender differences in officers' perception of danger in men's prisons. On the basis of previous research findings it was expected that, in addition to gender differences, men officers with more years of experience and officers assigned to maximum security prisons were more likely to perceive prisons to be too dangerous for women officers. The third purpose of this study was to test for gender differences in women officers' perceived job performance in men's prisons. In past studies researchers found that women officers were confident of their ability to work as well as men officers in men's prisons, but that confidence was not shared by men officers and supervisors, who were reluctant to assign women to the same responsibilities as men officers.

Method

Sample

Survey forms were distributed to all 112 women corrections officers and a random sample of 180 men officers employed in the adult male correctional facilities of the Minnesota Department of Corrections. Subjects were assured that their participation was voluntary, and all responses were confidential. A total of 162 survey forms were completed and returned [from 86 men and 76 women], a total response rate of 55 percent. . . .

Findings and Discussion

Women's Acceptance as Officers

Subjects' opinions about women's acceptance as COs, and the extent to which they believed women were accepted by inmates, are reported. Results supported previous findings of women's lack of acceptance by men officers (Peterson, 1982; Holeman and Krepps-Hess, 1983; Jurik, 1985a; Owen, 1985; Zimmer, 1986). More women (67 percent) than men (47 percent) believed that women were accepted by men officers in Minnesota prisons. More women (74 percent) than men (44 percent) believed most inmates accepted women as corrections officers. The women's perceptions of greater acceptance by inmates were consistent with previous research findings (Peterson, 1982; Holeman and Krepps-Hess, 1983). Fewer than half the subjects believed that there was resistance among men officers to employing women. Most men (80 percent) believed women should be hired, but that was significantly fewer than the nearly unanimous (96 percent) response of women.

Additional analyses controlling for officers' years of experience in the prison system revealed that significantly fewer male COs with six or more years of experience (72 percent) believed that women should be hired as COs in men's prisons (89 percent of male COs with 5 or fewer years of experience accepted women COs). Fewer of the more experienced men COs (77 percent) believed that acceptance of women COs in their prison was increasing (though the comparison with 84 percent for less experienced men COs was not a significant difference).

Perception of Prison Danger and Officers' Safety

Significant gender differences existed regarding the perception of danger of women working in men's prisons. Most men officers (61 percent) believed that women COs are in more danger, but less than one third (32 percent) of women believed they were in more danger. More men (37 percent) than women (16 percent) believed that men's safety was endangered when working with a woman officer. More men than women believed that men and women officers' personal safety was endangered when working alone in prison (67 and 64 percent men, compared to 43 and 41 percent women, respectively). Men and women clearly viewed the potential of danger in prison differently. Men officers either had a heightened sense of danger in prison, or women minimized the potential dangers. The gender differences in perception of danger raised the possibility that more of the men in the sample were employed in older, traditional maximum-security prisons and/or that more years of service had exposed them to more dangerous situations.

Women officers have relatively recently been hired and assigned to men's prisons, and the women in this sample had fewer years of experience than the men (45 percent of the men had six or more years of experience; 76 percent of women had less than five years experience). When controlling for years of experience, more men officers (66 percent) than women (19 percent) with six or more years of experience believed women officers were more in danger than men officers. More men (40 percent) than women (14 percent) with six or more years of service believed that men officers' safety is endangered when working with a woman officer. . . . Analyses revealed that significantly more men COs with six or more years of experience in the prison system believed that women COs were in more danger (68 percent agree compared with 53 percent of men COs with 5 or fewer years experience). Signifi-

cantly more of the older men COs (44 percent) than younger men COs (29 percent) also believed that they were endangered when working with a woman CO as a partner in the prison unit.

Gender differences in perception of danger are in part attributable to the security levels of the institutions in which the officers worked, even though nearly as many women in the sample (48 percent) as men (57 percent) were assigned to work in maximum security institutions. Additional analyses controlling for security level revealed significant differences between officers working in maximum compared with minimum or medium security facilities. More men (46 percent) and women officers (26 percent) working in maximum security facilities than men (30 percent) and women (11 percent) in minimum or medium security prisons believed men's safety was endangered when working with a woman officer. More men (71 percent) and women officers (56 percent) in maximum security prisons compared with men (63 percent) and women officers (33 percent) in minimum and medium security prisons believed women officers were in more danger when working in men's prisons. More men than women officers in the sample were assigned to the state's two older traditional maximum security prisons (66 percent compared to 30 percent of women). More of the women (18 percent) than men (9 percent) in the sample were assigned to the state's maximum security "new generation prison." Working in the older, traditional maximum security prisons may also partially explain the men's greater perceived danger. Researchers noted a relationship between officer attitudes and orientation and the organizational structure and working conditions in prisons (Jurik and Halemba, 1984; Jurik, 1985b). The findings of this study were also consistent with those of Van Voorhis et al. (1991) that maximum security officers reported significantly greater levels of perceived dangerousness in prison work.

Contrary to men officers' greater concern with prison safety, there was no evidence of increased inmate-officer assaults with the introduction of women officers to adult male prisons. Corrections department data showed that 49 officers were assaulted in 1992; 46 in 1993; and 48 in 1994 in Minnesota's ten prisons (with a 1994 prison population of about 4,300 inmates and supervised by about 1,100 officers). Not all of the assaults resulted in injuries and women were not assaulted or injured more frequently than men (Minnesota Department of Corrections, 1995). This was comparable to findings that women officers in California prisons were no more likely than men to be assaulted and injured by inmates (Holeman and Krepps-Hess, 1983; Shawver and Dickover, 1986).

Perceived Job Performance of Women Officers

. . . Women officers believed (nearly unanimously) that they can perform all custodial roles as effectively as men officers. Most of the men (but a significantly lower percentage than the women) agreed that women officers can effectively supervise, write reports, maintain personal control under stress, and control *verbal* confrontations of inmates. In situations requiring use of physical force, however, most men officers did not believe that women were as effective. Most of the men in this sample do not believe that women could effectively use sufficient force to control inmates or control a fight between inmates. Just slightly more than half (52 percent) believed that women officers could back up a partner in a dangerous situation.

When controlling for years of experience, significantly fewer of the more experienced men COs (26 percent) than less experienced men (56 percent) believed that women COs can effectively use sufficient force to control inmates, and 59 percent of men with more experience compared to 76 percent less-experienced men believed that women perform as effectively during incidents and other emergencies. Tenure on the job or age of men officers . . . made a significant difference in men officers' perception of women's ability to maintain personal control under stress (70 percent older men COs and 90 percent younger agreed); controlling a verbal confrontation between inmates (83 percent older compared with 90 percent of younger men); and only 30 percent of older men COs

compared with 61 percent of younger men agreed that women were equally as effective as men in controlling a fight between inmates. Controlling for security level of prisons in which the officers worked revealed significant differences between men (but not women) officers working in maximum versus minimum or medium security prisons. Significantly smaller percentages of the men officers in maximum security than men in minimum or medium security prisons agreed that women could effectively perform the job requirements discussed above. . . .

Among the men officers in this study, it was primarily the older men COs with more prison experience who responded similarly to men COs in previous studies. They expressed doubts that women have the physical and mental toughness considered necessary for working in men's prisons (Jurik, 1985a; Parisi, 1984). However, women officers expressed confidence in their ability to perform effectively in men's prisons and not be in any greater danger than men officers. And, the data indicated that they were not assaulted or injured more than men officers (Holeman and Krepps-Hess, 1983; Shawver and Dickover, 1986).

The final response item related to perceived job performance. It assessed subjects' beliefs about whether the presence of women officers improved the prison environment. Significantly more women (89 percent) than men COs (52 percent) in this sample agreed. Despite this difference, the data showed a greater level of men officers' support of women in men's prisons than has been reported in previous research.

Conclusions and Implications of the Study

One might question whether the findings of this study were generalizeable to other state prison systems. There are some variations in Minnesota. Only 9 percent of the officers were non-white (40 percent of inmates are non-white). Minnesota prisons had not experienced the severe overcrowding faced by many other prisons, though they were operating at or slightly above capacity, and Minnesota state prisons were accredited by the American Correctional Association. Despite active efforts to recruit and hire women, however, Minnesota ranked sixteenth in the United States for hiring women, who comprised just 14 percent of the state's corrections officers (Morton, 1991, p. 22). The results indicating low acceptance of women officers by men officers in Minnesota reflected similar findings in other states. The consistency of the findings with those of previous studies confirmed that the Minnesota prison system was not unique in this regard. Despite some differences in the size and racial composition of the prison population, the findings of this study appeared to be generalizeable to many other state prison systems.

The purpose of this study was to examine gender differences in women's acceptance as officers in men's prisons and the perceived danger and job performance of women COs. Significantly more women than men accepted the role of women officers in men's prisons, and fewer women than men officers believed they were in danger when working in men's prisons. Prison data on reported assaults and injuries to men and women officers supported women's belief that they were in no greater danger than men officers. Finally, significantly more women than men officers were confident of their ability to effectively perform the job responsibilities of officers in men's prisons.

The findings of the present study revealed significant gender differences in acceptance of women as officers in men's prisons. Most of the older men officers with more years of correctional experience were reluctant to accept women as coworkers. In contrast, many younger men officers with less correctional experience were more accepting and supportive of women COs in men's prisons. Analyses controlling for prison security level showed that more of the men officers assigned to maximum security facilities than men working in minimum and medium security prisons did not believe that women could work effectively in men's prisons without endangering themselves or other offi-

cers. The results reflected previous research findings showing that maximum security officers reported greater perceptions of dangerousness (Van Voorhis et al., 1991). Further research utilizing different measurements and employing longitudinal designs must be conducted to examine the effects of individual and prison variables on acceptance and perceived job performance of women corrections officers.

The results of this study supported findings of previous research that there was some resistance to women officers in men's prisons, particularly from older men officers with more years of experience in prison work. Such resistance is notable because it is likely to continue to place limitations on the role of women officers in corrections in the future.

References

Bowersox, M. S. (1981). Women in corrections: Competence, competition, and the social responsibility norm. *Criminal Justice and Behavior 8*, 491–499.

Chapman, J., E. Minor, P. Rieker, T. Mills, and M. Bottum. (1983). *Women employed in corrections*. Washington, DC: U.S. Dept. of Justice.

Clear, T. and G. Cole. (1994). *American Corrections* (4th ed.). Belmont, CA: Wadsworth Publishing.

Crouch, B. M. (1980). The book vs. the boot: Two styles of guarding in a Southern prison. In B. M. Crouch (ed.) *The Keepers* (pp. 207–223). Springfield, IL: Charles C. Thomas.

Crouch, B. M. (1985). Pandora's box: Women guards in men's prisons. *Journal of Criminal Justice, 13*, 535–548.

Crouch, B. M. and G. P. Alpert. (1982). Sex and occupational socialization among prison guards: A longitudinal study. *Criminal Justice and Behavior, 9*, 159–176.

Cullen, F. T., F. E. Lutze, B. G. Link, and N. T. Wolfe. (1989). The correctional orientation of prison guards: Do officers support rehabilitation? *Federal Probation, 53*(1), 33–42.

Fry, L. J. and D. Glaser. (1987). Gender differences in work adjustment of prison employees. *Journal of Offender Counseling, Services & Rehabilitation, 12*, 39–52.

Graham, C. (1981). "Women are succeeding in male institutions." *American Correctional Association Monographs, 1*, 27–36.

Holeman, H. and B.J. Krepps-Hess. (1983). *Women correctional officers in the California department of corrections*. Sacramento: California Department of Corrections.

Holland, T., M. Levi, G. Beckett, and N. Holt. (1979). Preferences of prison inmates for male versus female institutional personnel. *Journal of Applied Psychology, 64,* 564–568.

Horne, P. (1985). Female correctional officers. *Federal Probation, 49,* 46–54.

Jacobs, J. B. (1981). The sexual integration of the prison's guard force: A few comments on *Dothard v. Rawlinson.* In R. K. Ross (ed.) *Prison guard, correctional officer* (pp. 193–222). Toronto: Butterworths.

Jurik, N. C. (1985a). An officer and a lady: Organizational barriers to women working as correctional officers in men's prisons. *Social Problems, 32,* 375–388.

——. (1985b). Individual and organizational determinants of correctional officer attitudes toward inmates. *Criminology, 23*(3), 523–39.

Jurik, N. C. and G. J. Halemba. (1984). Gender, working conditions and the job satisfaction of women in a non-traditional occupation: Female correctional officers in men's prisons. *The Sociological Quarterly, 25,* 551–566.

Jurik, N. C. and R. Winn. (1987). Describing correctional-security dropouts and rejects: An individual or organizational profile? *Criminal Justice & Behavior, 14*(1), 5–26.

Kissel, P. and P. Katsamples. (1980). The impact of women corrections officers in the functioning of institutions housing male inmates. *Journal of Offender Counseling, Services, & Rehabilitation, 4,* 213–231.

Marquart, J. (1986). Prison guards and the use of physical coercion as a mechanism of prisoner control. *Criminology, 24,* 347–66.

Minnesota Department of Corrections. (1995). "Assaults on MCF Staff, 1992–94." (Unpublished department data memorandum). St. Paul, MN: Minnesota Department of Corrections.

Morris, N. and G. Hawkins. (1970). *The honest politician's guide to crime control.* Chicago: University of Chicago Press.

Morton, J. B. (1991). "Women correctional officers: A ten-year update." In J. B. Morton (ed.) *Change, challenge & choice: Women's role in modern corrections* (pp. 19–39). Laurel, MD: American Correctional Association.

Nicolai, S. (1981). The upward mobility of women in corrections. In R. K. Ross (ed.) *Prison guard, correctional officer* (pp. 223–238). Toronto: Butterworths.

Owen, B. (1985). Race and gender relations among prison workers. *Crime and Delinquency, 31,* 147–159.

Parisi, N. (1984). The female correctional officer: Her progress toward and prospects for equality. *The Prison Journal, 64,* 92–109.

Petersen, C. B. (1982). Doing time with the boys: An analysis of women correctional officers in all-male facilities. In B. Price and N. Sokoloff (eds.) *The criminal justice system and women* (pp. 437–460). New York: Clark Boardman.

Philliber, S. (1987). The brother's keeper: A review of the literature on correctional officers. *Justice Quarterly, 4,* 9–37.

Pollock, J. (1986). *Sex and supervision: Guarding male and female inmates.* New York: Greenwood Press.

Shawver, L. and R. Dickover. (1986). Research perspectives: Exploding a myth. *Corrections Today, 48* (August), 30–34.

Simpson, S. and M. White. (1985). The female guard in the all-male institution. In I. L. Moyer (ed.) *The changing roles of women in the criminal justice system* (pp. 276–298). Prospect Heights, IL: Waveland Press.

Szockyj, E. (1989). Working in a man's world: Women correctional officers in an institution for men. *Canadian Journal of Criminology, 31,* 319–328.

Toch, H. and J. Klofas. (1982). Alienation and desire for job enrichment among correction officers. *Federal Probation, 46*(1), 35–44.

Van Voorhis, P., F. T. Cullen, B. G. Link, and N. T. Wolfe. (1991). The impact of race and gender on correctional officers' orientation to the integrated environment. *Journal of Research in Crime and Delinquency, 28*(4), 472–500.

Walters, S. (1990). *Factors affecting the acceptance of female prison guards by their male counterparts.* Boulder, CO: National Institute of Corrections.

——. (1992). Attitudinal and demographic differences between male and female corrections officers. *Journal of Offender Rehabilitation, 18*(1/2), 173–189.

Zimmer, L. (1986). *Women guarding men.* Chicago, IL: The University of Chicago Press.

Zimmer, L. (1987). How women reshape the prison guard roles. *Gender and Society, 1,* 415–431.

Zupan, L. L. (1986). Gender-related differences in correctional officers' perceptions and attitudes. *Journal of Criminal Justice, 14,* 349–361.

——. (1992). The progress of women correctional officers in all-male prisons. In I. L. Moyer (ed.) *The changing roles of women in the criminal justice system* (pp. 323–343). Prospect Heights, IL: Waveland Press.

Practitioner Perspective

23

Working in a Male-Dominated World: Aggression and Women Correctional Officers

Denise L. Jenne
Robert C. Kersting

Focus Questions

1. How do women correctional officers handle aggressive encounters with prisoners?

2. Do women COs increase or decrease the rate of violence in prison?

3. How often is physical force really used by correctional officers?

4. In what situations, if any, did women COs respond more aggressively than men COs?

5. Did the findings in this study support previous research?

At a time when prison violence is becoming an increasing concern of most inmates and correction officers (COs) alike, the trend toward crossed-sex guarding generates much discord among practitioners, administrators, and policy makers, especially with regard to the growing use of women COs in male prisons. The controversy has been exacerbated by doubts regarding women's ability to handle volatile inmate situations. It is considered common knowledge, borne out by both "war story" experiences and existing empirical evidence (see, e.g., Holeman & Krepps-Hess, 1983) that women respond differently than men to violence. This difference is taken by many as indicative of women's ineffectiveness or unwillingness to contend with aggression. . . .

Yet research into gender differences suggests that the sexes generally do respond differently to external provocation, felt-anger, and their own aggressive behavior. Women tend to see the use of aggression as a loss of control and expect condemnation for such behavior, whereas men generally view it as gaining control in situationally justified circumstances (Campbell & Muncer, 1987). Thus women tend to engage in aggression less often and less extremely than men (Frodi et al., 1977, p. 637).

However, both men and women are more aggressive in the presence of and against a male over a female. Although men are more likely to initiate aggression, females are as likely to defend themselves against it (Maccoby & Jacklin, 1980). In fact, gender differences disappear when women are confronted with highly aggressive males because then women are "excused from the usual sex role requirement against retaliation" (Frodi et al., 1977, p. 655).

The finding that most violence by women is in retaliation or defense against male aggression is supported by case studies, ethnographies, survey data, and theory. Crimes by women seem to be "crimes of the powerless" committed in reaction to male supremacy, exploitation, and victimization (see, e.g., Daly & Chesney-Lind, 1988; Simpson, 1989, pp. 620–621).

The experiences of women in such violence-prone occupations as policing are consistent with these findings. Specifically, studies have found that women police officers respond to similar types of calls and deal with similar proportions of "dangerous, angry, upset, drunk or violent" citizens as their male counterparts (Morton. 1980, p. 25). Any existing gender differences regarding aggression and "control behavior" disappear in dangerous situations. However, there is no solid evidence that women defuse violence. Studies of police women provide contradictory data, although those with larger sample sizes indicate there are no significant differences due to gender (Linden & Minch, 1980).

Also, policing and guarding are not identical jobs, although the similarities between them are not negligible: Both are male-dominated occupations that stress their violence potential over their more routine service functions and the need for stereotypical masculine traits partially because they require aggressive responses to routine situations.

Available statistics on COs correspond with these findings: The increase in assaults on women COs parallels the increase in assaults on their male peers (Holeman & Krepps-Hess, 1983, p. 4). In other words, women officers are proportionally no more nor less likely to be attacked or injured by inmates than the men are.

Evidence conflicts regarding the relationship between the number of women COs in a facility and number of assaults on male officers. One study found no relationship (Zupan, 1992, p. 338), which suggests that women guards may be as likely as men to respond effectively to dangerous incidents and that gender differences disappear in dangerous situations; it also suggests that women are no more likely than men to defuse violence. However, a more recent research study found that as the proportion of women increases in a given institution, there appears to be a reduction in the number of assaults on staff (Rowan, 1996).

These and other findings raise several interesting possibilities about women in crossed-sex guarding: First, they suggest that if both sexes are more willing to aggress against men than women, COs regardless of gender might be more willing to aggress against male inmates. And, instead of diffusing violence in male prisons, women officers might be as aggressive with male inmates as their male counterparts.

Second, assuming that being a prison guard relieves women of the normal societal prohibition against their aggressing, it would seem reasonable to suggest that gender differences will disappear in dangerous situations behind bars, alleviating the need for concern about women guards' capabilities. In other words, the power relationships are redefined.

Third, it is possible that female COs are self-selected from among the more aggressive women in the population.

The issue of women's response to aggressive inmate encounters when crossed-sex guarding remains a salient concern, as yet unanswered by research. Although the existing literature on women in related fields suggests minimal gender differences, the attitudes of most practitioners and researchers maintain differences are significant. Thus the current study tests the following hypotheses: Women COs more frequently respond to inmate incidents in a less aggressive manner than male COs, and women COs see the use of violence as a loss of control, whereas male officers see it as gaining control.

Methodology and Sample

Mail questionnaires were sent, from November 1991 through June 1992, to individual officers of both genders working in six male penitentiaries within a northeastern state Department of Corrections (DOC). . . .

Eleven of the 16 critical incidents were used to compose an Aggression Scale:

1. You are given responsibility for awakening inmates for early duty. You awaken inmate X, whereupon he repeatedly tells you to "go fuck yourself."

3. An inmate has refused to let you give him a body search.

5. In a moderate tone of voice you have told an inmate to return to his work assignment. He replies: "Man, I wouldn't return to my work for the warden right now, and I'm damn sure not going to for you."

8. You are passing by the gym when a fight breaks out between two inmates.

9. You are working a housing unit where you fund several inmates gambling.

10. You are assigned to the dining room during the dinner meal. One inmate throws food at another, who retaliates. The first is preparing to return the counterattack.

11. In a routine, "spot" cell search, you discover narcotics in the cell of inmate Y.

12. While en route to your assigned post, you see an inmate smoking a cigarette in a "No Smoking" area.

13. While checking an inmate's pass, you discover it has been altered.

14. You politely ask inmate Z to move away from a group of inmates. He refuses by swearing at you.

15. While talking with an inmate in his cell, you spot something sticking out from under his mattress. You remove what appears to be evidence of an escape plan.

The female return rate was 34.9 percent of the original 229 contacted, providing a final N of 80 women COs. The return rate for male officers was 40.7 percent of the original 162, providing a final N of 66 men. The total N for both male and female COs is 146, or 37.3 percent of 391. For the follow-up interviews, a random sample of the 23 who agreed was contacted, resulting in 10 interviews, with at least 1 respondent from each facility. . . .

Quantitative Results

The two hypotheses explore gender differences regarding the aggressive tendencies displayed by correction officers. The responses for each critical incident were examined looking for gender differences using chi-square analysis, and an aggression scale was constructed from the incidents that provided potentially aggressive responses. Specifically, the responses for items in the Aggression Scale were dichotomized as aggressive or nonaggressive, making possible a score of 11 for aggressive individuals. Respondents' mean scores were 2.16 for women COs and 2.27 for men, which was not significant ($t = 0.63$, $df = 144$, $p = .53$). This finding suggests that men and women rate similarly on aggression and that neither is very aggressive.

Of the original 16 incidents, 9 elicited aggressive actions from respondents. Using chi-square statistics, the majority showed no significant differences between genders.

In three incidents, however, the differences were statistically significant. In each of these situations the difference was in the opposite direction than that hypothesized—that is, although still acting within the bounds of their legitimate authority, women were significantly more aggressive than their male counterparts. The three incidents that achieved significance were:

Incident 3—An inmate has refused to let you give him a body search;

Incident 7—You are assigned to the dining hall during noon feeding. An inmate deliberately dumps his tray on the floor; and

Incident 14—You politely ask inmate Z to move away from a group of inmates. He refuses by swearing at you.

Regarding responses to Incident 3, women tended to indicate they would most likely detain the inmate (73.0 percent), but men were less likely to respond this way (58.7 percent). Additionally, men were more likely to attempt to reason with the inmate than were women (17.5 percent and 4.0 percent, respectively). Also, women were twice as likely as men to threaten the inmate (10.8 percent and 6.3 percent, respectively).

In the situation where an inmate deliberately dumped his food tray on the floor, a variety of answers were provided. However, gender differences regarding these responses were most easily seen when they were collapsed into a dichotomous variable of aggressive or nonaggressive actions. Although men and women both tended toward an aggressive response, women were more likely to be aggressive then were men (76.3 percent versus 60.3 percent).

The most striking difference between gender was found in the situation where the inmate, politely asked [by the CO] to move away from a group of his peers, refused by swearing at the CO. Although both men and women most frequently indicated that they would order the inmate to move (50 percent and 76.9 percent, respectively), considerably more men than women (33.3 percent versus 11.5 percent) responded by talking with the defiant inmate. This difference was highly statistically significant ($p = .002$).

In contrast, when inmates were discovered gambling or in possession of narcotics, all the selected responses were aggressive actions, with the majority choosing to confiscate the contraband in both situations (70.8 percent and 61.496, respectively). Also, in situations that are in themselves aggressive, both male and female COs respond similarly. For example, when two inmates were found fighting, 88.3 percent of respondents indicated they would immediately call for backup. In the situation involving a food fight, the modal response was again to immediately call for backup (51 percent); however, 42.1 percent would order the inmates to stop, and 6.9 percent would use physical restraint.

It would seem, therefore, that men and women apply comparable interpretations to most inmate incidents and say they would respond in a similar fashion.

The second hypothesis was tested using the following three items from the control scale:

2. I feel most in control when I have physically restrained an inmate.	I feel least in control when I have to physically restrain an inmate.
9. Whenever trouble seems to be brewing with an inmate(s), I always call for backup.	If trouble seems to be brewing with an inmate(s), I try to handle it myself and only call for backup if necessary.
10. I find physical restraint is often the best way to handle inmates here and use it when the situation calls for it.	I find physical restraint is usually the worst way to deal with inmates here and use it only as a last resort.

. . . Neither men nor women indicated strong feelings of control when using physical restraint, but women seem to feel them slightly more than men. In the second item,. both genders indicated that they try to handle situations themselves and only call for help when necessary, with means of 5.5 for men and 5.3 for women. This difference was not significant ($t = .86$, $df = 140.51$, $p = .39$). Neither men nor women indicated, in the last item, that they found physical restraint an effective way of handling inmates. With means of 4.9 and 5.0 for men and women, respectively, and a significance of .88 ($t = .15$, $df = 130.55$), there was no significant difference between genders.

In conclusion, these findings provide no support for the second hypothesis, and at least one item gives marginal evidence that the relationship might actually be the opposite of that hypothesized. However, these findings are consistent with those presented above. Specifically, regardless of gender, COs tend to recognize the usefulness of strategies other than physical force in gaining inmate compliance and do not generally resort to its use. If there is a difference between genders, as marginally suggested by current findings, it is that women tend to feel more in control of an inmate situation once the prisoner is physically restrained than men do. To further understand these findings, the interviews will be examined next.

Qualitative Interviews and Discussion

The above findings apparently conflict with previous research and common assumptions regarding women in crossed-sex guarding. Hypotheses based on the existing literature were not supported. By exploring the issues from the eyes of the women themselves, we can delve into some possible explanations.

Aggressive Incidents

It was hypothesized that women COs more frequently respond to inmate incidents in a less aggressive manner than their male colleagues. Consistent with Zupan's (1992) finding that women COs tend to have fairly conservative sex role attitudes, the majority of interview respondents initially indicated agreement with this expectation because of perceived gender differences in "ego," machismo, "nature," and timidity. For example,

CO#1: Ah, I don't know, maybe females . . . ah, this might sound a little prejudice(d), but, as I see it, females, to me, seem a little bit more . . . um, what's the word I want to use, seem to encompass a little bit more before getting the job done.

Interviewer (I): And how do you think they do that?

CO# 1: Well, I guess it's just their initiative, in the way they go about it. Males deal with other males, and in that type of an environment, they probably go with a little more forceful manner than the female, who are totally the opposite.

I: Okay, so you think that men would be more aggressive then?

CO# 1: Probably . . . whether they truly mean it or not. Females tend to come from a female point of view, at the same time being firm and getting the job done.

I: Okay, and why do you think that difference would exist?

CO# 1: Because men are always macho, you know, they have to show their strength and all, this type thing, and that's not necessarily how you get it done. It's not necessarily the best and protective way. . . . Whereas, women speak to the human side, they go one person to another, whether they are incarcerated or not, a human being. Usually, in my opinion, [that's] more effective.

CO#2: Ah . . . from my experience, I find that a female is more diplomatic and . . . and . . . [better at] alleviating aggression.

I: Um hum. Why do you think that is so?

CO#2: Um . . . we don't have the macho ego . . . And, we prefer to um . . . um, reduce the levels, rather than accelerate.

CO#3: [Women] don't have a male ego. In order to feel that they did a good job, they don't have to get caught up in that ego, especially a female in a male institution.

As discussed, the findings did not support this prediction. Rather, they suggest that women officers are as aggressive as the men in most situations, and actually more aggressive in certain incidents.

When asked to explain the finding that overall there were few gender differences in aggression, most respondents expressed surprise. However, one offered the following explanation:

CO#1: Well, they are the same, because unlike the past, the department of corrections, when they saw a more forceful view is not necessary . . . Now, you more or less are to apply to the human side of a person. Even though they [inmates] committed . . . whatever, they are still a human being, somebody, person, a person. Try to understand the circumstance that caused whatever it is, and help the guy forward. Inside of that there is a human being, whether at some given time they act human or not. . . . So you more or less. . . . They far outnumber you. So, I would think that on the overall, the correction officer would reach for the human side. Because being a correction officer is unlike the street officer, you don't carry a weapon inside. Your weapon is your pen and your paper. So, therefore, you can't rely on your weapon here—you have to rely on your brain. So, I don't think . . . I think that's one of the major reasons you are able to relate to them more. You know, I mean treating them like people. Maybe some people don't choose to do it that way—but that's the best way.

This excerpt illustrates the potential dangers confronting those working behind bars and suggests that methods other than those that rely on muscle and force may be preferred. Similarly, it suggests that departmental policy, the occupational setting, and the exigencies of the job might be more critical than gender in determining officer behavior. Pollock (1995) proposed that similarities in the way male and female officers carry out their job may be due to two important trends in corrections—that is, strict adherence by prison management to formal and legalistic procedures and the increased use of standardized academy training of the guard force (pp. 112–113).

However, the role of gender is clearly not completely overridden by these other factors, as evidenced by the current finding that women officers do respond more aggressively than men in certain situations. One possible explanation for this finding might be attributed to the situation itself. For example, when asked to explain the finding that women COs were more likely than men to indicate an aggressive response to an inmate's refusal to be body-searched, one interview respondent suggested that because women are only allowed to conduct body searches in an emergency, an inmate's refusal to let her do so could be construed as a more critical situation than it would typically be for a male CO:

CO#4: Well, now as far as the body search, do you mean a strip search or pat search?

I: A body search.

CO#4: Well that is only done in an emergency situation . . . females are not allowed to strip search inmates of the opposite sex.

This respondent proceeded by suggesting another possibility:

CO#4: Ah (pause) . . . prob . . . ah . . . in my institution, I would say, because of being a female, you have to show that you are . . . because they look down on us, because society . . . the way it's been. The men are always the dominant one and the women have had to prove that they can actually do the job. And, when they are confronted, they've got to get more aggressive. And say, yes I can do it, and say, "This is what you are going to do."

Thus, because women traditionally are in the subordinate position in crossed-sex relationships, it might be that they feel a greater need than men to "take charge" by a show of aggression early in situationally specific encounters.

Although most prison violence is intra-inmate rather than inmate-to-guard (Clear & Cole, 1994, p. 271), it is while intervening in seemingly routine incidents that COs risk attack. In their daily work, guards must break up fights, take custody of rule violators, conduct shakedowns, and carry out other duties that can provoke the volatile or violence prone. Simultaneously and unpredictably, prisoners might challenge the guards' authority, make demands of their time or for quick decisions, push them to the limits of their power (Zimmer. 1986, p. 22), or open an attack on them despite the odds.

Gender and Power Issues

For a woman CO, who is more likely than her male counterparts to doubt her abilities (Kissel & Katsampes, 1980, p. 226) or to perceive the doubts of her peers or inmates, such challenges to her authority might evoke a greater sense of vulnerability than for the men. Actions such as refusing a body search or deliberately dumping a food tray in her presence could be interpreted as a direct challenge, a test that she must "pass" to survive. Thus she might be quicker to respond firmly than a male CO, who could perceive such behavior as a mere annoyance rather than a direct challenge. This explanation is consistent with the findings and received further support and elaboration from other respondents:

CO#5: I don't know. I can't really say for sure why that would happen. Other than maybe, I'm speaking for our prison, some of us haven't had as much one-to-one contact as the males. We haven't had the same details. Where we have six or eight inmates every day assigned to us. So maybe it would be quicker to, ah, call for backup, and whatever. I don't know.

I: So you would think, maybe it's, um, a question of feeling more confident calling someone else in?

CO#5: I think it's just not having as much experience, really. Because those jobs, those details things like that, they are . . . they only go to the officers with the most seniority. . . . I don't know. I have 10 years—but, that's not considered that much. I really couldn't say about other females. I don't think that too many have a whole lot more. But, I'm sure there's a few, but on average, I don't think they have too much more than that. . . . You might tend to call backup more quickly, than if he was one of your regular guys.

I: So you're saying, it's not so much time on the job, as experience working with inmates?

CO: Right.

CO#6: I don't know, I think we are expected, we are expected to be a little tougher, because men look at us as being weaker . . . so, we have to step it up a little bit, and be a little tougher.

I: Right. Okay, do you think those expectations come from the inmates, the other officers, or both?

CO#6: I would say from the other officers . . . because they watch us so closely.

CO#7: I think the women are pressured a little more so to do a good job. And the males there is somewhat of a bonding, they are not going to be nearly as rough with male inmates in a male institution. I think it prob . . . may be similar in a female institution . . . and, we are forced to be more aggressive in that field of work.

CO#3: I would be more aggressive because I have to stand my ground. I know I have to stand my ground. I let them . . . female-wise, if I allow them to think you can't win, they will all try it. So you can't let them see you back down. In the situation where you are polite and they are still act[ing] out of hand, then in that situation you have to really stand up to it. But, I don't know . . . why women were more aggressive, other than me myself . . . You can't get a reputation of backing down.

I: Do you think that's different for women than it is for men?

CO#3: Yes, because they think we are softer.

CO#1: Because I guess, being a female, first of all you are at a slight disadvantage when it comes to stress. So, females . . . it's just their nature, they don't back down or, as quick as a man, I don't think.

This vulnerability may be intensified when the challenge is made in front of other inmates, as evidenced by the high level of significance achieved in the situation where an inmate swears at the officer when standing with a group of inmates. The presence of others means the stakes are greater "in terms of self-image promotion and protection . . . than for either the inmate and officer alone." It is especially when in front of others that the guard is likely to give a strong show of force, reestablishing his authority, because group situations are considered the most dangerous (Lombardo, 1981, pp. 105–116) and the outcome of the encounter may be critical to both the present situation and future interactions with inmates.

No matter how improbable it is that an officer will be attacked, the possibility of being assaulted by one or more inmates, even in conducting the most ordinary tasks exists, and there is rarely, if ever, any way for the guard to foresee when it will materialize. Because so much of the violence behind bars seems to erupt over apparently trivial matters, its unpredictability is increased (Lombardo, 1981, p. 116), which, in turn, means the threat exists constantly. Put another way, regardless of its actual frequency, the symbolic importance of violence remains foremost in the minds of many guards and, perhaps, especially for women officers.

The bottom line is "the dominant position of the custodial staff is more fiction than reality" (Sykes, 1958, p. 45). In order to maintain its precarious position, the staff will convey the message that affronts to its authority will not be tolerated (Marquart, 1983, pp. 145, 147). Situations that end with violence may often be those in which there is a perceived threat—whether an inmate's perception of a threat to his dignity or autonomy or a guard's belief that his authority is in jeopardy. Because encounters between guard and inmate are generally seen by both as person-to-person transactions, the high level of tension between them may stem from both factions struggling to prove themselves. Violence is the end result of these "ego show-downs" (Zimmer, 1986, p.16).

Generally, current findings support previous evidence that "guards are motivated to use physical force sparingly because it carries with it the risk of being injured or killed themselves. Furthermore, force is simply less effective than other techniques" (Zimmer, 1986, p. 19).

Yet women officers, perhaps slightly more sensitized to their precarious position and challenges to their authority, could be more likely than men to respond sternly to an encounter that threatens their authority role.

This explanation is supported by the comments made by the interview respondents:

CO#8: You know, women would feel if there are other inmates around, they feel like they are being challenged, with the guys show off in front to their peers, if it has to deal with the women. So, then quite naturally, they are going to make sure the inmate follows the rule so that way the other guy observing is not going to try the same thing . . . Because, if that first inmate gets away with it, the second inmate's going to think, well, I can get away with it too, she let him get away with it, and might try the same thing.

CO#9: Anytime you tell an inmate . . . if you tell him with a group of people, he's not going to do it. Okay? . . . You have a tendency to have more problems with an inmate in a group of people than on one on one. It doesn't matter what inmate it is. If you do it one on one, you won't have so many problems because they know . . . you know, you are dealing with them directly, there is no one else. Like their peers for them to hang around and say, "She this, she that. . . ." Okay.

CO# 10: And an inmate drops his tray on the floor, guess what? . . . I'm not going to act like a real jerk and get aggressive with him. Because I have another 900–600 other inmates looking at me . . . I don't want to start an incident in the inmate dining room. . . . So an incident like that, I'm not getting aggressive in the inmate dining room. Anyone that said they did . . . is . . . I don't believe them. What you are going to do . . . what you are going to do is let him drop his tray, and you are going to kind of calmly just ask to see him a minute outside. Once you get him outside you can get a little more aggressive, but you are not going to get aggressive with him in the inmate dining room . . . If I walk up to an inmate and ask him to move away from a group of people, once again, I can't get too aggressive. If . . . if it's an incident that could erupt into a riot situation. . . .

It was also hypothesized that women officers perceive the use of violence as a loss of

control, in contrast to their male counterparts who would see it as gaining control. As shown above, this hypothesis was also rejected because neither men nor women indicated strong feelings of control when using physical restraint, but women tended to feel slightly more than men. This finding is suggestive: Although they generally apply similar interpretations to these situations, women might feel more control under particular circumstances.

Again, a partial explanation for this possibility may be the heightened sense of vulnerability that female COs experience due to their own self-doubts, which are fed by their coworkers and the conventional power relationships. Present findings indicate that women officers are as likely as their male colleagues to realize that not all situations are beyond their abilities to handle or require backup assistance and that physical force is not necessarily the best strategy in most situations. Once restraint is used, however, women are possibly more likely than men to feel the situation will not escalate out of their control.

Some evidence is found in the following interview excerpts:

CO#4: If I can control an inmate without physical restraints, I've got control of him. If you don't have control of him, then you surely aren't going to have much more control if he is restrained, because there he really can't do anything. And in order to have control of him without restraints shows that you have got the ability.

CO#5: Well, it's probably because the guys feel that, admit it or not, that they can control them without handcuffs. We know better. Ha Ha.

CO#8: Oh, I don't know, when it comes [to] that situation, the female's going to be more aggressive. You know, if you have to use restraint or anything . . . because, you know, usually if I have to take him somewhere I'm making sure the inmate follows the rules, and I cuff him and everything else, and I expect him to follow my commands . . . I don't know, for some reason, I guess once we feel you have cuffs on an inmate there's not much that they can do. Once in a while, you know, when we have an inmate cuffed, you may have a problem, and you may have to put leg irons on him. But, most of the time, once you cuff the inmates, the inmate seem to get more docile too.

CO 7: Oh, I think a lot of the inmates, once they are cuffed and all, they . . . at that point they submit, look for a figure to help. At that point the females are more, in their eyes, understanding. So, they comply easier to a female at that point.

CO#2: Ah, women are not used to using aggression . . . physical restraint. They are more so adept to talking to try to decelerate a situation, rather than using physical force to control a situation.

I: Um . . . but, once they have done so, they feel more in control of the situation?

CO#2: Yes.

I: Why?

CO#2: Because they were capable of doing so.

CO#6: Because a man is much more stronger than a woman.

I: So, it's just a matter of physical strength?

CO#6: Right!

CO#3: I don't know. If they can have them on cuffs, they have that leverage on them.

CO# 10: I can only speak from where I am at, right, and I um . . . this is a situation, of course, where anyone would feel more control, somewhat control, over the situation could get out of hand, and you finally got these cuffs on this person. Yes, you just feel like "whoo," if the situation could erupt, yes, you feel that way . . . yes, you feel somewhat in control . . . it makes you, you have to . . . who, who wouldn't? It's not something that females do that often.

These results are in direct conflict with Campbell and Muncer's findings that women view the use of aggression as a loss of control (1987; see, e.g., pp. 501–510). The differences might be found in a number of factors. First, in situations where aggression is expected, women may feel freer to use it than in normal circumstances where gender expectations are inhibitive. Indeed, as COs in male prisons, they might anticipate condemnation for not aggressing rather than for doing so. As previously stated, women tend to believe that anger-provoking encounters will lead to negative evaluations, whereas men generally view them as an exercise in social management, believing that aggression is situation appropriate. When women face the possibility of criticism for nonaggression, they might respond in ways resembling male behavior.

Similarly, where there is the possibility that they will be aggressed against, women are freed from the normal prohibitions. These findings concur with those of Frodi et al. who found, confronted with an aggressive male, women are as likely as men to aggress and find their behavior excused (1977, p. 642). They are also consistent with radical feminist theory, which maintains that women's aggression is a reaction to male dominance.

Conclusions and Implications

It would appear from the results of this study that women officers, for the most part, handle aggressive encounters in ways resembling those of male COs. The concern that women will not be able to handle situations requiring an aggressive response seems unwarranted. They not only tend to respond as aggressively as men, but, in particular situations, they respond more aggressively.

The findings suggest that women in crossed-sex guarding face the same exigencies as their male coworkers, combined with those barriers specific to women. For the most part, the occupational socialization they receive and the demands of the job counter any gender differences that might otherwise exist; that is, overall they do the job in ways similar to the men. What exceptions that do exist appear to result from the double bind of being token women in a male-dominated world within an organizational structure that is blind to the informal practices, including the sexist behavior, of its members. Doubting their preparedness or experience, yet feeling the need to prove themselves to the male eyes of both inmates and coworkers, women officers tend to respond more aggressively than the men in situationally specific encounters.

Whether real or perceived, the lack of confidence shown women officers from both the administration and their male *colleagues*, combined with the inadequate training all officers receive, might contribute to the current finding that women COs are more aggressive in situationally specific encounters. As noted, the women attribute their responses in particular incidents to such factors as lack of experience in direct-contact posts and the need to prove themselves as capable as the men of doing the job.

The research suggests that the presence of women COs in male penitentiaries may not significantly alter the situation found behind bars. Overall, the women neither increase nor decrease the rate of violence and are as effective at handling inmate incidents as are male officers. . . .

References

Campbell. A., & Muncer, S. (1987, December). Models of anger and aggression in the social talk of women and men. *Journal for the Theory of Social Behavior. 17(4).* 489–511.

Clear, T. R., & Cole. O. F (1994). *American corrections* (3rd ed.). Monterey. CA: Wadsworth.

Daly, K., & Chesney-Lind M. (1988, December). Feminism and criminology. *Justice Quarterly, 5(4),* 497–538.

Frodi, A., Macauley. J., & Thome P. R. (1977). Are women always less aggressive than men? A review of the experimental literature. *Psychological Bulletin 84(4),* 634–660.

Holeman, H., & Krepps-Hess B. J. (1983). *Women correctional officers in the California Department of Corrections.* Sacramento: California Department of Corrections.

Kissel, P., & Katsampes, P. (1980, Spring). The impact of women corrections officers on the functioning of institutions housing male inmates. *Journal of Offender Counseling, Services, and Rehabilitation, 4,* 213–237.

Linden, R., & Minch, C. (1980). *Women in policing: A review.* Manitoba: Ministry of the Solicitor General of Canada.

Lombardo, L. X. (1981). *Guards imprisoned: Correctional officers of work.* New York: Elsevier.

Maccoby, E., & Jacklin. C. N. (1980). Sex differences in aggression: A rejoinder and reprise. *Child Development, 51,* 964–980.

Marquart, J. W. (1983). Co-optation of the kept: Maintaining control in a southern penitentiary. *Dissertation Abstracts International, 45(1 A),* 307. (University Microfilms #AAC 8408457).

Morton, J. B. (1980). A study of employment of woman correctional officers in state level adult male correctional institutions. *Dissertation Abstracts International, 41(4A),* 1763. (University Microfilms #AAC 8023166).

Pollock, J. M. (1995). Women in corrections: Custody of the "caring ethic." In A. V. Merlo & J. M. Pollock (eds.), *Women, law and social control* (pp. 97–116). Needham Heights. MA: Allyn and Bacon.

Rowan, J. R (1996, April). Having more female officers reduces prisoner assaults on staff. *Overcrowded Times 7(2),* 2–3.

Simpson, S. S. (1989). Feminist theory, crime, and justice. *Criminology, 27(4),* 605–632.

Sykes, G. M. (1958). *Society of captives.* Princeton. NJ: Princeton University Press.

Zimmer, L. E. (1986). *Women guarding men.* Chicago: University of Chicago Press.

Zupan, L. L. (1992). The progress of women correctional officers in all-male prisons. In I. L. Moyer (ed.), *The changing roles of women to the criminal justice system* (2nd ed. pp. 323–343). Prospect Heights, IL Waveland.

24

Lady Hacks and Gentleman Convicts

Stephen C. Richards
Charles M. Terry
Daniel S. Murphy

Focus Questions

1. How does the convict subculture view the guard subculture?

2. What are the different viewpoints that male convicts have about women correctional officers?

3. Why is the presence of women correctional officers sometimes difficult for male prisoners?

4. How do women officers effectively deal with prisoners without being viewed as weak?

The three co-authors of this chapter are ex-convict academics, who in total have served more than 20 years in American prisons. Richards is an Associate Professor of Sociology and Criminology who served time in federal penitentiaries, correctional institutions, and camps. Terry is an Assistant Professor of Criminal Justice who spent 12 years in state prisons in California and Oregon. Murphy is a Ph.D. student and former federal prisoner.

As ex-convicts, our task is to explain the "convict perspective" (e.g., Murphy 2001; Terry 2000, 2001; Richards 1998, 2001; Ross and Richards 2001a, 2001b) on women guarding men. The discussion is based on our own experiences and that of male prisoners we knew in prison or have had the occasion to interview while conducting various research. We have also consulted with the Convict Criminologists, our ex-convict colleagues who are employed at different universities as professors of Criminology or Criminal Justice (Ross and Richards 2001a, 2001b). We will only briefly touch on the scholarly literature, which contains few references to convict concerns on this particular subject. Instead, this is our attempt to represent the general viewpoint of male prisoners concerning female prison staff.

Although many feminist readers may have difficulty with our discussion, and may take exception to our choice of words (e.g., lady, gentleman), we mean no offense and seek only to portray, as honestly as possible, how male prisoners perceive women correctional workers. After all, prisons are one-gender societies, socially backward, and culturally deprived.

Convict Perspective

A convict perspective reflects prison reality. The two most important issues for prisoners are time and space (Richards 1998, 139–140). Time is the sentence to be served—time down (completed) and time left to release. Space refers to the conditions of confinement, which may vary from the sensory deprivation of supermax disciplinary institutions to the everyday violence of "big house" maximum-security penitentiaries to the "gladiator school" medium-security correctional institutions for younger adult prisoners or the YMCA-like atmosphere of some minimum-security facilities or camps. The longer a person is incarcerated, and the more severe the conditions of confinement, the more likely it is that a prisoner will assume a convict perspective.

Prisoners want to live through the ordeal, do their time, and go home—the sooner the better. Even a man sentenced to death or a life sentence needs some hope of a reprieve, an appeal to a court that overturns or modifies a sentence or eventual parole. In the meantime, as the months and years pass by, he is concerned with day-to-day matters like personal safety, having suitable food and clothes, and some protection from the cold of winter and the heat of summer in cement and steel cellhouses.

Unfortunately, behind the wall there is a war going on between staff and convicts. Hacks and cons play their respective roles, each conforming to group expectations. Most men serving prison time develop a convict perspective in opposition to correctional managers. We say most, because not all prisoners are assimilated into the "convict culture," whose norms and values provide an active resistance and counter the oppression of prison. The prison is like a small city, populated with thousands of people, a diverse group that includes a wide variance in age, physical ability, mental capacity, and personal attitudes. In one cellblock there may be children barely old enough to shave, housed with elderly men who should be in nursing homes. Some prisoners are muscle bound and of sound health, while others are frail or dying from terminal illness. There may be cellblocks filled with individuals who are mentally ill or retarded. Conversely, there are convicts who are college educated. Some of the "short timers," and many of the most dysfunctional individuals, may even identify with the guards or solicit their favors. Nevertheless, most convicts, despite other distinctions, dislike guards.

Still, there are exceptions. Despite the brutality of prison, some prisoners learn that you cannot judge a person by their uniform. Many convicts tell stories about a decent guard who saved them from a violent confrontation, took their side in a disciplinary hearing, or got them out of the "hole" (solitary confinement). Conversely, correctional workers may relate how a prisoner defended them from attack or rescued them during a disturbance. Although prisoners and guards occupy rigid roles, over time, they may learn that you have to set aside the stereotypes and get to know people one at a time.

Definitions

Many people confuse jails with prisons. A jail is a community lock-up facility that holds prisoners after they are arrested, denied bail, during trial, or upon being convicted of misdemeanors (Irwin 1985). For each arrest or conviction, prisoners rarely spend more than a year in jail. Still, a few prisoners denied bail and standing trial may do more than a year in jail. In contrast, prison is an institution that incarcerates felons from one year to the end of life. Typically, as a result of mandatory minimums and harsh sentencing, many prisons are filled with men serving nickels, dimes, and quarters (5, 10, 25 years), with penitentiary convicts doing an average of ten or more years. Moreover, county or city jails are considered local or community facilities, while prisoners are transported far from home to distant penitentiaries. Doing jail time is only remotely related to serving prison time.

We will refer to men in prison as prisoners, convicts, or individuals. From a convict perspective, inmate is a managerial term that is used to insult prisoners. "Clients in prison are not considered persons, hence the word inmates" (Tewksbury and Clement 1999, 194). Generally, when convicts call another person an inmate it is a statement of disrespect. Inmates are understood to be prisoners who conform to institutional policy, follow the rules, obey orders, and are not to be trusted. They may be too familiar with or dependent on staff or may operate as snitches.

Prisoners, depending upon the prison system or region of the country, may label staff as guards, po-lice or cops, hacks, boss, turnkeys, or screws. "Guard" is the most common term used in both jails and prisons across the country. "Po-lice" are the many guards who behave like cop wannabees, patrolling cellblocks and looking to bust prisoners for disciplinary infractions. "Hack" is the term used exclusively in the federal system and stands for "hopeless assholes carrying keys" (Murphy 2001). "Boss" is used in many southern state prisons. "Turn-key" is an archaic term no longer used today (Richards 2001). "Screw" is the term used by old-time convicts to describe what they think of penitentiary guards. Rarely does a convict address a guard as "correctional officer" or "CO."

Women Guarding Men

The sparse prison literature that focuses on females working as guards in male prisons has generally ignored the convict perspective. Instead, attention has been given to topics such as the legal and social obstacles women encounter in pursuing equal employment opportunities in corrections (Alpert 1984), women's ability to respond as aggressively as men toward prisoners (Jenne and Kersting 1996), acceptance of women officers by their male counterparts (Zimmer 1986), and how men assume that women lack the physical and psychological strength to perform the job (Zupan 1992). Additional reasons for discrimination against women by male prison staff include the fear that they will threaten institutional security by having sex with prisoners or manage to get promoted by granting sexual favors to superiors (Jurik 1985; Owen 1985).

Most studies of women correctional officers are based on surveys or interviews of only correctional staff and usually emphasize employment opportunities and working conditions. The focus is on directly comparing the experience of female and male guards working in different correctional facilities, with little attention given to how male prisoners view women officers. The male prisoners have rarely been asked for their opinion. For example, research findings include indications that women officers are "conned" less often than male guards by prisoners (Peterson 1982), women correctional officers may do a better job in helping create a more relaxed atmosphere (Potter

1980), and as women they experience more hostility from the male guards than from prisoners (Belknap 1995). Exceptions include issues related to prisoner privacy (Jacobs and Zimmer 1983) and female officers' attitudes towards prisoners (Jurik and Halemba 1984; Zupan 1986).

This chapter is an effort to portray what having women working in male prisons is like for convicts. In so doing, it briefly illustrates the meanings, values, and ideas shared by prisoners. Without a brief discussion of the social world of convicts, any effort to understand how male prisoners perceive lady hacks would be nothing less than a misrepresentation of reality.

The Social World of the Male Prison

A wide range of people inhabit prisons. Their perspectives are influenced by their pre-prison identities as well as the way they adapt to the lifestyle of living behind bars (Irwin 1970; Newbold 1982/1985, 1989; Richards 1990, 1995, 1998; Lanier 1991, 1993, 1996; Jones 1995; Richards and Jones 1997; Terry 1997, 2000; Jones and Schmid 2000; Ross and Richards 2001a). Therefore, outlining a convict perspective about women working as guards in male prisons would be difficult to do without extensive interviewing of prisoners. As former prisoners, however, and participants of untold numbers of situations and events that included interactions with women guards, what we can do is relate what we saw, and what it was like for us.

Male prisons are the epitome of a hypermasculine environment. Similar conditions prevail in military combat situations or remote work camps, the difference being that prisoners may be confined in this all-male setting for many years, even decades, without reprieve. Convicts live day-to-day in a social world often characterized by violence, rage, racial tension, degradation, hopelessness, and animosity toward figures of authority. Prisoners do their best to survive the "pains of imprisonment," which include the deprivation of liberty, goods and services, autonomy and heterosexual relationships (Sykes 1958, 70–77; Johnson and Toch 1982). Like men who get together in a bar or locker room, convicts typically project images of toughness, fearlessness, and sexual virility in their everyday interactions. The major difference, of course, is that sex with women in prison is an uncommon event.

In the Company of Strangers

Doing prison time means living day to day in the company of strangers. A prison may be populated by several thousand men (big house penitentiaries) or a few hundred (minimum-security camps). This artificial environment is a social construction, where there are no families of women and children and life is dramatically different from that lived in the free world. This is a place where the men have little family responsibility, and the wisdom and compassion of women, if ever known, is a distant memory. Most prisoners receive few if any outside visits and rely on occasional phone calls or letters to keep up with family news. As the years pass in prison, they may be served with divorce papers, their children may grow up without them, and their parents may pass away. Meanwhile, the men live in the company of strangers, with a constant flow of new prisoners entering and old friends leaving the institution. The convict wakes up in the morning to find a new man in his cell, another lost soul with a prison number. His world is populated by strangers, homeless men with tall stories, who fill the corridors and walk the yard like rats in a maze or unwanted puppies in a dog kennel.

No Respect for Each Other

The prison defines the roles of both prisoner and guard. Despite the best intentions, both groups typically see each other as the enemy. Prisoners have little respect for most guards, be they male or female. The convict sees hacks as parking lot attendants, opening and locking doors, directing men into confined spaces. Many of the prisoners are urban outlaws, while the guards are rural hayseeds, each the product of different social environments. A better set-up for a culture clash would be hard to find. Despite their legal transgressions and mistakes in life, convicts pride themselves on being better than the guards, whom they view as conformists, persons who, if they had any self-respect, would find themselves an honest job.

The prisoners have little respect for guards because they see them standing around all day watching the clock, counting their overtime, and posturing like cops on a ghetto street corner, with little interest in improving prison conditions, getting to know individual people, or doing any real "corrections." Guards take no responsibility for producing a better "correctional product," that is, helping the prisoners obtain education, skills, and attitudes necessary to begin a legal life upon release. Unfortunately, very little effort is made by correctional staff to "correct" anybody.

Guarding prisoners is still a blue-collar occupation. Despite professional pretensions, rank, and uniform, guards are neither law enforcement nor military officers. Many are ex-military enlisted personnel, who may like to think of themselves as "officers" with troops to order around. Penitentiary convicts, however, because they are not soldiers, do not salute, march, perform close drill, or address them as "sir." Convicts follow orders only when they have to, and even then with little if any enthusiasm.

In turn, the guards, who may have misgivings about their chosen occupation, find solace in thinking of themselves as morally superior to the prisoners. Despite their own personal problems, or checkered history, they find comfort in knowing that they work eight-hour shifts and then go home. Some of them are honest enough to acknowledge that they are lucky, for they remember their own illegal activity, for which they were never arrested. Nevertheless, in every institution, a few correctional workers may try to do something for "inmates." Consequently, they may well suffer the retribution of "hard-line" staff. Prison takes its toll on everybody, both the keeper and the kept.

Prisoners Have Little Confidence in Prison Staff

The prisoners have little confidence in prison personnel who behave like cops or hacks. They know most of the staff hate their guts and do not care if they live or die or waste away slowly day by day. Convicts understand that the guards were trained to manage and control prisoners as if they were animals. Many prisoners complain about the poor food, inadequate medical attention (Murphy 2001), and decrepit overcrowded housing. For example, in many institutions food poisoning is common, uniforms are old rags, and men sleep in hallways, crowded dormitories, or ancient cellblocks.

The first concerns of guards are inmate management and security, which generally means running an orderly institution. They have little training in correctional counseling, rehabilitative services, or cultural diversity. As correctional officers, they have not been trained to encourage rehabilitation, nor is it perceived to be their responsibility within the guard subculture. Correctional counseling, if practiced at all, is left to a few case managers. It is rare to see a correctional officer suggest or promote vocational, educational, or recreational programs for the benefit of prisoners. They are afraid to advocate ideas that might please prisoners, as this would be understood by staff as giving comfort to the enemy. Instead, they act like cops, patrolling cellblocks filled with men they perceive to be no better than incorrigible criminals.

Dimensions of Sex and Compassion in Male Prisons

As human beings, we tend to magnify and dwell upon things we lack and desperately desire. Within the hypermasculine world of the male prison, sex is perhaps focused on to a greater degree than it is in the wider society, because of its inaccessibility. During daily conversations, which take place in public arenas like the yard, chow hall, or shower room, convicts regularly talk about sex. They talk about it in pornographic terms. For example, they delight in relating to their friends in detail what they would do sexually with the woman who starred in a movie they watched the previous evening, or with a fe-

male guard they all know. Their descriptions are graphic, raw, and indications of their unquenched thirst for sex, as well as their need to project a manly image to their peers.

Along with the lack of sexual affection, male prisons are basically devoid of feminine characteristics, such as kindness, the ability to express painful feelings, compassion, and understanding. Instead, these attributes are viewed as weakness, which can, if displayed, be grounds for ostracization or physical attack. Prison is not a place where a guy receives a "Dear John" letter from his wife and then shares his "pain" in the yard with his friends. Unmasculine emotions, when they are expressed, generally come out in humorous interactions (Terry 1997) or in letters, phone calls, and visits with females, if and when these forms of communication are possible. Women symbolize not only what is missing sexually, but also the potential for kindness and compassion.

Personal Encounters

Chuck Terry wrote about his own experiences with female correctional officers (CO). He remembers how the convicts were curious about the women's sexual orientation. Terry relates how this led to wild speculations:

From the time they first started using women as guards, until the day I got out of the joint (prison), I saw the whole scene change dramatically. More and more it appeared, the women hired seemed to be man haters. The convicts assumed they were lesbians, because of their short-cropped hair and attitudes that made the most antagonistic male guards seem like choirboys.

There were also the real feminine types who, whether they were good looking or not, were unable to fight off the advances of prisoners and guards alike. These women never seemed to last long. If they did, they generally went through some form of transformation in which they became more hardened and mean-spirited. Finally, there were a few who were able to maintain their femininity and do their jobs at the same time. For me, these were the ones who were most appreciated.

Terry's discussion demonstrates that convicts make assumptions about women based on their hairstyle and demeanor. Unfortunately, men in the free world may hold the same prejudices.

On the other hand, while convicts may appreciate women guards who maintain "Barbie doll" femininity, it may also make them uncomfortable. Terry recalls:

Personally, I came to regret the existence of female guards. Being a prisoner in a world devoid of sex I would rather not even see them, because it was frustrating to be around women who were off-limits and untouchable. There were occasions when a female guard was found having sexual relations with a prisoner, but these were rare events. For the most part, they were a reminder of what was missing, and in that regard, their mere presence was painful.

Of course, I was one of the lucky ones. I managed to make it out of that hellhole. Many are not so lucky. More and more, men are spending extraordinary amounts of time behind bars. For them, I think that having women guards around is more of a burden than anything else. I know one thing. If I were never getting out, I would not want them working in those places. In a world devoid of femininity and heterosexual relationships, the painfulness of their presence is something I would rather avoid.

These remarks alert us to the contradictions men have about female officers. On the one hand, they remind us that prisoners may have a difficult time accepting women as guards. On the other hand, prisoners may miss the women they once had in their lives—their mothers, sisters, daughters, wives, and sweethearts.

Male prisoners do not like women officers spying on them. In many correctional facilities, women officers are assigned to housing units, where it is their duty to supervise and monitor convicts. Prison toilet stalls and showers do not have doors; they are designed for easy staff surveillance. Terry remembers:

The awkwardness of having women work in male prisons was sometimes humiliating and at other times painful. It was never a welcome event to have women "monitoring" us in housing units or shower rooms. It was always weird taking showers and having one of them standing there checking you out.

Convicts maintain that women staff in bathroom areas is a demeaning and unnecessary violation of their privacy. This can be particularly difficult for young prisoners, who may be shy, or even virgins.

Prison can get boring. In order to break the monotony, prisoners may devise games and devious entertainment. Terry remembered a woman officer he refers to as "Raggedy Ann":

I remember when the first women CO got hired in the California Department of Corrections (CDC). The year was 1975, and I was doing time in a medium-security institution. One day, out of seemingly nowhere, I saw this good-looking blonde walking my way. For me, and the guys I was with, this was an almost surreal sight. What made it even more outrageous was the fact that she was dressed in a short skirt and blouse which had the colors and emblems of the CDC uniform. It was like being in the Twilight Zone or something. We wondered if we were seeing things. Female guards in here?

As it turned out, the name she was given by convicts was Raggedy Ann. Having her around was loads of fun. It was so strange having a female in that environment. She was nice, friendly, and great to watch. Keep in mind, male prisoners are continuously on the prowl for even the sight of a woman, and here was one right in our midst.

Raggedy Ann was not only an object of desire, but also the butt of prison humor. On more than one occasion, I saw her lured by a couple of friendly prisoners outdoors from inside the corridor, which linked the many dorms of the institution. Just as she stepped down onto the first or second stair of a very short stairwell, they would position themselves in a way that would block her from continuing forward, and coax her into a prolonged conversation. This little game was done for the sake of the one or two convicts crouched underneath the stairs, who were able to use this vantage point to look up her skirt. Meanwhile, guys up and down the hallway would be roaring with laughter.

The game was clearly at the expense of "Raggedy Ann." She probably did not appreciate the unsolicited attention.

Terry leaves us with this fond recollection of another women officer. He pays his respects to a woman who shared her smile and laughter:

> There was one female guard I remember well, who worked in the Oregon State Prison, several years before I was granted parole. She was decent looking, rather short, had a great personality, and was one of the few women who was able to maintain her femininity and do her job at the same time. For example, she was capable of being the person in charge of overseeing the chow line (making sure prisoners do not steal more food than they have coming) and, at the same time, be seen talking, smiling, and laughing with prisoners. For me, she was a pleasure to behold because she appeared to be the real deal. In other words, she was not projecting a tough, invulnerable image, like nearly everyone else in the place. She acted like a woman in an upside-down, unnatural social world, where softness, love, and kindness toward others was generally nonexistent. Unlike the majority of guards, male or female, she treated us like human beings and was greatly respected for doing so.
>
> Just prior to getting paroled, I approached this female guard and thanked her for working in that institution. I told her I appreciated seeing her smile every day, how good it made me feel, and that she acted as a reminder of what awaited in the outside world.

It should be noted that Terry, like many other convict criminologists, has mixed feelings about women guards. This should be no surprise, for as we all know, men have always been confused about the opposite gender.

Can Women Turn Hate to Love?

The introduction of women personnel into male prisons suggested some interesting possibilities, which require our thoughtful consideration. Do lady hacks provide a measure of civility to prisons? Maybe these officers force the male prisoners to behave like gentlemen? Greg Newbold, an ex-convict professor from New Zealand, suggests that lady hacks have improved prisons in his country:

> Over here [down under], the introduction of female staff into men's prisons in the late 1970s has pretty much been welcomed by convicts. Some are proper ladies, who by and large, have a maternal approach and have softened the prisons to quite an extent. So, a different type of relationship emerged. If a female screw pissed you off, you could not punch her out. There is negative stigma in that. You had to talk to her, which was a new experience for a lot of guys.

Newbold's discussion alerts us to the unique mystique and power that women may have over men. Locked in cages for years at a time, male prisoners may have lost the ability, if they ever had it, to control their anger and talk out their difficulties. The presence of women officers may encourage male prisoners to learn communications skills.

Then, again, men and women talking together may result in additional complications. Newbold recalls:

> There were also a few cases here of female screws literally being "good screws" and falling in love with an inmate. I actually testified [in court] as an expert in one such case in the 1980s and got the woman officer off a criminal charge.
>
> I've heard women screws say they would rather work with men than women convicts, because men are more straight forward, less emotional, and easier to handle. I think the women like being the only cat on the block, with all these sex-starved men about, who will comment on their new hairdo, and give them the little compliments their husbands stopped giving them years ago. And, they love the idea that they can tame these tough guys, and expose their inner souls.

Do ladies love outlaws? Some women like "bad boys" and may be attracted to wild and desperate guys. Hacks and cons are just human beings wearing different uniforms. It is not unusual for a lady hack to fall in love with a handsome convict.

An Act of Kindness

The Federal Bureau of Prisons operates a number of prisons that are filled with medical patients. These prisons are used to house prisoners with acute, chronic, or terminal medical conditions. These facilities are known for their high rate of death. Dan Murphy served a number of years in several of these facilities. Murphy reminds us, like Terry and Newbold, that male prisoners may prefer women who inspire male prisoners to act like gentlemen. He discussed his experience with lady hacks:

Over the course of my incarceration, which spanned 1992–1997, there were occasional bright spots. The vast majority of these were in dealings with women prison staff who conducted themselves as ladies. This, in turn, helped the prisoners to behave, more or less, as gentlemen. In describing such interactions, it is my hope to convey to the reader that prisoners are human beings, and if treated as such, may respond as gentlemen.

I had occasion to personally experience, as well as witness, how other convicts responded to the gracious hyper "ladylike" presentation of women working in the federal prison system. I must point out that this was the rare exception. The standard for women working in male prisons is to be hypermasculine. Those who presented themselves as ladies, within the parameters of the prison rules, were treated as ladies. Those who attempted to be manlier than those they guard were treated with disdain.

Acting as a lady enhanced prisoner compliance, whereas hypermasculine women were treated with defiance. Behaving like women, rather than men, they were afforded protection by prisoners. The respect they enjoyed was transformed into a protection network, with many prisoners looking out for their well-being. In contrast, the hypermasculine women fostered anger and rage, and consequently, may have become targets for prisoner aggression.

Unfortunately, gender role expectations remain relevant, maybe more so, in a place where women are still so rare. The male prisoners are tired of men; they want the female officers to act like women.

Murphy goes on to tell a story about a public health nurse, "Ms. Caregiver," who worked in a federal medical prison and provided him with medical attention. He discusses how she worked to care for many male prisoners who suffered the worst of fates, to die in prison:

One woman, in particular, over the course of my imprisonment, may have saved my life. She was a nurse struggling to give proper medical care, despite the medical neglect common in the federal prison system. Ms. Caregiver, as I will refer to her, was a compassionate person. As hard as she tried to secure proper medical care for many sick and dying prisoners, at every turn she was thwarted by prison policy. She knew many of us needed specialized medical care, did not give up, and fought the doctors to get us the attention we needed. This kind treatment, I believe, in many cases was stronger than any medicine. This nurse was polite and caring. I watched her help many men die with the dignity that should be afforded all human beings.

Approximately two years into my five-year term of imprisonment I became desperately ill. My weight dropped from 214 pounds to 154. I was passing blood, and feared dying. If not for Ms. Caregiver I very well may have. I will never forget one moment when Ms. Caregiver took my hand and pled with me to fight on. I became determined not to let her down.

Murphy reminds us that many women, besides guards, work in prisons. They may be doctors, nurses, teachers, psychologists, chaplains, wardens, case managers, correctional counselors, or clerical staff.

Conclusion

We have shared our reflections about lady hacks and gentlemen convicts. From our perspective, we most liked lady hacks who were able to maintain their femininity and still deal effectively with the prisoner population. For this we were grateful, because it helped humanize the prison. At the very least, lady hacks reminded us why we wanted to get out of prison and not return.

It should be no surprise that people do not like being locked up, kept in cages, or the guards that keep them there. Lady hacks have a tough role to play. How do they maintain their femininity without being "run over" or intimidated by male convicts? Every correctional officer will tell you that a prison is really run by the convicts. On any given day, the prisoners can take the place down. The secret to managing prisoners is learning how to talk with prisoners. Only the novice hack thinks the guards rule by force.

In a well-managed prison, women officers do not have to act like men. There is an unwritten social contract operating in every well-run prison. The institution functions in relative peace, with little violence, as long as the contract is honored. Prisoners must have decent food, reasonable living conditions, humane treatment, programs (paid work, vocational training, higher education opportunities, recreational activities), and a way to earn time off their sentence through "good time" credits. Violate this contract and all bets are off, and hell breaks loose. Do not blame this on the hacks or convicts. The fault belongs with the policymakers who thought they could operate safe prisons on meager budgets.

Women working in prisons do not have to be hacks that mimic men. As women have entered many occupations and professions, they have at first tended to learn their roles and routine from men. Over time, as more women are hired and promoted, they may challenge the work norms and transform the workplace. As ex-convicts, we hope for no less.

Women have strengths and skills that are needed in corrections. The male officers have made a mess of prisons, devising more elaborate ways to cage prisoners. The male model for corrections management is based on physical coercion, control architecture, and surveillance. A female model has yet to evolve. Nevertheless, we can learn a lot from the way women manage female prisoners. Women need to explore how communication, scheduled activities, and humane treatment may be used to manage male prisoners. Finally, setting aside hacks and cons, it might serve us all well to remember that male prisoners are not alien creatures; they are our fathers, sons, and brothers.

Acknowledgments

We would like to thank Richard S. Jones, Charles S. Lanier, Greg Newbold, and Jeffrey Ian Ross for their thoughtful comments and suggestions.

References

Abbott, Jack Henry. 1981. *In the Belly of the Beast: Letters from Prison*. New York: Random House.

Alpert, G. 1984. "The Needs of the Judiciary and Misapplications of Social Research: The Case of Female Guards in Men's Prisons." *Criminology* 22: 441–456.

Belknap, Joanne. 1995. "Women in Conflict: An Analysis of Women Correctional Officers." In B. R. Price and N. J. Sokoloff (eds.), *The Criminal Justice System and Women: Offenders, Victims and Workers*. New York: McGraw-Hill.

Irwin, John. 1970. *The Felon*. Englewood Cliffs, NJ: Prentice Hall.

———. 1985. *The Jail: Managing the Underclass in American Society*. Berkeley, CA: University of California Press.

Jacobs, J., and L. Zimmer. 1983. "Collective Bargaining and Labor Unrest." In J. Jacobs (ed.), *New Perspectives in Prisons and Imprisonment*. Ithaca, NY: Cornell University Press.

Jenne, Denise L., and Robert C. Kersting. 1996. "Aggression and Women Correctional Officers in Male Prisons." *Prison Journal* 76, 4: 442–461.

Johnson, Robert, and Hans Toch. (eds.) 1982. *The Pains of Imprisonment*. Prospect Heights, IL: Waveland.

Jones, Richard, S. 1995. "Uncovering the Hidden Social World: Insider Research in Prison." *Journal of Contemporary Criminal Justice* 11: 106–118.

Jones, Richard S., and Thomas J. Schmid. 2000. *Doing Time: Prison Experience and Identity Among First-Time Offenders*. Stamford, CT: JAI Press.

Jurik, Nancy C. 1985. "An Officer and a Lady: Organizational Barriers to Women Working as Correctional Officers in Men's Prisons." *Social Problems* 32: 375–388.

Jurik, Nancy C., and Gregory J. Halemba. 1984. "Gender, Working Conditions and the Job Satisfaction of Women in Non-Traditional Occupation: Female Correctional Officers in Men's Prisons." *Sociological Quarterly* 25: 551–566.

Lanier, Charles S. 1991. "Dimensions of Father-Child Interaction in a New York State Prison Population." *Journal of Offender Rehabilitation* 16: 27–42.

——. 1993. "Affective States of Fathers in Prison." *Justice Quarterly* 10, 1: 51–68.

——. 1995. "Incarcerated Fathers: A Research Agenda." *Forum on Corrections Research* 7, 2: 34–36.

——. 1996. "Children of Prisoners: Fathers' Issues." In Marilyn D. McShane and Frank P. Williams (eds.), *Encyclopedia of American Prisons*. New York: Garland.

Murphy, Daniel S. 2001. "Aspirin Ain't Gonna Help the Kind of Pain I'm In: Medical Care in the Federal Bureau of Prisons." In Jeffrey Ian Ross and Stephen C. Richards (eds.), *Convict Criminology*. Belmont, CA: Wadsworth.

Newbold, Greg. 1982/1985. *The Big Huey*. Auckland, NZ: Collins.

——. 1989. *Punishment and Politics: The Maximum Security Prison in New Zealand*. Auckland, NZ: Oxford University Press.

Owen, Barbara A. 1985. "Race and Gender Relations Among Prison Workers." *Crime and Delinquency* 31: 147–159.

Peterson, C. 1982. "Doing Time with the Boys: An Analysis of Women Correctional Officers in All-Male Facilities." In B. Price and N. Sokoloff (eds.), *The Criminal Justice System and Women*. New York: Clark Boardman.

Potter, J. 1980. "Should Women Guards Work in Prisons for Men?" *Corrections Magazine* 5: 30–38.

Richards, Stephen C. 1990. "Sociological Penetration of the American Gulag," *Wisconsin Sociologist* 27, 4: 18–28.

——. 1995. *The Structure of Prison Release: An Extended Case Study of Prison Release, Work Release, and Parole*. New York: McGraw-Hill.

——. 1998. "Critical and Radical Perspectives on Community Punishment: Lesson from the Darkness," In Jeffrey Ian Ross (ed.), *Cutting the Edge: Current Perspectives in Radical/Critical Criminology and Criminal Justice*. New York: Praeger.

——. 2001. "My Journey Through the Federal Bureau of Prisons," In Jeffrey Ian Ross and Stephen C. Richards (eds.), *Convict Criminology*. Belmont, CA: Wadsworth.

Richards, Stephen C., and Richard S. Jones. 1997. "Perpetual Incarceration Machine: Structural Impediments to Post-Prison Success." *The Journal of Contemporary Criminal Justice* 13, 1: 4–22.

Ross, Jeffrey Ian, and Stephen C. Richards. 2001a. *Convict Criminology*. Belmont, CA: Wadsworth Publishing.

——. 2001b. "The New School of Convict Criminology." *Social Justice.*.

Sykes, Gresham. 1958. *A Society of Captives: A Study of a Maximum Security Prison*. Princeton, NJ: Princeton University Press.

Terry, Chuck M. 1997. "The Function of Humor for Prison Inmates." *The Journal of Contemporary Criminal Justice* 13, 1: 23–40.

——. 2000. "Beyond Punishment: Perpetuation Difference from the Prison Experience." *Humanity and Society* 24, 2: 108–135.

——. 2001. "From C-Block to Academia: You Can't Get There From Here." In Jeffrey Ian Ross and Stephen C. Richards (eds.), *Convict Criminology*. Belmont, CA: Wadsworth.

Tewksbury, Richard, and Mary H. Clement. 1999. "Should Female Correctional Officers Be Used in Male Institutions?" In Charles B. Fields (ed.), *Controversial Issues in Corrections*. Needham Heights, MA: Allyn and Bacon.

Welch, Michael. 1996. *Corrections: A Critical Approach*. New York: McGraw-Hill.

Zimmer, Lynn E. 1986. *Women Guarding Men*. Chicago, IL: University of Chicago Press.

Zupan, Linda L. 1986. "Gender Related Differences in Correctional Officers' Perceptions and Attitudes." *Journal of Criminal Justice*, 14: 349–361.

——. 1992. "The Progress of Woman Correctional Officers in All-Male Prisons." In Imogene L. Moyer (ed.), *The Changing Roles of Women In the Criminal Justice System: Offenders, Victims, and Professionals*. Prospect Heights, IL: Waveland Press.

Chapter VIII
Discussion

Women Guarding Men

All three of these readings point to the difficulties that women experience when they work in a nontraditional job setting, supervising people who tend to view women in stereotyped roles. The real difficulty is being a female correctional officer in a violence-prone environment, where feminine qualities are viewed as weak and vulnerable. Prisoners despise the female correctional officer because she is a "hack," and many male officers may see her as a liability when use of physical force is needed to control an inmate (Lawrence and Mahan article). On the other hand, younger male officers with less experience working in prisons were more apt to accept and support women guards. She is rewarded by her peers for displaying masculine attributes, yet at the same time she is protected from having to break up violent fights and she is not required in some prisons to work in areas where men are showering or unclothed.

The reading by Richards, Terry, and Murphy reveals that convicts generally detest most, if not all, correctional officers of both sexes. Although most convicts resent taking orders from any correctional officer, women seem to find it more difficult than men to obtain prisoner compliance. This is because some male convicts refuse to let any woman tell them what to do, whether she is their wife, girlfriend, or a correctional officer. The more frequent challenges to authority may explain why Jenne and Kersting found that women correctional officers responded more aggressively in some situations than men officers.

Richards, Terry, and Murphy noted that male prisoners hold a wide variety of views about the presence of women guards. Some prisoners find it difficult to be around women officers because their existence reminds the prisoners of the women they have missed seeing in their own lives. Although the general sentiment is that females add compassion and "civility" to the prison environment, the prison environment as a whole has not become any less violent as a result of their presence. Some convicts may even regard women officers as a form of entertainment or sexual stimulation. So, while feminine qualities of communication and violence prevention are preferred over direct use of force for both men and women officers, Jenne and Kersting found that the prison environment is still violent, and women officers are altering their behavior to fit the male-dominated environment, rather than the reverse.

Part Four
Special Issues
Facing Corrections

Chapter IX
Introduction

Correctional Privatization

Common Assumptions	Reality
• A private prison is the same as a state or federal prison.	• A private company contracts with state and federal government to construct, manage, and/or provide services within a jail or prison facility. Some private facilities are 100 percent owned and managed by a private company. In other cases, the government may own the facility, but it is managed by a private company. State and federal governments retain ultimate legal liability for confinement conditions and treatment of prisoners.
• Private prisons are more abusive to prisoners than state prisons.	• No study to date has compared the use of excessive physical force in state and private prisons.

Punishment and legal liability of convicted offenders ultimately resides with federal, state, and local government (the public sector). Involvement of private companies in prison construction, prison management, or as a service provider has occurred in some form since the 1800s. Privatization seems like a new phenomenon to many people because the private sector has become increasingly involved in managing prison population growth since the early 1980s. Private companies contract out to state or federal governments to provide services inside state prisons (Shichor 1995). These services include food, medical care, drug and alcohol treatment, mental health, education, and transportation. Nineteen states contract out to private companies for food services, and thirty states use private medical care compa-

nies in some or all of their prisons (Camp and Camp 1999: 90).

A second way that private companies have been involved in corrections is through constructing and opening new (usually minimum or medium-security) prison facilities. Private companies may lease their bedspace to the government, with the option for the government to purchase the prison after the lease has expired. If the government purchases the prison, it has the option of retaining a private company to manage and operate the facility. Some private companies prefer to retain ownership, management, and operation after the lease period due to the potential for profit (Logan 1990). As of 1999, sixty private prisons were in operation under contract with the government at an average cost of $42.26 per prisoner per day, ranging from $25.86 in Mississippi to $83.18

in New Mexico (Camp and Camp 1999, 93). Corrections Corporation of America (CCA) operated the most private prisons (20), followed by Wackenhut (17), and then by Management Training Corporation (3). All other companies had one or two privately operating facilities (Camp and Camp 1999, 94–95). Private companies also operate jails, juvenile facilities, community centers, halfway houses, electronic monitoring devices, and other types of correctional technology.

As you read the selections, make a note of the arguments in favor of and against privatization. You will note that the dilemmas may be categorized into ethical, economical, legal liability and accountability, conditions of confinement, quality of services, and public safety and security. The main question to keep in mind as you read is: Should private businesses profit through the punishment of criminals?

Recommended Readings

Bowman, Gary W., Simon Hakim, and Paul Seidenstat, (eds). (1993). *Privatizing Correctional Institutions*. New Brunswick, NJ: Transaction.

Camp, Camille Graham, and George M. Camp. (1999). *Corrections Yearbook 1999*. Middletown, CT: Criminal Justice Institute.

Lanza-Kaduce, Lonn, K. Parker, and Charles Thomas. (1999). "A Comparative Recidivism Analysis of Releasees from Private and Public Prisons." *Crime and Delinquency* 45 (1): 28–47.

Lippke, Richard L. (1997). "Thinking About Private Prisons." *Criminal Justice Ethics* 16 (1): 26–39.

Logan, Charles H. (1990). *Private Prisons: Cons and Pros*. New York: Oxford University Press.

——. (1992). "Well-Kept: Comparing Quality of Confinement in Private and Public Prisons." *The Journal of Criminal Law and Criminology* 83 (3): 577–613.

Sechrest, Dale K., and David Shichor. (1997). "Private Jails: Locking Down the Issues." *American Jails* 11 (1): 21–36.

Shichor, David. (1995). *Punishment for Profit: Private Prisons/Public Concerns*. Thousand Oaks, CA: Sage.

——. (1999). "Privatizing Correctional Institutions: An Organizational Perspective." *The Prison Journal* 79 (2): 226–249.

Internet Websites

Correctional Services Corporation homepage. Available: *http://www.correctionalservices.com/*

Database of articles on private prisons by Oregon AFSCME Corrections. Available: *http://www.oregonafscme.com/corrections/private/aprivatearticlesholding.htm*

Logan, Charles, Professor of Sociology, Database comparing public and private prisons. Available: *http://www.ucc.uconn.edu/~wwwsoci/nmexsum.html*

Smith, Phil (1993). "Private Prisons: Profits of Crime." *Covert Action Quarterly*. Available: *http://www.mediafilter.org/MFF/Prison.html*

Thomas, C. W. (1999, October). Numbers of private facilities by geographical location. Available: *http://web.crim.ufl.edu/pcp/census/1999/Chart3.html*

An article titled: "The promise and peril of private prisons." Available: *http://www.gomemphis.com/newca/special/import/import3.htm*

Wackenhut Corporation Homepage. Available: *http://wackenhutcorp.com/*

25
Issues Concerning Private Prisons

David Shichor

Focus Questions

1. What different forms of privatization occurred between the thirteenth century and the end of the nineteenth century?

2. Who ultimately has legal liability for prisoners in state and private facilities?

3. What are some of the economic incentives that state governments may have if they work with a private company to construct, manage, and/or contract out for services?

4. How have private and public prisons performed when they have been evaluated against each other?

In the 1970s, America declared a "war on crime." A "war on drugs" followed in the early 1980s. These policies led to a dramatic increase in the size of the prison population. During the decade between 1980 to 1990 the number of inmates in state and federal prisons grew from 315,947 to 738,894 (an increase of 133.9 percent), and the incarceration rate (prisoners per 100,000 population) increased from 139 to 292. In 1992, the prisoner population reached 885,593 and the incarceration rate 329. Currently, the United States incarcerates the highest number of people per capita in the world. As a result, the cost of incarceration has skyrocketed. In 1984, total state expenditures on correc-

tional institutions were about $6 billion; in 1990, they were approaching $20 billion, an increase of 223 percent.

The large scale and rapid increase in incarceration resulted in prison crowding and serious financial problems. In 1988, thirty-nine states were under some kind of court order to limit their prison population unless they could increase their prison capacity. Often these orders brought an early release of inmates, a practice that clearly runs contrary to the prevalent "get tough" crime policies. In that situation there was a need to seek out alternative solutions to the problem. One that received considerable attention was prison privatization. In the early 1980s, thirty-eight states in the U.S. had some kind of contract with private companies to supply various correctional services. This trend coincided with President Reagan's administrative attempts to privatize many public services that traditionally were the sole responsibility of the government. These policies were supported by the American tradition of distrust of government and the strong belief in the efficiency of private enterprise.

In the early 1980s, private corporations started to operate entire prisons. In 1991, a census of private prisons in the U.S. indicated that forty-four correctional facilities were operated by fourteen companies, housing about 13,400 inmates (Thomas and Foard 1991). Two of those companies operated 50 percent of the private institutions; the other twelve operated one to three facilities each. There are several issues involved in the privatization of prisons, including conceptual, legal, contract-related economics, quality, and personnel issues.

Historical Background

Private involvement in the administration of punishment is not a new phenomenon in Western, especially English-American, tradition. In England, jails were operated by private entrepreneurs during the Middle Ages. Beginning in the thirteenth century, the crown gave the right to private citizens to manage jails in order to relieve itself of the responsibility. In some cases the right was sold; in other cases it was bestowed upon minor royal servants in lieu of a pension. The jailers made their living by extracting fees from prisoners for various services. Eighteenth-century records show that often special accommodations, including wine and women, were provided for those who could afford it. Most of the income came from selling beer, liquor, and tobacco to the inmates. Those who could not afford to pay had to work for the jail keepers, who often hired them out to work for others. In addition, payment for the incarceration of poor prisoners was made by the magistrates. Those payments were considerably below those paid by the well-to-do inmates. It was known to the authorities that the system was liable to abuse, but they accepted it because of its practicality. This practice created great differences between the treatment of those prisoners who could pay for services and those who could not.

The lucrativeness of operating jails was known, and in many instances, the office was subject to sale and purchase. Some families were involved in the occupation for generations. The abuses of this system were evident. The famous eighteenth-century penal reformer John Howard demanded the abolition of private fees in jails and government payments for the jailers. The fee system was abolished toward the end of the eighteenth century.

In America during the Colonial period, local jails were used mainly for detention and only on rare occasions held convicted prisoners. Generally, the jails were crowded and in poor condition. Escapes were frequent. The jailers were paid by the counties, but corruption was widespread, and many jailers embezzled public funds, extracted bribes from prisoners, sold whiskey to them, and physically abused them.

Penitentiaries

Toward the end of the eighteenth century, the penitentiary was born in the United States. Soon two competing types emerged. The Pennsylvania system was based on solitary confinement. Later, labor was introduced to the solitary cells, primarily to provide inmates with something to do. Prisoners were credited with "fair pay" and debited for their upkeep. In 1819, the Auburn (New York) penitentiary was opened. In that institution prisoners slept in separate cells, but during the day they worked and ate together under a strict rule of silence. Auburn soon became the leading model for prisons in America. One of its major attractions was that it lent itself to modern industrial production. Thus, the modern prison that developed during the industrial revolution fit into the system of mass production, which in turn provided ample opportunity for private involvement in prison industry.

It was not uncommon for manufacturers in the 1800s to contract with the prison for industrial production. The manufacturers supplied the materials, supervised the work, and paid for the finished goods. The Auburn penitentiary, for example, was not only self-supporting financially, but was even producing surplus revenue for the government. In some prisons, inmates were hired out to work outside the institution for private contractors. These arrangements gained widescale official and public support because many believed that in this way offenders could be punished, the community could be protected, potential offenders could be deterred, and all these results would come about without financial burden for the government. The entrepreneurs often made themselves a handsome profit. The contract system was the most widespread practice. In some prisons the industrial production was contracted out to several contractors, limiting the influence of any one of them. The contractors could interact with prisoners only to instruct them on the job.

The lease system, in which a private contractor operated the whole prison, was adopted in some states, mainly in the expanding frontier areas. The first such arrangement is traced to the state prison in Frankfort, Kentucky. In 1825, Kentucky, in a financial crisis, leased the prison to a businessman for five years for an annual rate of one thousand dollars. In several states, inmates were leased by private contractors to work outside the prison. Often these convicts were treated brutally; many of them escaped.

After the Civil War there was a great impetus in the South to expand leasing, because of the need to replace the liberated slaves with a cheap labor force with which to rebuild the devastated economy. The majority of Southern prisoners were black, and they were often kept by the private lessees in worse conditions than the slaves had been. This practice was discontinued at the end of the nineteenth century during an economic depression, when few contractors were ready to lease convicts.

enforcing minor institutional rules. While disciplinary hearings are conducted by governmental personnel, the disciplinary write-ups by employees of private companies may influence the conditions of confinement and even the date of release, by determining the "good time" earned by inmates.

Similarly, reports and evaluations of institutional behavior prepared by the staff may influence parole decisions. There is also the potential problem raised by critics that private companies have a financial interest in keeping the prison full at all times; therefore, they might overstate negative disciplinary reports when there is a decline in the prison population. So far, however, there had been no evidence of that during the 1980s and 1990s, when the prison population was growing rapidly.

Conceptual and Legal Issues

Punishment is a legally imposed deprivation or suffering. A core question concerning privatization is whether a private entity should profit from the punishment of lawbreakers. Supporters of privatization make a distinction between the sentencing of those who are found guilty in committing a crime and the actual administration of punishment.

Accordingly, the claim is made that the punishment remains under governmental authority, which supervises execution by a private party. In regard to the constitutionality of this arrangement, the federal courts have allowed the delegation of power to private contractors. The issue is more a concern of the states, because about 92 percent of inmates are in state prisons. State laws on the delegation of power, however, are confusing. Several states have therefore legislated laws that authorize the delegation of correctional functions to private parties.

One of the concerns is that, while formally the private company operating the prison is only administering the sentence and should not influence it, informally it does have an impact on the punishment, by setting and

Legal Liability

Legally, the government is responsible for what is happening in the prison. A private company's executive has stated this vividly: "The state can contract out duties, but it cannot contract away responsibility" (Fenton 1985, 44). Many state agencies would be ready to delegate legal liability to private companies, together with the management of the prison. As it stands, however, while the government does not have full control over the operations of private prisons, it does carry the ultimate liability. In that respect the government serves as a "safety net" for the private contractors. The issue is important in light of the large number of civil rights suits brought by inmates against the prison system. The fact that the government carries the ultimate liability may provide more security for the inmates in private prisons, because the company is liable to the government and thus in turn is liable before the courts (Logan 1990). This underlines the importance of the contract between the government and the private company and the effectiveness of its monitoring, as a safeguard against potential legal and financial problems for the state.

Issues of Contract and Monitoring

Contracting for the operation of prisons with private companies follows the contracting out of various governmental services such as garbage collection, data processing, building, and automobile maintenance. There are various services in many prisons that are contracted out (laundry, medical services, vocational and educational training, and so forth). The privatization of management of entire prisons, however, is qualitatively different from the provision of certain specific services.

A clearly written contract is a key element in the success of private prison operations. One issue is the term of the contract. Contracts are usually written for one to three years, in order not to commit money for the next budget period, to enable the government to change contractors, or to make changes in the contract. Short-term contracts are problematic for the contractors, because it is difficult to plan for such a short period.

The companies have an interest in long-term contracts, because of the up-front investments involved in privatization. A longer contract may be beneficial for the government as well, because changing contractors may involve a serious administrative and financial burden. The longer contract may also induce contractors to make more improvements to facilities or programs. And a longer contract may prevent bad publicity arising from frequent changes. Sometimes, changing contractors may be difficult because there are not many private prison companies available, and the government may not be in a position to take over prison operations after it becomes dependent on private providers. Thus, the advantages and disadvantages of both the short- and the long-term contracts have to be weighed when contracting is considered. The contract has to be flexible enough that its early termination is possible by either side if a valid and legitimate reason arises.

Monitoring Private Contracts and Facilities

Effective monitoring of prisons, private and public alike, is important. Prisons are not visible institutions, and the public rarely gets a glimpse of them except on occasions of unusual violence such as escapes or riots. There is a need to ensure that prisons follow operational guidelines not only because of the legal responsibility of the government, but also because in a democratic society inmates must be treated decently and according to the law. In addition, monitoring must make sure that private contractors operate in compliance with the contract.

Rigorous monitoring of private prisons may be expensive, because governmental agents must be on the premises. Also, the contracting agency may find little interest in monitoring, because the agency itself selected the firm and it may receive bad publicity if improprieties are discovered. On the other hand, the monitors may have little incentive to demand conditions beyond the minimum legal standards.

One possible way to make monitoring easier is to include in the contract incentives for positive performance in the form of bonuses or fines. It is likely that private contractors would respond to financial incentives.

An underlying concern of correctional privatization, that has implications for monitoring as well, is the entrenchment of correctional firms (Gentry 1986). To exercise effective monitoring, it is essential that the government have a backup ability and not be at the mercy of a handful of companies only. Therefore, it would be important that a free market evolve with the emergence of more private companies competing for the prison business. That would allow authorities to switch from one company to another if they are not satisfied with the services, or if they can find a less costly provider.

Another potential problem relates to the division of authority between the management of the private prison and the officials in charge of monitoring. "Unless care is taken to define the respective roles of public and private managers, two organizations are responsible, but neither may be clearly accountable" (Mullin et al. 1985, 75).

This kind of monitoring may confuse the chain of command in the prison, since lower-level state officials placed in the institution will have to approve decisions made by private executives and managers. "In the summary of this issue it is important to state that:

> To a large extent, the effectiveness of monitors . . . will depend upon the levels of sanctions that they can ultimately mobilize and the degree of critical autonomy that they can maintain from the organization being monitored" (Matthews 1989, 4).

Economic Issues

The major attraction of private prisons is economic. The claim is that private prisons can do the same job public prisons do, but less expensively. This can be accomplished, according to supporters, by the introduction of sophisticated private management techniques, more productive staff deployment and staff reduction (because they are not restricted by civil service regulations and union contracts), and by more effective and flexible procurement, which can cut expenses considerably. These companies can not only operate less expensively, they can also construct facilities faster and less expensively than government agencies can.

So far, there have been conflicting reports regarding the cost comparisons between public and private prisons. Some estimates indicate that private facilities are more cost effective, while others claim that private institutions are more expensive because of hidden costs that are hard to calculate. There are also those who find the cost comparisons inconclusive.

Cost estimates for government-run prisons are usually understated, because the operation often benefits from the services of other agencies. For example, education departments may run classes and government hospitals may care for sick prisoners. There may be hidden costs for the government in the operation of private prisons as well.

Those may include monitoring expenses; legal work involved in the preparation of contracts; costs that may accrue in unusual circumstances, such as the bankruptcy of private prison companies; maintenance of public services used in emergencies, such as in riots, fires, and natural disasters; and tax benefits given to companies and their investors. The major areas of cost comparisons are construction financing, the construction itself, and prison operations.

Construction Financing

In many states, the traditional method to raise money for prison construction is to issue bonds upon the voters' approval. During the 1980s, in the midst of an economic boom, the public tended to approve bond proposals. With the downturn of the economy, some proposals were turned down. In certain states, because of the legal debt ceiling the government could not take on any more financial obligations.

Private corporations may raise money through private sources. Often, the government and the private firm enter into a lease-purchase agreement according to which the governmental agency becomes a tenant in a facility owned by the company. At the end of an agreed-upon period, the ownership is transferred to the government. Payments under this arrangement are considered a part of the operating cost, thus the debt ceiling is not applicable. A major advantage of this arrangement is that the funds are raised much faster than through conventional methods. Private financing is usually costlier than public financing, because the government in general can obtain loans at lower interest rates than private companies can. This has to be included in the cost analysis.

Construction of Facilities

Private firms claim that they can site and build prisons faster and less expensively than the government does. The largest private company, Corrections Corporation of America (CCA), states that its construction price is only 80 percent of the government's cost (Logan 1990). Generally, it takes between two and three years to site and build a prison (maximum-security prisons may take five years). Some contractors, however, have designed, financed, and built a facility in six months (Logan 1990). Comparisons should be made on the same kind of institution. Also, the quality of construction is important. New materials and new methods of building should be carefully evaluated (Sechrest et al. 1987).

Prison Operations

According to the private companies, they can deliver the same services less expensively than the government does through "the side-stepping of government bureaucracy in building and operating prisons, better staff motivation, the utilization of modem management techniques, and increased flexibility in the hiring and firing of employees" (Borna 1986, 328).

Labor Costs

Corrections is a labor intensive industry. Between 60 and 80 percent of the cost is labor related. In order to operate prisons less expensively than the government does, and to make profit on them, private companies must cut their labor costs. They do so in various ways: paying lower salaries, providing fewer fringe benefits, limiting promotions, reducing staff, and providing less training.

Advocates of privatization claim that labor cost-cutting is achieved mainly through flexible staffing, using more electronic surveillance, and substituting profit sharing for fringe benefits (Crants 1991). Critics, on the other hand, believe that labor cost-cutting may result in reduced safety and security in prisons. Also, staffing formulas are often fixed in the correctional standards and labor contracts, making them hard to change.

It has also been suggested that differences in the managerial approach between the public and the private sectors affect prison costs: "Profit-and-loss incentives differ fundamentally from budget-driven bureaucratic incentives. Entrepreneurs are competitively motivated to provide maximum satisfaction at minimum cost. In contrast, bureaucrats are rewarded not so much for efficiency, but in direct proportion to the size and total budget of their agencies" (Logan 1990, 86).

Flexibility

Private companies are more flexible and can take advantage of more opportunities to cut costs than can public agencies. They can purchase supplies from any business that offers the best price. Their purchasing does not have to go through complex bureaucratic channels, and they are not bound by contracts with specific suppliers, as governmental agencies are. Using their centralized purchasing power, they can buy supplies nationwide and look for the best prices.

The public sector is known to be wasteful. For example, surplus money remaining in public institutions at the end of the budget year must be spent. If there are savings, the next year's budget may be smaller. Thus, prudent money management is penalized rather than rewarded. Consequently, there is no incentive for cost control. Private companies do have an interest in cutting expenses, because every dollar saved increases their profit. It is not ensured, however, that any part of the savings will be transferred to the government. There is also the question of whether substantial cost-cutting would lower the quality of incarceration.

Per Diem Payments

The most often used formula of payment for correctional services is a specified sum per day. One concern is that private firms will have an interest in keeping the prisons filled to capacity in order to receive maximum payments. That could result in lobbying efforts to promote policies of imprisonment and to abandon programs aimed at early release (Anderson et al. 1985).

The government must guarantee a certain occupancy level, below which the per diem rate goes up in order to provide the contractor with a "safety net" against losses. The addition of each inmate in private prisons adds the same amount to the expenses. In public prisons, however, the addition of an inmate will increase the total cost only marginally and can decrease the per capita cost. This may be a factor in the overcrowding of public prisons.

Quality of Service

Private companies contend not only that they can operate prisons less expensively than governmental agencies do, but that at the same time they can provide better quality of service. In the context of prisons, some refer to quality of service in terms of the quality and quantity of food, the variety of programs, and the professional background of staff. Others use indicators such as the condition of the buildings, escape rates, security and control procedures, the physical and mental health of the inmates, and the extent of recidivism.

The few available studies aimed at exploring the quality of services in private prisons seem to agree that the services are either at the same level as, or better than, those in public facilities. It will have to be seen whether this pattern will continue when larger and higher security institutions are privatized.

There is a need for continuous scrutiny of all penal institutions. In private prisons, it is a concern that the profit motive not override other considerations in the operation of the facility. Cutting costs, whether or not it results in the decline of quality, provides an opportunity to increase corporate profits, and it may be too tempting for some firms not to follow this policy.

Rehabilitation of offenders can be considered as a matter of quality of service, both for the inmates, in helping them to become a part of mainstream society, and for the community, as a way of correcting antisocial behavior. This emphasis on rehabilitation as a major goal of corrections has declined sharply since the early 1970s, but the public's desire for some efforts to rehabilitate offenders still exists. As mentioned, private companies do not have an incentive to implement successful rehabilitation programs. In fact, it may be a disadvantage for them, as the programs could lead to earlier release of inmates and sometimes to a loss of income. A clear set of criteria for rehabilitation included in the contract and tied to the amount of profits that the company can make could have some positive results in this matter.

Management and Personnel Issues

Corrections is labor intensive. Therefore, staff/inmate ratios and staff training have an important role in determining the cost of incarceration and the quality of services. Employees influence the quality of life in a prison through the level of order maintained. The training and personal characteristics of the staff are important to the general atmosphere in prison.

A considerable number of private prison workers are recruited from the unskilled labor force, and many of them work only part-time (Weiss 1989). Some of them are retired state correctional officers and retired military personnel. Private correctional workers often have fewer professional qualifications than public prison staff. For example, it was found in a California study that a private company that operated work furlough projects, community correctional programs, and INS detention facilities required no formal training from its line employees and paid the minimum wage to its new workers.

While that is not necessarily the case with every private company, there seems to be a pattern of lower pay, fewer benefits, and lower staffing formulas than in public prisons. Critics question whether well-qualified staff can be hired for such low pay. Private companies claim that they follow the correctional standards set by the American Correctional Association (ACA). Others suggest that certain private companies provide better and more effective training for their workers than public agencies do (Crants 1991). It is also claimed that effective personnel management can cut operating costs without cutting salaries. "Adequate and appropriate staffing, better working conditions, and more efficient procedures improve productivity and morale, decrease absenteeism and turnover, and reduce expensive reliance on overtime" (Logan 1990, 81).

Alan M. Schuman, director of the Social Service Division in the superior court of the District of Columbia, points out that lower wages and fewer fringe benefits in private prisons lead to the hiring of less qualified personnel and a high turnover rate. "Many of the best qualified private sector staff eventually apply for public sector probation positions that offer more job security and higher salaries. The high turnover rate must impact the quality of services that are provided, a factor that should be considered in cost analysis" (Schuman 1989, 32).

To alleviate staff problems, some companies, like the CCA, provide a stock option plan for "key employees" that usually does not include custodial personnel. There is also an Employee Stock Ownership Plan for all employees. Such plans are devised to substitute for the fringe benefits that are not provided by the companies. The effects of these programs will have to be evaluated.

Studies of Private Prisons

There have been relatively few studies of private prisons. The Silverdale facility in Tennessee, operated by the CCA, has been evaluated several times. Logan and McGriff (1989) compared the operational cost of that institution with the estimated cost if it were operated by the same agencies that ran the facility before privatization. An annual savings of at least 3 to 8 percent was shown. The authors claimed also that the services were better under private management, mainly because there were two full-time managers instead of one—the warden and the government monitor.

Another study of the same facility focused on the inmates' perceptions of the quality of services (Brakel 1988). Generally, inmates gave more positive than ambivalent or negative ratings to the services in the private facility. There were negative ratings concerning recreational opportunities and release procedures. Release procedures and good time credits, however, were handled by public authorities and not by the CCA. Six inmates were able to compare the prevailing situation in Silverdale with the conditions when it was operated by the county. Out of twenty-eight comparisons, twenty-four were favorable to private and four to county administration. This study had some major methodological problems. The most obvious

was that the questionnaires were distributed by the prison chaplain to inmates in a manner that was "random in all respects except that they [inmates] were known by him to be reasonably articulate" (Brakel 1988,180). This procedure hardly can be considered unbiased, random, and scientific.

Another study compared three private facilities (one of them Silverdale) with three public institutions. One of the comparisons was made between two secure juvenile institutions (Sellers 1989). The researcher had made three on-site visits and had interviewed administrators and staff members. The main findings of this study showed that in private facilities more programs were generally available to the inmates than in public ones, and that the cost in private institutions was substantially lower than in public facilities, mainly because the latter had higher staff-inmate ratios. The study concluded that the main motive for prison privatization is financial. It was recognized that some firms may deliberately submit low bids in order to obtain contracts (low-balling). For the long run, however, it was projected that eventually the competition among contractors will keep costs down. Another positive effect of privatization suggested by this evaluation was that its efforts have created more options for the public sector.

The fact that several studies focused on the Silverdale facility raises the question whether there is anything unique about this institution. It is noteworthy that these studies fail to mention that in 1986 there was a riot in this facility. The inmates demanded better food, more adequate recreation, and generally better treatment. A police SWAT team was called in to restore order.

The Urban Institute has conducted an evaluation of two private facilities, one in Kentucky and the other in Massachusetts, and compared them with two public institutions in the same states. In Kentucky, two minimum security prisons were compared. The private prison scored higher in the quality of programs and the delivery of services. The per diem cost in the private facility was 10 percent higher, but if the construction costs had been included the public prison would have cost 28 percent more. In Massachusetts, secure juvenile institutions were compared. The quality of services was somewhat better in the private one, but there were no significant differences in the cost (Hatry et al. 1989).

Two other evaluations were reviewed by Thomas and Logan in a paper presented to the American Society of Criminology at its 1991 meeting. One of them compared the quality of incarceration in a privately operated female prison in New Mexico with the same prison a year earlier, when it was operated by the state, and with a federal women's prison. The study found that the private prison outperformed the state and federal institutions in six out of eight measures of quality. In a separate analysis, however, it was found that, while the staff survey and the official records showed a higher quality of confinement in the private prison, inmates favored the conditions in the state prison. This divergence of opinions should be examined further. In terms of expense, the private facility cost 12.8 percent less than the state prison.

The Texas State Auditor's office issued a report in 1991 on four five-hundred-bed prisons contracted out to two private firms. The report indicated that private companies operate facilities 10 to 15 percent less expensively than the State Department of Corrections could.

There is a need for more studies to assess the consequences of prison privatization. The Government Accounting Office has concluded that private prisons have not yet been shown to have a substantial advantage over public prisons and, therefore, it did not make a recommendation for the privatization of prisons in the federal system.

Conclusions

The major push toward privatization of prisons came with the unprecedented growth of the inmate population during the 1980s, in the wake of the "get tough" crime control policies and the great increase in the cost of criminal justice.

This development should be seen in the framework of the American tradition that favors small government and free competition. There is a widely held public opinion that private sector management is more efficient than public sector management and that workers in private organizations work harder, are more motivated, and do a better job than workers in the public sector. The terms "bureaucracy" and "bureaucrat" have come to epitomize society's negative attitude toward governmental organizations and their employees.

Similar attitudes are held toward prisons, which often show a poor record in terms of violence, riots, waste, and abuse of prisoners. Along with the lure of cost savings, they contribute to the support for private prisons. Prisons are expected to protect society by keeping violent and harmful inmates incarcerated, but at the same time they must house them safely. The public perception of inefficient management, violence, lack of rehabilitation, physical deterioration, and inept staff, coupled with growing cost, results in a negative attitude about prisons. Many feel that "the situation cannot become worse" and that "it is worth it to try anything" to improve prison conditions. These attitudes provide fertile ground for the privatization of prisons, an idea that not only promises lower costs but also better services.

There are, however, some pitfalls with this policy. Privatization tends to support the crime control policies of the 1980s. It promotes the idea that massive incarceration can win the "war on crime" and that the major task is to make incarceration less expensive and more flexible. It also diverts attention from alternatives to the growing trend of incarceration. On the other hand, the idea of prison privatization has helped to focus on the problems of public prisons and on needed reforms both in those institutions and the correctional system as a whole. A continuous effort to introduce more effective methods of operation and more flexible administration, with the cooperation of employee unions, could help to alleviate some of the problems of public prisons.

As noted, punishment is largely a moral issue. It involves judgments of what is right and what is wrong. In the debate about privatization, however, there is an overemphasis on pragmatic considerations, mainly cost, and a considerable neglect of ethical and theoretical issues. There is already a great deal of private involvement in the penal process and in corrections. The key question is where should the line be drawn in privatization? One opinion is that the operation of entire prisons should not be delegated to private entities because the administration of punishment is inherently a public function. An opposing opinion holds that while the determination of punishment has to be made by public authorities, its administration can be delegated to private parties, who may do a better job in terms of cost and even in terms of quality.

In a social climate of increasing public concern about violent crime and such legislation as "three strikes, you're out," there is a strong likelihood that the prison population will continue to increase and that that will fuel the development of privately operated prisons.

References

Anderson, P., C. R. Cavoli, and L. J. Moriarty. (1985). Private corrections: Feast or fiasco? *Prison Journal 45*(2): 32–41.

Borna, S. (1986). Free enterprise goes to prison. *British Journal of Criminology, 26*(4): 321–34.

Brakel, S. J. (1988). Prison management, private enterprise style: The inmate's evaluation. *New England Journal of Civil Confinement 14*(2): 175–244.

Crants, R. (1991). Private prison management: A study in economic efficiency. *Journal of Contemporary Criminal Justice 7*(1): 49–59.

Fenton, J. (1985). A private alternative to public prisons. *Prison Journal 65*(2): 42–47.

Gentry, J. T. (1986). The Panopticon revisited: The problem of monitoring private prisons. *Yale Law Journal 96*: 353–75.

Hatry, H. P., P. J. Brounstein, R. B. Levinson, D. M. Altschuler, K. Chi, and P. Rosenberg. (1989). *Comparison of Privately and Publicly Operated Corrections Facilities in Kentucky and Massachusetts*. Washington, D.C.: Urban Institute.

Logan, C. H. (1990). *Private Prisons: Cons and Pros*. New York: Oxford University Press.

Logan, C. H., and B. W. McGriff. (1989). *Comparing Costs of Public and Private Prisons: A Case Study*. Washington, D.C.: National Institute of Justice.

Matthews, R. (1989). Privatization in perspective. In R. Matthews, ed. *Privatizing Criminal Justice*. London: Sage.

Mullen, J., K. J. Chabotar, and D. M. Carrow. (1985). *The Privatization of Corrections*. Washington, D.C.: National Institute of Justice.

Schuman, A. M. (1989). The cost of correctional services: Exploring a poorly charted terrain. *Research in Corrections 2*: 27–33.

Sechrest, D. K., N. Papas, and S. J. Price. (1987). Building prisons: Pre-manufactured, prefabricated, and prototype. *Federal Probation 51*(1): 35–A1.

Sellers, M. P. (1989). Private and public prisons: A comparison of costs, programs, and facilities. *International Journal of Offender Therapy and Comparative Criminology 33*: 241–56.

Thomas, C. W., and S. L. Foard (1991). *Private Correctional Facility Census*. Gainesville, Fla.: Center for Studies in Criminology and Law, University of Florida.

Weiss, R. P. (1989). Private prisons and the state. In R. Matthews, ed. *Privatizing Criminal Justice*. London: Sage.

26
A Comparison of Job Satisfaction Among Private and Public Prison Employees

Emmitt L. Sparkman
Kevin I. Minor
James B. Wells

Focus Questions

1. Why is it predicted that private employees will be less satisfied on the job than public employees?

2. How do state and private employees compare in terms of demographic characteristics?

3. How satisfied are employees working in state-run prisons compared with those in private prisons?

4. Does higher pay translate into increased job satisfaction with private and public employees?

Privately operated prisons have become increasingly common over the last two decades. According to one source, in the United States the total capacity of private facilities operated by 12 companies in 1999 was 122,871 beds. The trend toward privatiza- tion grows out of the difficulties govern- ments at all levels have faced in trying to af- ford adequate bed space for the unprece- dented growth of the prison population. At the end of 1998, there were over 1.3 million adults in state and federal institutions, com- pared to less than 774,000 at the end of 1990—a rise of almost 70 percent. The pri- vatization trend is also attributable to the enormous profit potential that privatization presents. The two largest firms, Corrections Corporation of America and Wackenhut Corrections, controlled over three-fourths of the U.S. market in 1999 and have built re- cords of solid performance on the New York Stock Exchange (Shichor 1999).

The growth of private prisons has sparked heated public controversies and increased media attention (e.g., Yeoman 2000). Mixed with this have been academic debates and a growing number of research studies devoted to the topic. For example, recent studies have compared private and public prisons on measures of cost effectiveness (Pratt and Maahs 1999) and recidivism (Lanza- Kaduce, Parker, and Thomas 1999). Other recent studies have explored the impact of privatization on prisons as organizations, with particular attention to how privatiza- tion may alter organizational goals and func- tioning (Ogle, 1999; Shichor 1999). Still other authors have commented on the legal liability issues introduced by the privatiza- tion movement (e.g., Josi and Sechrest 1998).

As Shichor (1999, 227) notes, "the prom- ise of privatization is that it is a vehicle that can finance and build correctional facilities faster and cheaper than government agen- cies, and that it can operate them for a lower cost without reducing the quality of services provided." However, studies have shown that privatization is not necessarily more cost effective (Pratt and Maahs 1999). And despite some evidence to the contrary (Logan 1992), there continues to be concern that private firms trim services for inmates as well as employee pay and benefits in order to maximize their profits (Bates 1999).

While private and public prisons have been compared on such dimensions as cost effectiveness, inmate recidivism, and quality of services, minimal research has compared the employees of public and private prisons. Specifically, not much has been known about how, if at all, public and private employees differ on basic demographic variables like ethnicity, education, and salary, and nothing has been known about whether these employees differ in their levels of job satisfaction. The present study addresses this gap in knowledge. The study examines differences between public and private prison employees on various demographic and work-related factors as well as differences on several measures of job satisfaction.

Job satisfaction is a critical factor in any agency or organization. Research shows that many correctional workers who are dissatisfied with their jobs will leave those jobs for other employment (Wright 1993), and in a field like corrections, high employee turnover can result in inefficient expenditures on training. Wright also found that correctional employees who quit their jobs tended to have higher performance ratings than those who remained. Studies show that dissatisfied employees cannot be expected to be committed and contribute their best efforts to the organization, and the logical implication is that organizational effectiveness will suffer (see Lambert, Barton, and Hogan 1999; Mottaz 1987).

The job satisfaction of public prison employees has been researched. For example, Hepburn and Knepper (1993) found job satisfaction to be related to the intrinsic rewards of the job among both program/treatment staff and security staff. In this same study, job satisfaction of treatment staff was related to the degree of perceived authority over inmates; staff who perceived themselves as having more authority were more satisfied. Likewise, Robinson, Porporino and Simourd (1997) found that correctional officers with college degrees expressed less job satisfaction than those without degrees.

To date, no studies have compared the job satisfaction of public and private prison employees. Yet as Lampkin (1991, 46) points out, "wages, benefits and working conditions are often different between publicly-operated and privately-operated prisons." She notes that privatization may "mean lower wages, reduced employee benefits, and higher employee turnover." To the extent that this is the case, private prison workers might be expected to display less job satisfaction than their public prison counterparts. Hence, the present study examines the job satisfaction of employees from three public and three private prison facilities located in a Southern state.

Method

Sample

The sample consisted of all employees with permanent full-time status in three minimum-security public facilities operated by the state Department of Corrections and three minimum-security private facilities operated by a private company under contract with the state (N=384). Permanent full-time status meant that employees had completed the training required for the position held and had been working for at least six months. The largest public facility had a capacity of just over 400 inmates and a workforce of about 100 employees, while the smallest had a capacity of less than 200 inmates and less than 50 employees (a 4:1 ratio in both cases). By comparison, the largest private institution had an inmate capacity of 500 and employed nearly 100 staff; the inmate capacity of the smallest private institution was 400, and this facility had just over 70 staff (a 5:1 and 6:1 ratio, respectively). Thus, inmate-to-staff ratios were narrower in the public facilities.

Measures

The instruments used to measure job satisfaction included the Job Descriptive Index (JDI) and the Job in General (JIG) scales. These instruments were chosen because they have been widely used in past research on job satisfaction and because the reading level is appropriate for the sample. Both instruments have been standardized in prior research and have demonstrated good reliability and validity (Balzer et al. 1997).

As the name suggests, the JIG measures an individual's overall level of satisfaction with his or her job. The JDI provides separate, more specific measures of satisfaction with the following aspects of a job: (a) the work itself, (b) pay, (c) promotion opportunities, (d) supervision, and (e) coworkers (see Figure 26.1). The possible point range on the JIG and on each of the five JDI scales is 0-54, with higher scores indicating greater job satisfaction.

Employees completing the JIG and JDI were also asked to furnish information about a variety of demographic and work-related variables on a separate sheet. These variables included gender, ethnicity, age, education, salary, job classification (security versus nonsecurity), length of time spent working at the present facility and in the field of corrections, and amount of contact with inmates.

Data collection procedure. The first author administered the survey (composed of the JDI, JIG, and the demographic sheet) to small groups of employees during each of three work shifts. At each administration, employees were given a standard introduction to the research and standard instructions for completing the survey. They were apprised that participation in the study was strictly voluntary and that responding would be anonymous. They were instructed to seal completed surveys without their names in an envelope and then deposit the envelope in a box.

In an effort to maximize the sample size, the first author made two trips to each of the six institutions. Any employee who did not complete the survey during one of these visits could not be included in the study. Of the total 384 public and private prison employees, 294 completed the survey, for a return rate of 76.6 percent. The response rate at individual prisons ranged from a high of 86.5 percent to a low of 65.7 percent. The average response rate across the private facilities (77.5 percent) was very similar to the average rate across the public prisons (75.1 percent).

Results

Subject Characteristics

Of the 294 survey respondents, 121 (41.2 percent) were public employees and the remaining respondents (58.8 percent) were employed in private prisons. The two panels of Table 26.1 summarize the demographic and work-related characteristics of these employees. The data in this table reveal that the majority of respondents were male (78.6 percent), white (92.5 percent), in their mid-thirties to early forties, and had slightly more than a twelfth-grade education. Over half (56.7 percent) of the entire sample reported having salaries at or below the median salary range, which was $15,001 to $17,500. (The salary range started at $10,000 and advanced by increments of $2,500.) Nearly 60 percent were classified as security personnel, and most were relatively experienced staff. Out of the entire sample (n=294), ten staff members had worked in both a public and a private prison; nine of these had transferred from a state facility to a private prison, while one began working for the state after receiving experience at a private facility.

Statistical testing revealed several significant differences between public and private employees in terms of the variables shown in Table 26.1. A greater proportion of private employees (98.3 percent) than public ones (84.3 percent) were white ($X^2 = 20.07$, df = 1, p .05). Likewise, public employees were on average older than private employees [t (287) = 5.64, p .05]. Compared to public prison staff, a greater proportion of private prison employees had security job classifications ($X^2 = 5.03$, df = 1, p .05) and salaries below the median range ($X^2 = 72.46$, df = 1, p .05). In fact, over 90 percent of private staff had salaries of $20,000 or less; this was true for under half (43.8 percent) of the public staff. Public staff had worked significantly more years at their present facilities [t (152.29) = 5.03, p .05] and also had signifi-

Table 26.1
Demographic and Work-Related Characteristics of Prison Staff

Panel A

Variable	Public Employees		Private Employees	
	n	%	n	%
Gender				
Male	95	78.5	136	78.6
Female	26	21.5	37	21.4
Ethnicity				
White	102	84.3	170	98.3
African American	19	15.7	3	1.7
Salary				
In or Below Median Range	33	27.3	133	77.3
Above Median Range	88	72.7	39	22.7
Job Classification				
Security	63	52.1	112	65.1
Non-Security	58	47.9	60	34.9

Panel B

Variable	Public Institution	Private Institution
Age		
Mean	42.5	35.7
SD	9.5	10.5
Years Education		
Mean	14.1	13.5
SD	1.9	1.7
Years at Present Facility		
Mean	7.0	4.1
SD	6.0	2.6
Years Working in Corrections		
Mean	9.3	4.8
SD	6.6	3.5
Number of Inmates Employee Has Contact with Daily		
Mean	76.1	89.4
SD	88.2	101.6

cantly more years of correctional experience overall [t (168.94) = 7.0, p .05].

Job Satisfaction

The possible point range on each measure of job satisfaction is 0 to 54, with higher scores indicating more job satisfaction. According to the developers of the JDI and JIG (Balzer et al., 1997), scores of 32 or greater demonstrate satisfaction with one's job, while scores of 22 or less show dissatisfaction; scores between 31 and 23 are in the neutral range. Figure 26.1 shows that the mean scores for employees of both public and private facilities were within the satisfaction range on the JIG as well as on the co-workers and supervision aspects of the JDI.

Private employees were in the satisfaction range on the work measure, and public employees had slightly lower scores. By contrast, both groups of staff were quite dissatisfied with pay, and public employees also expressed dissatisfaction with promotion opportunities; private staff fell in the neutral range on the promotion measure. There was only one significant difference found between job satisfaction scores of public and private staff members. T-tests revealed that staff members of private institutions were significantly more positive about their prospects for promotion than employees of public institutions.

The last step in the analysis was to investigate the relationship between job satisfac-

Figure 26.1
Job Satisfaction of Public and Private Prison Employees

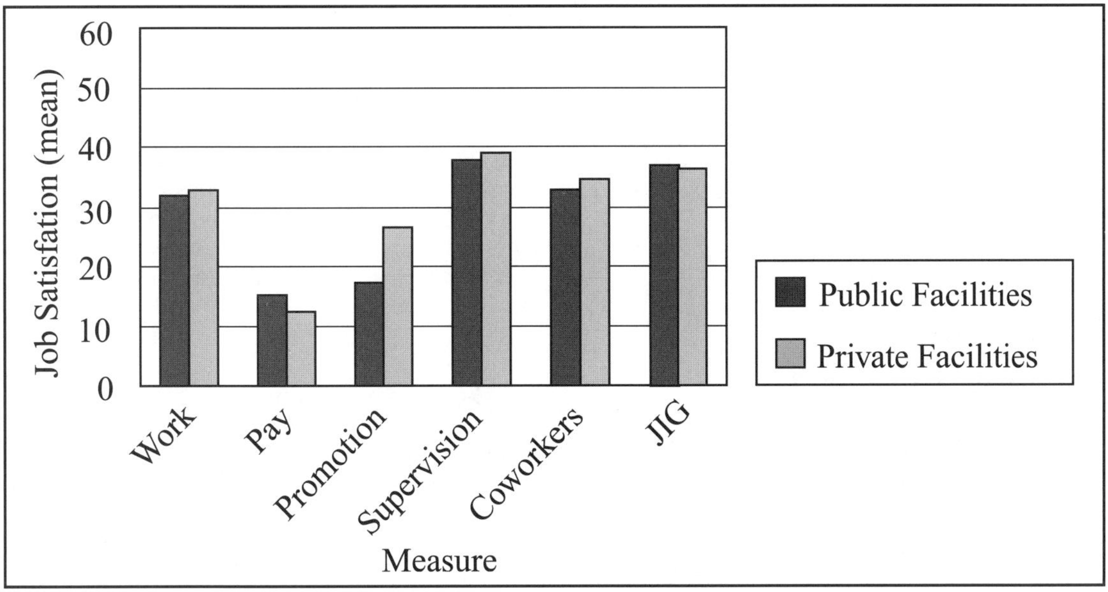

tion and pay for each type of facility in order to determine whether higher-paid employees exhibited greater satisfaction regardless of the type of facility in which they were working. Employees who made salaries above the median were compared with employees who were at or below the median. T-tests indicated that higher pay was associated with greater job satisfaction among private employees. Higher-paid private employees were significantly more satisfied with pay, promotion opportunities, coworkers, and with their jobs in general. However, this trend did not hold true for state prison staff. Higher-paid state prison staff exhibited greater satisfaction in being paid more, but they were no more satisfied on any other job satisfaction measure than public staff members who were paid less.

Discussion

This research uncovered several noteworthy differences between public and private prison employees on demographic and work-related variables. On average, public prison employees: (a) had higher salaries, (b) were more likely to hold nonsecurity jobs such as administrator or caseworker, (c) were older, and (d) had more job experience—both at their present facilities and in the field of corrections overall. These differences are undoubtedly interrelated to some extent. That is, most persons who hold nonsecurity jobs in prison earn more money than security staff, and they also tend to be older, more experienced staff who, in some cases, have advanced to their present positions from the security ranks.

This may partially explain why public prison staff displayed lower satisfaction toward opportunities for promotion. It is possible that a greater proportion of public than private employees had already received promotions and, as such, did not anticipate or expect as much by way of promotion for the future. Alternatively, because public employees were generally older and more experienced, they may have actually held greater expectations for promotion. If promotions were not forthcoming as staff anticipated or felt they deserved, these employees may have developed more negative perceptions of promotional opportunities than younger employees with less experience.

There are at least two other possible interpretations for the finding that private prison employees were significantly more positive toward promotion prospects than public employees, and these interpretations are not mutually exclusive. First, like any business, private prison companies actively seek contracts for new ventures and, by definition, create new job opportunities for their employees when contracts are obtained. Thus, private prison employees may actually have more advancement opportunities, particularly if they are willing to relocate to other areas of the state or nation.

Second, the promotion process can become bureaucratized and politicized in both the public and private sectors. In private business, however, profit is essential for survival and expansion, and employee job performance is a key factor in maintaining and increasing profits. Therefore, an employee's actual job performance might be expected to overshadow political or bureaucratic considerations that are only tangential to profit goals when promotion decisions are made. Because public prisons do not rely on profit to nearly the same degree, promotion decisions may be more vulnerable to being affected by the needs of the corrections bureaucracy and political patronage. This issue is in need of additional research.

Both public and private prison employees expressed satisfaction with respect to the nature of the work, their supervision, their co-workers, and their jobs generally. This is rather surprising in view of their considerable dissatisfaction with pay. There is no evidence that pay dissatisfaction carried over to cause dissatisfaction with the other areas. However, when considering pay satisfaction, it must also be noted that many of these employees (both public and private) resided in economically depressed rural areas where alternatives to prison work were neither plentiful nor promising. It is reasonable to think that when people form opinions about their jobs, they do so in view of the alternatives for employment that exist in their communities.

The data confirmed that employees of private prisons were generally not paid as well as employees of public facilities. Although over three-quarters of the private employees had salaries in or below the median salary range for the sample, this was true for only about one-quarter of the public prison employees. Interestingly, however, there were no significant differences between the two groups on the measure of pay satisfaction.

When the relationship between job satisfaction and pay was studied for public and private facilities separately, it was found that higher pay was associated with greater job satisfaction only among private prison employees. Public employees exhibited similar levels of satisfaction regardless of salary range. An implication of this finding is that pay may be linked to job satisfaction only when pay levels are relatively low. When salaries are higher, pay and job satisfaction may be largely independent of one another. The data from the public prison employees suggest that increasing salary is not necessarily a viable means of improving satisfaction with any aspect of the job except the pay aspect itself.

It has been suggested (Lombardo 1989; Johnson 1996) that corrections should be conceptualized as a human services field in which staff serve the needs of persons under correctional custody. This conception seems to presuppose that staff members feel their own needs are being served as correctional employees. There is concern that private prisons provide fewer and lower-quality services for their employees than public prisons, since private institutions have an incentive to cut employee pay and benefits to maximize profit. Past research implies that employee job satisfaction can significantly impact the effectiveness of an organization and the services it delivers to clients. Job satisfaction is obviously not a complete proxy for organizational effectiveness and the quantity or quality of services delivered. However, the logical implication of the finding that public and private prison workers differed only minimally in job satisfaction is that this general concern about private prisons may not be entirely founded; some qualifications may be in order. If future research confirms that private facilities generally do provide fewer and lower-quality employee services than public ones, the findings of this study imply that the differential in services may not translate into differences in employee job satisfaction.

Note

An earlier version of this chapter was presented at the annual meeting of the Academy of Criminal Justice Sciences, New Orleans, LA, March 2000.

References

Balzer, William K., Jenifer A. Kihm, Patricia C. Smith, Jennifer L. Irwin, Peter D. Bachiochi, Chet Robie, Evan F. Sinar, and Luis F. Parra. 1997. *Users' Manual for the Job Descriptive Index (JDI; 1997 Revision) and the Job in General (JIG) Scales*. Bowling Green, OH: Bowling Green State University.

Bates, Eric. 1999. "Prisons for Profit." In Kenneth C. Hass and Geoffrey P. Alpert (eds.), *The Dilemmas of Corrections* (pp. 592–604). Prospect Heights, IL: Waveland Press.

Hepburn, John, and Paul E. Knepper. 1993. "Correctional Officers as Human Services Workers: The Effect on Job Satisfaction." *Justice Quarterly* 10: 315–334.

Johnson, Robert. 1996. *Hard Time: Understanding and Reforming the Prison*. 2nd ed. Belmont, CA: Wadsworth.

Josi, Don A., and Dale K. Sechrest. 1998. *The Changing Career of the Correctional Officer: Policy Implications for the 21st Century*. Boston, MA: Butterworth-Heinemann.

Lambert, Eric G., Shannon M. Barton, and Nancy Lynne Hogan. 1999. "The Missing Link Between Job Satisfaction and Correctional Staff Behavior: The Issue of Organizational Commitment." *American Journal of Criminal Justice* 24: 95–116.

Lampkin, Linda M. 1991. "Does Crime Pay? AFSCME Reviews of the Record on the Privatization of Prisons." *Journal of Contemporary Criminal Justice* 7: 41–48.

Lanza-Kaduce, Lonn, Karen F. Parker, and Charles W. Thomas. 1999. "A Comparative Recidivism Analysis of Releasees From Private and Public Prisons." *Crime & Delinquency* 45: 28–47.

Logan, Charles H. 1992. "Well Kept: Comparing Quality of Confinement in Private and Public Prisons." *Journal of Criminal Law and Criminology* 83: 577–613.

Lombardo, Lucien X. 1989. *Guards Imprisoned: Correctional Officers at Work*. 2nd ed. Cincinnati, OH: Anderson.

Mottaz, Clifford J. 1987. "An Analysis of the Relationship Between Work Satisfaction and Organizational Commitment." *Sociological Quarterly* 28: 541–558.

Ogle, Robbin. 1999. "Prison Privatization: An Environmental Catch-22." *Justice Quarterly* 16: 579–600.

Pratt, Travis C., and Jeff Maahs. 1999. "Are Private Prisons More Cost-Effective Than Public Prisons? A Meta-Analysis of Evaluation Research Studies." *Crime & Delinquency* 45: 358–371.

Robinson, David, Frank J. Porporino, and Linda Simourd. 1997. "The Influence of Educational Attainment on the Attitudes and Job Performance of Correctional Officers." *Crime & Delinquency* 43: 60–77.

Shichor, David. 1999. "Privatizing Correctional Institutions: An Organizational Perspective." *The Prison Journal* 79: 226–249.

University of Florida. 1999. Census of Private Prisons. *http://web.crim.ufl.edu/pcp/census/1999/market.html*.

Wright, Thomas A. 1993. "Correctional Employee Turnover: A Longitudinal Study." *Journal of Criminal Justice* 21: 131–142.

Yeoman, Barry. 2000. "Steel Town: Corrections Corporation of America Is Trying to Turn Youngstown, Ohio, Into the Private-Prison Capital of the World." *Mother Jones* May/June: 39–45.

27
Six of One, Half-Dozen of the Other: Private Prisons and the Conditions of Confinement Debate

Alan C. Mobley

Focus Questions

1. What is most important to convicted prisoners in Mobley's view?

2. What purpose did the convict leasing system serve in history?

3. Why did private prisons reappear in the early 1980s?

4. What are unintended consequences of privatization?

5. In Mobley's view, why isn't the prison privatization debate more urgent for convicted felons?

Have you ever been inside a prison? I have. I lived in prison for nearly ten years. I worked there every day and slept there every night. Think about that for a minute. Where were you ten years ago? What were you doing? I was in prison. How about five years ago, or three? Prison. Think of the places you visited, the people you met, and all the new experiences of just the last year. It's almost overwhelming, isn't it? I spent nine years, eleven months, two weeks and one day, nearly a third of my life, in prison. My goal here is to give you the prisoner perspective on private prisons. I think you will agree that I am qualified, even if I am an ex-convict.

Doing Time

Some guys do their time in a virtual coma—the lights are on but nobody's home. Not me. Right from the beginning things were expected of me. Federal prosecutors had used the press to make me sort of famous—in the drug lord kind of way. So, ready or not, I had to be awake. That meant a certain level of awareness, of vigilance, on my part. The result was that I wasn't just in prison; I made a study of prison.

One of the first things they taught me was that you do the time, or the time will do you. Most convicts would say that "time is a motherfucker." It is relentless. If you dwell on where you are—and where you aren't—your own thoughts will become your worst enemy; they'll break you. Time will crawl and the suffering might lead you to betray friends, values, family, whatever, just to get out. I managed to survive by working on a bachelor's degree in economics and a master's in sociology. My studies really helped to pass the time.

Scholars and Cons

One hurdle I have had to overcome in writing this piece is my academic knowledge of private prisons. After my release from prison, I was accepted into graduate school at a major university. Right now I am in the final stages of writing a doctoral dissertation on prison privatization. When I graduate, I'll have an interdisciplinary Ph.D. in criminology, law, and society.

As a scholar, I have been trained to see things in a broad perspective, in a detached, ideal, or hypothetical way. The study of private prisons readily lends itself to such abstract analysis. For example, an evaluation of a competently run private facility will include the consideration of worst-case scenarios. In an earlier essay here, Shichor points to some of the temptations to exploit prisoners facing private prison operators. Delaying the release of inmates is one such possibility. Researchers studying privates have to question whether prudent business people might try to "milk every dime" out of their inmates by keeping them incarcerated longer. Public prisons, on the other hand, do not have this potentially corrosive motivation built into their portfolios.

Hypothetical situations mean little to prison inmates. Prisoners are all about the concrete here and now. Whether fighting their cases or pursuing policy changes, they have no time for theorizing; all they want is freedom. Some are politically aware of the finer points of penal politics, but for about 95 percent of prisoners, the important issues are those related to confinement conditions. In the eyes of most convicts, the more desirable joint to do time provides the best "three hots and a cot."

Conditions of Confinement

Being in any prison, public or private, is unpleasant by design. Prisons are intended to punish and they succeed in that very well. The basics of incarceration have not changed much over time, but the fundamental philosophies that support prisons have. At different times in American prison history, various ideas or ideologies have offered guidance. These ideas reflect the worldviews that prevailed in this country during those times.

One recurring theme in prison lore is the idea that prisons should be run exclusively by the state. State control of penal systems was thought to guarantee a higher, more humane quality of care. The state, however, has not hesitated to use the services of private, for-profit prison entrepreneurs when it was deemed necessary. Malcolm Feeley (1991) wrote that private prisons have been instrumental in easing state systems through transitions in penal philosophy. Feeley argues that contract prisons helped governments cope with changing conditions, such as overcrowding, by expanding and transforming the state's capacity to punish. Far from opposing privatization, the state used the presence of free-market jailers to plan and implement correctional policies. This intermittent sanctioning of private prisons illustrates well the American paradox involving morals and money. Many Americans want to be rich and morally right, but it is difficult to have it both ways.

In Colonial America, for example, Christianity was of primary importance because religion set the moral tone. Persons convicted of crimes against either civil or religious codes were placed in solitary cells and expected to reconnect with God. This arrangement in part replaced the colonies' first detention centers, an assortment of private, for-profit "gaols" that held persons of both sexes and all ages in filthy conditions. The change to a cleaner, more Spartan prison environment was thought to help spur the redemption process. Penal historians inform us, however, that solitude drove some inmates insane and others to suicide (Rothman 1980).

As science and rational thinking came to dominate the American mind, prisons were reoriented toward behavior modification. Instead of purifying the soul and allowing it to guide the mind and body, penology began to emphasize more direct physical and mental training. Prison populations grew, budgets soared, and many became like factories. Their purpose was to produce useful products and compliant, forthright citizens. Industrial prisons retained tightly regimented routines by employing timetables, strict standards, and officially sanctioned violence. Striped uniforms, enforced silence, and the lockstep march typified these institutions. Prisoners working hard labor were often contracted to private interests. These often cozy, politically expedient arrangements permitted the state to inculcate values and a proper work ethic while at the same time controlling costs or even turning a profit (Clear and Cole 2000). The infamous "convict leasing system," in particular, dominated Southern penal practices for decades following the Civil War.

Convict leasing in the postbellum South is often held up as exemplary of and a warning against the peculiar horrors of privatization. I believe there is much to learn from that tragic period, and at the same time I think the period should be recognized as the historic anomaly it was. The South was in the midst of a profound transformation, from a culture dependant on chattel slavery to one supported by prison slavery (Esposito and Wood 1982). Generations were to pass before many Southern societies felt secure in their postwar political economy and social relations. Only after regaining their financial footing did many Southern legislatures permit moral arguments to intrude on essentially racist imprisonment policies (Taylor 1999). In the meantime, much deprivation and death stalked the South's mostly black, laboring convict population.

Northern reformatory prisons were far less deadly than plantations, mines, timber camps, or chain gangs, but conditions were hardly more comfortable. Release decisions were left to self-interested prison administrators and arbitrary parole boards. Zebulon Brockway was warden at Elmira, the most highly touted reformatory. According to research conducted by Alexander Pisciotta, in the five years between October 1888 and September 1893, Brockway personally delivered 19,497 blows to 2,578 inmates using a 22-inch by 3-inch-wide leather strap. During the same period prisoners spent 7,609 days in "rest cure" solitary confinement (cited in Blomberg and Lucken 2000, 76–77). It appears that even in the "enlightened" North, only semantics separated punishment from reform.

Over the next half-century the onset of two world wars and a cold war demonstrated the limits of science to shape human lives in uniformly positive ways. Technological innovations transformed American society, yet "progress" did not bring an end to U.S. involvement in warfare, political assassination, racial discrimination, or social unrest. In fact, the rapid pace of social change enabled by technology actually added to the country's internal problems. By the 1960s, many writers feared that society itself was to blame for rising crime. Excepting the slow-to-change Old South, many prisons were reformulated to help criminals "find" themselves. Profit-oriented prisons had all but disappeared from the scene, and human relations experts decided that individualized, therapeutic treatment stood a better chance of rehabilitating offenders than did the standardized uniformity of the factory or reformatory.

New state and federal prisons constructed during this time were built to resemble campuses, and a wide-ranging series of educational and therapeutic programs were established. Still, most prisoners continued to live in cells, most remained racially segregated, and program participation was encouraged through coercive means. In many states, inmate enforcers were often used to maintain a semblance of order. Endemic staff corruption, systematic violence, inmate-on-inmate rape, and periodic riots, such as the slaughter at Attica in 1971, highlight this period, known without a trace of irony as the "rehabilitative ideal."

The mid-1980s saw the emergence of the latest prison trend: cost cutting. For the most part, penal strategies of the past, whether therapeutic, reformatory, rehabilitational, vocational, or spiritual, had been judged failures, and no new grand designs had been put forward. Placing criminal careers "on hold" via incapacitation moved to the top of correctional goals. Mass incarceration in warehouse prisons is presently aided by the construction of "correctional complexes" composed of several prisons sited on one location. This configuration is expected to achieve economies of scale and operational synergies. Supermax prisons hold especially troublesome inmates in isolation. Gangs, the spread of infectious disease, geriatric needs, race-based violence, official malfeasance, and staff brutality are of concern. Although not immune from traditional prison problems, privatized corrections management has been introduced in a large number of states to provide cost savings (Shichor 1995).

Private prison operations began to reappear in the early 1980s, advertising themselves as able to do the same job as public facilities but for a lower cost. This mission statement obviously holds little appeal to prisoners interested in improved conditions. In fact, nearly all private prison managers are hired away from public prison systems. Not surprisingly, the similarities between the two organizational orientations are much more noticeable than the differences. Still, the history of prisons reminds us that there is always the possibility, if not the inevitability, of reform. Private prison operators may once again find themselves the agents of change, willingly or not.

Prison Reform and Rhetoric

For our purposes, it is important to note that both prison yards and prison policies are highly contested ground. Each era of penal policy has seen competing factions battle to remedy the ills wrought by their foes and predecessors. Reform programs have improved targeted problem areas, but they have also, often innocently, created negative consequences of their own. These then serve as fodder for future reforms. Through tumultuous periods of reform and counter-reform, prisoners have remained committed to one goal: getting out. Besides the Holy Grail of release, inmates are mainly interested in doing their time as safely and comfortably as possible.

Interestingly, the simple goals pursued by prisoners often put them at odds with reformers on both sides of the political divide. Prison activists see themselves as agents of change, and inmates as their raw materials. Conservatives often want to punish or "save the souls" of offenders, while liberals are usually interested in "helping" or "fixing" them. Prisoners just want humane treatment, and to be left alone.

One reason prison inmates distrust prison activists of all stripes is the rhetoric they employ. Liberal prison activists typically decry the squalid conditions and predatory horrors of prisons, urging reform by warning the public to expect the worst from released felons. Although convicts appreciate the motives behind these pleas, many find that promoting images of inmate depravity and dangerousness worsens the already difficult task of post-release reintegration. Similarly, hard-line conservatives who see prisons as "soft" and "coddling" do cons no favors by portraying them as heavily muscled hulks, lazy, and morally reprehensible.

Reformers are currently drawing sides regarding privatization. Conservatives favoring free-market approaches to social life welcome the introduction of private-sector initiatives into corrections. These activists often fail to consider prisoners at all when discussing management or prison operations. For them, a suitable definition of "inmate" might be "bed-filler matter," since contractors get paid for each occupied prison bed. Liberals, on the other hand, complain about the questionable morality of profiting from the misery of others. They hold the state responsible for both the well-being and the suffering inflicted upon convicted criminals. Delegating the penal function to entrepreneurs is seen as distasteful, an abdication of responsibility, and ripe for abuse.

Prisoners tend to view such matters with a jaundiced eye. They suspect that well-connected people and institutions have been profiting from incarceration since the first penitentiary. With political conservatives currently ascendant, private prisons may find no shame in this latest, blatant financial exploitation of inmates. The very obviousness of their profiteering, however, may set the stage for their eventual undoing, as prisoners are always on the lookout for weaknesses in their keepers, and the need to turn a profit is a definite vulnerability. Prisoners with long sentences and little to lose may have found just the lever they need to force concessions on living arrangements from prison authorities.

Unintended Consequences of Privatization I: Increased Violence

Prisoners are aware of the ways in which those who detain them profit. Wardens and other upper-management figures in both public and private prisons have nice offices and secretaries and wear good suits. Inmates often work at jobs that pay a pittance, while the items they produce are sold at full market value. Should a prisoner feel resentment over his economic position, there is very little he can do about it. The government that convicted and sentenced him, and that now demeans and subjugates him, is so complex, multifaceted, and powerful that the futility of revenge is obvious.

When the state or federal government hires an outside agent to administer the punishment and degradation, however, the situation shifts. In the case of private prisons, inmates know that the company has a state contract paying a fixed amount per head. The private prison goes to great lengths to save money and increase profitability. If a prisoner can figure ways to waste money, he can effectively "get back" at the company, and through them, strike at government. If an inmate causes enough trouble, breaks enough equipment, damages enough property, threatens sufficient violence upon inmates and staff, he might even single-handedly drive the enterprise "into the red." If several convicts join together and quietly set about a program of subtle sabotage, the effects to the corporation could be devastating.

Unintended Consequences of Privatization II: Prisoner Empowerment

The possibility that inmates might knowingly and concertedly go about draining resources from a facility must be the bogeyman of private prison managers. Their institutions are designed and staffed in order to make money, and that means they often rely on dormitory housing and high inmate-to-staff ratios. Signs of trouble within the prison often provoke precautionary management measures, such as the deployment of additional officers. Such unplanned staffing drives up costs. Similarly, open inmate housing configurations make it difficult to restore order should a disturbance actually occur. Expensive-to-fix injuries and substantial property damages could pose dire fiscal consequences for a facility.

How can the risk-averse private prison manager guard against financial ruin at the hands of embittered or deviously clever inmates? Besides making impossibly expensive changes to the physical structure of an institution, it seems that the only alternative is to actually enlist the aid of inmates. If inmates feel that they have influence in prison operations and are empowered to create an environment that serves their needs, it stands to reason that the chances of their wrecking the place would be reduced. It seems to me that the savvy prison entrepreneur must work with prisoners to protect the company's investment, and that means some sort of power-sharing arrangement.

Almost all prisons operate on a basis of some level of cooperation between prisoners and staff, but the actual sharing of official power is different. Still, permitting inmates to participate in their own governance has been tried before. Southern prison plantations, or "farms," used to grant certain prisoners the authority to boss other inmates, even to carry firearms and guard perimeters. Such "inmate trustee" systems eventually got out of hand and became notorious for their abuses. According to prison managers, the system worked well for a long while (DiIulio 1987). For a time, California allowed an inmate union that elected representatives to serve in administrative advisory capacities. Prisoners could propose changes within the prison, and managers consulted with inmate leaders. Political pressures from beyond the walls brought the union experiment to an end. While it operated, however, the power-sharing scheme was considered highly progressive penology (Cummins 1994).

Involving prisoners in the governing of prisons has its risks, certainly, but financially pressed for-profit managers may be left with few alternatives. I have already seen one such scenario unfold. During my dissertation research, I saw a private prison facility go from staggering losses to profitability by employing inmates in supervisory roles. A standard inmate housing unit was transformed into an intensive drug-treatment program, and long-term inmates were trained as counselors. This type of unit is sometimes referred to as a therapeutic community (TC). Both private and public prison managers admire TCs for their relatively safe, trouble-free environments. In the case of private prisons, penal administrators who set up TCs are often able to levy additional charges for enhanced services, without incurring added personnel expenses. The private unit that I observed was managed by a former prisoner and staffed by current inmates. The prisoners I spoke with indicated a strong sense of common purpose or "family" and seemed committed to the program's success. The unit's discipline record was exemplary.

Could inmate-assisted housing units exist in public prisons? Surely, they can and do. But the remarkable thing about this situation was the way in which a set of structural liabilities—architecture literally set in stone and few funds for paid staff—was converted into a program asset. In quick succession, a besieged prison administration revamped its programs and surrendered some conventional penal control in favor of peace—and profits. Whether this particular configuration will remain a "win-win" situation is an open question. I suspect that inmates participating in the drug program may come to find the arrangement as oppressive as conventional imprisonment. Should that day come, hapless managers may find themselves facing insurrection once again.

Conclusion

In *The Perpetual Prisoner Machine*, Dyer (2000) found that most people who hear of prison privatization find the idea repugnant. The state, it is reasoned, ought to have an exclusive on the infliction of punishment. When told of the potential cost savings of privatized prisons, however, Dyer noticed that many views changed. Prisons are seen as necessary evils and dead weights on society. The consensus seems to be that if we must have them, we should at least minimize the economic drain.

For prisoners, the debate over privatization is not all that pressing. Besides arrest, the real drama happens in court. After you get sentenced, your sights turn to doing your time as painlessly as possible. If that means assignment to a private prison, fine. If things change and the private prison turns out bad, provoking improvements in living conditions inside a private prison may be easier than in conventional, state-run prisons.

Of course, anything that adds to or strengthens the burgeoning prison-industrial complex in America is a curse to prisoners. Sparkling new prisons may mean better living conditions, but they also mean no early releases to ease overcrowding. In the long run, the very availability of new prison space may trigger a bureaucratic project aimed at keeping it filled. That would mean the hiring of more cops and prosecutors, and the enactment of more laws and tighter parole rules. As Jerome Miller (1996) reminds us in his book *Search and Destroy: African-American Males in the Criminal Justice System*, the continuous widening of the "legal net" is making human targets of those whom we define as "outlaws." Excess prison capacity would only enhance our ability to do so.

One more thing about me. I was down about five years when a musical group came to the joint to perform. I loved it. They had women, it was outdoors on a beautiful spring day, and even though we were in Texas, I actually liked the music. The problem was I liked it too much. After one especially rousing song, the cheering finally stopped, and I noticed where I was. I was sitting on the concrete surrounded by prisoners, more concrete, steel, and bars. I was in prison. When "reality" hit me, when I came back to my body and noticed where I was, I realized that I had forgotten about prison for maybe the first time in five years. I felt tears in my eyes. They were partly in gratitude for the psychological and spiritual escape, and part in despair over my return. Prison is like that. Amenities and simple pleasures can make you feel good, and then really bad. And while lousy conditions may make you miserable, they also provide a basic dignity that feels strangely good.

It's confusing, both to talk about and to feel. Just remember that imprisonment is a debased way of living, period. As long as we continue to view prisons as solutions to our problems, from the prisoner perspective, it's hard to see that privatization matters.

References

Blomberg, Thomas G., and Karol Lucken. (2000). *American Penology: A History of Control*. Hawthorne, New York: Aldine de Gruyter.

Clear, Todd R., and George F. Cole. (2000). *American Corrections*, 5th ed. Belmont, CA: Wadsworth/West.

Cummins, Eric. (1994). *The Rise and Fall of California's Radical Prison Movement*. Stanford, CA: Stanford University Press.

DiIulio, John J., Jr. (1987). *Governing Prisons*. New York: Free Press.

Dyer, Joel. (2000). *The Perpetual Prisoner Machine: How America Profits from Crime*. Boulder, CO: Westview Press.

Esposito, Barbara, and Lee Wood. (1982). *Prison Slavery*. Washington, DC: Committee to Abolish Prison Slavery.

Feeley, Malcolm F. (1991). "The privatization of prisons in historical perspective." *Criminal Justice Research Bulletin*, 6(2):1—5.

Miller, Jerome. (1996). *Search and Destroy: African-American Males in the Criminal Justice System*. New York: Cambridge University Press.

Rothman, David J. (1980). *Conscience and Convenience*. Boston: Little, Brown.

Shichor, David. (1995). *Punishment for Profit*. Thousand Oaks, CA: Sage.

——. (1996). "Private Prisons." Pp. 364–372 in Marilyn McShane and Frank P. Williams (eds.), *Encyclopedia of American Prisons*. New York: Garland.

Taylor, William Banks. (1999). *Down on Parchman Farm*. Columbus, OH: Ohio State University Press.

Chapter IX
Discussion

Correctional Privatization

The reading by Shichor introduces many of the arguments in favor of and against privatization. Some of the concerns include the government's possessing legal liability but not having full control over private prisons, private business' interest with keeping their prisons at full capacity and cutting corners in staff salaries and benefits to maximize profits, and the relatively few studies that have been conducted comparing private and public prisons. On the other hand, private services may yield some cost savings to government, provide greater flexibility to expand and contract with changing markets (less bureaucracy), and provide quality services that (in one evaluation) outperform government services.

Sparkman, Minor, and Wells studied the employees at a total of six institutions: three minimum-security level state prisons and three minimum-security private prisons. The authors found that in comparison to public employees, private staff members were paid significantly less, had less work experience, and were less racially and ethnically heterogeneous (a higher percent of white staff members). Job satisfaction scores did not significantly vary between the two groups on any measure except promotional opportunities, which were seen as greater in private prisons than in public facilities. In addition, higher salaries were related to increased job satisfaction for employees working in private prisons, but more pay was unrelated to employee satisfaction in state prisons.

Mobley discusses the "unintended consequences of privatization" that were not discussed in any of the other readings. One negative consequence is increased violence (physical violence or property damage) by prisoners who feel resentment over private businesses profiting from their incarceration. One positive outcome of private prisons is the opportunity in some institutions for increased prisoner empowerment, or a new model of prison administration. The idea behind empowerment is to allow prisoners to participate in some self-governance so that violence and property destruction are decreased. Most readers may find it surprising that prisoners are actually less concerned about the privatization debate and more concerned with improving the conditions of confinement.

Chapter X
Introduction

Juveniles in Adult Corrections

Common Assumptions	Reality
• Juveniles tried in criminal court do longer sentences in adult prison than if they had remained in the juvenile system.	• Juveniles tried in criminal court receive longer sentences than they would have received in juvenile court (87 percent of the time). However, for all offenses (except rape), the average amount of time *actually served* was 3.5 years (or 27 percent of the original sentence), which is less time than the average sentence length served in the juvenile system (Redding 1999, 121).
• Incarcerating juveniles with adults will deter them from committing crimes in the future.	• No study exists to date that examines recidivism rates of juvenile offenders who were incarcerated in adult prisons with a matched control group. There have been, however, studies that have compared recidivism rates of youths (matched on prior record and offense) who were transferred to criminal court. When transferred youths were compared with youths who were tried in juvenile court, recidivism rates and time to re-offending were higher for transferred juveniles for seven different offense types (Bishop et al. 1996).

The juvenile justice system exists as a separate entity from the adult criminal justice system. Since the juvenile justice system began over a century ago, treatment and diversion became the core mission. Most juvenile offenders arrested today are nonviolent or petty offenders, and most are tried in juvenile courts under a more informal process than adult offenders.

In the last decade, two trends have emerged in the area of juvenile justice. The first trend is to change the way juvenile offenders are processed through the courts. To accomplish this change, many state jurisdictions have changed juvenile statutory laws in some way to more closely resemble the adult criminal justice system. These changes include requiring juveniles to be fingerprinted, opening juvenile records, opening juvenile court proceedings to the public, allowing victims to attend juvenile court, making offenders pay victim restitution, and obligating parents to take responsibility for their children's actions (Altschuler 1999).

The second trend in juvenile justice is the increased attention given to juveniles who commit violent crimes. To address this problem, many states have created the option for prosecutors or judges to "transfer," "waive," or "certify" a juvenile as an adult. The waiver process varies widely by state. Generally speaking, a juvenile waiver means that a transferred juvenile is tried and sentenced in an adult criminal court. For every 100 juvenile offenders who are formally adjudicated in juvenile court, one juvenile is waived to an adult criminal court (Stahl 1999). Some states even require that for certain crimes (e.g., first-degree murder) a juvenile must be automatically charged (no discretion) as an adult.

However, most states create options for where certified juveniles convicted in criminal court serve their time. Approximately half of all waived juveniles receive probation. For juveniles who will be incarcerated, most states hold one or more hearings at different stages to determine whether to retain the waived juvenile in a juvenile detention facility or to transfer the juvenile to an adult prison. Age and demeanor are among the factors that define if and when a certified juvenile is physically transported from juvenile detention to an adult prison. For example, the oldest age for which the juvenile justice system may retain jurisdiction over a waived juvenile varies from 17 to 56 years of age. Thus, some states may retain waived juveniles in juvenile detention until they reach the limit and must be transferred to adult prison. There are even five states that do not require a waived juvenile to serve any time in an adult institution (Altschuler 1999). Despite this, some states do not allow certain juveniles (habitual felons and/or violent juvenile offenders) to be housed with other juveniles. In this case, juveniles 17 or younger who are convicted as adults of violent crimes must be transferred directly to an adult prison. For example, "Georgia's 1994 law re-

quires mandatory transfer of juveniles 13 and older charged with specified serious crimes. If convicted, juveniles face a minimum 10-year term in Georgia's (adult) Department of Corrections" (Parent et al. 1997, 3–4).

It is clear that, given all the options, a very small number (0.25 percent) of all formally adjudicated juvenile offenders age 17 and younger actually serve time with adults in an adult institution. In the year 2000, there were 9,100 juveniles held in adult jails. Of this number, 5,475 were sentenced as "adults," while 3,625 were either pretrial detainees or were being held as a juvenile. Juveniles who have not been sentenced as adults cannot be integrated with adults.

In addition to jails, there were about 5,400 juveniles from 44 states under the age of 18 in adult prisons; 79 percent were 17 years of age, 18 percent were 16 years old, and 3 percent (162 juveniles) were between the ages of 13 and 15 at the time of admission to prison (Austin, Johnson, and Gregoriou 2000). Most of the offenders aged 13 to 15 were from Arkansas, Florida, Georgia, and North Carolina (Parent et al. 1997, 4). Juveniles in adult prisons comprise 0.5 percent of the state prisoner population. As a result of the constant admission and release of offenders, the number of juveniles actually admitted each year is much higher. In 1997 alone, 13,876 juveniles were admitted to an adult prison. Over half (57 percent) of juveniles are admitted to adult prisons for a violent crime, while 22 percent are admitted for a drug offense, and 21 percent for a property crime (Austin et al. 2000).

In 1994, only six states kept waived juveniles separate from adults; nine states housed transferred juveniles with adults ages 18 to 21; the remaining 36 states housed juveniles with adults of any age. In a nationwide study, Austin and his colleagues reported that one-third of juveniles in adult institutions are in protective custody (single-cell), while the vast majority of juveniles (51 percent) are housed in dormitories, and a small number (18 percent) share a cell with one cellmate. Other issues relevant to juveniles in adult prisons, such as treatment programs, education, dietary needs, and victimization are addressed in the readings that follow.

Recommended Readings

Altschuler, David M. (1999). "Trends and Issues in the Adultification of Juvenile Justice." In *Research to Results: Effective Community Corrections*, Patricia M. Harris (ed.). Lanham, MD: American Correctional Association.

Austin, James, Kelly Dedel Johnson, and Maria Gregoriou. (2000). *Juveniles in Adult Prisons and Jails: A National Assessment*. Washington, DC: U.S. Department of Justice.

Bishop, Donna M., Charles E. Frazier, Lonn Lanza-Kaduce, and Lawrence Winner. (1996). "The Transfer of Juveniles to Criminal Court: Does It Make a Difference?" *Crime and Delinquency* 42: 171–191.

Eisikovits, Z., and M. Baizerman. (1983). "Doin' Time: Violent Youth in a Juvenile Facility and In an Adult Facility." *Journal of Offender Counseling Services and Rehabilitation* 6: 5–20.

Glick, Barry, and William Sturgeon. (1998). *No Time to Play: Youthful Offenders in Adult Correctional Systems*. Lanham, MD: American Correctional Association.

Jensen, E., and L. Metsger. (1994). "A Test of the Deterrent Effect of Legislative Waiver on Violent Juvenile Crime." *Crime and Delinquency* 40: 69–104.

Maitland, A. S., and Richard D. Sluder. (1996). "Victimization in Prison: A Study of Factors Related to the General Well-being of Youthful Inmates." *Federal Probation* 60(2): 24–31.

Parent, Dale, Terence Dunworth, Douglas McDonald, and William Rhodes. (1997). *Transferring Serious Juvenile Offenders to Adult Courts*. Washington, DC: U.S. Department of Justice.

Redding, Richard E. (1999, April). "Examining Legal Issues: Juvenile Offenders in Criminal Court and Adult Prison." *Corrections Today* 92–95, 120–124.

Stahl, Anne L. (1999). *Delinquency Cases Waived to Criminal Court, 1987–1996*. Washington, DC: U.S. Department of Justice.

Internet Websites

April 1999 issue of *Corrections Today*—articles about juveniles in adult courts and adult prisons. Available: *http://www.corrections.com/aca/cortoday/april99/index.html*

The Impact of the Kansas Juvenile Justice Reform Act—Juveniles in Adult Prisons. Available: *http://www.jrsainfo.org/pubs/reports/sjsreport/kansas.html*

Increase of juveniles of minority groups held in adult prisons. Available: *http://www.apbnews.com/cjsystem/justicenews/2000/02/27/juveniles0227_01.html*

Juvenile Justice Database of Resources and Links. Available: *http://www.lib.msu.edu/harris23/crimjust/juvenile.htm*

PBS Forum: *On-Line News Hour: Kids and Crime*. Available: *http://www.pbs.org/newshour/forum/january00/kids_crime4.html*

Talbot, Margaret, September 10, 2000. "What's become of the juvenile delinquent?" *The New York Times* Available: http://www.newamerica.net/articles/Talbot/mtNYTimes9-10-00.htm

28
The Risks Juveniles Face in Adult Prisons

Jason Ziedenberg
Vincent Schiraldi

Focus Questions

1. What happens to youths when they are placed in adult prisons?

2. What is the juvenile offender suicide rate in juvenile facilities compared to that in adult facilities?

3. How many more juveniles reported getting sexually attacked or raped in an adult prison compared to a juvenile facility?

4. What did Fagan and his colleagues conclude is more likely to happen when juveniles in adult prisons are released after being victimized by violence?

Nearly a century ago, the juvenile justice system was created because children were subjected to unspeakable atrocities in adult jails and returned to society as hardened criminals. As the system developed, it became clear that housing young offenders and adult inmates together was self-destructive and self-defeating.

Despite the lessons of history, Congress stands poised to reunite adults and juveniles in the same prison system. The "Violent and Repeat Juvenile Offender Act" (S-10) calls for housing juveniles with adult inmates and would force states to transfer large numbers of young offenders to adult prisons in order to be eligible for federal funds. Child advocates, law enforcement officials, and criminologists have urged Congress to consider the destructive effects of placing youths in adult jails and prisons—a substantial body of research shows that placing youths in adult institutions accentuates criminal behavior after release.

In a recent full-page advertisement in *The Washington Times*, sheriffs, district attorneys, and legal professionals explained why they think the proposed legislation will make their jobs more difficult: "Lock up a 13-year-old with murderers, rapists, and robbers, and guess what he'll want to be when he grows up?" the advertisement read. Even John DiIulio, head of the conservative Council on Crime in America—a group that has provided much of the statistical analytical support for the juvenile crime bill—doesn't think locking children up with adults is a good idea. DiIulio wrote in *The New York Times*, "[M]ost kids who get into serious trouble with the law need adult guidance. And they won't find suitable role models in prison. Jailing youths with adult felons under Spartan conditions will merely produce more street gladiators (1996)."

The most disturbing aspect of the new bill is the fear that the thousands of young people slated to be placed in adult prisons and jails are more likely to be raped or assaulted, or to commit suicide. Surveys have documented the higher risk juveniles face when placed in adult institutions, and people who work with youths know the all-too-familiar stories: In Ohio, a 15-year-old girl is sexually assaulted by a deputy jailer after she is placed in an adult jail for a minor infraction; in Kentucky, 30 minutes after a 15-year-old is put in a jail cell following an argument with his mother, the youth hangs himself; in one year, four children being held in Kentucky jails—for offenses ranging from disorderly conduct to status offenses, like running away from home—committed suicide.

While groups as diverse as the American Jail Association and the American Civil Liberties Union have lobbied to keep youths out of the reach of adult inmates, the bills before Congress will result in substantially more children being imprisoned with adults. It is important to revisit the few statistics on how juveniles fare in adult institutions as Congress considers making these dramatic justice system changes.

Too Few Statistics

There is a dearth of data on rape, suicide, and assault rates among the 4,000 juveniles who are sentenced to adult prisons, as well as the 65,000 children who pass through the adult jail system every year. Some states lump suicide deaths under the category "unspecified cause," making the problem invisible. Other states and jurisdictions list rape among "inmate assaults"—effectively masking the problem. Academics in this field warn that any statistics on rape are "very conservative at best, since discovery and documentation of this behavior are compromised by the nature of prison conditions, inmate codes and subcultures, and staff attitudes." There also are obvious incentives for prison officials to under-report incidents of rape and suicide because they are administratively embarrassing to the prison system and could be used as evidence for lawsuits.

Even on the less politically charged measure of the number of "inmate-on-inmate" assaults, it is difficult to formulate a conclusive answer about whether offenders are more likely to be attacked in a juvenile institution or an adult prison. *The Corrections Yearbook*, an annual survey of the state of America's prisons compiled by the Criminal Justice Institute, suggests that assault rates vary from state to state. The yearbook's statistics show: Inmates are seven times more likely to be referred for medical attention due to an inmate assault in an adult prison in Connecticut than in one of the state's juvenile institutions: in Oklahoma, inmates are

10 times more likely to be referred; and in Kansas, they are 11 times more likely to see a medical professional due to an attack by another inmate. In other states, the difference seen here between reported assaults requiring medical attention in juvenile institutions and adult prisons is reversed.

Several academic surveys more clearly document what happens to youths who are placed in adult institutions.

Suicide

The most recent American study on juvenile suicide in adult institutions and youth facilities was conducted in 1980. Funded by the Office of Juvenile Justice and Delinquency Prevention, Michael G. Flaherty, a researcher with the Community Research Forum at the University of Illinois, surveyed the number of suicides in 1,000 jails and juvenile detention centers. The study found that the suicide rate of juveniles in adult jails is 7.7 times higher than it is in juvenile detention centers.

A more recent report on prison suicides completed by the British Prison Reform Trust supports the findings of the Flaherty study. Analyzing data collected by Her Majesty's Prison Service, the Trust found that while people ages 15 to 21 made up only 13 percent of the prison population, they comprised 22 percent of all suicide deaths.

These studies confirm what law enforcement officials have been telling Congress—children are abused more regularly and driven to desperation more quickly in prison facilities. Adult prisons and jails are not equipped to protect young offenders from these risks. Therefore, these juveniles are more likely to fall through the cracks.

Rape

A 1989 study by a team of researchers, led by Professor Jeffrey Fagan of Columbia University's School of Public Health, compared how youths at a number of juvenile training schools and those serving time in adult prisons reported being treated. Five times as many youths held in adult prisons answered yes to the question, "Has anyone attempted to sexually attack or rape you?" than those held in juvenile institutions. Nearly 10 percent of the youths interviewed reported that another inmate had attempted to sexually attack or rape them in adult prisons, while closer to 1 percent reported the same in juvenile institutions.

Another set of studies concurs that sexual assault is more prevalent in adult than in juvenile institutions. A group of researchers in 1983 found that, among the residents of six juvenile institutions, 9.1 percent of youthful offenders reported being victims of sexual attacks. But a 1996 study of adult inmates in Kansas found that 15 percent reported being "forced to have sex against their will."

Surveys in other countries have found similarly higher rape rates for young offenders in adult institutions. An Australian survey shows that of 183 inmates, ages 18 to 25, surveyed in a New South Wales prison, one-quarter reported being raped or sexually assaulted, and more than half said they lived in fear of it. A recent Canadian survey showed that, among 117 inmates surveyed in a federal prison, 65 incidents involving sexual assault were reported. Among those, the odds of victimization were eight times higher for a 20-year-old inmate than for the oldest inmates in the system. Compared to "nonvictims," the study reports that "victims tended to be younger, housed in higher security settings, and in the early part of their prison terms."

These statistics seem to fit with what some criminologists call the "prototype" prison rape victim: a young, if not the youngest, inmate within a given institutional system. Fagan points out that "because they are physically diminutive, they [juveniles] are subject to attack. . . . They will become somebody's 'girlfriend' very very fast."

Fagan's study, which found such alarming statistics on youth rape in prisons, also found that children placed with adults were twice as likely to report being "beaten up" by staff. Nearly one in 10 juveniles reported being assaulted by staff. The juveniles in adult prisons also were 50 percent more

likely to report being attacked with a weapon.

Conclusion

Whatever kind of threat you choose, be it rape, assault, or suicide, prison is a most dangerous place for young offenders. But the frightening character of these statistics raises a larger issue in terms of how effective the new juvenile justice bill will be from a crime control perspective. As Fagan's study notes, "Victimization by violence has well-established consequences for subsequent violence and crime, and victims of rape or sexual assault are more likely to exhibit aggression toward women and children." The authors write, "Although [juvenile] transfers decrease community risk through lengthy incapacitation of violent youngsters, the social costs of imprisoning young offenders in adult facilities may be paid in later crime and violence upon their release."

Each of the research areas represents crucial information currently being ignored by Congress. The present research bodes poorly for the large numbers of juveniles who will be transferred to adult prisons, as well as the children who will be jailed alongside adults under proposed legislation.

All 50 states have laws allowing juveniles to be tried as adults. During the past two years, 42 states have toughened those laws. Clearly, this is not an area that requires urgent federal intervention to spur the states into action.

The Justice Policy Institute recommends that Congress put much needed resources into a two-year, state-by-state evaluation of the changes in America's juvenile justice system. We further recommend that Congress hold off on sweeping and ill-advised legislation at this time. During that period, it is our recommendation that funds be specifically allocated to research:

- The different reoffense rates of similar groups of youthful offenders held in juvenile and adult institutions;

- The different rates of sexual and physical victimizations and suicides of juveniles in adult institutions, as compared to the rates in juvenile facilities; and

• A comparison of the different rates of juvenile crime in states with a large number of youthful offenders in adult jails, as compared to the rates of states with few or no juveniles in adult institutions.

No legislation that would reverse a century of juvenile justice reform and put thousands of young people into the adult prison system should be undertaken until this kind of research is conducted.

References

Bartollas, Clemens and Christopher M. Sieverdes. 1983. The sexual victim in a co-educational juvenile correctional institution. *The Prison Journal.* (Vol. 68, No. 1).

Cooley, Dennis. 1993. Criminal victimization in male federal prisons. *The Canadian Journal of Criminology.* (October).

The Corrections Yearbook: Adult Corrections 1995, p. 26–27.

DiIulio, John J., Jr. 1996. Crime where it starts. *The New York Times.* (13 July).

Donaldson, Stephen. 1995. *Rape of Incarcerated Americans: A Preliminary Statistical Look,* Seventh Edition. Stop Prison Rape. New York. (July).

Drummond, Robert W. 1992. The sexual assault of male inmates in incarcerated settings. *The International Journal of the Sociology of Law.*

Fagan, Jeffrey, Martin Forst, and T. Scott Vivona. 1989. Youth in prisons and training schools: Perceptions and consequences of the treat-ment-custody dichotomy. *Juvenile and Family Court.*

Flaherty, Michael G. 1980. *An Assessment of the National Incidence of Juvenile Suicide in Adult Jails, Lockups and Juvenile Detention Centers.* The University of Illinois, Urbana-Champaign, Ill.

Heilpern, David. 1995. Sexual assault of New South Wales prisons. *Current Issues in Criminal Justice.*

"Kids Behind Bars." 1997, *Investigative Reports,* A&E Network (14 June).

Lerner, S. 1984. The Rule of the Cruel. *The New Republic.* (15 October).

Richey, Warren. 1997. Teen crime trend puts them behind adult bars. *The Christian Science Monitor.* (2 June).

The Rising Toll of Prison Suicide. 1997. The Prison Reform Trust. London, England. (April).

Soler, Mark I. 1997. Remarks before the Senate Youth Violence Subcommittee, Senate Judiciary Committee on the core requirements of the Juvenile Justice Act and the Violent Juvenile and Repeat Offender Act of 1997. Washington, D.C. (June).

Struckman-Johnson, Cindy, and David Struckman-Johnson. 1996. Sexual coercion reported by men and women. *The Journal of Sex Research.*

29
Juveniles in Adult Prisons: Problems and Prospects

Frances P. Reddington
Allen D. Sapp

Focus Questions

1. What are the three ways that juveniles can be waived to adult criminal court status?

2. Were juvenile offenders in adult prisons viewed by administrators as being more likely than adult prisoners to be perpetrators or victims in disturbances?

3. Did correctional administrators view juveniles as easier or more difficult to deal with in adult prisons than in juvenile facilities?

4. What kinds of crimes did juveniles commit to get sentenced to adult prison?

5. Do juveniles receive additional treatment, beyond what adults receive, in adult prison facilities?

Introduction

The creation of the juvenile court was the culmination of a long-term reform movement to remove juvenile offenders from the adult criminal justice system and to ensure that troubled children were placed in a rehabilitative setting (Krisberg, 1988). The state, under the doctrine of *parens patriae*, acted in the place of a kindly parent towards the child. The juvenile court was a protector of children (Hahn, 1987). Since the creation of the juvenile court, there has been a system "safety valve" through a mechanism within the juvenile court to transfer unsalvageable youth into the adult system (Forst, 1995). However, such drastic measures were at odds with the underpinnings and goals of the juvenile system and were done with a reluctance and an acceptance of impending harm to the child (Sanborn, 1994).

In the late 1970s and early 1980s, many states "got tough" on juvenile crime in response to the public's growing concern and the failure of the juvenile justice system to eradicate juvenile crime or to seemingly even slow it down. The "new" answer was once again to turn to the adult system to deal with those youth who could not be rehabilitated within the juvenile system (Champion, 1989; Feld 1987). The result of this movement was twofold: First, legislation designed to get tough with juvenile crime focused on ways to expand transfer laws, especially with regards to age, offense requirements and the responsibility of who makes the decision to transfer (National Coalition of State Juvenile Justice Advisory Groups, 1993) and second, more juveniles were being transferred into adult court than at any previous time (Schwartz, 1989).

Transfer has again become the solution to seemingly out-of-control juvenile crime. The use of transfer, and the consequences of transfer, is one of the most pressing topics concerning juvenile offenders. The embracing of transfer as the answer to the juvenile crime problem raises questions that have been previously asked, though not answered. "The debate over the efficacy of criminal court transfer has been underway for at least 50 years" (Snyder and Sickmund, 1995:156).

Accordingly, in an attempt to examine the issue of transfer, there has been an increase in the philosophical and empirical research concerned with transfer and its processes. Philosophical questions have been raised regarding transformation of the juvenile court into an institution not envisioned by its creators (Feld, 1987). Some researchers posed questions regarding transfer policies (Sanborn, 1994). Empirical studies have included the examination of factors that impact the decision to transfer (Poulos and Orchowsky, 1994; Lee, 1994); dispositions of juveniles transferred to criminal court (Fagan, 1991; Houghtalin, and Mays, 1991; Champion, 1989); differences in the dispositions of certified and non certified juvenile offenders (Kinder et al, 1995); and the impact of juvenile transfer on violent juvenile crime (Jensen and Metsger, 1994). What is missing from the literature is research designed to determine the impact of juvenile transfer on the adult criminal justice system and an examination of the views of the adult correctional administrators who are faced with the increasing numbers of juveniles in the adult system.

First, this paper presents information about the incidence and reality of juvenile placement into adult facilities. In addition, this paper examines the attitudes of adult correctional administrators towards the transfer of juvenile offenders into adult prisons. These administrators can, in fact, validate if those concerns voiced in the literature about transferring juveniles into the adult system are borne out, as well as provide insight into any unintended results of the transfer movement.

However, before survey results are discussed, it is important to examine how the process of transfer works, how often the process is used, and what generally is the outcome of transfer. Related studies dealing with the treatment of juveniles in the adult system also will be discussed. Finally, the major findings of the present research will be presented and examined. In order to avoid confusion, the term *juvenile* is used throughout the paper to refer to juveniles who have been transferred by whatever method into the adult court, placed in adult facilities, and are viewed as adults in the eyes of the criminal justice system.

The Transfer Process

There are at least three ways that jurisdiction over juveniles can be waived by juvenile court judges and a juvenile can be processed by criminal courts. These are judicial waivers, prosecutorial waivers, and legislative waivers or automatic waivers or statutory exclusion. Different states may have several methods for transferring juveniles in their juvenile codes.

The Judicial Waiver

Historically, transfer was handled in early juvenile courts by judicial waiver, a practice that continues today in many juvenile courts (Snyder and Sickmund, 1995). The juvenile court judge makes the decision whether to transfer jurisdiction of the child to the adult system. The judge examines the individual circumstances of the child's case and makes a decision of transfer based upon that examination. The Supreme Court case, *Kent v. United States* (1966), which held that juveniles facing transfer have a right to a transfer hearing, also offered guidelines that judges should consider in the transfer hearing. Consideration is given by judges to the nature of the crime and the potential for rehabilitation within the juvenile justice system.

All states, except Nebraska and New York, currently provide for judicial waiver in their juvenile statutes (Snyder and Sickmund 1995). The request for the transfer hearing may come from a variety of sources, including the juvenile intake division, the prosecutor, and occasionally, the juvenile or their family (Sickmund, 1994). Most state statutes set criteria, usually concerning age and offense, for the use of waiver. However, in the get tough movement of the 1980s and 1990s, many states added or emphasized other provisions in the juvenile statutes which facilitate transfer to the adult system. In both methods described below, the prosecutorial waiver and the legislative waiver or statutory exclusion, the transfer hearing mandated by *Kent* does not have to take place.

The Prosecutorial Waiver

One of the other methods which results in juveniles being handled in the adult court is through the use of prosecutorial discretion.

One-fourth of the states allow for the prosecutor to determine the filing of the case in either adult or juvenile court without any judicial hearing (Snyder and Sickmund, 1995). The prosecutor holds concurrent jurisdiction over the juvenile and adult courts. In essence, the prosecutor will make the decision in which court the charges will be filed. Generally, the age of offender and the type of offense that is under the concurrent jurisdiction of the adult and juvenile court is limited by statute and is often limited to crimes that are violent or serious or where a pattern of repeated criminal activity is established (Sickmund, 1994). Philosophically, this has shifted the responsibility of transfer from a judicial decision based on individual assessment to a prosecutorial decision based on legal criteria and is in direct opposition to the philosophy of the original juvenile court (Bishop, Frazier, and Henrietta, 1989).

The Legislative Waiver or Statutory Exclusion

The third way that juveniles are handled in criminal court is through legislative statutes. The legislature may define certain criminal acts as automatically under the jurisdiction of the adult court. About half of the states have removed the jurisdiction for certain crimes or repeat activity out of juvenile courts and into the adult criminal courts. This process is not "typically" regarded as a type of transfer because the legislatures are in reality sending juveniles to the criminal court by "statutorily excluding them from juvenile court jurisdiction" Sickmund, 1994:3). In other words, because the juveniles committed certain illegal acts defined as criminal acts and not delinquent acts, the offenders are not juveniles in the eyes of the law. Many states have made legislative changes which basically take the decision to transfer out of the judicial system and move it into the legislative arena.

The Transfer Process and Numbers

Juveniles in Adult Court

It is estimated that between the years 1988 and 1992, the same years which saw an increase in violent juvenile crime, the number of juveniles judicially transferred to adult court increased dramatically (Snyder and Sickmund, 1995). It is estimated that 11,700 youth were judicially waived into the adult system in 1992, a 68 percent increase over 1988 (Sickmund, 1994). Yet, the total delinquency cases waived judicially in 1992 totaled less than 2 percent of all delinquency cases. Moreover, patterns of transfer changed in the same four-year period.

In 1992, more juveniles were waived for property crimes than crimes against persons, or crimes concerning public order or drugs. Forty-five percent of cases being waived judicially were for property crimes (Snyder and Sickmund, 1995). However, it is significant to note that over the four years, the increase in transfer was greatest in person crimes, (101 percent) drugs (91 percent) and public order crimes (90 percent) rather than property crimes (42 percent) (Sickmund, 1994). Demographically, the children that were transferred to the adult system were generally older; almost 90 percent were 16 or older. The majority of transferred youth, 96 percent, were male, and 53 percent were minorities (Snyder and Sickmund, 1995).

Options for Juveniles Transferred

When a juvenile is transferred to the adult court, the options available to the court in dealing with adult offenders are generally options for the juvenile. The imposition of the death penalty is limited in juvenile cases to those where the child is 16 or older.

Juveniles in Adult Facilities

A recent study by the U.S. Department of Justice suggests that the number of offenders under age 18 received in custody by the reporting state Departments of Corrections in 1993 totaled 6119, though some of these youth might have been put on probation, sent to some other community corrections program, or housed in youthful facilities (U.S. Department of Justice, 1995). However, most significantly, the juvenile population growth predicted in adult facilities over the next five years shows states predicting between a 1 percent increase and a 730 percent increase (U.S. Department of Justice,

1995). What the actual growth will be is difficult to access because of the new legislation in many states dealing with juvenile offenders and juvenile transfer. In many states the impact of the new legislation is, as yet, unknown.

Related Studies on the Impact of Waiver on the Juveniles in the Adult System

This section will examine two major issues regarding the impact of waiver on juveniles which results in incarceration in adult facilities or facilities under the direction of the states' department of corrections. These issues are safety issues and future behavior issues.

Safety Issues

Preliminary studies, although few in number, regarding the treatment of juveniles in adult institutions as opposed to those housed in juvenile facilities, indicate that juveniles in adult institutions are at a much greater risk regarding their safety and perceived safety. Research suggests that over 50 percent of youths in prison or in a juvenile facility are victims of property crime during their incarceration (Forst et al., 1989). However, the likelihood of being the victim of a violent crime increased in an adult prison (Forst et al., 1989). "Sexual assault was five times more likely among youth in prison than in training schools, beatings by staff nearly twice as likely, and attacks with weapons nearly 50 percent more common" (Forst et al, 1989:9). In addition, according to Eisikovits et al (1983:9), "[w]hile in prison, youths' major concern was their daily survival among older inmates."

Impact on Future Behavior

Another area of concern is the impact of prison on future behavior of juveniles after release from adult incarceration. One way this can be examined is to look at what types of programs are offered to youthful prisoners. Research suggests that juveniles in adult institutions will give more negative evaluations of the programs they encounter (treat-

ment, training, staff and services in general) than youth in juvenile training schools (Forst et al, 1989). For example, many juveniles in juvenile facilities perceived their health care, family relations programs, and counseling services to be of higher quality than did the youths in prison (Forst et al, 1989). According to Eisikovits et al. (1983), where a juvenile is housed will impact how juveniles "do time" and which will most likely impact their future behavior.

Methodology

This research was designed to examine the attitudes of adult correctional administrators towards the juvenile offenders who are transferred into the adult system, as well as to examine what resources juvenile offenders receive in adult facilities. The survey was conducted through a self-administered questionnaire mailed to the commissioners or directors of all state departments of corrections in the United States. A total of 44 surveys were returned for a return rate of 88 percent. Since one questionnaire was received after the analysis cut-off date, the results presented are based on the effective return rate of 86 percent. Since the study reflects the parameters of a population, all differences are real differences and, therefore, no inferential statistics are used. The data analysis relies on measures of central tendency and descriptive statistics. A series of questions were designed to deal with the safety issues that juveniles might pose in the adult system. In addition, the survey was designed to assess the quantity of prison programs designed to deal with the youthful offender. The results are presented below.

Results

Two of the major issues in the study focused on safety and future behavior of juveniles incarcerated in adult facilities or facilities under the control of the adult corrections system in the states. Each of these issues involved several parts. When asked what the single biggest problem that juveniles contributed in the adult facilities, prison administrators' most frequent response was *safety issues*. Interestingly, the mean age that respondents cited that juveniles belong in adult facilities is age 17.

Safety Issues

Safety issues can take on a number of meanings. The study attempted to determine the contribution of juveniles in adult facilities to disciplinary problems. Respondents were asked about juveniles' contribution to disturbances as both victims and perpetrators. . . . Responding prison administrators (27.0 percent) indicated that juveniles were the perpetrator of disturbances less often than adult inmates. Other administrators noted that juveniles were the perpetrators more often than adult inmates (21.6 percent) or about the same as adults (16.2 percent). Over one-third (35.2 percent) indicated they did not know.

Administrators reported that juveniles were victimized at about the same rate as adults (37.8 percent). Another 16.2 percent said they were more often the victims in disturbances and only 5.3 percent said juveniles were less often victimized. The lack of separate accounting for juveniles in state prisons contributed to the 40.7 percent who did not know whether juveniles were victimized more often than adults. . . .

Respondents were asked about the perception of correctional officers regarding juveniles in the facility. . . . More than one-half (52.8 percent) indicated juveniles were harder to deal with than adults and one-third (33.3 percent) said they were about the same as adults. Only 2.8 percent suggested that juveniles were easier to deal with than adult inmates. This question was not answered by 11.1 per cent of the respondents. . . .

Responses to the question of why the majority of certified juveniles were currently in the facilities were contradictory to the figures usually offered in the literature. The literature suggests that most juveniles transferred to adult correctional facilities are convicted of crimes against property. For example, a Bureau of Justice Statistics Report entitled *National Corrections Reporting Program, 1989* suggests that the percentage of juveniles under 18 years of age incarcerated in adult prisons for person crimes was only 38 percent, while property crimes accounted for 41 percent, drugs for 15 percent and other/unknown for 6 percent (Jones and Krisberg, 1994). The results of this study suggest an overwhelming percentage of the systems responding (78.4 percent) have a majority of their juveniles incarcerated for crimes against people. Only 5.4 percent of the respondents cited that the majority of the juveniles in their system were incarcerated for a crime against property.

When adult correctional administrators were asked what type of juvenile offenders should be held in a juvenile facility until they reached adulthood and then be transferred to an adult facility, there were some significant differences noted. Interestingly, 37.1 percent of the respondents felt that juveniles should be held in the juvenile facility until the age of adulthood for a property crime. The percentage dropped to 17.6 percent for a crime against person and 38.2 percent of the respondents stated that those juveniles belonged in the general population in adult facilities. Three (7.1 percent) of the administrators did not answer this inquiry.

Future Behavior Issues

Respondents were asked a series of questions designed to determine what programming . . . beyond what adults receive, juveniles currently receive in the adult facilities. Juvenile offenders receive additional treatment with career training (10.8 percent), prison survival (5.4 percent), and family counseling (2.7 percent) in only 18.9 percent of the responding adult systems. A total of 30 of the adult prison systems (69.5 percent) did not provide any additional treatment for juveniles incarcerated in adult facilities.

Additional comments indicated two states have special educational programs for youthful offenders, while one system offers alternative to violence workshops and an adjustment group. In one system additional alcohol and drug treatment is offered, and in one system additional counseling is offered to the youth.

Those responses change when asked what additional treatment juveniles *should* receive. Over one-half (54.1 percent) stated that prison survival training was needed and 45.9 percent called for career training. Family counseling was identified as a treatment juveniles should receive by 37.8 percent of the respondents. . . .

Other suggestions for additional treatment ranged from sex offender treatment programs, alternative dispute resolution, education (two respondents), mental health, substance abuse programs (four respondents), counseling for youthful offenders (three respondents), anger management, coping skills, adjustment counseling, values, and fetal alcohol issues.

Summary and Conclusions

The number of juveniles being certified and being incarcerated in adult facilities is increasing. In the most recent legislative session, a number of states have again changed their transfer laws by lowering transfer ages, and/or expanding the criminal acts which result in waiver, and/or initiating mandatory waiver laws, and/or expanding those who are given the discretion to determine waiver. Studies have focused on the process of waiver and the outcome of waiver. This study has shown that correctional administrators do have concerns about both the philosophical underpinnings of transfer and the actual day-to-day problems of dealing with juveniles in adult facilities. Correctional administrators indicate that juveniles present a number of unique safety issues in the institutions and that juveniles under the age of 17 should not be incarcerated in adult facilities.

Juveniles contribute to overcrowding which can be viewed as a safety issue, while at the other end of the continuum, juveniles may contribute negatively to the number and severity of confrontations in a facility. To quote one warden during a casual conversation when asked about the juveniles in his facility, he replied that juveniles were difficult to work with because "their mouths run much faster than their asses." Over half of the respondents feel that correctional officers find juveniles more difficult to deal with than adults.

These results also lead one to question if there is an issue here concerning the perception of juvenile offenders. Results indicate that most of the respondents claim that the vast majority of juveniles are in their facilities for violent crimes against people, an assumption not validated in the literature, at least through the numbers represented in judicial waiver. The numbers and crimes for other forms of transfer are not easily assessable. The rate of juveniles transferred for crimes against persons, however, is growing rapidly, which may be an explanation for the results found in this study.

It is also clear that juveniles have special programming needs and that those needs are not being met in most state adult facilities. The implications of incarceration of juveniles in adult prisons, with the resulting safety issues and the lack of needed treatment, does not bode well for the future behavior of those juveniles. When they are released from incarceration, they are likely to be even less equipped to deal with society than they were when they entered the adult system.

References

Bishop, D., C. Frazier, and J. Henrietta. (1989). "Prosecutorial Waiver: Study of a Questionable Reform." *Crime and Delinquency* 35: 179–201.

Champion, D. (1989). "Teenage Felons and Waiver Hearings: Some Recent Trends, 1980–1988." *Crime and Delinquency* 35: 577–585.

Eisikovits, Z. and M. Baizerman. (1983). " "Doin' Time': Violent Youth in a Juvenile Facility and in an Adult Facility." *Journal of Offender Counseling Services and Rehabilitation* 6: 5–20.

Fagan, J. (1991). "The Comparative Impacts of Juvenile and Criminal Court Sanctions on Adolescent Felony Offenders." *National Institute of Justice*, U.S. Department of Justice.

Feld, B. (1987). "Juvenile Court Meets the Principle of Offense: Legislative Changes in Juvenile Waiver Statutes." *Journal of Criminal Law and Criminology* 78: 471–533.

Forst, M. L. (1995). *The New Juvenile Justice.* Chicago: Nelson-Hall Publishers.

Forst, M., J. Fagan, and Scott (1989). "Youth in Prisons and Training Schools: Perceptions and Consequences of the Treatment-Custody Dichotomy." *Juvenile and Family Court Journal* 4: 1–14.

Hahn, Paul (1987). *The Juvenile Offender and the Law*. Cincinnati, Ohio: Anderson Publishing Company.

Houghtalin, M. and G. L. Mays. (1991). "Criminal Dispositions of New Mexico Juveniles Transferred to Adult Court." *Crime and Delinquency* 37: 393–407

Jensen, E. and L. Metsger. (1994). "A Test of the Deterrent Effect of Legislative Waiver on Violent Juvenile Crime." *Crime and Delinquency* 40: 69–104.

Jones, M. and B. Krisberg. (1994). *Images and Reality: Juvenile Crime, Youth Violence and Public Policy*. National Council on Crime and Delinquency.

Kent v. United States, 383 U.S. 54. (1966).

Kinder, K., C. Veneziano, M. Fichter and H. Azuma (1995). "A Comparison of the Dispositions of Juvenile Offenders Certified as Adults with Juvenile Offenders Not Certified." *Juvenile and Family Court Journal*, 37–41.

Krisberg, B. (1988). "The Juvenile Court: Reclaiming the Vision." National Council on Crime and Delinquency.

Lee, L. (1994). "Factors Determining Waiver in a Juvenile Court." *Journal of Criminal Justice* 22: 329–339.

National Coalition of State Juvenile Advisory Groups (1993). *Myths and Realities: Meeting the Challenge of Serious, Violent and Chronic Juvenile Offenders*. 1992 Annual Report.

Poulos, T. and S. Orchowsky (1994). "Serious Juvenile Offenders: Predicting the Probability of Transfer to Criminal Court." *Crime and Delinquency* 40:3–17.

Sanborn, J. (1994). "Certification to Criminal Court: The Important Policy Questions of How, When and Why." *Crime and Delinquency* 40: 262–281.

Sickmund, M. (1994). "How Juveniles Get to Criminal Court." Office of Juvenile Justice and Delinquency Prevention. Washington, D.C.: U.S. Department of Justice.

Snyder, H. and M. Sickmund (1995). "Juvenile Offenders and Victims: A Focus on Violence." Office of Juvenile Justice and Delinquency Prevention. Washington, D.C.: U.S. Department of Justice.

U.S. Department of Justice. (1995). "Offenders Under Age 18 in Adult Correctional Systems: A National Picture." Longmont, CO: National Institute of Corrections, Information Center.

30
Maximum-Security Offenders' Attitudes Toward Placing Juveniles in Adult Prisons

Martha L. Henderson

Focus Questions

1. According to the existing literature, what does society believe is the purpose of punishing juveniles as adults?

2. What do adult offenders perceive to be the purpose of juvenile corrections?

3. Do adult offenders accept juveniles in adult prison as a correctional policy?

4. What impact will prison programs have on juvenile prisoners housed in adult facilities?

5. Do adult prisoners believe that placing juveniles in prison with adults will deter young offenders from committing crime again in the future?

The general public appears to be convinced that there is a growing epidemic of violent juvenile offenses and recent juvenile arrest statistics seem to support this belief. In 1999,

law enforcement officers arrested approximately 2.5 million individuals under the age of 18 for criminal offenses (Snyder 1999). In addition, a growing number of these youth were arrested for violent crime index offenses of murder, non-negligent manslaughter, rape, robbery, and aggravated assault. In 1999, juveniles comprised 15 percent of all violent crime index arrests and 32 percent of all property crime index arrests (Snyder 1999).

The fear of victimization by violent juveniles has led members of the general public to argue that the criminal justice system needs to "get tough" on youthful offenders. The research literature also supports this shift in public attitudes. Several researchers have found increasing public support for the handling of certain juvenile cases in the adult system. For example, Meddis (1993) found that seven out of ten Americans favored trying violent juvenile offenders in adult criminal courts. In a similar study, two-thirds of the public supported waiver for juveniles who commit violent, property, and drug-related offenses (Wu 2000).

The public's demand for harsher punishments for violent juvenile offenders has resulted in several states increasing the number of youth who qualify for treatment in the adult system. By the end of 1996, 49 out of 50 states and the District of Columbia had statutes authorizing the prosecution of juveniles aged 14 or older charged with serious felony offenses in criminal courts instead of juvenile courts (Torbet and Szymanski 1998). Even the federal system has attempted to accommodate the public and permits children aged 13 and older who commit violent crimes with a firearm on federal property to be processed as an adult. Between 1992 and 1997, 44 states had made it easier to transfer a juvenile to adult criminal courts; 7 states established exclusion provisions; 28 states increased the number of offenses eligible for exclusion; and 7 states lowered age limits for exclusion (Torbet and Szymanski 1998). In fact, 22 States and the District of Columbia had at least one statute for transferring juveniles to criminal courts without a minimum age specification (Torbet and Szymanski 1998).

The negative impact of transferring juveniles to adult courts and ultimately to adult prisons has been established. Even the United States Supreme Court does not deny that transfer to the adult criminal system can have extreme consequences (*Kent v. United States* 1966, 554). For example, some studies indicate that serious and violent juvenile offenders receive longer and more severe sanctions when convicted in the criminal court and not adjudicated in the juvenile system (Fritsch, Caeti, and Hemmens 1996). Moreover, DiIulio has also argued that putting youthful offenders with adult prisoners will create "street gladiators" (DiIulio 1996). He points out the fact that both liberals and some conservatives fear that youthful offenders will become more criminal from taking up residence in adult penal institutions. Others have focused on the fact that youthful offenders are more likely to be raped or assaulted in adult institutions and to receive more disciplinary reports than adults in prison (Forst, Fagan, and Scott 1989). Recent studies have also indicated that juveniles in adult prisons are more likely to attempt and actually succeed in committing suicide (Ziedenberg and Schiraldi 1998).

Research conducted on the impact of juvenile transfers to adult institutions indicates that the influx of juveniles into the adult system has made the job of correctional administrators more difficult and more costly. Most state correctional facilities encounter the following problems with juvenile transfers: (1) a lack of funding to build separate facilities for juveniles; (2) inability to provide programming for juvenile offenders; (3) inability to train staff on how to deal with youthful offenders. Also, as a consequence of adding youthful offenders to the adult system, adult prison administrators must battle for funds with the juvenile justice system (Torbet et al. 1996).

Thus, after examining the available literature on juveniles transferred to the adult system, four points can be made. First, a current trend clearly indicates that an increasing number of juveniles will be transferred to the adult system. This increase is occuring because the general public and politicians are supportive of such policies. Second, juveniles who end up in adult prisons are negatively affected by the experience. Third, legislation increasing the number of juveniles in the adult system has the unintended consequence of overburdening an already inadequate adult prison system. Last, although the research has explored the attitudes of the public and the impact of juvenile transfer on adult corrections, it has not considered the perspective of adult prisoners, who are most likely to have their lives changed by an increase of juveniles in adult prison.

Ultimately, researchers have spent less time finding out what adult prisoners think about the juvenile justice system and their attitudes toward placing youthful offenders in adult prison. Adult prisoner perceptions are important for three reasons: (1) adult prisoners will determine how juvenile offenders will do their time—they can victimize or protect youthful offenders; (2) adult prisoners can provide insight on the usefulness and impact of prison programs with youthful offenders; and (3) prisoners are in a better position to assess the physical, mental, and social impact of imprisonment within an adult facility. Thus, the present study seeks to advance our understanding of adult prisoner perceptions by addressing the following questions:

1. What do adult offenders perceive to be the purpose of juvenile corrections?

2. Do adult offenders accept the placement of juveniles in adult prison as a correctional policy?

3. If juveniles are placed in prison, how should staff treat them?

4. What impact will prison programs have on juvenile prisoners housed in adult facilities?

5. Will placing juveniles in prison with adults stop these young offenders from committing crime in the future?

Methodology

The data used to examine offender perceptions of placing juveniles in adult prisons was collected by distributing a questionnaire to 500 male prisoners held in intake facilities in Ohio. The questionnaires were conducted during the winter and spring of 2000. A total of 450 surveys were completed. Fifty questionnaires were not eligible for analysis because of missing data. The data analysis presented here is the distribution of responses across items assessing prisoner perceptions of the purpose of juvenile punishment and the placement of youthful offenders in adult institutions.

The male prisoners who participated in the survey had certain demographic characteristics. A disproportionate number of respondents were nonwhite (59 percent). Respondents averaged 30 years old. Forty percent of the prisoners had dropped out of high school and 30 percent reported having earned a high school diploma. About one-third of the sample had completed some education beyond high school. In addition, over half (55 percent) of the offenders had never been married. Many prisoners who responded to the survey had had prior experience with juvenile prisons (64 percent), and about half (49 percent) had been sentenced to an adult prison prior to their current incarceration. Thus, the majority of the prisoners who responded to the survey had experience with the prison system as adults and as youth.

Results

Primary Goal of Juvenile Corrections

Prisoners were asked whether the primary goal of juvenile corrections should be punishment. Table 30.1 presents the results of prisoner perceptions on the research questions. The majority of the adult prisoners disagreed that the primary goal of juvenile corrections should be punishment (59.6 percent). In contrast, 40 percent of the prisoners were willing to accept that punishment should be the primary goal of the juvenile correctional system. One should note, however, that only 8.4 percent of the prisoners *strongly* agreed that the primary purpose of juvenile corrections should be punishment.

Perceptions of Placing Juveniles in Prison with Adults

A large number of the prisoners were opposed to placing juveniles in adult prison. Over 46 percent of the adult prisoners strongly disagreed with the statement that it

---

Table 30.1
Percentage Distribution of Prisoners' Perceptions Regarding Juveniles in Adult Prison (N = 450)

Statement	Strongly Agree	Agree	Slightly Agree	Slightly Disagree	Disagree	Strongly Disagree
Q.1 The primary goal of juvenile corrections should be punishment.	8.4	17.3	14.7	9.8	20.9	28.9
Q.2 It is okay to place juveniles in prison with adults.	5.6	10.4	12.0	8.0	17.6	46.4
Q.3 The same rules should apply for juvenile and adult offenders.	7.3	15.3	13.1	13.6	18.2	32.4
Q.4 Prison programs are more likely to help juveniles than adults.	12.2	17.8	17.1	11.4	21.2	20.2
Q.5 Juveniles placed in adult prison should have their own programs.	32.4	32.7	11.8	5.1	10.7	7.3
Q.6 Prison will stop juveniles from committing crime again in the future.	8.2	10.7	18.2	12.2	23.3	27.3

was okay to place juveniles in prison with adults. Another 25 percent of the adult prisoners disagreed or slightly disagreed with putting juveniles in the same institutions as adults. Thus, it is not surprising that in general less than 30 percent of the adult prisoners surveyed believed that placing juveniles in prison with adults is a good idea.

The issue of placing juveniles in prison with adults also raises concerns about whether juveniles in adult prison should be treated the same as their adult prisoner counterparts. The respondents to this questionnaire were asked whether they agreed or disagreed with having the same rules apply for both adult and juvenile prisoners. Over 60 percent of the prisoners did not agree that the same rules should be used for adult and juvenile prisoners in adult institutions. Only 7.3 percent strongly agreed that the same rules and regulations should be applied across the board.

Adult Prisoner Perceptions of Prison Programs for Juveniles

The respondents were asked two questions to determine adult prisoner perceptions of prison programs. The responses to the statement that prison programs are more likely to help juvenile offenders than adult offenders reveals a split in adult prisoner perceptions. More than half (52.8 percent) of the prisoner sample disagreed with the statement that prison programs are more likely to help juveniles than adults. In fact, 20 percent strongly disagreed with the statement, whereas only 12 percent strongly agreed that prison programs are more likely to help juvenile prisoners rather than adult prisoners. Thus, the adult prisoners did not think that prison programs were more likely to help juvenile offenders.

Surprisingly, an overwhelmingly large number of these prisoners did agree that juveniles in adult prison should have their own programs. Over 30 percent of the sample strongly agreed with granting juveniles in prison their own programs. Only 7 percent of the prisoners strongly disagreed with this arrangement.

Perceptions of What Can Be Gained From Juvenile Incarceration in Adult Prisons

The placement of juveniles in adult prison has typically been justified on the basis of "getting tough on crime" and teaching juveniles a lesson. The respondents to this survey were asked whether placing juveniles in adult prison would prevent these young offenders from committing crime again in the future. Over 27 percent of the respondents strongly disagreed in some manner with the statement that the prison experience would stop juveniles from committing crime again. Another 23 percent disagreed and 12 percent disagreed slightly. Surprisingly, very few respondents strongly agreed that placing juveniles in prison with adults would reduce future criminality. Thus, the adult prisoners did not think that prison would lead to significant reductions in the future criminality of juvenile offenders incarcerated in adult prison.

Discussion

Whereas the general public has supported the transfer of youthful offenders to the adult system, correctional administrators have recognized that there are pitfalls to such policies (see Reddington and Sapp 1997 for discussion). The results here indicate that adult prisoner perceptions of the impact of placing juveniles in adult prison also differ from the attitude held by the general public. The prisoners in this study did not believe that the primary purpose of juvenile corrections should be punishment, nor did they think that adult prison was a proper place for juvenile prisoners. Although the prisoners in the current study were not directly asked about why this was a bad idea, one could speculate that their reasoning is the same or similar to that of the correctional administrators examined in the Reddington and Sapp study. Several of the prisoners wrote on their surveys that young prisoners are nothing but trouble in prison and indicated that these young prisoners belonged elsewhere. As one inmate stated, "these young ones, all they want is to give lip. They are loud and give you no peace."

A secondary consideration is whether juveniles placed in prison with adults should follow the same rules and procedures as their adult counterparts. The prisoners in this study did not believe that the same rules for adult prisoners should apply to juvenile offenders incarcerated in adult facilities. In fact, over 75 percent of the prisoners agreed that juveniles in prison should have their own programs. Prisoners disagreed, however, on whether prison programs were more likely to help juveniles than adult prisoners (52 percent did not agree that prison programs were more beneficial for juveniles).

The general public and politicians have increasingly supported policies placing young violent offenders in prison with adults on the basis of deterrence. The public believes that prison time will teach juveniles a lesson and prevent future criminality. The prisoners in the current study did not believe that prison would stop young offenders from committing crime again in the future. This attitude might reflect the belief that (as held by the early positivist criminologists), the cause of crime lies in the failures of society. In the nineteenth century, the positivists viewed crime as an act that individuals were propelled into as a result of social, economic, biological, and mental forces beyond their individual control. The positivists thus did not have faith that incarceration alone would rehabilitate or change offenders. In order to reduce rates of crime, the positivists argued that alternative methods for dealing with offenders were necessary. "One size could not fit all." Essentially, their argument was that because the cause of crime is unique to the individual, incarceration might work for some and psychological therapy for another. Thus, crime-prevention efforts needed to be broadened to address individual offender needs.

The prisoners in the present study also appeared to view environmental factors, such as poor schools, lack of jobs, and lack of money, as the cause of juvenile offending. To quote one prisoner, "Society is the problem. Having no jobs is the problem. Having no future is the problem. Prison is not the problem or the solution." As another offender reported on the survey, "If they can't learn in school, they sure as hell are not going to learn in here about doing the right thing. Prison doesn't teach you how to make it on the outside." Thus, the responses from offenders in this study suggest that these offenders, like the early positivists, would view education, job placement, and better opportunities on the outside as having a greater impact on juvenile crime than incarceration alone.

An alternative explanation for the negative views that prisoners hold about the impact of prison on youthful offenders could be traced back to their views of the purpose of prison for themselves. In a study conducted by Henderson (2000), prisoners appeared to be evenly divided in their beliefs as to the purpose of punishment. On one side, there exist a large number of offenders who perceive that prison serves a purpose, such as rehabilitation, deterrence, or just desert. These offenders thought that they could get help for their problems in prison and admitted that prison had taught them a lesson. On the other side are those offenders who believe prison serves no purpose. These offenders were quick to state that nothing can be gained by doing prison time. It is possible that some of the offenders in the present study fall into this latter group, which perceives prison to serve no functional purpose. Ultimately, such offenders would see very few benefits to placing juveniles in prison with adults when prison will do little to change their own perceptions.

An additional problem arises for offenders who perceive that prison serves a rehabilitative function for them. These offenders believe that prison can offer the opportunity for change and reductions in future criminality but state that the structure of prison programming precluded this possibility. As one offender stated, "Yeah, prison has some programs that can help you make it on the outside. You just can't get in them. The wait list for the education program here is six months and most of us will leave here by then." Thus, some offenders in the current study might have been unlikely to view prison as a place that can help juveniles. Even if juveniles wanted help, staff shortages and waiting lists or the unavailability of treatment programs would prevent them from getting the help that they need.

The present study is just the beginning for understanding the impact of placing juvenile offenders in prison with adults. It is clear that adult prisoners have a problem with this correctional policy. Future research should focus on specific issues that arise as a result of young offenders in an adult prison setting and if young prisoners change the structure and routine of prison life.

References

DiIulio, J. (1996, July 13). "Crime Where It Starts." *The New York Times* (July 13, 1996).

Forst, M., J. Fagan, and V. T. Scott. (1989). "Youth in Prisons and Training Schools: Perceptions and Consequences of the Treatment-Custody Dichotomy." *Juvenile and Family Court Journal* 40 (1):1–14.

Fritsch, E. J., T. J. Caeti, and C. Hemmens. (1996). "Spare the Needle but Not the Punishment: The Incarceration of Waived Youth in Texas Prisons." *Crime and Delinquency* 42(4): 593–609.

Henderson, M. L. (2000). "The Meaning of Punishment: What Do Inmates Expect From Prison?" Unpublished doctoral dissertation. The University of Cincinnati.

Meddis, S. (1993, October 29). "Poll: Treat Juveniles the Same as Adult Offenders." *USA Today*: 1A.

Reddington, F. P., and A. D. Sapp. (1997). "Juveniles in Adult Prisons: Problems and Prospects." *Journal of Crime and Justice* 20:139–152.

Snyder, H. (1999). *Juvenile Arrests, 1999*. Washington, DC: Office of Juvenile Justice and Delinquency Prevention.

Torbet, P., and L. Szymanski. (1998). *State Legislative Responses to Violent Juvenile Crime: 1996–1997 Update*. Washington, DC: Office of Juvenile Justice and Delinquency.

Torbet, P., R. Gable, H. Hurst, I. Montgomery, L. Szymanski, and D. Thomas. (1996). *State Responses to Serious and Violent Juvenile Crime*. Washington, DC: Office of Juvenile Justice and Delinquency Prevention.

Wu, B. (2000). "Determinants of Public Opinion Toward Juvenile Waiver Decisions." *Juvenile and Family Court Journal* 50:9–20.

Ziedenberg, J., and V. Schiraldi. (1998). "The Risks Juveniles Face: Housing Juveniles in Adult Institutions Is Self-Destructive and Self-Defeating." *Corrections Today* 60(5): 22.

Court Cases

Kent v. United States, 383 U. S. 541 (1966)

Chapter X
Discussion

Juveniles in Adult Corrections

A larger number of juveniles have come under the jurisdiction of adult institutions, and many institutions have not made any special accommodations. In many states a juvenile sent to an adult penitentiary is treated no differently than an adult. On the other hand, the juvenile goes to the adult prison *as punishment*, not for more punishment. Ziedenberg and Schiraldi discuss statistics showing that juveniles do "hard time" in adult prisons. Juveniles in adult institutions suffer higher rates of assault, rape, and suicide than juveniles in youth facilities.

Whereas Ziedenberg and Schiraldi compared juveniles in adult settings with juveniles in juvenile institutions, correctional administrators in Reddington and Sapp's reading compared juveniles with adults in adult prisons. Most administrators responded that juveniles were victimized as much or more often than adults, yet there were a wide variety of responses on the rate that juveniles are involved as perpetrators in prison disturbances. Most adult institutions, as of 1997 (70 percent), did not provide additional treatment for juveniles. These data correspond with the concerns voiced in both of the other articles—by Henderson and Ziedenberg and Schiraldi—that juveniles may not receive the support they need to address their problems. Most correctional administrators and prisoners were opposed to juveniles being incarcerated in adult prisons. In Henderson's article, prisoners agreed that the adult prison experience would not deter juveniles from committing crimes in the future. In addition, most prisoners thought that some concessions of leniency could be made for incarcerated juveniles.

The most interesting finding about the practitioner's point of view was the large number of correctional administrators who did not seem to have accurate data on juveniles in their facilities (as calculated by the high number of "don't know" responses). This is somewhat disturbing, given the increased number of juveniles being tried in criminal courts today and the lack of programs to aid in the maturation of young minds. After having contact with more experienced criminals while incarcerated, and being at risk for victimization, most waived juveniles will be released from prison without additional treatment. Furthermore, juveniles will not have "aged out" of crime yet, so a high level of recidivism is predicted.

Chapter XI
Introduction

On Death Row

Common Assumptions	Reality
• A capital punishment sentence is racially discriminatory against the offender.	• The decision to seek the death penalty is more likely in cases where the victim's race/ethnicity is white than if the victim is a member of any other race/ethnicity (Deiter 1998, Ralph, Sorensen, and Marquart 1992). However, offenders on death row, irrespective of their race, are more likely to be economically disadvantaged.
• The death penalty significantly deters other people from committing murder.	• The relationship between deterrence of homicide and capital punishment is inconsistent. More recent studies suggest that the death penalty contributes to an *increase* in homicide (Bowers and Pierce 1980; Cochran, Chamlin, and Seth 1994), while other research found *no deterrent effect* (Peterson and Bailey 1991). Still, a handful of studies found a *deterrent effect* (Ehrlich 1975). Nevertheless, the Ehrlich study has been criticized for its methodological flaws.

The death penalty is one of the most controversial issues in the field of American corrections. Capital punishment has been promoted in this country, in part, by public opinion polls suggesting that there is a high level of public support (75 to 80 percent of people) favoring the death penalty. In 2000, Gallup polls showed public support had decreased to 64 percent, which was the lowest level in nineteen years. Public support decreased further to between 41 and 56 percent when respondents were provided with other options, such as imprisonment for life without parole or prison for a mandatory 25 years (Death Penalty Information Center 2000).

Political figures have actively begun to question errors made in capital cases. For example, in 2000, George Ryan, governor of Illinois, temporarily suspended capital punishment in his state so that an appointed commission could investigate errors that may have been made in capital cases. In that same year, one study identified 87 people who, between 1973 and 2000, had been freed from death row because they were innocent of the crime for which they had been sentenced to death (Death Penalty Information Center 2000). Radelet and his colleagues identify 23 people who, between 1900 and 1985, were executed and later found to be innocent of the crime (Radelet, Bedau, and Putnam 1992).

In the face of this controversy, over 3,700 people currently remain on death row nationwide. Since capital punishment was reinstated in 1976, the United States has carried out approximately 650 executions, 80 percent of which were completed in Southern states. Offenders wait an average of nine years from the time they are sentenced to death to the time of their execution. This is because of the lengthy court appeals process. It is interesting to note that nearly 40 percent of inmates sentenced to death are removed from death row in some other way besides execution. Most offenders removed from death row get their case overturned, while a small number die of natural causes or get their sentences commuted.

Most people have developed an opinion in favor of or against the death penalty. Capital punishment retentionists believe one or more of the following issues to be true. The death penalty carried out by the government:

- Prevents individual vigilantism (private individuals who carry out the sentence of death of a person suspected of murder).

- Creates closure for the victim.

- Prevents the offender from killing again (specific deterrence).

- Deters others from committing murder (general deterrence).

- Ensures that the offender pays for his or her crime (just deserts).

- Is listed in the Bible as "An eye for an eye. . . ." This means that for taking a life, you pay with your own life (retribution).

On the other hand, death penalty abolitionists believe one or more of the following about the death penalty:

- It is imposed in an arbitrary and disproportionate manner. (Only 4.3 percent of all murderers are sentenced to death; poor black men who live in the South and have killed a white victim are the most likely to receive the death penalty.)

- It has no significant deterrent value in the commission of homicide.

- It may increase violence (brutalization hypothesis).

- The death penalty is final. Innocent people have been convicted and executed.

- Juveniles ages 16 and 17 and mentally ill adults can be executed.

- Life in prison without parole is an efficient and more cost-effective sentencing option.

- The Bible says "Thou shalt not kill." The state should not be exempt from this commandment.

The three readings here focus on the process of capital punishment from the eyes of the participants. As you read, think about the validity of the arguments for and against the death penalty.

Recommended Readings

Arthur, John. (1998). "Racial Attitudes About Capital Punishment." *International Journal of Comparative and Applied Criminal Justice* 22 (1):131–144.

Bailey, William. (1998). "Deterrence, Brutalization, and the Death Penalty: Another Examination of Oklahoma's Return to Capital Punishment." *Criminology* 36(4):711–733.

Bowers, William J., and Glen L. Pierce. (1980). "Arbitrariness and Discrimination Under Post-Furman Capital Statutes." *Crime and Delinquency* 26:563–635.

Cochran, John, Mitchell Chamlin, and M. Seth. (1994). "Deterrence or Brutalization," *Criminology* 32 (1):107–134.

Deiter, Richard. (1998). *The Death Penalty in Black and White.* Washington, DC: Death Penalty Information Center.

Ehrlich, I. (1975). "The Deterrent Effect of Capital Punishment: A Question of Life and Death." *American Economic Review* 65: 397–417.

Haines, Herbert. (1996). *Against Capital Punishment.* New York: Oxford University Press.

Peterson, Ruth D., and William C. Bailey. (1991). "Felony Murder and Capital Punishment." *Criminology* 29:367–395.

Radelet, Michael L., Hugo A. Bedau, and Constance E. Putnam. (1992). *In Spite of Innocence: Erroneous Convictions in Capital Cases.* Boston: Northeastern University Press.

Ralph, Paige, Jon Sorensen, and James W. Marquart. (1992). "A Comparison of Death-Sentenced and Incarcerated Murderers in

Pre-Furman Texas." *Justice Quarterly* 9 (2): 185–209.

Sorensen, Jon, and D. Wallace. (1999). "Prosecutorial Discretion in Seeking Death." *Justice Quarterly* 16(3): 559–578.

van den Haag, Ernest, and J. Conrad. (1983). *The Death Penalty: A Debate.* New York: Plenum.

Internet Websites

Amnesty International. (2000). Facts and figures on the death penalty. Available: *http://www.amnesty.org/alib/airpub/*

Amnesty International–USA. (1999). Killing with prejudice: Race and death penalty in the USA. Available: *http://www.amnesty-usa.org/rightsforall/dp/race/summary.html*

Amnesty International is dead wrong. (1999, 22 May). *New York Post* [Online]. Available: *http:/www.nypostonline.com/052299/editorial/8114.htm*

Death Penalty Information Center. (2000). The Death Penalty in 2000: Year end report (December). Available: *http://www.deathpenaltyinfo.org/yrendrpt00.html*

Freedberg, S. P. (1999, 4 July). Freed from death row. *St. Petersburg Times* [Online]. Available: *http://www.sptimes.com/News/70499/news_pf/State/Freed_from_death_row.shtml*

Harrington, J. (1999, 11 February). Work of Protest, students free death row inmate. *Northwestern Observer* [Online]. Available: *http://www.nwu.edu/univ-relations/media/observer/category/1998-99*

Mills, S., and Armstrong, K. (1999, 18 May). Yet another death row inmate cleared. *Chicago Tribune* [Online]. Available: *http://www.chicagotribune.com/news/metro/chicago/article/0,1051,ART-28731,00.html*

Radelet, M. L. (1999). Post-Furman botched executions. Available: *http://www.essential.org/dpic/botched.html*

Streib, V. L. (1999a, June). Death penalty for female offenders, January 1973 to June 1979. Available: *http://www.law.onu.edu/faculty/streib/femdeath.pdf*

Streib, V. L. (1999b, June). The juvenile death penalty today: Death sentences and executions for juvenile crimes, January 1973–June 1999. Available: *http://www.law.onu.edu/faculty/streib/juvdeath.pdf*

31
Death Work: A Modern Execution Team

Robert Johnson

Focus Questions

1. What are the goals of the deathwatch team during the execution process?

2. How do deathwatch team members feel about capital punishment?

3. How does the deathwatch team cope with work-related stress?

4. What purpose do physical isolation and secrecy serve?

5. What advantages and disadvantages do the correctional officers report about being a member of the deathwatch team?

The execution of Gary Gilmore, carried out in 1977, marked the resurrection of the modern death penalty. The event was big news and was commemorated in a book by Norman Mailer, *The Executioner's Song,*[1] later made into a movie. The title is deceptive. Like others who have explored the death penalty, Mailer tells much about the condemned but very little about the executioners. Indeed, if we examine Mailer's account more closely, the executioner's story is not only unsung, it is also distorted.

Gilmore's execution was quite atypical, even if his crime was not. He was sentenced to death for killing two men in cold blood, for

no apparent reason. Viewed from the outside, his own death had a similar ring of nihilism. Gilmore, unrepentant and unafraid, refused to appeal his conviction—under a then-untested capital statute. There is no doubt that he could have contested his case for years, as many condemned prisoners have done since his death. But Gilmore, who had already served some twenty-two years of his young life behind bars, would have none of that. To him, prison was death; life in prison was a kind of living death in its own right. Death by firing squad gave him a chance to offer blood atonement for his awful crimes (a notion that resonated with his dark Mormon obsessions[2]), as well as a kind of immortality as the man who put the executioner back to work.

Relishing his notoriety and his perverse power, Gilmore dared the state of Utah to take his life, and the media repeated the challenge until it became a taunt that may well have goaded officials to action. (There was even a *Saturday Night Live* skit depicting him fixing his make-up in preparation for his execution.) His brother Mikal, who spoke with Gary near the end, states that "Gary remained fierce and unswerving in his determination to die," and to use lawyers for the state of Utah, primarily, but death penalty advocates as well, to bring about his death. Gilmore transformed them into his servants: men who would kill at his bidding, to suit his own ideas of ruin and redemption. By insisting on his own execution—and in effect directing the legal machinery that would bring that execution about—Gary seemed to be saying: *There's really nothing you can do to punish me, because this is precisely what I want, this is my will. You will help me with my final murder.*[3]

A failed suicide pact with his lover staged only days before the execution, using drugs she delivered to him by a kiss in an intimate visit, added a hint of sex and melodrama to the already compelling human drama.

Gilmore's final words, "Let's do it," seemed to invite—even, perhaps, command—the lethal hail of bullets from the firing squad. That nonchalant phrase, at once fatalistic and brazen, became Gilmore's epitaph. It clinched his outlaw-hero image and found its way onto tee shirts that confirmed his celebrity status.

As befits a celebrity, Gilmore was treated with unusual leniency by prison officials during his confinement on death row. He was, for example, allowed to hold a party on the eve of his execution, during which he was free to eat, drink, and make merry with his guests until the early morning hours. As we have seen, this was not unprecedented: Notorious English convicts of centuries past would throw farewell balls in the prison on the eve of their executions. . . . For the record, Gilmore served Tang, Kool-Aid, cookies, and coffee, later supplemented by contraband pizza and an unidentified liquor. Periodically, he gobbled drugs obligingly supplied by the prison pharmacy. He played a modest arrangement of rock music albums but refrained from dancing.

Gilmore's execution, like his parting fete, was decidedly out of step with the tenor of modern executions. Most condemned prisoners fight to save their lives, not to have them taken. They do not see their fate in romantic terms, and they do not host farewell parties of any sort. Nor are condemned prisoners, with the exception of some slated for lethal injection, given medication to ease their anxiety or gain their compliance. The subjects of typical executions remain anonymous to the public and even to their keepers. They are very much alone at the end.

The focus of my research, in contrast with Mailer's account, is on the executioners themselves as they carry out typical executions. In my experience, executioners—not unlike Mailer himself—can be quite voluble, and sometimes quite moving, in expressing themselves. I draw on their words to describe the death work they perform in our name.

Death Work and Death Workers: Defining Parameters

Executioners are not a popular topic of social research, or even of conversation at the dinner table or cocktail party. We simply don't give the subject much thought. When we think of executioners at all, we imagine men of questionable character who work stealthily behind the scenes to carry out their grim labors. We picture hooded forms hiding in the shadow of the gallows, or anonymous figures lurking just out of sight behind an electric chair or a firing blind or outside a gas chamber, or, most recently, beyond a curtained partition, syringe in hand, in an execution chamber made to look like a hospital room. We wonder who would do such grisly work and how they sleep at night.

This image of the executioner as a sinister and often solitary person is, of course, a holdover from earlier times, when executions were public and executioners were scorned as evil, contaminated by the death work that was their livelihood. Their lives might be placed in jeopardy by an angry crowd, by relatives of the condemned, or by superstitious neighbors. They were often afforded a hood or cloak while at work to protect their identities, which would offer them a token shield against harm. Some of these execution traditions, or at least remnants of them, linger on even today. Thus it is that a few states hire freelance executioners and engage in macabre theatrics. Executioners may be picked up under cover of darkness at lonely country crossroads; some still wear black hoods to hide their identity. They slip into the prison unnoticed, do their work, then return to their civilian lives.

In Florida, this scenario is played to the hilt. A hooded executioner is picked up before daybreak at a designated spot and driven to the prison by a corrections official. He wears the hood at all times—before, during, and after the execution. He is escorted to the execution chamber at the prescribed time (which in Florida is at sunrise), and, on cue, he pushes a button that activates the electric chair. When the man is dead, the executioner, hood still in place, "is driven back and paid"—in cash, to further protect his anonymity. (In some states, the doctors who administer lethal injection are afforded an "executioner's cloak"—official anonymity, not a garment to protect their identities; they, too, can be paid in cash to further shield them from scrutiny.[4]) Florida's executioner meets with no man face-to-face. "You won't be seeing him," a Florida Department of Corrections official told a journalist. "Not on this side of life."[5]

Some executioners forgo secrecy. For example, the executioner's name is a matter of public record in Alabama and Mississippi. In these states, " 'the dirty little secret' of capital punishment is neither fetishized nor veiled."[6] Here we find no hooded figures, no blood money collected in cash. These executioners—in Alabama, the warden; in Mississippi, a ranking correctional officer—are popular figures in the community, told by passersby on the street to "Keep up the good work."[7] Sam Jones, Louisiana's civilian executioner responsible for nineteen deaths, was initially reluctant to be photographed; however, he eventually went public, allowing interviews with local newspapers and *Playboy* magazine, even appearing on television. These men see themselves as doing a job, as professionals who approach their work without passion or prejudice. Matter-of-fact, Jones describes himself as "a normal John Doe that walks the streets every day. I work and live a normal social life."[8] How ironic that an executioner would characterize himself in such a way—as a John Doe, a nameless corpse—as if in subconscious recognition that it takes a dead (dehumanized) man to kill other men in cold blood for a living.

The very presence of an official executioner, particularly when drawn from outside the ranks of the prison system, may give comfort to skittish prison administrators. In one warden's words, "We can honestly say that we didn't do it."[9] The warden's point almost seems to be, "Nobody did it—no one is responsible—if we don't know who did it or if he is not one of us." That warden, of course, is spouting sheer nonsense. Correctional officials are always involved in executions, even if they themselves do not directly carry out the killing. The plain fact is that formal executioners, whether shrouded in secrecy or working more or less as public figures, do not orchestrate the execution process. The warden or his designate does. As former warden Cabana notes, "my hand was on the lever as well. The executioner could not, would not, proceed until I gave the

order."[10] Neither the warden nor the executioner can go to work until after the prisoner has been escorted to the death chamber and fastened to the execution apparatus. At that key juncture, the executioner merely flips a switch, pulls a lever, or pushes a button, "something a child, an animal, or even a machine could do."[11]

Formal executioners are almost peripheral to the modern execution process. This process starts on death row, the bleak and oppressive "prison within a prison" where the condemned are housed for years awaiting execution . . . and culminates in the deathwatch, a brief period, usually twenty-four to forty-eight hours long, that ends when the prisoner has been executed. This final period, the deathwatch, is supervised by a team of correctional officers—variously known as the tactical squad, the strap-down team, the deathwatch team, or simply the execution team—who typically report directly to the prison warden. It is generally the warden who reads the death warrant; as noted above, he signals the executioner to start the machinery of death. The warden, depending on his personal proclivities, may be more or less involved with the condemned prisoner over the period of his confinement and execution.[12]

The warden or his representative presides over the execution. In many states, it is a member of the execution team, acting under the warden's authority, who plays the role of executioner. Though this officer may technically work alone, his teammates are apt to view the execution as a shared responsibility. As one member of a deathwatch team told me in no uncertain terms,

> We're all as a team, together. We all take a part of the killing, the execution. So, this guy that pulled the switch shouldn't have more responsibility than the guy that cut his hair or the guy that fed him or the guy that watched him. We all take a part in it; we all play 100 percent in it, too. That take[s] the load off this one individual [who pulls the switch].

The formal executioner—in this case, the head of the deathwatch team—concurred. "Everyone on the team can do it," he said, "and nobody will tell you I do it. I know my team." My research confirmed these claims.

The correctional officers who serve on deathwatch teams are expressly selected and trained to carry out executions. They are executioners, in my view, even when they are assisted by an outsider who is hired to complete the formalities of the execution—to flip a switch or push a button, thus taking the life of a prisoner he may have never even seen. By contrast, the deathwatch team officers must serve, observe, and control the prisoner, then escort him to the death chamber and secure him for execution—if they do not also perform the execution themselves. It is they who are the most active in the conduct of executions; it is they who carry the heaviest psychological burden.

The officers of these deathwatch teams are, for all intents and purposes, our modern executioners. I studied one such team, composed of eight seasoned male officers of varying ranks. (A ninth officer, a woman, seated the witnesses but was not otherwise involved in the execution. The team is very much a man's world.) The team had carried out five electrocutions when I began my research. I interviewed each officer on the team after the fifth execution, following the same general format that I had used with the death row officers.[13] Again, my aim was to elicit and explore the officers' perceptions of their work by allowing them to delineate the execution process as they saw and participated in it. At the start of each interview, I posed open-ended questions about each officer's role in the execution process. These questions, in turn, led to others about how the officer was trained to do his job, about how he felt about and perceived the executions he had helped to carry out, about his observations of the prisoners as their executions drew near, and about the effects on him personally of his involvement with executions. I then served as an official witness at the team's sixth execution and as a behind-the-scenes observer during their seventh, at which point I informally reinterviewed each of the officers.

I also interviewed the warden, the prison's operations officer, and a member of the prison's treatment unit who had advised a condemned prisoner who was later executed. In these interviews, again focused but using open-ended questions, I probed the dimensions of each person's role in the execution process, their perceptions of the individual condemned inmates they had observed, and the effects, if any, their involvement in the execution process may have had on them as individuals. In addition, I interviewed a counselor affiliated with a prison reform organization. The counselor had assisted both of the men whose executions I'd observed, in each case staying with them through all but the final minutes of the deathwatch. I also interviewed a journalist who had spoken with one of the condemned prisoners both before and, by telephone, during his deathwatch. These latter interviews were almost exclusively aimed at reconstructing the experiences of condemned prisoners during their final hours. After the publication of [this article], I observed yet another execution—as a behind-the-scenes observer—and interviewed the officers and warden again. (By this time, two officers had left the team; I interviewed their replacements.[14]) . . .

The Deathwatch Team

Members of the deathwatch team referred to themselves, with evident pride, as simply "the team." This pride was shared by correctional officials. The warden praised them as solid citizens—in his words, "country boys." (Some of the officers were in fact from urban areas and about half were African Americans, but they all qualified as country boys in the warden's eyes because of their reliable characters.) These men, the warden assured me, could be counted on to do the job of execution and do it well, however unpleasant they might find the experience to be. As a fellow administrator put it, "it takes a certain amount of grit" to serve on the execution team. Continuing, he mused,

What's the expression? "When the going gets tough, the tough get going." A certain amount of professionalism [is required] there. . . . An execution is something [that] needs to be done, and good people, dedicated people who believe in the

American system, should do it. And there's a certain amount of feeling, probably one to another, that they're part of that—that when they have to hang tough, they can do it, and they can do it right. And that it's just the right thing to do.

In the eyes of the warden and other prison officials, an execution is a good man's burden, shouldered stoically for us all.

The official view of an execution is that it is a job that has to be done, and done right. The death penalty is, after all, the law of the land. In this context, "done right" means that an execution should be proper, professional, and dignified. In the words of a prison administrator,

It was something, of course, that had to be done. We had to be sure that we did it properly, professionally, and [that] we gave as much dignity to the person as we possibly could in the process. . . . You gotta do it, and if you've gotta do it, it might just as well be done the way it's supposed to be done—without any sensation.

In the language of the respondents, "proper" refers to procedures that go off smoothly, and "professional" means without personal feelings that intrude on the procedures in any way. The phrase "without any sensation" no doubt expresses a desire to avoid media sensationalism, particularly if there should be an embarrassing and undignified hitch in the procedures—for example, a prisoner who breaks down or becomes violent and must be forcibly placed in the electric chair as witnesses, some from the media, look on in horror. Or, perhaps worse, a botched execution.[15] Still, the phrase may also be a revealing slip of the tongue. For executions are indeed meant to occur without any human feeling, without any sensation. A profound absence of feeling would seem to embody the bureaucratic ideal for the modern execution.[16]

There is, to be sure, no room for passion or even for emotion in the professional execution sought by prison administrators. Condemned prisoners are not supposed to be dragged kicking, screaming, or weeping to their deaths. They are meant to go to their deaths with dignified dispatch, if not decorum ("graciously," to quote one of the execu-

tion team officers). The point is, I suppose, that an execution should be, or should at least appear to be, a punishment to which one submits voluntarily, if reluctantly, rather than a calculated act of violence one resists at all costs. It boils down to a matter of appearances, and appearances matter to everybody on the scene, particularly the officials. There is, then, an execution etiquette. Part of death work is making sure that this etiquette is observed.

The view of executions held by the officers of the team parallels that of correctional administrators but is somewhat more restrained. The officers are closer to the killing and dying and are less apt to wax abstract or eloquent in describing the process. Listen to one man's observations:

I look at it like it's a job. I don't take it personally. You know, I don't take it like I'm having a grudge against this person and this person has done something to me. I'm just carrying out a job, doing what I was asked to do. . . . This man has been sentenced to death in the courts. This is the law, and he broke this law, and he has to suffer the consequences. And one of the consequences is to put him to death.

From where the deathwatch officers sit, the important yet "dirty" job of execution must be done in a workmanlike manner. No one is proud of the blood or the mess, the sights and smells of violent death. As one officer observed, "It's nothin' to be proud of; it's just a job to do, one way or another."

The job of execution offers many opportunities for abuse. The prisoner could, for example, be strapped in the chair in an intentionally demeaning or painful way. But no one on the execution team seeks to inflict suffering on the condemned prisoner. Their reasons are rooted in a practical notion of humaneness: Abuse is not only unprofessional but impractical, because it is likely to trigger resistance. Accordingly, the officers have modified equipment, such as the face mask, to reduce both the prisoner's discomfort and the likelihood of shifting or squirming; the team members try to cinch down the body straps gently to avoid causing pain as well as to avoid provoking any struggle from the prisoner. All the officers, like the prison administrators, want a smoothly orchestrated, professional execution. In their view, however, such executions are neither acts of patriotism (as some of their administrative supporters would have it) nor acts of murder (as some of their free-world critics would have it). Rather, executions are, in the team's eyes, lawful and arguably humane penal sanctions. For the men of the deathwatch team, that is enough.

Which is just as well, since only a few members of the execution team support the death penalty outright and without reservation. Having seen executions close up, some of the team officers have lingering doubts about the justice or wisdom of this sanction. What puts these officers off is not so much the violence of execution—violence comes with the territory in the penitentiary. Besides, many of the officers have encountered violence in the military or in the free world. But violence in prison and elsewhere is usually situational and reactive, occurring when there seems to be no alternative. Such violence need not be justified, in the eyes of the officers. Executions are different because they are arranged. When asked, "Does being part of a planned life-taking process trouble you?" two men responded as follows:

- (Sigh) That's a good question. That's a real good question. (Sigh and long pause) It do, in a sense, and it don't. It probably—if it do, it's 'cause every person that's put on this earth, I feel, is created equal, you know, and they [are] put on this earth to do, to handle some type of problems and whatever. They got to live to do that. But my old grandfather had a saying, you know, "Do unto others what you want them to do unto you." So when you kill somebody, you should be killed. . . . [But] the execution, the killing itself, don't bother me. I was in the service eighteen months in Nam. I was on body patrol, far as when they dropped napalm and you went in and picked up dead bodies and stuff, put 'em in body bags. I guess another part of it, I live in a ghetto. I see a lot of life and death over there, you know. It really don't bother me, you know. Even inmates here get killed, you know. I've saved a couple of inmates here who

have been cut up real bad as well as taken the dead bodies out from here that been killed. So the killing, it really don't bother me.

- There is turmoil, even for someone that I didn't like per se and might not care if he lives or dies, okay? But the violence doesn't bother me. Out in population, you may have to subdue someone or whatever. Certainly, if you subdue someone improperly, you could give them a lethal blow or whatever. So, then, you know, working on the tower, we have firepower. Okay, push may come to shove and we may have to use it. . . . [But with an execution] I ask myself, "Am I doing the right thing? Is this just or unjust? Do we have the right to take a man's life?"

A number of their colleagues entertain similar concerns. Nevertheless, the members of the deathwatch team can be counted on to do the difficult job of execution, because all of them accept without question the authority of the law and hence conclude that the matter is essentially out of their hands. Somebody's got to do it, say these men in unison and with conviction, because it's the system. And if we're the ones to do it, they continue, at least we'll do it right. One officer put the matter this way:

I've seen it. I know what it is. I've smelled it. I've tasted it. I've felt it. . . . I'm not sure the death penalty is the right way. I don't know if there is a right answer. So I look at it like this: If it's gotta be done, at least it can be done in a humane way, if there is such a word for it. 'Cause I know it can be a nasty situation. Executions have been here for a long time. And for a long time it's been done, you know, unprofessionally and for primitive reasons. The only way it should be done, I feel, is the way we do it. It's done professionally; it's not no horseplaying. Everything is done by documentation. On time. By the book.

Executions by the Book

Arranging executions that occur "without any sensation" and proceed "by the book" is no mean task, but it is a task the execution team undertakes in earnest. The tone of this enterprise is set by the team leader, a man who takes a hard-boiled, no-nonsense approach to correctional work in general and death work in particular. "My style," he says, "is this: If it's a job to do, get it done. Do it and that's it." He seeks out kindred spirits, men who see killing as a job—a dirty job one does reluctantly, perhaps, but above all a job one carries out dispassionately. In his words,

I wouldn't want to put a man on the team that would like it. I don't want nobody who would like to do it. I'd rather have the person not want to do it than have a person who wants to do it. And if I suspected or thought anybody on the team really's gettin' a kick out of it, I would take him off the team. . . . I would like to think that every one of them on the team is doin' it, is doing it in the line of duty, you know, carryin' out their duties.

Not all officers are candidates for death work. Only volunteers are sought, and though a fair number step forward, only a few are chosen.[17] The team leader screens the volunteers carefully. He knows the officers at the prison from his long years of service there, and his friendly, down-home country style invites them to admit any difficulties they may experience. Reluctant or squeamish candidates are encouraged to move on to different assignments without fear of sanction or prejudice.

I would know what type of officer you have been, because I've been working with you and seen the way you conducted yourself. I'd sit down and talk to you and tell you what, what we gonna do and what's expected of you, and ask you, "Do you think you could handle it?" And if you told me you thought you could, why, I'd start training you. And then if I saw a weakness or something, that you're falling back, why then I'd ask you, you know, "Do you have a problem with it?" And then I would take you back and sit you down and tell you, if you did have a problem with it, had anything against it or you thought you had anything against it, you ought to just drop out. And nothing would ever be said. We'd just carry it on through.

Those volunteers who are selected to serve on the team are, by all accounts, the cream of the correctional officer corps. They are seasoned, mature, and dependable officers; level-headed types who have proven time and again that they know how to cope with the daily tribulations of work in the prison. Physically and emotionally strong, they take orders well but can also be counted on to use discretion. Common sense and cell-block finesse enable them to relate to and understand convicts. In the warden's words, these officers "can look condemned prisoners in the eye and tell them 'no' when they have to and not get them upset." Some of the officers credit military combat experience as their baptism of fire. All have proven that they can keep cool and handle the pressure that is endemic to the prison community. The observations of one officer, confirmed by the team leader, substantiate this last point:

I volunteered because of my [military] service background and my job background here. They were looking at experience, more or less, number one. And they were also looking for (pause) the people who had been through a lot of stress—stress from inside the institution—that could handle stress more. The overall thing was to deal with the stress and pressure. . . . As long as I've been here, I have been used, more or less, as the person to handle the big problems and straighten them out.

Executions always have the potential to become big problems, so this officer feels he has found his niche on the deathwatch team.

In part to avoid any problems, big or little, the deathwatch team has been carefully drilled in the mechanics of execution. The execution process has been broken down into simple, discrete tasks and practiced repeatedly. The team leader described the division of labor in the following exchange with me:

The execution team is a nine-officer team and each one has certain things to do. When I would train you, maybe you'd buckle a belt; that might be all you'd have to do. . . . And you'd be expected to do one thing, and that's all you'd be expected to do. And if everybody do what they were taught, or what they were trained to do, at the end the man would be put in the chair and everything would be complete. It's all come together now.

So it's broken down into very small steps?

Very small, yes. Each person has one thing to do.

I see. What's the purpose of breaking it down into such small steps?

So people won't get confused. I've learned it's kind of a tense time. When you're executin' a person, killing a person—you call it killin', executin', whatever you want, the man dies anyway—I find the less you got on your mind, why, the better you'll carry it out. So it's just very simple things. And so far, you know, it's all come together; we haven't had any problems.

This division of labor allows each member of the execution team to become a specialist in one specific task, an expert technician who takes pride in his work. Here's how two officers saw their specialized roles:

- My assignment is the leg piece. Right leg. I roll his pants leg up, place a piece [an electrode] on his leg, strap his leg in. . . . I've got all the moves down pat. We train from different posts; I can do any of them. But that's my main post.

- I strap the left side. I strap his arms and another man straps his legs and another one puts his head in the cap. But my job is strapping his left arm in. . . . I was trained with those straps. The way those straps is on the chair, see, I have to know, you know, exactly where each thing is.

The implication is not that the officers are incapable of performing multiple or complex tasks but simply that it is more efficient to focus each officer's efforts on one easy task. "Every man I got down there can carry the job," the team leader maintained. "We may cross-train . . . but when it comes down to, to the time a man goes into the chair, everybody does only one thing and that's it."

On-the-Job Training

An integral part of the training is realistic rehearsals, with team members cast as recalcitrant surrogate prisoners, or "dummies," so that the team can anticipate problems and practice the restrained use of force.

We might set up a training, and I might be the dummy, you know, the dummy. And I sit in the chair, they put on the arm straps and stuff, and I might buck, you know, whatever, resist them putting me in the chair. So we can practice this. We go through stuff like this. And we have had one officer that nearly got his arm broke in the practice. . . . We have different people we use for dummy. We might carry a small person through, or a big person, or somebody, you know, trying to basically size the person [the prisoner] up. If you've got a man that's scheduled to go and he's gonna be big, I'd use myself or somebody else big.

Each inmate presents a different set of physical characteristics that must be not only "sized up," to quote the officer, but also accommodated. Straps must be adjusted so they will be tight enough; exact placement across an inmate's body will vary as well, so a rehearsal with a similar-sized "dummy" allows the team to determine, in one officer's words, "where exactly the straps have to go, and to make adjustments."

Serving as the dummy during execution rehearsals at once demands and promotes trust in one's peers. Imagine the role: Officers march you into the death chamber, strap you in an electric chair, and fasten your arms, chest, and legs. With you pinioned, they affix a cap to your head and cover your face with a leather mask. Electrodes are then connected to the cap and your right leg. All this occurs in an electric chair that, though obviously not activated at the moment, is the real McCoy, capable of shooting twenty-five hundred volts of electricity through your body.

The team leader, who routinely plays the role of surrogate prisoner, described the experience as "peculiar." Explaining, he observed, "Well, when I first started, it was peculiar, you know, because when they put the mask on me, you know, you can't really tell what the person is doing. You feel helpless." Another officer on the team, more voluble than his leader, chose the word "weird." He, too, stressed the helplessness he felt when strapped in the chair.

> It's kind of weird. You feel totally helpless, you can't move, you can't see, you can't speak. It's total darkness. All you can hear are sounds around you. It's definitely weird. It's kinda like puttin' you in another world.... You get a little queasy, I guess from being helpless. You can't fight it. This is total helplessness.

According to the team leader, the officers submit to this stressful procedure[18] out of trust and commitment. "You have to trust your peers. You have to trust people. And like I said, it's a team, and you trust and love one another, so you go on and do it for the team." Each of the deathwatch officers shares the leader's devotion to the team: At some point, each has volunteered to play this trying role, doing so quite consciously out of dedication to the team.

Practice is meant to produce a confident group that is capable of fast and accurate performance under pressure. Time is crucial in the execution trade: The less time spent securing a prisoner for execution, the less opportunity there is for things to go wrong. A smooth execution drill unfolds rapidly and conforms to institutional operating procedures (IOPs). Practically speaking, doing an execution right means, perhaps above all else, doing it fast.

> We've got a time schedule for everything that we do. The head man has got to see that everything is going according to the clock. The clock—we're timed on everything. There's a certain time—you gotta go by the IOPs on the thing, and each thing has gotta be done at a certain time.... You know everything you've got to do. You just got to, you just got to do it in a certain time, a certain time you got to do this. The schedule is boss. You've got to break it down to the schedule, every last minute.

The rewards of practice are reaped in improved performance. Executions take place with increasing efficiency and, eventually, with precision. "The first one was grisly," a team member confided to me. He explained that. a certain amount of fumbling made the execution seem interminable. There were technical problems as well: The generator was set so high that the body was mutilated. The execution chamber stank of burnt flesh, described as having a greasy odor reminiscent of fatty pork. (Air fresheners were subsequently installed throughout the death house.) But that is the past, the officer assured me. "The ones now, we know what we're doing. It's just like clockwork."[19]

Team Cohesion

'We're a Family'

In the execution training, individual tasks are emphasized and the team members are called upon to function as automatons. The team itself, however, is a warm and even intimate primary group, a close-knit group its members can trust at all costs. The team's work environment—the death house—is a home away from home: The officers of the team work together to handle the problems and pressures posed by death work. In their words,

- The team is very close. I guess we're probably . . . closer than any of the officers in here. . . . Comes from working close together. It's real, real close, you know. We really don't have nobody [else] to talk to. And we'll share ideas and things, we'll go off and sit down and just talk and share ideas. How we feel or how it's affecting us. We, I guess, have confidence in one another, trust. Just a good group of people.

- There's more closeness than in any other group I've seen in the system, as far as working together. And one thing we do—we got this thing with the team—we talk to each other. If we got a problem, we go and talk to each other first about it before we go off [and get upset]. . . . Everything that we do stays there [and gets worked out], you know what I'm sayin'? That's the way we operate.

- We are very, very close-knit. When we got a problem from an execution, we all go down in the basement, the execution chamber—we call that our home— draw the curtains, and go in the back, and we'll talk. One guy may say, "I don't think I can make it tonight." And we'll sit down and say, "C'mon, what's the problem? Let's talk it out. . . ." Then we have to remind him, "the law says that this is what has to be done, and we have to do it."

As one officer succinctly put it, "We're not a team, we're a family. In the prison, we fuss, cuss, and threaten each other constantly. But down there [in the death house], we're a family."

At first blush, such sentimentality may seem strained or fabricated, but it is neither. Individual people may function as cogs and, in groups, may be deployed in mechanical fashion as the sum total of those cogs. But this is almost never the whole story. Such arrangements violate essential human needs for purposiveness in action and relationships with others, needs the team members meet through the primary-group relations that exist among them. Each and every officer comes to see himself as a man among men he likes and admires, working together to complete a critical task in service of the larger social good. The team thus functions as a psychological safe harbor and a moral reference point which is to say, a source of support and direction as the officers go about the business of death work. In the niche provided by the team, officers feel more confident and assured; the demands of death work become a manageable routine. In one officer's words,

When I first started, I was nervous. I told them I was nervous. I think they could sense it anyway, but I told them I was nervous. I was scared to death of my reactions, of how I was gonna react to seeing a man executed. Would I get so excited I might pass out, maybe embarrassing everyone? That would be unprofessional. I didn't know how I'd react. I didn't know once the switch threw whether I'd lose everything in my stomach or not. . . . I didn't [lose control], because I had the family.

They were there. They gave me all the support I needed through the first one. Then after that it just became a job. It just became a normal job. You build up your self-confidence so that when the time comes, you just do what you got to do.

"Now," the officer concluded with evident satisfaction, executions "seem like something we do every day."

The Private World of the Execution Team

The team that binds these men as a primary group operates in a world of its own, a world that is tailored to promote and reward the efficient conduct of executions. In a number of ways, the team is actually, and not just symbolically, set apart from the rest of the world during practice sessions and particularly during the deathwatch. For one thing, the death house in which the team carries out its duties is located in the basement of a building on the periphery of the prison compound. Though the death house is within the prison's massive walls, it is removed from the daily ebb and flow of life in the penitentiary.

You just get down there and you're pretty much left alone. . . . It's physically located in the basement. And even the windows— they have windows, but there's an earth mound outside and you can look up and you only see the bottom of people's feet as they're walking by (laughing). And you're isolated, you know. People sometimes tend to forget about you, too.

Team members work in pairs during the deathwatch. These pairings (four in all) have evolved into stable partnerships. The formal reason for pairing the officers is to promote security, but the resulting partnerships strengthen each officer's bonds to the whole team as well as to his individual partner. When any given pair of officers is on duty during the twenty-four hours of the deathwatch, the remainder of the team sets up camp in the officers' lounge. This, once again, removes the execution team officers from interaction with the regular prison community.

We set up a place to sleep, almost a camp here. Because we got to rotate, you know, at night, through the night. When some of us are sleeping in [one area], we can walk and come up here [to another area] and drink coffee and eat, whatever.

These arrangements allow for continuing interaction between partners, reinforcing a sense of teamwork and shared purpose. Particularly as the time of execution draws near, the team uses its camp as a place to build esprit de corps and to get ready—"psyched up"—for the execution.

The team's camp also shelters the officers from potentially harsh scrutiny by outsiders, whether in the prison or from the larger community. Paradoxically, most prison inmates most of the time are indifferent to the workings of the execution team.

[Inmates] think that the people that is going to be electrocuted have deserved it. They went through all the process of the courts, and some of them been on death row for five or six years, and they figured they've, they've been fair to them.

Fellow officers, however, can be another matter. They may show jealousy and resentment, approval, or disapproval. In any case, the team considers these reactions distracting, and best ignored.

Your fellow workers back here is more harder on you than maybe the inmates. You know, they give you the ol' silent treatment. Funny vibes you get from them, I don't know. . . . Some of 'em disapprove, and some of 'em pat you on the back. I really learnt don't pay no attention to it. Pay no attention one way or another.

The team also sees the media as a critical audience that must be kept at bay. Reporters are said to lurk outside the prison waiting to interview people involved with the execution, so the officers are content to stay where they are until the execution is over. Then, they know they will be free to go about their business. "News people are funny," said the team leader. "They'll run over the top of you to get a story. But after the story is over with, they'll, they'll leave just as quick as they come in, you know." Meanwhile, according to another officer, "Being up there together and isolated from everybody gives us a little better feeling."

Physical isolation is complemented by the social isolation of self-imposed secrecy. Team members do not want others to know the details of their involvement in executions. Said one officer, "We look for a person who is very secretive, you know, and can keep things to himself. 'Cause this is very secretive, you know, what my part is and what his part is." Officers do not speak of their activities to outsiders. Their presumption is that outsiders simply wouldn't understand because, in one officer's blunt reckoning, "They hadn't been there." (I became an insider, it would seem, because I offered the officers a chance to speak openly and anonymously about their concerns. From the start, the officers encouraged me to attend an execution to form my own assessment of their operations.) Officers are even hesitant to let members of their families know any details of the execution process or their roles in it: "Well, we, we were sworn to secrecy. When I first got on the team, I wouldn't even tell my wife what I was doing. The deal was, keep it among ourselves. Whatever we say or do down here has got to stay down here, you know." Team members particularly fear that if the person who plays the formal role of executioner were to be identified as an individual, he would be stigmatized by others for what is really a team activity, and perhaps singled out and abused by vengeful convicts.

An Elite Unit

The deathwatch team, set apart physically and by its self-imposed social isolation, quite explicitly sees itself as an elite. As one officer observed, "It's an honor among ourselves to be on the team. I wouldn't go out on the street and broadcast that I'm on the execution team, but I'm proud of it." And rightly so. As befits an elite unit, the team receives privileges and perks. The officers are not paid a separate fee for carrying out executions, but the long hours mean overtime pay. Isolation from the regular prison routine allows small but special freedoms: the extra smoke or cup of coffee when they want it, the chance to mingle with their colleagues and to be their own boss much of the time. (Being isolated in the death house means being on their own a lot.) The camp mentality mentioned earlier lends itself to a suspension of normal work routines. There is a sense that on the deathwatch the officers are liberated from the mundane constraints of daily prison work.

Clearly, the team is an important group engaged in an important enterprise. After all, those who work at matters of life and death are protected from the hassles of everyday prison work. Furthermore, a direct line of command connects the team with the warden, which attests to the gravity of the team's task and gives the officers the heady sense that finally they can stand or fall on their collective merits.

> One thing that relieved us of a lot of stress was [that] we worked for the warden. When he activated us, we worked for him; that's who our orders came from. Came, you know, through the team leader and then to us. Anybody else, they couldn't come and, you know, disrupt you. So everybody knew what they had to do, and they just did what they had to do. You know, if you did it wrong, you did it wrong. You know what I'm sayin'?

In the prison work environment, one is subject to the conflicting directives and evaluations of various sector and shift commanders, and the rules of the game are often a hodgepodge one negotiates at one's peril.[20] Being on "the warden's team," entrusted with a special and clearly defined mission, is a privilege. "That team works on their own," confirmed the warden. "I never interfere. They know what they're doing. If they can't solve a problem, they'll bring it to me." In correctional circles, this is more than a job. It is almost, one suspects, an adventure.

These gratifying arrangements motivate the team members to do their work well. The officers think of themselves as skilled deathwork technicians. Functioning as an autonomous team allows them to focus their technical skills to good result. Away from the madding crowds of the cell block and yard, following an explicit procedure and reporting to a single, supportive boss, the team is free to do well what it feels it does best:

> We think of ourselves as a special team. And I even heard one of [the officers] remark one time—tension got bad in the back and we were having a lot of problems [with the regular prisoners], and he walked up to me and he said, "When are we going to go back down in the basement and do what we do best?" Said, "Hell, I'd rather do the work down there than back here."

"We like to think we're the best in the nation," added another officer. "Nobody," he assured me, "does a better execution than we do."

A Modern Execution Team

This team was, to my knowledge, the first execution team to be studied and described. A study of Missouri's execution team was [later] undertaken by Steve Trombley and published in a book fittingly entitled *The Execution Protocol: Inside America's Capital Punishment Industry.*[21] The dynamics of Missouri's execution team, using lethal injection, offer an exact parallel to those of the execution team I studied using the electric chair. There is a detailed protocol in which every step in the execution process is laid out clearly, broken down into small steps, and rehearsed so that things go off like clockwork. Trombley reports that "During the execution, each event is timed with a stopwatch and logged by the operations officer, who is in the death chamber."[22] There is even a rehearsal with an officer from the team similar in size to the prisoner to be executed so that problems in the management of the offender can be simulated.[23] The focus is on teamwork and on the maintenance of morale; all members take responsibility for the execution and all members stress humaneness, defined as the "desire to ensure that the inmate's suffering is reduced to a minimum."[24] Close custody prevails during the death watch, with one or more officers observing the condemned prisoner in his solitary cell at all times.[25] Prisoners are told what to expect, "step by step," so there are "no surprises."[26] The prisoners cooperate, following the ritual, submitting to social control. "So far, we have not had to manhandle an inmate to get him in there to put him down."[27] The shared view is that "The constant practice, the breaking down of the process into specific roles, the clear understanding on the part of staff precisely what their role is," yields an execution procedure that is "competent, professional, and stress-free."[28]

My research and that of others reveals that bonds of solidarity are an essential feature of modern execution teams.[29] Established and nurtured in the private world of the deathwatch team, these ties are forged in commitment to a common purpose and tested in countless rehearsals. These human connections are the psychological cement that holds an execution team together under the pressures of death work. "It's really a team when you get down to the last hour, you know. You've got to be in, in conjunction. You've got to be ready to work together, to know this man's gonna be with me when I go down there to the death house." The men stress their professionalism as agents or instruments of the state and their respect for one another's skills, which have been tested in the ultimate context of the taking of life. When officers are called upon to take a prisoner to his death, they all draw strength from the knowledge that they are part of a modern execution team.

Notes

1. N. Mailer, *The Executioner's Song* (Boston: Little, Brown, 1979).

2. Gilmore was much influenced by his mother, who early on saw her son as the criminal of the family. She also passed along a version of Mormonism that brought with it a preoccupation with violence. States Mikal, "They saw themselves not only as God's modern chosen people, but also as a people whose faith and identity had been forged by a long and bloody history, and by outright banishment. They were a people apart—a people with its own myths and purposes, and with a history of astonishing violence." A central tenet of Mormonism, at least at the outset and as understood by the Gilmores, was blood atonement. "If you take a life, or commit any comparable ultimate sin, then your blood must be shed. Hanging or imprisonment would not suffice for punishment or restitution. The manner of death had to be one in which your blood spilled onto the ground, as an apology to God." M. Gilmore, *Shot in the Heart* (New York: Doubleday, 1994), 10, 17.

3. Ibid., xi.

4. See, for example, A. A. Skolnick, "Physicians in Missouri (but not Illinois) Win Battle to Block Physician Participation in Executions," *Journal of the American Medical Association* 274 (7):524 (August 1995).

5. I. Solotaroff, "The Last Face You'll Ever See," *Esquire* 124 (2):93 (August 1995).

6. Ibid., 95.

7. Ibid., 95.

8. W. Rideau and R. Wikberg, *Life Sentences: Rage and Survival Behind Bars* (New York: Times Books, 1992), 4–5, 316–317.

9. E. Johnson, "Some States Prepare for First Executions in Twenty Years or More," *Wall Street Journal*, 6 November 1984, 1. Lesy described the division of labor associated with executions, beginning at the top, with the warden, as a series of psychological "cutouts" that the individuals performing the labor use to minimize or even deny their involvement in executions. See M. Lesy, *The Forbidden Zone* (New York: Farrar, Straus & Giroux, 1987), 135–157. This warden exemplifies Lesy's point. Yet the warden and the officers of the execution team I studied did take responsibility, individually and collectively, for the executions they carried out. They asserted that executions are lawful sanctions, and as agents of the law they have nothing to hide from themselves or others. How they prepared themselves psychologically to carry out their perceived duty is a more complicated matter, often involving elements of psychological denial (especially of the humanity of the victim), but they did not deny or downplay their responsibility for executions.

10. D. A. Cabana, *Death at Midnight: The Confession of an Executioner* (Boston: Northeastern University Press, 1996), 17.

11. Rideau and Wikberg (n. 8), 317.

12. There are marked variations on this score. The warden of the prison I studied kept his distance from the process. He showed up to read the death warrant and signal the start of the execution but was otherwise uninvolved with the execution process. Donald Cabana reports that he was very much involved with the execution process, including being present for rehearsals; he was very much involved in the lives of the condemned prisoners, even during their final hours and minutes. See Cabana (n. 10).

13. For a discussion of focused interview procedures, see Chap. 3, Note 57.

14. One officer retired, the other died. To date, the team has had no dropouts, and morale remains high.

15. The team I studied was more concerned about losing control of the situation and having to use violence than they were with the prospect of a technically botched execution. Experience suggests, however, that when an execution is botched, the staff are deeply affected. "I remember the scene vividly," reports Commissioner Thigpen, present at a botched execution in Alabama's Atmore Prison. "I could not find adequate words then or later to express how much I regretted what had taken place. The members of the execution team who had failed to connect the chair correctly to its power source apologized time and again for their error. Steps were taken immediately following that event to eliminate the possibility of the same error occurring again. Still, that does not relieve you of the fact that you know a mistake had occurred that caused unnecessary suffering." See M. L. Thigpen, "A Tough Assignment—A Former Commissioner's Thoughts on Carrying Out Executions," *Corrections Today* 55(4): 58 (July 1993). At this execution, it was apparent to all involved that the execution had been botched. In other situations, outside observers may see an execution as flawed while the execution team does not, particularly if they conclude, rightly or wrongly, that no added distress was caused by any problems of implementation.

16. This view is widely shared by those associated with execution teams. As Warden Charlie Jones of Alabama's Atmore Prison put it, "You want to do it right. You've got to do it, and you want to do it in the most humane way possible. The least little annoyance in the routine can throw the whole thing out of kilter." See G. E. Goldhammer, *Dead End* (Brunswick, ME: Biddle Publishing Company, 1994), 107. For other expressions of these and related sentiments, see the various articles under the heading, Special Focus—Managing Death Row, *Corrections Today* 55(4): 56–99 (July 1993).

17. Great care in the selection of execution team members is the norm in the field, though it is not always the team leader who selects the officers on the team. See, for example, Cabana (n. 10), and Special Focus—Managing Death Row (n. 16).

18. The words of the officers are testimony to the stressful nature of the experience. As it happens, there is also objective evidence. Cabana reports that one of his officers, who served as a volunteer for a gas chamber rehearsal, showed a "heart rate [that] was wildly erratic." See Cabana (n. 10), 161. We can only imagine what condemned prisoners experience when they are secured to the execution machinery. The notion of "total helplessness" used by one of my respondents would seem appropriate, though perhaps "total terror" would be even more apt.

19. Terms like *clockwork* or *machine-like precision* are commonly used to describe executions carried out by well-trained teams of officers. See for example S. Trombley, *The Execution Protocol: Inside America's Capital Punishment Industry* (New York: Anchor Books, 1993), and Special Focus—Managing Death Row (n. 16).

20. L. X. Lombardo, *Guards Imprisoned: Correctional Officers at Work*, 2/e (Cincinnati: Anderson, 1989).

21. Trombley (n. 19), esp. 104–116. Donald Cabana's *Death at Midnight* (n. 10) examines executions in Mississippi's Parchman Prison. Cabana places more emphasis on his role as warden in charge of the execution process and less on the role played by the execution team. To the extent that the workings of the team are examined—the protocol, practice, rehearsals, etc—the parallels are once again exact.

22. Trombley (n. 19), 112.

23. Ibid., 116.

24. Ibid., 107.

25. Ibid., 108–109.

26. Ibid., 114.

27. Ibid., 114.

28. Ibid., 223.

29. The group dynamics of execution teams have not been explicitly discussed in the literature to any great extent, though the bonding of execution team officers is now well known to practitioners. The remarks of Warden Martin of Broad River Correctional Facility in South Carolina are instructive on this score: "As the execution date drew closer and the preparation grew more intense, our team became extremely close." See G. N. Martin, "A Warden's Reflections—Enforcing the Death Penalty with Competence, Compassion," *Corrections Today* 55(4): 62 (July 1993). In my occasional work

as a consultant on execution related matters, I have found that recognition of this bonding effect is quite common. See, generally, Trombley (n. 19).

32 Managing Death Row: A Tough Assignment

Morris L. Thigpen

Focus Questions

1. After witnessing eight executions, what are Thigpen's general sentiments about the death penalty?

2. What was the Catholic priest's reaction to witnessing an execution?

3. What are some of the problems that Thigpen mentions about the death penalty?

This past January at the ACA [American Correctional Association] Winter Conference in Miami, I attended a workshop that focused on death penalty procedures. Listening to the discussions and presentations, one could have concluded that executions occur in a sterile environment, devoid of any feelings or emotions.

As one who has witnessed eight executions, I know that nothing could be further from the truth. It seems that no one wants to talk about what an execution does to the staff responsible for carrying them out. With this article, I want to try to do just that. It is difficult to transpose my feelings into words—perhaps that is why there is so little writing or discussion about an execution's impact on staff.

I often have heard individuals who have never participated in an execution say they would be more than willing to pull the switch, drop the pellet, or inject the needle. On the other hand, I never have heard anyone who has participated in an execution say, "I would like to do that again." For most of the members of the execution team, the procedure is a gut-wrenching, highly emotional experience. Watching death occur under any circumstances is most unpleasant. As commissioner of the Alabama Department of Corrections from 1987 to May 1993, I witnessed eight human beings move from life to death in less than 120 seconds. Those experiences remain indelibly imprinted in my mind.

When the death penalty was reinstated in the 1970s, a circus-like atmosphere surrounded many of the first executions. In Alabama, we did our best to carry out executions in an atmosphere of dignity and respect. The condemned inmates, their families, and their friends deserve that.

Every effort is made to ensure that each execution is done without mistakes. This requires the execution team to go through numerous practice sessions before the actual execution. In spite of these efforts, however, sometimes errors are made.

In at least one case in Alabama, the first attempt at electrocution failed as a result of human error. I remember the scene vividly. The warden came into the viewing room where I was standing and told me what had happened. With the condemned man's father and his principle attorney standing less than two feet away, I remember telling the warden we would have to proceed with a second attempt. Both were commenting, "They are torturing him."

I could not find adequate words then or later to express how much I regretted what had taken place. The members of the execution team who had failed to connect the chair correctly to its power source apologized time and again for their error. Steps were taken immediately following that event to eliminate the possibility of the same error occurring again. Still, that does not relieve you of the fact that you know a mistake had occurred that caused unnecessary suffering.

Some victim advocates have criticized any expression of compassion for the condemned inmate as conveying a lack of respect for the victim. That certainly is not the case. I made a point of reviewing the file of every inmate before the execution. The crimes they have committed are heinous. However, I still feel compassion for them. I wonder what events in their lives led them to commit a capital offense. Was there some point at which intervention of some type might have changed the course of events?

In the last execution performed under my leadership in Alabama, we allowed a Catholic priest to witness the execution at the inmate's request. We had made numerous concessions in allowing the priest to spend as much time as possible with the inmate. In spite of that, upon emerging from the witness room, the priest turned to several of my employees and remarked that he had just "witnessed a group of barbarians in action." His comment hurt the staff members deeply and made all of us very angry. After the media reported the priest's statement, he repeated it at the inmate's funeral. We realized there was little we could do except to accept the fact that the comment came from an uninformed person.

Another troubling aspect of capital punishment for me is the length of time inmates spend on death row. I found that the person we were executing may not be the same type of person who committed the crime.

One particular case that still troubles me was an inmate who had been on death row for seven or eight years. During that time he underwent a significant change in his life. His was not a last-minute acknowledgment of Christian redemption but one that occurred several years previously. While strapped in the electric chair just moments before the death penalty was carried out, the inmate asked permission to pray. He prayed for his own forgiveness, for those who were about to execute him, and for his victim's family.

I believe that individuals do have the ability to change and that over the course of time they spend on death row, some rather dramatic changes occur. I always will wonder about the good this man might have accomplished if his sentence had been commuted to life without parole. After the media reported that I was obviously disturbed by this execution, a female death row inmate asked to speak to me. "Commissioner," she said, "you should not feel any guilt about what you have to do. We put ourselves where we are today." That is true, but I still am unable to reconcile certain questions in my own mind.

Questions also surface involving plea-bargained capital crimes. I am troubled when two or more offenders are involved in the same capital crime and one testifies against the other. One life is spared, the other is taken. Does this represent true justice?

One of my own very personal conflicts centers on how accountable I will be for my role in executions at the end of my life on this earth. I fully understand that what I have done is legal under the laws by which we are governed. However, my religious beliefs cause me to question my actions. After each execution, I felt as though I left another part of my own humanity and my spiritual being in that viewing room.

Holman Prison, where Alabama's executions are carried out shortly after midnight, is about a two-hour drive south of Montgomery, where I live. I almost always drove home alone after an execution. Sleep was out of the question. I found I needed to be alone for a while. During this time I wrestled with myself. Is the world a safer, more just place because of what has taken place tonight?

Reprinted from: Morris L. Thigpen, "Managing Death Row: A Tough Assignment." In *Corrections Today*, (July, 1993): 56–58. Copyright © 1993 by the American Correctional Association, Lanham, MD. Reprinted by permission.

33
Walker's Requiem

Anthony Ross

Focus Questions

1. Compare the nature of Walker's relationship with the psychiatrist to his relationship with the lawyer.

2. What responsibilities do members of the deathwatch team have prior to the execution?

3. What procedures occurred over the course of Walker's last day?

4. What were Walker's perceptions of dying, as noted in his poem and his dreams?

[Editor's Note: This selection was written by a man currently on death row to depict what the last day before execution might be like].

I could see myself in the dark mahogany coffin. How I had gotten there and why was something I couldn't remember. I could hear the hum of an organ playing softly in the background, as mourners began filling the pews of the small church. Most of the faces I didn't recognize, but there were a few mugs I was happy to see, homeboys from the old neighborhood—Big J. T., Lowdown, Spoony, and Spoony's little brother, Klepto, who, at the ripe old age of ten, was already a professional thief. I thought it was strange that they were wearing white dinner jackets and carrying serving plates. Then again, these were guys who'd wake up in the morning and smoke weed for breakfast. They probably thought there were going to be some eats after the funeral. I didn't blame them; these things can be pretty boring. I saw my family seated in the front row. My lawyer, with his secretary, Dora, was sitting behind them. My mother, who never dreamed she would outlive any of her children, looked on, stricken. I felt a pang of guilt.

The sound of the organ began to fade and the faint hush of whispers among the mourners slowly subsided.

Whack! "Now put that back!" I heard Spoony say, as he popped Klepto upside the head. Then they all began to stare hypnotically at the dark-robed figure standing ominously behind the wooden podium. His face was obscured by a large hood, and his hands were gloved. Man, this guy is straight outta the comic books, I thought.

When he spoke, his voice seemed to resonate off the walls of the church, sending icy chills through my skin like an arctic breeze.

"Let us all rejoice in the holy offering!" he bellowed.

Offering? What offering? I thought.

"Let us give thanks to the blessed one," he commanded, as everyone in the church began nodding their heads in unison and shouting, "Thank you, Lord! Thank you, Lord!"

Whooooaaaa! Back up, mister! What fucking offering? This is my goddamn funeral, not a—

"We shall partake of the sacrifice!" he thundered on, followed by another joyous chorus of "That's right, Lord. Thank you, Lord!"

Hey! What the hell is going on here? I tried to scream, but couldn't make a sound. He then beckoned to everyone to gather around the casket, and I could feel them pressing and pushing up against the sides, peering in at my lifeless body, lovingly . . . almost hungrily. Panic set in, and I tried to get up and run, but I couldn't move. *Aw, c'mon—let me outta here,* I pleaded. *I ain't no offering.*

I felt hands caressing and poking my body. Then I saw my little sister and Klepto licking their lips and my lawyer's secretary wiping off her silverware. The dark figure walked to the head of the casket and pulled back his hood. His face was hideous: There was no skin, just bone and pieces of rotting flesh. His mouth was twisted and mangled as he grinned, displaying rows of sharklike teeth, and his eyes were only gaping holes filled with maggots. I frantically looked around and saw everyone changing into grotesque and disfigured creatures. My mother was barely recognizable as she grabbed me by the throat with a clawed hand and began to lift me straight from the coffin. Filled with the horror of what was about to happen, I tried to close my mind to the gruesome scene. . . . I couldn't.

"Now! Let us all feast!" the robed thing said, as he snapped off one of my arms like a chicken wing.

Noooooo! I screamed in my mind, just as the thing that used to be my little sister dislodged one of my eyeballs from its socket with her Easybake oven fork and greedily gobbled it down.

My eyes flew open and I quickly sat up in the bunk to survey the small cell. Everything was still. "Damn!" I whispered to myself. "You gotta get a grip, man." Dreaming is one thing, but this shit is ridiculous. Some would claim this was guilt eating away at my conscience . . . fuck them! I bet that prison shrink would have a field day analyzing my dream. *Fuck him, too.*

I looked out the small window directly in front of my cell. It was dark outside, making things seem almost peaceful. But that was an illusion. There was nothing peaceful about prison, nothing serene about death row, and at that very moment certain preparations were being carried out that placed me at the center of it all.

My name is Nathan Cole Walker, Nat Cole for short, a nickname my grandmother gave me on account of her fondness for the singer Nat King Cole. Personally, I can't hit a note and rap music is my thing. I must admit, I did have a smooth style that infatuated the young ladies. But that was eons ago and a helluva lot has changed since those days.

In less than twenty-four hours it will be my twenty-fifth birthday, but there will be no celebrating, no party, no happy nothin'. Because I'm not gonna live to see it.

Six years ago, I was sentenced to death. The whys don't matter now, and the particulars aren't important. Today I have run out of time, destiny has come kicking at my door, and I am scheduled to be executed promptly at eleven thirty Wednesday night. It is now Wednesday morning . . . my last day on Earth.

I tried to shake the dream from my head, before beginning my routine of pacing the six-by-ten cell. It's a mode of controlling the rage of the half-man, half-animals we've become. A silent way of expressing our malediction at being caged. It is never escape—respite, maybe—but never escape.

"Anything wrong, Walker?" the guard who was posted outside my cell asked. He had been watching me from the moment I woke up, jotting down his observations on paper.

"Naw, nothin' I can't deal with," I shot back in disgust.

"What time is it?" I asked the guard. He glanced up from the *Playboy* he had stashed between the pages of a *National Geographic*, rubbed his eyes, and looked at his watch.

"It's almost six thirty." He yawned. "Just about time for me to be gettin' outta here," he added, with apparent relief. Six thirty was the shift change; another guard would be taking his place for second watch in a few minutes. I resumed my pacing.

Anyone put on death watch is provided with around-the-clock security and scrutiny, compliments of the Department of Corrections, just in case you decide to skip the scenic route to the gas chamber, in an attempt to cheat the state out of its judicial duty to personally kill you. The guard who would be coming on for second watch was named Ford. I had known Ford over the years; he was okay, as guards go. Sometimes we'd get in a game or two of chess, or shoot the breeze to break the monotony. When you're waiting to die, the boredom alone could kill you.

I could hear Ford locking the door.

"How's it going, Ford?" I said, still looking up at the ceiling.

"Not too bad, Walker. And you?"

"Same old tune." There was silence for a moment.

"You wanna get in a game of chess later?" he asked, trying to sound cheerful. We both knew we'd played our last game.

"I don't know—maybe."

"Well, if you do, just holler." He turned to his paperwork and I shut my eyes in a futile attempt to shield out reality. My mind was like a movie screen.

"Nigger, you got somethin' to say before I end your black ass life?" I didn't say a word as I watched the cop pull his pants leg and reach for the gun that was strapped to his ankle. I let the Glöck slide easily down my sleeve and into my hand. By the time the cop realized a gun was pointing at him, it was too late. The first bullet tore through the front of his neck and the second one entered his right eye. He died before hitting the ground. The scene repeated itself over and over. After all these years, that one event still seemed like it happened yesterday.

The ringing of the phone brought me back. "I'll ask him, hold on. Walker, it's Chaplain Graves," Ford said, with an ear-to-ear grin. "You wanna see him?"

"Fuck him!" I said. I sat up on the bunk and grabbed a book from the pile on the floor. It was Ralph Ellison's *Invisible Man*. I could relate to the main character, because all my life I've been invisible to folks. The only time they seemed to take notice was when I got into trouble. No one really knew me, not even my family—hell, I didn't even know myself. Everything I did brought me close to death, toward this very moment. I once read somewhere that desperate men are always running out of time. Well, right now, I must be truly desperate.

I must have read for almost an hour before putting the book down. I was just about to close my eyes when Ford asked, "Say, Walker? If you want, I can call the Muslim chaplain or something. I mean, in case you wanted to speak to someone."

"Thanks, but no thanks."

"Well, I just thought you might want to talk to somebody who can understand—well, who can relate to—you know what I mean?"

"I know what you mean, Ford."

"Say, Walker? Are you afraid of dying? I mean, I can't even imagine how I would feel in your place."

I thought about it for a moment, but I already knew my answer.

"Naw, I ain't afraid of dying. Dying is something I've been doing all my life. But when you know when and how it's gonna happen, all it takes is that one step over the edge inside your head—then bam! That's why most men are able to walk to their execution. They're already dead inside their heads."

"That's a helluva way of looking at it, Walker."

"I don't need to get nothing off my chest. And if there is a God out there, then he's gonna have a lot of fucking explaining to do when I reach the hereafter."

We both laughed; then there was a long pause. Empty of anything else to say, we both went back to what we were doing. I was tossed back to old times, and it wasn't long before I dozed off.

"Hey, Walker! Walker!" I heard my name being called from far away.

"Whaaat . . ." I mumbled, still half in the dream state.

"Walker. Someone here to see you," Ford said apologetically.

"Who?" I demanded, fully awake now.

"Doctor Cohen."

"Doctor Cohen?" I tried to place the name. Cohen was the prison shrink. This was his third visit; the first two times I simply ignored his ass.

He pulled the extra chair from the desk and planted it in front of the cell. We were face-to-face with the cell bars between us.

"What's up, Doc?" I smiled.

"How are you feeling today, Walker?" He always started off with the same stupid ass question, trying to sound as sincere as possible.

"Well, you caught me in a good mood today, Doc. I was just about to start playing with my dick . . . but what can I do for you?"

"I came by to see how you are doing."

"For cryin' out loud, all of a sudden everyone is concerned about my fucking welfare. What gives?"

"I'm just doing my job, Walker," he stated matter-of-factly.

"And what is that, Doc?" He looked at me, puzzled.

"Well, to talk, mainly."

"About what?"

"About emotions you're feeling, about things that may be going through your mind, or dreams you may be having." His mention of dreams caught me off guard, and I wondered if I had talked in my sleep.

"Dreamt I walked on water, Doc," I said sarcastically.

"Walker, I understand that under the circumstances it's normal to feel anger, but you don't have to be confrontational."

"Wrong! That's my style, man, plus I like testing seersuckah-suit mothafuckahs like you, just to see that geek look you get on your face." I burst out laughing; he just sat there, turning beet red. His mouth opened and closed, as if he were trying to find something to say.

"Okay, Walker, you crazy bastard!" he whispered through clenched teeth, trying vainly to maintain his clinical composure. "If you want to play fucking games—"

I immediately stopped laughing and sprang to my feet, cutting him off. I had him and he knew it.

"Game! Naw, this is far from a fucking game, Doctor. Here the stakes are much higher."

"Well, then, what would you call it?"

"I call it . . . my personal responsibility to upset bullshit mental tacticians like yourself. You waltz in here doing your friend routine, thinking you'll become famous at my expense by getting me to expose the juicer morsels of my brain—so you can jump in front of the camera seconds after I'm dead, claiming you were the only one I would talk to, the only one I trusted."

"Walker, that's not true," he said, nervously shaking his head. "I would never do anything like that."

"Tell me, Doc, when were you planning on cutting a book deal—while the dirt was still moist on my grave, or after it dried?"

"I'm telling you, Walker, no such thing has ever crossed my mind. Nothing that's mentioned here will go beyond these walls. I'm a professional doctor, for Christ's sake!"

"When you look at me, all you see is an experiment . . . some data that might make you famous. But you sit there confident, grinning inside, never realizing that by trying to look into my head, you incriminate yourself, just like all the others who will watch me suffocate, watch me slowly, painfully, pass into nonexistence. My death will render me not guilty, but it illuminates your guilt, your savage necrophilia. I'm every bit as human as those who seek to strip me of my humanity."

He sat there looking like a kid who just got busted bang with his hand in the cookie jar. If I had been in doubt, his eyes convinced me that my words had hit their mark.

He stood abruptly, began to walk toward the door, hesitated, and then left. I lay back on the bunk with my hands behind my head, staring at the ceiling.

"What time is it, Ford?" I called out.

"Ten twenty," he called back.

My lawyer, Duncan Brock, would be coming around noon, as he did every day. He was the only person I still cared to talk to. "Ten twenty," I said to myself. *You're gonna be a statistic, Nat Cole, in less than fifteen hours.*

The phone rang. Ford answered it.

"Walker, your attorney is here. They're on their way to pick you up."

"All right, thanks."

Two guards escorted me to the small room where they allowed me to visit. When I walked in, Duncan Brock stood up to greet me. We shook hands warmly, then sat at the small table. He looked tired, and I knew he had probably slept only a few hours in the last four days. His otherwise immaculate suit was rumpled, his hair halfheartedly combed, and there were noticeable dark spots beneath his eyes.

"How are you holding up, Nat?"

"So-so, but you look like you been mugged." We both smiled. Duncan was one of the few people left in the world I truly respected. Over the years we'd had our share of differences but always managed to work them out. It made us respect each other as persons, as friends. I felt sorry for him. He had done his best, yet I thought he was always going to feel that there was something more he could have done. Even in these final hours, Duncan was optimistic.

We talked about how my family was doing, and about the people outside the prison protesting my execution. Then he began to tell me about the legal strategies he was trying.

"Listen, Nat, I filed a new writ with the Ninth Circuit Court challenging—"

My thoughts began to drift, and images floated through my mind. "Son, where are you going?" "To basketball practice; Momma—"

"I talked to one of my law professors and he thinks—"

"Momma, Nat hit me—"

"—also the Supreme Court could—"

"Homeboy! Nat Cole is straight crazy—"

"—other options that legally—"

"Mrs. Walker, we've arrested your son for—"

"—the main thing is the constitutionality of—"

"You are hereby sentenced to be put to death in the—"

Like a motion picture the scenes came and went, until one thing remained: the words *The End*.

We sat there exchanging small talk until a guard showed up at the gate, announcing it was time for me to go back. We stood and embraced each other.

Then the guard motioned me to him. I walked over, turned around, and he put the cuffs on and opened the gate to escort me back upstairs.

"Take care, Duncan," I said.

"I'm not going to give up, Nat!" he said strongly. I didn't answer. I knew this was the last time we would see each other.

Back at my cell, it was a little after four o'clock. The phone had been installed right outside, a direct link to my lawyer for good news . . . or bad.

It was almost six o'clock when Ford called to me. At first my mind couldn't compute the reality of his question. I was stunned by its finality, even though I knew they would ask me.

"Walker, the warden wants to know what you'd like for your last meal."

I didn't say anything. My mind locked on the question. The concept loomed like a giant neon sign, pushing all other thoughts to the side, until it alone remained. Last meal! Hell, how in the fuck was I supposed to enjoy something like that? My stomach did some gymnastics and I knew there was no way I was going to be able to eat anything. The very thought of crapping on myself while choking to death was enough to deter me from eating. When they pulled me out of the chamber, my drawers were going to be clean.

"Fuck that, man. I don't want nothin'!" I told Ford.

"Sure?"

"Absolutely. I don't want shit!" I could imagine the warden's expression. He'll probably try to send that shrink over here. But I doubt he wanted to see me again. I got off the bunk and began pacing again. I also started singing every song I knew in my mind, but after a while, I would sing the first verse, then nothing . . . hum a few notes, then nothing. It was like the words were just vanishing from my memory. Verses got mixed up, songs became intertwined. I finally gave up.

"What time you got, Ford?"

"Seven thirty-five."

"I need to use a pencil and paper."

"No problem." He went in his desk and got out some sheets of paper and a small pencil that had been broken in half, for my supposed safety.

I rolled my mattress back so I could use the flat steel bunk as a table. I was going to write one last letter, but instead found myself just sitting there, staring at the paper. After about an hour of scribbling on several sheets of paper and tossing them into the toilet, I finally wrote something. I titled it *A Seminar in Dying*. It was a poem, the kind only a desperate man could write.

Imagine seeing the flash of a camera, and in that same instant you witness the most violent and brutal scene of your life.

Imagine seeing a contorted face, broken limbs, blood flowing.

Imagine the terrified screams, the unbearable pain, the pleas for help, the tears.

Imagine death, as you fall to your knees, embracing a dying body . . . your body.

Imagine that last look, that last word, that last touch . . . that last breath.

Imagine life the day after, the week after, the year after . . . the hereafter.

Imagine seeing that camera flash in your sleep and your waking moments . . . over and over, every second, every minute, every hour, in your mind.

Imagine seeing the end . . . your end, every day, until you die . . . imagine.

It was all I had left in me. I folded the paper, got an envelope from Ford, and addressed it to my lawyer.

"Make sure he gets this after—you know, when things are over."

"He'll get it, don't worry."

Sometime later, the phone in front of my cell rang. I just stared at it, uncertain of what to do.

"Answer it," Ford said, enthusiastically. I reached gingerly through the bars and picked it up.

"Yeah?" I whispered.

"Nat?" It was Duncan. He sounded exhausted.

"Yeah?" I whispered again.

"Nat, the courts turned us down, but—"

I put the phone down, not hanging it up, just laying it on its side. I could hear Duncan still calling my name, but there was nothing else to say, nothing else to hear.

"What time you got, Ford?"

"Eleven-o-five." Just then, the phone on his desk rang. The sudden change of his expression told me everything.

"Walker," he said solemnly, as he hung up the phone.

"Yeah, I know." They were on their way to get me. This was it—time to face the matador.

"You want some more orange juice or something, Walker?"

I just looked at him. I knew he was trying to break the overwhelming sense of dread that had started to condense like storm clouds around us. I looked down at my feet. I didn't recognize them. They seemed like independent machines separate from my body, and they would of their own volition lead me right to the gas chamber. Looking away, I thought, *would hate to have to whack you guys off.* I put my shoes on and splashed some cold water on my face. I took a piss, washed my hands, and combed my hair—but as I was combing it, I was struck by the realization that everything I was now doing would be my last time doing it. I suddenly felt completely alone; my heart started to thump somewhere in my throat.

"Walker, it's time to go." The warden and two guards were waiting like stone sentinels. I walked over to the bars, consciously controlling each step. One guard put the cuffs on through the tray-slot. Ford opened the gate and, as I stepped out, I nodded to him slightly. He nodded back. I walked slowly, my breath hard. The sound of it echoed in my head like giant waves. I turned to the warden.

"Do me a favor, Warden?"

"What is it?" he asked, bewildered.

"Well, do you think we could make this long walk short?"

"How?" He looked even more confused.

"By running!" I said and burst out laughing.

They all looked at me like I had just snapped, Ford included. They stood there, uncertain of what to do next.

"Aw, c'mon guys, it's a joke," I said. "I'm just trying to ease the gloom. Hell, the way you dudes look, a person would think you're the ones about to get x'ed out."

"Walker, how can you joke at a time like this?"

"Yeah, you're right, Warden. So when do you think would be a good time for me to joke?"

Then, looking him straight in the eye, I asked him seriously, "Warden? When was the last time you been to a circus?" But I didn't give him time to answer. "Let's go," I said. "There's one waiting for us."

We walked out into a long, narrow hallway.

The warden stuck a key into a slot where the buttons should have been and turned it.

It took a few seconds for the door to open and I could hear the elevator lumbering toward the top. The door opened suddenly with a whoosh, and we all stepped in. The guards positioned themselves behind me, while the warden remained at my side. It had all been rehearsed, their roles, the parts they would play. I imagined them practicing it. I wondered who they got to play me.

The elevator stopped and the door whooshed open. We stepped into a smaller hallway, made a right, and walked toward a large green steel door. I thought I could hear a murmur of voices on the other side and I imagined rows of people drinking soda, eating popcorn, and chanting, "Kill him, kill him, kill him!"

The warden pressed a button this time, and a few seconds later the door popped open. As we walked in, my entire body grew hot and the palms of my hands started to sweat. The first thing I saw was the gas chamber.

Everything became dreamlike and every second was an eternity., My mind went numb, my throat bone dry. This was my first real look at the chamber—I stood there, my eyes transfixed on the cylindrical shape and the chair sitting directly in the middle. The feeling of déjà vu hit me again, this time much stronger. Now don't get the wrong impression—I didn't all of a sudden get religion. But when dying is the central theme of your life, your perspective on things can change. I don't think it's an issue of whether or not we're afraid of dying—it's more like being afraid of not having existed, you know what I mean? I guess that's why people tend to believe in things like reincarnation, heaven, and transmigration, because those things offer a sense of continuity or immortality. Hey, life after death sure beats ashes to ashes.

"Let's go, Walker," the warden said, taking hold of my arm. We walked to the door of the chamber. One of the guards pulled open the door and, as I stepped in, the air was stale and oppressive. I swear I could sense the men who had gone before me—that somehow I could feel them still in that room. If my mind was playing a trick on me, it was a damn good one.

I sat down hypnotically. The chair was hard and cold. The two guards began immediately to strap me in, wrists first, then my waist and legs. My eyes were wide, alert, as if trying to suck in the last images of life. They darted around the chamber seeking anything . . . everything. The cubicle was spotless, almost as if all trace of reality itself had been vacuumed out. It was the only place I had ever been inside prison where there was absolutely no graffiti . . . no "Kilroy was here," no "Jesus loves you," no gang writing, not so much as a scratch. I guess anyone coming in here ain't in a position to do nothing but die—and the only thing that will ever deface these walls will be the souls of dead men. The warden double-checked the straps after the guards had finished. Then in a well-practiced monotone, he asked, "Do you have any last words, Walker?"

Ignoring his question, I swallowed the large lump that had formed in my throat and stared straight ahead at the dark glass window in front of me. I knew there would be people sitting on the other side, waiting to watch my death. *Well, enjoy the show, folks,* I said to myself. The warden asked me again if I had any last words. I said nothing, still staring at the window. He then proceeded to tell me in the same flat voice how the sentence of death was being carried out by order of the court. When he had finished, he and the two guards left without looking back. I heard the latch locking the door, and except for my breathing, there was absolute silence. I pulled against the strap—nothing. I knew it was useless at this point, but still . . .

I could feel my muscles tightening, as my pulse vibrated throughout my entire body. An eternity seemed to pass as I sat there, waiting for something to happen. I kept thinking that they were going to come through the door at any second. My eyes were frantically searching the window for any movement. Finally, I closed them and let my head fall back. I felt some sweat or a tear rolling off my cheek. I opened my eyes just in time to catch it falling from my face, and as I watched it fall in slow motion, I suddenly tasted something bitter and acidic in my mouth, and my lungs seemed to ignite into flames. Without even thinking about it, I quickly held my breath and, at that very moment, I knew that once I let it go, it would all be over.

With each second, the pain in my chest grew more unbearable—inside I was on fire. I began spinning and tumbling, my head falling backward and forward. I could feel the explosion in my chest heaving upward, as the pain began to burst into a billion pieces of light . . . and then I was falling, falling toward the sky, higher and higher, until I could no longer see beneath the clouds, until darkness began to engulf me. It was almost over. "C'mon, Nat, warp speed, man." *Yeah,* I

thought, *I do have something to say* . . . then I felt the rush of warm wind, and I breathed out.

1995, California State Prison—San Quentin
San Quentin, California

Reprinted from: Anthony Ross, "Walker's Requiem." In *Doing Time: 25 Years of Prison Writing*, Bell Gale Chevigny (ed.), pp. 308–319. Copyright © 1999 by Anthony Ross. Reprinted by permission of Arcade Publishing, New York, NY.

Chapter XI
Discussion

On Death Row

The three readings in this chapter focus on the experiences that prisoners and practitioners have while living and working on death row. Prisoners with a sentence of death are considered high escape risks, and extra precautionary measures must be taken at all times. Death row prisoners are on a restricted status—they never mix with general population inmates, and they must wear handcuffs and be accompanied by a correctional officer whenever they are outside their cells (except while taking a shower and while exercising in a special recreation yard). With some exceptions, most death row inmates spend an average of 22 hours a day in a cell by themselves. They are allowed visits but typically must request that legal materials be delivered to their cells.

All three of the readings discuss some aspect of the deathwatch team. It should be noted that in most states, the prison where death row inmates are housed is different from the facility where the execution occurs. This change of location is intentional, so that the correctional officers who have worked with death row inmates for years are not the same officers who are members of the deathwatch team. The deathwatch team is composed of seasoned officers who have not formed a bond with the death row inmate waiting to be executed. It is interesting to note, however, that the execution process is to be performed properly and with the utmost respect and professionalism. This professionalism ensures that the procedure is completed correctly, legally, and with least resistance from the prisoner. Johnson has described the process as mechanical, with all the simple tasks practiced repeatedly.

Even with these procedures in place, some staff members found it difficult to separate their professional role from their personal feelings. For example, after witnessing eight executions, Thigpen shared the conflict he had with his role in the state deaths of prisoners. In his reading, Thigpen mentions the arbitrariness of the death penalty, and how he believes that even the worst prisoners have the ability to change their ways over time. Thigpen is not alone in his views. Donald Cabana, former warden in Missouri, expresses similar sentiments. In the reading by Johnson, he found that some members of the deathwatch team expressed concerns over the death penalty—whether it is the "right thing to do."

The final reading by Anthony Ross depicts Nathan Cole Walker's last day on earth before his execution in the gas chamber. This reading is most likely a portrayal of the experience Ross believes he himself will have on his last day, if and when his execution date draws near. Even though this account is fictional, the procedures and feelings prior to the execution are realistic. It is interesting that Walker has a momentary flashback of his crime—killing a police officer—but, like many offenders, there is no discussion of the pain the victim and the victim's family suffered as a result of the murder. Most of the attention is self-centered on the offender and his pain. This selection illustrates how central the concept of death and dying is to death row inmates, even in a dream state. In one of Walker's dreams, it seems that Walker perceives that he has caused his own family anguish while being on death row. He mentions that he isn't afraid to die because he is already dead. In other words, he has given up hope for his own future even before his execution.

Part Five
Getting Out

Chapter XII
Introduction

Release From Prison: Parole

Common Assumtions	Reality
• Parole and probation are basically the same kind of sentence.	• Parole is community reentry from prison by mandatory or discretionary release. Probation is a community sentence imposed by the judge in place of prison. Parolees and probationers do have similar conditions of supervision, however.
• Parole is revoked only when a new crime is committed in the community.	• Parole can be revoked for either a new crime or a "technical violation." A technical violation is a breach of one or more parole conditions, such as using illegal drugs while on parole or failing to report to the parole officer. Parolees usually must commit a number of technical violations over time before they are in violation.

Parole is defined as the conditional release of a convicted felon from a correctional institution to serve the remainder of his or her sentence in the community under state supervision. Eighty percent of all prisoners reenter the community from prison either by mandatory release or discretionary parole. Individuals on mandatory release (otherwise known as "postrelease supervision" or "supervised release") do not go before a parole board. Rather, they reenter the community *automatically* at the expiration of their maximum term *minus* credited time off for good behavior. In other words, mandatory release is not decided by a parole board but by legislative statute or good-time laws.

In contrast to mandatory release, individuals released on discretionary parole reenter the community because members of a state parole board have decided that the prisoner poses a minimal community risk and has earned the privilege to be released from prison while still remaining under supervision. Parole board members use various assessment tools to estimate the future risk that the parolee may pose to the community upon release. Before making their decision, many parole boards review the records maintained by prison officials, and they also interview the offender in person or by closed circuit television (Cromwell, del Carmen, and Alarid 2002).

Currently, about the same number of prisoners are released annually on discretionary parole as on mandatory supervision. Parolees on mandatory release or discretionary parole are supervised by a parole officer and adhere to similar conditions. In both cases, if release conditions are not followed, offenders can be returned to prison (Cromwell et al. 2001).

Thirty years ago, discretionary parole was the most common form of release from prison. In the mid-1970s, rehabilitation, indeterminate sentencing, and parole were heavily criticized because of the correctional system's failure to reduce the steadily increasing crime rate and its inability to reduce recidivism, rehabilitate offenders, or make predictive judgments about offenders' future behavior. The pendulum swung toward a "just deserts" approach—stressing a punishment-oriented correctional system that included decreasing or eliminating the discretion of parole boards to release prisoners. Many states substituted mandatory or automatic release in place of discretionary release (Griswold and Wiatrowski 1983).

Burke (1995) provides the following information about mandatory versus discretionary release:

- Parole boards (discretionary release) can impose prisoner participation in treatment programs as incentives for release. With automatic release, there are no more incentives for prisoners to better themselves while behind bars.

- Parole boards have improved their techniques for more objective and open decision making through parole guidelines.

- Victims can attend parole board hearings to convince the board not to release their offender, but victims have no say in mandatory or automatic release situations.

- Release from prison is a right under automatic supervision rather than a privilege under discretionary parole.

- Release decisions are made by computer under automatic release rather than by a human parole board, which can keep prisoners in prison if it feels the offender will remain a danger to society.

- Abolishing discretionary parole does *not* mean that prisoners will serve their full sentence; it does *not* prevent prisoners from getting out, and it does *not* necessarily increase public safety.

Whether the type of release is mandatory or discretionary, Williams, McShane, and Dolny (2000) explain the functions of parole supervision today:

> [P]arole is tasked primarily with protecting the public from released offenders. This goal is accomplished in three general objectives: (1) by enforcing restrictions and controls on parolees in the community, (2) by providing services that help parolees integrate into a noncriminal lifestyle, and (3) by increasing the public's level of confidence in the effectiveness and responsiveness of parole services through the first two activities (i.e., in part a reduction in fear of crime).

At the beginning of 2000, the nationwide parolee (mandatory and discretionary) population totaled over 712,000 prisoners, or 352 people per 100,000 adults. Most parolees are men, but women comprise nearly 11 percent of offenders on parole. According to Petersilia (2000a), one-fifth of all felons receive no supervision whatsoever after they leave prison because they have served their full sentence in prison.

The challenges facing parole agencies today are that they are operating with fewer resources to both monitor and aid parolees in meeting their parole conditions. Furthermore, public tolerance of parole has decreased. At this time, most parole agencies have only one option for parole violators—return them to prison. Statistics show that over 60 percent of all persons admitted to state prisons are parole violators, which represents a significant problem for prison crowding. There is significant motivation at this juncture for parole agencies and constituents to reexamine other options for how corrections can respond differently to parole violators (Petersilia 2000b).

Recommended Readings

Burke, Peggy B. (1995). *Abolishing Parole: Why the Emperor Has No Clothes*. Lexington, KY: American Probation and Parole Association, and California, MO: Association of Paroling Authorities, International.

Cromwell, Paul F., Rolando V. del Carmen, and Leanne F. Alarid. (2002). *Community Based Corrections*, 5th Edition. Belmont, CA: Wadsworth.

Griswold, David B., and Michael D. Wiatrowski. (1983). "The Emergence of Determinate Sentencing," *Federal Probation* (June):28–35.

Petersilia, Joan. (2000a). "When Prisoners Return to the Community: Political, Economic, and Social Consequences," *Sentencing and Corrections: Issues for the 21st Century.* Washington, D.C.: U.S. Department of Justice.

———. (2000b). "Parole and Prisoner Reentry in the United States, Part II." *Perspectives* (Fall): 40–47.

Williams, Frank P., Marilyn D. McShane, and H. Michael Dolny. (2000). "Developing a Parole Classification Instrument for Use as a Management Tool," *Corrections Management Quarterly* 4(4):45–59.

Internet Websites

Parole Watch, an organization that provides information on when violent offenders will be released from prison. Available: *http://www.parolewatch.org/*

A Convict's View of Why Criminals Recidivate. Available: *http://www.prisonzone.com/writers/inside.html*

Snider, E. (1999, June). The road to freedom. Available: *http://www.exoffender.org/road_to_freedom.html*

United States Parole Commission. An overview of the United States Parole Commission. Available: *http://www.usdoj.gov/uspc/overview.htm*

34
The Current State of Parole in America

Norman Holt

Focus Questions

1. Why did parole come under attack in the 1970s?

2. What changes in sentencing structure led to a decrease in parole discretion?

3. What are parole guidelines?

4. What are the problems with having too many parole conditions?

5. How have parole agencies responded to improve their accountability?

Parole is both a procedure by which a board administratively releases and returns inmates to prison and a provision for post-release supervision. Parole has gone through two decades of turbulent change. Indeterminate sentencing and discretionary release came under near fatal attack in the late 1970s as the cohesive philosophy of rehabilitation, and the accompanying coalition of powerful interest groups who supported it, began to dissolve. State after state enacted sentence "reforms," which stripped parole boards of their most important powers. This article is the story of how parole has changed in response to these pressures and the critical issues and opportunities it now faces.

Parole in a Rapidly Changing Environment

Earlier attacks on parole focused on its shortcomings in practice and its failure to live up to its lofty ideals. But in the 1970s, the attacks were also against the basic principles and assumptions of parole and indeterminate sentencing.

Attack on Parole Board Practices

The traditional criticisms of parole boards and their releasing practices grew louder as the old faultfinders found some new liberal friends. Critics pointed out that there were seldom any professional requirements to become a board member, and when legislative guidelines were established, they were usually ignored in favor of patronage. Boards were viewed as meeting in secret, operating beyond public scrutiny, and exercising unfettered discretion while refusing to provide the simplest documentation of the reasons for their case decisions. Absent [of] any standards, direction, or feedback, parole decisions were often arbitrary, capricious, and inherently flawed. What was intended as a systematic, scientific inquiry, in practice was the simplest of common questioning having little to do with the causes of crime. The parole dockets (preboard reports) were threadbare documents in many states, often little more than an arrest report. It was probably just as well. In a lawsuit against the California parole board in 1974, board members gave depositions that they relied heavily on the psychological evaluation in making their release decisions. When the plaintiff's attorney read excerpts from typical reports in open court, none of the members could explain what the excerpts meant. But the deficiencies of the dockets were overshadowed by the speed with which cases were dispatched—three to six minutes was not uncommon (Rothman, 1980, p. 165). Even more detrimental was the charge that there was no scientific basis for determining readiness for release in the first place.

Attacks on Field Supervision (the Other Parole)

Field supervision practices did not stand up to scrutiny much better. Caseloads were often outrageously large, well beyond most agents' abilities to provide a reasonable semblance of supervision. The national average budgeted caseload in 1979 was seventy-one parolees. Computations of the agent's available time, after administrative duties, usually revealed only a few minutes a month for each parolee. A study of federal probation showed seven minutes a week per case. Another in Georgia showed eight minutes per week. Moreover, most were superficial contacts in the office, amounting to little more than empty formalities (Rhine et al., 1991, p. 24). Outsiders and control agencies were often told that parole work was so esoteric it could not be explained to laypersons. In practice, it often resembled a set of customs or traditions more than science or craft. Management was by sporadic case reviews combined with a detailed sifting of major parolee incidents to discover any agent errors in judgment (McCleary, 1978; Simon, 1993).

Still, most agents had some formal casework training, saw themselves as professionals, and were well paid compared with county probation officers or local police. The disorganization, although considerable, may not have been as detrimental in practice as it seemed at a distance. Parole supervision during this period is probably best described as operating on an "assistance model," brokering services from the wealth of federally funded War on Poverty and Great Society programs.

Intellectual Foundation for a Retribution Model

While the demise of indeterminate sentencing was probably due largely to various shifting social currents, the intellectual foundation for its demise was laid by a few academics. The results were alliances of liberal and conservative legislatures each using the abolition of parole to pursue very different ends. For liberals, the problem was the unfettered discretion of parole boards. A justice model seemed more honest and humane. For conservatives, it was the early release of inmates and frustration over the inability to enact legislation with a real impact on prison terms. It seemed senseless to enact laws increasing penalties when the results were neutralized by parole board decision (Burke, 1988; Holt, 1995).

"Nothing works." Robert Martinson struck the first serious academic blow in 1974 with an article titled, "What Works? Questions About Prison Reforms." The article summarized the results of a larger work that reviewed the effectiveness of 231 treatment programs and found little or no evidence of positive effects. The equivocal result from treatment programs was known and documented for some time but failed to find a receptive audience until the mid-1970s (Kassebaum et al., 1971; Robison and Smith, 1971). Martinson's overdrawn and strident conclusions were widely and regularly paraphrased as "nothing works," a position he refuted himself in 1979, particularly in reference to the use of probation and parole as alternatives to incarceration (Martinson and Wilks, 1977). The broad dissemination and acceptance of Martinson's earlier conclusion dealt a near fatal blow almost overnight to the rehabilitation concept. If rehabilitation could not be legitimated by science, there was nothing to support the "readiness for release" idea, and therefore no role for parole boards or indeterminate sentencing.

"Just desserts." What was needed for the final blow was a seemingly neutral ideological substitute for rehabilitation. The concept was furnished in a report by the Committee For the Study of Incarcerations, authored by Andrew von Hirsch. The report, entitled *Doing Justice: The Choice of Punishments* (1976), argued that the discredited rehabilitation model should be replaced with a simple nonutilitarian notion that sentencing sanctions should reflect the social harm caused by the misconduct. Certainly justice requires consideration for differences in culpability and blameworthiness, but the sanction should fit the offense, not the offender.

Criminal conduct similarly situated should suffer similar results.

Determinate Sentencing

The promise of equitable sentencing was necessary because there was no logical reason why doing justice should lead to expanded sanctions. One might even think a system devoid of any rehabilitative pretenses would deprive fewer people of their liberty for shorter periods and be even less expensive. But, under determinate sentencing structures, the conservative just deserts allies were rapidly increasing the number and length of prison sentences to the point of dangerously overcrowding prisons. Determinate sentencing was intended to solve the capriciousness of sentencing and to ensure that defendants served the time intended. Most observers would agree it has done neither. Sentencing went from a "stealth" system well insulated from daily politics and the passions of the moment to a structure that was very visible and easily changed. Some critics feared that determinate structures would become a "Christmas tree" for legislators to hang their favorite crime bills on like shiny ornaments and would raise in lawmakers the endless and irresistible urge to "tinker." States that adopted determinate sentencing discovered they also lost their ability to equalize justice between jurisdictions and manage unusual or heinous cases. Equally important, along with the loss of releases, the states lost their safety valve to prison overcrowding.

Major Changes in Sentencing Structures

Between 1975 and 1985 the criminal justice system went from a system in which the sentencing codes of every state had some form of indeterminacy to a situation where every state had revised, replaced, or seriously considered replacing its codes with determinate sentencing. Between 1976 and 1979, seven states abolished all or most of the paroling authority's discretion (Ringel et al.,1993). These were joined by six more states by 1990. New Jersey and Pennsylvania abolished indeterminate sentencing without abolishing parole. From 1990 to 1993, three additional states had considered but rejected abolishing parole (Burke, 1995, p. 16). Illinois, California, and Minnesota, among the first to alter parole, are examples of states that adopted fixed sentences but retained post-release supervision. Connecticut, Washington, Maine, and Florida abolished both discretionary release and field supervision. Delaware abolished determinate sentencing in 1990.

Decrease in parole release authority. Short of abolition, many legislatures continue to decrease the authority of parole boards by changing sentencing rules. Changes take several forms.

1. Parole consideration has been prohibited until the inmate serves all of the minimum term, such as in Michigan and Massachusetts.

2. Sentences of life without parole for certain offenses have been mandated in five states and the District of Columbia.

3. "Three strikes" laws requiring extremely long minimum terms for certain repeat offenders have been enacted by the federal government and several states such as Washington and California.

4. Laws requiring that a specified proportion of the total sentence be served in prison have passed in many more states, such as Missouri, Nebraska, Montana, and Texas. Maryland recently increased the 25 percent requirement for parole to 50 percent of the sentence.

5. Some states have increased prison time requirement for violent offenses to as much as 85 percent in order to qualify for construction funds under the Federal Violent Crime Control and Law Enforcement Act of 1994. This not only effectively eliminates parole but also most "good time."

In the last five years, a dozen parole boards have lost some or all of their releasing authority. In 1993, Kansas developed sentencing guideline grids for drug- and nondrug-related crimes and Arizona abolished discretionary release. Virginia and North Carolina abolished parole releases in

1994. Mississippi and North Carolina followed suit in 1995. Ironically, the Ohio parole board, whose releasing authority ended July 1, 1996, was to assume a new role of extending terms for prison misconduct (National Institute of Corrections, 1995). Adding time, of course, is just the opposite of where parole boards began in the 1800s.

Current status of parole release. In November 1995, thirty-five states retained some form of discretionary release of inmates but nineteen of these were limited to certain kinds of offenses. In New York, for example, the board's discretion over second-term violent felons was curtailed. Sixteen other states have paroling authorities that continue to hear only those cases committed before indeterminate sentences were abolished. Although parole release was largely abolished in only seventeen jurisdictions, several are among the largest (California, Florida, Illinois, plus the U.S. Parole Commission) (National Institute of Corrections, 1995, pp. 3–10). This, combined with increasing restrictions placed on numerous other boards, caused the dramatic decline in the percent released by way of parole from 71.9 percent in 1977 to 38.8 percent in 1993.

Release by parole remained the most common form of release in 1993 but by only a slight margin. By the end of 1996, parole releases were less frequent than mandatory supervision.

Responding to Changes

"Abolish parole" became a popular political slogan and began to symbolize a wide variety of complaints with the criminal justice system and the demand that offenders be held strictly accountable for their crimes. As a campaign slogan, "abolish parole" is simple; abolishing parole in practice is very complicated. Parole departments reacted to the attacks first by increasing accountability for what both boards and field supervisors did and why. Boards became more open, promulgated formal policies, adopted term-setting guidelines, and made special efforts to open the process so that victims could have their say. Virtually every board now has

procedures to notice victims of hearings, decisions, and release dates and to take and consider their testimony in release decisions. Some provide for victim attendance at release hearings. Parole field agencies developed new parole supervision models and programs.

Parole Term-Setting Guidelines

The parole release and supervision decisions were traditionally arrived at by the case study method, also referred to as clinical judgments. In this process, the board member, caseworker, or parole agent collects as much information as possible, combines it in unique as well as traditional ways, mulls over the results, and arrives at a decision (Holt and Glaser, 1985). The problems with this method and the superiority of statistical prediction have been known for some time (Wiggins, 1973), and criminologists had urged parole boards to use actuarial devices (Glaser, 1962).

Early guidelines. The U.S. Parole Commission's Salient Factors Score was the first of a new generation of such "risk assessment" or predictive instruments (Hoffman and Adelberg, 1980). The score was arrived at by summing the points assessed for various background factors. This total was then combined with an offense severity scale to form a matrix or grid. Those inmates sentenced for the least serious crimes and also the least likely to reoffend (statistically) were the first to be released, and so forth. The federal system was followed by a National Institute of Corrections (NIC) term-setting model that was widely disseminated in the 1980s (Burke et al., 1989). By 1988, virtually all boards had developed or borrowed some system of guidelines or other devices to make parole decision-making more objective (Champion, 1994, p. 62), and 40 percent used a risk prediction instrument. Guidelines may also be a few simple written but nonbinding rules.

Problems applying guidelines. It is unclear, however, just how these devices are used (Rhine et al., 1991). To be effective, instruments should be uniformly applied and consistently followed, except in very unusual cases. Merely adding a statistical prediction as one more piece of information to a clinical judgment process does not work. Even the most structured decision-making allows for exceptions, which tend to increase to the point where they become the rule. For example, parole decisions in Utah in 1985–1986 departed from the guidelines 61 percent of the time and mostly for longer terms (Rhine et al., 1991, p. 74). Members sometimes feel that using numbers and checking boxes trivializes the important decisions they must make. New members sometimes feel they represent special constituencies and bring a long overdue fresh perspective to the board, and they may take pride in making different decisions. There may be a structured instrument in place but members are told, as in New York, that the ranges of time "are merely guidelines." Whatever form they take, guidelines require that decisions be audited to be most effective. But it is doubtful whether more than a few systems collect and aggregate information in a way that would allow actions of hearing panels or individual members to be systematically examined.

Value of guidelines. Nevertheless, at a minimum, guidelines direct the members' attention to specific crime-relevant information and away from idiosyncratic concerns in decision-making. They also make some standard for decision review possible, provide a basis for consensus building, raise relevant policy issues, and help members appreciate their role as policymakers as well as case reviewers.

The Changing Role of Parole Boards

Parole boards have always served as "back door" population managers in times of crisis. Few observers missed the fact that states that were quick to abolish discretionary parole soon had major prison overcrowding problems. The population crisis became the single most important factor derailing the movement to eliminate parole in the 1980s (Burke, 1988). It probably still is. The board's role in helping to manage the population crisis is more important now than ever. This is done formally through laws and administrative changes or informally through directions from the governor and members' personal concern for the crisis.

Managing overcrowding. Michigan became the first state to pass emergency overcrowding legislation in 1981. By 1988, twenty-one states had adopted an Emergency Powers Act, while Florida, Hawaii, Oklahoma, and Rhode Island have since developed emergency release mechanisms. The act usually provides that inmate eligibility for parole be advanced when overcrowding reaches a predetermined level. The parole board then selects inmates for early release from this new pool of eligibles. In other states, boards have adjusted their guidelines to more nearly reflect the prison bed space available (National Institute of Corrections, 1995, pp. 3–9). The Oregon board, for example, was reported to use a flexible term-setting matrix that moved time up or down based on the level of new prison intake. Several states reinstated discretionary release or the functional equivalent. For example, Florida has now reconstituted its board. In some states, such as Texas, boards were informally instructed to establish a parole quota system so that releases would approximate admissions. Until recently when new construction was completed, North Carolina had gradually revested the board with release authority for certain offenders. Even Maine, the first state to abolish parole, has expanded the role of the clemency advisory board to process the greater number of reviews in response to overcrowding (Burke, 1988).

Apart from formal procedures, board members are well aware of the desperate need for beds and court injunctions lurking just around the corner. But "backdoor management" is not an easy task, or one that boards always relish. As gubernatorial appointees, members are part of and empowered by the same political process that causes the overcrowding in the first place.

Parole violators add to the overcrowding problem. The hope of parole as the backdoor population manager has another, darker side, however. Agents recommend and boards decide whether to return parolees to prison for violating the conditions of their release. Ironically, boards help create the same overcrowded conditions they are supposed to cure. [T]he percentage of prison admissions that were parole violators increased from 19.6 to 30.2 in ten years. Technical violators alone accounted for about 17 percent of all prison admissions in 1993—the great majority of these people would not be in prison had they not been on parole. Yet boards are even more vulnerable to criticisms for continuing a violator on parole than for releasing an inmate before the term expires. In the public's view, the parolee has already had one break by being paroled. Every serious felony committed by a continued parole violator will be viewed as a crime that would have been prevented if the board had just done its job. Never mind that the same parolee would have committed the same or similar crime after a six-month $12,000 return to prison.

Unrealistic parole conditions. Unfortunately, parole conditions serve as much to comfort agencies and parole boards and help the release decision withstand public scrutiny as to establish realistic expectations for the parolee. In a 1982 survey, 135 different conditions of parole were recorded with an average number of "standard" conditions of 14.8 (Rhine et al., 1991, p. 120). Boards were asked in 1988 to indicate from a list of fourteen items which were standard conditions in their state. The most common, of course, was "obey all laws." However, 78 percent required "gainful employment" as a standard condition, 61 percent "no association with persons of criminal records," 53 percent "pay all fines and restitution," and 47 percent "support family and all dependents," none of which can consistently be met by most parolees (Rhine et al., 1991, pp. 102–107). Thus, we design systems so that almost all parolees are likely to fail at some point.

Conditions that might work. Realistic standard conditions would be limited to "report to your parole agent," "obey laws," and "receive permission to leave the county or state." But even realistic conditions are commonly violated. Should violators go to prison for missing a drug test, an appointment with their agent, or visiting a girl friend across the county line?

Need for intermediate sanctions. The second obstacle to successful guidelines is that most jurisdictions have few program or procedural options between reprimand and return to prison. Whether intermediate sanctions will reduce crime in the long run is doubtful, but they are important in legitimating the agent's recommendation and the board's decision to leave the violator in the community. Sanctions demonstrate that parole conditions are taken seriously and violations have consequences for the offender, consequences that are at least inconvenient if not painful. Since 1990, sixteen states have formulated new responses to parole violations (National Institute of Corrections, 1995, pp. 8–9). Several jurisdictions, including California and the U.S. Parole Commission, have established standards for the revocation time parolees should serve for different types of violations (Burke et al., 1990, p. 19). Others have developed guidelines for revocation and alternative dispositions. More successful attempts, such as in Washington, have used a formal decision matrix for violation dispositions or, as in Oregon, extraordinary program moneys are made available or agents have access to county jail beds for short-term incarceration. But more often, the resources to operate progressive discipline and intermediate sanctions successfully aren't there. Many jurisdictions have such limited resources that they control little more than the conditions of parole. Several states allow agents to restructure parole conditions and impose local sanctions for minor violations without board review. While it may meet a need to demonstrate that "something" was done, it's hard to see how increasing the number or stringency of conditions will prevent future violations by parolees who fail to meet the previous conditions.

Response of Parole Field Supervision

While many legislatures may have been happy to see discretionary parole release disappear, the same cannot be said for parole supervision, which has actually increased. After twenty years of sentence "reform," almost all states have retained or reinstated post-release supervision (called conditional release when it follows a fixed prison term). . . . [T]he dramatic drop in parole releases was not matched by a decline in supervision. The total percent of releases under parole-type supervision in 1993 was 83.4 percent, about 1 percent above the highest point for discretionary releases in 1977. Illinois, California, and Minnesota are examples of states that adopted determinate sentences but retained post-release supervision. Several states that originally abolished supervision reintroduced a supervision component. These include Florida, Connecticut, and Washington, where supervision returned four years later after heavy lobbying by local law enforcement (Ringel et al., 1993, p. 15). Maine developed an interesting twist on supervision. When supervision was eliminated in 1976, judges began giving "split sentences." Offenders are sentenced to a prison term, part of which is suspended, followed by a probation period. Violators are returned by the court for the suspended part of the sentence.

New Supervision Models

The first response of the parole field agencies was to improve their accountability by adopting new models of supervision. These models were intended to:

1. provide an objective way of evaluating the offender's public risk and personal needs.

2. allocate resources based on need.

3. direct the agent's time by prioritizing cases.

4. provide a management information system to evaluate the process.

The models are described as "management tools," not as devices to reduce recidivism directly. Almost all states now classify parolees and almost all of these systems include an assessment of the risk posed to the public and the parolee's needs. The risk assessment devices are based on research predicting the likelihood of failure, which usually means re-arrest or revocation, supplemented by nonpredictive policy items. Most are additive checklist systems. Case factors are assigned point values. The total points determine the classification level. The majority of systems in use were adapted from the state of Wisconsin model (Baird et al., 1989).

Problems Applying Risk Assessment Scales

The new supervision models and their risk assessment instruments pose several problems for operations staff. Most scales are not purely predictive, largely because violent crimes do not predict recidivism. Even the Wisconsin model includes points for a violent commitment offense, although not supported by research (Burke et al. 1989). As Gottfredson and Gottfredson (1986) remarked, "Severity of the instant offense has rarely been found to be a useful predictor of danger to the public, but has been consistently used for that purpose anyway." The dilemma for risk assessment is that property and drug offenders have higher re-arrest rates (Burke et al., 1990, p. 17). Thus, predictions are not focused on those offenders of most concern to the public. . . .

Responding to the Attack with New Programs

The second response to the attack on parole was to create new programs to reduce overcrowding and position field supervision closer to the retribution and deterrence philosophy. In keeping with these changes, agencies began allowing agents to carry concealed firearms in the 1980s. Firearms are now provided by thirty-three jurisdictions and represent a major investment of training resources, agent time, and administrative oversight. The programming innovations likewise represent a theme of control and supervision rather than service and assistance. Parolees are held more accountable and for a broader range of behavior, including alcohol and substance abuse, restitution, curfews, and service fees. Parole aims to earn its way by providing a tough legitimate alternative to continued or renewed incarceration and by enhancing public safety through rigorous rule enforcement and deterrence. Innovations include home confinement and electronic monitoring, day reporting centers, intensive supervision, boot camps, and specialized caseloads. Unfortunately none of the innovations has proved very successful.

Concluding Remarks

If the last twenty years has been a period of new models and program innovations, it has also been a period lacking in focus or direction. Agencies scrambled to force old organizations into new philosophies, creating disjunctive values, goals, and activity. Many are still struggling to contribute without a coherent conceptual basis of operation or a clear sense of purpose. In one sense, these innovations are attempts to solve serious social structural problems with simple technologies and thus avoid the deep divisive issues that plague criminal justice. While much emphasis is placed on decision rules, classifications, and numbering systems, it's by no means certain that the answer lies in better numbers. Indeed, better numbers may serve only to cloud the real issues. Some managers, for example, have mistaken parolee classification for parole work itself, as if the work is done once the proper category is determined (Clear and Gallagher, 1985). At the same time, while we are creating elegant categories, many agents are not sure what to do after they ring the doorbell. Counting contacts becomes a substitute for good casework and avoids the larger issue of whether the process itself contributes anything to the social good.

References

Baird, Christopher, Richard Prewstine, and Brian Klockziem. 1989. "Revalidation of the Wisconsin Probation/Parole Classification System." San Francisco: National Council on Crime and Delinquency.

Burke, Peggy. 1988. "Current Issues in Parole Decisionmaking: Understanding the Past; Shaping the Future." Justice Institute COSMOS Corp., Washington, DC.

———. 1995. *Abolishing Parole: Why the Emperor Has No Clothes*. Lexington, KY: American Probation and Parole Association.

Burke, Peggy, Linda Adams, and Becki Ney. 1990. "Policy for Parole Release and Revocation: The National Institute of Corrections 1988, 1989 Technical Assistance Project." Longmont, CO: National Institute of Corrections.

Burke, Peggy, Chris Hayes, Helen Connelly, Linda Adams, and Becki Ney. 1989. "The Institute of Corrections Model Case Management and Classification Project: A Case Study in Dissemination." Longmont, CO.: National Institute of Corrections.

Bureau of Justice Statistics. 1984, 1988, 1994. *Sourcebook of Criminal Justice Statistics*. Washington, DC: U.S. Department of Justice.

Champion, Dean. 1994. *Measuring Offender Risk: A Criminal Justice Sourcebook*, Westport, CT: Greenwood Press.

Clear, Todd, and Kenneth Gallagher. 1985. "Parole and Probation Supervision: A Review of Current Classification Practices." *Crime and Delinquency* 31: 423–43.

Glaser, Daniel. 1962. "Prediction Tables as Accounting Devices for Judges and Parole Boards." *Crime and Delinquency* 8: 239–58.

Gottfredson Stephen, and Don Gottfredson. 1986. "The Accuracy of Prediction Models." In *Criminal Careers and Career Criminals*, Vol. 2, edited by Alfred Blumstein et al. Washington, DC: National Academy Press.

Hoffman, Peter, and Sheldon Adelberg. 1980. "The Salient Factor Score: A Non Technical Overview." *Federal Probation* 44(1).

Holt, Norman. 1995. "California's Determinate Sentencing: What Went Wrong?" *Perspectives* 19(3).

Holt, Norman, and Daniel Glaser. 1985. "Statistical Guidelines for Custodial Classification." In *Correctional Institutions*, edited by Robert Carter, Daniel Glaser, and Leslie Wilkins, 3rd ed. New York: Harper and Row.

Kassebaum, Gene, David Ward, and Daniel Wilner. 1971. *Prison Treatment and Parole Survival*. New York: John Wiley.

Martinson, Robert. 1974. "What Works? Questions About Prison Reforms." *Public Interest* 35: 22–54.

———. 1979. "New Findings, New Views: A Note of Caution Regarding Sentencing Reform." *Hofstra Law Review* 7:243–58.

Martinson, Robert, and Judith Wilks. 1977. "Save Parole Supervision." *Federal Probation* 41(3).

McCleary, Richard. 1978. *Dangerous Men: The Sociology of Parole*. Beverly Hills, Calif.: Sage.

National Institute of Corrections. 1995. "Status Report on Parole, 1995: Results of an NIC Survey." Longmont, CO: National Institute of Corrections.

Rhine, Edward, William Smith, and Ronald Jackson. 1991. *Paroling Authorities: Recent History and Current Practices*. Laurel, MD: American Correctional Association.

Ringel, Cheryl, Ernest Cowles, and Thomas Castellano. 1993. "The Recasting of Parole Supervision: The Causes and Responses of

Systems Under Stress." Southern Illinois University. Paper presented at the Academy of Criminal Justice Science Conference, Kansas City, MO. Also in *Critical Issues in Crime and Justice,* edited by A.R. Roberts. Newbury Park, CA: Sage, 1994.

Robison, James, and Gerald Smith. 1971. "The Effectiveness of Correctional Programs." *Crime and Delinquency* 17(1).

Rothman, David. 1980. *Conscience and Convenience: The Asylum and its Alternatives in Progressive America.* Boston: Little, Brown.

Simon, Jonathon. 1993. *Poor Discipline: Parole and the Social Control of the Underclass, 1890–1990.* Chicago: University of Chicago Press.

von Hirsch, Andrew. 1976. *Doing Justice: The Choice of Punishments.* New York: Hill and Wang.

Wiggins, Jerry. 1973. *Personality and Prediction.* Reading, Mass.: Addison Wesley.

35

Perspectives on Parole: The Board Members' Viewpoint

Ronald Burns
Patrick Kinkade
Matthew C. Leone
Scott Phillips

Focus Questions

1. What did parole board members think was the most important purpose of corrections?

2. What were the most serious problems facing the board?

3. What areas of change did members think would most improve the parole board process?

4. What rationales did parole board members use to justify parole granting and/or continuing parole?

5. What specific factors did board members consider to be important parole release criteria?

The origins of parole date back to the 19th century, when the practice of "giving mark" was established by English and Irish prison reformers (Clear & Cole, 1990). Under these early systems, prisoners were granted a release from incarceration if they accumulated a designated number of "marks" by following institutional rules and working toward self-improvement. The extension of parole as a correctional practice into the United States was linked to the adoption of the indeterminate sentencing models of the early 20th century. Under these models, the correctional system's primary function was to reform the prisoner. Once this reformation was completed, it made sense to release inmates back into society since the correctional system had diverted them from their criminal tendencies. It was the parole board that exercised this discretion in terms of these releases, deciding whether the incarcerated had, indeed, been reformed.

Over the last 20 years, however, the nature of parole has changed. The political constituencies of many jurisdictions began to view indeterminate sentencing as too lenient and opted to shift to determinate sentencing. Using this form of sentencing, the courts prescribe an upper limit of years that the offender must serve with a set rate of "good time credit" the offender may earn for following institutional rules and for meeting personal treatment goals. The discretion for release, then, was removed from the parole board and retained by the judiciary through the process of charging the offenders for their crimes. The parole board, however, maintained the responsibility for parole revocation hearings, deciding if the offender should be reinstitutionalized for violating court-prescribed conditions for release.

Currently, the increasing number of offenders under correctional supervision has affected all members of the criminal justice system, including parole boards. Jackson, Rhine, and Smith (1989) report that between 1970 and 1988 the number of inmates in United States prisons roughly tripled. These figures are corroborated by Joo, Ekland-Olson, and Kelly (1995), who note that incarceration rates have nearly tripled since 1980. At the end of calendar year 1996, the total number of adults under correctional supervision—incarcerated or in the community—reached a new high of 5.5 million (Brown & Beck, 1997). The criminal justice system has responded in traditional fashion by increasing parole (Joo et al., 1995) and changing the methods by which parole is granted. For instance, California parole is considered automatic, and the parole board serves only to deny, rather than grant, release. Many states have even utilized Emergency Powers Acts, which increase parole eligibility in order to meet court-mandated prison population limits (Jackson et al., 1989). The resulting increase in the parole population has been staggering as the number of parolees has swelled from 220,000 in 1980 to 457,000 in 1989 (Joo et al., 1995).

More recently, in 1996, there was a 3.7 percent increase in the overall parole population, with eight states reporting increases of at least 10 percent in their parole populations. New Hampshire (up 35.8 percent) and Alaska (up 20.5 percent) experienced the greatest increases (Brown & Beck, 1997). Similarly, between 1985 and 1996, there was a 134.7 percent increase in the number of persons released on parole (Brown & Beck, 1997). Currently, about 12.4 percent of individuals under correctional supervision are on parole (U.S. Department of Justice, 1996). The problems associated with such rapid parole population growth include overwhelmed community support services, such as substance abuse counseling and halfway houses, increased caseloads for parole board members and a concomitant decrease in the quality of community supervision, and an inability to revoke parole caused by crowded county jails and overburdened state prisons (Jackson et al., 1989).

In the United States, then, there are primarily two forms of parole currently in use: discretionary parole, by which the parole board grants release, and mandatory parole, by which the judiciary defines release as a function of sentencing. Until recently, discretionary parole was most commonly used, although in 1996 mandatory parole was used slightly more often (48 percent compared to 46 percent respectively) than discretionary parole (U.S. Department of Justice, 1996). However, use of the parole board as a release mechanism is likely to increase in coming years. Indeed, despite the general public's distaste for parole and parole's perceived leniency, conditions in prisons are forcing correctional officials to use early release mechanisms to keep their institutions within the constitutional standards defining "cruel and unusual punishment" (Jackson et al., 1989).

Given parole's common use, and the likelihood that such use will expand in the coming years, the nature of the parole decision-making process should come under academic scrutiny. Standards for release are, at best, ill defined and irregularly applied. In one of the best studies on this topic, Talarico (1975) suggests that parole board release is not based on "a detailed clinical assessment of treatment effects that parole theory and model are based on" (p. 136). Instead, the decision is an interplay between a variety of external factors about which parolees and the public are misinformed. The net result is a public that is frightened about a perceived threat from the paroled offender and an incarcerated population frustrated about the perceived caprice within the parole process.

Goals and Objectives

Despite both the pivotal role and dynamic nature of parole in the criminal justice system, few research efforts have been directed at understanding parole board decision-making processes. The goal of this research was to collate a data set that will begin to detail how and why parole is granted in individual parole cases across the United States, as well as provide greater insight into the primary actors in the parole process. Prior work on this topic is sparse and has become dated. This study specifically will add to the literature on parole board decision-making processes by determining: 1) parole board members' perceptions of the most important purpose of corrections; 2) parole board members' perceptions of the most serious problem facing parole boards; 3) parole board members' perceptions of the most important areas of change that might improve the parole board process; 4) parole board members' primary rationales used to justify parole as an early release mechanism; 5) the importance of various rationales parole board members use as justification for the continuance of parole; and 6) the importance of various release criteria as justification for parole board members to grant parole.

Methodology

This study employed a survey methodology. Parole board members were selected as the appropriate respondent group on these issues because of their familiarity with the parole decision-making process. . . .

The Population

The sample frame has been compiled as The 1995 Directory of Juvenile and Adult Correctional Departments, Institutions, Agencies and Paroling Authorities. This volume provides a current list of the names, addresses, and phone numbers of all parole board members in the United States. The final respondent group of 351 was drawn from this list. In that there are relatively few parole board members in the United States, the population as a whole can be surveyed, eliminating both sampling error and bias.

Respondent Demographics

The median age for the respondent group was 52 with a range of 35 to 78. Approximately 70 percent of the respondents were male and 30 percent were female. Approximately 80 percent of the respondents were Caucasian. Twelve percent had no more than a high school diploma, 35 percent had a bachelor's degree, and 53 percent had an advanced degree. Approximately 65 percent identified themselves as politically conservative and 35 percent identified themselves as politically liberal. The median number of years of experience in the criminal justice system was 19 and the median number of years in parole was 7. . . .

Results

The first question in the survey asked the parole board members what they thought was "the most important purpose of corrections." Five options were provided: 1) rehabilitation (training offenders to lead noncriminal lives); 2) deterrence (preventing crime by showing potential offenders the serious consequences of committing a criminal offense); 3) incapacitation (protecting the public by removing offenders from the community, where they might commit additional crimes); 4) retribution (simply making offenders pay for the crime they have committed: "an eye for an eye"); and 5) restitution (creating a situation whereby inmates work to restore those damaged by their act). Of the five options, incapacitation was most often ranked as the first or second most important purpose (71.8 percent). In order of perceived importance, the other options were rehabilitation (63.4 percent), deterrence (47.7 percent), and restitution (22.7 percent). Retribution was ranked a distant fifth, with only 12.4 percent noting it as their first or second most important purpose. . . .

The second question asked the respondent to rank by seriousness the problems currently facing parole boards. Seven options were given: 1) lack of commitment by parole board members; 2) burnout among parole board members; 3) lack of support for the parole process by government officials; 4) lack of support for the parole process by the public; 5) media coverage of parole board activities; 6) excessive caseload demands; and 7) lack of support for the parole board by other correctional officials. Interestingly, the percentage of respondents who noted lack of public support (69.9 percent) and lack of government support (51.9 percent) as the first or second most important problem in parole far surpassed the percentage who noted that excessive caseload demands (37.1 percent) were most important. . . .

The third question asked the subjects what they considered the most important area of change that could improve the parole board process. The options included were: 1) better systems of inmate classification; 2) more treatment-based programs within the prison; 3) more programming options available outside the prison; 4) better trained parole board members; 5) better developed guidelines for paroling decisions; and 6) better public understanding of the parole process. In general, the need for better public understanding of the parole process and more treatment-based programs within prison (both at 56.6 percent) were most commonly cited as the first or second most important problem in the parole process while the need for more programming options available outside the prisons (48.2 percent) appeared to be of high importance as well. . . .

The fourth question asked the respondents about the primary rationale they used to justify parole as an early release mechanism. The six options were: 1) reintegration (It creates circumstances whereby offenders are aided in their transition from institutional life back into society.); 2) incentive (It helps to maintain order within the institution by giving the correctional official a reward to offer for "good behavior."); 3) prison overcrowding (It helps to maintain court-mandated prison population caps by lowering the number of incarcerates.); 4) rehabilitation (It allows prisoners who have demonstrated change in their tendencies to begin restructuring their lives in society at large); 5) sentencing disparities (It allows for the criminal justice system to reconcile arbitrary differentials in punishment levied against offenders who have committed the same crime.); and 6) punishment (It allows the criminal justice system to continue to impose a sanction against offenders who might otherwise simply be released.). The two options that were perceived as being of greatest importance (either first or second option) were rehabilitation (74.7 percent) and reintegration (59.9 percent). . . .

The fifth question addressed the respondents' perceived importance of several rationales according to their appropriateness as justifications for the continuance of parole. The rationales included: 1) "helps reintegration to society"; 2) "works as incentive for good behavior in prison"; 3) "helps relieve prison overcrowding"; 4) "works toward the end of rehabilitation"; 5) "helps to remove sentencing disparities between prisoners"; and 6) "extends the length of punishment possible." Based on the responses, it appears that parole board members use parole because they believe that it helps reintegration to society (95.4 percent rate it as very, or somewhat, important), that it works toward the end of rehabilitation (89.9 percent), and because it works as an incentive for good behavior in prison (86.9 percent). . . .

The sixth question asked the respondents to rate the importance of each of the following release criteria in their decision to grant parole: the nature and circumstances of the inmate's offense; the inmate's prior criminal record; the inmate's attitude toward family responsibilities; the inmate's attitude toward authority; the inmate's attitude toward the victim; the inmate's institutional adjustment; the inmate's community support; the inmate's financial resources; the inmate's physical health; the inmate's psychological health; the inmate's insight into the cause of his or her past criminal conduct; the adequacy of the inmate's parole plan; the attitude of the offender's victims about the offender's release; prison conditions; public sentiment about the offender or the offense type; public notoriety of the case; and the inmate's age. . . .

In general, it appears that parole board members feel that the nature of the inmate's offense, as well as the inmate's prior criminal record, attitude toward the victim, institutional adjustment (as measured by the inmate's participation in prison programs), and insight into the causes of past criminal conduct are the most important factors in the decision to grant parole. In contrast, the board members appear to feel as though the inmate's physical health and age, prison conditions, and the public notoriety of the case are of lesser importance in the decision to grant parole.

Discussion

Each of the survey questions raises several significant areas of discussion based on the responses of the parole authorities.

Thus, the following discussion addresses several of the issues within the context of each question.

The first question asked the respondents what they thought was the most important purpose of corrections. It appears that the parole board members included in the present study believe that correctional practices should be designed to protect society and rehabilitate offenders, as opposed to punishing offenders. Such a finding could be explained through the nature of parole decision-making. For example, because they may bear the brunt of the responsibility for releasing an offender on parole who subsequently commits a serious crime, these board members may be more concerned about the well-being of the individual offender and society than about inflicting punishment upon the offender. It could be argued that releasing an offender who has been punished, yet not "corrected," is of little interest to parole board members.

Based upon the responses to the second question, which asked the subjects what they thought was the most serious problem facing parole boards, it appears that parole board members perceive a lack of support from both the public and government. Because one of the limitations of survey research is the inability to further "pry" into subject responses, future research should be directed toward a better understanding of why, and to what extent, parole board members perceive a lack of support from both groups, as well as how the situation can be improved. Nevertheless, the present research findings suggest that, given the significance of their decision-making roles, parole board members do not feel as though they should be solely responsible for the entire parole process. In other words, similar to the recent movement in law enforcement toward greater involvement of the community in addressing crime, parole board members recognize the need for, and encourage help from, those typically outside of the parole process.

Similarly, based on the finding that a lack of government support was noted as the second most important problem facing parole boards, it is not surprising that excessive caseloads was noted as the third most important problem facing parole boards. Such findings lead to speculation that parole board members believe that their workload could be reduced through a greater concern for the roles they play in the correctional process. Yet, despite the perceived lack of support these officials receive and their excessive workload, the subjects appear to believe that parole board members are quite committed to their job and that burnout is not a problem. In other words, the problems facing parole boards have little to do with parole board personnel, but with other factors instead.

In general, the responses to the third question were consistent with the responses to the first and second questions. For example, respondents frequently noted that the most important area of change that might improve the parole board process involved both the need for more treatment based programs within prison and a better public understanding of the parole process (the percentages of respondents who cited these responses as the first or second most important area of change were exactly the same). The high number of responses suggesting the need for more treatment-based programs within prisons is consistent with responses to previous questions, which found that parole board members are concerned about the well-being of the offenders and society, and the answers to the fourth question, which suggests that 74.7 percent of the parole board members felt that rehabilitation was a highly important rationale to justify parole as an early release mechanism. The results also resemble responses to previous questions in that board members noted that they were not necessarily concerned about the punishment of the offender and that they perceived a lack of government support. Accordingly, the need for more programming options available outside of prisons was selected as the third most important area of change. Because the respondents rated the need for better treatment programs and programming options as more important than the needs for better developed guidelines and a better classification system (ranked fourth and fifth in importance, respectively), we can begin to see where the need for government support would be required. Nevertheless, additional research obviously is necessary.

The finding that parole board members believe that one of the most important areas of change to improve the parole process requires the public to better understand the parole process also is consistent with the finding in the second question, which suggested that parole board members would like greater public support. Finally, it does not appear that parole board members perceive the problems of the parole board process to involve parole board members, as the response suggesting the need for better parole board members was least often cited by the subjects.

The fourth question of the survey concerned the respondents' primary rationale used to justify parole as an early release mechanism. In accordance with the responses to several of the previous questions, parole board members suggested that the well-being of the offender and the safety of society were of utmost importance. By most often noting rehabilitation and integration as the most important factors in their primary rationales used to justify parole, respondents demonstrated consistency in their concerns about the parole process. Interestingly, punishment, which previously was ranked low in importance by the parole board members, was noted by the respondents as the third most important rationale used to justify parole as an early release mechanism. Although the percentage of respondents who supported punishment as an important rationale to justify parole was significantly lower than those who felt reintegration and rehabilitation were most important (a difference of roughly 35 and 50 percent, respectively) and nearly half (48.9 percent) of the respondents ranked it last or second to last in importance, punishment was selected as more important than incentive, sentencing disparities, and prison overcrowding, the latter being the least often used rationale to justify parole as an early release mechanism. These findings appear to be in contrast to previous research which suggests that parole has been employed

pragmatically to promote prison discipline (i.e., incentive) and reduce prison overcrowding (e.g., Abadinsky, 1978).

The fifth question addressed the parole board members' perceptions of various rationales for the continuance of parole. Once again, many of the results are in accordance with the responses to the previous questions in the present research. For example, once again parole board members appear to be concerned about the reintegration and rehabilitation of the parolees (which were most often noted as "very" or "somewhat" important) while the continuance of parole as a justification for helping to relieve prison-overcrowding and as an extension of the length of punishment were most often noted as somewhat, or very unimportant. Interestingly, in contrast to previously noted results which suggested that parole board members generally do not support parole as an incentive for good behavior in prison, 86.9 percent of the responses to this question noted that respondents felt that the continuance of parole was either very, or somewhat important as an incentive for good behavior in prisons. Thus, it appears that as a rationale to justify parole, parole board members are slightly more supportive of the rationale of punishment than that of incentive for good behavior. Yet, with regard to the rationale for the continuance of parole, the opposite is true. Further research in this area could shed greater insight into why such is the case.

A great deal of research has focused upon the issue addressed in the sixth and final question of the present research, which concerned the subjects' perceived importance of various criteria in the decision to grant parole. In general, with regard to the issue being addressed/measured in the present question, many of the findings in the present research have been suggested by previous research in the area. For example, the criteria that were most often (at least 90 percent) cited as very, or somewhat, important were as follows (in order of noted importance): 1) the inmate's prior record; 2) the nature and circumstances of the inmate's offense; 3) the inmate's institutional adjustment; 4) the inmate's attitude toward the victim; 5) the inmate's insight into the causes of his or her past criminal conduct; 6) the adequacy of the inmate's parole; and 7) the inmate's psychological health. Other release criteria noted in the present research and consistent with previous research that were found to be somewhat, or very important, although not to the extent as the previously noted criteria (at least 80 percent but less than 90 percent), were the inmate's support in the community and the inmate's attitude toward authority, which were noted as being of equal importance.

The factors that appeared to be of least importance to parole board members in their decision to grant or deny parole also were consistent with the previous literature and, in part, with the above-noted research findings in the present study. For example, prison condition was the release criterion that was generally noted as least important in parole decision-making. This finding is consistent with the findings of the present research and, by its absence in the previous literature concerning the factors related to parole decision-making, is consistent with prior research. An inmate's health and public notoriety of the case also appear to be of little consideration in the parole decision-making process, and they, too, are absent in the previous research. Finally, based on the present results, an inmate's age does not appear to be an overly important release criteria although Heinz et al. (1976) noted that the relationship between age and parole is curvilinear with the youngest and oldest having the greatest chance of parole.

Conclusion

. . . Through obtaining a better understanding of parole decision-makers, we hope that we can obtain a better grasp of the current state of parole and of how parole board members wield their discretion. Although we would like to think of such personnel as automatons who consistently make unbiased, accurate, and consistent decisions each time they are presented with a case, such a case is highly unlikely. As Gottfredson and Ballard (1966, p. 112) ask, "Are differences in parole decisions associated not only with the characteristics of the offenders themselves (or their crime) but also with the persons responsible for the decisions?"

It is quite likely that despite our attempts to limit parole board member discretion—for example through parole guidelines—the answer to Gottfredson and Ballard's question is "Yes, the characteristics of parole board members do play a role in the parole process." As such, the present research has attempted to obtain a better grasp of the beliefs, perceptions, and values of those largely involved in the decision-making process, with the ultimate goal of furthering our understanding of the parole process.

Working in a branch of corrections, parole board members often face the difficult task of deciding if an offender is ready to return to society. They must determine if the person is "corrected." The innumerable variables in predicting human behavior can quite easily lead to an incorrect decision. When that incorrect decision results in physical harm or even loss of life, it becomes easy to point fingers at the persons responsible, whether directly or indirectly, for this harm. Yet, such is the role parole board members play daily. With such decision-making powers and the amount of discretion inherent in the position, the need for understanding what "makes these people tick" becomes vital. We hope that we have added to this understanding.

References

Abadinsky, H. (1978). Parole history: An economic perspective. *Offender Rehabilitation,* 2(3): 275–278.

Brown, J.M., & Beck, A.J. (1997). *Nation's probation and parole population reached almost 3.9 million last year.* Washington, DC: Bureau of Justice Statistics.

Clear, T.R., & Cole, G.F (1990). *American corrections* (2nd. Ed.). Pacific Grove, CA: Brooks/Cole.

Gottfredson, D.M., & Ballard, K.B. (1966). Differences in parole decisions associated with decision-makers. *Journal of Research in Crime and Delinquency* 3: 112–119.

Heinz, A., Heinz, J., Senderowitz, S., and Vance, M. (1976). Sentencing by parole board: an evaluation. *Journal of Criminal Law and Criminology* 67: 1-31.

Jackson, R.W, Rhine, E., & Smith, W. (1989). Prison crowding: A policy challenge for parole. *Corrections Today* 51: 118–123.

Joo, H.J., Ekland-Olson, S., & Kelly, W. (1995). Recidivism among paroled property offenders released during a period of prison reform. *Criminology* 33:389–1110.

Talarico, S.M. (1975). *Patterns of decision-making in the judicial process: The special case of probation and parole.* Ph.D. dissertation, University of Connecticut.

U.S. Department of Justice, Bureau of Justice Statistics. (1996). *Sourcebook of criminal justice statistics.* Washington, DC: Government Printing Office.

36
Making It in the 'Free World': Women in Transition From Prison

Patricia O'Brien

Focus Questions

1. How many women in this group had been on parole before?

2. What were some of the problems women experienced while on parole supervision?

3. What additional problems do mothers on parole face, as in Mandi's situation?

4. Why did women parolees attribute their own success on parole to the type of parole officer they had?

5. What factors did women parolees believe inhibited their success on parole?

I had a lot of time to think, and I thought, Now look where I'm at and what am I gonna do to get out of here . . . I gotta do something positive or somethin' better.

—Nicole

Prison, for some people, is better than where they lived.

—Jeanette

Get up, brush yourself off, and just go on. You gotta walk for the rest of your life.

—Nan

Exiting prison is a crucial time for women in transition to the community, or "free world." Sykes (1958) notes various pains of imprisonment including deprivation of freedom, familial relationships, choice of associates, status, and material supports. But women also face an array of personal, social, cultural, and structural issues in reestablishing themselves within their communities. This chapter addresses some of the challenges formerly incarcerated women face as women, such as socialization to role functions and gender-specific identity as well as issues related to becoming an "ex" (Ebaugh 1984). . . .

The 'Ex-Offender' Label

Goffman (1961) described the transition into the world of the inmate in mental institutions in which there is a deep initial break with past roles, dispossession of property and self-identity, an appropriation of privacy, and an enforcement of regimentation by bureaucratic surveillance. This disculturation in the total institution results in the loss of or failure to acquire some of the habits required to live in the wider society. When women are released from the institution, numerous challenges lie ahead for them in their efforts to return to or establish a conventional life, due in part to their necessary adaptation to the institution (Jose-Kampfner 1990; Larson and Nelson 1984).

The 'Ex' Role

"Ex-offender" is an example of an emerging "ex" role, as the incarceration of women has become more widespread over the last several decades. Only a few studies (Chambliss 1984; Shover 1983; Snodgrass 1982) have focused on the lives of ex-offenders, and all sampled only males. These studies centered on the effects of prior attributes and activities on their subsequent lives. Only one study (Adler 1992) examined the factors affecting lawbreakers' reintegration into society. Other sociological studies (Ebaugh 1984; Herman 1993; Warren 1991) have examined the process involved in other types of role transition.

Becker's (1963) discussion of the internalization of deviant labels implies that transforming deviant identities is extremely complex. An ex-offender not only has to construct a new self based on the personal desire to create a noncriminal life, but also has to deal in some way with others' expectations. Such expectations are often derived from ignorance, outdated notions, or judgmental preconceptions. The person who is trying to harmonize self and role, therefore, has the added difficulty of remolding and reformulating others' expectations of him or her self. . . .

Managing the Intrusion

Similar to Goffman's (1961) description of life in a total institution, many of the women described peers who had grown dependent on the prison for making their everyday decisions and meeting their survival needs and therefore were sometimes unable to make their own decisions after leaving prison. Anita, who did not make it the first time she was released, expressed it this way:

> They pay the bills. You don't have to worry about your lights. I think that's why a lot of people get institutionalized, and they come out here, and you go to try to fill out for an apartment, and they turn you down, and then they get frustrated, and then they say, "Forget it. I'm goin' to smoke" or whatever they're doin', and they just say "To H-E-L-L with it."

Elizabeth, who says that she was quickly "institutionalized," recalled a time soon after her release when she was at a discount store and had the awful feeling of being out of place. Her feelings of being institutionalized extended to the community after her release so that she had difficulty in regaining autonomy.

> I'm not where I'm supposed to be, and it's all over now. A policeman on the road, if I'm driving, even if I wasn't speeding or wasn't sliding through a stop sign, there was that, "Where am I supposed to be? Is everything right? Do I have my pass?" It [that feeling] stayed for a long time.

The extension of the institutional control is maintained through the system of supervision. All inmates on release to the community are assigned a supervision status for a designated length of time based on their offense history and sentence. The terminology depends on whether the ex-offender is supervised through the Federal Office of Probation and Parole or a state office of parole. Ex-inmates in the state system, for example, are referred to as parolees and are supervised by parole officers. Ex-inmates on the federal level may be referred to as parolees or probationers, or as "cases in custody under supervision," depending on whether the individual is completing a term under old or new sentencing guidelines. Federal and state sentencing guidelines passed on the federal level in 1987 and implemented in Kansas in 1993 also have an effect on the length of parole or supervision. However this period of monitoring is specified for the individual, all the study participants had some time after their release in which they had to meet certain conditions in order to become eligible for discharge from the system in which they had been convicted (also called "getting off paper" by the participants).

Table 36.1 identifies the participants' supervision status at the time of the interviews. For some participants, the interview was conducted some time after the completion of parole or supervision, while, for others, they were continuing to negotiate the systems' monitoring of their day-to-day activities. Of the ten participants who continued under supervision, six are federal ex-inmates who were convicted of drug-related crimes (possession, trafficking, conspiracy, sales).

The ways by which women negotiated meeting their conditions of supervision and their relationship with their parole or probation officer were instrumental to the women's transition. Since seven of the participants had been incarcerated previously, they were even more cognizant of the difficulties of getting through this initial part of the transition.

Racque, who essentially married out of her life on the streets by moving from Oakland, California, to a small town in Kansas, recalls that in her long history of repeated incarceration for property and disorder offenses, there were several times when she was only able to stay out for a night before she was arrested on a new charge or for violation of her parole. At the time that she met the man she eventually married, she had only been out a month and realized her chances of staying out were slim. Racque reported that she was "watching [her] back and more or less bein' sneaky, and tryin' not to get caught doin' whatever [she] was doin'." Racque attributed her problems to the fact that she hung around with the wrong crowd and did not have a support system in

the area that could assist her in getting a new start. However, she recognized that she needed a change if she was going to make it out of the cycle of one incarceration after another.

> I was tired of living that life. I stood a chance of goin' back to prison for a long time and never getting' out or I might ended up dead somewhere. If you're gonna change your life, you ought to be able to do it around the environment you was dealin' with then. But, then, it didn't work for me. It took me to where I had to leave California in order to change my whole life around, but it worked out for the better and we're happy.

However, moving to Kansas placed Racque in jeopardy with the California criminal justice system because she was adjudicated to have absconded from their custody while on parole. She was able to solve that problem with her "understanding" parole officer.

> I just took the chance and came over here, and then called 'em when I got over here, and then had to go back to California to straighten that mess out. The parole officer I had in California. He was pretty cool. He was understanding.

No other participant had such a geographical opportunity for a new start. Most of the women returned to the area where they had previously lived or were near to the

Table 36.1
Participants' Supervision Status[1]

Release from Federal Incarceration	Released from State Incarceration
Ashley—on federal supervision	Anita—on parole
Demi—on federal supervision	Margi—on parole
Elena—on federal supervision	Susan—on parole
Jeanette—on federal supervision	
Nan—on federal supervision	Bernie—discharged from parole
Rene—on federal supervision	Elizabeth—discharged from parole
	Mandi—discharged from parole
Deeni—discharged from federal supervision	Racque—discharged from parole
	Regina—discharged from parole
	Sadie—discharged from parole
	Suzy—discharged from parole

[1]At time of interview.

towns in which they had grown up. The rules or parole conditions under which the women were placed are meant to provide ex-inmates with the motivation to steer clear of former criminal associates in their previous settings. However, participants often found that the expectations were overwhelming and, sometimes, impossible to meet.

Nan described her frustration in a typical day in her life that she describes as being "under the roof" of her supervision after her release from Dismas House.

> I work 11 P.M. to 7 A.M., I have a Code-A-Phone number I need to call Monday through Saturday to see if I need to come in and leave a UA [urinalysis]. So, I'm responsible for makin' sure I remember to call every day, workin' a job. I have five children. Then on Thursday, I go for a counselin' session up at Research. Right now I'm not free, even though I left the halfway house and I felt I was free, because I was away from their jurisdiction. They had their own rules and regulations. I had to abide by them. I felt like, "Okay, I'm goin' to the house, and I'm on my own." I'm not. You know, I have three years paper. So, until that three years of paper is up, I'm not actually free. I'm always up under the roof.

Other women also expressed the frustration of being free as a consequence of being outside of prison, but still feeling confined or controlled because they were still accountable to the correctional system.

Participants who were currently on parole or supervision at the time of the interview often described a feeling of being overwhelmed by the conditions imposed on them. Mandi not only had to meet conditions placed on her for her parole period, but also had to meet court-imposed conditions to demonstrate her ability to parent her children in order to regain physical and legal custody that she had lost previous to her incarceration. Many of Mandi's initial obstacles in meeting her conditions of parole related to her precarious financial condition.

> Well, getting a job and getting there. I had to walk from home. When I was in my own house, I didn't have a car. I found a house within walking distance from Taco Bell. It was probably about a mile. Obstacles were no vehicle. Trying to meet the parole requirements. Like, I had to report once a month by phone; however, I couldn't have a phone in my name because of an outstanding bill, so I couldn't get a phone in my house, but I had to report once a month by phone and you get charged for that. So, finances were a real big struggle, getting to work without a vehicle, trying to go see the parole officer without a vehicle.

As summarized by the following quote, Mandi described some of the conditions that she had to meet to address both the parole conditions and the court to regain custody of her children. She described a strategy she used of taking it one step at a time in order to mediate her feeling of being regularly overwhelmed. She exhibited some of the same dogged persistence she had shown in cracking the computer codes while incarcerated to manage her process of reintegration, although she did not immediately perceive the advantages of doing so.

> I went to court . . . like a week after I got out of prison. So, I went, the judge was like, "You can't have 'em back, because you don't even know where you're gonna live tomorrow." The judge gave me a list of things I had to do to get the kids back. So, I remember during that week, and I remember especially since I was reminded a few months ago, when I went back to court, how when I went home and I got the list in the mail. It was just so overwhelming, because here I am thinkin' how there was this whole list to do to get my kids back and I got this whole list to do for my parole officer, and I thought, "How am I gonna do all this thing?" I was like court ordered to AA meetings three times a week. I was court ordered for parenting class once a week. I was court ordered for intensive psychotherapy at least once a week, plus I was court ordered to have a full-time job, and I was court ordered to maintain my own home. I was court ordered to do everything. I thought, "If I'm gonna maintain a full-time home, I'm gonna have to work two jobs. If I work the two jobs, when am I gonna go to the meetings, and when am I gonna go to [see her children]." . . .

Mandi met all her conditions, but not without some cost to her personally, and at great risk to her parole. She tearfully recounted how she relapsed by smoking crack on two different occasions during the first year of her release, after she had started employment and was attempting to do it all. With the assistance of an understanding employer, she was able to acquire the substance abuse treatment she needed, successfully regained legal and physical custody of her children, and received a discharge from parole supervision.

Negotiating Demands of Supervision

Many of the women in the sample attributed their success and/or difficulties in part to the type of parole officer or supervisor they had. Table 36.2 summarizes the women's perceptions of negative or positive responses of the parole officers toward them.

Study participants had positive relationships with parole officers who treated them as a person rather than a number; left them alone, without daily intrusions into their lives; willingly responded to changing circumstances by modifying conditions when appropriate; provided specific information

about the parole process when requested; and in several cases, requested early discharge from parole. Among the participants, four of the Kansas parolees shared the same parole officer and two of the federal parolees had the same officer. In each of these cases, the participants made positive observations about the ways in which their parole officer had promoted their transition.

Mandi, who as described earlier, faced many obstacles in dealing with all the conditions placed on her, negotiated with her parole officer a modification of her condition for attending AA/NA meetings.

I told my parole officer that I wasn't making it to three meetings a week because I was going to parenting group, I was goin' to therapy besides working two jobs. My parole officer agreed that if I didn't work and make my income, that I would lose my house and, therefore, I'd be back on the streets. So, she ended up changing my conditions to go to meetings basically as desired.

In addition, when Mandi did not have the transportation to report to the parole office to report in to her parole officer, the parole officer met Mandi at her house and gave her a ride to one of her jobs. Mandi recounts how she made the request:

Table 36.2
Continuum of Parole Officer's Response to Participants

Inhibits Progress	Neutral	Promotes Progress
Invades privacy	Does her job	Treats me with respect
Arbitrary in making decisions	Tells me what I need to do	Can be flexible based on my individual situation
Goes by the book		
Doesn't believe me	Manages the paperwork	Believes in me
Forced me to work outside the home	Left me alone	Proud of me
		Wants me to succeed
		Knows that I am different
		Provides information about resources in the community
		Modified my conditions based on my changing needs
		Requests early discharge from parole

I was reportin' to her. I wasn't just reporting by phone. It was by phone and reporting to her once a month. Like, one day she came to my house. I called her up, and I was like "I just don't know how I'm gonna get over there." She said, "Well, you have to report." I said, "Well, I have an idea. How about you meet me in the morning?" because it was kind of cold that week, I remember. I had to walk, so I asked if she could come over to my house and see where I was livin', and give me a ride to work. I think she kind of chuckled and said, "Okay, I'll do that." So, she did. She came in, and I took her through the house. I said, "I work right down this way." We visited in the car in the parking lot for a little bit. She told me she thought I was doin' good. Definitely, she knew I did have a home, she definitely knew that I had a job.

Nicole recalled that the same parole officer treated her with respect and praised her progress on parole:

I think she looked at me for the person that I was instead of where I'd been. I mean, you can pretty much talk to a person and tell what their situation might be, and I think she just knew that it was something I had to go through. But, I think she seen that I was determined, and I was not gonna go back, and so she knew right off the bat that I was gonna be easy to work with.

When Sadie got into a personality dispute with coworkers who put her at risk of revocation because they made a complaint to her parole officer, the same parole officer checked it out, and when she found that the accusations were false, immediately requested an early discharge for Sadie.

... this deal happened with these two people trying to making all these phone calls to her telling her that I was crazy and that I was violent and that I was doing drugs. She thought they were the ones that were crazy, fortunately for me. It could have been the opposite, it could have been totally the opposite but I think she felt confident about me. Then she did it immediately, about a month later I got my [discharge] and I got a nice letter from her with it.

Sadie felt as though she had developed a good relationship with her parole officer, which helped her when she had problems. That relationship probably evolved in part due to Sadie's perception that she was willing to take responsibility for her behavior.

I think I was probably a little different than a lot of people she had dealt with. Maybe it was kinda like a breath of air, to not have to be dealing with a lot of problems, a lot of stuff, excuses for not showing up, excuses for not sending in this or excuses for why you moved and never said anything, whatever.

Elena was primed by other ex-inmates to have difficulties with her parole officer but became aware that it would be her own behaviors that would "send her back:"

Yeah, I thought she was out to send me back. I didn't trust her. I didn't like her. My mom fell in love with her when she first met her. And, I just heard stories about her from other girls at the halfway house, but later on I found out that they ended up usin' and they send their ownselves back. She didn't send 'em back. They sent their ownselves back. That's one thing she don't tolerate is drug usin'. She's even told me that if I ever had a dirty UA or anything that she was sendin' me back. But, like, if I have any problems or any questions, I can call her up and talk to her and she's very understanding.

Study participants reported that they sometimes had difficulties in dealing with their parole officers, and in two cases the women felt that the parole officer hindered their successful progress on parole. Negative characteristics mentioned by the women included arbitrary interpretation of the rules, excessive intrusion in their lives, and a lack of understanding of the obstacles they had to address coming out of prison. When Suzy was first discharged from prison, she was assigned to a parole officer whom she described as having no backbone when a mental health provider reported her resistance to a course of recommended treatment.

One of the conditions of my release was mental health. I didn't have no problem with that. I knew that, so I had to contact

Mental Health. I started goin' there, and the therapist that I had, was, you know, I was havin' problems adjustin' to bein' a wife again and bein' a mother again. So, she was tryin' to tell me that I needed to go to counseling for my family and for my son, and parenting classes and all this stuff. She wanted me to do this, and I didn't have any money. I had just gotten home. My husband was on a low paying job. I told her I couldn't afford it, so she called my PO. She called my PO twice tellin' him that I couldn't do it, and I was refusin' to do it. So, he was ready to send me back.

At the same time that Suzy was struggling with these expectations from "mental health," she and her husband moved across county lines where she was assigned another parole offcer who was more responsive to her situation. She recalls that he also treated her respectfully by validating her work as a mother:

Yeah, and I met up with Don S. He was great to me. He treated me like a person, and he treated me right. He allowed me to stay home. He asked what I wanted out of life. I told him I wanted to stay home and I wanted to be a mom. He let me stay home and be a mom. I went to mental health, and I had no problem. Anytime I needed to talk to him—he gave me his pager number, and I just picked it up and called him. He was always there for me anytime I had a problem or just wanted to talk. Most people bitch about their POs, because they treat 'em like they're just a damned convict or disrespectful. Don never treated me like that. I was his only female parolee, and he was proud of me.

Although most participants found some way to manage their conditions and develop a mutually respectful relationship with their parole officer, Ashley in particular expressed frustration about what she considered arbitrary intrusion into the choices she made in her daily life. She felt, for example, that her officer projected his moral standards on her relating to her sexual behavior. She related several conversations she had with her officer about his expectation that he be able to know her whereabouts at all times. She recalls asking him several years ago, "I understand you're married, but I like sex. I can't go to a hotel and have sex?" To which the parole officer answered, "No, you have to be at your house." Another conflict erupted again when she attempted to assert her rights to privacy:

About three months ago, he called me and said, "Meet me at your house. We need to talk." Okay, he comes over here. Now, there were several reasons why he wanted to talk. One was that he came by my (house) at 6:30 in the morning and did not see my car and wanted to know where the hell I was. Well, sometimes I leave to go to work early. "Well, you don't have to be to work until 7:00." "Well, I get there at 6:20 or 6:30 or 6:40 or 6:55 or 6:59. It just depends on how I feel that morning. I might have left early." "But, you weren't here." "Well, I was at work." So, he really believed that I was sleeping somewhere else. And, I think that's hard to ask an adult. I brought that to his attention. I said, "What if I liked somebody and wanted to spend the night at their house." "You have to call me and get permission." This past Thanksgiving and this past Christmas, two days before the holiday, I had to call and get permission to go spend the night at my mom's house out of fear he would violate me if he happened to pass by and didn't see my car.

Ashley protested what she considered was an unfair extension of control over her individual choices and discovered that she was accountable for her location and that the parole officer could decide how to enforce that accountability.

I called his supervisor a couple of days after Christmas to discuss this issue with him, and he said that it's more of the parole officer's initiative as to how far they can take it. He didn't have any guidelines, but he said, "It's up to your parole officer." I didn't think that was fair at all, because that's not in my manual, but I'm not gonna test y'all and fuck with y'all. So, I'm gonna go with what he's sayin'. So, I don't spend the night anywhere. If I have to have sex, it has to be here. I do not go into your house, and I'm not goin' to a hotel. I mean, I think that's just takin' it to the extreme, to the utmost extreme. . . . And, I think that a lot of times he oversteps his boundary. But, I'm not in a position to push it.

Rene observes that it is difficult sometimes to follow the rules even when you know what the rules are, want to be responsive to the rules, and are behaving in a way that is consistent with the rules. As federal ex-inmates move through the levels of supervision, eventually they are assigned a number they are required to call on a daily basis that randomly identifies anyone who has a drug abuse history to report for a urine analysis. Failure to make the daily call can result in a revocation, even if, as in Rene's case, it was an inadvertent mistake. She recalled that she was working and doing her best and still felt scared that she could be reincarcerated due to what she characterized as a human error.

> I worked, and that's why you work, and you save so much of your own money, and you get a place. You know, I was already doin' my part for the home. Just, basically, stayin' clean, goin' by the rules, and just knowin' that I wasn't gonna go back the life I was. When you're clean and you want to do right, it's a lot easier than to have a guilty conscience when things aren't—like, I missed a UA and I got into panic. It could cost me my freedom, and I'm not even doing drugs or anything. Now, that's what scares you to death, you know. It's just, you might not be doin' anything, and you can lose your freedom. There are things that you have to do. That call. What happened that day was I had to go to the unemployment office, and my schedule got off track. I usually call at 7:30, and I forgot—totally forgot. But see, they don't care. You're not allowed to be human. You're not allowed to make an error, and that error could cost me my freedom. That's my main stressor there is that number I got to call on Monday through Saturday.

Many of the participants described the parole or supervision process as "doing what I have to do." The process was facilitated by parole officers, most of whom the women described as promoting their transition, despite the context of supervision and control they represented in their daily lives.

References

Adler, P. 1992. The 'post' phase of deviant careers: Reintegrating drug traffickers. *Deviant Behavior* 13: 103–126.

Becker, H. 1963. *Outsiders: Studies in the Sociology of Deviance.* New York: Free Press.

Chambliss, W. J. 1984. *Harry King: A Professional Thief's Journey.* New York: Wiley.

Ebaugh, H. R. F. 1984. Leaving the convent: Role exit and self-transformation. In *The Existential Self in Society*, eds. J. A. Kotarba and A. Fintana, 156–176. Chicago: University of Chicago Press.

Goffman, E. 1961. *Asylums.* Garden City, NY: Anchor Books.

Herman, N. J. 1993. Return to sender: Reintegrative stigma-management strategies of ex-psychiatric patients. *Journal of Contemporary Ethnography* 22(3): 295–330.

Jose-Kampfner, C. 1990. Coming to terms with existential death: An analysis of women's adaptation to life in prison. *Social Justice* 17(2): 110–125.

Larson, J. H., and J. Nelson. 1984. Women's friendship and adaptation to prison. *Journal of Criminal Justice* 12(4): 601–615.

Shover, N. 1983. The later states of ordinary property offenders' careers. *Social Problems* 31: 208–218.

Snodgrass, J. 1982. *The Jack-Roller at Seventy: A Fifty-Year Follow-Up Study.* Lexington, MA: Lexington.

Sykes, G. 1958. *A Society of Captives.* Princeton, NJ: Princeton University Press.

Warren, C. A. B. 1991. *Madwives: Schizophrenic Women in the 1950s.* New Brunswick, NJ: Rutgers University Press.

Chapter XII
Discussion

Release From Prison: Parole

O'Brien's reading is a detailed study of the struggles and challenges eighteen adult female prisoners face when they are released from state and federal institutions. The interviews were conducted at different points in their transitions, to depict how women "negotiated" their parole conditions. Most women returned to the same community they had lived in before their incarceration because their support structures and children lived there. Yet, women found it financially difficult and emotionally stressful to meet all the expected responsibilities and conditions. Many women are tempted to return to old habits (e.g., drug use) to deal with the stress of being on parole and the idea that they may be separated from their children if they violate their parole conditions.

The reading by Holt explains why discretionary parole was replaced by mandatory and automatic release practices in some states. Discretionary parole boards have, however, improved their objectivity through their use of risk assessment instruments. Holt also mentions a significant problem facing parolees on community supervision—parolees are expected to abide by too many conditions simultaneously. Although parole officers routinely work with parolees who do not abide by their conditions, we return to Holt's question posed earlier: When it comes to the number of conditions we expect prisoners to perform, how *realistic* are these parole expectations after prisoners leave an environment where, for years, they have had virtually no responsibility? Upon release, the parolee is faced with so many rules to follow and tasks to complete that the situation may be overwhelming. Have we designed a system of conditions so rigid and pressure-filled that parolees are destined to fail? This may explain, in part, why a significant number of parole violators are returned to prison, many of whom have *not* posed a dangerous community threat but have only accumulated too many technical violations.

The article by Ronald Burns and colleagues provides a more optimistic view of the future of parole. Findings suggest that parole rates will increase in the next decade, although it is unclear whether resources to handle the numbers will follow. Parole board members do not perceive that their role is or should be affected by prison crowding. However, board members seemed keenly aware that parole lacks public and government constituent support. The article touches on the important need to educate the public about discretionary and mandatory release. This may provide the first step in alleviating the burgeoning prison populations that are currently full of parole violators.